ORACLE®

Oracle Press

Oracle *9i* SQLJ Programming

Nirva Morisseau-Leroy
Martin K. Solomon
Gerald P. Momplaisir

Osborne/**McGraw-Hill**

New York   Chicago   San Francisco
Lisbon   London   Madrid   Mexico City
Milan   New Delhi   San Juan
Seoul   Singapore   Sydney   Toronto

Osborne/**McGraw-Hill**
2600 Tenth Street
Berkeley, California 94710
U.S.A.

To arrange bulk purchase discounts for sales promotions, premiums, or fund-raisers, please contact Osborne/**McGraw-Hill** at the above address. For information on translations or book distributors outside the U.S.A., please see the International Contact Information page immediately following the index of this book.

Oracle 9*i* SQLJ Programming

1234567890 CUS CUS 01987654321

Book p/n 0-07-219059-0 and CD p/n 0-07-219094-9
parts of
ISBN 0-07-219093-0

Publisher	**Copy Editor**
Brandon A. Nordin	Paul Medoff
Vice President & Associate Publisher	**Proofreader**
Scott Rogers	Linda Medoff
Acquisitions Editor	**Indexer**
Jeremy Judson	Jack Lewis
Project Editor	**Computer Designers**
Jenn Tust	George Toma Charbak, Lauren McCarthy
Acquisitions Coordinator	**Illustrators**
Ross Doll	Michael Mueller, Alex Putney, Lyssa Sieben-Wald
Technical Editor	**Series Design**
Ekkehard Rohwedder	Jani Beckwith

This book was composed with Corel VENTURA™ Publisher.

About the Authors

Nirva Morisseau-Leroy, MSCS, is an Oracle Database Administrator and Application Developer with over sixteen years' database and object-oriented analysis, design, implementation, and component-based modeling experience. Trilingual (French, Spanish, and English), Morisseau-Leroy is also one of the winners of the "Best Java Implementation" award presented by the NOAA's High Performance Computing and Communications (HPCC) at NOAATech2000, Silver Spring, MD, in October 1999. Morisseau-Leroy can be reached at nmorisseauleroy@data-i.com.

Dr. Martin K. Solomon is an Associate Professor of Computer Science and Engineering at Florida Atlantic University. His major areas of research include the design, implementation, and theory of database systems, computational complexity theory, and the philosophical aspects of computability. Dr. Solomon has published articles on these topics in such prestigious journals as *ACM Transactions on Database Systems*, *Communications of the ACM*, *Journal of Symbolic Logic*, and *British Journal for the Philosophy of Science*. He has a strong professional interest in all aspects of the Oracle RDBMS and is a frequent contributor to the South Florida Oracle Users Group Newsletter. Dr. Solomon can be reached at marty@cse.fau.edu.

Gerald P. Momplaisir is an Oracle consultant for the J2EE Architectural and Development group of the Advance Technology Systems at Oracle Corporation. He is a member, designer, and developer of the Oracle Cleveland Foundation framework. He can be reached at gerald.momplaisir@oracle.com.

Contents

PART I
Basic Oracle9*i* SQLJ

PART II
Advanced SQLJ for Relational Processing

PART III

SQLJ and Object Deployment

Foreword

J ava has emerged as the primary language for building applications due to its power, portability, and productivity. It is the only modern, object-oriented programming language designed for the Internet. To build enterprise applications in Java, application developers needed two facilities—a highly scalable server environment in which to run Java and a simple, easy to program link between Java and SQL, the language in which most of the world's data is defined and stored.

Oracle recognized the emergence of the Internet Computing model and these two fundamental needs and made major strategic investments: Oracle Java Virtual Machine (JVM) and SQLJ. To provide developers with the industry's most scalable, highly available, and high-performance Java server environment—Oracle JVM—we designed a highly specialized Java Virtual Machine directly into Oracle9*i*, our Internet database. While complying completely with Java standards, Oracle JVM is able to support thousands of concurrent clients and scales excellently across a wide range of hardware configurations.

Oracle's other investment—SQLJ, or embedded static and dynamic SQL in Java— provides the simplest and most elegant way to build database applications in Java. An industry standard accepted by the ANSI/ISO standards bodies and supported by all the major database vendors, SQLJ provides a portable way to build a variety of different types of programs—database stored procedures, triggers, Enterprise JavaBeans, CORBA services, and even applets. With Oracle's comprehensive support for SQLJ, you can quickly and efficiently build applications combining Java and the Oracle database and deploy them on the Internet.

*Oracle9*i *SQLJ Programming*, by Nirva Morisseau-Leroy, Martin K. Solomon, and Gerald P. Momplaisir, is precisely the tool you need to master SQLJ programming. It begins by introducing you to why SQLJ is useful and how to get started building applications in SQLJ. It then provides a number of more detailed chapters that succinctly provide you with the necessary background to the core of SQLJ programming—including how it can be combined with SQL, PL/SQL, Java, and JDBC. Finally, as you grow in your use of SQLJ, it provides a number of superbly written advanced programming chapters that deal with such topics as server-side programming in SQLJ, combining SQLJ with the Oracle database's object-relational facilities, and distributed systems development in SQLJ involving Remote Method Invocation (RMI), CORBA Services, and Enterprise JavaBeans.

I really enjoyed the practical nature with which all the material was presented and the very rich examples on how to use SQLJ in building real applications. I am very excited about the publication of this book. I know that you will find it an indispensable guide as you learn to use SQLJ and Oracle JVM.

Thomas Kurian
Vice President/Oracle 9ias and e-business
Oracle Corporation

Preface

L et's cut right through to the heart of the matter:

Do you want to use the best, most productive computer language, directly accessing the best database system to write applications that can be deployed and run on the client, in the server, and in the middle tier? And do you want to accomplish that in the easiest, most efficient, and productive way?

If so, then this book is the answer for you.

- **Java** is the revolutionary, productive, and portable programming language for enterprise computing that is being taken very seriously by proponents and (if we may consider imitation as the sincerest form of flattery) detractors alike.

- **Oracle** is *the* database, and **SQL** is *the* language to access and manipulate the data that lives in it. Oracle 9*i* gives users a whole spectrum of features to model their business data, from large object types to full object-relational capabilities. Moreover, you can utilize the Oracle 9*i* JavaVM inside the database server to run your Java programs, or to implement Stored Procedures or Triggers in Java. Thus your choice of *where* you run your application: client, server, or middle tier becomes somewhat orthogonal to *which* of the Java programming models (such as direct database access, CORBA, EJB, or JSP) you want to choose, providing you with a maximum of flexibility.

- **SQLJ** combines the two by embedding SQL directly in Java programs. This is the easiest and most productive way to write concise, reliable Java programs that access the database directly through SQL. With SQLJ you can focus with laser-sharp precision on *what* you want to say without being detracted by the *how*. Low-level details and the checking of your SQL statements are delegated—and rightly so—to the computer and not to you.

My fingers are itching to provide you an example of a SQLJ statement to demonstrate—if you will—the essence of SQLJ. This assumes a passing acquaintance of SQL and Java.

```
int no;  String name = "SMITH";
#sql { SELECT empno INTO :no FROM emp WHERE ename=:name };
```

See also Appendixes A and B for brief introductions to SQL and Java.

What Is New in This Edition?

This book covers the Oracle 9*i* SQLJ release, which I am very excited about! Previous SQLJ versions provided only support for *static SQL*—in a static SQL statement everything except the data values of the bind variables must be determined at translate time. For *dynamic SQL* statements you would have had to revert to the JDBC API, which means having to learn that, too (let alone shelling out more money for another 500-page tome). What is the big advantage of using the easier, more productive SQLJ paradigm if you end up having to switch to JDBC anyway (even if only from time to time)?

Well, no more—get out of the way, JDBC! SQLJ 9*i* supports practically all requirements for dynamic SQL directly. Programmers get the best of both worlds: conciseness of embedded SQL as well as the power of dynamic SQL, whenever required. Can you guess what the following SQLJ statement does?

```
double money;  String name="SMITH";
String column = "sal";  String table = "emp";
#sql { SELECT :{column} INTO :money FROM :{table} WHERE ename=:name };
```

Now don't get me wrong about JDBC. If you have started out programming in JDBC, you may feel like having been neglected by SQLJ folks. And yes, we are guilty as charged, having focused mostly on the embedded SQL part. Once more though, with Oracle 9*i* this is no longer the case. You can immediately recast any of your original JDBC logic directly and more concisely in 9*i* SQLJ. One more code example (the last one in this preface, I promise). This will look strangely familiar to JDBC programmers.

```
double min = 1500.0; String name; int no;
ResultSetIterator rsi;
#sql rsi = { SELECT ename, empno FROM emp WHERE sal > :min };
while (rsi.next()) {
    #sql { FETCH CURRENT FROM :rsi INTO :name, :no }; …
}
rsi.close();
```

So, What Do I Get?

All right, already. SQLJ is simple, straightforward, and demands less typing. Why in the world would you want to buy such a voluminous book as *Oracle 9*i *SQLJ Programming*? Couldn't you just give us the fundamentals on two pages (or maybe five) and we will be off our merry ways, programming?

Not so quick! You *do* get that summary of SQLJ in Appendix D. But this book has much more to offer than just the fundamentals of SQLJ. It is chock-full of example programs and solutions that permit you to hit the ground running. Re-use instead of re-invent, and start learning from a plethora of working programs! This book also covers an amazing number of features. The authors left (almost) nothing out, whether it be SQLJ functionality (such as dynamic SQL, all of the flavors of iterators, the various contexts, etc.), a feature in Oracle SQL (they cover LOB types, collection types, user-defined object types, and many others), or any one of the many Java programming models (applications, applets, use of RMI, CORBA, EJB, Java Server Pages, and Java Stored Procedures). Oh, and did I mention that you are also introduced to the basics of the different Oracle Java tools from the integrated JDeveloper development environment to the SQLJ and JPublisher command line utilities and others that you need during program development and deployment? This is an eminently practical and invaluable resource for all programmers working with Java and SQL!

Finally, some words on my own behalf: Keep giving Oracle feedback and suggestions on SQLJ, so that we can make it even better. We do wish you as much enjoyment in *using* SQLJ as we had in *creating* it. See you on the Oracle Technology Network (technet.oracle.com)!

Ekkehard Rohwedder
SQLJ Lead Developer
Java Platform Group
Oracle Corporation

Acknowledgments

Our book was made possible because of many people. I specially appreciate their support, advice, and feedback during the development of this project. I would like to acknowledge the excellent technical suggestions of Ekkehard Rohwedder, SQLJ Manager, Oracle Corporation, Braden N. McDaniel, and Dr. Maryse Prezeau. Many special thanks to my coauthors, Martin K. Solomon and Gerald P. Momplaisir. Thanks to Dr. Mark D. Powell, Atmospheric Scientist, and his H*WIND team at the NOAA's Hurricane Research Division (HRD), Dr. Joseph Prospero, Professor and Director, Cooperative Institute for Marine and Atmospheric Studies (CIMAS), University of Miami, Dr. Hugh Willoughby, Director of HRD, Jeremy Judson, acquisitions editor, Ross Doll, Jenn Tust, Paul Medoff and Linda Medoff of the Osborne/McGraw-Hill editorial staff.

Nirva Morisseau-Leroy
Miami, Florida
June 2001

I would like to acknowledge the excellent technical suggestions of Ekkehard Rohwedder, SQLJ Manager, Oracle Corporation, the invaluable help of Ross Doll, Jenn Tust, Paul Medoff and Linda Medoff of the Osborne/McGraw-Hill editorial staff, and the editorial leadership of Jeremy Judson. I also thank my wife Abby for her tireless typing contributions. I give special thanks to my coauthors, Nirva Morisseau-Leroy and Gerald P. Momplaisir, for being such a pleasure with whom to work.

Marty K. Solomon
Miami, Florida
June 2001

I would like to express many thanks to my coauthor Nirva Morisseau-Leroy for her vision, inspiration, and tireless support. I appreciate the advice, suggestions, and the superb technical review of Mr. SQLJ, Ekkehard Rohwedder, for this edition. Oops, I think I blew your cover Mr. SQLJ. He should be called Mr. Detail because nothing gets by him. I am grateful for all the hard work of the staff of Osborne/McGraw-Hill: Jeremy Judson, Ross Doll, Jenn Tust, Paul Medoff and Linda Medoff. I cannot forget Marc Horowitz, Chad Naeger, Sam Pizzuto, Jason Stallings, and the original Luis Amat from the Oracle Cleveland Framework development team at Oracle Corporation. Finally, special thanks go to my wife Tara for providing data writing the SQL scripts used for this book and her endless small contributions.

Gerald P. Momplaisir
Miami, Florida
June 2001

Introduction

In Parts I and II of the book, you will develop SQLJ programs that manipulate a "pure" relational database, that is, a financial schema called the Purchase Order schema. The Purchase Order relational database schema is part of a database design presented in the *Design of a Financial Administrative System Using the Semantic Binary Model*. In Part III, you will develop SQLJ programs that manipulate an object-relational database, that is, a scientific schema called the Observation schema. The Observation object-relational database schema is part of the scientific database design presented in the *Atmospheric Observations, Analyses, and the World Wide Web Using a Semantic Database*. Note that all the programs that you will develop in this book have been tested against the Oracle8*i* database server releases 8.1.5, 8.1.6, and 8.1.7 and some of them have been deployed in the Oracle9*i* Internet Application Server (Oracle9*i* AS). The book also covers some new concepts (in particular the support of dynamic SQL in Oracle SQLJ) implemented only in the Oracle9*i* SQLJ upcoming release.

The Purchase Order and the Observation schemas were designed for the Atlantic Oceanographic and Meteorological Laboratory (AOML), Miami, Florida, an Environmental Research Laboratory (ERL) of the National Oceanic and Atmospheric Administration (NOAA), part of the U.S. Department of Commerce (DOC). In particular, the Observation schema was designed for the Hurricane Research Division (HRD) at AOML and is currently being implemented by HRD as part of the H*WIND system that produces real-time surface wind analyses to National Hurricane Center's (NHC) forecasters and the FEMA Hurricane Liaison Team at NHC.

How the Book Is Organized

This book takes your hand and leads you through well-integrated and step-by-step coverage of SQLJ and the Oracle9*i* JavaVM, progressing through more advanced scenarios at a comfortable pace, and leaving you in a better place where you're ready to begin using your fresh SQLJ techniques in the real world.

Other facets of the book that should appeal to you include

- Treatment of traditional relational and object-relational usage scenarios

- Complete, realistic programs, with line-by-line inspection

- Comprehensive deployment scenarios: client-side, server-side, client/server, and n-tier

- Demonstrations of the tight integration between SQLJ and the Oracle9*i* JavaVM

- A tutorial on the basics (for those new to Oracle or Java)

Part I: Basic Oracle9*i* SQLJ

This introductory section leads off with a view of SQLJ from 30,000 feet, gradually descending below cloud cover to reach ground level. The basics of SQLJ syntax, tools, implementation, and deployment are covered in great detail and reinforced by comprehensive real-world sample code. By the end of this section, you should have a firm grasp of how to write SQLJ programs that modify and retrieve data from the database, as well as how to create and drop database objects. Chapters include

- Chapter 1: Introduction to Oracle9*i* SQLJ

- Chapter 2: SQLJ Program Development

- Chapter 3: Basic SQLJ Programming

Part II: Advanced SQLJ for Relational Processing

In Part II, you'll learn to build truly robust, scalable SQLJ-based solutions by taking advantage of SQLJ's tight integration with Oracle9*i*. SQLJ joins PL/SQL (Oracle's proprietary procedural SQL language) as Oracle9*i*'s stored procedure language. This section will instruct you in the myriad ways in which to build 100 percent Java database solutions via SQLJ stored procedures and triggers. Chapters include

- Chapter 4: Developing SQLJ Stored Procedures and Triggers

- Chapter 5: Advanced SQLJ Deployment

- Chapter 6: Advanced SQLJ Functionality

- Chapter 7: Advanced SQLJ Features

Part III: SQLJ and Object Deployment

Java brings application-level object-oriented design and development to the masses. Oracle9*i*'s object-relational model allows object orientation to take place at the logical level as well. Part III covers the object-relational features of Oracle9*i*, and how to interface with them via SQLJ-based methods and components. Chapters include

- Chapter 8: Object-Relational Processing Using SQLJ

- Chapter 9: SQLJ Business and Scientific Object Deployment

Part IV: Effective Use of SQLJ

Building upon your newfound understanding of how to design, implement, and deploy your SQLJ code, Part IV will help you refine your solutions to be ready for prime time. Learn proven techniques to optimize your SQLJ methods and components, exploiting the robust and highly tunable Oracle9*i* platform. And if you didn't think that SQLJ was enough of a productivity boost, you'll also learn how to ease your development burden even further via Oracle tools designed expressly for Internet computing and e-business solutions. Chapters include

- Chapter 10: SQLJ Applications: Performance Tuning

- Chapter 11: Oracle9*i* Development Tools

Part V: Appendixes

For experienced Java and Oracle application developers, these appendixes will be a welcome reference that you can access whenever the need arises—typically when you least expect it in the wee hours of the morning as you stare bleary-eyed at a computer screen full of code listings, wondering if it's worth the effort to swill the sludge (some might call it coffee) left warming in a pot in the kitchen. The rest of you will get a quick and dirty introduction to the mechanics of Oracle SQL, Java, JDBC, and SQLJ. The Appendixes include

- Appendix A: Oracle SQL Basics

- Appendix B: Java Basics

- Appendix C: Introduction to Java Database Connectivity (JDBC)

- Appendix D: SQLJ Quick Reference Guide

Intended Audience

The traditional audience for this book will be application developers and database designers, the two groups most likely to take advantage of SQLJ in solutions (application developers) or as stored procedures and triggers (database designers). These groups also include those who aspire to the ranks of designers and implementers, including students in undergraduate and graduate programs studying The Next Best Thing in computing paradigms.

JDBC programmers will not only become comfortable with SQLJ very quickly but also obtain an immediate productivity boost. Now they can say what they mean directly without an API getting in the way. As an added bonus SQLJ offers to check SQL code at compile time rather than at runtime.

We also encourage experienced Java programmers who haven't had much database exposure to broaden their minds by wringing every last bit of information from this text. SQLJ eases the transition from monolithic, non-persistent Java programs to n-tier, database-driven e-business solutions. Take the next step in the evolution of your skills by joining the SQLJ community.

Though this book caters to programmers and database designers, we have no wish to be exclusionary. If you would like to learn about the nexus between Java and SQL, we hope that you'll also be interested in this book regardless of your background. You never know where your career might lead given the right opportunity and catalyst.

SQL Scripts to Create the Financial Purchase Order Schema

Use the following `createposchema.sql` SQL script to create the Purchase Order schema in the Oracle8*i* database:

```
-- File Name:  createposchema.sql
DROP TABLE DEPARTMENT_LIST CASCADE CONSTRAINTS
/
CREATE TABLE DEPARTMENT_LIST(
deptno        NUMBER(5),
```

```
shortname      VARCHAR2(6),
longname       VARCHAR2(20))
/
DROP TABLE ACCOUNT_LIST CASCADE CONSTRAINTS;
/
CREATE TABLE ACCOUNT_LIST (
accountno      NUMBER(5),
projectno      NUMBER(5),
deptno         NUMBER(5)),
PRIMARY KEY ( accountno ))
/
DROP TABLE EMPLOYEE_LIST CASCADE CONSTRAINTS
/
CREATE TABLE EMPLOYEE_LIST(
employeeno     NUMBER(7),
deptno         NUMBER(5),
type           VARCHAR2(30),
lastname       VARCHAR2(30),
firstname      VARCHAR2(30),
phone          VARCHAR2(10))
/
DROP TABLE CREDITCARD_LIST
/
CREATE TABLE CREDITCARD_LIST (
cardno             VARCHAR2(15),
employeeno         NUMBER(7),
expirationdate     DATE)
/
DROP TABLE CHECKACCOUNT_LIST
/
CREATE TABLE CHECKACCOUNT_LIST(
accountno      NUMBER(5),
employeeno     NUMBER(7))
/
DROP TABLE VENDOR_LIST
/
CREATE TABLE VENDOR_LIST(
vendorno      NUMBER(6),
name          VARCHAR2(30),
address       VARCHAR2(20),
city          VARCHAR2(15),
state         VARCHAR2(15),
vzip          VARCHAR2(15),
country       VARCHAR2(15))
/
DROP TABLE PROJECT_LIST
/
CREATE TABLE PROJECT_LIST (
projectno          NUMBER(5),
```

```
projectname        VARCHAR2(20),
start_date         DATE,
amt_of_funds       NUMBER,
PRIMARY KEY( projectno );
/
DROP TABLE PURCHASE_LIST
/
CREATE TABLE PURCHASE_LIST (
requestno          NUMBER(10),
employeeno         NUMBER(7),
vendorno           NUMBER(6),
purchasetype       VARCHAR2(20),
checkno            NUMBER(11),
whenpurchased      DATE)
/
DROP TABLE LINEITEM_LIST
/
CREATE TABLE LINEITEM_LIST (
requestno          NUMBER(10),
lineno             NUMBER(5),
projectno          NUMBER(5),
quantity           NUMBER(5),
unit               VARCHAR2(2),
estimatedcost      NUMBER(8,2),
actualcost         NUMBER(8,2),
description        VARCHAR2(30))
/
```

Use the following to create constraints for the Purchase Order schema:

```
-- File Name: poconstraints.sql
alter table DEPARTMENT_LIST
  ADD CONSTRAINT deptno_pk PRIMARY KEY(deptno)
  USING INDEX TABLESPACE INDX
/
ALTER TABLE ACCOUNT_LIST
  ADD CONSTRAINT acc_deptno_fk
  FOREIGN KEY(deptno)
  REFERENCES DEPARTMENT_LIST(deptno)
  USING INDEX TABLESPACE INDX
/
ALTER TABLE EMPLOYEE_LIST
  ADD CONSTRAINT employeeno_pk PRIMARY KEY(employeeno)
  USING INDEX TABLESPACE INDX
/
ALTER TABLE EMPLOYEE_LIST
  ADD CONSTRAINT emp_deptno_fk
  FOREIGN KEY(deptno)
  REFERENCES DEPARTMENT_LIST(deptno)
```

```
  USING INDEX TABLESPACE INDX
/
ALTER TABLE CREDITCARD_LIST
  ADD CONSTRAINT cardno_pk PRIMARY KEY(cardno)
  USING INDEX TABLESPACE INDX
/
ALTER TABLE CREDITCARD_LIST
  ADD CONSTRAINT credit_employeeno_fk
  FOREIGN KEY(employeeno)
  REFERENCES EMPLOYEE_LIST(employeeno)
  USING INDEX TABLESPACE INDX
/
ALTER TABLE CHECKACCOUNT_LIST
  ADD CONSTRAINT accountno_pk PRIMARY KEY(accountno)
  USING INDEX TABLESPACE INDX
/
ALTER TABLE CHECKACCOUNT_LIST
  ADD CONSTRAINT check_employeeno_fk
  FOREIGN KEY(employeeno)
  REFERENCES EMPLOYEE_LIST(employeeno)
  USING INDEX TABLESPACE INDX
/
ALTER TABLE vendor_list
  ADD CONSTRAINT vendorno_pk PRIMARY KEY(vendorno)
  USING INDEX TABLESPACE INDX
/
ALTER TABLE Purchase_list
  ADD CONSTRAINT requestno_pk PRIMARY KEY(requestno)
  USING INDEX TABLESPACE INDX
/
ALTER TABLE LINEITEM_LIST
  ADD CONSTRAINT lineno_pk
  PRIMARY KEY(requestno,lineno,projectno)
  USING INDEX TABLESPACE INDX
/
```

Use the following to create sequences for the Purchase Order schema:

```
-- File Name: posequences.sql
CREATE SEQUENCE deptno_SEQ
  START WITH 200
  INCREMENT BY 1
/
CREATE SEQUENCE projectno_SEQ
  START WITH 300
  INCREMENT BY 1
/
CREATE SEQUENCE employeeno_SEQ
  START WITH 100
  INCREMENT BY 1
```

```
/
CREATE SEQUENCE accountno_SEQ
  START WITH 1000
  INCREMENT BY 1
/
CREATE SEQUENCE cardno_SEQ
  START WITH 311200
  INCREMENT BY 1
/
CREATE SEQUENCE vendorno_SEQ
  START WITH 400
  INCREMENT BY 1
/
CREATE SEQUENCE requestno_SEQ
  START WITH 500
  INCREMENT BY 1
/
CREATE SEQUENCE lineno_SEQ
  START WITH 1
  INCREMENT BY 1
/
```

SQL Scripts to Create the Scientific Observation Schema

Use the following `createobjschema.sql` SQL script to create the scientific Observation schema in the Oracle8i database:

```
-- File Name:  createobjschema.sql
DROP TABLE passed_observation_list
/
DROP TYPE passedObsArray
/
DROP TYPE passedObs
/
DROP TABLE oceanic_observation_list
/
DROP TYPE oceanic_observation_TYPE
/
DROP TYPE oceanic_observation
/
DROP TABLE QC_EVENT_LIST
/
DROP TYPE QUALITY_CONTROL_TYPE
/
DROP TABLE ATMOSPHERIC_EVENT_LIST
/
DROP TYPE ATMOSEVENT
```

```
/
DROP TABLE SCIENTIST_LIST
/
DROP TYPE SCIENTIST
/
DROP TABLE PLATFORM_TYPE_LIST
/
DROP TYPE PLATFORM_TYPE
/
CREATE TYPE PLATFORM_TYPE AS OBJECT(
key_id        NUMBER(8),
type          VARCHAR2(50),
description  VARCHAR2(50))
/
CREATE TABLE PLATFORM_TYPE_LIST OF PLATFORM_TYPE
/
CREATE TYPE SCIENTIST AS OBJECT(
usr_id          NUMBER(6),
lastname        VARCHAR2(20),
firstname       VARCHAR2(20),
platform_id     NUMBER,
for_platform    REF PLATFORM_TYPE)
/
CREATE TABLE SCIENTIST_LIST OF SCIENTIST
/
CREATE TYPE atmosevent AS OBJECT(
key_id          NUMBER(8),
when_t          DATE,
name            VARCHAR2(30),
type            VARCHAR2(20),
refkey          NUMBER(8),
transformed_to  REF atmosevent)
/
CREATE TABLE atmosevent_list OF atmosevent
/
CREATE TYPE oceanic_observation AS OBJECT(
latitude_deg          NUMBER(10,4),
longitude_deg         NUMBER(10,4),
windspeed_mps         NUMBER(10,4),
adj_windspeed_mps     NUMBER(10,4),
wind_direction_deg    NUMBER(6),
pressure_mb           NUMBER(6))
/
CREATE OR REPLACE TYPE oceanic_observation_type AS OBJECT(
obs_id          NUMBER(8),
when_t          DATE,
at_time         CHAR(8),
station_id      NUMBER(6),
produced_id     NUMBER(8),
```

```
produced_by          REF PLATFORM_TYPE,
obsobj               oceanic_observation)
/
ALTER TYPE oceanic_observation_type REPLACE AS OBJECT (
obs_id               NUMBER(8),
when_t               DATE,
at_time              CHAR(8),
station_id           NUMBER(6),
produced_id          NUMBER(8),
produced_by          REF PLATFORM_TYPE,
obsobj               oceanic_observation,
    member function get_platform_type
      return platform_type,
    pragma restrict_references( get_platform_type, wnds, wnps ) );
/CREATE OR REPLACE TYPE BODY oceanic_observation_type IS
  member function get_platform_type RETURN PLATFORM_TYPE IS
    pt platform_type;
  begin
    -- Select the PLATFORM_TYPE_LIST record whose OID matches the OID
    --   in the produced_by field of the oceanic_observation_type instance.
    --
    -- VALUE(pt1) returns the object type record from the
    --   table.  * wildcard or list of platform_type fields
    --   would be incompatible with pt variable.
    --
    SELECT VALUE(ptl ) INTO pt FROM PLATFORM_TYPE_LIST ptl
      WHERE REF( ptl ) = produced_by;
    return pt;
  end;
end;
/
-- List of all oceanic observations by date, time, and platform type
CREATE TABLE OCEANIC_OBSERVATION_LIST OF OCEANIC_OBSERVATION_TYPE
/
— use qc_id_seq to update QUALITY_CONTROL_EVENT qc_id
CREATE TYPE QUALITY_CONTROL_EVENT AS OBJECT(
qc_id                NUMBER(8),
when_t               DATE,
at_time              CHAR(8),
event_id             NUMBER(8),
for_event            REF atmosevent,
whom_id              NUMBER(6),
by_whom              REF scientist)
/
CREATE TABLE QC_EVENT_LIST OF QUALITY_CONTROL_EVENT
/
CREATE TYPE PASSEDOBS AS OBJECT(
obsid         NUMBER(8),
passed        CHAR(1))
```

```
/
CREATE TYPE PASSEDOBSARRAY AS TABLE OF PASSEDOBS
/
CREATE TABLE PASSED_OBSERVATION_LIST(
passed_id       NUMBER(5),
qcid            NUMBER(8),
when_t          DATE,
at_time         CHAR(8),
idobj           passedObsArray)
NESTED TABLE idobj STORE AS pobsid_list
/
ALTER TABLE POBSID_LIST
STORAGE (MINEXTENTS 1 MAXEXTENTS 20)
/
```

Use the following to create constraints for the Observation schema:

```
-- File Name: objconstraints.sql
ALTER TABLE PLATFORM_TYPE_LIST
 ADD CONSTRAINT PT_KEY_ID_PK PRIMARY KEY(KEY_ID)
 USING INDEX TABLESPACE INDX
/
ALTER TABLE SCIENTIST_LIST
 ADD CONSTRAINT SL_USR_ID_PK PRIMARY KEY(USR_ID)
 USING INDEX TABLESPACE INDX
/
ALTER TABLE ATMOSEVENT_LIST
 ADD CONSTRAINT AL_KEY_ID_PK PRIMARY KEY(KEY_ID)
 USING INDEX TABLESPACE INDX
/
ALTER TABLE OCEANIC_OBSERVATION_LIST
 ADD CONSTRAINT O_OBS_ID_PK PRIMARY KEY(OBS_ID)
 USING INDEX TABLESPACE INDX
/
ALTER TABLE QC_EVENT_LIST
 ADD CONSTRAINT QC_ID_PK PRIMARY KEY(QC_ID)
 USING INDEX TABLESPACE INDX
/
ALTER TABLE QC_EVENT_LIST
 ADD CONSTRAINT qc_whom_id_fk
 FOREIGN KEY(whom_id)
 REFERENCES SCIENTIST_LIST(usr_id)
 ON DELETE CASCADE
/
ALTER TABLE PASSED_OBSERVATION_LIST
 ADD CONSTRAINT passed_id_pk PRIMARY KEY (passed_id)
 USING INDEX TABLESPACE INDX
/
```

```
ALTER TABLE PASSED_OBSERVATION_LIST
 ADD Constraint po_qc_id_fk
 FOREIGN KEY(qcid)
 REFERENCES QC_EVENT_LIST(qc_id)
 ON DELETE CASCADE
/
ALTER TABLE PASSED_OBSERVATION_LIST
ADD CONSTRAINT passed_qcid_ukey UNIQUE(qcid)
 USING INDEX TABLESPACE INDX
/
ALTER TABLE PASSED_OBSERVATION_LIST
 MODIFY (qcid NOT NULL)
/
```

Use the following to create sequences for the Observation schema:

```
-- File Name: objsequences.sql
-- key_id sequence for PLATFORM_TYPE
CREATE SEQUENCE PT_key_SEQ
 START WITH 1
 INCREMENT BY 1
/
-- usr_id sequence for SCIENTIST
CREATE SEQUENCE USERSEQ
 START WITH 1
 INCREMENT BY 1
/
-- key_id sequence for ATMOSEVENT
CREATE SEQUENCE atm_key_seq
 START WITH 1
 INCREMENT BY 1
/
CREATE SEQUENCE OBSID_SEQ
 START WITH 1
 INCREMENT BY 1
/
-- qc_id sequence for QUALITY_CONTROL_EVENT
CREATE SEQUENCE qc_id_seq
 START WITH 1
 INCREMENT BY 1
/
-- passed_id sequence for PASSED_OBSERVATION
CREATE SEQUENCE passed_id_seq
 START WITH 1
 INCREMENT BY 1
/
```

Conventions Used in This Book

This book uses the following conventions:

- Classes are set in Courier typeface.
  Example The standard Java class `Java.lang.*`

- Datatypes are set in Courier typeface.
  Example The `REF CURSOR` datatype

- Filenames and extensions are lowercase and are set in Courier typeface.
  Examples `.class` files; the `.ser` extension

- Functions and procedures are set in Courier typeface.
  Examples `InsertPurchaseOrder()`; a function `GetObsId()`

- SQL keywords are all capital letters and are set in Courier typeface.
  Examples `CREATE TABLE; INSERT; DELETE`

- Database table names are all capital letters and are set in Courier typeface.
  Example `PASSED_OBSERVATION`

- Java keywords in paragraphs are boldface and are set in Courier typeface.
  Example **`public`**

Providing Feedback to the Authors

The authors welcome your comments and suggestions on the quality and usefulness of this book. Your input is important to us. You can send comments to us via e-mail:

- Nirva Morisseau-Leroy at nmorisseauleroy@data-i.com

- Martin K. Solomon at marty@cse.fau.edu

- Gerald P. Momplaisir at gmomplaisir@data-i.com

Retrieving Examples Online

The schema scripts and program source code can be found on the CD-ROM, at www.data-i.com, and at http://www.osborne.com.

Disclaimer

The programs presented here are not intended for use in any inherently dangerous applications. It shall be the reader's responsibility to take all appropriate fail-safe, backup, redundancy, and other measures to ensure the safe use of such applications.

About the CD-ROM

The CD included with Oracle9i SQLJ Programming contains a number of code samples from the chapters of the book. These include the following:

Chapter 2: Learn how to write SQLJ programs that insert data into database tables and use SELECT statements to retrieve data from database tables. Also, learn about the SQLJ translation process, the structure of the sqlj command line, and how to use properties files (instead of the sqlj command line) to set translator options.

Chapter 3: Learn how to declare and use SQLJ named and positional iterators and code SQLJ executable statements: SQLJ DDL, SQLJ non-SELECT DML commands, SQLJ transaction control commands, SQLJ executable statements in anonymous PL/SQL blocks and stored procedure and function calls, SQLJ SELECT statements.

Chapter 4: Learn how to develop SQLJ Stored Programs and Triggers.

Chapter 5: Learn how to declare and use SQLJ ConnectionContext instances, use javax.sql.DataSource objects in SQLJ programs, and deploy SQLJ programs in the client (Java/SQLJ applets and Java/SQLJ applications), middle-tier, and in the Oracle database.

Chapter 6: Learn how to declare and use SQLJ ResultSetIterator, scrollable named, positional, and ScrollableResultSetIterator iterators. Also, learn how to code dynamic SQL in SQLJ statements.

Chapter 7: Learn how to use SQLJ stream classes, create multithreaded SQLJ programs, the interactions between SQLJ and JDBC, and subclassing of SQLJ iterators.

Chapter 8: Learn how to define Oracle*8i/9i* SQL user-defined object types and user-defined collection types, processing SQL object types and SQL collection types in Oracle*9i* SQLJ, and using SQLData in SQLJ programs.

Chapter 9: Learn how to design and develop a SQLJ component-based object, deploy a SQLJ component using the Java Remote Method Invocation (RMI), deploy an Enterprise JavaBeans component object using a SQLJ implementation, and deploy a CORBA component object using a SQLJ implementation.

Chapter 10: Learn about the support features of Oracle performance enhancements, develop efficient SQLJ programs that implement the Oracle performance enhancements, and tune SQL statements from SQLJ with the Oracle Optimizer. (Disabling the auto-commit mode, Row prefetch, Update batching, Statement caching, Column definitions, and Parameter size definitions.)

Chapter 11: Learn how to use Oracle JDeveloper to develop SQLJ programs.

Appendix B: Learn Java constructs to develop Java applications and applets that access an Oracle database.

Appendix C: Learn Java constructs to develop JDBC applications and applets that access an Oracle database.

Appendix D: This appendix gives you a summary of SQLJ. Go there to look up SQLJ syntax, refresh your memory on concepts that you learned in the different chapters of the book, or get an overview of the fundamentals of SQLJ.

PART

I

Basic Oracle9*i* SQLJ

CHAPTER
1

Introduction to
Oracle9i SQLJ

QLJ is a version of embedded SQL that is tightly integrated with the Java programming language, in which embedded SQL is used to invoke SQL statements within "host" general-purpose programming languages such as C, C++, Java, Ada, and COBOL. In an embedded SQL program, SQL statements appear as if they are directly supported as host program constructs. C and C++ can also invoke SQL statements through host language function calls via the open database connectivity (ODBC) interface. Similarly, Java programs can invoke SQL statements through the Java database connectivity (JDBC) method calls. However, as you shall see, such function call interfaces reside at a much lower level than the embedded SQL interfaces. The SQL statements in the traditional embedded SQL are passed as string arguments to functions instead of being directly coded within the host program.

The Oracle relational database management system (Oracle RDBMS) is an object-relational database that heavily emphasizes the Java programming language and the development of Internet/intranet database applications. One of the important features of Oracle8*i* and 9*i* is the full and efficient support of SQLJ. Starting with Oracle8*i* release 8.1.5 (April, 1999) and following up with Oracle8*i* release 8.1.6 (December, 1999), Oracle8*i* release 8.1.7 (July, 2000), and the upcoming release Oracle9*i* (early 2001), Oracle furnishes Java programmers with an end-to-end Java solution for creating, deploying, and managing Java applications.

The Oracle solution consists of client-side and server-side programming interfaces and a Java virtual machine integrated with the Oracle8*i* and 9*i* database servers. More importantly, Oracle provides several tools for building Java-based components that can reside anywhere on a network (client-side components) and others (server-side components) that can reside inside application or database servers. All of these products are 100 percent compatible with Java standards. As with Oracle8, Oracle8*i* and 9*i* not only provide powerful support for relational database processing, but also support such object-relational structures as collection types, user-defined types, and object types. In Chapter 8, you will learn about object-relational processing using SQLJ.

SQLJ consists of a set of syntax and programmatic extensions that define the interaction between SQL and Java. The term *SQLJ* refers to a series of specifications for ways to embed SQL in the Java programming language. In 1999, SQLJ was defined as static embedded SQL for the Java programming language; in other words, a SQLJ program is a Java program containing static embedded SQL statements. Notice that in static embedded SQL, all the SQL statements embedded in the program are known at compile time, while in dynamic (embedded) SQL at least some SQL statements are not completely known until run time.

Prior to Oracle9*i* release, SQLJ complemented the JDBC dynamic embedded SQL model with a static embedded SQL model. JDBC provided (and does up to today) a dynamic SQL interface for Java, whereas SQLJ provided a static embedded SQL interface. Thus, with the availability of SQLJ, Java programmers had two different programming interfaces between Java and SQL: JDBC and SQLJ. With the upcoming release of Oracle9*i*, Oracle SQLJ will provide static and dynamic embedded SQL access for Java. Consequently, application developers can use one single interface between Java and SQL: SQLJ.

Programming languages such as C, C++, FORTRAN, COBOL, and Ada share essentially the same embedded SQL, whereas SQLJ has been specified for Java as a somewhat different embedded SQL standard by the ANSI (part 10 of the ANSI Standard: X3.135.10-1998) standards organization and also by ISO: (ISO/IEC 9075-10:2000). This raises the question of why Java has its own embedded SQL, while all the other programming languages share essentially the same embedded SQL. One reason is that SQLJ is more tightly coupled to Java than in other programming languages. In particular, Java classes can be used as the types for the columns in SQL tables. Also, SQLJ provides a strongly typed version of the cursor construct, called an *iterator*. This iterator construct is nicely integrated into the Java language, where an iterator is represented by a Java class. Note also that, like embedded SQL for the other programming languages, Oracle9*i* SQLJ permits both static and dynamic SQL constructs.

In this chapter, which provides an overview of SQLJ in the Oracle8*i* and Oracle9*i* environments, you will learn the following:

- The relation of the Java language to database processing on the Internet.

- The tight integration of Java and the Oracle8*i* and Oracle9*i* database servers (Oracle Java VM, formerly called Oracle JServer). Note that throughout the book, Oracle Java VM and Oracle JServer JVM will be used interchangeably, and both terms will refer to the JVM embedded in the Oracle database server.

- The static and dynamic embedded SQL model for Java: SQLJ. Note that the static embedded SQL model applies to Oracle8*i* releases 8.1.5, 8.1.6, and 8.1.7 Also note that 8.1.5, 8.1.6, and 8.1.7 are called Oracle 8*i* release 1, Oracle 8*i* release 2, and Oracle 8*i* release 3, respectively, whereas the embedded SQL model that applies to Oracle9*i* includes both static and dynamic embodiment of SQL in the Java programming language.

- The deployment of SQLJ in thick and thin client-side and server-side applications.

- How SQLJ compares to other embedded SQL languages such as Pro*C and PL/SQL.

Relation of the Java Language to Database Processing on the Internet

Java is a modern object-oriented programming language that borrows heavily from the syntax and semantics of the C and C++ programming languages. Its initial popularity came from its capability for developing client-based applications and adding dynamic content to Web pages. Over the last several years, however, Java has matured from a programming language used to develop client-based programs, in particular Graphical User Interface (GUI) programs, to a platform for developing and deploying applications at all levels of an organization by distributing applications over networks using Internet/intranet capabilities (that is, enterprise applications).

Java facilitates the development of robust and portable programs. As with most modern programming languages, Java is object oriented from the ground up. This contributes to the robustness of applications developed in the language. Additionally, Java provides mechanisms that help developers produce robust code, including early (compile-time) checking, later dynamic (run-time) checking, and a pointer model that eliminates the possibility of overwriting memory and corrupting data. Some of Java's other features that contribute to robustness are automatic storage management (referred to as *garbage collection*) and type safety. Such features make Java ideal for server-side programming, in which a server crash can be quite costly in terms of time and money. Java defines both a language and a set of standard class libraries (Java packages) that ensure that applications can be constructed to run on any Java Virtual Machine (JVM). The JVM is an interpreter for Java; therefore, a program can be ported from one machine architecture to another with minimal change. The JVM is responsible for controlling the Java execution environment and obtaining resources from the computer hardware. Java programs are compiled into compact intermediate hardware-independent code (Java's bytecode). Also, the fact that Java is interpreted makes it easier for the system to perform run-time error checking, further enhancing the robustness of Java programs.

Traditional design and development strategies create *monolithic systems*. A monolithic system corresponds to a single application, running or executing on a single computer. Business and scientific applications are becoming far more complex than they have ever been. Therefore, their designers are turning to techniques such as distributed systems in response to the increased pressure to better manage and manipulate information. Java provides a platform and framework for developing and deploying applications for today's complex information systems. The Java language, with its component-based models, enables users to assemble, partition, and distribute application components across a network. Java's components consist of a set of platform-independent services, such as Remote Method Invocation (RMI), JavaBeans, and Enterprise JavaBeans (EJB). RMI is a standard Java facility that makes it possible to invoke Java methods remotely, whereas EJB is an architecture for developing transactional applications as distributed components in Java. See Chapter 9 for a tutorial on building RMI, EJB, and CORBA objects.

Java facilitates Internet/intranet development applications. Its virtual-machine–based organization defines a highly compact set of bytecodes, which can be efficiently transported in the Internet/intranet environment. Java offers the power to unify the infrastructure of today's computing environment, where mission-critical and industrial-strength servers are still heterogeneous. Distributed applications with components that need to communicate across multiple systems in a network can use Java to do so. Java supports many standard communication protocols, including TCP/IP (Transmission Control Protocol/Internet Protocol), HTTP (Hypertext Transfer Protocol), and IIOP (CORBA's Internet Inter-ORB Protocol).

Java applets, servlets, and applications are appearing all over the Web, bringing rich functionality to what before was a static medium. Leading hardware vendors, infrastructure providers, and software vendors provide support for building extensible applications across all tiers, as well as tools to Web enable existing client/server applications. Leading browser platforms are building Java Virtual Machines into their systems. Database vendors, such as Oracle and Informix, are integrating Java Virtual Machines with their data servers.

Tight Integration of Java and the Oracle9*i* Database Server

Prior to Oracle8*i*, Oracle application developers used PL/SQL to develop server-side applications that have tight integration with SQL data. PL/SQL is an Oracle RDBMS procedural language extension to SQL. The language integrates features such as exception handling, overloading, and a limited amount of information hiding (accomplished by declaring variables and types in a package body instead of a package specification). In addition to providing these capabilities, PL/SQL subprograms (procedures and functions) and triggers can be stored in the Oracle database server. A subprogram consists of a set of PL/SQL statements that are grouped together as a unit to perform a set of related tasks. They are created and stored in compiled form in the database. Additionally, application programmers can create PL/SQL *packages*. Packages provide a method of encapsulating and storing related procedures, functions, variables, and other packages constructed together as a unit in the data server. All objects are parsed, compiled, and loaded into memory once. Stored procedures and packages, because of their central location, can be called and executed by users and other database applications. These capabilities offer increased functionality, network traffic reduction, and application and system performance. See Appendix A for a tutorial on PL/SQL.

Since 1999, starting with the release of Oracle8*i*, the Oracle Relational Database Management System (RDBMS) supports two major programming languages: Java and PL/SQL. Embedded in the Oracle8*i* and Oracle9*i* database servers is the Oracle Java Virtual Machine (JVM). This JVM is a Java 2–compliant (Oracle8*i* release 8.1.6 and higher) Java execution environment and Java 1.1.*x* compliant in Oracle8*i* release 8.1.5. Beginning with the Oracle9*i* Internet Application server (4th quarter of 2000) or Oracle9*i* AS, Oracle supports Java in the middle tier. Oracle9*i* AS is a scalable, secure, middle-tier application server. It enables you to deliver Web content, host Web applications, connect to back-office applications, and access your data on wireless devices. Oracle9*i* AS is distributed with the Oracle release 8.1.7.

In the Oracle8*i* and Oracle9*i* database servers, both Java and PL/SQL languages seamlessly interoperate and complement each other. SQL and PL/SQL can call Java methods. A Java *stored procedure* is a program written in Java to execute in the Oracle Java VM. Java stored procedures can be called directly with products such as SQL*Plus or indirectly with a trigger and can be accessed from any Net8 client— OCI, PRO*, JDBC, or SQLJ. Java can also call SQL and PL/SQL, via either JDBC or SQLJ. Since the Oracle Java VM provides a fully compliant implementation of the Java programming language and Virtual Machine, Java developers can develop Java programs independent of PL/SQL.

Oracle JavaVM: Overview

Oracle8*i* was the first commercial database system to offer an integrated JVM. The Oracle8*i* and 9*i* JVMs are embedded in the Oracle RDBMS and include a Java Virtual Machine (JVM) and a Java execution environment. Since Java is an interpreted language (interpreted by the JVM), it faces a performance penalty when compared to languages like C or C++. A Java program can run very slowly, and this can be a real problem for Java applications. To address this problem, Oracle delivers the core Java classes, Aurora/ORB (Object Request Broker), and JDBC code in natively compiled form. Standard Java classes, such as `java.lang`, `java.io`, `java.net`, `java.math`, and `java.util`, exist in shared libraries. Thus, the developer's Java code, which is loaded in the Oracle JVM, is interpreted, while the standard classes on which this code relies are fully compiled.

The JVM is embedded in the Oracle data server with native compilation and optimization and is compatible with the Java standard. The Java Virtual Machine executes Java programs on the Oracle8*i* and 9*i* database servers. Java applets and applications can access the Oracle8*i* and Oracle9*i* via JDBC and/or SQLJ. The integration of the Java Virtual Machine in the data server expands Oracle's support for Java into all tiers of applications, allowing Java programs to be deployed in the client, server, or middle tier. Using Java, the Oracle8*i* or Oracle9*i* database server, and Oracle9*i* AS, Java programmers can build and deploy server-based Java applications shared by all clients. These applications can easily be distributed across networks, providing access to Oracle data from any computer that supports Java.

Java programmers can access relational and object-relational databases via JDBC. JDBC consists of two parts: the high-level API and multiple low-level drivers for connecting to different databases. The JDBC API is a standard Java interface for connecting to relational databases from Java. It specifies Java interfaces, classes, and exceptions to support database connections; SQL Database Manipulation Language (DML) and SQL Data Definition Language (DDL) statements; processing of data result sets; database metadata; and so on. The JDBC standard was defined by Sun Microsystems. In this scenario, all Java program components such as business logic, GUI (Graphical User Interface), and JDBC drivers reside on the client side (see Figure 1-1).

The Oracle Java VM is a standard, compatible Java environment that will execute any 100 percent pure Java program. It allows programmers to manipulate data with Java and SQLJ directly in the database. The Oracle Java VM supports Java and SQLJ logic in the form of stand-alone stored procedures, Enterprise JavaBeans (EJB) components, and CORBA components. Note that Java and/or SQLJ components can reside in the clients, in application servers (for example Oracle9*i* AS), or in the database server. Also note that the stored procedures and components that you develop are reusable at both client and server levels.

To ensure fast execution in the Oracle database, Java or SQLJ stored procedures have access to the same server-internal structures as SQL and incorporate low-level compilation and optimization, which enhance application performance. Furthermore, the Java stored procedures provide better performance, because they are compiled once and stored in bytecode form in the data server. Procedure calls from Oracle JVM are quick and efficient. Browser-based, middle-tier (that is, application server) Java or

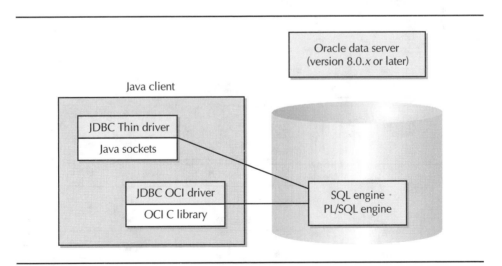

FIGURE 1-1.   *JDBC API to connect to database*

CORBA clients can communicate with server-side Java/SQLJ procedures and EJB components via an object-based protocol such as IIOP.

As explained in *Oracle9i Java Stored Procedures and Developer's Guide, the Oracle JVM* (shown in Figure 1-2) consists of

- ◼ Oracle's Aurora Java Virtual Machine, the supporting run-time environment, and Java class libraries (Oracle8*i* and 9*i* release)

- ◼ A tight integration with PL/SQL and Oracle RDBMS functionality (Oracle8*i* and 9*i* releases)

- ◼ An Object Request Broker (the Aurora/ORB) and Enterprise JavaBeans support. Oracle JVM comes with a built-in CORBA 2.0–compliant ORB

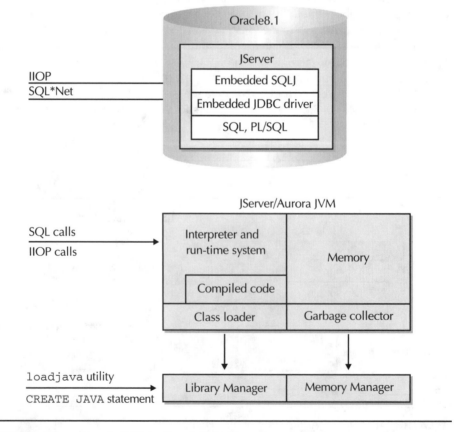

FIGURE 1-2. *Oracle JVM in Oracle8i/9i Data Server*

and support for EJB. The ORB and some of the CORBA services supplied with Oracle8*i* and Oracle9*i* JVM are based on VisiBroker for Java code licensed from Inprise. Programs developed in any language can communicate directly, via the Aurora/ORB, with the Oracle8*i* database through a version of the IIOP (Internet Inter-ORB Protocol) protocol, the standard wire protocol defined by the Object Management Group (OMG), a standardization group for object-oriented systems.

Main Components of the Oracle JVM

The Oracle Java Virtual Machine (JVM) of Oracle8*i* release 8.1.5 is a complete Java 1.1.8–compliant Java execution environment, whereas the Oracle8*i* releases 8.1.6 and 8.1.7 and Oracle9*i* are Java 2 compliant. Also notice "the Oracle JVM runs in the same process space and address space as the RDBMS kernel, sharing its memory heaps and directly accessing its relational data. This design optimizes memory use and increases throughput."

Some of the main components of the Oracle9*i* JVM:

■ **A Library Manager**   Used to store Java classes in the Oracle database. Oracle provides the command-line utility `loadjava` to load Java `.class` and `.java` files in the database. Application developers can use this tool to upload Java files in the database.

■ **A Memory Manager**   Uses memory allocation techniques, that is, automatic garbage collection, to tune object lifetimes.

■ **A standard Java 2 compiler**   In Oracle8*i* releases 8.1.6, 8.1.7, and Oracle9*i* only, and a Java 1.1.*x*-compliant compiler for Oracle8*i* release 8.1.5.

■ **A Java bytecode interpreter**   With its associated Java run-time system, it is provided to execute standard Java class files.

■ **A class loader**   Used to locate, load, and initialize Java classes stored in the database.

■ **A verifier**   Used to prevent the inadvertent use of Java class files.

■ **A server-side JDBC internal driver**   Complies fully with the Sun Microsystems JDBC specification. This driver is tightly integrated with the RDBMS; it supports Oracle-specific datatypes, NLS character sets, and stored procedures.

■ **A server-side SQLJ translator**   Enables application developers to embed SQL statements in Java programs. The SQLJ translator, highly optimized, runs directly inside the RDBMS, where it provides run-time access to Oracle data using the server-side internal JDBC driver.

■ **An Oracle JVM accelerator** A native-code compiler that speeds up the execution of Java programs by eliminating interpreter overhead. It translates standard Java class files into specialized C source files that are processed by a platform-dependent C compiler into shared libraries, which the Oracle JVM can load dynamically. The Oracle Accelerator is portable to all OS and hardware platforms. To speed up your applications, the Oracle JVM has natively compiled versions of the core Java class libraries, ORB, SQLJ translator, and JDBC drivers. Note that the core JDK classes and supplied Oracle classes that the programs use are natively compiled. Although the Java programs you load into the database are interpreted, they use natively compiled facilities. Note that the Oracle accelerator is available in Oracle8*i* database release 8.1.7 and in Oracle9*i*.

In addition to the Aurora JVM, the Oracle8*i* and Oracle9*i* Java programming environments consist of

■ **Java stored procedures and PL/SQL subprograms** You can call a Java stored procedure from a PL/SQL package; you can call PL/SQL procedures from a Java stored procedure.

■ **JDBC and SQLJ interface to access SQL** Java developers can use a combination of either JDBC or SQLJ, or both, to access SQL or simply SQLJ (Oracle9*i* only) for dynamic and static embodiment of SQL in Java.

■ **Object Request Broker (the Aurora/ORB)** Use this for distributed enterprise application development and Enterprise JavaBeans support.

■ **Dynamic HMTL** Use dynamic HTML to page through Servlets and JavaServer Pages (Oracle8*i* release 8.1.7. and Oracle9*i* only).

■ **Tools and scripts** These are used in assisting in development, class loading, and class management.

Oracle offers client-side and server-side programming interfaces to Java developers using JDBC and SQLJ (see Figure 1-3).

For client applications, Oracle provides two different JDBC drivers:

■ **JDBC Oracle Call Interface (JDBC OCI)** For developers writing client-server applications or Java-based middle-tier server

■ **JDBC Thin** For those writing pure Java applications and applets

For server-side applications running inside an Oracle database, Oracle provides two specialized versions of JDBC:

■ **JDBC Server-Side Thin Driver**   For Java programs that need to access a
remote Oracle server from an Oracle server acting as a middle tier.

■ **JDBC Server-Side Internal Driver (formerly, JDBC-KPRB)**   Supports any
Java code that runs inside an Oracle database—Java stored procedures,
Enterprise JavaBeans, or CORBA objects—that must access the same database.
This driver allows the Java Virtual Machine (JVM) to communicate directly
with the SQL engine. See Chapter 2 for SQLJ programs using Oracle
JDBC-OCI, JDBC-Thin, and JDBC-KPRB drivers.

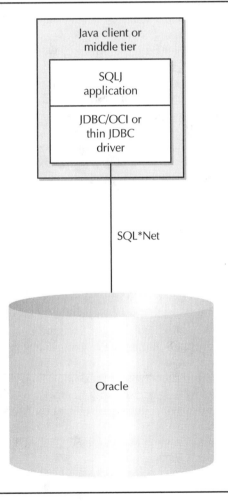

FIGURE 1-3.   *SQLJ and/or JDBC to access Oracle JVM*

Static and Dynamic Embedded SQL Model for Java: SQLJ

SQL is a relational database language that is used to operate on data stored as tables in relational and object-relational database systems. While the origins of the language date from IBM's SEQUEL, the official name is SQL (pronounced *S-Q-L*). The ANSI/ISO standard follows this usage. SQL is an industry standard, being the most widely used relational database language. In particular, the major RDBMSs, such as Oracle, Sybase, Informix, and Microsoft SQL Server, are all based on SQL.

SQL supports statements to set up the structure of the database (DDL statements) and statements to manipulate the database (DML statements). The CREATE TABLE and CREATE VIEW are examples of DDL statements, and the INSERT, DELETE, UPDATE, and SELECT statements are the principal DML statements. See Appendix A for a tutorial on SQL.

Embedded SQL is a method for combining the computing power of host languages such as Java, C/C++, FORTRAN, COBOL, and Ada with the database processing capabilities of SQL. The term "embedded" SQL literally refers to SQL statements being placed within an application program. Most SQL statements can be placed directly in the source code of application programs, preceded by identifying tokens such as EXEC SQL or #sql. Embedded SQL is supported by most RDBMSs.

Two types of embedded SQL programs exist: dynamic and static. You will learn these concepts next.

Dynamic SQL

Unlike static embedded SQL programs, dynamic SQL programs involve the execution of at least some SQL statements that are not completely known until run time. Such dynamic SQL statements are not directly embedded in the source program. Instead, they are stored in character strings input into, or built by, the program at run time.

Dynamic SQL (see Figure 1-4) allows you to create general and flexible applications because the full text of the SQL statement does not have to be known at compile time. A dynamic SQL program can contain a SQL statement that operates on a table whose name is not known until run time. SQL statements can be built interactively with input from users having little or no knowledge of SQL.

Dynamic SQL programs can be used to implement such systems as general-purpose load utilities and query processing systems for users with no knowledge of SQL. In particular, stand-alone SQL systems, such as Oracle SQL*Plus, and vendor-supplied load utilities, such as Oracle SQL LOADER, are typically implemented as dynamic SQL programs.

Static Embedded SQL

In static embedded SQL programs, the SQL commands used by the application program are known at compile time. With static embedded SQL, all data definition information, such as table definitions referenced by the SQL statements, are known at compile time. Thus, the analysis and optimization of the static embedded SQL programs can be performed at compile time. Consequently, static embedded SQL programs show significant speed improvement over dynamic SQL programs, where both analysis and optimization must be performed at run time.

Overview of SQLJ

SQLJ is a new standard that has emerged as a result of a multivendor effort. The language specification is a joint specification supported by leading database-tool vendors and database vendors including IBM, Compaq/Tandem, JavaSoft, Oracle, Sybase, and Informix. At the very beginning of its conception, SQLJ provided support to embed static SQL in Java programs. Prior to Oracle9*i*, a "pure" SQLJ program was only static because all SQL statements were known at compile time.

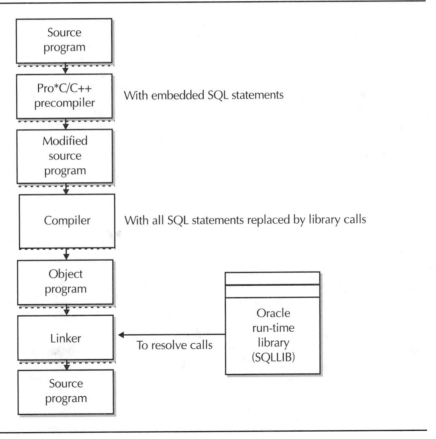

FIGURE I-4. *Dynamic embedded SQL using Oracle Pro*C tool*

However, with the upcoming release of Oracle9*i*, Oracle SQLJ will provide support for both static and dynamic embedded SQL. Additionally, SQLJ can be used to implement stored procedures, triggers, and classes within the Oracle JVM environment, as well as being used with Enterprise JavaBeans and CORBA.

SQLJ consists of a set of clauses that extend Java programs. SQLJ provides a way to develop applications, both on the client side and in the middle tier, that access databases and the data server using Java. SQLJ applications are portable and can communicate with databases from multiple vendors using standard JDBC drivers.

When writing a SQLJ program (source code), you write a Java program and embed SQL statements in it following certain standard syntactic rules that govern how SQL statements can be embedded in Java source code. Then, you run a SQLJ translator to convert the SQLJ program into a standard Java program. An Oracle SQLJ translator is conceptually similar to other Oracle embedded SQL pre-compilers. A SQLJ translator performs the following tasks:

- Syntactic checking of the embedded SQL constructs

- Java and SQL data type checking

- Schema checking

At translation time, the SQLJ translator replaces the embedded SQLJ statements with calls to the SQLJ run-time library, which implements the SQL operations. The result of such a translation is a Java source program that can be compiled using any Java compiler. Once the Java source is compiled, the Java executables can be run against any database.

The SQLJ run-time environment consists of a thin (that is, one containing a small amount of code) SQLJ run-time library, which is implemented in pure Java, and which in turn calls a JDBC driver targeting the appropriate database.

A SQLJ program can be executed in many environments. You can write a SQLJ program that will execute on a "thin" client, such as a Web browser or a network computer, as a client application on a workstation or PC, as part of a middle-tier application, and as a server-side application. Because of this locational transparency, you can easily port SQLJ programs from location to location and from system to system. The diagram in Figure 1-5 shows how the SQLJ translator interacts with the Java compiler and run-time system to produce a SQLJ program.

JDBC is the primary API for universal access to a wide range of relational and object-relational databases. You will now turn your attention to the basic concepts of JDBC, since an understanding of those concepts is essential for you to develop Java database applications. See Appendix C to learn more about JDBC program development.

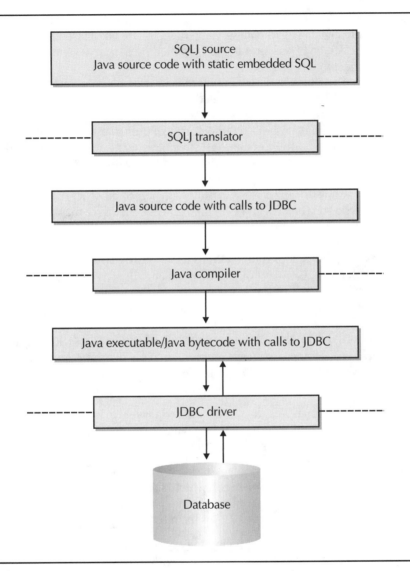

FIGURE 1-5.   *SQLJ interaction with Java compiler*

Basic JDBC Concepts

The JDBC API, whose specification was defined by JavaSoft, is a standard data access interface developed by Sun and its partners that incorporates Java technology.

It is a Java application programming interface, not vendor specific, that lets Java programs communicate with a data server. JDBC is made up of a set of Java interfaces that specify the API and of several drivers supplied by database vendors that let Java programs connect to a database.

The JDBC API defines Java classes that represent database connections, SQL statements, result sets, and database metadata. JDBC classes are modeled after ODBC structures. These classes provide standard features. These features include transaction management, queries, manipulation of precompiled statements with bind variables, calls to stored procedures, streaming access to long column data, access to the database dictionary, descriptions of cursors, and simultaneous connections to several databases.

Java applications that need to issue SQL statements and process the results use the Java API to do so. The Java API is implemented via a driver manager that can support multiple drivers connecting to different databases. JDBC drivers can either be entirely written in Java so that they can be downloaded as part of an applet, or they can be implemented using methods to bridge to existing database access libraries. For example, Oracle provides two sets of JDBC drivers: JDBC-Thin for Java applets and JDBC-OCI for Java applications.

JDBC drivers fit into one of four categories (see *A Brief Overview of JDBC* [1]):

- **JDBC-ODBC bridge** Provides JDBC access via most ODBC drivers. This driver is most appropriate on a corporate network or for application server code written in Java in a three-tier architecture. ODBC binary code must be loaded on each client machine that uses this driver.

- **Native-API, part-Java, technology-based driver** Converts JDBC calls into calls on the client API for DBMS such as Oracle, Sybase, and DB2. This style of driver requires that some binary code be loaded on each client machine.

- **Native-API, all-Java, technology-based driver** Translates JDBC calls into a DBMS-independent net protocol, which is then translated to a DBMS protocol by a server. This net server middleware is able to connect all of its Java clients to many different databases. This is the most flexible JDBC driver.

- **Native-protocol, all-Java, technology-based driver** Converts JDBC calls into the network protocol used by the DBMS directly. Since many of these protocols are proprietary, the database vendors themselves will be the primary source for this style of driver. Several database vendors have these in progress.

Here is an example of a JDBC program (see Appendix C to learn more about JDBC programs):

```
import java.sql.*;
class OceanicObservation{

    public static void main(String[] args)
            throws SQLException {

        // Load the Oracle JDBC driver
        DriverManager.registerDriver(
                    new oracle.jdbc.driver.OracleDriver() );

        // Create an instance of the JDBC Connection class
        Connection conn;

        // Connect to the Oracle database using Oracle driver
        // Note that in Oracle9i and later the subprotocol is
        // oci and not oci8. However oci8 is supported for
        // backward compatibility.
        DriverManager.getConnection (
                "jdbc:oracle:oci8:@datai_com", "scott", "tiger");
        // Create a Statement
        Statement stmt = conn.createStatement ();

        // Select observation id from ObservationList table
        // and store the query result in a JDBC ResultSet
        ResultSet rset =
                stmt.executeQuery ("SELECT Obs_id
                                    FROM ObservationList");

        // Iterate the result
    }
}
```

Oracle provides two means by which Java database application developers can access relational and object-relational data servers: JDBC, as described previously, and SQLJ. A SQLJ program can contain both Java and SQLJ statements, as well as JDBC calls. Next, you will learn the basic concepts of SQLJ.

Basic SQLJ Concepts
SQLJ has two major components:

- **The SQLJ translator** A precompiler, written in pure Java, that developers run after creating SQLJ source code. The translator supports a programming syntax that allows you to embed SQL operations inside SQLJ statements. When invoked, the SQLJ translator produces a .java file and one or more SQLJ profiles that contain information about the SQL operations. SQLJ then automatically invokes a Java compiler to produce .class files from the .java file. Note that with Oracle9*i* SQLJ, the creation of profile files is optional—the new front-end setting -codegen=oracle generates direct calls to the Oracle JDBC driver, obviating the need for separate profile files.

■ **The SQLJ run-time library** This component is invoked automatically at run time. The SQLJ run-time library is written in pure Java. It implements the desired actions of the SQL operations and accesses the database using a JDBC driver. Unlike Oracle SQLJ, non-Oracle SQLJ does not require that a SQLJ run-time library use a JDBC driver to access the database. The Oracle SQLJ run-time library is a thin layer of pure Java code that runs above the JDBC driver (Figure 1-5, earlier in the chapter). An Oracle SQLJ translator translates the SQLJ source code and generates run-time classes that act as equivalent JDBC classes providing special SQLJ functionality.

An additional SQLJ component is the *customizer.* SQLJ automatically invokes a customizer to tailor your SQLJ profiles for a particular database implementation and any vendor-specific features and data types. Oracle SQLJ uses the Oracle customizer for applications that use Oracle-specific features.

A SQLJ *profile* is a set of entries, in which each entry maps to one and only one SQL operation. Each entry specifies a corresponding SQL operation describing each of the parameters used in executing this instruction. A profile implements the embedded SQL operations in the SQLJ executable statements. SQLJ profiles are not produced if there are no SQLJ executable statements in the SQLJ source code.

A SQLJ translator generates a profile for each *connection context* class in the application. A connection context class corresponds to a particular type of database schema to which your program connects. The SQLJ profiles are serialized Java objects. Profiles are vendor specific; therefore, they must be customized. By default, SQLJ profile filenames end in the .ser extension. Optionally, profiles can be converted to .class files instead of .ser files.

SQLJ-generated profile files feature binary portability and, therefore, are portable across platforms. Thus, a profile generated by a Java application developed on Oracle can be used as is with other kinds of databases or in other environments. For example, a profile compiled on NT against Oracle8*i* may be moved to DB2 for OS/390, *customized* and bound into a DB2 package or plan with limited modification of any source code.

This is true of generated .class files as well. A note of caution: The standard SQLJ translator addresses only the SQL92 (late SQL89 or early SQL92) dialect of SQL, but allows vendors' extensions beyond that. For example, Oracle SQLJ supports Oracle's SQL dialect, which contains non-SQL92 constructs. Therefore, to assure that their programs are portable, developers should avoid using SQL syntax and SQL types that are not in the standard. Vendor-specific SQL types might not be supported in all environments.

Development Tools

Oracle JDeveloper, a Windows-based visual development environment for Java programming, can be used to develop Oracle SQLJ programs. JDeveloper invokes the translator, semantics checker, compiler, and customizer. A stand-alone SQLJ-to-Java translator can also process SQLJ. Since SQLJ runs on top of the JDBC API, a driver compliant with the database to be used must be installed in your system. The current version of SQLJ has been tested with the production release of Oracle JDBC drivers and the JDBC-ODBC available from JavaSoft. See Chapter 11 to learn more about Oracle development tools.

Basic Features of SQLJ Standard

Most SQL constructs can appear in SQLJ programs. In addition to SQL constructs, Oracle PL/SQL constructs can appear in Oracle SQLJ source code. Here is a partial list of these SQL and PL/SQL constructs:

- **SQL DML statements**   For example, SELECT, INSERT, UPDATE, and DELETE.

- **SQL transaction control statements**   For example, COMMIT and ROLLBACK.

- **SQL DDL statements**   For example, CREATE TABLE and DROP TABLE.

- **Calls to Oracle PL/SQL stored procedures, functions, and packages** Assume a procedure named InsertPurchaseOrder() and a function GetObsId() have been created and stored in an Oracle database.

  ```
  // Procedure call
  CALL InsertPurchaseOrder ( :newOrderNbr );
  VALUES ( GetObsId ( :obsId ) );  // Function call
  ```

- **Session directives**

   See Chapter 4 to learn more about SQLJ calling PL/SQL procedures and functions.

SQLJ Statements

SQLJ statements can be divided into two main categories: declarations and executable statements. Each SQLJ statement starts with the token #sql.

Declaration Statements   These statements are used for creating Java classes for iterators or connection contexts. A SQLJ *iterator* is similar to a JDBC result set. There are two types of SQLJ iterators: a *named* iterator and a *positional* iterator. *Connection contexts* (see Chapter 5) are used to establish database connections to different kinds of schema. A SQLJ declaration consists of the #sql token followed by the

declaration of a class. See Chapter 3 for additional information about
SQLJ declaration.

```
// syntax: Iterator declaration
#sql <modifier> iterator Iterator_ClassName ( type declarations );

// syntax: connection context declaration
#sql <modifier> context Context_ClassName;
```

Examples of SQLJ declaration statements are

```
// Use the SQLJ iterator called OceanObs to select data from
//a database table
// with corresponding observation id and platform type of matching
// names (obsId and fromPlatform ) and datatypes ( NUMBER and CHAR )

#sql public iterator OceanObs ( int obsId, String fromPlatform );

// Use the connection context DeclaredConnectionContext to connect to
// two different schemas residing on the same data server: localhost.
// As a result of this statement, SQLJ translator generates a public
// class DeclaredConnectionContext.

#sql public context DeclaredConnectionContext;
```

Executable Statements   These statements are used to execute embedded SQL
operations. The SQLJ clause is the executable part of a statement (everything to the
right of the #sql token).

```
// Syntax: For a statement with no output, like INSERT
#sql { SQL operation };

// Syntax: For a statement with output, like SELECT
#sql result = { SQL operation };
```

Examples of SQLJ connection context declaration are

```
// User defined connection context declaration

#sql context DeclaredConnectionContext;

// Create an instance of the following
// DeclaredConnectionContext class
```

```
// specifying an URL, username, password,
// and set the auto-commit flag.

DeclaredConnectionContext anInstanceCtx =
          new DeclaredConnectionContext
             ("jdbc:oracle:thin@localhost:1521:ORCL",
                "username", "userpassword", false);

// Instances of the DeclaredConnectionContext class can be used
// to create database connections to different schemas, in this
// case: observation and besttrack

DeclaredConnectionContext observationCtx =
          new DeclaredConnectionContext
        ("jdbc:oracle:thin@localhost:1521:ORCL", "observation",
               "obspassword", false);

DeclaredConnectionContext besttrackCtx =
       new DeclaredConnectionContext
        ("jdbc:oracle:thin@localhost:1521:ORCL",
            "besttrack", "bestpassword", false);

// Explicit association of an instance of the
// connection context class, DeclaredConnectionContext
// class, with a SQLJ executable statement.

#sql [besttrackCtx] result = { SQL operation };
```

See Chapter 5 to learn more about associating an instance of a SQLJ connection context class in an executable statement.

Java Host Variables

SQLJ uses Java host expressions to pass arguments between Java source code and SQL operations. Host expressions are interspersed within the embedded SQL operations in SQLJ source code. A host expression can be any valid Java expression. A host variable is always preceded by a colon. Host expressions can represent any of the following:

- Local variables. Some host examples:
  ```
  :hostvariable, :INOUT hostvariable,
  :IN (hostvariable1+hostvariable2),
  :(hostvariable1*hostvariable2),
  :(index--), and so on
  ```
- Declared parameters

- Class attributes (such as `QualityControlActions.onOceanicObs`)
- Static or instance method calls
- Array elements

Examples of local host variables:

```
// Java variable declaration
int obsId = 11111;
String fromPlatform = "AIRCRAFT";
...


// SQLJ executable statement using host
// variables obsId and fromPlatform
#sql {UPDATE OceanicObservationList
          SET platformtype =
            :fromPlatform WHERE obs_id = :obsId};

// SQLJ executable statement calling a
// stored function and using host variables
#sql {UPDATE OceanicObservationList
          SET platform_id = :(getPlatformId (fromPlatform))
      WHERE obs_id = :obsId};

// SQLJ executable statement using many types of expressions
/*
Syntax: #sql [connctxt_exp, execctxt_exp] result_exp =
                  { SQL with host expression };
*/


// SQLJ executable statements setting host variables
/*
Syntax:
#sql { SET :hostvariable = expression };
*/

// Declare a Java array of type integer
int[] generatedObsId = new int[30];

// Declare two variables: indexCtr and idNo
int idNo = 1000;
int indexCtr = 1;

// Use SQLJ statement to fill the array called generatedObsId.
// The use of the "++" suffix attached to indexCtr
// variable increments the value of this variable by 1.
// In the expression, :( idNo + indexCtr),
```

```
// the content of idNo is added to the content
// of indexCtr and the resulting value is assigned to
// the array cell indicated by indexCtr++.

#sql { SET :( generatedObsId [indexCtr++] ) = :( idNo + indexCtr) };
```

Oracle PL/SQL Blocks in SQLJ Executable Statements

PL/SQL blocks can be used within the curly braces of a SQLJ executable statement just as SQL operations can. Using PL/SQL in your SQLJ code would prevent portability to other platforms because PL/SQL is Oracle specific.

```
/*
Syntax:
#sql { <DECLARE>  … > BEGIN  …  END; };
*/


// SQLJ executable statement setting host variables using PL/SQL block
#sql {
    BEGIN
        SET :( generatedObsId[indexCtr++] ) := :(idNo + indexCtr);
    END;
    };


// SQLJ executable statement using an Oracle anonymous PL/SQL block
// to create observation ids in the OceanicObservationList table
#sql {
    DECLARE
       incrementNo  NUMBER;
    BEGIN
       incrementNo := 1;
       WHILE incrementNo <= 100 LOOP
            INSERT INTO OceanicObservationList(obs_id)
                 VALUES (2000 + incrementNo);
              incrementNo := incrementNo + 1;
       END LOOP;
    END;
    };
```

SQLJ Statement for Single-Row Query Results

SQLJ allows you to assign selected items directly to Java host expressions inside SQL syntax. This is done by using the SELECT INTO statement. The syntax is as follows:

```
/*
Syntax:
#sql { SELECT expression1,..., expressionN INTO
           :host_exp1,...,  :host_expN
```

```
            FROM datasource <optional clauses> };
*/
// SQLJ statement using SELECT .. INTO to select a single
// row from OceanicObservationList
String platformName = null;
String platformDescription = null;

// SQLJ executable statement
#sql { SELECT platform_name, platform_description
        INTO :platformName, :platformDescription
        FROM OceanicObservationList
        WHERE obs_id = 1111
    };
```

SQLJ Statement for Multiple-Row Query Results Using the SQLJ Iterator

A SQLJ iterator is a strongly typed version of a JDBC result set and is associated with an underlying database cursor (see Appendix A for a brief explanation of cursors). SQLJ iterators are used first and foremost to take query results from a SELECT statement.

```
/* Syntax for a named iterator:
#sql iterator IteratorName ( type declaration );  */

// Declare an iterator
#sql iterator OceanicObs ( int obsId, float lat,
                           float lon, String obsTime);

// Executable code
class ObservationQueryManager {
    ...
    void GetOceanicObservation () throws SQLException {
        // Declare a variable
        String platformType = "MOORED_BUOY";
        // Declare an iterator oceanicObs of type OceanicObs
        // and initialize it
        OceanicObs oceanicObs = null;
        #sql oceanicObs =
            { SELECT O.obs_id AS obsId,
               O.latitude AS lat, O.longitude AS lon,
                            O.obs_time AS obstime
              FROM OceanicObservationList O
              WHERE O.platform_type = :platformType
            };
        ...
    }
```

```
}

/* Syntax for a positional iterator:
#sql <modifier> iterator Iterator_ClassName ( type declarations ); */

// Declare a positional iterator.  Data items in the table
// must be in the same order as the iterator
#sql iterator OceanicObs ( int, float, float, String);

// Executable code
class ObservationQueryManager {
    …
    …
    void GetOceanicObservation () throws SQLException {

        // Declare a variable
        String platformType = "MOORED_BUOY";

        // Declare an iterator oceanicObs of type OceanicObs
        // and initialize it
        OceanicObs oceanicObs = null;

        // Execute the query and store the result in
        // the SQLJ oceanicObs iterator.
        #sql oceanicObs =
            { SELECT O.obs_id, O.latitude,
                    O.longitude, O.obs_time
              FROM OceanicObservationList O
              WHERE O.platform_type = :platformType
            };
        …
    }
}
```

SQLJ Statement Calling Stored Procedures

SQLJ provides syntax for calling stored procedures and stored functions in the
database. These procedures and functions can be written in Java, SQLJ, PL/SQL
(Oracle RDBMS database only), or any other language supported by the database.

```
/*  Syntax to call Java, SQLJ, PL/SQL procedure:
#sql { CALL PROC1 ( <parameter list> ) };  */



/* Syntax to call a PL/SQL function:
#sql result = { VALUES ( FUNC1 ( <parameter list> ) ) };  */
```

SQLJ Iterator as Stored Function Return: Oracle REF CURSOR

The Oracle SQLJ translator allows the use of a SQLJ iterator as a return type for a stored function, using a REF CURSOR type in the process. The REF CURSOR datatype is a PL/SQL cursor variable, a pointer similar to a C/C++ pointer. See the *PL/SQL User's Guide and Reference* [40] to learn more about PL/SQL cursors.

NOTE
In Oracle9i and later, Java Stored Procedures can also return REF CURSORs. Prior to that, only PL/SQL stored procedures and PL/SQL blocks could return a REF CURSOR.

Assume that a PL/SQL package, named QualityControlQueries, has been stored in the Oracle database. Note that exception handling has been removed from the package for the sake of clarity.

```
CREATE OR REPLACE PACKAGE QualityControlQueries AS
    TYPE observationtype IS REF CURSOR;
    FUNCTION getObservations ( p_date VARCHAR2 )
    RETURN observationtype;
END QualityCOntrolQueries;

CREATE OR REPLACE PACKAGE BODY QualityControlQueries AS
    FUNCTION getobservations ( p_date VARCHAR2 )
    RETURN observationtype IS
        v_date DATE := TO_CHAR(p_date,'MM-DD-YYYY');
        refcursor observationtype;
    BEGIN
        OPEN refcursor FOR SELECT O.obs_id, O.latitude,
                    O.longitude, O.obs_time
                    FROM OceanicObservationList O
                    WHERE O.when_t = v_date;
        RETURN refcursor;
    END getobservations;
END QualityControlQueries;
```

The following example uses a SQLJ iterator to call the function getobservations:

```
// SQLJ iterator declaration
#sql iterator Observations ( int obsId, float lat,
                             float lon, int obsTime );
...
Observations anObservation = null ;
```

```
...
// Get all observations for specific :aDate
#sql anObservation =
        { VALUES
          ( QualityControlQueries.getobservations ( :aDate ) )
        };
// Iterate to access each observation
while ( anObservation.next() ) {
        int obsno = anObservation.obsId();
        float latitude = anObservation.lat();
        float longitude = anObservation.lon();
        String obstimestamp = anObservation.obsTime();
}
anObservation.close();
...
```

Overview of Oracle and ISO Extensions to SQLJ ANSI Standard

In the "Basic Features of SQLJ Standard" section of this chapter, you learned some of the features of SQLJ constructs. Most of these constructs are defined in the SQLJ ANSI standard, which requires only JDK 1.1.*x*. Beginning with Oracle8i release 8.1.7, Oracle SQLJ supports the SQLJ ISO specification, a superset of the SQLJ ANSI standard, which requires a JDK 1.2 or later environment that complies with J2EE. The Oracle SQLJ translator (Oracle8*i* release 8.1.7 and Oracle9*i*) accepts a broader range of SQL syntax than the ANSI SQLJ standard specifies. We will present here a partial list of new features in the Oracle SQLJ since Oracle8*i* release 8.1.5. As you go through this book, you will develop SQLJ programs that implement these features.

New features from Oracle8*i* release 8.1.7 to Oracle9*i* release (early 2001) are

■ Embedding dynamic SQL source directly in SQLJ statements.

■ FETCH directly from "untyped" `ResultSetIterator`
`ScrollableResultSetIterator`.

■ Direct generation of Oracle JDBC code, for example, `-codegen=oracle`,
This means no more `.ser` files, no more profile customization, and no
need for `-ser2class`. This kind of support generates smaller, thus
faster, programs.

New features from Oracle8*i* release 8.1.5 to Oracle8*i* release 8.1.7
(Sept. 15, 1999):

■ JDBC 2.0 features as defined in the SQLJ ISO specification, such as

    ■ Connection context type maps for reading and writing user-defined
    types, such as instances of `java.sql.SQLData`. Note that this feature
    requires JDK 1.2 and the SQLJ file `runtime12.zip`.

- Scrollable named and positional iterators. The ISO standard for SQLJ has adopted support for scrollable iterators, which is patterned after the JDBC 2.0 specification for scrollable JDBC ResultSets. (See Chapter 6.)

- Association of connection contexts with DataSources. (See Chapter 5.)

- Control of batching and row prefetch through the ExecutionContext. (See Chapter 10.)

- Support for JDBC 2.0 connection pooling. (See Chapter 10.)

- Java object serialization in RAW and BLOB columns, using connection context type maps. (See Chapter 7.)

- "FETCH CURRENT FROM . . ." syntax for positional iterators. This feature allows you to preserve the program logic when migrating from java.sql.ResultSet objects to SQLJ iterators. (See Chapter 6.)

- Several different SQLJ run-time libraries, such as runtime11.zip and runtime12.zip, are applet enabled and optimized for use with the Oracle JDBC 8.1.7 and later drivers; runtime.zip provides compatibility with all Oracle JDBC drivers.

- Use of IMPLEMENTS clause in connection context declarations.

- Semantics checking of your connection context usage.

- Subclassing iterators. Oracle SQLJ provides the ability to subclass iterator classes. This feature is very useful, particularly if you wish to add functionality to your queries and query results. (See Chapter 7.)

- Type maps (Oracle-specific only, not part of ISO standard).

- Statement caching. By default, the SQLJ run-time caches the last five SQL statements that it executes on a given JDBC connection. You can use the -P-Cstmtcache=NN flag to set the statement cache size to NN. Setting the size to 0 disables statement caching. See Chapter 10 to learn more about statement caching.

- Update-batching (part of ISO standard). With Oracle update-batching, instead of the JDBC driver executing a prepared statement each time its executeUpdate() method is called, the driver adds the statement to a batch of accumulated execution requests. The driver will pass all the operations to the database for execution once the batch value is reached. The Oracle JDBC drivers use a caching mechanism to store temporarily sets of SQL operations. The number of SQL operations is based on the preset batch value. Once this value is reached, all SQL operations are sent to the database and processed in one trip. See Chapter 10 to learn how to write SQLJ programs that use the update batching features.

■ Data sources (Oracle specific only, not part of ISO standard). JDBC 2.0 extended API specifies the use of data sources, a standard way for creating objects for specifying databases or other resources to use. A data source is a portable alternative to the current mechanism offered by `java.sql.DriverManager` for obtaining JDBC connections. The data source functionality does not require your application to register the vendor-specific JDBC driver class name, and you can use logical names for URLs and other properties. Data sources can be bound to Java Naming and Directory Interface (JNDI) entities so that you can access databases via logical names. Note that JNDI is JDK1.2-compliant. See Chapter 5 to learn about JDBC data source and Chapter 9 to learn about JNDI.

■ Auto commit mode for `DataSource` connections.

■ Fetch limit (Oracle specific only, not part of ISO standard).

■ Oracle-specific features such as writing/reading serializable Java objects in `RAW` and `BLOB` columns and support for `FETCH CURRENT` functionality to permit use of movement commands with positional iterators.

■ Advanced transaction control. Oracle SQLJ supports the SQL `SET TRANSACTION` statement to specify the access mode and isolation level of any given transaction. Standard SQLJ supports `READ ONLY` and `READ WRITE` access mode settings, but Oracle JDBC does not support `READ ONLY`. (You can set permissions to have the same effect, however.) Supported settings for isolation level are `SERIALIZABLE`, `READ COMMITTED`, `READ UNCOMMITTED`, and `REPEATABLE READ`. Oracle SQL, however, does not support `READ UNCOMMITTED` or `REPEATABLE READ`.

SQLJ Versus JDBC

JDBC is a way to use dynamic SQL statements in Java programs. Java programs use JDBC to query and update tables, where details of the database object such as the column names, number of columns in the table, and table name are known only at run time.

Many applications do not need to construct SQL statements dynamically because the SQL statements they use are fixed and static. In these cases, SQLJ can be used to embed static SQL in Java programs. In static SQL, all of the SQL statements are complete or "textually evident" in the Java program. That is, details of the database object are known at compile time. SQLJ programs result in faster execution at run time than dynamic SQL and provide greater opportunity for certain optimizations.

Some of the advantages that SQLJ offers over coding directly in JDBC include the following:

- Since SQLJ programs require fewer lines of code than JDBC programs, they are easier to debug.

- SQLJ can perform syntactic and semantic checking on the code, using database connections at compile time. A SQLJ clause is associated with a connection type, which represents the kind of schema where that clause will be executed.

- SQLJ provides strong type checking (compatibility of Java and SQL expressions at translation time) of query results and other return parameters, while JDBC values are passed to and from SQL without having been checked at compile time.

- SQLJ provides a simplified way of processing SQL statements. Instead of having to write separate method calls to bind each input parameter and retrieve each select list item, you can write one SQL statement.

- SQLJ is at a higher level than JDBC. In particular, SQLJ comes closer to satisfying the dual mode of use principle (see *An Introduction to Database Systems, Sixth Ed.*), which asserts that embedded SQL statements should be the same as stand-alone SQL statements. In a SQLJ program, one can clearly see the SQL statements. They are not hidden in method calls as in JDBC.

SQLJ can be used to write multithreaded applications. The SQLJ run time supports multiple threads sharing the same connection context. However, SQLJ programs are subject to synchronization limitations imposed by the underlying JDBC driver implementation. If a JDBC driver mandates explicit synchronization of statements executed on the same JDBC connection, then a SQLJ program using that driver requires similar synchronization of SQL operations executed using the same connection context.

While connection contexts can be safely shared between threads, execution contexts should not be shared. If an execution context is shared, the results of a SQL operation performed by one thread will be visible in the other thread. If both threads are executing SQL operations, a race condition might occur in which the results of an execution in one thread are overwritten by the results of an execution in the next thread before the first thread has processed the original results. Furthermore, if a thread attempts to execute a SQL operation using an execution context that is currently being used to execute an operation in another thread, a run-time exception is raised. To avoid such problems, each thread should use a distinct execution context whenever a SQL operation is executed on a shared connection context.

See Chapter 2 to learn how to develop basic SQLJ programs, and see Chapters 3 and 6 to create complex SQLJ programs using the most advanced features of SQLJ.

Deployment of SQLJ in Thick and Thin Client-Side and Server-Side Applications

SQLJ code can run in several scenarios:

- Thin and thick client applications, from Java applets or Java applications.

- Server-side applications, that is, running the SQLJ translator in the data server. For example, Oracle8*i* JVM includes a SQLJ translator. Additionally, Oracle SQLJ can run against an Oracle Lite database.

See Chapter 5 to learn how to deploy SQLJ in client-side applets and applications (Java applications and applets, and SQLJ applications and applets), and server-side applications (Java and SQLJ applications).

Thick Client Applications

Most Java applets on the Web today fall into the fat (or thick) Java client category, as shown in Figure 1-6. In these implementations, all components live in the client with only the persistent domain data residing on the server. Web browser users know the pain of waiting for large Java applets to download across the Internet or an intranet. The size of Java applets can make or break the success of an application. In the fat clients, referred to as one- or two-tier applications, most, if not all, of the application or business logic is downloaded to the client and requires no server application to service client requests. The thick client includes all of each of the following:

- Graphical User Interface (GUI) widgets needed to present the application to the user

- Controllers needed to handle user input

- Application domain objects and logic

- JDBC classes to support the database access

- JDBC drivers (required protocols for Java programs to communicate with a database)

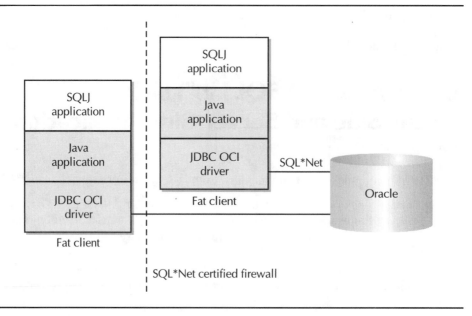

FIGURE 1-6.   *Thick SQLJ and Java clients*

Thin Client Applications

The thin-client computing concept is gaining importance. In the thin Java clients, the application must separate the presentation (GUI widgets) from the application logic. The thin client architecture, shown in Figure 1-7, distributes much of the design to the server, leaving as little code as possible on the client. These multiple-tier client/server designs limit the number of components on the client and move the application domain objects, the logic, the database objects, and the database drivers to the server. In this scenario, the Java thin client networked application results in faster Java applet downloads and less client RAM. Existing distributed protocols, such as RMI (Remote Method Invocation) and CORBA/IIOP, can be used in the thin client architecture to distribute the components across a network of machines.

Server-Side Applications

At the present time, server-side SQLJ applications, shown in Figure 1-8, can run on the Oracle8*i* and Oracle9*i* data servers. SQLJ code can run on the server in the form of stored procedures, stored functions, triggers, and methods (see Chapter 4), as well as Enterprise JavaBeans or CORBA objects. Server-side access is done via the Oracle

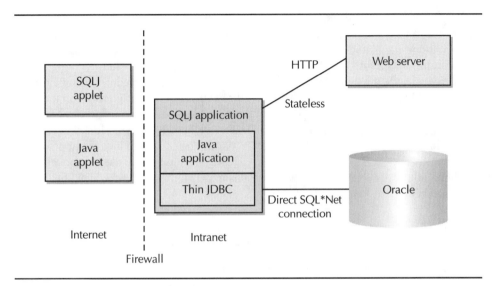

FIGURE 1-7. *Thin SQLJ client*

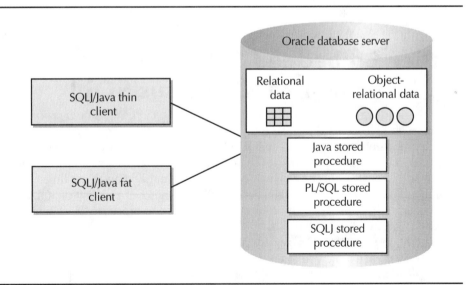

FIGURE 1-8. *SQLJ in Oracle8*i*/9*i* *data server*

JDBC server-side JDBC-KPRB driver. Oracle JVM includes an embedded SQLJ translator in the Oracle8i server so that SQLJ source files for server-side use can optionally be translated directly in the server. Loaded SQLJ source code on the server is translated and compiled by the server's embedded translator.

Server-side SQLJ source code can be translated and compiled on either a client or the Oracle server. Generated classes and resources from compilation on the client can then be loaded into the server. Client-side classes and resources can be pushed into the server via the Oracle `loadjava` utility. Server-side classes can be pulled from the server using SQL commands and SQLJ and Java client programs.

There is very little difference between coding for server-side use as opposed to client-side use. Some of the differences (as explained in *Oracle8i/9i SQLJ Developer's Guide Reference* are

- SQLJ client-side applications can establish many concurrent connections (see Chapter 5). Server-side applications only have one connection.

- The connection must be to the database in which the code is running.

- The connection is implicit (does not have to be explicitly initialized, unlike on a client).

- The connection cannot be closed—any attempt to close it will be ignored.

Additionally, the JDBC server-side driver does not support autocommit.

Other Embedded SQLs, such as PL/SQL and Pro*C, Versus SQLJ

Oracle PL/SQL is a procedural language that extends SQL. PL/SQL stored procedures, functions, and packages allow the application programmer to develop server-side applications using static embedded SQL. One of the advantages of static embedded SQL is that the SQL statements do not change from execution to execution. The full text of the SQL statements is known at compile time, rather than at run time. Additionally, PL/SQL allows developers to build and process a variety of SQL statements at run time. Application programs that need to process SQL statements on-the-fly can use PL/SQL to do so.

In addition to PL/SQL, Oracle also provides a set of programming tools called *precompilers* that enable you to embed dynamic SQL statements in programming languages such as C, C++, FORTRAN, COBOL, and so on. An Oracle precompiler allows you to embed SQL statements in a high-level source program. The precompiler accepts the source program as input, translates the embedded SQL statements into standard Oracle run-time library calls, and generates a modified source program that you can compile, link, and execute. Precompiling adds a step to the application development process, but it saves programmers time because the precompiler, not the programmer, translates the embedded SQL statements.

The programming tools, with the exception of PL/SQL stored procedures, can only be used in client or middle-tier database applications. SQLJ and Java are the only tools that offer the flexibility of building client-side and server-side applications. SQLJ provides a powerful way to develop both client-side and middle-tier applications that access databases from Java. Java developers can combine SQLJ programs with JDBC and use it in stored procedures, triggers, and methods within the Oracle JVM environment, as well as with EJB and CORBA. Today, leading database vendors deliver support for Java industry standards within their data server. For example, data servers, such as Oracle8i and Oracle9i JavaVMs, and Informix Dynamic Server include JDBC and SQLJ. These initiatives are part of the vendors' overall strategy of providing a Java product suite that enables customers to build Java enterprise applications.

CHAPTER
2

SQLJ Program Development

he purpose of this chapter is to give you the basic information you need to write, translate, and run simple SQLJ applications. You will use three SQLJ programs as vehicles for understanding the basic components of a SQLJ program and the basic steps in the SQLJ development process. In particular, you will

- Use a SQLJ program that loads a table from a data file to gain an understanding of how to connect to the database using a specific JDBC driver; how to execute a standard SQL statement (other than a SELECT statement) from a SQLJ program; and how to translate, compile, and run a SQLJ program.

- Use a SQLJ program that prints account information for accounts involving an input project to gain an understanding of how to execute a SELECT statement from a SQLJ program using a named iterator.

- Use a modification of the preceding SQLJ program to gain an understanding of SELECT statement processing in SQLJ using positional iterators.

- Learn about the SQLJ translation process.

- Learn about the structure of the sqlj command line, and how to use properties files (instead of the sqlj command line) to set translator options.

Executing Non-SELECT SQL Statements from a SQLJ Program

There are two types of SQLJ statements:

- SQLJ declarations that are used to declare connection context classes and iterator classes.

- SQLJ executable statements that are used to execute SQL statements, such as INSERT and DELETE statements, that do not return results and SQL statements, such as SELECT statements, that do return results.

In this section, after learning how to connect to a database, you will learn about SQLJ executable statements that do not return results. In particular, you will see a LoadAccountList program that contains such a SQLJ statement. In the sections of this chapter entitled "Executing SELECT Statements from a SQLJ Program Using

Named Iterators" and "Executing SELECT Statements in SQLJ Programs Using Positional Iterators," you will learn about iterator declarations and executing SELECT statements from SQLJ programs. In Chapter 5, you will learn about connection context declarations.

Connecting to a Database

Before a SQLJ program can do anything with a database, it must first connect to the database. Probably the easiest way to connect to a database is to use the connect() method of the oracle.sqlj.runtime.Oracle class. This method creates a DefaultContext instance and initializes it with a specified connection URL (which indicates JDBC driver and database), Oracle username, and Oracle password. SQLJ programs use either an instance of a user-declared connection context class or an instance of the sqlj.runtime.ref.DefaultContext class to establish a database connection. Note that the Oracle.connect() method initializes the static default context with an instance of the oracle.sqlj.runtime.Oracle class also. Additionally, the Oracle.connect() and Oracle.getConnection() methods register the Oracle JDBC driver automatically.

For programs that require only a single connection, it is best to use the DefaultContext class. The connect() method has several signatures, but the signature that uses a properties file to indicate connection URL, username, and password is the simplest to use.

In the subsequent LoadAccountList.sqlj program, Oracle.connect (getClass(),"connect.properties") passes two arguments: the Class object that describes the class LoadAccountList initiating the connection, which is returned by the getClass() method inherited from the Java Object class; and the name of the properties file that the program uses for the connection. Importantly, note that the relevant point here is not that the LoadAccountList class initiates the connection. The point is that the specified properties file is available on the CLASSPATH in the same package as the LoadAccountList class specified here. Note that getClass(), being a nonstatic method of the application class LoadAccountList, cannot be called directly from a static method of LoadAccountList. If the connect() method were invoked from a static method of LoadAccountList (such as main()), LoadAccountList.class would be used instead of getClass() to return the Class object for LoadAccountList:

```
Oracle.connect( LoadAccountList.class, "connect.properties" )
```

Another connect() signature allows you to explicitly pass connect information directly instead of using a properties file. For example, use the Oracle JDBC thin driver, host name, port number, username, and password as an input parameter to the `Oracle.connect()` method to establish a database connection:

```
// Use the Oracle JDBC thin driver
Oracle.connect
        ( "jdbc:oracle:thin:@data-i.com:1521:ORCL","scott","tiger" )
```

The first argument is the URL that identifies the JDBC driver, host machine, and database for the connection. The format of the URL depends on the JDBC driver that will read it. However, the Oracle JDBC `thin` and `oci` drivers expect the following format:

Listing 2-1

```
// Oracle JDBC thin format:
driver:@host:port:databaseSID
// for example:
jdbc:oracle:thin:@data-i.com:1521:ORCL

// Oracle JDBC oci format. Note the absence
// the port number and the Oracle SID
driver:@host
// For example:
jdbc:oracle:oci8:@data-i.com
```

NOTE
In Oracle9i and later, you can also say oci instead of saying oci8.

In Listing 2-1, the JDBC driver selected is the `jdbc:oracle:thin` driver, the host machine for the database is `data-i.com`, the SQL*Net server connection port is `1521`, and the SID (system identifier) of the database is `ORCL`. The last two arguments are the username `scott` and password `tiger` for the connection.

You can obtain a `connect.properties` file from your SQLJ demo directory (on UNIX, `[OracleHome]/sqlj/demo`, on PC Windows, `[OracleHome]\sqlj\demo`, where in either case `[OracleHome]` designates the Oracle home directory). You must then edit `connect.properties` to specify the correct URL, username, and password. The following `connect.properties` file has been edited to specify the URL for the JDBC Thin driver on the `data-i.com` system, as well as specifying the username `scott`, and the password `tiger`:

```
# The connection below uses the thin connection for
# the data-i.com server.

# Fill in the correct username and password for your login.
sqlj.url=jdbc:oracle:thin:@data-i.com:1521:ORCL
#sqlj.url=jdbc:oracle:oci8:@
```

```
#sqlj.url=jdbc:oracle:oci7:@

# Username and password here.
sqlj.user=scott
sqlj.password=tiger
```

Note that the original file contained commented lines (with #) for the three JDBC client-side drivers: JDBC Thin, JDBC OCI7 (for the Oracle7 call interface), and JDBC OCI8 (for the Oracle8 call interface). You uncomment and fill in the line for the appropriate driver (in our example, JDBC Thin), as well as filling in the appropriate username and password.

At this point, the role of the JDBC driver in SQLJ processing and the different types of Oracle9*i* JDBC drivers are discussed. First, observe that the SQLJ run-time (system) accesses a database using a JDBC driver, as does the SQLJ translator, when it checks the semantics of SQLJ statements against the database structures (you will see that the run-time JDBC driver and translator JDBC driver can be different). Thus, the JDBC driver is critical for SQLJ processing.

Oracle9*i* supports three types of drivers: JDBC Thin, JDBC OCI Fat (for Oracle7, Oracle8, and Oracle9*i*), and a server-side KPRB (Kernel PRogram Bundled calls) driver. JDBC Thin is a 100 percent Java implementation. It is perfect for downloadable applications, such as applets, and in fact is the required driver for coding SQLJ applets.

The JDBC OCI Fat drivers are somewhat faster than the JDBC Thin driver, since the OCI driver does a lot of its data processing in C (OCI is a call-level interface for invoking SQL from C programs). The JDBC OCI Fat driver is good for Java middle-tier applications, such as ones used with the Oracle9*i* Application Server (Oracle9*i* AS).

The JDBC KPRB server is used for server-side applications such as implementing triggers, stored procedures, user-defined type methods, Enterprise JavaBeans, and CORBA objects. See Chapters 4, 7, and 8 for presentations of server-side SQLJ applications.

SQLJ Executable Statements That Do Not Return Results

A SQLJ executable statement has the following syntax:

```
#sql { sqlj clause };
```

A `sqlj clause` can be an assignment clause—that is, a clause that *contains* a result expression because the clause delivers output (such as a clause that contains a `SELECT` statement)—or a statement clause that *does not* contain a result expression because it does not deliver output (such as a clause that contains an `INSERT` or `DELETE` statement). Assignment clauses are discussed in the section of this chapter entitled "Executing `SELECT` Statements from a SQLJ Program Using Named

Iterators," and are treated in more detail in Chapter 3. It is recommended that the SQLJ clause not terminate with a semicolon, but, of course, a semicolon is required after the right brace at the Java level.

A statement clause can be any SQL DDL or SQL transaction control command, and any SQL DML command except a SELECT statement, as well as other statements to be discussed in Chapter 3. These commands can contain host variables, just like in embedded SQL (see Appendix A).

```
#sql { INSERT INTO ACCOUNT_LIST VALUES
            ( :accountno, :projectno, :departmentno) };
```

is an example from the subsequent LoadAccountList.sqlj program of a SQLJ executable statement containing a statement clause. The row that is inserted into ACCOUNT_LIST gets its values from host variables—that is, from Java variables, in this case, fields from the LoadAccountList class. In general, a host variable can be any Java expression, that is, a Java declared parameter or a Java class field. Note that if the host variable/expression does not consist of a single identifier, it must be enclosed in parentheses (...).

A host variable in a SQLJ clause must be preceded by a colon, along with IN (optional-default), OUT (default in the INTO clause of the SELECT INTO statement), or INOUT, depending on whether the host variable is an input variable, or output variable, or both. The preceding INSERT statement could have been coded with IN explicitly specified:

```
#sql { INSERT INTO ACCOUNT_LIST VALUES
            ( :IN accountno, :IN projectno, :IN departmentno ) };
```

Note that a SQLJ clause does not terminate with a semicolon (;). Instead, the semicolon (;) follows the right brace (}) of the SQLJ executable statement.

SQLJ Load Program: LoadAccountList.sqlj

The following is a SQLJ program that inserts records into the ACCOUNT_LIST table from a data file called acct_data. The source file containing this program is named LoadAccountList.sqlj. All SQLJ source files must have the extension .sqlj, and the base names of such files must be the same as the public class contained in the file (in this application, LoadAccountList), if such a public class exists. If there is no public class in a source file, it is recommended that the base name of the source file be the same as the first class that is contained in the file. This recommendation stems from the way the server-side SQLJ/Javac compiler behaves.

The LoadAccountList class uses a user-defined Java class called TokSequence, which provides convenient methods for extracting ints, doubles, and Strings from an input line. Note that the Pro*C version of LoadAccountList can be found in Appendix A as load_acctlist.pc. There are two reasons why the SQLJ version is somewhat longer than the Pro*C version. First, the Java catch clause, which is used in the SQLJ program to trap SQL errors and file IO errors, takes more space than an if statement testing a variable (such as SQLCODE) or testing a value returned by a function (such as fopen). Also, the lack of direct support in Java for formatted input and the decomposition of the input into a stream of tokens forces you to implement these features yourself, using the Integer and Double wrapper classes and the StringTokenizer class.

```
/*
** Program Name:  TokSequence.java
**
** Purpose:  TokSequence.java contains the TokSequence class
**           for returning ints, doubles, and Strings from a
**           StringTokenizer object.
**
*/
/* java.util contains the StringTokenizer class, which supports
   the nextToken() method for sequentially extracting white space
   separated token strings from an input string.
*/
import java.util.*;

public class TokSequence {
  private StringTokenizer tk;
  /* TokSequence constructor initializes StringTokenizer field tk
     to StringTokenizer object for input string to be scanned.
  */
  public TokSequence( StringTokenizer tk1 ) {
    tk = tk1;
  }

  /* getInt() method extracts the next token from tk as a String,
     invokes the static Integer.valueOf() method to return an Integer
     object initialized to the integer represented by the token, and
     invokes the Integer.intValue() method on that Integer object to
     return the int value of the Integer object.
  */
  public int getInt() {
    int n = Integer.valueOf( tk.nextToken() ).intValue();
    return n;
  }

  // getDouble() method is similar to getInt(), but for doubles.
  public double getDouble() {
```

```
      double d = Double.valueOf( tk.nextToken() ).doubleValue();
      return d;
   }

   // getString() returns next token as String.
   public String getString() {
      return tk.nextToken();
   }
}

/*
** Program Name:  LoadAccountList.sqlj
**
** Purpose:  Load the ACCOUNT_LIST table from the text file acct_data.
**
*/
/* java.io contains FileReader class, for reading character files,
   and BufferedReader class that supports line-at-a-time input from
   character files.
*/
import java.io.*;

// java.util contains StringTokenizer class.
import java.util.*;

// Required SQLException class for SQL errors.
import java.sql.SQLException;

/* oracle.sqlj.runtime.Oracle class contains connect() method for
   connecting to database.
*/
import oracle.sqlj.runtime.Oracle;

// Define application class LoadAccountList.
class LoadAccountList {
   // BufferedReader class allows line-at-a-time input.
   private BufferedReader input;

   /* The following three fields hold input from data file record
      (that is, line).
   */
   private int accountno;
   private int projectno;
   private int departmentno;

   /* Initialize database connection and open data file within the
      constructor of the application class.
   */
```

```
public LoadAccountList() {
  connectDB();
  openFile();
}

public static void main( String args[] ) {
  /* Invoke LoadAccountList constructor to connect to database and
     open data file.
  */
  LoadAccountList maincode = new LoadAccountList();

  /* The runLoadAccountList() method executes the main body
     of code for the application.
  */
  maincode.runLoadAccountList();

  // You must close your oracle connection
  // to efficiently release all SQLJ and JDBC resources
  Oracle.close();
}

public void runLoadAccountList() {
  /* For each line of input in data file, read the line into String b,
     use the readRec() method to place accountno, projectno, and
     departmentno values into class fields, and insert row into
     ACCOUNT_LIST getting the row values from the class fields,
     and commit insert.
  */
  try {
    // (See Note 1.)
    for ( String b = input.readLine();
          b != null;
          b = input.readLine() ) {
      readRec(b);
      insertRow();
      commitInsert();
    }
  }

  // Catch any IO exceptions raised when reading file.
  catch( IOException e ) {
    System.err.println( "Error reading data file. \n" + e );
    closeFile();
    System.exit(1);
  }

  // Close data file.
  closeFile();
```

```
      System.out.println( "Program complete. \n" );
  }

// Method to connect to database.
private void connectDB() {
    try {
      Oracle.connect( getClass(), "connect.properties" );
    }

    // Catch SQL exceptions raised when connecting to database.
    catch( SQLException e ) {
      System.err.println( "Error connecting to database. \n" + e );
      System.exit(1);
    }
  }

// Method to open data file.
private void openFile() {
    try {
      // (See Note 2.)
      input = new BufferedReader( new FileReader( "acct_data" ) );
    }

    // Catch any IO exceptions raised when opening data file.
    catch( IOException e ) {
      System.err.println( "File not opened properly. \n" + e );
      System.exit(1);
    }
  }

/* Method to extract accountno, projectno, departmentno from input
   string, and place them in class fields.
*/
// (See Note 3.)
private void readRec( String line ) {
    StringTokenizer tk = new StringTokenizer( line );
    TokSequence g = new TokSequence( tk );
    accountno = g.getInt();
    projectno = g.getInt();
    departmentno = g.getInt();
  }

// Method to insert row into ACCOUNT_LIST table.
private void insertRow() {
    try {
      #sql {
            INSERT INTO ACCOUNT_LIST VALUES
              ( :accountno, :projectno, :departmentno )
          };
```

```
    }

    /* Catch SQL exceptions raised when inserting row into ACCOUNT_LIST
       table.
    */
    catch( SQLException e ) {
      System.err.println( accountno + projectno + departmentno +
                          " could not be inserted. \n" + e );
    }
  }

  // Method to commit insert.
  private void commitInsert() {
    try {
      #sql {
            COMMIT WORK
          };
    }

    // Catch SQL exceptions raised when committing insert.
    catch( SQLException e ) {
      System.err.println( "commit on " + accountno +
                          " failed. \n" + e );
    }
  }

  // Method to close data file.
  private void closeFile() {
    try {
      input.close();
    }

    // Catch IO exceptions raised when closing data file.
    catch( IOException e ) {
      System.err.println( "File not closed properly. \n" + e );
      System.exit(1);
    }
  }
}
```

Notes on `LoadAccountList.sqlj`:

1. The `readLine()` method of the `BufferedReader` class returns the next line of characters from the input file as a string, if such a line exists, and returns null otherwise.

2. The `BufferedReader` class implements a buffered character input stream as a filter. By a filter, it is meant that a `BufferedReader` object must be

composed with an already open input stream in our program. The acct_data file is opened through the `FileReader` object, and that object is specified as the argument to the `BufferedReader` constructor. The principal reason that `BufferedReader` is used in this program is that it provides the `readLine()` method for line-at-a-time input.

3. The `StringTokenizer` class is used to extract the accountnos, projectnos, and departmentnos as strings, from the input line, and convert them into `ints` (in C and C++ this would be accomplished through formatted input). The `StringTokenizer` constructor takes the input line as its argument, and successive calls to `nextToken()` from the `TokSequence.getInt()` method, and returns the desired `int` values of accountno, projectno, and departmentno.

NOTE
In real life, such a program should use the SQLJ update batching facility. To learn more about SQLJ update batching, see Chapter 9. As an excellent exercise, we recommend that you modify this sample program to take advantage of batching.

Translating and Executing the `LoadAccountList.sqlj` Program

In this section, you will learn how to translate and execute client-side SQLJ application programs manually. In Chapter 10, you will learn how to develop programs using the JDeveloper Integrated Development Environment (IDE). In Chapter 5, you will learn how to deploy compiled Java class files from applets and in the Oracle9*i* Server. Please note that in the subsequent discussion, it is assumed that the CLASSPATH environment variable has been set, indicating the directories in which .class files may be located. See Appendix D for information on setting CLASSPATH. Note that all the programs listed in the book are on the accompanying CD-ROM. For updated information and errata, go to http://www.data-i.com and http://www.osborne.com.

Of course, you must first enter **LoadAccountList.sqlj** and **TokSequence.java** using your favorite text editor.

As a first step in translating `LoadAccountList.sqlj`, you can compile `TokSequence.java` into a bytecode `TokSequence.class` file by entering

```
javac TokSequence.java
```

You can then translate `LoadAccountList.sqlj` into a Java source file by entering

```
sqlj LoadAccountList.sqlj
```

Another alternative is to use the SQLJ translator to compile both the SQLJ and Java source files:

```
sqlj TokSequence.java LoadAccountList.sqlj
```

If there are no errors in the SQLJ program, the SQLJ translation will generate a `LoadAccountList.java` file. By default, the SQLJ translator then sends this Java source file to a Java compiler, which translates this Java source file into a bytecode file, `LoadAccountList.class`. If you had set the `-compile` flag to false on the `sqlj` command line (see the section later in this chapter entitled "`sqlj` Command-Line Options and Properties Files"), you would have to manually compile the Java source file by entering

```
javac LoadAccountList.java
```

You next execute the main method in the `LoadAccountList` class by entering

```
java LoadAccountList
```

You can now check that the program worked by signing on to SQL*Plus and entering

```
SELECT * FROM ACCOUNT_LIST;
```

to see if the new rows were inserted.

In a subsequent section of this chapter, you will take a closer look at the SQLJ translation process; and in the section after that, you will consider the options available on the `sqlj` command line.

Executing `SELECT` Statements from a SQLJ Program Using Named Iterators

There are two types of declaration statements in SQLJ: strongly typed iterator class declarations and connection context declarations. Connection context declarations were briefly discussed in Chapter 1, and will be discussed in more detail in Chapter 5. A *strongly typed iterator* is a strongly typed version of the embedded SQL cursor (see Appendix A) and is used to receive `SELECT` statement output. There are two categories of strongly typed iterators, *named iterators* and *positional iterators*. The current section deals with the former, the next section with the latter. Oracle9*i* SQLJ also provides support for a weakly typed version of an iterator that is called a *result set iterator*, which does not require an iterator class declaration. You will learn about this kind of iterator in Chapter 3. You will also learn in Chapter 3 about scrollable named, positional, and result set iterators. Scrollable iterators provide more flexibility in the navigation through the set of rows that populates the iterator instance.

Named Iterator Processing

The following steps summarize named iterator processing:

- Use a SQLJ declaration to define the iterator class.

- Declare an instance of the iterator class.

- Populate the iterator instance with the output from a compatible `SELECT` statement in a SQLJ executable statement.

- Use the `next()` method of the iterator class to retrieve the next row from the iterator instance.

- Extract the column values from the current iterator row by using the iterator class accessor methods.

- Deactivate the iterator instance by invoking the `close()` iterator class method.

These steps are now considered in more detail.

Iterator Class Declarations

The first step in iterator processing is to define the iterator class in a SQLJ declaration. An iterator class declaration specifies a Java class that SQLJ constructs for you. The SQLJ translator replaces a SQLJ iterator declaration with a Java declaration for a class with the same name as the iterator. For example, in the subsequent SQLJ program, you will find the following iterator declaration:

```
#sql iterator DnoAno( int departmentno, int accountno );
```

A DnoAno iterator instance can be populated by any `SELECT` statement whose set of `SELECT` list elements (that is, the expressions that follow the keyword `SELECT`) is a subset of the set of DnoAno attributes. That is, a DnoAno instance can be populated by any `SELECT` statement whose `select_list` consists of the two columns `departmentno` and `accountno`. The criterion is that both the departmentno and the accountno columns exist in the select list. Additional columns are also permitted.

The SQLJ translator will translate the SQLJ DnoAno iterator declaration into a Java declaration for a Java class DnoAno. This DnoAno Java class will contain

- A next () method that retrieves data from the iterator row by row.

- Accessor methods departmentno () and accountno () that return the values of the departmentno and accountno columns in the row currently being processed.

- A close () method that deactivates the iterator instance.

A simplified syntax for a named iterator declaration (you will see the full syntax in Chapter 3) is

```
#sql iterator iteratorname( list_of_attribute_declarations ) ;
```

where an attribute_declaration consists of a Java type, followed by an attribute name, and the elements of the list are comma separated.

Under JDK 1.1.*x*, SQLJ declarations—that is, iterator declarations and connection context declarations—are restricted to appear at the top level of a compilation unit (with the import statements), at the class level (with the fields, methods, and nested classes of a class), and at the nested class level (with the fields, methods, and nested classes of a nested class). Thus, under JDK 1.1.*x*, SQLJ declarations cannot appear locally within a method. However, under JDK 1.2 or later, SQLJ declarations can appear locally within a method.

Iterator Instance Declarations

After declaring an iterator class, the next step is to declare an instance variable for that iterator class. The iterator class instance is the object that will be populated by (that is, will hold the output from) a SELECT statement that is consistent with the attributes in the iterator declaration. In the subsequent AcctsForProjs.sqlj program, you will find the declaration

```
DnoAno aDnoAno;
```

which declares aDnoAno as an instance variable for the DnoAno iterator class. Note that this iterator instance declaration is a Java declaration, not a SQLJ declaration. Thus, an iterator instance is a first-class Java object, which can be used in any way that any Java object can be used. For example, you can declare an array of iterators (you will see this in the next chapter) or, in fact, place an iterator in a data structure as complex as you like. Note that embedded SQL cursors are not first-class objects in the host language. Hence, SQLJ is superior to embedded SQL in this respect, suffering less of an impedance mismatch. See *An Introduction to Database Systems, Sixth Edition* for a discussion of the impedance mismatch problem.

Populating an Iterator Instance with Output from a SELECT Statement

Next, you will populate the iterator instance with the output from a compatible SELECT statement in a SQLJ executable statement:

```
#sql aDnoAno = { SELECT departmentno, accountno FROM ACCOUNT_LIST
                    WHERE projectno = :projectno };
```

aDnoAno is then thought of as containing the output rows from the SELECT statement that returns account numbers and department numbers from accounts involving the project whose project number is in the host variable projectno. More precisely, when this SQLJ statement is executed, a new DnoAno object will be allocated and populated with the output rows from the SELECT statement, and the aDnoAno variable will be set to reference this new DnoAno object.

The names and the data types of the columns selected must match the names and the data types of the iterator attributes (however, for named iterators, the position of the column in the select_list is irrelevant). Note that for named iterators, you can have more attributes in the iterator attribute_list than columns in the select_list. That is, you can have attributes "left over" (we do not have that situation in our example).

The syntax of a SQLJ statement that populates an iterator instance with a SELECT statement output is

```
#sql iterator_instance = { select_statement };
```

A SQLJ executable statement has this form:

```
#sql { sqlj_clause }
```

where a sqlj_clause has the form:

```
{ sql_operation }
```

or

```
result = { sql_operation }
```

The former type sqlj_clause is called a *statement clause*. The latter type sqlj_clause is called an *assignment clause*. Therefore, you populate an iterator

instance with SELECT statement output using an executable SQLJ statement
containing an assignment clause. The INSERT statement in the preceding program
LoadAccountList.sqlj was contained in a statement clause.

Retrieving Row and Column Values from the Iterator Instance and Closing the Iterator Instance

Now that the iterator class instance has been populated, you can use the next()
method of the iterator class to retrieve the next row from the iterator instance. The
row is conceptually held in the iterator instance, from which you extract the column
values using the iterator accessor methods. The next() method returns false when
there are no more rows to retrieve, and true otherwise. In the subsequent program,
AcctsForProjs.sqlj, you will extract the departmentno and accountno
values by invoking aDnoAno.departmentno() and aDnoAno.accountno().

Finally, you deactivate the iterator (releasing all iterator resources) by invoking
the iterator close() method—for example, aDnoAno.close().

A SQLJ Retrieval Program That Uses a Named Iterator: AcctsForProjs.sqlj

The following SQLJ program repeatedly reads a project number, and prints the department
numbers and account numbers for accounts involving that project. When the program
reads -1, instead of a valid project number, it terminates. A Pro*C version of this
program can be found in Appendix A as accts_for_projs.pc.

```
/*
** Program Name:   AcctsForProjs.sqlj
**
** Purpose:   Reading project numbers from standard input, one project
**            number per line, and printing the department numbers and
**            account numbers for accounts involving those projects.
**
*/
// java.io contains BufferedReader and InputStreamReader classes.
import java.io.*;

// java.util contains StringTokenizer class.
import java.util.*;

// Required SQLException class for SQL errors.
import java.sql.SQLException;

/* oracle.sqlj.runtime.Oracle class contains connect() method for
```

```
    connecting to database.
*/
import oracle.sqlj.runtime.Oracle;

/* Declare iterator class DnoAno to be consistent with the SELECT
   statement from which its instance will receive output.
*/
// (See Note 1.)
#sql iterator DnoAno( int departmentno, int accountno );

// Define application class AcctsForProjs.
class AcctsForProjs {
  // BufferedReader class allows line-at-a-time input.
  private BufferedReader input;

  /* aDnoAno is an iterator class instance that will receive output
     from the SELECT statement.  Note that aDnoAno is declared in a
     Java declaration, not in a SQLJ declaration.
  */
  private DnoAno aDnoAno;

  /* Initialize database connection and direct System.in to a
     BufferedReader stream within application class constructor.
  */
  public AcctsForProjs() {
    connectDB();
    openInput();
  }
  public static void main( String[] args ) {
    /* Invoke AcctsForProjs constructor to connect to database and
       direct System.in to a BufferedReader stream.
    */
    AcctsForProjs maincode = new AcctsForProjs();
    /* The runAcctsForProjs() method executes the main body of code
       for the application.
    */
    maincode.runAcctsForProjs();
  }
  private void runAcctsForProjs() {
    int accountno, departmentno, projectno;
    String line;

    /* Main loop of program.  In each iteration, prompt user for,
       and read from standard input, a project number (or -1 to
       terminate), select into aDnoAno account numbers and department
       numbers for accounts involving the input project number,
       retrieve rows from aDnoAno using next() method, and retrieve
       and print fields from each row using the iterator class DnoAno
       accessor methods.
```

```
*/
try {
  for ( ; ; ) {
    System.out.println( "Please enter a project number" +
                        " (enter a -1 to terminate) >> " );
    // Read input line.
    line = input.readLine();
    /* Invoke getProjectno() method to extract projectno from
       input line.
    */
    projectno = getProjectno( line );
    // If projectno = -1 terminate program.
    if ( projectno == -1 ) {
      System.out.println( "Bye" );
      System.exit(1);
    }

    /* Invoke select() method to populate aDnoAno with accountno's
       and departmentno's for accounts with the input projectno.
       If select() didn't detect problems with the SELECT
       statement, proceed with row processing of aDnoAno.
    */
    if ( select( projectno ) == 0 )
      /*  For each row retrieved into aDnoAno, use the accessor
          methods accountno() and departmentno() to print the
          accountno and departmentno in that row.
      */
      while ( aDnoAno.next() ) {
        System.out.println( "Account number = " +
          aDnoAno.accountno() + " Department number = " +
            aDnoAno.departmentno() );
      }
    /* Close aDnoAno so that it can be repopulated in next
       iteration of main loop.
    */
    closeIter( aDnoAno );
  }
}
/* Catch any IO exceptions raised when reading standard input
   with the readLine() method.
*/
catch( IOException e ) {
  System.err.println( "Error reading input. \n" + e );
  closeInput();
  System.exit(1);
}

// Catch any SQL exceptions raised when accessing aDnoAno.
catch( SQLException e ) {
```

```
      System.err.println
        ( "Error getting data from iterator. \n" + e );
      closeInput();
      System.exit(1);
    }
  }

/* Method to direct System.in to a character stream, and to direct
   that character stream to a BufferedReader stream.
*/
// (See Note 2.)
private void openInput() {
  input = new BufferedReader( new InputStreamReader( System.in ) );
}

/* Method to connect to database.  See the previous program
   LoadAccountList.sqlj.
*/
private void connectDB() {
  try {
    Oracle.connect( getClass(), "connect.properties" );
  }

  // Catch SQL exceptions raised when connecting to database.
  catch( SQLException e ) {
    System.err.println( "Error connecting to database. \n" + e );
    System.exit(1);
  }
}

/* Method to use the StringTokenizer class and TokSequence class
   from the previous LoadAccountList.sqlj example to extract projectno
   from input line.
*/
private int getProjectno( String line ) {
  StringTokenizer tk = new StringTokenizer( line );
  TokSequence g = new TokSequence( tk );
  return g.getInt();
}

/* Method to populate iterator class instance aDnoAno with output
   from SELECT statement.
*/
private int select( int projectno ) {
  try {

    /* The order of the fields in the SELECT list is irrelevant,
       since we are dealing with a named cursor.
    */
```

```
      #sql
        aDnoAno = { SELECT accountno, departmentno FROM ACCOUNT_LIST
                      WHERE projectno = :projectno
                  };
      return 0;
    }
    // Catch SQL exceptions raised when populating aDnoAno.
    catch( SQLException e ) {
      System.err.println( "Cannot execute SELECT statement. /n" + e );
      return -1;
    }
  }
  // Method to close aDnoAno.
  private void closeIter( DnoAno aDnoAno ) {
    try {
      aDnoAno.close();
    }
    // Catch SQL exceptions raised when closing aDnoAno.
    catch( SQLException e ) {
      System.err.println
        ( "Cannot close iterator. \n" + e.toString() );
      closeInput();
      System.exit(1);
    }
  }

  // Method to close buffered stream.
  private void closeInput() {
    try {
      input.close();
    }

    // Catch IO exceptions raised when closing buffered stream.
    catch( IOException e ) {
      System.err.println
        ( "Cannot close buffered stream. \n" + e.toString() );
      System.exit(1);
    }
  }
}
```

Notes for `AcctsForProjs.sqlj`:

1. If you are concerned that the SELECT statement will return NULL values
   for the departmentno column (the accountno column is NOT NULL
   because it is the primary key of the ACCOUNT_LIST table), you should
   declare the departmentno attribute of DnoAno as being of type
   Integer (the Java wrapper class) instead of int. If you do that,

aDnoAno.departmentno() will return NULL if the departmentno
column retrieved by the SELECT statement was NULL. However, if you
keep the int declaration, the SQLNullException will be raised when
you try to populate aDnoAno with a NULL departmentno column value.

2. It is desired to read System.in a line at a time. In order to accomplish
this, System.in (a byte stream) is directed to InputStreamReader, a
character stream, which is then directed to BufferedReader, a character
stream that provides line-at-a-time input.

Executing SELECT Statements in SQLJ Programs Using Positional Iterators

In this section, you will consider the differences between processing positional
iterators and processing named iterators, followed by a SQLJ program that illustrates
positional iterators.

Differences Between Named and Positional Iterators

The following summarizes the differences between processing positional iterators
and processing named iterators:

- The iterator class declaration is different. Since the correlation between the
  iterator attributes and a SELECT list is done by position, not by name, the
  names of the attributes are omitted from the positional iterator declarations,
  and only their types are listed. For example:

```
#sql iterator DnoAno2( int, int );
```

- Rows are retrieved from positional iterators using a SQLJ FETCH statement
  instead of the next() method. For example:

```
#sql { FETCH :aDnoAno2 INTO :accountno, :projectno };
```

This is similar to the fetching from embedded SQL cursors (see Appendix A).
However, note that the positional iterator instance aDnoAno2 is prefixed with a
colon (:) because an iterator instance is a Java variable, and is hence treated as
a host variable in the FETCH statement. Note that the FETCH statement does two
actions: move to the next row (if any) and populate the variables (if it was able to
move to a row).

■ Since, with positional iterators, you will fetch the column values into Java host variables, there is no need for iterator accessor methods. Note that the iterator attributes are matched up with the SELECT list columns by position, and the number of attributes must exactly match the number of SELECT list columns.

■ With positional iterators, end-of-data is tested using the boolean-valued endFetch() iterator method. Roughly speaking, endFetch() returns true if and only if there are no more rows to be fetched from the indicated iterator. More precisely, endFetch() returns true before any FETCH statements have been executed against the indicated iterator for the current SELECT statement, false once a row has been successfully fetched, and then true again after the last row has been fetched.

In general, named iterators are more flexible than positional iterators, since with named iterators you don't have to worry about the position of a host variable in a FETCH statement or a column in a SELECT list. Also, with named iterators, the number of iterator attributes must be greater than or equal to the number of SELECT list elements; but with positional iterators, they must be exactly equal. On the other hand, positional iterators are processed more like embedded SQL cursors, and so some developers may be more comfortable with the positional iterators.

A SQLJ Retrieval Program That Uses a Positional Iterator: AcctsForProjs2.sqlj

The following SQLJ program has been obtained by modifying the AcctsForProjs. sqlj program from the earlier section of this chapter entitled "A SQLJ Retrieval Program That Uses a Named Iterator: AcctsForProjs.sqlj," so that a positional iterator instead of a named iterator is used. Recall that the program repeatedly reads a project number, and prints the department numbers and account numbers for accounts involving that project. When a project reads –1 instead of a valid project number, it terminates. Observe that AcctsForProjs2.sqlj is very similar to AcctsForProjs.sqlj. The statements in AcctsForProjs2.sqlj that differ from the corresponding statements in AcctsForProjs.sqlj by more than identifier names are each displayed in bold.

```
/*
** Program Name:  AcctsForProjs2.sqlj
**
** Purpose:  Reading project numbers from standard input, one project
**           number per line, and printing the department numbers and
**           account numbers for accounts involving those projects.
**
```

```
*/
// java.io contains BufferedReader and InputStreamReader classes.
import java.io.*;

// java.util contains StringTokenizer class.
import java.util.*;

// Required SQLException class for SQL errors.
import java.sql.SQLException;

/* oracle.sqlj.runtime.Oracle class contains connect() method for
   connecting to database.
*/
import oracle.sqlj.runtime.Oracle;

/* Declare positional iterator class DnoAno2 to be consistent with
   the SELECT statement from which its instance will receive output.
*/
#sql iterator DnoAno2( int, int );

// Define application class AcctsForProjs2
class AcctsForProjs2 {

  // BufferedReader class allows line-at-a-time input.
  private BufferedReader input;

  /* aDnoAno2 is an iterator class instance that will receive output
     from the SELECT statement.  Note that aDnoAno2 is declared in a
     Java declaration, not in a SQLJ declaration.  Since DnoAno2 is
     a positional iterator, the DnoAno2 attributes and SELECT list
     columns will be matched up by position instead of by name.
  */
  private DnoAno2 aDnoAno2;

  /* Initialize database connection and direct System.in to a
     BufferedReader stream within application class constructor.
  */
  public AcctsForProjs2() {
    connectDB();
    openInput();
  }
  public static void main( String[] args ) {
    /* Invoke AcctsForProjs2 constructor to connect to database
       and direct System.in to a BufferedReader stream.
    */
    AcctsForProjs2 maincode = new AcctsForProjs2();

    /* The runAcctsForProjs2() method executes the main body of code
       for the application.
```

```
    */
    maincode.runAcctsForProjs2();
  }
private void runAcctsForProjs2() {
    /* Host variables, like accountno and departmentno, that will
       be fetched into must be initialized, since the Java code
       into which the SQLJ FETCH statement is translated will not
       necessarily initialize the host variables.
    */
    int accountno = 0, departmentno = 0, projectno;
    String line;

    /* Main loop of program.  In each iteration, prompt user for,
       and read from standard input, a project number (or -1 to
       terminate), select into aDnoAno2 account numbers and department
       numbers for accounts involving the input project number, fetch
       from iterator into host variables (break out of loop if no row
       was fetched), and print values of host variables if row was
       fetched.
    */
    try {
      for ( ; ; ) {
        System.out.println( "Please enter a project number" +
                            " (enter a -1 to terminate) >> " );
        // Read input line.
        line = input.readLine();
        /* Invoke getProjectno() method to extract projectno from
           input line.
        */
        projectno = getProjectno( line );
        // If projectno = -1 terminate program.
        if ( projectno == -1 ) {
          System.out.println( "Bye" );
          System.exit(1);
        }

        /* Invoke select() method to populate aDnoAno2 with
           accountno's and departmentno's for accounts with the
           input projectno.  If select() didn't detect problems
           with the SELECT statement, proceed with row processing
           of aDnoAno2.
        */
        if ( select( projectno ) == 0 )
          /*  Use FETCH statement instead of next() and accessor
              methods to extract row data from positional iterator.
          */
          for ( ; ; ) {
            #sql {
              FETCH :aDnoAno2 INTO :departmentno, :accountno
```

```
            };
        if ( aDnoAno2.endFetch() ) break;
        System.out.println( "Account number = " + accountno +
          " Department number = " + departmentno );
      }
          /* Close aDnoAno2 so that it can be repopulated in next
        iteration of main loop.
      */
      closeIter( aDnoAno2 );
    }
  }
  /* Catch any IO exceptions raised when reading standard input
     with the readLine() method.
  */
  catch( IOException e ) {
    System.err.println( "Error reading input. \n" + e );
    closeInput();
    System.exit(1);
  }

  // Catch any SQL exceptions raised when accessing aDnoAno2.
  catch( SQLException e ) {
    System.err.println
      ( "Error getting data from iterator. \n" + e );
    closeInput();
    System.exit(1);
  }
}
/* Method to direct System.in to a character stream, and to direct
   that character stream to a BufferedReader stream.
*/
private void openInput() {
  input = new BufferedReader( new InputStreamReader( System.in ) );
}

// Method to connect to database.
private void connectDB() {
  try {
    Oracle.connect( getClass(), "connect.properties" );
  }

  // Catch SQLExceptions raised while connecting to database.
  catch( SQLException e ) {
    System.err.println( "Error connecting to database. \n" + e );
    System.exit(1);
  }
}

  /* Method to use the StringTokenizer class and TokSequence class
```

```
      from the LoadAccountList.sqlj example to extract projectno
      from input line.
  */
  private int getProjectno( String line ) {
    StringTokenizer tk = new StringTokenizer( line );
    TokSequence g = new TokSequence( tk );
    return g.getInt();
  }

 /* Method to populate iterator class instance aDnoAno2 with output
   from SELECT statement.
*/
private int select( int projectno ) {
  try {
    /* Note that the order of the fields in the SELECT list must
       match the order of the host expressions in the subsequent
       fetch statement, and must provide type agreement by
       position with the declaration of the positional iterator
       class.
    */
    #sql
      aDnoAno2 = { SELECT departmentno, accountno FROM ACCOUNT_LIST
                  WHERE projectno = :projectno
                };
    return 0;
  }
  // Catch SQL exceptions raised when populating aDnoAno2.
  catch( SQLException e ) {
    System.err.println( "Cannot execute SELECT statement. /n" + e );
    return -1;
  }
}
// Method to close aDnoAno2.
private void closeIter( DnoAno2 aDnoAno2 ) {
  try {
    aDnoAno2.close();
  }
  // Catch SQL exceptions raised when closing aDnoAno2.
  catch( SQLException e ) {
    System.err.println
      ( "Cannot close iterator. \n" + e.toString() );
    closeInput();
    System.exit(1);
  }
}

// Method to close buffered stream.
private void closeInput() {
  try {
```

```
      input.close();
    }

    // Catch IO exceptions raised when closing buffered stream.
    catch( IOException e ) {
      System.err.println
        ( "Cannot close buffered stream. \n" + e.toString() );
      System.exit(1);
    }
  }
}
```

SQLJ Translation Process

In this section, you will consider the various steps in the SQLJ translation process.

As you have seen, a SQLJ source file contains a combination of standard Java source code, along with SQLJ declarations and SQLJ executable statements that contain SQL operations. This source code must be located in a file with the extension .sqlj. After you have entered the SQLJ source file using your favorite text editor, you run the sqlj command to translate the SQLJ source file into a Java source file and generate other output files described subsequently. The sqlj command runs as a script in UNIX and as an executable file in PC Windows, and invokes a Java VM (see Chapter 1), passing its arguments to the Java VM. The Java VM then invokes the SQLJ translator, which performs syntax analysis on the SQLJ source file, checking for incorrect SQLJ syntax.

The SQLJ translator next invokes the semantics checker, which checks the semantics of the executable SQLJ statements. If the online checking option was selected on the sqlj command line (by using the –user option, as discussed in an upcoming section), the semantics checker will connect to the database and check that the usage of database objects, such as tables and stored procedures, is consistent with the structure of the corresponding objects stored in the database. If offline semantics checking was selected (by the absence of the –user option on the sqlj command line), only simple checking that doesn't require connection to the database will be performed.

The SQLJ translator then performs its code generation step by converting SQLJ executable statements into SQLJ run-time calls and generating a separate profile for each connection class in the SQLJ source file. The results of this step are a Java source file (with the extension .java) that was translated from the SQLJ source, and the generated profiles. The .java file contains the following:

- Any Java code from the SQLJ source file.

- Class definitions created as a result of SQLJ declarations in the SQLJ source file, such as iterator class definitions.

- A class definition for the profile-keys class that SQLJ generates and uses in conjunction with the profiles.

- A SQLJ run-time call for each SQLJ executable statement. Note that the SQLJ run-time uses the specified JDBC driver to access the database.

Each generated profile is placed, by default, in a serialized `.ser` file. However, you can specify that SQLJ converts the `.ser` files to `.class` files by setting the `-ser2class` flag on the `sqlj` command line (for example, `sqlj -ser2class LoadAccountList.sqlj`).

The information for all the SQL operations executed against a connection context class is contained in the profile for that connection context class. If there are no SQLJ executable statements in the SQLJ source file, no profiles will be generated.

As a default, the Java VM invokes the Java compiler (usually the standard `javac`) to compile the `.java` file generated. If you wish to suppress this compilation, you specify `-compile=false` on the `sqlj` command line. The Java compiler compiles the `.java` file into `.class` files, as usual. You will get a `.class` file for each class you defined in your SQLJ source file, as well as a `.class` file for the SQLJ-generated `profile-keys` class.

The Java VM then invokes the Oracle SQLJ customizer to customize the generated profiles in an Oracle-specific way.

For the `LoadAccountList` application in the earlier section of this chapter entitled "SQLJ Load Program: `LoadAccountList.sqlj`," the SQLJ translator generates the output files `LoadAccountList.java` and `LoadAccountList_SJProfile0.ser`. In addition, the Java compiler invoked by the Java VM will generate a `LoadAccountList.class` file and a `LoadAccountList_SJProfileKeys.class` file. In general, the SQLJ translator will produce a Java file with the same base name as the SQLJ file and at least one profile (assuming the SQLJ file contains SQLJ executable statements). A profile filename is obtained by concatenating the SQLJ base filename with `SJProfilen`, where n is a number that indicates that the context connection class for the profile was the nth one encountered in the SQLJ source file, and makes the profile filename unique. In the `LoadAccountList` application, there is only one profile corresponding to the `DefaultContextClass`, so $n=0$ is used in the profile filename: `LoadAccountListSJProfile0.ser`. Also, the SQLJ translator will generate a profile-keys class named `sqljsourcename_SJProfileKeys` (`LoadAccountList_SJProfileKeys` in the `LoadAccountList` application), for which the Java compiler will generate a `.class` file (`LoadAccountList_SJProfileKeys.class` in the `LoadAccountList` application). Similarly, a `.class` file will be generated for each iterator class and connection context you defined in the SQLJ source file. The base name of these files will be the same as the name of the corresponding iterator or context connection class.

When you run your application, the SQLJ run-time reads the profiles and creates "connected profiles," which incorporate database connections. The following steps are then executed each time the application accesses the database:

■ The SQLJ-generated code executes methods in the profile-keys class to access the connected profile and read the relevant SQL operations, which it passes to the SQLJ run-time.

■ The SQLJ run-time then invokes the JDBC driver, passing it the SQL operation for execution.

■ The JDBC driver will send any data to the program that the SQL operation requires.

NOTE
With Oracle9i or later, you can also choose to generate Oracle-specific JDBC code directly, rather than code that calls the SQLJ run-time and that accesses the profile file(s) at run time. You can achieve this by supplying the option -codegen=oracle *on the command line. In this case, the* _SJProfileKeys.class *and the* .ser *files will not be created, and the additional profile customization step is not needed, either.*

`sqlj` Command-Line Options and Properties Files

In this section, you will learn how to specify options to SQLJ via the command line and via properties files. Please see Chapter 8 of *Oracle9i SQLJ Developer's Guide and Reference* for more information on SQLJ options and properties files. See Appendix D of this book for a list of SQLJ options.

`sqlj` Command-Line Options

After learning about the structure of the `sqlj` command line, you will see examples of several important command-line options.

Structure of the `sqlj` Command Line
The syntax of the `sqlj` command line is

```
sqlj [ option_list ] file_list
```

option_list is a sequence of blank-separated SQLJ options. file_list is a sequence of blank-separated .sqlj, .java, .ser, and .jar files.
In the simplest command line, one SQLJ file and no options will be passed:

```
sqlj LoadAccountList.sqlj
```

Additional SQLJ files are necessary if you wish to declare public iterator and connection context classes. Also, if you have .sqlj files and .java files that each require access to code in the others, you must enter all of them in the command line for a single execution of SQLJ. You cannot specify them for separate executions of SQLJ.
.jar files and .ser files are provided as input to the profile customizer. See Chapter 10 of *Oracle9i SQLJ Developer's Guide and Reference* for more information on these types of files. The general form of a SQLJ option is

```
-optionname=value
```

If an option is Boolean valued, it is called a *flag* and can be set to true by specifying

```
-flagname=true
```

or simply

```
-flagname
```

The only way to set the flag to false is by specifying

```
-flagname=false
```

The -J, -C, or -P prefix is attached to the left of an option to indicate that the option should be sent to the Java VM (-J), the Java compiler (-C), or the SQLJ profile customizer (-P). For example, in the sqlj command line

```
sqlj -compile=false -ser2class -P-backup LoadAccountList.sqlj
```

you specify, using the -compile flag, that the Java compiler should not be invoked after the translation phase (-compile=false). The default setting of the -compile option is true (that is, invoke the Java compiler to generate a .class file). You specify, using the -ser2class flag, that .ser profiles should be converted to .class files. The default setting of the -ser2class option is false.

You specify using the −P prefix with the −backup flag that the −backup flag should be passed to the customizer (this flag indicates that the profiles should be backed up before they are customized).

Not so widely known is that SQLJ options may appear anywhere on the command line, even after names of files. This can be useful if your command shell has a history facility, and you want to change the SQLJ translator setting and recompile quickly.

Some Important SQLJ Options

Several important SQLJ options are now discussed through examples.

```
sqlj -user=scott -password=tiger
-url=jdbc:oracle:thin:@data-i.com:1521:ORCL LoadAccountList.sqlj
```

The specification of −user enables online semantics checking and specifies that username scott should be used when connecting to the database. If this option is not specified, no online semantics checking occurs. The −password option indicates the password to use when connecting (the password can also be indicated on the −user option: -user=scott/tiger), and the URL option indicates the JDBC driver and database to use in the connection. This URL can also be specified in the −user option:

```
-user=scott/tiger@JDBC:oracle:thin@data-i.com:1521:ORCL
```

These connection values do not have to be the same for the SQLJ translator (the values specified on the sqlj command line) as they do for SQLJ run-time (the values passed to connect methods in the SQLJ source code). For example, if you are developing in a different environment than the one in which you will deploy, the connections may be different.

```
sqlj -driver=sun.jdbc.odbc.JdbcOdbcDriver LoadAccountList.sqlj
```

The −driver option indicates the driver classes (comma separated) to register for interpreting JDBC connection URLs for online semantics checking. The default class is OracleDriver, which supports the Oracle OCI, thin, and server-side drivers.

```
sqlj -props=newprops.properties LoadAccountList.sqlj
```

indicates that SQLJ options can be found in the properties file newprops. properties that you created. Translation time properties files are discussed in the next section, entitled "Specifying SQLJ Options with Properties Files."

```
sqlj -help
sqlj -help-long
```

To receive help in using the `sqlj` command-line options, you execute the `sqlj` command with no options or files specified, or with only –help specified to give you a synopsis of the most frequently used SQLJ options and a listing of the additional –help flag settings available. –help-long gives a complete list of SQLJ options information. The `sqlj -version` and, more importantly, the `sqlj -version-long` are important options. In particular, the `sqlj -version-long` command tells you everything about the SQLJ version, the JDBC driver version, and the JDK under which you are running. It is very useful in diagnosing issues with the SQLJ configuration.

```
sqlj -linemap LoadAccountList.sqlj
```

Specifying –linemap (that is, -linemap=true) causes run-time Java error messages to be labeled with SQLJ source line numbers instead of Java source line numbers. Thus, the error will be related to code that you wrote, instead of code that was generated by the SQLJ translator. The default value for this flag is false, that is, line numbers refer to generated `.java` source.

Specifying SQLJ Options with Properties Files

In this section, you will see that instead of using the command line to specify options to the SQLJ translator, Java compiler, and SQLJ profile customizer, you can use *properties files.* However, you cannot use properties files to set the following SQLJ options, flags, and prefixes: -classpath, -help, -help-long, -help-alias, -C-help, -P-help, -J, -n, –passes, -props, -version, -version-long, and -vm. Also, properties files can only be used with client-side applications, as there is a different mechanism for specifying options to SQLJ in the server.

First, you will learn about the structure of a properties file. Then you will consider the order in which options are set. In particular, you will consider the processing of `sqlj.properties` files.

Structure of Properties Files

Option settings in a properties file are placed one per line, and lines with SQLJ options, compiler options, and customizer options can be interspersed because they are parsed by the SQLJ front end and handled appropriately. Each option has the following form:

```
target.optionname=value
```

where `target` is `sqlj`, `compile`, or `profile`, and `optionname` is the name of the option being set. For example:

```
sqlj.linemap=true
```

A flag can be enabled by entering it without a setting. For example:

```
sqlj.linemap
```

As you have seen, the SQLJ `props` option indicates the properties file to be used for the translation:

```
sqlj -props=myprops.properties LoadAccountList.sqlj
```

Please consider the following properties file `myprops.properties`:

```
sqlj.user=scott
sqlj.password=tiger
sqlj.url=jdbc:oracle:@data-i.com:1521:ORCL
sqlj.linemap
```

`myprops.properties` specifies the username, password, and URL needed to connect to the database for the purpose of online semantics checking, and that line numbers in error messages should refer to SQLJ source and not Java source.

Default `sqlj.properties` Files and the Order of Setting Options

Before discussing default properties files, the `SQLJ_OPTIONS` environment variable is introduced. Any option that can be set on the `sqlj` command line can alternatively be set using the `SQLJ_OPTIONS` variable. SQLJ inserts the `SQLJ_OPTIONS` settings, in order, at the beginning of the `sqlj` command line, before any other command-line setting. For example, using your operating system's specific method for setting environment variables, `SQLJ_OPTIONS` can be set to

```
-linemap=true -compile=false
```

These options will then be automatically inserted at the beginning of any subsequently executed `sqlj` command line.

Even if you specified a properties file in a `-props` option, the SQLJ front end still searches for files named `sqlj.properties`, the default properties files. The following indicates the order in which SQLJ takes option settings, where each step overrides settings from the previous steps, and the options on the `sqlj` command line are set from left to right.

- Set default settings for options.

- Set settings for options found in the `sqlj.properties` file in the Java home directory (if such a properties file exists).

- Set settings for options found in the `sqlj.properties` file in the user home directory (if such a properties file exists).

- Set settings for options found in the `sqlj.properties` file in the current directory (if such a properties file exists).

- Extract settings for options in the `SQLJ_OPTIONS` environment variable, inserting them at the beginning of the `sqlj` command line, and set those settings.

- Extract settings for properties file set in the `-props` option and place them on the command line where `-props` appears.

- Set option settings found on the command line, with later settings overriding earlier settings.

A sample `sqlj.properties` file can be found in your SQLJ demo directory `[OracleHome]/sqlj/demo`, with sample option lines commented out. You can then edit this file to remove the appropriate comment symbols and enter desired option values. An example of such an edited `sqlj.properties` file is this one:

```
###
### Settings to establish a database connection for online checking
###

### turn on checking by uncommenting user
### or specifying the -user option on the command line
sqlj.user=scott
sqlj.password=tiger

### add additional drivers here
#sqlj.driver=oracle.jdbc.driver.OracleDriver<,driver2...>

### Oracle JDBC-OCI7 URL
#sqlj.url=jdbc:oracle:oci7:@

### Oracle JDBC-OCI8 URL
#sqlj.url=jdbc:oracle:oci8:@

### Oracle JDBC-Thin URL
#sqlj.url=jdbc:oracle:thin:@<host>:<port>:<oracle_sid>
sqlj.url=jdbc:oracle:thin:@data-i.com:1521:ORCL
```

The preceding `sqlj.properties` file specifies username, password, and URL for the semantics-checking database connection.

In this chapter, you examined SQLJ programs that illustrated how to connect to the database and execute non-SELECT and SELECT SQL commands from your SQLJ program. You also considered the SQLJ translation process, and how to influence that process through the SQLJ command line and through properties files. In Chapter 3, you will encounter an extensive treatment of the different types of SQLJ statements that can be embedded in your SQLJ program. In particular, you will consider how host expressions and result expressions can be used in your executable SQLJ statements, more about the strongly typed named and positional iterators and the weakly typed result set iterators (including the scrollable versions of these different kinds of iterators), as well as considering the Oracle9*i* (versions 9.0.0 and later) support for dynamic SQL.

CHAPTER
3

Basic SQLJ Programming

There are two types of SQLJ statements: SQLJ declarations and SQLJ executable statements. Also, there are two types of SQLJ declarations: connection context declarations and iterator declarations. In addition, there are two types of executable SQLJ statements: statements that return values and thus contain result expressions to hold those values, and statements that do not contain result expressions. There are two types of result expressions: iterator expressions that hold the result returned by a SELECT statement and expressions that hold the result returned from a stored procedure invocation. Therefore, it appears that SQLJ follows Noah's Ark "two by two" model.

In Chapter 5, connection context declarations are discussed. In Chapter 6, scrollable iterators are discussed, along with dynamic SQL in SQLJ executable statements. In Chapter 7, JDBC interoperability features—iterator conversion executable SQLJ statements, which convert a JDBC ResultSet to an iterator, and subclassing iterator classes—are discussed. In this chapter, you will learn about the other SQLJ statements. In particular, you will encounter

- Executable SQLJ statements without result expressions: SQLJ DDL and SQLJ non-SELECT DML commands

- Executable SQLJ statements without result expressions: SQLJ transaction control commands

- Executable SQLJ statements without result expressions: anonymous PL/SQL blocks and stored procedure calls

- Executable SQLJ statements without result expressions: SET, FETCH, and SELECT INTO statements

- Executable SQLJ statements with result expressions: SQLJ SELECT statements

- Executable SQLJ statements with result expressions: stored function calls

- Evaluation of host expressions and result expressions at run time

- JDBC and SQLJ exception classes

- Other useful JDBC and SQLJ classes

A SQLJ executable statement can appear any place a Java block statement can appear, namely, within method definitions and static initialization blocks. The syntax of a SQLJ executable statement depends on whether or not the statement involves a result expression. The syntax of a SQLJ executable that does not contain a result expression is

```
#sql { sql_operation } ;
```

The syntax of an executable statement that contains a result expression is

```
#sql result_expression = { sql_operation } ;
```

In either case, a SQLJ clause is the executable part of a statement (that is, everything to the right of the #sql token). A SQLJ clause that does not contain a result expression is called a *statement clause*. A SQLJ clause that contains a result expression is called an *assignment clause*. A result expression can be any legal Java expression that is assignable.

A *statement clause* can consist of any SQL command except a SELECT statement. In particular, a statement clause can consist of any SQL DDL command, any SQL transaction control command, or any SQL DML command except a SELECT statement. In addition, a statement clause can consist of the following SQLJ-specific statements: a SELECT INTO statement, a FETCH statement, a stored procedure call, and an anonymous PL/SQL block.

An *assignment clause* can consist of a query clause (that is, a SQLJ SELECT statement) that selects data into a SQLJ iterator, a stored function call, a SET statement, or an iterator conversion clause.

In this chapter, you will learn about all of these statement clauses and assignment clauses except the iterator conversion clause.

Executable SQLJ Statements Without Result Expressions: SQLJ DDL and Non-SELECT DML Commands

In this section, you will examine the structure of SQLJ DDL and non-SELECT SQLJ DML commands. In particular, you will see how host expressions, that is, Java expressions, can be incorporated into DML commands.

SQLJ DDL Commands

A SQLJ DDL command is a SQLJ statement that consists of a SQL DDL command. A SQL DDL command is used to set up the structure of the database (see Appendix A). All SQL DDL commands start with one of the keywords CREATE, DROP, ALTER, ASSERT, DEFINE, GRANT, REVOKE, DROP, or REPLACE. A SQLJ statement clause can consist of any DDL command. Such statement clauses are particularly simple because they cannot contain Java expressions, that is, host expressions. You will see in the next section, "SQLJ DML Commands," that host expressions can appear anywhere in a SQLJ DML command that an expression can appear, as well as in the target lists of FETCH and SELECT INTO statements and in other places.

An example of a SQLJ CREATE TABLE statement is

```
#sql { CREATE TABLE ACCOUNT_LIST (
           accountno     number( 5 ),
           projectno     number( 5 ),
           departmentno  number( 5 ),
           PRIMARY KEY   ( accountno ),
           FOREIGN KEY   ( projectno )    REFERENCES PROJECT_LIST,
           FOREIGN KEY   ( departmentno ) REFERENCES DEPARTMENT_LIST )
     };
```

SQLJ DML Commands

A SQLJ DML command is a SQLJ statement that consists of a SQL DML command.
A SQL DML command is used to manipulate the database (see Appendix A). The
SQL DML commands are the INSERT, DELETE, UPDATE, and MERGE statements,
and query statements such as SELECT and SELECT WITH. Unlike the SQLJ DDL
commands, the SQLJ DML commands can contain host expressions. These SQLJ
host expressions are discussed next.

SQLJ Host Expressions

SQLJ uses Java host expressions to pass arguments between SQLJ DML commands,
SELECT INTO statements, FETCH statements, PL/SQL blocks, SET statements, SELECT
statements, stored procedure calls, stored function calls, and the Java code that
surrounds these statements.

The simplest kind of host expression consists of only a non-dotted Java identifier.
This is called a *host variable*, which you encountered in Chapter 2. In general, any
valid Java expression can be used as a host expression. These include expressions
that contain fields, class variables, Java method calls, array elements, and arithmetic
expressions. Any Java variable whose type is SQL convertible (see Appendix D for
a table correlating SQL and Java types) and that is legal in the Java scope where the
SQLJ executable statement appears can be used as a host expression. There is no
limitation on the types you can use in a host expression, provided that the entire
host expression is of a type that is SQL convertible.

Any of the following Java identifiers can be used as SQLJ host variables or in
SQLJ host expressions:

- Local variables

- Declared parameters

- Class fields (such as `ClassName.classField`). When qualified like here
  with a class name, the class field must be a host expression.

- Method calls (`static` or instance method call). Syntactically not possible to be used as a host variable, it must be a host expression.

Host expressions, like the host variables described in Chapter 2, can have mode `IN`, `OUT`, or `INOUT`. The syntax for a host variable is

```
:[ mode ] host_variable
:[ mode ] ( host_expression )
:( ( a + b ) * c )
```

This is legal, whereas

```
:( a + b ) * c
```

is not legal.

The default mode is `OUT` for host expressions in the `into_list` of a `FETCH` statement, the `into_list` of a `SELECT INTO` statement, and the assignment host expression of a `SET` statement. The default mode is `IN` for all other host expressions.

Java expressions can be used as any of the following:

- Connection context expression (optional; evaluated to specify the connection context instance to be used)

- Execution context expression (optional; evaluated to specify the execution context instance to be used)

- Result expression (when appropriate: to receive results from a stored function, for example)

- Host expression

NOTE
It is perfectly fine and perfectly portable if the host variable is only used in an IN expression. If the same host variable occurs in multiple OUT or INOUT positions, or in an IN position as well as one or more OUT or INOUT positions, then the semantics may not be portable between different databases. Specifically, every occurrence would, by default, be treated as a separate occurrence, rather than assuming that all occurrences use one and the same variable. (This is the way the SQLJ standard treats it, since SQLJ is based on JDBC and JDBC does not permit binding multiple occurrences as if they were the same variable.)

Here is an example of SQLJ DML command using the `Insert  SQL  DML` command:

```
#sql { INSERT INTO ACCOUNT_LIST
          SELECT accountno, projectno, departmentno
             FROM NEW_ACCOUNTS WHERE departmentno = :departmentno
       };
```

A SQLJ DML command using the `DELETE  SQL  DML` command:

```
#sql { DELETE FROM ACCOUNT_LIST WHERE accountno = :oldaccountno };
```

A SQLJ DML command using the `UPDATE  SQL  DML` command:

```
#sql { UPDATE ACCOUNT_LIST
          SET departmentno = :newdepartmentno
            WHERE accountno = :acc
       };
```

Using Host Variables and Expressions in SQLJ

In this section you will develop the `InsertWithHostExpressions.sqlj` program. The `InsertWithHostExpressions` class consists of the `addAccounts()` method, an overloaded method that illustrates how to use host variables and host expressions in SQLJ executable statements. The `addAccounts(departmentno, projectno)` method demonstrates how to use host variables in SQLJ, whereas the `addAccounts(anAccount)` method uses the `AccountRec` class to teach you how to use host expressions.

Here is the definition of the `Account  Rec` class followed by the `InsertWithHostExpressions` class:

```
/*
** Program Name:  AccountRec.java
**
**
*/
public class AccountRec {
  private int accountno;
  private int departmentno;
  private int projectno;

  /* The AccountRec constructor is used to initialize the AccountRec
     instance with an account number (iaccountno), department number
     (idepartmentno), and project number (iprojectno).
  */
  public AccountRec
```

```
       ( int iaccountno, int idepartmentno, int iprojectno ) {
         accountno = iaccountno;
         departmentno = idepartmentno;
         projectno = iprojectno;
     }

   /* Since the accountno, departmentno, and projectno fields are
      private, accessor methods getAccountno(), getDepartmentno(),
      and getProjectno() are provided to return those respective
      values.
   */
   public int getAccountno() {
     return accountno;
   }
   public int getDepartmentno() {
     return departmentno;
   }
   public int getProjectno() {
     return projectno;
   }
}


/*
** Program Name:  InsertWithHostExpressions.sqlj
**
** Purpose:  Insert data into the ACCOUNT_LIST table
**           using host variables and expressions.
**
*/
package chapter02;

import sqlj.runtime.*;
import sqlj.runtime.ref.*;
import java.sql.*;
// Import the AccountRec class
import AccountRec;

/* oracle.sqlj.runtime.Oracle class
   contains connect() method for
   connecting to database.
*/
import oracle.sqlj.runtime.Oracle;

public class InsertWithHostExpressions {
    public InsertWithHostExpressions() throws SQLException {
        Oracle.connect( "jdbc:oracle:thin:@localhost:1521:ORCL",
                           "scott","tiger" );
```

```
      } // End of constructor
      public static void main( String args[] ) throws SQLException {
        InsertWithHostExpressions app =
                           new InsertWithHostExpressions();
       // Create some variables
       int projectno = 300;
       int departmentno = 200;
       int accountno;
       // Create an AccountRec object
       AccountRec anAccount =
             new AccountRec (accountno, departmentno,projectno);
       try { // Create a new account using Host variables
           app.addAccounts(departmentno,projectno);
       }  // End of try
       catch (SQLException ex) {
           System.out.println("unable to create new account!!"
                              +ex.getMessage());
           System.exit(1);
       }  // End of catch
       try { // Create a new account using Host expressions
           app.addAccounts(anAccount);
       }  // End of try
       catch (SQLException ex) {
           System.out.println("unable to create new account "
                  +"using host expressions!! " +ex.getMessage());
           System.exit(1);
       }  // End of catch
       finally {
          // Close the database connection
          Oracle.close();
       } // End finally()

    }  // End of main()

    public void addAccounts(int departmentno, int projectno)
             throws SQLException {
      int accountno;
      try {
          accountno = createNewAccountNo();
      }  // End of try
      catch (java.lang.NullPointerException ex) {
          // quit. I need an accountno
          throw new java.lang.NullPointerException(ex.getMessage());
      }  // End of catch()

      // System.out.println("I came back from create ");

      // Usage of Host variables in the SQLJ
```

```
    // Executable statement
    #sql { INSERT INTO ACCOUNT_LIST
          VALUES (:accountno, :projectno, :departmentno )
    };

    // System.out.println("I am inside first add: "
    //                    +accountno);
    // commit the changes
    #sql {COMMIT WORK};
} // End addAccounts() method

public void addAccounts(AccountRec anAccount)
        throws SQLException {
    int accountno;
    try {  // Get a new account no
        accountno = createNewAccountNo();
    }  // End of try
    catch (java.lang.NullPointerException ex) {
        // quit. I need an accountno
        throw new java.lang.NullPointerException(ex.getMessage());
    }  // End of catch()
    // Create a AccountRec object
    AccountRec aNewAcc =
        new AccountRec(accountno,anAccount.getDepartmentno(),
                anAccount.getProjectno());

    // Usage of Host expressions in the SQLJ
    // Executable statement
    #sql {INSERT INTO ACCOUNT_LIST
          VALUES (
                :( aNewAcc.getAccountno() ),
                :( aNewAcc.getProjectno() ),
                :( aNewAcc.getDepartmentno() ) )
    };
    // System.out.println("I am inside second add: "
    //                    +accountno);
    // commit the changes
    #sql {COMMIT WORK};
} // End addAccounts() method

// Method that creates a new account no.
private int createNewAccountNo ( ) throws SQLException {
    int accountno;
    try { // Using host variable in SQLJ
        #sql {SELECT ACCOUNTNO_SEQ.NEXTVAL INTO :accountno
                FROM DUAL
            };
    }  // End of try
```

```
catch (java.lang.NullPointerException ex) {
   // quit. I need an accountno
   throw new java.lang.NullPointerException(
     "Unable to create accountno, see DBA " +ex.getMessage());
}  // End of catch()

return accountno;
}  // End of createNewAccountNo()

}  // End of InsertWithHostExpressions class
```

The InsertWithHostExpressions class illustrates the general point that a SQLJ clause that involves complicated host expressions can always be rewritten as a SQLJ clause involving only simple Java variables, as long as extra assignment statements are placed before the SQLJ statement containing that clause (for IN expressions), after that statement (for OUT expressions), or before and after that statement (for INOUT expressions).

Executable SQLJ Statements Without Result Expressions: SQLJ Transaction Control Commands

A *SQLJ transaction control command* is a SQLJ statement that consists of a SQL transaction control command. A *transaction* is a sequence of SQL statements that the DBMS server treats as a single unit. In case of a system crash, all transactions that have committed will be redone, all others will be undone. When several transactions (from different programs) are concurrently executing, their effect on the database, at least theoretically, is such that they each appear to be executing in isolation from each other—that is, they do not appear to be executing concurrently, but instead it seems as if one transaction finishes before another begins.

A SQLJ program is divided into transactions in the following way. A transaction begins with the first executable SQLJ statement after the execution of a connection to the database, a COMMIT, or a ROLLBACK. A transaction ends with the explicit or implicit execution of a COMMIT or a ROLLBACK. Executing a COMMIT makes permanent all changes made to the database in the current transaction. Executing a ROLLBACK cancels all changes to the database made in the current transaction. A COMMIT can be accomplished by explicitly executing a COMMIT command:

```
#sql { COMMIT };
```

or

```
#sql { COMMIT WORK };
```

or it can be executed automatically, as indicated in the following.

In Oracle, all DDL commands are automatically and immediately committed. Thus, the execution of a DDL command terminates the current transaction. In addition, you can specify that all INSERT, DELETE, and UPDATE statements be automatically and immediately committed by enabling the auto-commit flag. You will learn how to enable auto-commit in the next section, "auto-commit."

A rollback occurs when a ROLLBACK statement is explicitly executed:

```
#sql { ROLLBACK };
```

or

```
#sql { ROLLBACK WORK };
```

or when a program terminates without having the final transaction committed.

NOTE
If you have enabled auto-commit, you cannot execute any explicit COMMIT or ROLLBACK statements.

Next you will learn about

- auto-commit
- The SET TRANSACTION statement

auto-commit

You can enable auto-commit (which is disabled by default) either when you define a SQLJ connection, or by using the setAutoCommit() method on an existing connection object. For example, you can enable auto-commit by using the connect() method of the oracle.sqlj.runtime.Oracle class with the signature that takes URL (String), username (String), password (String), and auto-commit flag (boolean):

```
Oracle.connect(
  "JDBC:oracle:thin:@data-i.com","scott","tiger",true);
mycontext.getConnection().setAutoCommit(true);
```

There are certain disadvantages:

- You cannot ROLLBACK changes.

■ Because a separate COMMIT will be executed for each INSERT, DELETE, and UPDATE statement as soon as they are executed, you will suffer a loss of runtime performance due to this increased "COMMIT overhead."

NOTE
You cannot enable auto-commit in server applications.

SET TRANSACTION **Statement**

The SQL-92 standard includes a SET TRANSACTION statement to allow an increase in concurrency of transactions, the downside being that these transactions may interfere with each other.

Oracle SQLJ supports a version of the SET TRANSACTION statement. The SQLJ SET TRANSACTION statement has the following syntax:

```
#sql {
   SET TRANSACTION [ access_mode ] [ , ]
     [ ISOLATION LEVEL isolation_level ]
       };
```

The two access_mode settings are read only and read write. read write is the default setting that allows INSERT, DELETE, and UPDATE statements, as well as SELECT statements, to be executed. The read only setting does not allow INSERT, DELETE, UPDATE, or SELECT FOR UPDATE statements to be executed in the transaction. However, DDL commands are allowed in Oracle. The only DML command allowed is the SELECT statement. Note that Oracle JDBC does not support the access mode READ ONLY. You will receive an SQLException if you specify it.

Specifying the read only setting guarantees that the transaction will enjoy transaction-level consistency instead of statement-level consistency. This means that all queries in the current transaction will only see changes made by other transactions that were committed before the current transaction began. read only can be very convenient for reports that contain more than one query, involving the same tables that are being updated at the same time by other users. This is actually the default behavior of the Oracle READ COMMITTED transaction isolation level, which is also the default setting.

The isolation_level settings are SERIALIZABLE and READ committed. SERIALIZABLE is the default setting in the SQL-92 standard (not in Oracle) and will guarantee that executing transactions that are running concurrently will not interfere with each other—that is, that it appears that one will finish before another one begins. Note that most applications running against Oracle actually use the READ COMMITTED setting, because that is quite a bit faster than the SERIALIZABLE setting.

Concurrent transactions are regulated in Oracle by locking rows and (in the case of the SQL `lock table` command) locking entire tables. Locking a unit, say, a row, means that the server reserves the row for a particular transaction, and it will not let any other transaction access that row until the lock is released (`SELECT` statements only lock out `INSERT`, `DELETE`, and `UPDATE` statements; `INSERT`, `DELETE`, and `UPDATE` statements lock out `SELECT` statements as well). Serializability is enforced by the server holding all locks until the entire transaction completes.

The `read committed` setting for a transaction is the default setting in Oracle, and it guarantees that an uncommitted change made by another transaction will not be read by the current transaction. However, two types of interference between other concurrent transactions with the current transaction will be allowed with this setting, namely, nonrepeatable reads and phantom reads. Because of this, a transaction running under the `read committed` setting does not really satisfy the theoretical definition of a transaction given, for example, in *Transaction Processing: Concepts and Techniques,* by J. Gray and R. Andreas.

A *nonrepeatable read* in the current transaction occurs when the current transaction reads a record once and then reads the same record again, only to encounter different data. This can happen when the Oracle server releases the lock that the current transaction has on the record as soon as the statement that is reading the record completes, instead of holding the lock until the entire transaction completes. Thus, two different locks are held on the record for the current transaction at two different points in time. As a result, another transaction is allowed to update the record in between those two points in time.

`read committed` is enforced by only holding locks for the duration of a SQL statement, not for the duration of the whole transaction. The non-repeatable read interference is allowed in order to gain run-time performance (the updating transaction will not be held up until the entire reading transaction completes).

The *phantom read* phenomenon is similar to the nonrepeatable read phenomenon, but deals with sets of records returned by `SELECT` statements instead of field values of individual records. The phantom read phenomenon occurs when a transaction executes the same `SELECT` statement twice but encounters new "phantom records" the second time.

You can refer to *Transaction Processing: Concepts and Techniques,* by J. Gray and R. Andreas, for an excellent treatment of transaction processing in general. The *Oracle8i/9i SQL Reference Manual* offers more information on the `SET TRANSACTION` command.

An example of a `SET TRANSACTION` command that declares a transaction to be `read only` and disallows nonrepeatable and phantom reads is

```
#sql { SET TRANSACTION read only, ISOLATION LEVEL serializable };
```

NOTE
READ ONLY is not supported by Oracle SQLJ, and thus Oracle JDBC.

Executable SQLJ Statements Without Result Expressions: Anonymous PL/SQL Blocks and Stored Procedure Calls

In this section, you will consider invoking the following from SQLJ programs:

- Anonymous PL/SQL blocks
- Stored procedures

Anonymous PL/SQL Blocks

A PL/SQL block can appear within the curly braces of a SQLJ executable statement in the same manner that a SQL DDL, DML, or transaction control command can. Note that the final end of the PL/SQL block must have a terminating semicolon. For example, consider the following PL/SQL block, which inserts some rows into the ACCOUNT_LIST table:

```
#sql {
  begin
     INSERT INTO ACCOUNT_LIST VALUES ( 10000, 20000, 30000 );
     INSERT INTO ACCOUNT_LIST VALUES ( 40000, 50000, 60000 );
     INSERT INTO ACCOUNT_LIST VALUES ( 70000, 80000, 90000 );
  end;
     };

int z, x = 0;
#sql {
  begin
     :OUT x := 5;
     :OUT z := :x;
  end;
     };
System.out.println( "x = " + x + " z = " + z );

#sql {
  begin
    SELECT COUNT(*) INTO :OUT x FROM ACCOUNT_LIST;
  end;
     };
```

Is equivalent to:

```
#sql { SELECT COUNT(*) INTO :x FROM ACCOUNT_LIST };
```

A performance advantage of embedding a PL/SQL block in your SQLJ program instead of embedding the SQL statements from the block individually is that all those SQL statements will be sent to the server in one call.

Stored Procedure Calls

A *stored procedure* is a procedure that has been stored in the database with a command, such as the Oracle SQL CREATE PROCEDURE statement (see Appendix A). Stored procedures can be coded in PL/SQL, Java, or any other language that the DBMS allows. In Chapter 4, you will learn about coding stored procedures in SQLJ. In this section, you will consider stored procedures coded in PL/SQL. In any case, the syntax for a SQLJ stored procedure call is

```
#sql { call procedure_name [ ( parameter_list ) ] };
```

procedure_name is the name of the procedure, which can optionally take a list of parameters. If the procedure does not have any parameters, this can be indicated by omitting the parentheses or by having empty parentheses:

```
#sql { call hit };
```

or

```
#sql { call hit() };
```

However, only the former method is compatible with Oracle7.

```
CREATE PROCEDURE
    deleteacct( acctno ACCOUNT_LIST.accountno%type,
                worked out NUMBER ) as
  x integer;
  begin
    /* Check if account record exists. */
    /* When selecting into a PL/SQL variable (like x), the PL/SQL
       variable is not prefixed with a ":"
    */
    SELECT COUNT(*) INTO x FROM ACCOUNT_LIST
      WHERE accountno = acctno;
    /* If it does not exist, set worked to false and return. */
    if x = 0 then worked := 1;
    return;
    end if;
```

```
    /* If it does exist, delete the account, commit the delete,
       and set worked to true.
    */
    DELETE FROM ACCOUNT_LIST WHERE accountno = acctno;
    COMMIT WORK;
    worked := 0;
  end deleteacct;
```

```
#sql { call deleteacct( :accountno, :OUT status ) };
```

Here, you use host variables to pass in the account number of the account to be deleted and to receive the Boolean status of the deletion. Recall that PL/SQL supports modes in, out, and in out for subprogram parameters, just as SQLJ supports modes IN, OUT, and INOUT for host expressions. If you are using host expressions in the procedure call, the mode of the host expression must be the same as the mode of the corresponding formal parameter in the procedure. Also, of course, the types of the host expressions must be compatible with the types of the corresponding formal parameters in the procedure.

In any case, the ability to invoke stored subprograms from your SQLJ programs allows you conveniently to reuse code that already exists, instead of having to recode it again.

Executable SQLJ Statements Without Result Expressions: SET, FETCH, and SELECT INTO Statements

In this section, you will consider the three types of SQLJ statements that can contain host expressions with default mode OUT:

■ The SET statement

■ The SELECT INTO statement

■ The FETCH statement

■ The endFetch() method

SET Statement

The SET statement is used to compute the value of an expression and assign that value to a host expression. The syntax for the SET statement is

```
#sql { set :host_expression = expression };
```

The `host_expression` has default mode `OUT` and must be a Java l-value.
Do not try to specify an `IN` or `INOUT` mode for the `host_expression`. That
will result in a translation-time error. The `SET` clause is equivalent to a PL/SQL
block clause:

```
#sql {
   begin
     :OUT host_expression := expression;
   end;
      }
```

Thus, the `expression` to the right of the = in a `SET` statement can contain anything
that is legal in an expression that is located in a PL/SQL block without a `DECLARE`
section. In particular, the `expression` can contain several stored function calls.
In fact, the major application of the `SET` statement is to perform such a computation
easily in one SQLJ statement. Without the `SET` statement, either you would have to
invoke a PL/SQL block, or you would have to invoke several SQLJ statements, each
statement capturing one of the stored function values. Stored function call statements
are discussed in a subsequent section of this chapter.

```
#sql {
      SET :nfailed = emppak.insertemp
        ( 1000, 'Jones', 'Joe',   '(305)999-9999', 1050 ) +
        ( 2000, 'Smith', 'Damon', '(212)999-9999', 1050 ) +
        ( 3000, 'Cohen', 'Naomi', '(212)888-8888', 1050 )
      };
```

SELECT INTO Statement

The `SELECT INTO` statement, which is also supported in PL/SQL and embedded SQL,
is used to retrieve a single row from the database and place data from that row in host
expressions. The syntax for the `SELECT INTO` statement is the same as the syntax
for a `SELECT` statement with the addition of a `list_of_host_expressions`
following the `select_list` of the `SELECT` statement. The number of elements in
the `list_of_host_expressions` must be the same as the number of elements
in the `select_list`. The default mode for the host expressions in the `list_of_`
`host_expressions` is `OUT`.

Note that an attempt to specify the mode as `IN` or `INOUT` will result in a translator
error. A `SELECT INTO` statement that returns more than one row will result in an
execution-time error. A `SELECT INTO` statement that computes the number of
`ACCOUNT_LIST` records for the project whose number is in the host variable pno is

```
#sql {
      SELECT COUNT(*) INTO :num_of_accts FROM ACCOUNT_LIST
        WHERE projectno = :pno
      };
```

NOTE
Host variables in the WHERE *clause have
default mode* IN.

FETCH Statement

The FETCH statement is used to retrieve a row from a positional iterator instance.
Use a FETCH INTO statement together with the endFetch() method to test through
the rows of a positional iterator and retrieve the data. Do not explicitly use the
next() method in a positional iterator unless you are using the special FETCH
CURRENT syntax introduced in Oracle SQLJ release 8.1.7. FETCH CURRENT is
used when you have an existing JDBC program that you want to rewrite in SQLJ
with very minimal modification. See the "Result Set Iterators" section of Chapter 6
to learn more about the FETCH CURRENT statement.

The syntax for a FETCH INTO statement is

```
FETCH iterator_host_expression INTO list_of_host_expressions
```

where iterator_host_expression references an iterator instance and has
default mode IN. The host_expressions in the list_of_host_expressions
have default mode OUT. An attempt to designate modes IN or INOUT for the latter
host_expressions will generate a translator error. The number of elements in
the list_of_host_expressions must be the same as the number of attributes
in the positional iterator attributes, and the host_expressions in the list and the
iterator attributes are matched up by position. Note that the host_expressions in
the list must be initialized, or you will get a Java compiler error indicating that they
may never get assigned (the FETCH statement will only assign values if a row was
fetched). In earlier releases of Oracle8i, the FETCH INTO statement would implicitly
call accessor methods named according to iterator column numbers. Starting
with Oracle8i release 8.1.7, this factoid is *not* true when you use the setting
-codegen=oracle. In this case, SQLJ generates assignments to appropriate
getter invocations on the underlying Oracle JDBC result set. The SQLJ generation
of a positional iterator class defines an accessor method for each iterator column,
where each method name corresponds to the column position. An example of a
FETCH INTO statement, taken from the AcctsForProjs2.sqlj program in
Chapter 2, is

```
#sql { FETCH :aDnoAno2 INTO :accountno, :projectno };
```

where that program had these declarations:

```
#sql iterator DnoAno2( int, int );
     DnoAno2 aDnoAno2;
     int accountno, projectno;
```

The `endFetch()` method

The problem with FETCH is that you really have to understand endFetch() to use it properly and fully grasp what is going on.

As noted in the previous section, a FETCH INTO statement works together with the endFetch(). FETCH does a motion, like the next() method, and then a population. Note, however, that FETCH will silently not populate if the move takes it outside of a valid table row. The endFetch() method will return false if and only if we are currently not positioned on a valid row. Specifically, before issuing a FETCH, the test endFetch() will return true, since we are before any valid rows. Importantly, the endFetch() method determines whether you have reached the last row of a positional iterator. It is very important to understand what the test endFetch() accomplishes and that you do not deviate from the straight and narrow path of its proper usage. It is not uncommon to see someone process every other row, or see him or her process the last row twice. Use endFetch() to test whether you have reached the last row of a positional iterator:

```
while (true) {
    // Use the FETCH INTO to get the data
    #sql { FETCH :aPosIter
           INTO :accountno, :projectno, :deptno };

    // This test must be AFTER fetch,
    // but before results are processed.
    // Test to see if you have reached the
    // last row of the aPosIter positional iterator.
    // If you have, quit processing.
    if (aPosIter.endFetch()) break;

    printIterators(accountno, projectno, deptno);
}  // End of while
```

Executable SQLJ Statements with Result Expressions: `SELECT` Statements

The processing of multirow SELECT statements in SQLJ requires a strongly typed version of a cursor called an *iterator*, as seen in Chapter 2. In this section, you will learn additional information about iterators. Specifically, you will consider

- The full syntax of iterator declarations

- The full syntax of query clauses (except for connection expressions)

- A SQLJ retrieval program `UsingNamedAndPositionalIter.sqlj` that illustrates result expressions

- Populating iterators with nested cursor output

- Support for `REF CURSOR` types in SQLJ

NOTE
Connection expressions will be discussed in Chapter 5.

Syntax of Iterator Declarations

As you saw in Chapter 2, there are two types of iterators: named and positional. In this section, you will learn how to declare and use these types of iterators. In Chapter 6, you will learn how to declare scrollable named, positional, and `ResultSetIterator` iterators.

When you declare a named iterator class, the SQLJ translator generates a class that implements the `sqlj.runtime.NamedIterator` interface. Classes implementing the `NamedIterator` interface have functionality that maps iterator columns to database columns by name, as opposed to by position.

However, when you declare a positional iterator class, the SQLJ translator generates a class that implements the `sqlj.runtime.PositionedIterator` interface. Classes implementing the `PositionedIterator` interface have functionality that maps iterator columns to database columns by position, as opposed to by name. Notice that both the `NamedIterator` interface and the `PositionedIterator` interface, and therefore all generated SQLJ iterator classes as well, implement or extend the `sqlj.runtime.ResultSetIterator` interface. The `ResultSetIterator` is a weakly typed iterator. Use this iterator when you need to convert it to a JDBC result set and, more importantly, when you do not need named or positional iterator functionality.

The `ResultSetIterator` interface specifies the following methods for all named and positional SQLJ iterators:

- `close()`   Closes the iterator. Use the `close()` method to close any iterator once you are done with it.

- `getResultSet()`   Extracts the underlying JDBC result set from the iterator. This method is central to SQLJ-JDBC interoperability that you will learn in Chapter 7.

- `isClosed()`   Determines if the iterator has been closed.

- `next()`   Moves to the next row of the iterator.

Additionally, the `PositionedIterator` interface adds the following method specification for positional iterators:

- **`endFetch()`** Determines whether you have reached the last row of a positional iterator.

Named Iterator Declarations

The syntax for named iterator declarations is

```
#sql [ modifiers ] iterator iterator_class_name [ implements_clause ]
    [ with_clause ] ( type_name_list );
```

`modifiers` is a sequence of Java class modifiers such as `public`, `private`, `protected`, and `static`. `iterator_class_name` is the name of the iterator class being defined, and the `type_name_list` is the list of iterator attribute names and types with which any `SELECT` statement that populates the iterator instance must be compatible. An example illustrating `modifiers` is given before examining the `implements_clause` and `with_clause`:

```
#sql public iterator DnoAno3( int departmentno, int accountno );
```

This declaration is similar to the one that appears in the `AcctsForProjs.sqlj` program in Chapter 2. However, in that program the `public` modifier was absent. With the `public` modifier present, SQLJ will generate DnoAno3 as a `public` class. Because DnoAno3 is defined as a `public` class, its iterator declaration should be contained in its own SQLJ file, and translated and compiled before any program can use it. This is in conformance with the Java practice of putting a `public` class declaration in its own source file. Alternatively, you can declare the iterator nested inside of a class. In this case, use the modifiers `public static`.

```
DnoAno3 dx;
#sql dx =
    { SELECT ano AS accountno, dno AS departmentno
        FROM OLD_ACCOUNTS WHERE pno = 55555
    };
```

Here the `OLD_ACCOUNTS` table has column names ano, dno, and pno for account number, department number, and project number, respectively. Thus, accountno and departmentno are assigned as column aliases to ano and dno, causing the select_list to match up by name with the attributes of DnoAno3. More important, how do the column alias (name) and the name in the type map list match up? It is *always* in a *case-insensitive* way. Also, you will have to explicitly use a column alias for computed columns (their default alias names do not make for good Java names).

The SQLJ implements Clause

The implements_clause lists Java interfaces that the iterator class will implement. Recall that a Java interface, like a Java abstract class, defines a set of methods or constant declarations with no implementation of the method bodies. Unlike the abstract class, however, all the method declarations of the interface are automatically abstract and public. A class that implements an interface must provide the method bodies for all the methods advertised by the interface. Consequently, if an iterator implements an interface, it must provide the implementation for all the methods listed in the interface. Recall that, when you declare a named iterator class, the SQLJ translator generates an accessor method for each column defined in the iterator class. If you want to restrict access to certain columns of a named iterator, you can create an interface with only a subset of the accessor methods, and then expose instances of the interface type to the user instead of exposing instances of the iterator class type. For example, suppose you want to hide the departmentno() accessor method from certain applications. You can code an interface, Ano, which only contains an accountno() accessor method, have DnoAno3 implement that interface, and only expose Ano to the application. The InterfaceExample SQLJ program demonstrates how to declare the Ano interface and a named iterator class, DnoAno3, which implements the Ano interface. Another use of the implements clause is for two predefined interfaces: sqlj.runtime.ForUpdate (iterator that can be used for positional update/delete, though this functionality is not supported in Oracle SQLJ) and sqlj.runtime.Scrollable (see Chapter 6 to learn more about sqlj.runtime.Scrollable).

Here is the definition of the InterfaceExample SQLJ program:

```
/*
** Program Name:  InterfaceExample.sqlj
**
** Purpose:  Illustrate the use of iterator class implements clause
**           to accomplish hiding.
**
*/
// Required SQLException class for SQL errors.
import java.sql.SQLException;

/* oracle.sqlj.runtime.Oracle class contains connect() method for
   connecting to database.
*/
import oracle.sqlj.runtime.Oracle;

/* Interface Ano will be used to hide the departmentno field from
   the main() method.
*/
```

```
/* All the iterator methods that main needs must be declared in the
   interface.
*/
/* Since the SQLJ generated iterator methods accountno(), next(),
   and close() throws SQLException, the corresponding interface
   methods must do the same.
*/
interface Ano {
  int accountno() throws SQLException;
  boolean next() throws SQLException;
  void close() throws SQLException;
}

// Declare the iterator class.
#sql iterator DnoAno3 implements Ano
  ( int departmentno, int accountno );

// Define application class InterfaceExample.
/* Quick and dirty example where methods throw exceptions (that is,
   propagate them back to the calling method) instead of catching
   them (one or the other has to be done since SQLException is a
   checked exception class).
*/
public class InterfaceExample {
  public static void main( String[] args ) throws SQLException {
    // Invoke InterfaceExample constructor to connect to database.
    InterfaceExample e = new InterfaceExample();

    /* Invoke getIterInst() method to create iterator instance and
       return it as interface instance.
    */
    Ano ax = e.getIterInst();

    // Retrieve row from iterator.
    ax.next();

    /* Use accountno() accessor method to retrieve account number
       from row, and then print that account number.
    */
    System.out.println( "Account number = " + ax.accountno() );

    // Close iterator.
    ax.close();
  }  // End of main()

  // Initialize database connection within constructor.
  public InterfaceExample() throws SQLException {
    Oracle.connect( getClass(), "connect.properties" );
```

```
}   // End of constructor

/* This method populates iterator instance and returns it as
   interface instance, hiding the departmentno() accessor method
   from the calling method.
*/
public Ano getIterInst() throws SQLException {
  DnoAno3 dx;
  #sql dx = { SELECT departmentno, accountno FROM ACCOUNT_LIST };
  return( (Ano) dx );
}   // End of getIterInst()
}   // End of InterfaceExample class
```

The SQLJ with Clause

The `with_clause` enables you to define and initialize constants that will be included in the definition of the generated iterator class. These constants are `public static final`. In standard SQLJ, there is a predefined set of constants, mostly involving cursor state options, which can be defined in a `with_clause`, and these are the only constants that can be so defined. In Oracle SQLJ, a predefined set of standard SQLJ constants can be defined in a `with` clause. However, not all of these constants are meaningful to an Oracle8i/9i database or to the Oracle SQLJ run-time. More importantly, attempts to define constants other than the standard constants is legal with an Oracle8i/9i database, but may not be portable to other SQLJ implementations and will generate a warning if you have the `-warn=portable` flag enabled. To learn more about the –warn flag, see Appendix D and the *Oracle8i/9i SQLJ Developer's Guide & Reference*.

The syntax for the `with_clause` is

```
with ( var1 = value1, var2 = value2, ..., varn = valuen )
```

where the `varn`'s are the constant names, and value 1 is the value for constant varn.

In Oracle9i SQLJ, you can use a `with` clause to associate a type map with the iterator class in an iterator declaration. For example, use the following fragment code to declare the `PlatformTypeIter` and associate it with the `PlatformTypeMap` type map:

```
#sql iterator PlatformTypeIter with (typeMap="PlatformTypeMap")
        (PlatformType platform);
```

Note that if you use Oracle-specific code generation (through the translator setting `–codegen=oracle`), and you use type maps in your application, then your iterator and connection context declarations must use the same type map(s).

The other predefined constants in the SQLJ standard, also not yet supported by Oracle SQLJ, are

- **Returnability (values: true/false)** This specifies whether an iterator can return JDBC result sets from a stored procedure call.

- **Holdability (values: true/false)** This specifies whether iterator position will be held after a COMMIT is executed.

- **Sensitivity (values: sensitive, asensitive, or insensitive)** This specifies whether an open cursor is guaranteed to be insensitive to the changes made by other SQL statements in the same transaction, whether it is guaranteed to be sensitive to the changes made by other SQL statements made in the same transaction, or whether there are no guarantees either way (asensitive). This is actually supported on Scrollable iterators in Oracle 9.0.1 and later.

- **UpdateColums** This is a String literal containing a comma-separated list of column names.

Note that an iterator declaration with a with clause that specifies updateColumns must also have an implements clause that specifies the sqlj.runtime.ForUpdate interface.

Positional Iterator Declarations

The syntax of the positional iterator declaration is

```
#sql modifiers iterator iterator_class_name
    [ implements_clause ] [ with_clause ] ( type_list )
```

The only difference between the positional iterator declaration and the named iterator declaration is that the former contains a type_list, a list of types, while the latter contains type_name_list, a list of attribute names and types. This is because when a SELECT statement populates an instance of a positional iterator class, the elements of its select_list are matched up with the iterator attributes by position; whereas when the SELECT statement populates a named iterator class instance, the elements of its select_list are matched with the iterator attributes by name. The following positional iterator declaration appeared in the AcctsForProjs SQLJ class from Chapter 2:

```
#sql iterator DnoAno2( int, int );
```

Syntax of Query Clauses

You have already seen several query clauses. For completeness, we recap the syntax here:

```
#sql result_expression = { select_statement };
```

The `result_expression` can be any Java expression that is an I-value and that references an iterator instance.

For example, the subsequent program `UsingNamedAndPositionalIter.sqlj` contains the following statement:

```
#sql aNamedIter = { SELECT ACCOUNTNO AS accountno,
                           PROJECTNO AS projectno,
                           DEPTNO AS departmentno
                    FROM ACCOUNT_LIST
     };
```

A SQLJ Retrieval Program: `UsingNamedAndPositionalIter.sqlj`

This program demonstrates how to use SQLJ named and positional iterators in your program. The `UsingNamedAndPositionalIter` class consists of the following:

■ Two SQLJ iterators, The `NamedIter` named iterator and the `PosIter` positional iterator, whose definitions are as follows:

```
// Declare a named iterator
   #sql public static iterator NamedIter (int accountno,
                             int projectno, int departmentno);

   // Declare a positional iterator
   #sql public static iterator PosIter (int, int, int);
```

■ The `usingNamedIter()` method uses a SQLJ named iterator to query data.

■ The `usingPosIter()` method uses a SQLJ positional iterator to query data.

Here is the definition of the `UsingNamedAndPositionalIter` class:

```
/* Program Name: UsingNamedAndPositionalIter
**
** Purpose:      A SQLJ program that teaches how
**               to use SQLJ Named and Positional iterators.
**
*/
```

```
import sqlj.runtime.*;
import sqlj.runtime.ref.*;
import java.sql.*;

import oracle.sqlj.runtime.Oracle;

public class UsingNamedAndPositionalIter {

  // Declare a named iterator
  #sql public static iterator NamedIter (int accountno,
                          int projectno, int departmentno);

  // Declare a positional iterator
  #sql public static iterator PosIter (int, int, int);

  public UsingNamedAndPositionalIter()
          throws SQLException {
    Oracle.connect( "jdbc:oracle:thin:@data-i.com:1521:ORCL",
                                        "scott","tiger" );
  }  // End of contructor

  // Method that illustrates how to use named iterators
  private static void usingNamedIter()
        throws SQLException {

    System.out.println("Using a Named SQLJ Iterator!!");

    // Declare a NamedIter
    NamedIter aNamedIter;

    // query data using aNamedIter object
    #sql aNamedIter = { SELECT ACCOUNTNO AS accountno,
                              PROJECTNO AS projectno,
                              DEPTNO AS departmentno
                        FROM ACCOUNT_LIST
    };

    while (aNamedIter.next()) {
        printIterators(aNamedIter.accountno(),
            aNamedIter.projectno(), aNamedIter.departmentno());
    }  // End of while

    // Always close the iterator
    aNamedIter.close();

  }  // End of usingNamedIter()

  // Method that illustrates how to use named iterators
```

```
private static void usingPosIter()
        throws SQLException {

  int accountno = 0;
  int projectno = 0;
  int deptno =0;

  System.out.println("Using a Positional SQLJ Iterator!!");

  // Declare a PosIter
  PosIter aPosIter;

  // Use the PosIter to query the database
  #sql aPosIter = { SELECT accountno, projectno, deptno
                    FROM ACCOUNT_LIST
  };

  while (true) {
      // Use the FETCH INTO to get the data
      #sql { FETCH :aPosIter
             INTO :accountno, :projectno, :deptno };

      // This test must be AFTER fetch,
      // but before results are processed.
      if (aPosIter.endFetch()) break;

      printIterators(accountno, projectno, deptno);
  }  // End of while

  // Always close the iterator
  aPosIter.close();

}  // End of usingPosIter()

public static void main( String args[] )
        throws SQLException {

  // Connect to the database
  UsingNamedAndPositionalIter app =
        new UsingNamedAndPositionalIter();

  // Use a SQLJ Named iterator
  usingNamedIter();
  // Use a SQLJ Positional iterator
  usingPosIter();

  // Always close the connection
```

```
        Oracle.close();

    }   // End of main()

    private static void printIterators(int accountno,

                int projectno, int deptno) throws SQLException {

        System.out.println("Account #: "+accountno +" Project #:
                        "+projectno +" Department #: " +deptno);
    }   // End of printScrollable()

}   // End of UsingNamedAndPositionalIter class
```

Populating Iterators with Nested Cursor Output

The material covered in this section is specific to Oracle and is not part of the SQLJ standard. In Oracle8, a *nested cursor* designates a set of rows that can appear in the select_list of a SELECT statement. For example:

```
SELECT projectno, cursor
   ( SELECT accountno FROM ACCOUNT_LIST
       WHERE PROJECT_LIST.projectno = ACCOUNT_LIST.projectno )
   FROM PROJECT_LIST
```

This SELECT statement prints the project number of each project, followed by the set of account numbers of accounts that involve that project. Sample output obtained by executing this SELECT statement in SQL*PLUS for a PROJECT_LIST table that contains three projects (with project numbers 10000, 20000, and 30000), and an ACCOUNT_LIST table that contains accounts 1 and 2 for project 10000, accounts 3 and 4 for project 20000, and no accounts for project 30000 is shown here:

```
PROJECTNO CURSOR(SELECTACCOUNT
---------- --------------------
     10000 CURSOR STATEMENT : 2

CURSOR STATEMENT : 2

   ACCOUNTNO
   ---------
           1
           2

     20000 CURSOR STATEMENT : 2

CURSOR STATEMENT : 2
```

```
     ACCOUNTNO
     ----------
             3
             4

      30000  CURSOR STATEMENT : 2

CURSOR STATEMENT : 2

no rows selected
```

In this section, you will learn two ways to retrieve nested cursor data in SQLJ using iterators:

■ Selecting a nested cursor into an iterator.

■ Populating a nested iterator with a nested cursor.

Selecting a Nested Cursor into an Iterator

A SELECT INTO statement that contains a nested cursor in its select_list can contain an iterator instance in its into_clause. The following program, NestedCursorExample.sqlj—which prints the name of project 10000, followed by the set of account numbers of accounts that involve project 10000—contains such a SELECT INTO statement.

```
/*
**
** File Name:   AnosForPnos.sqlj
**
** Purpose:   If an instance of an iterator class will be used in a
**            host expression, that iterator class must be declared
**            public, hence have its declaration be contained in
**            its own file.  An AnosForPnos instance will hold a set
**            of account numbers.
**
*/
import sqlj.runtime.*;
import sqlj.runtime.ref.*;
import java.sql.*;

// Declare a Named iterator
#sql public iterator AnosForPnos( int acountno );
```

Here is the definition of the `NestedCursorExample` class:

```
/*
** Program Name:  NestedCursorExample.sqlj
**
** Purpose:  To illustrate selecting nested cursor output into
**           an iterator.
**           Due to a bug in the JDBC thin driver, the
**           program will fail on the second project with
**           an invalid cursor error message.
**
*/
package chapter03;
import sqlj.runtime.*;
import sqlj.runtime.ref.*;
import java.sql.*;

// Required SQLException class for SQL errors.
import java.sql.SQLException;
/* oracle.sqlj.runtime.Oracle class contains connect() method for
   connecting to database.
*/

import oracle.sqlj.runtime.Oracle;
// Define application class NestedCursorExample.
public class NestedCursorExample {

    /* SQLExceptions, like all checked exceptions, must be caught
       or thrown (that is, propagated back to the calling method).
    */
    public static void main( String[] args ) throws SQLException {
        // Invoke NestedCursorExample to connect to database.
        NestedCursorExample maincode = new NestedCursorExample();

        /* The runNestedCursorExample() method executes the main body
           of code for the example.
        */

        runNestedCursorExample();
        // Always close the connection
        Oracle.close();

    }  // End of main()

    // Initialize database connection within constructor.
```

```
public NestedCursorExample() throws SQLException {
    Oracle.connect( getClass(), "connect.properties" );
}  // End of constructor

private static void runNestedCursorExample() throws SQLException {
  /* Declare iterator variable anAnosForPnos that will be
       populated by SELECT INTO statement.
  */

  AnosForPnos anAnosForPnos;
  String projectName;

  /* Select project name into projectName variable and nested cursor
     output (namely, the account numbers for accounts that involve
     project 10000) into anAnosForPnos.  Of course anAnosForPnos is
     a host variable here.
  */

  #sql {
      SELECT projectName, cursor
        ( SELECT accountno FROM ACCOUNT_LIST
           WHERE PROJECT_LIST.projectno = ACCOUNT_LIST.projectno )
             INTO :projectName, :anAnosForPnos
             FROM PROJECT_LIST WHERE projectno = 10000
  };

  System.out.println( "Project Name = " +projectName );
  System.out.println( "Accounts for project 10000 is = " );

  /* Retrieve rows from the anAnosForPnos iterator, and print the
     account numbers in those rows using the accessor method
     accountno().
  */

  while ( anAnosForPnos.next() ) {
      System.out.println( anAnosForPnos.accountno() );
  }  // End of while

  // Close iterator.
  anAnosForPnos.close();

} // End of runNestedCursorExample()

} // End of NestedCursorExample class
```

Populating a Nested Iterator with a Nested Cursor

A *nested iterator* is an iterator that is an attribute of another iterator. Iterators that contain nested iterators as attributes can be populated by SELECT statements that contain nested cursors, with the output from the nested cursor going to the nested iterator. For example, consider the following program NestedCursorExample2.sqlj that contains such a nested iterator. NestedCursorExample2.sqlj prints each project number, followed by the account numbers of accounts that involve that project. The same output, in a different format, was produced by the stand-alone SQL statement at the beginning of the section "Populating Iterators with Nested Cursor Output."

The corresponding sample output from NestedCursorExample2.sqlj is

```
Project number = 10000
Account numbers =
1
2
----
Project number = 20000
Account numbers =
3
4
----
Project number = 30000
Account numbers =
----


/*
** Program Name: NestedCursorExample2.sqlj
**
** Purpose:   Illustrate nested iterators.
**
*/
// Required SQLException class for SQL errors.
import java.sql.SQLException;

/* oracle.sqlj.runtime.Oracle class contains connect() method for
   connecting to database.
*/
import oracle.sqlj.runtime.Oracle;

/* Declare named iterator class PnoAno so that a PnoAno instance will
   hold a set of rows consisting of a project number and a set of
   account numbers.  The set of account numbers will be held in the
   nested iterator anos.
*/
```

```
#sql iterator PnoAno( int projectno, AnosForPnos anos );
public class NestedCursorExample2 {
  public static void main( String[] args ) throws SQLException {

    // Invoke NestedCursorExample2 to connect to database.
    NestedCursorExample2 maincode = new NestedCursorExample2();

   /* The runNestedCursorExample2() method executes main body of
      code for example.
    */
    runNestedCursorExample2();

     // Always close connection
     Oracle.close();
  }  // End of main()

  // Define application class NestedCursorExample2.
  public NestedCursorExample2() throws SQLException {

    // Initialize database connection within constructor.
    Oracle.connect( getClass(), "connect.properties" );
  }
  public static void runNestedCursorExample2() throws SQLException {

    // Declare "outer" iterator variable aPnoAno.
    PnoAno aPnoAno;

    /* Populate aPnoAno with SELECT statement output.  The SELECT
       statement returns, for each project, the project number of
       that project and the set of account numbers of accounts which
       involve that project.  The nested cursor output from the SELECT
       statement goes to the nested iterator anos in aPnoAno.
       (See Note 1.)
    */
    #sql aPnoAno =
      { SELECT projectno, cursor
          ( SELECT accountno FROM ACCOUNT_LIST
              WHERE PROJECT_LIST.projectno = ACCOUNT_LIST.projectno )
          AS anos
            FROM PROJECT_LIST
      };

    // Retrieve rows from aPnoAno using next() method.
    while ( aPnoAno.next() ) {
      /* Retrieve project number from aPnoAno row using projectno()
         accessor method, and print the project number.
      */
      System.out.println
```

```
                ( "Project number = " + aPnoAno.projectno() );
      /* Retrieve nested iterator output from aPnoAno row using
         anos() accessor method, and populate AnosForPnos instance
         variable anAnosForPnos with that output.
      */
      AnosForPnos anAnosForPnos = aPnoAno.anos();
      System.out.println( "Account numbers = " );

      // Retrieve rows from anAnosForPnos using next() method.
      while ( anAnosForPnos.next() ) {

        /* Retrieve account number from anAnosForPnos row using
           accountno() accessor method, and print account number.
        */
        System.out.println( anAnosForPnos.accountno() );
      }   // End of while

      // Close anAnosForPnos iterator.
      anAnosForPnos.close();
      System.out.println( "----" );

    }   // End of while

    // Close aPnoAno iterator.
    aPnoAno.close();
  }   // End of runNestedCursorExample2()

} // End of NestedCursorExample2 class
```

Note for NestedCursorExample2.sqlj: the column alias anos is required in
the SELECT statement so that the nested cursor column matches up by name with
the anos attribute of aPnoAno.

```
/*
** Program Name: NestedCursorExample3.sqlj
**
** Purpose:   Illustrate a named iterator nested within a positional
**            iterator.
**
*/
// Required SQLException class for SQL errors.
import java.sql.SQLException;

/* oracle.sqlj.runtime.Oracle class contains connect() method for
   connecting to database.
*/
import oracle.sqlj.runtime.Oracle;
```

```
/* Declare positional iterator class PnoAno2 so that its instances
   can hold the same type of data as iterator Pnoano instances held
   in the preceding program NestedCursorExample2.sqlj.  Note the
   nested iterator in PnoAno2 is of type AnosForPnos, and hence is
   a named iterator.
*/
#sql iterator PnoAno2( int, AnosForPnos );

// Define application class NestedCursorExample3.
public class NestedCursorExample3 {
  public static void main( String[] args ) throws SQLException {

    // Invoke constructor NestedCursorExample3 to connect to database.
    NestedCursorExample3 maincode = new NestedCursorExample3();

    /* The runNestedCursorExample3() method executes main body
       of code for example.
    */
    runNestedCursorExample3();

    // Always close connection
    Oracle.close();
  }   // End of main()

  public NestedCursorExample3() throws SQLException {

    // Initialize database connection within constructor.
    Oracle.connect( getClass(), "connect.properties" );
  }   // end of constructor
  public static void runNestedCursorExample3() throws SQLException {

    // Declare outer positional iterator variable aPnoAno.
    PnoAno2 aPnoAno;

    /* Populate aPnoAno with SELECT statement output.  The
       nested cursor output from the SELECT statement goes to
       the nested named iterator in aPnoAno.
       (See Note 1.)
    */
    #sql aPnoAno =
      { SELECT projectno, cursor
          ( SELECT accountno FROM ACCOUNT_LIST
              WHERE PROJECT_LIST.projectno = ACCOUNT_LIST.projectno )
          FROM PROJECT_LIST
      };

    // Loop to process outer iterator rows.
```

```
for ( ; ; ) {
  /* Variables to be fetched into must be initialized.
     anAnosForPnos is initialized to null since it is
     a class instance.
  */
  int projectno = 0;
  AnosForPnos anAnosForPnos = null;

  /* Fetch from positional iterator into host variables.
     Named iterator instance anAnosForPnos will hold output
     from nested iterator.
  */
  #sql { FETCH :aPnoAno INTO :projectno, :anAnosForPnos };

  // If at end of data, terminate program.
  if ( aPnoAno.endFetch() ) break;

  /* Otherwise, print project number and set of account numbers
     that was fetched.
  */
  System.out.println( "Project number = " + projectno );
  System.out.println( "Account numbers = " );

  /* Retrieve rows from iterator instance anAnosForPnos using
     next() method.
  */
  while ( anAnosForPnos.next() ) {
    /* Use accountno() accessor method to retrieve account
       number from row, and print that account number.
    */
    System.out.println( anAnosForPnos.accountno() );
  }

  // Close iterator anAnosForPnos.
  anAnosForPnos.close();
  System.out.println( "----" );
}
// Close iterator aPnoAno.
aPnoAno.close();
} // End of runNestedCursorExample3()
} // End of NestedCursorExample3 class
```

Note for `NestedCursorExample3.sqlj`: Unlike the SELECT statement in the preceding program `NestedCursorExample2.sqlj`, a column alias is not needed here because the SELECT columns and positional iterator attributes are matched up by position and not by name.

Support for REF CURSOR Types in SQLJ

See the *PL/SLQ User's Guide and Reference* for detailed information on ref cursors. A REF CURSOR *variable* is a variable that references a cursor. A ref cursor variable can be dynamically attached to different SELECT statements in a PL/SQL block at run-time, using the PL/SQL open for statement. This attachment of a ref cursor variable to a SELECT statement must be accomplished in PL/SQL. However, iterator variables can receive their output sets from REF CURSOR variables. There are, in fact, four ways that a SQLJ iterator variable can be attached to the output set of a REF CURSOR variable. These include the iterator instance being

- An OUT host expression in a PL/SQL block.

- The actual parameter passed to an OUT formal parameter of a PL/SQL procedure or function.

- An OUT host expression in the INTO clause of a SQLJ SELECT INTO or FETCH INTO clause. You have already seen these clauses in the preceding section, since nested cursors are actually implicit REF CURSOR types.

- The result expression in a SQLJ stored function call. You will consider this case in the upcoming section on stored function calls.

- It can be retrieved from a SELECT-list column.

In this section, you will develop the Pnos.sqlj program that demonstrates how to use REF cursor types. We present first the curpak.sql scripts that create the curpak package:

```
/*
** Program Name: curpak.sql
**
** Purpose:   Package curpak contains the definition of the specific
**            ref cursor type to be used in procedure pnoscur, and
**            also contains that procedure pnoscur.  All ref cursor
**            variables must be declared to be of a specific named
**            type that was defined by a PL/SQL type statement.
**
*/
CREATE PACKAGE curpak AS
  type pcur is ref cursor;
  procedure pnoscur( p out pcur );
end curpak;
/
CREATE PACKAGE BODY curpak AS
```

```
  /* The parameter p must be declared to be of mode OUT so that the
     iterator that will be passed to p can be changed.
  */
  procedure pnoscur( p out pcur ) is
  begin

     /* The PL/SQL open for statement attaches a SELECT statement to
        a ref cursor variable, executes the query, and identifies the
        result set.
     */
     open p for SELECT projectno FROM ACCOUNT_LIST;
  end;
end curpak;
```

Here is the definition of the Pnos class:

/

```
/*
** Program Name:  Pnos.sqlj
**
** Purpose:  If an instance of an iterator class will be used in a
**           host expression, that iterator class must be declared
**           public, hence its declaration must be contained in
**           its own file.  A Pnos instance will hold a set of project
**           numbers.
**
*/
#sql public iterator Pnos( int projectno );


/*
** Program Name: RefCursorExample.sqlj
**
** Purpose:  To retrieve the set of project numbers from the
**           ACCOUNT_LIST table two ways: using an embedded
**           PL/SQL block containing an open for statement, and
**           using a stored procedure containing an open for
**           statement.
**
*/
// Required SQLException class for SQL errors.
import java.sql.SQLException;

/* oracle.sqlj.runtime.Oracle class contains connect() method for
   connecting to database.
```

```
*/
import oracle.sqlj.runtime.Oracle;

// Define application class RefCursorExample.
public class RefCursorExample {
  public static void main( String[] args ) throws SQLException {

    // Invoke constructor to connect to database.
    RefCursorExample maincode = new RefCursorExample();

    /* The runRefCursorExample() method executes the main body
       of code for the example.
    */
    runRefCursorExample();
  }  // End of main()

  // Initialize database connection within constructor.
  public RefCursorExample() throws SQLException {
    Oracle.connect( getClass(), "connect.properties" );
  }  // End of constructor

  public static void runRefCursorExample() throws SQLException {

    /* Declare px to be an array of references to Pnos iterators,
       and assign an array with two slots to px.
    */
    Pnos[] px = new Pnos[2];
    /* Execute a PL/SQL block that opens a ref cursor for the set
       of project numbers in the ACCOUNT_LIST table, and populates
       px[0] with the result set from that ref cursor.  px[0] is an
       OUT host variable expression here, so that its value can be
       changed by the PL/SQL block, that is, it can reference
       the appropriate result set.
    */
    #sql {
      begin
        open :out ( px[0] ) for SELECT projectno FROM ACCOUNT_LIST;
      end;
        };

    /* Another way to get the same output is to call the procedure
       pnoscur stored in the package curpak, passing the OUT host
       expression, :out px[1] as a parameter to pnoscur.  Note that
       the mode of the host expression must match the mode of the
       pnoscur parameter.
    */
    #sql {
      CALL curpak.pnoscur( :out ( px[1] ) )
        };
```

```
/* A for loop is used to retrieve the data from px[0] and px[1]
   (the output for both will be the same).
*/
for ( int i = 0; i < 2; i++ ) {
  // Use the next() method to retrieve the next row from px[i].
  while ( px[i].next() ) {
    /* Use the projectno() accessor method to retrieve the project
       number from the row, and then print that project number.
    */
    System.out.println( px[i].projectno() );
  }  // End of while

  // Close the px[i] iterator.
  px[i].close();
  System.out.println( "----" );
}  // End of for loop

} // End of runRefCursorExample()
}
```

Executable SQLJ Statements with Result Expressions: Stored Function Calls

The syntax for a stored function call embedded in a SQLJ program is

```
#sql result_expression =
    { values ( function_name ( parameter_list ) ) };
```

Note that the outer parentheses around the function call are optional in Oracle SQLJ. The `result_expression` can be any Java I-value expression that is compatible with the return type of the function. The syntax and semantics of the `parameter_list` are the same as those described for stored procedure calls. The following SQLJ executable statement calls the function `insertemp` from the package `emppak`, described in an earlier section of this chapter "`SET` Statement," which inserts a row into the `EMPLOYEE_LIST` table using the data passed as its arguments. `insertemp` returns 0 if the insert was successful, and 1 otherwise:

```
int status;
#sql { status = values( emppak.insertemp
        ( 1000, 'Smith', 'Joe', '(999)999-9999', '1050' ) )
    };
```

If the stored function does not take any arguments, you can use either empty parentheses, `function_name()`, or no parentheses, `function_name`.

NOTE
Do not use any empty parentheses if you wish your code to be compatible with Oracle7.

For example, suppose that the PL/SQL package `curpak` coded in the preceding section contains the following function:

```
function dfunc return pcur is
p pcur;
begin
  open p for SELECT projectno FROM ACCOUNT_LIST;
  return  p;
end;
```

Then, the following code fragment assigns the output set from p to the iterator instance px:

```
#sql iterator pno( projectno int );
Pnos px;
#sql px = { values( curpak.dfunc ) };
```

Evaluation of Host Expressions and Result Expressions at Run Time

Since Java expressions (such as ++x) can have side effects, the order in which these expressions, in particular host and result expressions, are evaluated can affect their values. The following indicates the order in which host and result expressions in a SQLJ statement are evaluated:

1. If there is a connection context expression, then it is evaluated immediately (before any other Java expressions are evaluated).

2. If there is an execution context expression, then it is evaluated after any connection context expression, but before any result expression.

3. If there is a result expression, then it is evaluated after any context expressions, but before any host expressions.

4. After evaluation of any context or result expressions, host expressions are evaluated from left to right as they appear in the SQL operation. As each host expression is encountered and evaluated, its value is saved to be passed to SQL.

Each host expression is evaluated once and only once.

5. IN and INOUT parameters are passed to SQL, and the SQL operation is executed.

6. After execution of the SQL operation, the output parameters (Java OUT and INOUT host expressions) are assigned output in order from left to right as they appear in the SQL operation. Each output host expression is assigned once and only once.

7. The result expression, if there is one, is assigned output last.

NOTE
Host expressions in PL/SQL blocks are evaluated before the block is sent to be executed, and each host expression in a PL/SQL block is evaluated exactly once. See the example given in the earlier section "Anonymous PL/SQL Blocks."

JDBC and SQLJ Exception Classes

In this section, you will consider the SQLException classes, and its subclasses, and how to extract information from those classes. The SQLException class was defined for JDBC, and is a subclass of the Java Exception class. You have already seen that printing a SQLException object will print an error message identifying the error that caused the exception to be raised.

SQLException also contains two methods that can provide additional information: getSQLState() and getErrorcode(). The exact information provided by these two methods depends on where the exception was raised. If the exception was raised from Oracle SQLJ runtime, getSQLState() returns a five-digit string containing the SQLState—that is, a string identifying the error according to X/Open standard conventions. If the exception was raised by the Oracle server, getErrorCode() returns the *xxxxx* portion of the ORA-*xxxxx* error code. In all other cases, the methods do not return anything of use.

Useful subclasses of SQLException are SQLNullException and SQLWarning. sqlj.runtime.NullException is a SQLJ exception that is raised when a null value might be returned to a Java primitive variable. java.sql.SQLWarning are attached to the SQLJ ExecutionContext, and can be queried/extracted with the getWarnings() method. Note, however, that the Oracle JDBC driver does not generate any SQLWarnings, so that, in practice, you would never have to use this method. To learn more about ExecutionContext methods, see Chapter 10.

You can print the message that goes along with the preceding exceptions by printing the exception object, as you do with `SQLException` objects. Also, you should place the `catch` blocks for the subclass exceptions before the `SQLException` catch, so that they will be handled first, carrying out special operations appropriate to the subclass type of exception.

Other Useful JDBC and SQLJ Classes

You may need `java.sql` classes besides `SQLException`, such as `java.sql.ResultSet` (if you are using Java `ResultSets` instead of, or in addition to, iterators).

You have already used `java.sqlj.runtime.Oracle`, which contains the `connect()` method. Other `sqlj.runtime` classes you may need are in the `sqlj.runtime.ref` package (the `sqlj.runtime.ref.DefaultContext` class, to be discussed in Chapter 5, is defined in this package). Some important run-time classes that are directly in the `sqlj.runtime` package are `sqlj.runtime.AsciiStream` and `sqlj.runtime.BinaryStream` (these are SQLJ `Stream` classes that will be discussed in Chapter 7), `sqlj.runtime. ResultSetIterator` (also to be discussed in Chapter 7, along with other topics regarding the interoperability of JDBC and SQLJ), and `sqlj.runtime. ExecutionContext` (to be discussed in Chapter 5).

In this chapter, you learned about the different types of executable SQLJ statements. Specifically, you learned that there are two types of executable SQLJ statements:

- **Executable SQLJ statements without result expressions**   In the sections that dealt with this type, you learned how to construct the executable statement with SQLJ DDL and SQLJ non-`SELECT` DML commands; SQLJ transaction control commands; and `SET`, `FETCH`, and `SELECT INTO` statements. Importantly, you learned how to code executable statements in anonymous PL/SQL blocks and stored procedure calls.

- **Executable SQLJ statements with result expressions**   In the sections that dealt with this type, you learned how to code executable statements with SQLJ `SELECT` statements and stored function calls.

In Chapter 4, you will learn how to code stored procedures and functions in SQLJ, instead of in PL/SQL, and how to code database triggers in SQLJ.

PART
II

Advanced SQLJ for
Relational Processing

CHAPTER
4

Developing SQLJ Stored Programs and Triggers

S tored subprograms are procedures and functions that are either directly stored in the database with the SQL CREATE PROCEDURE and CREATE FUNCTION statements, or are stored in the database by being contained in PL/SQL packages and user-defined object types that are stored in the database. In Chapter 3, you saw that stored procedures and functions could be invoked from SQLJ programs. The stored subprogram examples in Chapter 3 were all coded in PL/SQL. In this chapter, you will learn how to code stored procedures and functions in SQLJ. Such stored subprograms can be used in exactly the same way as the stored subprograms implemented in PL/SQL: they can be invoked from SQL statements, as well as from PL/SQL blocks, and can be contained in PL/SQL packages, as well as being members of user-defined SQL object types. Also, just as is the case for PL/SQL subprograms, SQLJ stored procedures (that is, SQLJ methods that return void) can be invoked from SQL*Plus, Pro*C, database triggers, and SQLJ statement clauses using the SQL CALL statement. Also, SQLJ stored functions (that is, SQLJ methods that have a non-void return type) can be invoked directly from SQL DML commands, as well as from SQLJ assignment clauses and, using the SQL CALL statement, from SQL*Plus and Pro*C.

In this chapter, you will consider

- The development of SQLJ stored programs on the client side

- Creating call specifications in PL/SQL packages

- The invocation of SQLJ stored subprograms from SQL statements and PL/SQL blocks in various environments

- The loading and translation of SQLJ source in the server

- Dropping Java schema objects with the dropjava utility

- Advantages and disadvantages of implementing stored subprograms in SQLJ, as opposed to implementing them in PL/SQL

In Chapter 5, you will learn how to invoke stored programs from Java and SQLJ applets, and Java and SQLJ applications. In Chapter 9, you will consider the invocation of stored subprograms from CORBA objects and Enterprise JavaBeans.

Development of SQLJ Stored Programs on the Client Side

There are two approaches to developing SQLJ stored subprograms. One approach is to translate and compile the SQLJ source on the client side and then load the generated class and resource files into the server. The other approach is to load the SQLJ source into the server and then translate and compile it using the server-side translator. This is all a single step to the user, though. The former approach is probably the best, since the client-side translator has better support for option setting and error processing, and that approach is the subject of the current section. More important, you can first compile/test/debug the Java program on the client before deploying it in the server. In order to do that, you have to be clear about the differences between server- and client-side code. Fortunately, there are not many; actually, it is possible to write code that runs unchanged both on the client and in the server. Specifically, in this section you will consider

- Overview of Oracle server-side JDBC drivers

- SQLJ coding considerations for server-side applications

- `EmpInsert.sqlj`: an example server-side application

- Translating SQLJ source files on the client side

- Loading classes and resources into the server

- Checking that schema objects have been loaded in the server

- Creating call specifications for stored procedures using PL/SQL

- `FuncTest.sqlj`: a simple application that invokes a stored subprogram

- Summary of development steps

Overview of Oracle Server-Side JDBC Drivers

In Chapter 1, you learned about the Oracle JDBC drivers. As a reminder, we present here a brief overview of the JDBC drivers. See the *Oracle8i/9i JDBC Developer's Guide and Reference* to learn more about these drivers.

Oracle Client-Side JDBC Drivers

For client applications, Oracle provides two different JDBC drivers:

- **JDBC Oracle Call Interface (JDBC-OCI)**   For developers writing client-server applications or Java-based middle-tier server.

- **JDBC THIN**   For those writing pure Java applications and applets.

NOTE
The Oracle client-side JDBC drivers are JDK 1.x and JDK 1.2 compatible.

Oracle Server-Side JDBC Drivers

For server-side applications running inside an Oracle database, Oracle provides two specialized versions of JDBC: JDBC server-side thin driver and JDBC server-side driver. The server-side internal driver allows the Oracle8*i*/9*i* JVM to communicate directly with the SQL engine. The server-side internal driver is the default JDBC driver for SQLJ code running as a stored procedure, stored function, trigger, Enterprise JavaBeans, or CORBA object in the Oracle8*i*/9*i* server.

- **JDBC server-side thin driver** For Java programs that need to access a remote Oracle server from an Oracle server acting as a middle tier. URLs typically have the form

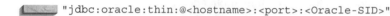

```
"jdbc:oracle:thin:@<hostname>:<port>:<Oracle-SID>"
```

- **JDBC server-side internal driver (formerly, JDBC-KPRB)** Supports any Java code that runs inside an Oracle database—Java stored procedures, Enterprise JavaBeans, or CORBA objects— and must access the same database. This driver allows the Oracle8*i*/9*i* Java Virtual Machine (JVM) to communicate directly with the SQL engine. The server-side internal driver supports only JDK 1.2.*x*. URLs typically have the form

```
"jdbc:oracle:oci8:@<tns-aliasname>"
```

Note that the Oracle 7.3.*x* JDBC drivers use `oci7` instead of `oci`; and in Oracle 9*i* and later, you can write `oci` instead of `oci8`, though these drivers still support `oci8` for backward compatibility.

NOTE
Starting with Oracle8i release 8.1.6, the Oracle JVM is JDK 1.2 compatible. Thus, the Oracle server-side JDBC drivers are only JDK 1.2 compatible.

Connecting to the Database with the Server-Side Internal Driver

Unlike client-side SQLJ programs, Java stored procedures using SQLJ implementations do not have to connect to the database, explicitly. The connection is implicit, that is, the connection does not have to be explicitly initialized.

Java stored procedures using JDBC implementations, as opposed to server-side SQLJ programs, have to connect to the database, explicitly. The server-side internal driver runs within a default session. There are two methods you can use to access the default connection:

- Use the static `DriverManager.getConnection()` method, with either the `jdbc:oracle:kprb` or the `jdbc:default:connection` as the URL string. For example:

```
DriverManager.getConnection("jdbc:oracle:kprb:");
// or
DriverManager.getConnection("jdbc:default:connection:");
```

- Use the Oracle-specific `defaultConnection()` method of the `OracleDriver` class. Oracle recommends that you use the `defaultConnection()` method.

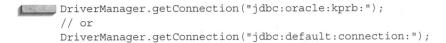

NOTE
With Oracle8i release 8.1.6 and higher, you are not required to register the `OracleDriver` class for connecting with the server-side internal driver. You can do so if you want. More importantly, the `OracleDriver` class is not required for either the `getConnection()` method or the `defaultConnection()` method to make the connection. Also, note that you do not need a user name and password to connect to the Oracle internal driver. Any user name or password you include in the URL string is ignored in connecting to the server default connection. One thing that you have to do, though: you must add the colon (`:`) after `kprb`, or this driver protocol will not be recognized.

Exception Handling for the Server-Side Internal Driver

To handle error conditions, the Oracle JDBC drivers throw SQL exceptions, producing instances of the `java.sql.SQLException` class or its subclass. You learned about `SQLException` in the "JDBC and SQLJ Exception Classes" section of Chapter 2. Recall that you can retrieve basic error information with the following `SQLException` methods:

- **`getMessage()`**   If the error originates from a JDBC driver, this method returns the error message with no prefix. If the error occurs in the RDBMS, it returns the error message prefixed with the corresponding `ORA` number.

- **`getErrorCode()`**   This method returns a five-digit `ORA` number for either the driver or the database.

■ **getSQLState()** This method returns useless information if the error is generated from the JDBC driver. If the error is generated in the database, the method returns a five-digit code indicating the SQL state.

The server-side internal driver, in addition to the preceding capabilities, offers extended features via the `oracle.jdbc.driver.OracleSQLException` class. This class is a subclass of the `java.sql.SQLException` class and is not available to the client-side JDBC drivers or the server-side `thin` driver:

■ **SQLException getNextException() (standard)** This method returns the next exception in the chain (or `null` if no further exceptions).

■ **int getNumParameters() (Oracle extension)** This method returns the number of parameters included with this error.

■ **Object[] getParameters() (Oracle extension)** This method returns a Java `Object[]` array containing the parameters included with this error.

The following fragment demonstrates how to use these methods:

```
...
try {
...
} // end try
catch (OracleSQLException e){
      System.out.println(e.getMessage());
      System.out.println(e.getNumParameters());
      Object[] params = e.getParameters();
      System.out.println(params[0]);
} // End catch
```

Coding Considerations for Server-Side Applications

Because stored subprograms run in the Oracle8*i*/9*i* server, when implementing a SQLJ subprogram you have to take into account the differences between writing code that will execute on the client and writing code that will execute in the Oracle8*i*/9*i* database server. Fortunately, there are only the following small number of differences to consider:

■ The connection is implicit, that is, if you want to use the (default) session connection. You can also use the thin JDBC driver inside the server to connect out to other servers. In this case, you need to have been granted specific privileges by the system administrator—to open sockets and to connect to other hosts.

■ The server-side driver operates within a default session and default transaction context. The default session is the session in which the JVM was invoked. This is different from the client side, where there is no default session. Client-side SQLJ programs must explicitly connect to the database.

■ You only have one database connection, namely, to the database in which the code is running. That connection is implicit. You do not explicitly connect to the database (that is, you will not have an explicit call to a method like `connect()`).

■ This connection cannot be closed. Any attempt to close it will be ignored, but no error will be generated. More important, you must make sure to close connection context instances that you have typically created with `KEEP_CONNECTION`. For example:

```
DefaultContext ctx = new DefaultContext(OracleDriver.getConnection());
```

Use the following syntax:

```
ctx.close(ConnectionContext.KEEP_CONNECTION);
```

The reason for using this code is that it permits the SQLJ run-time to garbage collect the context object, as well as any statements in the context's statement cache. If you only ever use the one static `DefaultContext` instance, then you need not worry about this— the cleanup will happen when the session gets disconnected.

■ For server-side SQLJ programs, there is no SQLJ class that the user must import for the benefit of the generated code, ever, because in the generated code, everything is referenced in a fully qualified way. Note that, for client-side and server-side SQLJ programs, you must import the `oracle.sqlj.runtime.Oracle` class if and only if your own code explicitly references the Oracle class.

■ You must be very careful about closing iterators when you are done with them, because the JDBC server-side internal driver does not release cursors for an iterator until the iterator is closed. The cursors will persist across calls to the stored subprogram. If you do not close your iterators, you could run out of available cursors, causing your subprogram to fail.

■ The JDBC server-side internal driver does not support `auto-commit`.
You must, therefore, explicitly commit all your updates, either in the stored
subprogram or the client that invokes the stored subprogram. For example,

```
// Commit the changes, explicitly:
#sql {COMMIT};
// Undo all changes, explicitly:
#sql {ROLLBACK};
```

Note that in a Java class, any public static method, including `main()`, whose Java
types are compatible with some SQL type can be used to define a stored subprogram.
Also, note that any such method can invoke any other accessible method in the
same class or in another accessible class that is stored on the server.

The default output device in the Oracle8i/9i Java VM is the current trace file.
If you wish to redirect your output to the screen, you have two alternatives. One
alternative is to execute the PL/SQL `dbms_output.put_line` procedure from
your SQLJ subprogram code, which will direct your output to the `dbms_output`
buffer. Such a call must be preceded by a call to `dbms_output.enable`, which
will enable your program to place output into the buffer. A client program can then
read this output from the buffer by first calling `dbms_output.enable` and then
calling the `dbms_output.get_line` procedure to read a line of output from the
buffer. The other alternative for getting output from a stored subprogram is to invoke,
in the stored subprogram, the PL/SQL procedure `dbms_java.set_output`,
which will direct subsequent Java output (from methods such as `System.out.println`)
to the `dbms_output` buffer. This invocation must be followed by a call to
`dbms_output.enable`. The client program can then read this output from
the `dbms_output` buffer using `dbms_output.get_line`, just as in the first
alternative. Both these alternatives will be illustrated with the upcoming program,
`EmpInsert.sqlj`.

Observe that the first method must also be used in any SQLJ program (client side
or server side) to get the output from an embedded PL/SQL block that contains a call
to `dbms_output.put_line`, since the call to `dbms_output.put_line` will not
directly send output to the screen when invoked from SQLJ. You must precede the call
to `dbms_output.put_line` in the PL/SQL block with a call to `dbms_output.enable`,
so that the output will go to the `dbms_output` buffer. The information must then be
read in the SQLJ program from the buffer using `dbms_output.get_line`:

```
#sql { begin
        /* The enable procedure accepts as its parameter
           the desired size of the buffer.
           enable must be called before you output to (the
           situation we have here) or input from the buffer.
```

```
          */
          dbms_output.enable( 500 );
          dbms_output.put_line( 'Hello' );
       end;
     }
String x;
int status;

/* The enable procedure must be called before you output to
   or input from (the situation we have here) the buffer.
*/
#sql { CALL dbms_output.enable( 500 ) };

/* The get_line procedure accepts two OUT parameters: the string to
   hold the input line, and the integer variable that is set to 0 if
   the line was successfully read, and is set to 1 otherwise.
*/
#sql { CALL dbms_output.get_line( :OUT x, :OUT status ) } ;
System.out.println( x );
```

EmpInsert.sqlj: An Example of a Server-Side Application

The following program, EmpInsert.sqlj, contains a method insertEmp()
that will insert a new employee record into the EMPLOYEE_LIST table. The method
insertEmp() will return 1 if the record could be inserted and 0 otherwise, as
well as printing an error message in the latter case. A PL/SQL function insertemp
that is similar to insertEmp() appears in the section "PL/SQL Subprograms" of
Appendix A. EmpInsert.sqlj is written with the preceding coding considerations
in mind, since it is intended subsequently to use the insertEmp() method to define
a stored function. Of course, one reason to use 1 and 0 here for boolean values is
that the PL/SQL BOOLEAN type (like all other PL/SQL-only types) is not supported for
Java stored procedures.

Here is the definition of the EmpInsert SQLJ class:

```
/*
** Program Name:  EmpInsert.sqlj
**
** Purpose:  Define a method insertemp() to insert a record into
**           EMPLOYEE_LIST table, returning 0 on success and 1 on
**           failure.
**
*/
import java.sql.SQLException;
import oracle.jdbc.driver.OracleSQLException;
```

```
// Looks like overkill, since OracleSQLException
// subclasses SQLException. In real life, you would choose
// one or the other.  This example illustrates how you can
// use the OracleSQLException class

public class EmpInsert {
  public static int insertEmp( int empno, int deptno,
                               String type, String lastname,
                               String firstname, String phone )
     throws SQLException, OracleSQLException {
    try {
      #sql { INSERT INTO EMPLOYEE_LIST VALUES( :empno, :deptno,
                                               :type, :lastname,
                                               :firstname, :phone )
            };

      /* Return 0 if insert was successful, that is, SQLException
         wasn't raised.
      */
      return 0;
    }  // End of outer try

    // Handle SQLException raised during insert.
    catch(OracleSQLException e ) {
      try {

        /* Enable access to dbms_output buffer, and print error
           message in buffer.
        */
        #sql { CALL dbms_output.enable( 500 )
              };
        #sql { CALL dbms_output.put_line( :( "Insert failed. "
              +e.getMessage()
              + " Parameter No. : " +e.getNumParameters() )
            };
        // (See Note 1.)

        // Since exception was raised during insert, return 1.
        return 1;
      }  // End of inner try

      // If exception was raised during calls, return 1.
      catch(OracleSQLException ex ) {
        return 1;
      }  // End of inner catch
    }  // End of outer catch
  } // End of insertEmp()
}  // End of EmpInsert()
```

Note for `EmpInsert.sqlj`:

I. If you wish to implement the second alternative for redirecting output to the
`dbms_output` buffer, you would replace the following lines of code:

```
#sql { CALL dbms_output.enable( 500 ) };
#sql { CALL dbms_output.put_line( :( "Insert failed. " + e ) )
    };
```

with

```
/* The set_output procedure accepts as its parameter
   the desired buffer size.
*/
#sql { CALL dbms_java.set_output( 500 ) };
#sql { CALL dbms_output.enable( 500 ) };
System.out.println( "Insert failed. " + e );
```

However, the calling code would remain the same.

Translating SQLJ Source Files on the Client Side

Oracle recommends that you upload in the database-generated `.class` files
instead of `.sqlj` or generated `.ser` files. For server-side programs, you must
use the `-ser2class` option of the translator to compile your source code. The
problem is that early versions of the server-side JVM were not dealing correctly
with `.ser` files. Even in the upcoming Oracle9*i* release 9.0.1, there is still one
problem when you use `typeMaps` and the `.ser` files get customized. The
workaround in this case is the use of the `-ser2class option`, which
prevents the server from performing customization. Actually, using the
`-ser2class` option will increase the size of the application and memory
usage. In Oracle9*i* the antidote would be the `-codegen=oracle` option.

The following command will translate and compile the preceding
`EmpInsert.sqlj` program:

```
sqlj -ser2class EmpInsert.sqlj
```

Loading Classes and Resources into the Server

The Oracle client-side utility `loadjava` is used to convert `.class` files into database
library units, called *Java class schema objects*, that are stored in the server, and to
convert `.ser` files (if any) into similar units, called *resource schema objects*, that are
also stored in the server. Note that `loadjava` also loads `.java` and `.sqlj` source
files as easily as `.class`, `.ser`, and `.properties` files. A distinct schema object
is created for each `.class` file and each `.ser` file. See the section "SQLJ Translation
Process" in Chapter 2 for information on files generated by the SQLJ translator.

On the `loadjava` command line, you can specify each `.class` or `.ser` file separately, or you can first combine them into a `.jar` (Java archive) file and then just specify that `.jar` file on the `loadjava` command line. Combining `.class` and `.ser` files in a `.jar` file is the preferred way.

Prior to Oracle8*i* release 8.1.6, if you submitted to `loadjava` all your `.class` and `.ser` files as a `.jar` file, you had to make sure that `.jar` did not compress your files, since `loadjava` did not support compressed files. Presently, Oracle8*i* releases 8.1.6 and higher and Oracle9*i* support compressed jar files.

The following command line creates an uncompressed file called `EmpInsert.jar` for all the output files from the translation of `EmpInsert.sqlj` (note that there are no .ser files, due to the use of the `sqlj -ser2class` option):

```
jar -cvf0 EmpInsert.jar EmpInsert.class
   EmpInsert-SJProfileKeys.class EmpInsert_SJProfile0.class
```

This can be expressed more succinctly as

```
jar -cvf0 EmpInsert.jar EmpInsert*.class
```

Note that

- The c option creates a new and empty archive, the v option generates verbose output on `stderr`, and the f option indicates that the archive is to be placed in a file (the next argument) instead of on standard output.

- Passing a 0 option to `.jar` suppresses compression.

- You can not use the succinct "wildcard" version of the `loadjava` command line if you have other files, unrelated to the desired class output, that start with `EmpInsert`.

Next, you will consider the `loadjava` command line to load the `.class` files for `EmpInsert.sqlj` into the server as class schema objects. The default driver for `loadjava` is the JDBC OCI driver, which does not require a URL in the -user option setting. However, suppose instead that you desired the JDBC thin driver, which does require a URL. This can be specified by using the `-thin` option and indicating a URL on the -user option:

```
loadjava -resolve -verbose -thin -user scott/tiger@data-i.com:1521:ORCL
EmpInsert.jar
```

The `-resolve` option directs `loadjava` to immediately resolve class references, instead of later when the subprogram is first executed. The `-verbose` option prints a step-by-step report on the `loadjava` command execution.

If you instead prefer the default OCI driver, you execute `loadjava`, as shown in the Listing 4-1.

Listing 4-1

```
loadjava -user scott/tiger EmpInsert.jar
```

Checking That Schema Objects Have Been Loaded in the Server

From SQL*Plus, you can query the `user_objects` view to determine whether `loadjava` successfully loaded your schema objects. To do this, you need to know how schema objects are named. There are two types of schema objects produced: class objects and resource objects (if you specified the `-ser2class` option to `sqlj`, only class objects are produced, simplifying naming). After the execution of `loadjava`, as shown in Listing 4-1, use the following SQL statement to check whether the `EmpInsert.class` file has been uploaded correctly in the Oracle data server:

```
// Use SQLPLUS or svrmgrl
SELECT object_name || ''|| object_type
|| ''|| status FROM USER_OBJECTS
  WHERE object_name = dbms_java.shortname( 'EmpInsert' );
```

The execution of the preceding SQL statement generates the following output:

```
OBJECT_NAME||''||OBJECT_TYPE ||''||STATUS
EmpInsert JAVA CLASS VALID
```

If the `.class` files were uploaded incorrectly, you would get the following output:

```
OBJECT_NAME||''||OBJECT_TYPE ||''||STATUS
EmpInsert JAVA CLASS INVALID
```

If the `.class` or `.ser` files that you are uploading are qualified with a package, the class schema object *full name* is produced by taking the class name, fully qualified with its package path, and substituting slashes (/) for dots (.). For example, if a fully qualified class name is `A.B.C.D.EmpInsert`, the full name of the corresponding schema object would be `A/B/C/D/EmpInsert`.

The naming scheme for resource objects (that is, schema objects for `.ser` files) is somewhat more complicated, providing a reason for converting all `.ser` files to `.class` files with the `sqlj -ser2class` option. However, if the `loadjava` or `jar` command, on which the `.ser` file is specified, is executed from the directory specified by the `sqlj -d` option (that is, the top-level directory in which `.class` and `.ser` files are to be placed), and if that directory is in your `CLASSPATH`, then the full name of the `.ser` file is the `.ser` filename (including the `.ser` extension), prefixed with the package path for the corresponding application class. For example, the full name of the `.ser` file for the class `A.B.C.D.EmpInsert` would be `A/B/C/D/EmpInsert_SJProfile0.ser`.

If the full name of a schema object exceeds 31 characters or contains illegal characters, a *short name* is generated for the schema object, and the schema object is loaded under that name. However, when querying the `user_objects` view, you do not need to know whether the full name or the short name is used—because the `dbms_java.shortname` function will take a long name as its argument and return a short name, if there is one, for the object, or the full name if there isn't a short name. Thus,

```
SELECT object_name FROM USER_OBJECTS
   WHERE object_name = dbms_java.shortname( 'A/B/C/D/EmpInsert' );
```

will tell you whether a schema object is loaded for `A.B.C.D.EmpInsert`, and whether a short name was used for loading that schema object or not.

The next section discusses creating call specifications using PL/SQL.

Creating Call Specifications for Stored Procedures Using PL/SQL

The final step in the development of a SQLJ subprogram is to create a top-level *call specification* (or *call spec*), that is, a SQL wrapper for the stored subprogram. A call specification declares a Java method or a third-generation language (3GL) routine so that it can be called from SQL and PL/SQL. The call specification tells Oracle which Java method, or which named function in which shared library, to invoke when a call is made. It also tells Oracle what type conversions to make for the arguments and return value. It is the call spec, written in PL/SQL, that makes the SQLJ subprogram appear, and it is used in invoking the subprogram from SQL statements and PL/SQL blocks. In this section, you will learn how to create a *top-level call spec* (that is, one that is not contained in another unit, such as a PL/SQL package) by using the SQL `CREATE PROCEDURE` and `CREATE FUNCTION` statements. In a subsequent section, you will learn how to create wrappers as part of PL/SQL packages.

Call Specifications: Requirements

A call spec and the Java method it publishes must reside in the same schema unless the Java method that is being advertised has a `PUBLIC` *synonym*. A synonym is an alternative name for a table, view, sequence, procedure, stored function, package, materialized view, Java class schema object, or another synonym. `PUBLIC` synonyms are accessible to all users. When you are defining a call spec, you can declare it as

■   Stand-alone PL/SQL function or procedure

- Packaged PL/SQL function or procedure

- Member method of a SQL object type

Because a call spec exposes a Java method's top-level entry point to Oracle, you can only publish `public static` Java methods. One exception to this rule is member methods of an Oracle object `TYPE`.

Oracle8*i*/9*i* provide new syntax options for the SQL `CREATE PROCEDURE` and `CREATE FUNCTION` statements (see Appendix A for the original syntax). These options allow you to associate the stored subprogram you are creating with a Java method in a Java class that you have already loaded into the server with the `loadjava` utility (that is, to create a SQL wrapper for your Java method). In such CREATE commands, you specify the parameter types and return type (if you are creating a stored function) of the stored subprogram, as well as the argument types and return type (if non-void) of the corresponding Java method. The stored subprogram parameter types must be SQL types, and must be compatible (see Appendix D) with the Java types of the corresponding (by position) arguments of the Java method. The SQL return type of a stored function must be compatible with the Java return type of the Java method. The Java method can return void (indicated by an absent return clause for the Java method) if and only if a stored procedure is being created.

For example, the `CREATE FUNCTION` statement, shown in Listing 4-2, creates a wrapper for the `EmpInsert.insertEmp()` Java method previously considered.

Listing 4-2

```
CREATE OR REPLACE FUNCTION insertemp( employeeno number,
                                      deptno number,
                                      type varchar2,
                                      lastname varchar2,
                                      firstname varchar2,
                                      phone varchar2 )
                                        return number AS
    LANGUAGE java
    NAME 'EmpInsert.insertEmp( int, int, java.lang.String,
                    java.lang.String, java.lang.String,
                    java.lang.String )
    return int';
```

The preceding SQL statement creates a stored function named `insertemp` having the indicated SQL return type and the indicated parameters. The stored function corresponds to a method written in Java having the fully qualified name `EmpInsert.insertEmp`. Note that the fully qualified specification must be given for any Java type (such as `String`) that is defined in a Java package. In Oracle8*i*/9*i* data server, although the `java.lang` package is automatically available to Java programs stored in the database, you must name it explicitly in your call specs. This is a common source of errors.

As a rule, Java names and call spec parameters must correspond one to one. However, that rule does not apply to the `main()` method. The `String []` parameter of the `main()` method can be mapped to multiple `CHAR` and/or `VARCHAR2` Oracle types call specs parameters. For example, the following fragment code creates a Java/SQLJ class:

```
public class PublishingMain {
    public static void main ( String [] args ) {
        int arraySize = args.length();
        String databaseAction = args[0];
        String objectType     = args[1];
        ...
        String nextArgument    = args[arraySize];

    }   // End of main()
}   // End of PublishingMain class
```

Use the following call spec to publish the `PublishingMain` class:

```
CREATE OR REPLACE PROCEDURE publishing_main (
    arg1    VARCHAR2,
    arg1    VARCHAR2,
    arg1    VARCHAR2)
AS LANGUAGE JAVA
NAME ('PublishingMain.main(java.lang.String[])';
```

Notice also that there are two major differences between the CREATE FUNCTION shown in Listing 4-1 and the CREATE FUNCTION for the PL/SQL version of `insertemp` given in Appendix A:

- The `insertemp` here returns number, whereas the `insertemp` in Appendix A returns `boolean`. You could not declare the `insertemp` here to return `boolean`, even if you were willing to have the `EmpInsert.insertEmp()` Java method return `boolean`. The reason is that PL/SQL subprograms can have PL/SQL types (which include SQL types and some other types) for their parameter and return types, whereas SQLJ stored subprograms must have SQL types for their parameter and return types. Since `boolean` is a PL/SQL type, but not a SQL type, it can be a return type for a PL/SQL stored function, but not for a SQLJ stored function. If you recoded the Java method `EmpInsert.insertEmp` to return `boolean` and then coded your CREATE FUNCTION so that `insertemp` returned `boolean`, you would still get an inconsistent data type error message any time you tried to call `insertemp`, even from SQLJ.

■ The Appendix A version of the CREATE FUNCTION used the %type attributes to define the parameters of `insertemp`, whereas the version given here uses the explicit types `number` and `varchar2`. Although neither PL/SQL nor SQLJ stored subprograms can use explicit constrained types as parameter and return types, PL/SQL subprogram parameter and return types can be specified using the %type attribute for a table field that is of a constrained type. If you use such a %type attribute when you define your SQLJ subprogram, you get a "Can't have constrained type" error message when you execute your CREATE FUNCTION statement.

The stored function `insertemp` can be invoked from a SQLJ program via the following SQLJ executable statement that contains an assignment clause:

```
int error;
// Where all fields preceded with ":" are host variables
#sql error = { VALUES(insertEmp ( :empno, :deptno, :type,
                              :lastName, :firstName, :phone ) )
        };
```

If you wish the calling program to read the output deposited by `insertemp` in the `dbms_output` buffer, follow the #sql statement with

```
int status;
String z;
#sql { CALL dbms_output.enable( 500 ) };
#sql { CALL dbms_output.get_line( :OUT z, :OUT status ) };
if ( status == 0 ) System.out.println( z );
```

The next section of this chapter, "`FuncTest.sqlj`: A Simple Application That Invokes a Stored Subprogram," contains a fully coded, simple SQLJ program that invokes the `insertemp` stored function.

The syntax of the CREATE FUNCTION and CREATE PROCEDURE statements for defining SQL wrappers for Java methods is given by the *Oracle8i/9i Java Stored Procedures Developer's Guide*:

```
CREATE
{ PROCEDURE procedure_name [ ( param[, param]... ) ]
  | FUNCTION function_name [ ( param[, param]... ) ] RETURN sql_type }
  [ AUTHID { DEFINER | CURRENT_USER } ]
  [ PARALLEL_ENABLE ]
  [ DETERMINISTIC ]
  { IS | AS } LANGUAGE JAVA
```

```
NAME 'method_fullname (java_type_fullname [, java_type_fullname ]...)
   [ return java_type_fullname ]';
```

where param stands for

```
parameter_name [ in | out | in out ] sql_type
```

Note that

- Constraints, such as the maximum number of digits in a number type or maximum length of a varchar2, cannot be specified for subprogram parameters. This is also the case for any PL/SQL subprogram formal parameter.

  The stored subprogram parameter list element param can contain the PL/SQL modes in, out, and in out. If a parameter has mode out or in out, the corresponding argument of the Java method must be an array. A SQL caller (which includes a Java caller that goes through the SQL call spec) will not be handling or passing in an array. However, if you have to call the actual method from Java, you will, of course, have to pass in a one-element array (more elements are fine, though they will not be changed). For example, the method setOne in the following class ExampleOut sets its argument to 1:

```
//Program Name:  ExampleOut.sqlj
public class ExampleOut {
  public static void setOne( int [] x ) {
    x[0] = 1;
  }
}
```

The following creates a wrapper for the method (after the class has been compiled and loaded into the server):

```
CREATE PROCEDURE setone ( x out   number ) AS
   LANGUAGE java
     NAME 'ExampleOut.setOne( int [] )';
```

setone can be invoked from the following SQLJ fragment:

```
int y = 5;
#sql { CALL setone( :OUT y ) };
System.out.println( y );
```

The preceding `println` will print 1, not 5.

A restriction you should note is that stored functions with `in out` and `out` parameters cannot be invoked from SQL DML commands.

- The `authid` clause indicates whether the stored subprogram executes with the privileges of its `definer` or its `invoker`. The default is the `invoker`.

- The `parallel_enable` option allows a stored function to be used in slave sessions of parallel DML evaluations.

- The `deterministic` hint instructs the optimizer that the value returned by a stored function depends only on the values of its arguments. The optimizer, therefore, can store and reuse the results of past function calls.

- The `method_fullname` must be fully qualified with the name of the class containing the method and the complete package path for the class—for example, `A.B.C.D.classname.methodname`.

   Except when the Java method is the `main` method of the class, the subprogram parameters and the method arguments must be in one-to-one correspondence. The `String[]` argument of `main` can be mapped to multiple `char` and `varchar2` subprogram parameters:

```
class Example {
   public static void main( String[] args ) {
      ...
   }
}
CREATE PROCEDURE nothing ( x1 varchar2,
                           x2 varchar2,
                           x3 varchar2,
                           x4 varchar2 ) AS
   LANGUAGE java
   NAME 'Example.main( java.lang.String[] )'
```

- If the Java method does not have any arguments, an empty parameter list (`f()`) is coded for it in the name clause. However, the procedure or function call contains no parameter list at all (`f`).

- Semantic errors in the `CREATE PROCEDURE` and `CREATE FUNCTION` statements are not reported until the procedure or function is invoked. Thus, if there was a type mismatch between the type of a procedure parameter and the corresponding Java method argument, it would not be reported when you executed the CREATE PROCEDURE statement, but when you first tried to invoke the procedure.

Note that in the Oracle9i release, Oracle is providing several utilities in the [ORACLE_HOME]/sqlj/demo/server/contrib directory that are useful when developing Java stored procedures. Some of them are a Javap program; a Java program to call the main() entry point of .class files; a bare-bones Java interpreter (Javafn); and the SqlWrappers.java program, which can be used to produce a first cut version of the SQL Wrapper script for the static methods of a particular class.

FuncTest.sqlj: A Simple Application That Invokes a Stored Subprogram

The following listing, FuncTest.sqlj, is a SQLJ class that illustrates how to invoke a stored subprogram:

```
/*
** Program Name:  FuncTest.sqlj
**
** Purpose:   Test the insertemp stored function, and report the error
**            message placed by insertemp in the dbms_output buffer in
**            the case that the insert failed.
**
*/
package chapter04;
import java.sql.SQLException;
import oracle.sqlj.runtime.Oracle;

public class FuncTest {


  // Some comment is in order on Oracle.connect():
  // if a SQLJ connection context has already been initialized
  // (which is the case in the server), then Oracle.connect()
  // behaves essentially like a no-op. This permits you to
  // use the same code, both on the client and in the server.
  public FuncTest() {
    // Initialize database connection within FuncTest constructor.
    try {
      Oracle.connect( getClass(), "connect.properties" );
    }
    catch( SQLException e ) {
      System.out.println( "Connection failed. " + e.getMessage() );
      System.exit(1);
    }  // End of catch
```

```java
}  // End of constructor
public static void main( String[] args )
     throws SQLException {
 // Invoke FuncTest constructor to connect to database.
 FuncTest f = new FuncTest();
 int error = 0;
 int output = 0;
 String errmess;
 /* Invoke insertemp to insert record.  Store return code in
    error variable.
 */
 int empno = 1946;
 int deptno = 204;
 String type = "Supervisor";
 String lastName = "Jones";
 String firstName = "Joe";
 String phone = "3059999999";
 try {
     // Calling a PL/SQL function from SQLJ
     // (See Note 1.)
     #sql error = { VALUES(insertEmp ( :empno, :deptno, :type,
                         :lastName, :firstName, :phone ) )
     };
 }  // End of try
 // Handle SQLException raised during function call.
 catch( SQLException e ) {
     System.out.println( "Error in call to FuncTest. " + e );
     System.exit(1);
 }  // End of catch
 // If no error, commit insert.
 try {
     if ( error == 0 ) {
         #sql { COMMIT WORK };
         System.out.println( "Example complete." );
     } // End if
 }  // End of try
 // Handle SQLException raised during commit.
 catch( SQLException e ) {
     System.out.println( "Error in commit. " + e );
     System.exit(1);
 }  // End of catch
 /* Otherwise, enable access to dbms_output buffer, read message
    from dbms_output buffer using get_line procedure, and print
    the message.
 */
 if ( error != 0 ) {
     try {
         #sql { CALL dbms_output.enable( 500 )
```

```
            };
            #sql { CALL dbms_output.get_line
                  ( :out errmess, :out output )
            };
            if ( output == 1 ) {
                System.out.println( "Insert failed." );
            } else {
                System.out.println( errmess );
            }
            // Disable access to dbms_output buffer.
            #sql { CALL dbms_output.disable };
        }   // End of try
        // Handle SQLException raised during buffer read.
        catch( SQLException e ) {
            System.out.println( "Error in reading buffer. " + e );
            System.exit(1);
        }   // End of catch
    } // End if
    // Close the connection
    Oracle.close();
  }   // End of main()
} // End of FuncTest class
```

Note on the `FuncTest` class:

1. This statement calls the `insertEmp` PL/SQL procedure, whose implementation is a SQLJ stored procedure. In "Creating Call Specifications in PL/SQL Packages," later in this chapter, you will create the `emppak2` PL/SQL package, in which you will define again the `insertemp` PL/SQL function that you created in this section.

Summary of Development Steps

In this section, the previously given development steps for client-side stored subprogram development are summarized, using the `insertemp` example.

1. Create the SQLJ source file, `EmpInsert.sqlj`, for the class `EmpInsert`, which contains the method `insertEmp` that will be "converted" into a stored subprogram.

   Translate and compile the SQLJ source file `EmpInsert.sqlj`, specifying that generated `.ser` files be converted to `.class` files:

   ```
   sqlj -ser2class EmpInsert.sqlj
   ```

2. Combine the `.class` files generated in the previous step into a `.jar` file:

   ```
   jar -cvf0 EmpInsert.jar EmpInsert*.class
   ```

3. Load the `.class` files contained in the `.jar` file `EmpInsert.jar` into the Oracle8*i*/9*i* server:

```
loadjava -thin -resolve -verbose
 -user scott/tiger@data-i.com:1521:ORCL EmpInsert.jar
```

4. Check in SQL*Plus that server schema objects were created for the classes loaded in the previous step:

```
// Use SQLPLUS or svrmgrl
SELECT object_name || ''|| object_type
|| ''|| status FROM USER_OBJECTS
  WHERE object_name = dbms_java.shortname( 'EmpInsert' );
```

CAUTION
Make sure that when you query the USER_OBJECTS table, the status attribute displays VALID before proceeding.

5. Create a wrapper in SQL*Plus for the stored subprogram:

```
CREATE OR REPLACE FUNCTION insertemp( employeeno number,
                           deptno number, type varchar2,
                           lastname varchar2, firstname varchar2,
                           phone varchar2 )
  return number AS LANGUAGE Java
    NAME 'EmpInsert.insertEmp
       ( int, int, java.lang.String, java.lang.String,
         java.lang.String, java.lang.String )
    return int';
/
```

6. Invoke the stored subprogram `insertemp`:

```
int x;
int empno = 1946;
    int deptno = 204;
    String type = "Supervisor";
    String lastName = "Jones";
    String firstName = "Joe";
    String phone = "3059999999";
    // Calling a PL/SQL function from SQLJ
    #sql error = { VALUES(insertEmp ( :empno, :deptno, :type,
                             :lastName, :firstName, :phone ) )
        };
```

Creating Call Specifications in PL/SQL Packages

As described in Appendix A, a PL/SQL package consists of a package specification, which contains (among other things) the specifications of subprograms that are available for use by clients of the package, and a package body that contains (among other things) the implementation (specification and body) of each subprogram declared in the package specification. Such an implementation can consist of a SQL wrapper for a SQLJ stored subprogram, instead of a fully coded PL/SQL subprogram.

For example, consider the following package emppak2, in which the CREATE PACKAGE and the CREATE PACKAGE BODY statements for emppak2 are each contained in their own SQL*Plus script, which is similar to the package emppak from Appendix A.

```
--
-- Program Name:  emppak2.sql
--
-- Purpose:  Define a package specification for PL/SQL package
--           emppak2.  emppak2 contains the insertemp
--           function that you developed in the previous
--           sections of this chapter.
--
--
CREATE OR REPLACE PACKAGE emppak2 is
FUNCTION insertemp( employeeno number, deptno number, type varchar2,
                                lastname varchar2, firstname varchar2,
                                phone varchar2 )
   return number;
end emppak2;
/


--
-- Program Name:  emppak2body.sql
--
-- Purpose:  Implement emppak2.insertemp
--           by providing wrappers for the Java methods
--           EmpPak2.insertEmp().
--
--
CREATE PACKAGE BODY emppak2 is
    -- Wrapper for EmpPak2.insertEmp().
    -- Remember to use only unconstrained types for insertemp
    -- parameter types and return type.
```

```
FUNCTION insertemp( employeeno number,
                             deptno number, type varchar2,
                             lastname varchar2, firstname varchar2,
                             phone varchar2 )
  return number AS LANGUAGE Java
    NAME 'EmpPak2.insertEmp
        ( int, int, java.lang.String, java.lang.String,
          java.lang.String, java.lang.String )
    return int';
End emppak2;
/
```

If you wish, you can create your subprogram wrappers in your package specification, which can eliminate the need for a package body. This is illustrated by the SQL*Plus script emppak3 . sql:

```
--
-- Program Name:  emppak3.sql
--
-- Purpose:  Provide wrappers for the Java methods
--           EmpPak2.insertEmp() in the package specification,
--           eliminating the need for a package body.
--
--
CREATE OR REPLACE PACKAGE emppak3 is
 FUNCTION insertemp( employeeno number,
                             deptno number, type varchar2,
                             lastname varchar2, firstname varchar2,
                             phone varchar2 )
  return number AS LANGUAGE Java
    NAME 'EmpPak3.insertEmp
        ( int, int, java.lang.String, java.lang.String,
          java.lang.String, java.lang.String )
    return int';
End emppak3;
/
```

The stored subprograms defined in emppak2 can be invoked by qualifying the subprogram names with the package name emppak2, as shown in Listing 4-3.

Listing 4-3

```
int x;
int empno = 1947;
    int deptno = 204;
    String type = "Supervisor";
```

```
String lastName = "Doe";
String firstName = "John";
String phone = "3059999999";
// Calling a PL/SQL function from SQLJ
#sql error = { VALUES(emppak2.insertEmp ( :empno, :deptno, :type,
                           :lastName, :firstName, :phone ) )
};
```

To test the fragment code shown in Listing 4-3, use the `FuncTest` SQLJ program that you developed in the "`FuncTest.sqlj`: A Simple Application That Invokes a Stored Subprogram" section of this chapter. Make the changes shown in Listing 4-4 and recompile the program:

Listing 4-4

```
// Replace the following SQLJ statement from the FuncTest.sql
#sql error = { VALUES(insertEmp ( :empno, :deptno, :type,
                           :lastName, :firstName, :phone ) )
};

// with the SQLJ statement shown in Listing 4-3
#sql error = { VALUES(emppak2.insertEmp ( :empno, :deptno, :type,
                           :lastName, :firstName, :phone ) )
};
```

The Invocation of SQLJ Stored Subprograms from SQL Statements and PL/SQL Blocks

In this section, you will learn how to invoke stored subprograms from SQL statements and PL/SQL blocks in the SQL*Plus, Pro*C, and SQLJ environments, as well as from database triggers.

You will consider these topics in the following order:

■ Invocation of stored subprograms from PL/SQL blocks.

■ Invocation of stored functions from SQL DML commands.

■ Invocation of stored procedures from SQLJ, SQL*Plus, Pro*C, and database triggers using the SQL CALL statement.

- Invocation of stored functions from SQL*Plus and Pro*C using the SQL `CALL` statement.

- Invocation of stored functions from SQLJ using assignment clauses.

You will see that the nice thing about SQLJ stored subprograms is that, because of the SQL wrappers, their invocation is exactly the same as the invocation of PL/SQL stored subprograms. You can say that stored subprogram usage is independent of the language in which the subprogram is written (subject to a few restrictions on SQLJ stored subprograms that are discussed in the last section of this chapter).

Invocation of Stored Subprograms from PL/SQL Blocks

Since SQLJ stored subprograms are invoked exactly the same way as PL/SQL stored subprograms, SQLJ stored functions and procedures can appear the same way in a PL/SQL block as can any PL/SQL function and procedure. For example, the following PL/SQL block invokes the subprograms from the `emppak2` package:

```
begin
   if emppak2.insertemp( 1948, 124, 'Nurse Lead', 'Jones', 'Joe',
                         '4619999999') = 1
   then dbms_output.put_line( 'Insert rejected.' );
   end if;
   exception
     when others then
       dbms_output.put_line( 'Unable to insert data.' );
end;
```

Note that PL/SQL blocks can be executed from SQL*Plus, Pro*C, SQLJ, and database triggers. Thus, SQLJ stored subprograms can be indirectly invoked in all these environments by being invoked from PL/SQL blocks that are being executed in these environments.

Invocation of Stored Functions from SQL DML Commands

A stored function can be invoked from anyplace in a SQL `INSERT`, `DELETE`, `UPDATE`, or `SELECT` statement that an expression of the same type as the function return type can appear. In particular, stored functions can be invoked from the select_list and where_clause of a SELECT statement. For example, suppose a stored function projamt takes a project number as its parameter and returns the amount of money invested in the project with that project number. projamt appears in the select_list and where_clause of the following SELECT statement, which prints the project number and project amount for each project that has an amount greater than $100,000:

```
SELECT projectno, projamt( projectno )
  FROM PROJECT_LIST WHERE projamt( projectno ) > 100000
```

SQL DML statements that invoke stored functions can be executed from SQL*Plus, Pro*C, PL/SQL blocks, SQLJ, and database triggers.

Note that you cannot invoke a stored function from a SQL DML command if

- The DML command is a SELECT statement and the function modifies any tables.

- The DML command is an INSERT, a DELETE, or an UPDATE statement, and the function queries or modifies tables that are modified by the statement.

- The function executes transaction control or DML commands.

These rules are intended to control harmful side effects. Violation of these rules generates a run-time error when the DML command is parsed.

Invocation of Stored Procedures Using the SQL CALL Statement

You have already seen in Chapter 3 how to execute PL/SQL stored procedures from SQLJ programs using the SQL CALL statement. By the principle of independence from the implementation language of stored subprogram invocation, these PL/SQL stored procedures might as well have been SQLJ stored procedures. The usage is exactly the same. For example, you have seen that the procedure emppak2.insertemp can be invoked from a SQLJ program as here:

```
#sql error = { VALUES(emppak2.insertEmp ( :empno, :deptno, :type,
                                :lastName, :firstName, :phone ) )
    };
```

Also, being a bona fide SQL statement, the CALL statement can be invoked from SQL*Plus and Pro*C (although not from PL/SQL).

You will now consider the invocation of stored procedures from

- SQL*Plus
- Database triggers
- Pro*C

Invocation of Stored Procedures from SQL*Plus Using the SQL `CALL` Statement

Calling stored procedures from SQL*Plus is essentially the same as calling them from SQLJ. The following invocation of `emppak2.deleteemp` (see "Creating Call Specifications in PL/SQL Packages," earlier in this chapter) from SQL*Plus illustrates this sameness. Note that this invocation causes an error to be generated in the case that the delete failed, indicating that an uncaught Java exception was thrown in the procedure.

```
SQLPLUS> CALL emppak2.insertEmp ( 2000, 124, 'Nurse Manager',
                                  'Timer', 'Yanick', '3059999999' )
```

Invoking the SQL `CALL` Statement from Database Triggers

A *database trigger* consists of an action (that is, a block of code) that is stored in the database and is *fired* (that is, automatically executed) whenever an event occurs (that is, the execution of a `DELETE`, an `INSERT`, an `UPDATE`, or a DDL command on a specified table) and a specified condition is satisfied. Triggers are very useful for propagating updates on one table into related data in other tables. In particular, triggers can be used to enforce the consistency of the database.

Database triggers are created with the SQL `CREATE TRIGGER` statement. Prior to the release of Oracle8*i*, the action in an Oracle database trigger had to be a PL/SQL block. In Oracle8*i*, the action can be either a PL/SQL block or a stored procedure call. See the *Oracle8i/9i SQL Reference Manual* for the full syntax of the `CREATE TRIGGER` statement.

The following SQL `CREATE TRIGGER` statement (to be executed in, say, SQL*Plus) implements the SQL-92 `SET NULL` referential action for the `EMPLOYEE_LIST` table. Recall from Appendix A that the referential integrity rule states that no foreign key can reference a nonexistent record. The `EMPLOYEE_LIST` table contains the departmentno field as a foreign key that references the `DEPARTMENT_LIST` table. The default way (as described in Appendix A) of enforcing the referential integrity rule for deletes and updates on the referenced table (here, the `DEPARTMENT_LIST` table) is to prevent such commands from executing that would violate referential integrity. This is called NO ACTION in the SQL-92 standard. There are three other *referential* actions (that is, means of enforcing referential integrity for deletes and updates on the referenced table) in the SQL-92 standard: CASCADE, SET NULL, and SET DEFAULT. Oracle supports the CASCADE action as an option on the CREATE TABLE and ALTER TABLE statements, but does not support the SET DEFAULT or SET NULL actions. The SET NULL referential action indicates that when a DELETE or UPDATE statement is executed on the referenced table, the foreign-key values on all matching records in the referencing table are set to NULL. So, the SET NULL referential action applied to the EMPLOYEE_LIST table causes the deletion of a department from the DEPARTMENT_LIST table to force each employee in that department to have their deptno field set to NULL.

```
CREATE OR REPLACE TRIGGER setnulldept
  BEFORE DELETE OR UPDATE OF deptno
    on DEPARTMENT_LIST
      FOR EACH ROW
begin
  if deleting or :old.deptno != :new.deptno
    then UPDATE EMPLOYEE_LIST
      SET deptno = NULL
        WHERE deptno = :old.deptno;
  end if;
end;
/
```

Note the following:

■ The CREATE TRIGGER statement specifies the name of the trigger (setnulldept), the *time* that the trigger is to be fired (before, as opposed to after, the delete or update on the row is complete), the *event* that will fire the trigger (either a delete on DEPARTMENT_LIST or an update of the deptno field of DEPARTMENT_LIST), the *granularity* of the trigger (the trigger will be fired once for each row affected by the DELETE or UPDATE command, as opposed to being fired once for the entire DELETE or UPDATE statement), and the *action* of the trigger (the indicated PL/SQL block).

■ The deleted row is referenced by the *correlation variable* :old.

■ The row before the update is referenced by :old. The row after the update is referenced by the *correlation variable* :new.

■ The predefined PL/SQL boolean functions, *deleting* and *updating*, indicate whether the triggering event was the execution of a DELETE or an UPDATE statement. If the delete and update cases are to be handled somewhat differently, these functions are quite convenient. For example, in the setnulldept trigger, the matching deptno in EMPLOYEE_LIST will be set to NULL in the update case only if the updated deptno field in DEPARTMENT_LIST has a different value than the original value, whereas it will be unconditionally set to NULL in the delete case.

■ This trigger does not contain the optional when_clause, which specifies a condition that must be satisfied in order for the trigger to be fired. Thus, this trigger will be unconditionally fired whenever the indicated delete and update are executed.

Now suppose that you wish to implement the trigger action by a SQLJ stored procedure call. One way to do this is to invoke the procedure from the PL/SQL block. However, the new CREATE TRIGGER statement syntax in Oracle8*i*/9*i* allows you to bypass the PL/SQL block entirely:

```
CREATE OR REPLACE TRIGGER setnulldeptd
   BEFORE DELETE ON DEPARTMENT_LIST
      FOR EACH ROW
         CALL setnulltrig( 0, :old.deptno, 0 )
/
```

Here, setnulltrig is a stored procedure that corresponds to the method Trig.setNullTrig() in the program Trig.sqlj.

```
/*
** Program Name:  Trig.sqlj
**
** Purpose:  The class Trig contains the method setNullTrig() that
**           will be used to define the trigger procedure setnulltrig.
**
*/
package chapter04;
import java.sql.SQLException;
public class Trig {
   // For the method setNullTrig():
   /* The argument dmlcommand indicates whether the event that fired
      the trigger was a delete statement (dmlcommand == 0) or an update
      statement (dmlcommand == 1).
      The argument olddepartmentno is the number of the department
      that was deleted (if the firing event was a delete statement)
      or the deptno before the update (if the firing event was
      an update statement).
      The argument newdepartmentno is zero (if the firing event was
      a delete statement) or the deptno after the update (if
      the firing event was an update statement).
```

```
*/
/* Need throws clause because the raise_application_error call
   will raise a SQLException.
*/
public static void setNullTrig( int dmlcommand,
  int olddepartmentno, int newdepartmentno )
throws SQLException {

  /* If the firing event was a delete or the firing event was
     an update that actually changed the department number to
     something different, set the departmentno field in all
     matching EMPLOYEE_LIST records to NULL.
  */
  if ( dmlcommand == 0 || olddepartmentno != newdepartmentno ) {
    try {
      #sql { UPDATE EMPLOYEE_LIST SET deptno = NULL
             WHERE deptno = :olddepartmentno
          };
    }
    /* If a SQLException was raised in the update command, call
       the DBMS_STANDARD.raise_application_procedure passing
       in an error number of -20100 and an
       error message 'Referential integrity action failed'.
       Notice that you must fully qualify packaged PL/SQL
       procedures and functions that you use in your
       stored procedures.
       (See Note 1.)
    */
    catch( SQLException e ) {
      #sql { CALL DBMS_STANDARD.raise_application_error
             ( -20100, 'Referential integrity action failed.' )
          };
    } // End of catch
  }  // End if
}  // End of setNullTrig()
}  // End of Trig class
```

Note on the `Trig` class:

1. The `DBMS_STANDARD.raise_application_error` call will terminate
   the trigger, roll back the effects of the DML command that caused that trigger
   to be fired, and report to the client program an error code and error message.
   Note that you must fully qualify packaged PL/SQL procedures and functions
   that you use in your stored procedures. If the client was coded in PL/SQL or
   Pro*C, the error code can be obtained from the `SQLCODE` variable, and the
   error message can be obtained in PL/SQL from the `sqlerrm` variable and

in Pro*C from the `sqlca.sqlerrm.sqlerrmc` variable. If the client was coded in SQLJ, the error code can be obtained by invoking the `SQLException` instance method `getErrorCode()`, and the error message can be obtained by invoking the `SQLException` instance method `getMessage()`. Unfortunately, for all these clients, if the stored subprogram was coded in SQLJ instead of PL/SQL, the error code will be for the generic "Java call terminated by uncaught Java exception" (–29532 in PL/SQL and Pro*C, 29532 in SQLJ), instead of the error code (such as –20100) that was passed as a parameter into the `raise_application_error` procedure. Thus, even if a SQLJ stored subprogram contains several calls to `raise_application_error` corresponding to different errors, passing in different error codes to help the client trap these errors, the client will always get back the same error code. This caveat is an instance of the exception problem pointed out in the note to the program `EmpPak2.sqlj`, in "Creating Call Specifications in PL/SQL Packages," earlier in this chapter. However, the error code number and message passed into `raise_application_error` will be part of the error message (along with the "Java call terminated by uncaught Java exception" message) that is passed back to the client, which is why the `raise_application_error` call is present in this method.

NOTE
When using packaged PL/SQL procedures or functions in your stored procedures, you must fully qualify them as you did for the DBMS_STANDARD.raise_ application_error procedure.

After loading the `Trig` class into the server, you can create the following wrapper for the `setnulltrig()` method in SQL*Plus:

```
CREATE PROCEDURE setnulltrig( dmlcommand number,
    olddepartmentno number, newdepartmentno number ) AS
  LANGUAGE java
  NAME 'Trig.setNullTrig( int, int, int )';
/
```

A similar trigger, using the same stored procedure, `setNullTrig`, can be defined for the update case. Unfortunately, if you are implementing the action as a stored procedure call and if you want the two cases to be handled somewhat differently by the action, you cannot define the same trigger for both delete and update. This is because Oracle will not allow you to invoke the deleting and updating

predicates in the stored procedure call. Thus, the following is illegal, even if
`setNullTrig` was coded in PL/SQL so that the first parameter could be boolean:

```
CREATE TRIGGER setnulldeptu
  BEFORE DELETE OR UPDATE OF deptno ON DEPARTMENT_LIST
    FOR EACH ROW
    // Illegal:
    CALL setNullTrig( DELETING, :old.deptno, :new.deptno )
/
```

Here is the (legal) separate update trigger:

```
CREATE TRIGGER setnulldeptu
  BEFORE UPDATE OF deptno ON DEPARTMENT_LIST
    FOR EACH ROW
      CALL setnulltrig( 1, :old.deptno, :new.deptno )
/
```

As you may have observed from the preceding examples, in the `CALL` format of
the `CREATE TRIGGER` statement, you do not place a semicolon (`;`) after the stored
procedure call.

Note that whenever a feature, such as the `CASCADE` referential action, is
available as a declarative option of a SQL statement, you are better off using
that declarative option, instead of implementing the feature yourself as a trigger.
The trigger will complicate your system, is riskier than the declarative feature,
and will probably underperform the declarative feature. Please see the *Oracle8i/9i
Application Developer's Guide—Fundamentals* for information on the proper use of
database triggers.

Invocation of Stored Procedures from Pro*C Using the SQL `CALL` Statement

The SQL `CALL` statement also provides the mechanism for directly invoking stored
subprograms from Pro*C. The following `exec sql` statement will invoke the
`deleteemp` stored program that is contained in the PL/SQL package `emppak2`:

```
exec sql CALL insertEmp ( :empno, :deptno, :type,
            :lastName, :firstName, :phone )
```

The C host variable `empno` and the other variables are passed as parameters to
`emppak2.insertemp`. These host variables must be declared in the declare
section for the Pro*C program. For example,

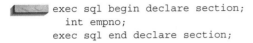

```
exec sql begin declare section;
   int empno;
exec sql end declare section;
```

Invocation of Stored Functions from SQL*Plus and Pro*C Using the SQL CALL Statement

There are two formats for the SQL CALL statement: one for calling stored procedures and one for calling stored functions. The format for calling stored functions contains an into_clause (such a CALL statement will be referred to as a CALL INTO statement) indicating the host variable in which to place the value returned by the function. Note that the CALL INTO statement is illegal in SQLJ programs (assignment clauses or, perhaps, SET clauses are used to call stored functions), and both forms of the CALL statement are illegal in PL/SQL.

You will now consider the usage of the CALL INTO statement in SQL*Plus and Pro*C.

Invocation of Stored Functions from SQL*Plus Using the SQL CALL Statement

The function insertEmp() from the earlier section "Coding Considerations for Server-Side Applications" is used in the following example. Note that you must first declare a SQL*Plus bind variable to receive the output from the function:

```
SQLPLUS> set serveroutput on
SQLPLUS> variable n number
SQLPLUS> CALL emppak2.insertEmp ( 2000, 124, 'Nurse Manager',
                                  'Timer', 'Natasha', '3059999999' ) INTO :n;
SQLPLUS> print n
```

The serveroutput flag is turned on so that the output from emppak2.insertemp that was directed to the dbms_output buffer can be printed. Unlike SQLJ and Pro*C, it is not necessary in SQL*Plus to call dbms_output.enable or dbms_output.get_line to enable and extract the buffer contents for printing. Also, if a PL/SQL block containing a call to emppak2.insertemp were submitted to SQL*Plus, in order to print the output from emppak2.insertemp, it would suffice to set serveroutput on in SQL*Plus before executing the PL/SQL block:

```
set serveroutput on
declare
n integer;
begin
```

```
   n := emppak2.insertEmp ( 2001, 124, 'Nurse Director',
                                'Momplaisir', 'Tara', '3059999999' );
   dbms_output.put_line( n );
end;
/
```

Invocation of Stored Functions from Pro*C Using the SQL CALL Statement

Calling a stored function from Pro*C is identical to calling a stored procedure from Pro*C, except that the CALL INTO statement is used, as here:

```
exec sql begin declare section;
   int employeeno, departmentno, status, n;
   varchar2 type[40] last[40], first[40], phone[20], s[100];
exec sql end declare section;
exec sql CALL insertemp( :employeeno, :departmentno,
                         :type, :last, :first,
                         :phone) INTO :n;
if (n == 1) {
  exec sql CALL dbms_output.enable( 500 );
  exec sql CALL dbms_output.get_line( :s, :status );
  if ( status == 0 ) printf( "%s\n", s);
}
```

   Note that like SQLJ, but unlike SQL*Plus, the client must enable access to the dbms_output buffer and then get_line from it to display the information that emppak2.insertemp wrote into the buffer.

Invocation of Stored Functions from SQLJ Using Assignment Clauses

This was already discussed in Chapter 3. For example, the following SQLJ code fragment invokes the stored function emppak2.insertemp:

```
#sql error = { VALUES(emppak2.insertEmp ( :empno, :deptno, :type,
                                :lastName, :firstName, :phone ) )
   };
```

The Loading and Translation of SQLJ Source Files in the Oracle8*i*/9*i* Server

Since the client SQLJ translator supports many more options, and the option setting and error processing are more convenient for the client translator, it is recommended that the SQLJ source for stored subprograms be translated and compiled (and also tested/debugged to the extent possible) using the client SQLJ translator instead of the server translator. However, for completeness, this section provides a discussion of the usage of the server SQLJ translator. In this approach, you will load your SQLJ source into the server and have the embedded SQLJ translator in the Oracle8*i*/9*i* Java VM process your source.

The `loadjava` utility is used to load, translate, and compile your SQLJ (and Java) source:

```
loadjava -resolve -thin -user scott/tiger@data-i.com:1521:ORCL
   EmpInsert.sqlj
```

The `loadjava` command without the `-resolve` option will merely load the SQLJ source into the server, creating a source schema object for it, which is analogous to the class schema objects and resource schema objects created when `.class` and `.ser` files (respectively) are loaded into the server. The source will then be implicitly translated, compiled, and customized the first time an attempt is made to use a class that is contained in the source. However, the `-resolve` option causes

- The embedded SQLJ translator to automatically translate, compile, and customize the SQLJ source

- Any translation or compilation error messages to be output to your screen

- The resolution of external references in each generated class

Classes are loaded into the server when the source is loaded, and the resources are loaded into the server when the source is translated. Thus, a separate `loadjava` execution for these steps is not necessary.

TIP
One problem that people encounter is first uploading
`.class` files and then trying to upload the same in
source form (or vice versa). The server-side SQLJ
translator will notice conflicts (some, but not all
of the files that, taken together, form a unit and
are to be overwritten). In this case, you need to
use `dropjava` (see the following) first to drop
the classes (or sources) that were loaded before
reloading them in a different manner. One other
point is that, in most cases, classes should be
transitively closed: they should not reference classes
that have not been loaded (or that are not being
loaded) into the server. The `-resolve` option also
helps enforce this at load time, instead of deferring
it to run time.

The remaining step in the creation of the stored subprogram—namely, the creation of top-level or packaged SQL wrappers for the subprogram—is done exactly as described when the source was translated by the client-side translator in "Creating Call Specifications for Stored Procedures Using PL/SQL" and "Creating Call Specifications in PL/SQL Packages," earlier in this chapter. Note that

- Once you load classes and resources from a source file, you cannot subsequently reload the classes and resources directly unless you first use the `dropjava` command to drop the SQLJ source. See "The `dropjava` Utility," later in this chapter, for more information.

- You can put multiple SQLJ source files into an uncompressed `.jar` file, and submit that `.jar` file to `loadjava`.

Next, you will now learn about

- Options supported in the server translator

- Setting options for the server translator

- Generated output from the server translator and `loadjava`

- Error output from the server translator

Options Supported in the SQLJ Server Translator

Only the following options are supported by the server translator: `encoding`, `online`, and `debug`.

- The `encoding` option specifies that NLS encodings, such as SJIS, be applied to your `.sqlj` and `.java` source files and your `.java` generated files when they are loaded in the server. See the *Oracle8i/9i SQLJ Developer's Guide and Reference*, and Appendix D of this book, for information about the encoding option.

- Setting the `online` flag to true (the default value) enables online semantics checking. Setting it to false specifies offline checking. See "SQLJ Translator Process" in Chapter 2 for some information on semantics checking.

- The `debug` option is equivalent to the `javac -g` option, and directs debugging information to be output when the SQLJ source is compiled. The capability to perform a fuller form of debugging is placed into/compiled into the generated `.class` files. You would then typically use JDeveloper or any other tool to debug the SQLJ and Java programs that you have loaded into the server.

Setting Options for the Server Translator

Since there is no command line and no properties files for the server translator, options are held in a table called `java$options`. Options are queried and entered into this table through subprograms in the package `dbms_java`:

- `get_compiler_option` is a function that returns the setting for the indicated option in the indicated source.

```
CALL dbms_java.get_compiler_option( 'EmpInsert', 'online') INTO :x;
```

- `set_compiler_option` is a procedure that sets the indicated option to the indicated value in the indicated source.

```
CALL dbms_java.set_compiler_option( 'EmpInsert', 'online', 'false' );
```

■ `reset_compiler_option` is a procedure that resets the indicated option to its default value in the indicated source.

```
CALL dbms_java.reset_compiler_option( 'EmpInsert', 'online' );
```

Generated Output from the Server Translator and `loadjava`

In addition to the class and resource schema objects already discussed for `loadjava` when the source is translated and compiled on the client, a source schema object is generated for the SQLJ source. The full name of this source schema object is obtained from the fully qualified package path of the first class defined in the source, with slashes (/) used instead of dots (`.`).

For example, if `classname` is in package `x.y.z` and is the first class defined in its source, the source schema object would be called: `s/y/z/classname`.

Error Output from the SQLJ Server Translator

SQLJ errors are directed into the `USER_ERRORS` table of the user schema. A `SELECT` statement that returns the text field of this table will report the message for an error:

```
SELECT text FROM USER_ERRORS;
```

The `dropjava` Utility

The `dropjava` utility is the inverse of the `loadjava` utility; it is used to remove class, resource, and source schema objects from the Oracle8i/9i server. You can identify the schema objects to be dropped by listing the `.sqlj`, `.class`, `.ser`, and `.jar` files that generated them, or you can list the schema object names (full names) directly. It is probably simpler to list the filenames, so that the `dropjava` commands resemble the `loadjava` commands that created the schema objects. For example, to remove the schema objects loaded for the `EmpInsert.sqlj` file, you would enter the following when it was translated and compiled on the client side:

```
dropjava -thin -user scott/tiger@data-i.com:1521:ORCL EmpInsert.jar
```

You should drop schema objects for dependent classes before the classes on which they depend.

Note that if you reload a class that is already loaded and the new version differs from the version that is already loaded, the new version will automatically replace the already loaded version. Thus, in that case, dropping the already loaded version is unnecessary. The problem is that if you load `.class` files and then load sources, or vice versa, then you must use `dropjava`.

Advantages and Disadvantages of Implementing Stored Subprograms in SQLJ Versus Implementing Them in PL/SQL

In this chapter, you learned how to implement stored subprograms in SQLJ and how to invoke stored subprograms from SQL and PL/SQL in SQLJ, SQL*Plus, Pro*C, and database triggers. Note that such stored subprograms can also be coded in pure Java and JDBC. In fact, the SQLJ stored subprogram is just a special case of the Java stored subprogram. Please refer to the *Oracle8i/9i Java Stored Procedures Developer's Guide* for information on implementing Java stored subprograms, http://technet.oracle.com/tech/java/sqlj_jdbc/htdocs/faq.html, and the *Oracle8i/9i SQLJ Developer's Guide and Reference* for information on implementing SQLJ stored subprograms, in particular.

At this point, it is desirable to say a few words about the relative advantages of implementing a stored subprogram in SQLJ, as opposed to PL/SQL.

The individual non-SQL statements are probably executed more efficiently in Java than in PL/SQL. However, the SQL call overhead is higher for SQLJ than it is for PL/SQL.

Subprograms implemented in PL/SQL cannot be ported to other database systems, since PL/SQL is proprietary to Oracle. However, standardization of SQLJ should ensure portability across many different database management systems.

It is clearly more convenient to develop a SQLJ subprogram than a PL/SQL subprogram. There are more development tools (IDEs, and so on) available for Java than for PL/SQL. Also, when you code in SQLJ, you reap the well-known benefits of developing your subprograms in a full-scale object-oriented programming language (see, for example, the Introduction to *Java with Object-Oriented Programming and World Wide Web Applications,* by Paul S. Wang). Also, don't forget that you can often make a deployment choice rather than a development choice, for example, moving logic among server, middle tier, and client.

Using stored procedures has its disadvantages:

- Java stored procedures only support SQL types, not PL/SQL types (such as index-by tables, BOOLEAN, and the like.)

- In Oracle database releases prior to Oracle9*i* release 9.01, Java stored procedures do not permit REF CURSOR parameters to be returned as OUT parameters. In 9.0.1, you can return a java.sql.ResultSet through a REF CURSOR parameter. However, you need to use an Oracle-specific API when opening that ResultSet. Support for SQLJ iterators is not provided in 9.0.1, though it is planned for future releases.

- While SQL and PL/SQL exceptions become manifest in a Java stored procedure as a SQLException, there is no mechanism to pass a SQLException from a Java stored procedure to SQL or PL/SQL and have it turn back into the original exception. Instead, all Java exceptions turn into an Uncaught Java Exception error.

- Conversions are costly.

- Creating connections and starting up JavaVMs are relatively costly (connection caching from middle tier).

- You definitely should use batching when looping over DML statements (such as inserts).

If your application consists largely of Java programs, then implementing your stored subprograms in SQLJ instead of PL/SQL will reduce the overall complexity of your system by reducing the number of languages used in the implementation. However, if your subprogram will be mostly called from PL/SQL, there are advantages to be gained by implementing the subprogram in PL/SQL. For one thing, as you have seen in "Creating Call Specifications for Stored Procedures Using PL/SQL," earlier in this chapter, PL/SQL subprograms can use PL/SQL parameter and return types, whereas SQLJ subprograms must use only SQL types. Thus, a PL/SQL function can return a boolean, but a SQLJ subprogram cannot. More precisely, a PL/SQL function returning a boolean can be successively invoked from a PL/SQL block, whereas a SQLJ function that returns a boolean cannot be successfully invoked from any environment, not even from SQLJ: an incompatible types error message is generated when the function is invoked. Note that a PL/SQL function returning a boolean cannot be invoked from SQLJ. The preceding error message will be generated.

Another advantage of coding your subprograms in PL/SQL is that the raise_application_error procedure can be used to report errors conveniently back to the caller, whether the caller is implemented in PL/SQL, Pro*C, or SQLJ. Unfortunately, as was pointed out in the section "Invoking the

SQL `CALL` Statement from Database Triggers," `raise_application_error` does not have a very useful behavior when called from a SQLJ stored subprogram. The error code returned to the caller is the code for the generic "Java call terminated by uncaught Java exception," instead of the error code that the subprogram passed to `raise_application_error`. This caveat greatly reduces the usefulness of `raise_application_error` in trapping different errors in the client program that were generated in the subprogram, and it is expected that the caveat will be removed in a subsequent release of Oracle9*i*.

Another point in favor of PL/SQL is that SQL is more seamlessly integrated into PL/SQL than into SQLJ. This causes SQLJ to suffer more from the impedance mismatch problem than PL/SQL. For example, the following PL/SQL loop from the section "PL/SQL Block" of Appendix A presents a more natural way of processing `SELECT` statement output than does the iterator construct:

```
for i in ( SELECT departmentno FROM DEPARTMENT_LIST )
  loop
    SELECT COUNT( DISTINCT projectno ) INTO nprojsd
      FROM ACCOUNT_LIST
        WHERE deptno = i.deptno;
    if nprojs = nprojsd
      then dbms_output.put_line( i.deptno );
    end if;
  end loop;
```

However, as was remarked in the section "Iterator Instance Declarations" of Chapter 2, the iterator construct is certainly more tightly coupled to Java than is the cursor construct to embedded SQL host languages, causing the cursor to generate more impedance mismatch on the host language side than does the iterator.

A situation in which it is preferable to code your subprogram in SQLJ is when you decide to move certain already existing client code, implemented in SQLJ, into the Oracle8*i*/9*i* server as stored subprograms. If you also code your subprograms in SQLJ, you will get away with making, at most, minor coding changes, as opposed to the situation in which you code the subprograms "from scratch" in PL/SQL.

In this chapter, you learned the following:

- How to develop SQLJ stored procedures that reside in an Oracle8*i*/9*i* database server. You learned how to code it on the client side and load it in an Oracle database.

- How to use the `loadjava` tool to upload SQLJ stored procedures into an Oracle database.

- How to create SQL call specifications in PL/SQL packages.

■ How to invoke SQLJ stored subprograms from SQL statements and PL/SQL blocks in various environments.

■ How to remove Java schema objects with the `dropjava` utility.

In Chapter 5, you will see an example of migrating client-side code into the Oracle8*i*/9*i* server and invoking stored subprograms in advanced scenarios, such as invoking them from applets. You will also learn about connection contexts and execution contexts in that chapter.

CHAPTER
5

Advanced SQLJ
Deployment

JDBC program connects to a database via an instance of the Java `Connection interface`, whereas a SQLJ program connects to a database via an instance of a `sqlj.runtime.ConnectionContext` interface. The Java `Connection interface` is part of the `java.sql` package, which is distributed with the JDBC 2.0 API, and the `ConnectionContext interface` is part of the `sqlj.runtime` package.

In the previous chapters, you learned the basic features of SQLJ and some of its advanced features. In this chapter, you will learn how to use these features and deploy SQLJ in many complex scenarios, specifically how to

- Use a SQLJ connection context to establish database connections
- Use the SQLJ `DefaultContext` class to connect to databases
- Manage multiple database connections with SQLJ
- Deploy SQLJ in an application: SQLJ application
- Deploy SQLJ in a thick client: SQLJ thick client
- Deploy SQLJ in an application server: SQLJ middle tier
- Deploy SQLJ in a thin client: SQLJ thin client
- Deploy SQLJ in a Java application: Java application
- Deploy SQLJ in a Java applet: Java applet
- Deploy SQLJ in an applet: SQLJ applet
- Deploy SQLJ in an Oracle8*i*/9*i* data server: SQLJ stored procedure
- Deploy SQLJ in the Oracle9*i* Internet Application Server (Oracle9*i* AS)
- Use `javax.sql.DataSource` objects in SQLJ programs

Using SQLJ Connection Context for Database Connections

SQLJ programs can use the following types of class instances to establish a database connection (see Appendix C for a discussion on the concept of a class versus an instance of a class):

- The instances of a declared connection context class

■ The instances of the `sqlj.runtime.ref.DefaultContext` class. The `DefaultContext` class is the only "predefined" class that is part of the SQLJ run-time that implements this `interface`.

First, you will learn how to declare a SQLJ context class, and then you will develop SQLJ programs to implement your declared SQLJ context class.

Connection context classes provide strongly typed connections for use with different sets of SQL entities. A set of SQL entities is a set of tables and stored procedures used in a particular database schema. For example, you can declare connection context classes to connect to a database and to use the set of SQL entities that you defined in the `PurchaseOrder` schema or the `Scientific Observation` schema.

Declaring a connection context class results in the SQLJ translator defining a Java class for you in the translator-generated code. Instances of the generated Java class allow a SQLJ program to establish a single connection or multiple connections to a single database server. Additionally, these instances can be used by a program to connect to several Oracle and non-Oracle databases located on different servers.

The following syntax declares a connection context class:

```
#sql <modifiers> context Context_Classname <implements clause> <with clause>;
```

This declaration results in the SQLJ translator generating a class that implements the `sqlj.runtime.ConnectionContext` interface. Additionally, the SQLJ translator will extend some (vendor-specific) base classes that also implement the `ConnectionContext` interface. Note that expressions and clauses within closed angular brackets are optional. Next, you will learn the meaning of these expressions and clauses, and how to use them in the declaration of your connection context classes.

SQLJ *modifiers* can be any standard Java class modifiers such as `public`, `private`, `protected`, `static`, and `final`. The SQLJ modifier rules correspond to the Java modifier rules. See Appendix B for a tutorial on Java.

The following is an example of a declared SQLJ connection context class using a Java modifier:

```
#sql public context LocalHostConnectionContext;
```

As a result of this statement, the SQLJ Translator creates a Java `public` `LocalHostConnectionContext` class. A SQLJ program that specifies this class can use its instances to establish database connections to schemas stored in a data server.

If you are writing Java programs and you wish to use the instance of a declared SQLJ connection context class, you should define the SQLJ connection context class in a separate file. That holds for top-level public classes. You could also define nested public static classes. Often this is much more convenient, since you can keep your class declarations in the same file. The `javac` compiler provided with the Sun JDK requires that each `public` class be defined in a separate file. For example, specify the declared SQLJ connection context class, the `LocalHostConnectionContext` class, in a separate file called `LocalHostConnectionContext.sqlj`.

Semantics Checking of the Connection Context

In the "SQLJ Translation Process" section of Chapter 2, you learned about the various steps in the SQLJ translation process. Recall that at translation time the SQLJ translator invokes the semantics checker, which checks the semantics of the executable of SQLJ statements. Here, you will learn about semantics checking of the connection context usage.

SQLJ programs can connect to a database either at application run time or at translation time. This feature provides semantics checking at different levels. Semantics checking at translation time is very useful because it allows you to discover program errors at translation time, helping you avoid generating run-time errors.

A significant feature of SQLJ is strong typing of connections. At translation time, this strong typing allows SQLJ semantics checking to verify that you are using your SQL operations correctly with respect to your database connections. To enable online semantics checking during translation, use the SQLJ `-user`, `-password`, and `-url` options and provide an exemplar schema if you do not wish to use your run-time schema. Remember, though, that the SQL entities of your exemplar schema must have the same names and datatypes as defined in your run-time schema.

During semantics checking, the SQLJ *translator* connects to the specified schema via the connection context class and performs two specific tasks:

- It examines the construct of each SQLJ statement specified by an instance of the connection context class and checks its SQL operations such as `SELECT`, `UPDATE`, `INSERT`, and `DELETE`. Schema object definitions (tables, views, stored procedures, and so on) also undergo semantics checking.

- It verifies that the objects referenced in the SQL operations match the objects in the specified schema. In other words, the schema objects referenced in the SQL operations must also exist in the database.

NOTE
You can use a schema example—that is, a test schema—instead of a production schema, as long as they each have the same schema object definitions.

You may use the same connection class to connect to several database servers, related SQL entities, and unrelated SQL entities. Remember, though, that a connection context class declaration does not define a set of SQL entities.

If you use qualified SQL names in your SQLJ programs, such as SCOTT.PURCHASE_LIST, the application user must have permission to access resources by these fully qualified names.

You can use a single connection context class to access non-Oracle databases. In this scenario, remember that these schema entities must have the same names as the entities of your schema example you tested and that they must use compatible datatypes.

The SQLJ implements Clause

When you declare a connection context class, you can also specify one or more interfaces to be implemented by the generated class. For example, the implements clause and the with clause specify additional interfaces to implement and variables to define and initialize. Use the following SQLJ statement to declare the Context_Classname context class with the implements clause:

```
#sql <modifiers> context Context_Classname
        implements InterfaceClass1,…, InterfaceClassN;
```

In the implements clause, the portion implements InterfaceClass1,…, InterfaceClassN, derives one class from a Java interface. Each part of the implements clause for the connection context —InterfaceClass1,…, InterfaceClassN— must be a user-defined Java interface. However, in addition to a user-defined interface, a SQLJ iterator that uses the implements clause in its declaration can also implement the SQLJ interface sqlj.runtime.ForUpdate. The SQLJ implements clause corresponds to the Java implements clause (see Appendix B for the definition and examples of the Java implements clause).

Recall that you learned about the implements and with clauses in Chapter 3. The implements clause is useful in a SQLJ iterator declaration, in particular, iterators that implement either the sqlj.runtime.Scrollable interface or sqlj.runtime.ForUpdate interface. Like in the declaration of a SQLJ iterator, you can use the SQLJ with clause in the declaration of a connection context class.

The SQLJ with Clause

The SQLJ with clause allows you to declare a SQLJ connection context class with a list of constants. At translation time, these constants are specified and initialized and are included in the definition of the generated class. Note that the constants that are produced are always public static final.

Here is the syntax for a connection context declaration using the with clause:

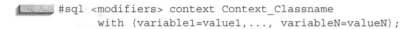

```
#sql <modifiers> context Context_Classname
     with (variable1=value1,..., variableN=valueN);
```

Note that the concept of the with clause, with (variable1=value1,…, variableN=valueN), is unique to SQLJ. There is no Java clause that corresponds to the SQLJ with clause. Also note that the with clause has nothing to do with the SQL-99 WITH query clause WITH…SELECT….

There is a predefined set of standard SQLJ constants that can be defined within a with clause. The SQLJ standard constants involve cursor states and can only take particular values (see Chapter 3 for a discussion of the SQLJ cursor). Note that the definitions of constants other than the SQLJ standard constants are vendor specific and might not be portable from one database to another. In fact, the SQLJ translator will generate error warnings when translating a SQLJ program that specifies nonstandard SQLJ constants.

NOTE
The list of constants for the with clause must be enclosed in parentheses, whereas the implements list does not require parentheses. See Chapter 3 and Appendix D to learn more about the SQLJ implements clause.

SQLJ allows you to place both the implements clause and the with clause in the declaration of a SQLJ connection context class, but the implements clause must precede the with clause:

```
#sql <modifiers> context Context_Classname
          implements InterfaceClassi ( i = 1,…,N)
     with (aSqljStandardConstant=…);
```

NOTE
If you include both the implements clause and the with clause in the declaration of SQLJ connection context, remember that the implements clause always comes before the with clause.

`DataSource` **Support**

One way for a Java application to connect to a database is by using the JDBC driver manager. The `java.sql.DriverManager` class is the management layer of JDBC and works between the user and the driver. It keeps track of the drivers that are available and handles establishing a connection between a database and the appropriate driver. One drawback to using this approach is that usually your program must use the JDBC driver of a specific vendor, which can make the code that loads the driver specific to a vendor's product—therefore, not portable.

You can solve the preceding problem by using the Java Naming and Directory Interface (JNDI) and JDBC 2.0 API. The JDBC 2.0 extended API specifies the use of DataSource and JNDI as a portable alternative to the current `java.sql.DriverManager` mechanism for obtaining JDBC connections. It allows database connections to be established through a JNDI name lookup. This name is bound to a particular database and schema prior to program run time through a `DataSource` object. The name can be bound to different physical connections without much source code changes by just rebinding the name in the directory service. A nice feature of the JDBC 2.0 extension API is that you can use data source objects for specifying other resources. For example, you can use the API to specify printers that are on your network. The JDBC 2.0 API is part of the Java 2 Platform, Standard Edition, v1.2.2 API Specification. The complete JDBC API includes both the `java.sql` package (the JDBC 2.0 core API) and the `javax.sql` package (the JDBC Standard Extension API).

A `DataSource` object is a Java object that implements the `javax.sql.DataSource interface`. It is a factory for `java.sql.Connection` objects. Beginning with Oracle8*i* release 8.1.7, the Oracle database supports data sources. We present here a very brief overview of how Oracle supports this concept. To learn more about Oracle's implementation and `DataSource` objects, see the *Oracle8i JDBC Developer's Guide and Reference, Release 3 (8.1.7)* (or the 9*i* JDBC) technical manual and the *JDBC 2.0 Standard Extension API* (http://java.sun.com/ products/jdbc/ jdbc20.stdext.pdf), respectively.

An object that implements the `DataSource interface` will typically be registered with a JNDI service provider. A service provider is a set of modules that together satisfy JNDI API requests. As defined by the JDBC 2.0 extended API, data sources can also be implemented using a connection pool or distributed transaction service. Note that the JNDI classes are distributed with JDK 1.3. Thus, you can use `DataSource` objects and JNDI in the JDK 1.3 environment. However, you can also use `DataSource` and JNDI in a JDK 1.2 or JDK 1.1.*x* environment. You do so with the Java Extension classes. To use JNDI in earlier JDK 1.3 environments, include in your CLASSPATH the `jndi.jar` file. You can download the `jndi.jar` from Sun (http://java.sun.com/products/jndi/ #DOWNLOAD12).

Here is a partial definition of the `javax.sql.DataSource interface`:

```
public interface DataSource {

    // Establish a connection to the database
    public java.sql.Connection getConnection()
        throws SQLException;
    // Overloaded method to establish a connection
    public java.sql.Connection getConnection( String username,
        String password) throws SQLException;
    // Get the DataSource log writer
    public java.io.PrintWriter getLogWriter()
        throws SQLException;
    // Set the DataSource log writer
    public void setLogWriter(java.io.PrintWriter out)
        throws SQLException;
    // Set the maximum time (in seconds)
    public void setLoginTimeout(int seconds)
        throws SQLException;
    // Get the maximum time in seconds
    public int getLoginTimeout()
        throws SQLException;

} // End of interface DataSource
```

Like other interfaces in the JDBC API, such as `java.sql.Connection` and `java.sql.ResultSet`, implementation of `javax.sql.DataSource` is provided by JDBC driver vendors as part of their JDBC 2.0 products. Oracle implements the `javax.sql.DataSource` interface with the OracleDataSource class in the `oracle.jdbc.pool` package. The OracleDataSource class provides a set of properties that you can set in your program in order for your application to establish a connection to a particular data source. For example, The OracleDataSource class provides the overloaded `getConnection()` method that returns an OracleConnection instance, optionally taking a username and password as input. The OracleDataSource class and all subclasses implement the `java.io.Serializable` and `javax.naming.Referenceable` interfaces. See the *Oracle8i JDBC Developer's Guide and Reference Release 3 (8.1.7)* (or the 9i JDBC) to learn more about the `oracle.jdbc.pool package`. For a complete definition of the OracleDataSource class, see [ORACLE_HOME]/ jdbc/doc/javadoc.zip. This directory is created for you when you install Oracle8i release 3 (8.1.7).

Here is a partial definition of the `OracleDataSource` class:

```
public class OracleDataSource  extends java.lang.Object
        implements javax.sql.DataSource,
```

```
                    java.io.Serializable,
                    javax.naming.Referenceable {
 // Establish a connection to the database
 public java.sql.Connection getConnection()
            throws SQLException;
// Overloaded method to establish a connection
public java.sql.Connection getConnection( String username,
            String password) throws SQLException;
...
...
// This method works only for JDBC OCI driver
public void setTNSEntryName(java.lang.String dbname);
// This method works only for JDBC OCI driver
public void getTNSEntryName();
// Set the data source name
public void setDataSourceName(java.lang.String dsname);
// Get the data source name
public void getDataSourceName();
// Set the name for a database server
public void setDatabaseName(java.lang.String dsname);
// Get the name for a database server
public void getDatabaseName();
// Get the name of the database server
public java.lang.String getServerName()
// Set the name of the database server
public java.lang.String setServerName(java.lang.String sn);
// Set URL from which connections have to be obtained
public void setURL(java.lang.String url);
// Get URL from a data source
public void getURL()throws SQLException;
// Set the user name
public void setUser(java.lang.String user)
// Get the user name for the data source
public void getUser();
// Set the user password
public void setPassword(java.lang.String pd);
// Get the user password
public void getPassword();
// Set the JDBC driver (OCI, thin, or kprb);
public void setDriverType(java.lang.String dt);
// Get the JDBC driver (OCI, thin, or kprb)
public void getDriverType(;)
// Set network protocol, default TCP
public void setNetworkProtocol(java.lang.String np);
// Get network protocol
public void getNetworkProtocol();
// Set port number
public void setPortNumber(int pn);
// Get port number
```

```
public void getPortNumber();
// Get getReference in interface javax.naming.Referenceable
public javax.naming.Reference getReference()
  throws javax.naming.NamingException;

} // End of the OracleDataSource class
```

Oracle SQLJ (release 8.17 and 9*i*) uses a mechanism similar to the one that JDBC 2.0 API uses to create connection context instances. In SQLJ, you can associate a connection context class with a logical schema in a similar manner as you associate the name of a `DataSource` in a JDBC connection. In a SQLJ program, you can combine both concepts by adding the `DataSource` name to your connection context declaration.

For example, if you create a data source named `jdbc/Test`, you can declare a connection context class and associate it with your `jdbc/Test` data source. When you do so, the connection context class that you declare with the `DataSource` property provides new constructors and omits some of the constructors provided by the `java.sql.DriverManager` class. Use the following syntax to declare the `TestCtx` context class and associate it with the named `jdbc/Test` data source:

```
#sql context TestCtx with (dataSource="jdbc/Test")
```

The `TestCtx` connection context class that you declare with the property of the `jdbc/Test` `DataSource` provides the following new constructors:

- `public TestCtx()` looks up the `DataSource` for `"jdbc/Test"` and then calls the `getConnection()` method on it to obtain a connection.

- `public TestCtx(String user, String password)` looks up the `DataSource` for `"jdbc/Test"` and then calls `getConnection (user,password)` on it to obtain a connection.

- `public TestCtx(ConnectionContext ctx)` delegates to the `ctx` object to obtain a connection.

The `TestCtx` context class will omit the following `DriverManager`-based constructors:

- `public TestCtx(Connection conn)`

- `public TestCtx(String url, String user, String password, boolean autoCommit)`

- `public TestCtx(String url, boolean autoCommit)`

- `public TestCtx(String url, java.util.Properties info, boolean autoCommit)`

■ `public TestCtx(String url, boolean autoCommit)`

Note that, like the connection context class, you can also associate the `DefaultContext` class to a `DataSource` object. Also, note that you do not really have an option: this "association" is done whether or not you want it. The only way to avoid this association is to initialize the `static DefaultContext` instance. Also note that in the server, we do not use this default data source: the default context is always initialized to the session connection. For example, if your SQLJ program uses a `DefaultContext` object and the default context object is null, then the SQLJ run time will use the *SQLJ default data source* to connect to the database. The SQLJ default data source is bound to a default name `jdbc/defaultDataSource`. In the "Using `DataSource` in SQLJ Programs" section, later in this chapter, you will write a SQLJ program in which you will declare the `TestCtx` connection context class that you will associate with the `jdbc/Test` data source.

Auto-Commit Mode for `DataSource` Connections

The new `DataSource`-based constructors, unlike the `DriverManager`-based constructors they replace, do not include an explicit auto-commit parameter. They always use the `auto-commit` mode defined by the data source. Data sources are configured to have a default auto-commit mode depending on the deployment scenario. Data sources in the server and application server or middle tier typically have auto-commit off. For example, data sources in the Oracle database server and in the Oracle9*i* Internet Application server have `auto-commit` off; those on the client may have it on. However, it is also possible to configure data sources with a specific auto-commit setting. This is a nice feature that allows you to configure data sources for more-specific applications and deployment scenarios. Note that you can write your programs so that they can verify and possibly override the current auto-commit setting with the JDBC connection that underlies their connection context.

You should be aware of the following:

■ If you use the Oracle class, then `auto-commit` is off, unless you specify it explicitly.

■ If you use the `DefaultContext` or a connection context with DriverManager-style constructors, then the `auto-commit` setting must always be specified explicitly.

■ If you use the `DataSource` mechanism, then the auto-commit setting is inherited from the underlying `DataSource`. In most environments, the `DataSource` object originates from JDBC, and the `auto-commit` option is on. To avoid unexpected behavior, always check the `auto-commit` setting.

In order for you to use data sources, you must import into your program
the following:

- The `javax.sql.*` package

- The `javax.naming.*` package

- The `InitialContext` interface. This is a required interface that
  allows your SQLJ program to obtain the JNDI context in which the SQLJ
  run-time can look up the `DataSource` object. See Chapter 9 to learn
  more about the `InitialContext` interface and how to use it in
  SQLJ programs.

Note that all the Oracle SQLJ run-time libraries support `DataSource`. Recall
that, starting with Oracle8*i* release 8.1.6, Oracle SQLJ is distributed with several
SQLJ run-time libraries, such as

- **`runtime11.zip, runtime12.zip`** Applet enabled and optimized
  for use with the Oracle JDBC 8.1.7 drivers. Note that `runtime11.zip`
  is for JDK 1.1 and Oracle 8.1.7 JDBC, and `runtime12.zip` is for JDK 1.2
  and Oracle 8.1.7 JDBC. Actually, `runtime11.zip` (obtained from SQLJ
  X.Y.Z) is meant to be used with JDBC X.Y.Z (and similarly for JDBC). Do
  not use the 9*i* `runtime11.zip` with 8.1.7 JDBC.

- **`runtime.zip`** Provides compatibility with all Oracle JDBC drivers.

- **`runtime12ee.zip`** For `DataSource` object usage.

Remember that if you use the `runtime12ee.zip` you always need to have
`javax.sql.*` and `javax.naming.*` in your CLASSPATH or the run-time will
not load. The other libraries, such as `runtime.zip`, `runtime11.zip` and
`runtime12.zip`, use reflection to retrieve `DataSource` objects. See the
"Using `DataSource` in SQLJ Programs" section of this chapter to learn how
to use `DataSource` objects in SQLJ programs.

Instances of a declared connection context class or of the `DefaultContext`
class can be associated with an instance of the `ExecutionContext` class. Next,
you will learn about this class and its relation to the `ConnectionContext` class.

Relation of the Execution Context to the Connection Context in the SQLJ Executable Statement

In a SQLJ program, all statements that are used for database access are in SQLJ
clauses. An executable statement is a SQLJ clause that contains a SQL operation.

Remember that SQLJ executable statements are used to execute embedded SQL operations (see Chapters 1 and 3). Also note that SQLJ executable statements can only execute embedded SQL operations that are supported by the JDBC driver that a SQLJ program uses. Thankfully, JDBC drivers support most SQL operations (DML, DDL, and transaction control statements).

A SQLJ executable statement consists of a #sql token followed by a SQLJ clause:

```
#sql { SQL operation };
```

A SQLJ operation is always associated with an instance of the ExecutionContext class. An execution context is an instance of the sqlj.runtime.ExecutionContext class. Unlike connection context classes, there is only one ExecutionContext class. Note that if you do not associate an execution context object explicitly with your SQLJ clause, SQLJ will implicitly associate the default instance of this class that is associated with the connection context you are using with the SQLJ clause. Use the following syntax to retrieve the default ExecutionContext instance of your connection context instance:

```
ExecutionContext anEC =
        DefaultContext.getDefaultContext().getExecutionContext();
```

Use the following syntax to create a new ExecutionContext instance:

```
ExecutionContext aNewEC = new ExecutionContext();
```

An execution context provides a context in which SQL clauses are executed. An ExecutionContext can be described as

- A template for the statement(s) you are executing, in which you can supply the desired settings for your statements (timeouts, fetch sizes, fetch limits, batching, and so on).

- A container in which your statement is executed and that receives the statement "outputs," such as update counts, batch counts, batching state, warnings, and so on, and that—for statement batching—is also keeping track of the current statement batch.

Importantly, the ExecutionContext class contains methods that can help you control the execution of your SQL operations. The available methods are categorized as status methods, control methods, cancellation methods, and the update-batching methods. See Appendix D for detailed explanations of all the methods of the ExecutionContext class.

The methods of an `ExecutionContext` object are as follows:

- **Status methods** for getting the results of the most recent SQL operation.

- **Control methods** for modifying the semantics of future SQL operations.

- **Cancellation methods** to cancel or terminate operations in situations in which multiple SQL operations are occurring on the same underlying connection object (see Chapter 7).

- **Update-batching** methods include enabling and disabling batching, setting the batch limit, and getting update counts. See Chapter 10 to learn how to use these methods in SQLJ programs.

Note that `ExecutionContext` methods are all synchronized methods. This means that when a SQLJ executable statement tries to use an execution context object currently in use by another SQLJ operation, it will be blocked (that is, it will wait) until the other statement completes. However, such blockage can be avoided by creating several execution context instances. In Chapter 7, you will develop Multithreading SQLJ programs in which you will declare a separate execution context instance for each thread that you use.

NOTE
Explicit synchronization on execution contexts is not performed with the setting `-codegen=oracle`. *In this case, the user needs to ensure that every active thread uses its own execution context instance (or its own connection context instance) for executing SQLJ statements. Also note that the blockage of a statement that tries to use an execution context instance already in use does not apply to recursive calls being executed inside the database server. Multiple SQLJ statements caused by recursive calls can simultaneously use the same execution context instance without being blocked.*

An example is when an SQLJ stored procedure (or function) calls another SQLJ stored procedure (or function). In this scenario, both SQLJ stored procedures (or functions) can simultaneously use the same execution context instance without being blocked.

Each SQLJ executable statement requires a connection context instance, declared either implicitly or explicitly. A SQLJ executable statement can specify a particular connection context instance (either of `DefaultContext` or of a declared connection context class) for its database connection. Alternatively, it can omit the connection context specification, and thereby use the default connection (an instance of `DefaultContext` that you previously set as the default). The connection context is an optional expression and is delimited surrounded by square brackets. An instance of this class indicates the location of the data server where the SQL operation will execute:

```
#sql   [aConnectionContextInstance] { SQL operation };
```

For example, the following SQLJ clause (see Listing 5-1) executes a `SELECT` statement at the database located on `data-i.com` (see the `SingleDefaultContext` SQLJ application in the upcoming section "Using the SQLJ `DefaultContext` Class."

Listing 5-1

```
#sql [dataiConnCtx] lineItems =
     { SELECT requestno, projectno, quantity, unit,
         estimatedcost, actualcost, description
       FROM LINEITEM_LIST
       ORDER BY requestno };
```

In the SQLJ executable statement here, the explicit connection context instance, `dataiConnCtx`, is associated with the SQLJ clause. Note that each connection context object implicitly has its own execution context instance. Since no explicit instance of the `ExecutionContext` class is associated with the SQLJ operation, SQLJ associates a default instance of the `ExecutionContext` class to this clause.

The execution context is an optional expression and, like the connection context, is delimited and enclosed in square brackets:

```
#sql [anExecutionContextInstance] { SQL operation };
```

Listing 5-2 demonstrates the explicit association of an instance of the `ExecutionContext` class with the SQLJ clause. The connection context instance, `dataiConnCtx`, specifies the data server on which to perform the SQL operation.

Listing 5-2

```
// First import the ExecutableContext class.
import sqlj.runtime.ExecutionContext;

// Create an instance of the above class using
// the constructor of the ExecutionContext class
ExecutionContext anExecutionContext = new ExecutionContext();
```

```
// Associate the instance to an SQLJ executable statement.
#sql [dataiConntCtx,anExecutionContext] lineItems =
    { SELECT requestno, projectno, quantity, unit,
        estimatedcost, actualcost, description
      FROM LINEITEM_LIST
      ORDER BY requestno };
```

Be aware of the following:

■ In the absence of a specified ExecutionContext instance, your SQLJ
program will implicitly use the default execution context instance of your
declared or default connection context instance.

■ If you create an ExecutionContext instance and you do not explicitly
associate it with a connection context instance, SQLJ will associate with
the default connection context instance of your program.

■ In scenarios in which you specify no connection context instance and
no execution context instance, SQLJ uses the default connection context
instance of your application and its associate execution context instance.

■ When explicitly specifying a connection context and an execution context,
the first context listed must be the connection context. It must be separated
from the execution context with a comma.

Typically, a single ExecutionContext instance is sufficient for a connection
context instance. However, there are some circumstances in which you would need
to create more than one instance.

Use multiple execution context instances with a single connection context
instance in the following situations:

■ Multithreading—each thread must have its own ExecutionContext instance.

■ To have better execution control operations on different SQLJ statements.
This is particularly useful in situations in which you want to perform batching.

■ To retain different sets of SQL status information from multiple SQL operations.

See the listing of the MultiDeclaredConnectionCtx.sqlj application in
the "Managing Multiple Database Connections with SQLJ" section of this chapter
for an example of how to use instances of the ExecutionContext class and its
methods in a SQLJ program.

In the next section, you will use instances of the SQLJ DefaultContext class
to connect to databases. Remember that instances of this class are used to create
single or multiple connections to a single database.

Using the SQLJ
`DefaultContext` Class

If you need to establish a single database connection to a specific schema type, you can use the `getConnection()` method of the `DefaultContext` class to do so. Typically, you will use a `DefaultContext` object for a single connection or multiple connections to database schemas that use SQL entities with the same names and datatypes.

When you construct the `DefaultContext` object, you specify the database URL, username, and password:

```
// Declaration of two DefaultContext instances
// to connect to:
// 1.  two separate database servers
// 2.  two separate Oracle database schema
//     located on the same database server
DefaultContext aDefaultContext1;
DefaultContext aDefaultContext2;

// 1. Connecting to two separate database servers
// Assignment of both instances to databases located at
// data-i.com and haiti respectively
aDefaultContext1 = getConnection
        ("jdbc:oracle:thin:@data-i.com:1521:ORCL",
                "scott","tiger",boolean value);
aDefaultConnection2 = getConnection
        ("jdbc:oracle:thin:@haiti:1521:ORCL",
                "scott","tiger",boolean value);

// 1. Connecting to two separate Oracle database schema
// Assignment of both instances to the database located at
// data-i.com
aDefaultContext1 = getConnection
        ("jdbc:oracle:thin:@data-i.com:1521:ORCL",
                "scott","tiger",boolean value);
aDefaultConnection2 = getConnection
        ("jdbc:oracle:thin:@data-i.com:1521:ORCL",
                "scott","tiger",boolean value);

// NOTE: These could also be associated to the
// same underlying connection.
```

In this example, both `DefaultContext` objects, `aDefaultContext1` and `aDefaultConnection2`, use the Oracle JDBC Thin driver to connect user `scott` (password `tiger`) to a database on the machine `data-i.com` and `haiti` through port `1521`, where `ORCL` is the SID of the database to connect on that machine. As an alternative to the Oracle `thin` driver, you can use the Oracle JDBC-OCI driver to connect to a database. For example:

```
jdbc:oracle:oci8:@ORCL
jdbc:oracle:oci8:@
```

Note that SQLJ programs that use instances of the `DefaultContext` class must import the `sqlj.runtime.ref.DefaultContext` class or the whole `sqlj.runtime.ref.*` package. This listing of the `SingleDefaultContext.sqlj` application is an example of how to implement a `DefaultContext` instance:

```
/*                              (See Note 1.)
** Program Name:       SingleDefaultContext.sqlj
**
** Purpose:
** SQLJ application that implements a single SQLJ default
** context to connect to one database server. Also,
** this program uses a named SQLJ iterator to query a
** relational database table in Oracle8i and
** the Oracle.connect() method to set the DefaultContext
** instance.
** Required classes: none
**
*/
// Required SQLJ classes for any SQLJ program
import sqlj.runtime.*;          // (See Note 2.)
import sqlj.runtime.ref.*;

// Required Java classes for any application
// that needs to access a database
import java.sql.*;

// Required Oracle classes for Oracle database
import oracle.sql.*;
import oracle.sqlj.runtime.Oracle;
import oracle.jdbc.driver.*;

public class SingleDefaultContext {
     // Declare a named SQLJ iterator: LineItemIterator()
     // This iterator will access data from dataiConnCtx
     #sql public static iterator LineItemIterator   // (See Note 3.)
        (int requestno, int projectno, float quantity,
         String unit, float estimatedcost,
          float actualcost, String description);
```

```
      // Declare one protected static variable of type
      // DefaultContext. Variables must be static.
      // This is a Java requirement.
   protected static DefaultContext dataiConnCtx;// (See Note 4.)

      // Constructor
      public SingleDefaultContext () {
          try {
            // Instantiate Default Context for the specific host
            // (See Note 5.)
              dataiConnCtx = Oracle.getConnection
                  ("jdbc:oracle:thin:@data-i.com:1521:ORCL",
                          "scott","tiger",false);
          } // end try
          catch (SQLException ex) {        // (See Note 6.)
             System.err.println("Error from dataiConnCtx  "
                           +"SingleDefaultContext: "  +ex);
             String sqlMessage = ex.getMessage();
             System.err.println("SQL Message: " + sqlMessage);
          } // end catch
      }   // end constructor

   // Main entry point
   public static void main(String[] args) throws SQLException {

      // Instantiate SingleDefaultContext constructor
      // to create one connection context of type
      // DefaultContext
      SingleDefaultContext app = new SingleDefaultContext();

      // Stop execution if we cannot connect.
      if   (dataiConnCtx == null) {
          System.out.println("I cannot connect to "
                  + "the database - Stop execution.");
          System.exit(1);
      }
      try {
        // Run the application (See Note 7.)
        app.runSingleDefaultContext(dataiConnCtx);
      }  // end try
      catch (SQLException ex) {
             System.err.println("Error running "
                 +"runSingleDefaultContext: " + ex);
             String sqlMessage = ex.getMessage();
             System.err.println("SQL Message: " + sqlMessage);
      }  // end catch
   }  // end main()
```

```
void runSingleDefaultContext(DefaultContext dataiConnCtx)
        throws SQLException {

    //  Set DefaultContext to dataiConnCtx   (See Note 8.)
    DefaultContext.setDefaultContext(dataiConnCtx);

    /* Instantiate the named SQLJ iterator
       and initialize it to null.   */
    LineItemIterator lineItems = null;      // (See Note 9.)

    /* obtain all lineItems info from the default context */
    #sql [dataiConnCtx] lineItems =      // (See Note 10.)
        { SELECT requestno, projectno, quantity, unit,
                 estimatedcost, actualcost, description
          FROM LINEITEM_LIST
          ORDER BY requestno };

    /* Use iterator methods to get the values from
       the table columns. (See Notes 11 and 12.) */
    while (lineItems.next()) {
            System.out.println("Request No: " +
                        lineItems.requestno() );
            System.out.println("Project No: " +
                        lineItems.projectno() );
            System.out.println("Quantity: " +
                        lineItems.quantity() );
            System.out.println("Unit: " +
                        lineItems.unit() );
            System.out.println("Estimated Cost: " +
                        lineItems.estimatedcost() );
            System.out.println("Actual Cost: " +
                        lineItems.actualcost() );
            System.out.println("Description: " +
                        lineItems.description() );
    } // End while
    // Close the iterator
    lineItems.close();     // (See Note 13.)
} // End of runSingleDefaultContext()
} // End SingleDefaultContent class
```

Notes on the `SingleDefaultContext.sqlj` application:

1. Program documentation. This section is optional but is highly
   recommended.

2. These statements import the SQLJ, JDBC, and Oracle packages that are used by SQLJ.

3. This iterator declaration clause declares a named iterator, LineItemIterator, which is used to select rows from the LINEITEM_ LIST table. When you specify an iterator in the SQLJ application, SQLJ generates a class named LineItemIterator. You must then ensure that LineItemIterator is a valid Java class name that is unique within its scope.

4. This statement creates a DefaultContext instance named dataiConnCtx.

5. This statement uses the Oracle thin driver to set up a connection to the Oracle database at URL address data-i.com, listening on port 1521 (default port number for Oracle database), using ORCL as the Oracle SID. The connection will be established using "scott" and "tiger" as the username and password, respectively, and the auto-commit feature will be set to off.

6. These statements allow you to catch any raised exceptions and print a corresponding SQL error message.

7. This statement invokes the method runSingleDefaultContext() while specifying a DefaultContext instance as its parameter.

8. This statement sets up the instance dataiConnCtx to be the default for the SQLJ execution statement that will select the rows from the LINEITEM_ list table.

9. This statement declares lineItems as an instance of the named iterator LineItemIterator class and initializes it to null.

10. This assignment clause executes the SELECT statement, constructs an iterator object that contains the result table for the SELECT statement, and assigns the iterator object to variable lineItems. Note that an execution context instance is associated implicitly with this SQL operation. Also, because the application is using a default connection, it is not necessary to specify a connection context instance. For example, the following statement would have selected the data from the LINEITEM_LIST table located at dataiConnCtx even though the context instance is not specified.

```
#sql lineItems =
    { SELECT requestno, projectno, quantity, unit,
             estimatedcost, actualcost, description
      FROM LINEITEM_LIST
      ORDER BY requestno
    };
```

11. The next () method, which belongs to the generated class, LineItemsIterator, advances the iterator to successive rows in the SQLJ result set. This method is similar to the next () method for the Java JDBC ResultSet. The next () method returns a value of true when a next row is available or a value of false when all table rows have been fetched from the iterator.

12. The accessor methods lineItems.requestno(), lineItems. projectno(), lineItems.quantity(), lineItems.unit(), lineItems.estimatedcost(), lineItems.actualcost(), and lineItems.description() retrieve the values of the table columns from the current row of the result table.

13. The close() method, which also belongs to the generated class, LineItemIterator, closes the iterator and frees any database resources being held by the iterator.

SQLJ programs can use the connect() method from the oracle.sqlj. runtime.Oracle class to set the value of the static default instance of the DefaultContext class. This class provides two basic methods: the getConnection() and the connect() methods. The getConnection() method is used to create a new database connection and return a handle to it in the form of a connection context instance. The getConnection() method is used when you wish to create multiple connection context instances, explicitly. The connect() method is somewhat similar to the getConnection() method in that it creates a new database connection. Sometimes, but not always, it will only create a new connection if the static connection context has not already been initialized. This means that server-side connect() is turned into a no-op, since the static (session) connection has already been established. Also, note that the connect() method, additionally, installs the new connection as the static default context. The latter function can only be used with Oracle databases because the SQLJ program needs to import an Oracle-specific class to use the connect() method. Note that the Oracle class was meant to be used with Oracle databases, since it also automatically tries to register the Oracle JDBC driver. If you need to access non-Oracle databases, you should use an instance either of a declared connection context class or of the sqlj.runtime.ref.DefaultContext class to establish database connections.

You should be aware of the following:

■ Oracle.connect() will not set your default connection if one has already been set. In that case, it returns null. (This functionality allows you to use the same code on a client or in the server.) If you do want to override your default connection, use the static `setDefaultContext()` method of the `DefaultContext` class, as described in the next sections.

■ The `Oracle.connect()` method defaults to a false setting of the `auto-commit` flag; however, it also has signatures that let you set it explicitly.

■ You can optionally specify `getClass()`, instead of MyClass.class, in the Oracle.connect() call, as long as you are not calling `getClass()` from a static method.

Both methods, `getConnection()` and `Oracle.connect()`, have several overloaded signatures that allow you to pass the URL, username, and password as parameters to the methods. You may also set these parameters indirectly via the `connect.properties` file provided by Oracle. If you wish to use a `connect.properties` file, you must import `oracle.sqlj.runtime.Oracle` class, edit the properties file appropriately, and package it with your application. See Chapter 2 for a discussion on the Oracle `connect.properties` file. The following is an example of a properties file:

```
#  File Name:       connect.properties
# Users should uncomment one of the following URLs or add their own.
#sqlj.url=jdbc:oracle:thin:@localhost:1521:orcl
#sqlj.url=jdbc:oracle:oci8:@
#sqlj.url=jdbc:oracle:oci7:@
# User name and password here
sqlj.user=scott
sqlj.password=tiger
```

See the `UsingSqljDefaultContext.sqlj` and the `SqljClientAccessJavaStoredProc.sqlj` for examples on how to use the `Oracle.connect()` method with a properties file. See Chapter 2 to learn more about the `Oracle.connect()` method with a properties file and the `UsingSqljDefaultContext` SQLJ application in the section "Using the SQLJ `DefaultContext` Class," earlier in this chapter. Here is the syntax:

```
// The Oracle.connect() method using a properties file.
Oracle.connect(class_name.class, "connect.properties");

// class_name.class can be replaced with getClass
Oracle.connect(getClass(), "connect.properties");
```

The class provided here specifies the package in which the properties file is accessible in the application. Note that if a default connection has been set, the `Oracle.connect()` method will not reset it. You may, however, use the setDefaultContext() method of the DefaultContext class in order to override a default connection that has been previously set. The following is a list of the various Oracle.connect() overloaded signatures and their input parameters (see the *Oracle8i/9i SQLJ Developer's Guide and Reference* for a complete listing for both methods, the getConnection() and the connect() methods.

```
// The method declaration followed by its parameter list
public static DefaultContext connect ( list of parameters )
                  throws SQLException
```

Here are the various signatures:

- URL (String), username (String), password (String)

- URL (String), username (String), password (String), auto-commit flag (boolean)

- URL (String), java.util.Properties object containing properties for the connection

- URL (String), java.util.Properties object, auto-commit flag (boolean)

- URL (String) fully specifying the connection, including username and password

- URL (String), auto-commit flag (boolean)

- java.lang.Class object specifying package from which to load properties file, name of properties file (String)

- java.lang.Class object, name of properties file (String), auto-commit flag (boolean)

- java.lang.Class object, name of properties file (String), username (String), password (String)

- java.lang.Class object, name of properties file (String), username (String), password (String), auto-commit flag (boolean)

- JDBC connection object

- SQLJ connection context object

You should be aware of the following:

- A connection context class and the `DefaultConnection` class have constructors for opening a connection to a database schema. The list of input parameters described previously is used by the `DefaultConnection` class and a connection context class.

- Do not initialize a connection context instance with a null JDBC `Connection` object. In other words, constructors of the `DefaultConnection` class or a connection context class that take a JDBC `Connection` object require a non-null object.

- The `auto-commit` flag determines whether SQL operations are automatically committed.

Associating a `DataSource` with the `DefaultContext`

Like with the connection context class, you can also associate a `DataSource` object with the `DefaultContext` class. If the SQLJ program accesses the default connection context, and the default context has not been set, then the SQLJ run-time will use the SQLJ default data source to establish its connection. The SQLJ default data source is bound to the name:

```
jdbc/defaultDataSource
```

This mechanism provides a portable means to define and install a default JDBC connection for the default SQLJ connection context. See the "Using DataSource in SQLJ Programs" section, later in this chapter, to learn how to associate a `DataSource` object with the `DefaultContext` class.

Next, you will write several SQLJ programs that will teach you how to use a properties file to establish a connection to an Oracle database.

The `UsingSqljDefaultContext.sqlj` Program

The following SQLJ applications use the `Oracle.connect()` method associated with a `connect.properties` file to create database connections:

- The `UsingSqljDefaultContext.sqlj` application uses the following syntax:

```
Oracle.connect(getClass(), "connect.properties");
```

■ The `SqljAppletCallsSqljSP.sqlj` applet (see the "Deploying SQLJ in an Oracle8*i*/9*i* Data Server: SQLJ Stored Procedures" section, later in this chapter) uses the following syntax:

```
Oracle.connect(class_name.class(), "connect.properties");
```

Furthermore, the SQLJ applet uses the `ConnectionManager` Java class to create a `DefaultContext` database connection.

Here is the definition of the `UsingSqljDefaultContext.sqlj` program.

```
/*
** Program Name:        UsingSqljDefaultContext.sqlj
*/
// Required SQLJ classes for any SQLJ program
import sqlj.runtime.*;
import sqlj.runtime.ref.*;

// Required Java classes for any application
// that needs to access a database
import java.sql.*;

// Required Oracle classes for Oracle database
import oracle.sql.*;
import oracle.sqlj.runtime.Oracle;
import oracle.jdbc.driver.*;

public class UsingSqljDefaultContext {

    // Declare a named SQLJ iterator. LineItemIterator()
    #sql public iterator LineItemIterator
        (int requestno, int projectno, float quantity, String unit,
         float estimatedcost, float actualcost, String description);

    // Constructor
    public UsingSqljDefaultContext () {
      try {
          // set the default connection to the URL, user,
          // and password specified in your
          // connect.properties file (See Note 1.)
            Oracle.connect(getClass(), "connect.properties");
      } // end of try
      catch (Exception ex) {
        System.err.println("Error from constructor "
                        + "UsingSqljDefaultContext: " + ex);
      } // end of catch
    }  // end constructor
```

```
    // main entry
    public static void main(String[] args) throws SQLException {

        // Instantiate UsingSqljDefaultContext
        UsingSqljDefaultContext app = new UsingSqljDefaultContext();

        // Cannot connect to database, stop program execution.
        // (See Note 2.)
        if (DefaultContext.getDefaultContext() == null ) {
            System.out.println("I cannot connect to the database "
            + "-- Stop Execution.");
            System.exit(1);
        }
        try {
            // Run the application
            app.runUsingSqljDefaultContext();
        }  // end try
        catch (SQLException ex) {
            System.err.println("Error running " +
                    runUsingSqljDefaultContext: " + ex);
            String sqlMessage = ex.getMessage();
            System.err.println("SQL Message: " + sqlMessage);
        }  // end catch
        finally {
                Oracle.close();
        } // End of finally() method
    }  // end main

  void runUsingSqljDefaultContext() throws SQLException {
      LineItemIterator lineItems = null;
      #sql lineItems =
              { SELECT requestno, projectno, quantity, unit,
                    estimatedcost, actualcost, description
                FROM LINEITEM_LIST
                ORDER BY requestno };
...
...
// The remaining SQLJ source code is the same as the
// SingleDefaultContext.sqlj
```

Notes on the UsingSqljDefaultContext.sqlj application:

1. This statement uses the Oracle.connect() method to set an instance
of the DefaultContext class. The method installs the new connection
as the static default context. The database connection uses the parameters
listed in the properties file: the JDBC driver, the URL, the listener port, the
Oracle SID, the username, and the user password.

2. This statement retrieves the default connection that the `connect()` method had previously installed. Use the `connect()` method when you need to create a single connection context implicitly.

Managing Multiple Database Connections with SQLJ

Recall that instances of the `DefaultContext` class are typically used for single or multiple connections to a single database. SQLJ, also, supports connecting to multiple databases within the same program at the same time. You can create multiple instances of the `DefaultContext` class to connect to databases located at different sites.

The `MultiDefaultCtx.sqlj` application uses two `DefaultContext` objects to access two databases located on `data-i.com` and `haiti` servers. In the case where the application needs to create multiple connections to different types of database schemas, you should use connection context declarations (see the "Using SQLJ Connection Context for Database Connections" section, earlier in this chapter) to define your own connection context classes so that SQLJ can do more rigorous semantics checking of your code.

The `FireWallMultiDefaultCtx.sqlj` application demonstrates making multiple database connections to an Internet data server and an intranet data server (see listing at http://www.osborne.com). This SQLJ application creates two instances of the `DefaultContext` class to replicate platform data from an Oracle database (version 8.0.4) located outside of a firewall (on the Internet) to an Oracle8*i* database located inside of that firewall (in an intranet). (See the "How Firewalls Work" section in the *Oracle8i/9i JDBC Developer's Guide*, A64685-1):

```
/*
** Program Name:       MultiDefaultCtx.sqlj
**
** Purpose:        SQLJ application that implements
** two sqlj default context to connect to two databases located
** on two different Oracle servers. Also, this program uses
** a named SQLJ iterator to query a relational database table.
*/

// Required SQLJ classes for any SQLJ program
import sqlj.runtime.*;
import sqlj.runtime.ref.*;

// Required Java classes for any application that needs to
// access a database
import java.sql.*;
```

```
// Required Oracle classes for Oracle database
import oracle.sql.*;
import oracle.sqlj.runtime.Oracle;
import oracle.jdbc.driver.*;

public class MultiDefaultCtx {

    // This iterator will access data from data-i.com
    #sql public iterator LineItemIterator (int requestno,
        int projectno, float quantity,String unit,
          float estimatedcost,float actualcost,String description);

    // PlatformIter() will access haiti
    #sql public iterator PlatformIter (int aPlatformId, String aType,
                                       String aDesc);

    // Declare two protected static variables of type DefaultContext
    // Variables must be static. Java requirement.
    protected static DefaultContext dataiConnCtx;  // (See Note 1.)
    protected static DefaultContext haitiConnCtx;
    // Constructor
    public MultiDefaultCtx () {

        try {
            // Instantiate Default Context for each host
            // (See Note 2.)
              dataiConnCtx = Oracle.getConnection
                ("jdbc:oracle:thin:@data-i.com:1521:ORCL",
                    "scott","tiger",false);
            haitiConnCtx = Oracle.getConnection
                ("jdbc:oracle:thin:@haiti:1521:ORCL",
                            "scott","tiger",false);
        } // end try
        catch (Exception ex) {
                System.err.println("Error from " +
                    "haitiConnCtx/dataiConnCtx " +
                    "MultiDefaultCtx: " + ex);
        } // end catch

    }  // end constructor

    public static void main(String[] args) throws SQLException {

        // Instantiate MultiDefaultCtx constructor to create
        // two connection contexts of type DefaultContext.
        MultiDefaultCtx app = new MultiDefaultCtx();

        // We cannot connect to the database, stop program execution.
```

```
   if   (dataiConnCtx == null) {
        System.out.println("I cannot connect to the " +
             "data-i.com database - Stop execution.");
        System.exit(1);
    } // end if
   if   (haitiConnCtx == null) {
        System.out.println("I cannot connect to the " +
         "haiti database  - Stop execution.");
        System.exit(0);
    } // end if

 try {
 // Run the application (See Note 3.)
    app.runMultiDefaultCtx(haitiConnCtx, dataiConnCtx);
    } // end try
 catch (SQLException ex) {
     System.err.println("Error running" +
          " runMultiDefaultCtx: " + ex);
     String sqlMessage = ex.getMessage();
     System.err.println("SQL Message: " + sqlMessage);
 }  // end catch
 // Close the DefaultConnection Context object
 finally {
     // Close the database connection
     Oracle.close();
 } // End finally()
} // end main

void runMultiDefaultCtx(DefaultContext haitiCtx,
          DefaultContext dataiCtx  )  throws SQLException {

   /*      ** Set DefaultContext to haitiCtx       */
   DefaultContext.setDefaultContext(haitiCtx);  // (See Note 4.)

   LineItemIterator lineItems = null;
   #sql [haitiCtx] lineItems =     // (See Note 5.)
       { SELECT requestno,projectno,quantity,
           unit,estimatedcost,actualcost,description
         FROM LINEITEM_LIST
         ORDER BY requestno };

   while (lineItems.next()) {
      System.out.println("Request No: " + lineItems.requestno() );
      System.out.println("Project No: " + lineItems.projectno() );
      System.out.println("Quantity: " + lineItems.quantity() );
      System.out.println("Unit: " + lineItems.unit() );
      System.out.println("Estimated Cost: " +
              lineItems.estimatedcost() );
```

```
        System.out.println("Actual Cost: " +
                lineItems.actualcost() );
        System.out.println("Description: " +
                lineItems.description() );
};  // end while

// Close iterator
lineItems.close();

/* ** Set DefaultContext to dataiCtx   */
DefaultContext.setDefaultContext(dataiCtx); // (See Note 6.)
PlatformIter platform = null;   // (See Note 7.)

#sql [dataiCtx] platform =      // (See Note 8.)
    { SELECT P.key_id AS aPlatformId,
      P.type AS aType,P.description AS aDesc
      FROM PLATFORM_TYPE_LIST P };

while (platform.next()) {
  System.out.println("Platform id: " + platform.aPlatformId() );
  System.out.println("Type: " + platform.aType() );
  System.out.println("Description: " + platform.aDesc() );
}  // end while
// Close iterator
platform.close();

  }   // End runMultiDefaultCtx()
}  // End MultiDefaultCtx class
```

Notes on `MultiDefaultCtx.sqlj` application:

1. This statement and the one that follows it create two `DefaultContext` instances named `dataiConnCtx` and `haitiConnCtx`, respectively.

2. These statements use the `getConnection()` and the Oracle thin driver to set up connections to two databases located on `data-i.com` and `haiti`, respectively. The `getConnection()` method is used when multiple or explicitly passed connection contexts are required.

3. This statement invokes the method `runMultiDefaultCtx()` while specifying two `DefaultContext` instances as its parameters.

4. This statement sets up the instance `haitiCtx` as the default for the SQLJ execution statement that will select the rows from the `LINEITEM_LIST` table located at URL address `haiti`. The static `setDefaultContext()` method of the `DefaultContext` class sets a specific database connection as the default connection. Use this method when an application needs to perform

several SQL operations on a specified database. There is no need to specify a connection class instance for an SQL operation in this case. For example, the SQLJ clause in Listing 5-3 executes a SELECT on the LINEITEM_LIST table located on haiti and uses an explicit connection context instance called haitiCtx; whereas in Listing 5-4, the SQLJ clause uses an implicit connection context instance to perform the same SQL operation.

Listing 5-3

```
// SQLJ iterator instance using explicitly a DefaultContext
instance
#sql [haitiCtx] lineItems =
    { SELECT requestno, projectno, quantity, unit,
            estimatedcost, actualcost, description
      FROM LINEITEM_LIST
      ORDER BY requestno
    };
```

Listing 5-4

```
// SQLJ iterator instance using implicitly a DefaultContext
instance
// after calling the setDefaultContext() method.
#sql lineItems =
{ SELECT requestno, projectno, quantity, unit, estimatedcost,
    actualcost, description
  FROM LINEITEM_LIST
  ORDER BY requestno };
```

5. This assignment clause executes a SELECT statement, constructs an iterator object that contains the result table for the SELECT statement, and assigns the iterator object to the lineItem variables. The iterator accesses the table located on haiti.

6. This statement sets up the instance dataiCtx as the default for the SQLJ execution statement that will select the rows from the PLATFORM_TYPE_list table located at URL address data-i.com.

7. This statement creates an instance of the iterator PlatformIter class and initializes it.

8. This iterator instance accesses a table located on data-i.com.

Next, you will use a user-defined SQLJ declared connection context class to connect to a single database, as well as to several databases located at different remote sites. Recall the SQLJ syntax in "Using SQLJ Connection Context for Database Connections," earlier in this chapter:

```
#sql <modifiers> context Context_Classname;
```

Because a connection context class implements the
`sqlj.runtime.ConnectionContext` interface, it must implement all of its
methods. See Oracle8i/9i *SQLJ Developer's Guide and Reference Release 8.1.5*:

- **close(boolean CLOSE_CONNECTION/KEEP_CONNECTION)** Use this
  method to close a connection and release all resources.

- **getConnection()** This method returns the underlying JDBC Connection
  object for this connection context instance.

- **getExecutionContext()** A method that returns the default
  `ExecutionContext` instance for this connection context instance.

In addition to these methods, each declared connection context class defines its
own methods:

- **getDefaultContext()** This is a static method that returns the default
  connection context instance for a given connection context class.

- **setDefaultContext (the specified connection context
  object)** This is a static method that defines the default context instance
  for a given connection context object.

The SQLJ translator generates a Java class for the user-defined connection
context class in the `MultiDeclaredConnectionCtx.sqlj` application:

```
// A declared SQLJ connection context class
#sql context DeclaredConnectionContext;
```

Listing 5-5 shows a list of the methods that the SQLJ translator generates for the
user-defined `DeclaredConnectionContext` class. Method implementations
are omitted for the sake of clarity.

Listing 5-5

```
class DeclaredConnectionContext
        extends sqlj.runtime.ref.ConnectionContextImpl
            implements sqlj.runtime.ConnectionContext {

  public DeclaredConnectionContext(java.sql.Connection conn)
      throws java.sql.SQLException;

  public DeclaredConnectionContext(java.lang.String url,
            java.lang.String user, java.lang.String password,
            boolean autoCommit) throws java.sql.SQLException;
```

```
public DeclaredConnectionContext(java.lang.String url,
        java.util.Properties info, boolean autoCommit)
                throws java.sql.SQLException;

public DeclaredConnectionContext(java.lang.String url,
        boolean autoCommit) throws java.sql.SQLException;

public DeclaredConnectionContext
        (sqlj.runtime.ConnectionContext other)
            throws java.sql.SQLException;

public static DeclaredConnectionContext getDefaultContext();

public static void setDefaultContext
        (DeclaredConnectionContext ctx);

private static DeclaredConnectionContext defaultContext = null;

public static java.lang.Object getProfileKey
        ( sqlj.runtime.profile.Loader loader,
        java.lang.String profileName )
                throws java.sql.SQLException;

private static final sqlj.runtime.ref.ProfileGroup profiles =
                    new sqlj.runtime.ref.ProfileGroup();

public static sqlj.runtime.profile.Profile
            getProfile(java.lang.Object profileKey);
}
```

The following SQLJ application, `MultiDeclaredConnectionCtx.sqlj`,
associates explicitly an instance of the `ExecutionContext` class to each
connection context instance.

```
/* ** Program Name:        MultiDeclaredConnectionCtx.sqlj
** Purpose:          SQLJ application that implements
** two instances of a declared SQLJ connection context class to
** connect to two databases located on two different Oracle servers:
*/
// Required SQLJ classes for any SQLJ program
import sqlj.runtime.*;
import sqlj.runtime.ref.*;

// Required SQLJ class to use instances of the ExecutionContext class
import sqlj.runtime.ExecutionContext;   // (See Note 1.)

// Required Java classes for any application that needs
```

```
// to access a database
import java.sql.*;

// Required Oracle classes for Oracle database
import oracle.sql.*;
import oracle.sqlj.runtime.Oracle;
import oracle.jdbc.driver.*;

// Import the user-defined SQLJ connection context class
// import DeclaredConnectionContext;
#sql context DeclaredConnectionContext;   // (See Note 2.)

public class MultiDeclaredConnectionCtx {

    // Declare a named SQLJ iterator. LineItemIterator()
    // This iterator will access data from haiti
    #sql public iterator LineItemIterator (int requestno,
        int projectno,float quantity,String unit,float estimatedcost,
          float actualcost,String description);

    // PlatformIter() will access data-i.com
    #sql public iterator PlatformIter (int aPlatformId, String aType,
                                    String aDesc);
    // Constructor
    public MultiDeclaredConnectionCtx () {
    }  // end constructor

    public static void main(String[] args) throws SQLException {

        /* If you are using an Oracle JDBC driver and call the
        standard Oracle.connect() method to create a default
        connection, then SQLJ handles this automatically.
        Oracle.connect() registers the
        oracle.jdbc.driver.OracleDriver class. */
        //(See Note 3.)
        DriverManager.registerDriver
              (new oracle.jdbc.driver.OracleDriver());

        MultiDeclaredConnectionCtx app =
              new MultiDeclaredConnectionCtx();
        // (See Note 4.)
        DeclaredConnectionContext haitiConnCtx =
           new DeclaredConnectionContext("jdbc:oracle:thin:" +
            "@haiti:1521:ORCL","scott","tiger",false);
```

```
        // Stop program execution if we cannot
        // connect to the database
        if  ( haitiConnCtx == null ) {
              System.out.println("I cannot connect to the database "
                        + " - Stop execution");
              System.exit(1);
        }  // end if


        // Create an instance of an ExecutionContext class for haiti
        ExecutionContext haitiExecCtx =
                            new ExecutionContext(); // (See Note 5.)

        try {           // Run the application
        app.runMultiDeclaredConnCtxHaiti(haitiConnCtx,haitiExecCtx);
         }  // end try
         catch (SQLException ex) {
             System.err.println("Error running "
                         + "runMultiDeclaredConnCtxHaiti: " + ex);
             String sqlMessage = ex.getMessage();
             System.err.println("SQL Message: " + sqlMessage);
         }  // end catch


        // Instantiate a connection to second host
        DeclaredConnectionContext dataiConnCtx =
           new DeclaredConnectionContext("jdbc:oracle:thin:" +
                   "@data-i.com:1521:ORCL",
                        "scott","tiger",false); // (See Note 6.)

        if  (dataiConnCtx == null ) {
              System.out.println("I cannot connect to the database "
                        + " - Stop execution");
              System.exit(1);
        }  // end if


        // Create an instance of an ExecutionContext
        // class for data-i.com
        ExecutionContext dataiExecCtx =
                            new ExecutionContext();    // (See Note 7.)

   try { // Run the application
        app.runMultiDeclaredConnCtxDatai(dataiConnCtx,dataiExecCtx);
   }  // end try
   catch (SQLException ex) {
        System.err.println("Error running "
```

```
                                  + "runMultiDeclaredConnCtxDatai: " + ex);
            String sqlMessage = ex.getMessage();
            System.err.println("SQL Message: " + sqlMessage);
        }  // end catch
        finally {
            // Close the database connection
            if (haitiConnCtx != null) haitiConnCtx.close();  // (See
Note 8.)
            if (dataiConnCtx != null) dataiConnCtx.close();
        } // End finally()

    }  // end main

    public void runMultiDeclaredConnCtxHaiti
            (DeclaredConnectionContext haitiCtx,
             ExecutionContext haitiExCtx )  throws SQLException {

        LineItemIterator lineItems = null;
        #sql [haitiCtx, haitiExCtx] lineItems =     // (See Note 9.)
            { SELECT requestno,projectno,quantity,unit,
                     estimatedcost,actualcost,description
              FROM LINEITEM_LIST
              ORDER BY requestno };

        while (lineItems.next()) {
            System.out.println("Request No: " +
                    lineItems.requestno() );
            System.out.println("Project No: " +
                    lineItems.projectno() );
            System.out.println("Quantity: " +
                    lineItems.quantity() );
            System.out.println("Unit: " +
                    lineItems.unit() );
            System.out.println("Estimated Cost: " +
                    lineItems.estimatedcost() );
            System.out.println("Actual Cost: " +
                    lineItems.actualcost() );
            System.out.println("Description: " +
                    lineItems.description() );
        }  // end while
        // Close iterator
        lineItems.close();

    }  // End runMultiDeclaredConnCtxHaiti()
```

```
public void runMultiDeclaredConnCtxDatai
        ( DeclaredConnectionContext dataiCtx,
            ExecutionContext dataiExCtx ) throws SQLException {
    PlatformIter platform = null;
#sql [dataiCtx,dataiExCtx] platform =
        { SELECT P.key_id AS aPlatformId,P.type AS aType,
                P.description AS aDesc
          FROM PLATFORM_TYPE_LIST P };

    while (platform.next()) {
        System.out.println("Platform id: " +
                platform.aPlatformId() );
        System.out.println("Type: " +
                platform.aType() );
        System.out.println("Description: " +
                platform.aDesc() );
    }  // End while loop

     // Close iterator
     platform.close();

  }  // End runMultiDeclaredConnCtxDatai()
}
```

Notes on `MultiDeclaredConnectionCtx.sqlj` application:

1. This class is required if you wish to create explicitly instances of the `ExecutionContext` class.

2. This statement creates a declared connection context class.

3. This statement registers the Oracle JDBC driver. If you are using an Oracle JDBC driver and you call the standard `Oracle.connect()` method to create a default connection, this method registers the `oracle.jdbc.driver.OracleDriver` class automatically for you. If you are using an Oracle JDBC driver but do not use `Oracle.connect()`, then you must manually register the `OracleDriver` class. In the event that you are using a non-Oracle JDBC driver, you must register this driver prior to creating an instance of the connection context class. Failure to register the JDBC driver generates a "driver not available" error at run time.

4. This statement creates an instance of a declared connection context class named `haitiConnCtx` and uses one of the constructors generated by the SQLJ translator to connect to the database on `haiti` (see Listing 5-5 for a listing of the generated Java class and its methods).

5. This statement creates an instance of the `ExecutionContext` class named `haitiExecCtx`. The instance is associated explicitly with the `haitiConnCtx` instance. A SQL operation will use both instances to execute a query on the `LINEITEM_LIST` table located on `haiti`.

6. This statement creates an instance of a declared connection context class named `dataiConnCtx` and uses one of the constructors generated by the SQLJ translator to connect to the database on `data-i.com`.

7. This statement creates an instance of the ExecutionContext class named `dataiExecCtx`. A SQLJ executable statement uses both instances, the `dataiConnCtx` and the `dataiExecCtx`, to execute a query on the `PLATFORM_TYPE_LIST` table located on `data-i.com`.

8. This statement and the one that follows it close the database connections to the data servers located on `haiti` and `data-i.com`, respectively. It is advisable to close your connections before exiting your program. You do so preferably in a `finally` clause. The code within a `finally` clause is guaranteed to execute, even when your application terminates abnormally. The `close()` method releases all resources used in maintaining this connection and closes any open connected profiles, so it's important that you close all the connection context instances.

9. This assignment clause executes the `SELECT` statement, constructs an iterator object that contains the result table for the `SELECT` statement, and assigns the iterator object to variable `lineItems`. This iterator accesses the table located on `haiti`. The SQLJ executable statement explicitly uses an instance of the connection context class and an instance of the execution context class. With this construct, SQLJ does more rigorous semantics checking of your code. Furthermore, developers have better control over SQL operations that are being executed on a particular server.

CAUTION
Before delving into more SQLJ applications, it is
worth talking about Oracle customization options
for SQLJ connections.

Connection for Customization

Oracle customization does not require a database connection. However, Oracle SQLJ supports `customizer` connections. Recall that the Oracle SQLJ installation includes a front-end utility that automatically runs the Oracle SQLJ translator, your Java compiler, and the Oracle profile `customizer`. In SQLJ, customization is optional. During the customization step, a default or specified `customizer` processes the `.ser` files (profiles) to allow use of vendor-specific features.

However, note that means it really is not optional if your program uses an Oracle-specific feature, such as an Oracle-specific type, being able to pass result sets or iterators from the database, and so on. Prior to Oracle9*i* database beta release, at translation time, the Oracle SQLJ translator would produce one or more `.ser` serialized resource files containing the application "profiles" which contain information about all your SQL statements. In Oracle9*i* SQLJ, the translator optionally will no longer generate `.ser` files. Only Java `.class` files will be generated, provided you use the setting `-codegen=oracle`.

Customizer connections are useful in two scenarios:

- A connection is required when you use the Oracle `customizer` with the `optcols` option. The `optcols` option is specific to the Oracle `customizer`. This option allows iterator column type and size definitions for performance optimization.

- In Oracle SQLJ, the online checker is true by default. If you are using the `SQLCheckerCustomizer`, specialized `customizer` that performs semantics checking on profiles, and an online checker, then a connection is required.

Deploying a SQLJ Application

A SQLJ application is a Java application with static or dynamic embedded SQL statements. SQLJ applications are stand-alone programs that run independently of any browser. Recall from Chapter 1 that when you compile SQLJ source code, the SQLJ translator converts the program into a standard Java program. A SQLJ application then behaves like a regular Java application. A Java program can be called a Java application if there is a `main()` method entry point in the source code (see Appendix B).

The `main()` method in SQLJ, similarly in Java, controls the flow of the program, allocates whatever resources are needed, and runs any other methods that provide the functionality for the SQLJ application, just as in plain Java.

NOTE
The SQLJ programs listed in the previous sections are all SQLJ applications.

Deploying a SQLJ Thick Client

Typically, a thick SQLJ application includes the following:

- All domain objects and logic to manipulate the database, such as DML, DDL, and transaction control statements

- SQLJ classes to support the database access

- Imported JDBC drivers

The decision to design a thick SQLJ client program over a thin SQLJ client depends not only on the application requirements, but also on the availability of hardware resources. Resources are typically scarce in small information technology (IT) shops. For example, at the Atlantic Oceanographic & Meteorological Laboratory (AOML) in Miami, one of the Environmental Research Laboratories (ERL) of the National Oceanic and Atmospheric Administration (NOAA), where many of the SQLJ programs for this book were designed and implemented, the limited resources initially imposed the design of SQLJ/Java thick clients versus thin clients. With the release of Oracle8*i* JServer, the design strategy has changed so that more database logic will be removed from the thick client and moved to the Oracle data server, freeing the client from database processing that can be done more efficiently by the server. Another advantage of removing database processing from the client is the reduction of network traffic. Consequently, SQLJ client programs gain performance. See the "Deploying SQLJ in an Oracle8*i*/9*i* Data Server: SQLJ Stored Procedures" section later in this chapter to learn how to move database logic into the Oracle9*i* data server.

Several design strategies and techniques exist that can help in reducing database processing in SQLJ clients. One of them is the distributed system (see Chapter 1). Next, you will learn how to distribute application logic between a client and an application server (middle tier).

Deploying SQLJ in an Application Server (Middle-Tier Server)

Conventional two-tier systems (see Figure 5-1) put most database operations and business logic in the client tier. This is often due to the limited hardware resources and the constraints of current tools. A significant amount of code, in addition to having to speak to a database, puts a burden on a client. In an effort to reduce the client's size, database and hardware vendors have introduced the *three-tier* or *middle-tier* model, commonly referred to as an *application server* model. The middle-tier model is a logical layer (often, a physical layer) between a client and a database, as Figure 5-2 illustrates.

In a three-tier system, the client program communicates with the middle tier, and the middle tier communicates with the database. Given this scenario, the application server is the only entity that talks to the database. Moving some of the code to an application server reduces the SQLJ thick client-side code. For example, most, if not all, of the DML, DDL, and transaction control statements, and the JDBC

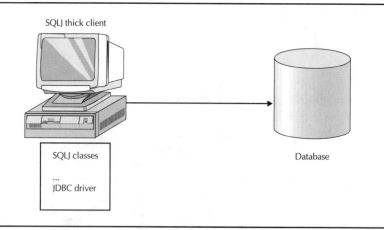

FIGURE 5-1. *Conventional two-tier system*

driver can be placed in the middle-tier server. In fact, you can move entire SQLJ applications to the application server, thereby freeing the client, now a *thin* client, from database processing code. In the "Deploying SQLJ in Oracle9*i* AS" section of this chapter, you will learn how to write a SQLJ application and deploy it in the Oracle9*i* AS application server.

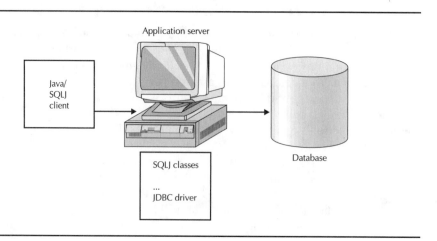

FIGURE 5-2. *SQLJ logic in the application server*

Deploying a SQLJ Thin Client

The advantages of the industry's trend toward smaller Java programs are twofold:

- The applications are small, and they can be downloaded much faster.
- Java applications are a good fit for the Internet, where bandwidth is limited.

NOTE
See the `SqljAppletCallsSqljSP.sqlj` *applet at the end of the chapter for an example of SQLJ thin client.*

Deploying SQLJ in a Java Application

Java applications can call Java methods from other Java classes. In a similar manner, Java programs can also call SQLJ methods. To call SQLJ methods from a Java source:

1. Create a stand-alone SQLJ application.

2. Compile the SQLJ application using the SQLJ Translator.

3. Run the SQLJ application.

4. Write the Java application. Call the SQLJ method like you would call a Java method. For example:

   ```
   sqljProc.addLineItem (aRequestno, aQuantity, aProjectNo,
               aUnit, anEstimatedcost, anActualcost, aDescription);
   ```

   where `sqljProc` is an instance of the SQLJ `PIManager` class, followed by the SQLJ `addLineItem()` method of the class.

5. Compile the Java application.

6. Run the Java application.

Note that all program source code (SQLJ and Java code) should be placed in the same directory hierarchy. The following examples illustrate the preceding steps:

Step 1   Create the SQLJ application: `PIManager.sqlj`.

```
/* Program Name:    PIManager.sqlj
**
*/
// Required SQLJ classes
```

```
import sqlj.runtime.*;
import sqlj.runtime.ref.*;

// Required Java classes
import java.sql.*;

// Required Oracle classes
import oracle.sql.*;
import oracle.sqlj.runtime.Oracle;
import oracle.jdbc.driver.*;

// A java utility class that creates a JDBC connection
import ConnectionManager;  // (See Note 1.)

public class PIManager {

    // Constructor to establish database connection
    public  PIManager () {
        try {  // Establish a Connection
            ConnectionManager.initContext();   // (See Note 2.)
        }
        catch (Exception ex) {
            System.err.println("Unable to connect "
                    + "ConnectionManager : " + ex);
        }
    }  // End Constructor

    public static void main (String argv[])
                    throws SQLException  { // Main entry

        PIManager sqljApp = new PIManager();    // (See Note 3.)

        // cannot connect to the database, stop program execution.
        if  (DefaultContext.getDefaultContext() == null ) {
            System.out.println("I cannot connect to the database "
                        + "-- Stop Execution.");
            System.exit(1);
        }

        // Create host variables
        int aRequestno = 501;    // (See Note 4.)
        int aQuantity = 20;
        int aProjectNo = 300;
        String aUnit = "04";
        double anEstimatedcost = 10000;
        double anActualcost = 7000;
        String aDescription = "FAU-Consulting";

        // Call the SQLJ method (See Note 5.)
```

```
      sqljApp.addLineItem (aRequestno,aQuantity,aProjectNo,
          aUnit, anEstimatedcost, anActualcost, aDescription);
} // End Main

public static void addLineItem (  // (See Note 6.)
      int aRequestno,int aQuantity,int aProjectNo, String aUnit,
      double anEstimatedcost, double anActualcost,
       String aDescription ) throws SQLException {

      int aLineNo = 0;
      #sql {SELECT lineno_seq.NEXTVAL
            INTO :aLineNo FROM DUAL };  // (See Note 7.)

        if  (aLineNo > 0) {
            try {
              // (See Note 8.)
              #sql {
                    INSERT INTO LINEITEM_LIST
                    ( requestno,lineno,projectno,quantity, unit,
                    estimatedcost, actualcost, description )
                    VALUES
                    (
                      :IN aRequestno,:IN aLineNo,
                      :IN aProjectNo,
                      :IN aQuantity,:IN aUnit,
                      :IN anEstimatedcost,
                      :IN anActualcost,
                      :IN aDescription
                    )
                  };
            } // End of try
            catch (SQLException er) {
                    System.err.println(er.getMessage());
            }   // End catch
      }  // End if

      try {
          // Commit
          #sql {COMMIT};  // (See Note 9.)
      }
      catch (SQLException ex) {
          System.err.println(ex.getMessage());
      }

    } // End addLineItem

} // End PIManager
```

Notes on `PIManager.sqlj` application:

This application establishes a database connection using the `initContext()` method from the `ConnectionManager` class and inserts data into the `LINEITEM_LIST` table.

1. This statement imports a Java utility class that returns a JDBC connection.

2. The constructor connects to the database using the `initContext()` method from the `ConnectionManager` class.

3. This statement creates an instance of the `PIManager` class and automatically connects to the database.

4. This statement and the six others that follow it create several Java variables.

5. This statement calls the SQLJ `addLineItem()` method. This method is called with an implicit `DefaultConnection` context created by the `PIManager()` constructor. Note that this call and all the host variables (in step 4) can be removed after the SQLJ application has been tested.

6. This statement declares the SQLJ `addLineItem()` method. Note that this method has been declared `public static` (see Appendix B for an explanation of Java `public static` methods).

7. This statement selects the next available line number to be inserted into the `LINEITEM_LIST` table.

8. This statement inserts a row of data into the `LINEITEM_LIST` table using host variables as input parameters to the `INSERT` statement.

9. This statement commits the changes to the database.

Step 2 Compile/translate the SQLJ application: `PIManager.sqlj`.

```
// At the command line, type the following command:
sqlj PIManager.sqlj ConnectionManager.java
```

Step 3 Run the SQLJ application.

```
// At the command line, type the following command:
java PIManager
```

Step 4 Create the Java application: `DeploySqljAppInJavaApp.java`.

```
/*
** Program Name:        DeploySqljAppInJavaApp.java
**
** Purpose:             Java application that calls an SQLJ method.
```

```
**
*/
// Required Java classes for any application
// that needs to access a database
import java.sql.*;

// Import the SQLJ class
import PIManager;       // (See Note 1.)

public class DeploySqljAppInJavaApp {

  public static void main(String[] args) throws SQLException  {

    PIManager sqljProc = new PIManager();      // (See Note 2.)

    // Stop program execution if we cannot connect to the database
    if  (DefaultContext.getDefaultContext() == null ) {
            System.out.println("I cannot connect to the database "
                          + "-- Stop Execution.");
            System.exit(1);
    }

    // Set Host Variables
    int aRequestno = 501;     // (See Note 3.)
    int aProjectNo = 300;
    int aQuantity = 30;
    String aUnit = "04";
    double anEstimatedcost = 15000;
    double anActualcost = 8500;
    String aDescription = "Datai-Consults";

    try {
        // Call the SQLJ method from
        // the Java application (See Note 4.)
        sqljProc.addLineItem (aRequestno, aQuantity, aProjectNo,
            aUnit, anEstimatedcost, anActualcost, aDescription);
    }  // end try
    catch (SQLException ex) {
          System.err.println("Error calling the SQLJ"
              + " addLineItem() method : " + ex);
            String sqlMessage = ex.getMessage();
            System.err.println("SQL Message: " + sqlMessage);
    }  // end catch
  }   // End main()

}  // End DeploySqljAppInJavaApp class
```

Notes on DeploySqljAppInJavaApp.java application:
This Java application calls a SQLJ method to insert data into the LINEITEM_
list table.

1. This statement imports a SQLJ class. The SQLJ `PIManager.sqlj` application is used in this example.

2. This statement creates an instance of the `PIManager` SQLJ class and connects to the database using its constructor. This database connection is done using the Oracle JDBC Thin driver.

3. These statements set the host variables. Note that you can create a user interface to accept these variables as input parameters.

4. This statement calls the `addLineItem()` SQLJ method contained in the Java application.

Step 5   Compile the Java application: `DeploySqljAppInJavaApp.java`.

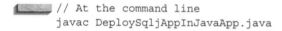
```
// At the command line
javac DeploySqljAppInJavaApp.java
```

Step 6   Run the Java application: `DeploySqljAppInJavaApp`.

```
// At the command line, run the DeploySqljAppInJavaApp.class
java DeploySqljAppInJavaApp
```

Deploying SQLJ in a Java Applet

A Java applet is a Java program that can start program execution in a Java-compatible browser via an `init()` method. It does not contain a `main()` method (see Appendix B). Every applet is implemented by creating a subclass of the `Applet` class. The steps to deploy SQLJ in a Java applet are similar to those of deploying SQLJ in a Java application. In addition to the steps in the "Deploying SQLJ in a Java Application" section of this chapter, you must translate the SQLJ `.ser` files (see Chapter 4) into regular Java .class files:

1. Create a stand-alone SQLJ application.

2. Compile the SQLJ application using the SQLJ Translator.

3. Run the SQLJ application.

4. Write a Java applet. Include a Java statement to call the SQLJ method.

5. Recompile the SQLJ application with the Java applet.

6. Translate the SQLJ `.ser` files into regular Java `.class` files. Create a root directory and retranslate the SQLJ `.ser` files. Make sure that you set up your path to point to this root directory. You may also need to put a copy of the JDBC driver and the SQLJ Translator into that directory. Failure to do so will generate the run-time error `applet not initialized`.

7. Copy the SQLJ `runtime11.zip` and `classes111.zip` in the same directory from step 6.

8. Set your system CLASSPATH to point to this directory.

9. Create an HTML file for the Java applet.

10. Run the Java applet by calling appletviewer.

The SQLJ runtime.zip run-time makes *very* extensive use of reflection. This is something that some browsers (most notably Netscape) are not very fond of, since this constitutes a security hole. When you use runtime11.zip instead, you cut down on the amount of use of reflection. Finally, if you use runtime11.zip, the Oracle 9*i* JDBC driver, and the setting -codegen-oracle, you will be able to eliminate Java reflection altogether. Even if you heavily use Oracle-specific features (such as SQL object types) that would require reflection in a standard SQLJ run-time, there are no .ser files to worry about, and this should be the recommended configuration. Keep checking technet.oracle.com for updates on the -codegen-oracle flag.

Steps 1–3   These steps are identical to steps 1–3 in the "Deploying SQLJ in a Java Application" section of this chapter. Next you will create the Java applet that will invoke the addLineItem() method from the PIManager SQLJ class.

Step 4   Write a Java applet. Include a Java statement to call the SQLJ method. The following is the source code for the Java applet, the SqljInJavaApplet.java.

```
/*
** Program Name:        SqljInJavaApplet.java
*/
// Import the JDBC classes
import java.sql.*;

// Import the java classes used in applets
import java.awt.*;
import java.io.*;
import java.util.*;

// Import the SQLJ class
import PIManager;

public class SqljInJavaApplet extends java.applet.Applet {

  // The button to call the SQLJ addLineItem() method
  Button execute_button;

  // The place to dump the applet actions
  TextArea output;

  // Create the User Interface
  public void init ()   {
```

```
      this.setLayout (new BorderLayout ());
      Panel p = new Panel ();
      p.setLayout (new FlowLayout (FlowLayout.LEFT));
      execute_button = new Button ("Insert Line_Item");
      p.add (execute_button);
      this.add ("North", p);
      output = new TextArea (10, 60);
      this.add ("Center", output);
}   // End of init()

public boolean action (Event ev, Object arg)  {

   if (ev.target == execute_button){
      // Clear the output area
       output.setText (null);

     // Connect to the database
      PIManager sqljProc = new PIManager();
       output.append ("Connecting to database" +
           " using SQLJ " + "\n");

       // Stop program execution if we cannot connect to the database
       if  (DefaultContext.getDefaultContext() == null ) {
            System.out.println("I cannot connect to the database "
                            + "-- Stop Execution.");
            System.exit(1);
       }

       // Set Host Variables
       int aRequestno = 501;
       int aProjectNo = 300;
       int aQuantity = 30;
       String aUnit = "04";
       double anEstimatedcost = 15000;
       double anActualcost = 8500;
       String aDescription = "Oracle-Support";

       output.append ("Calling PIManager.addLineItem()" + "\n");
       output.append("with req# = 501 " + "\n");
       output.append("with proj# = 300 " + "\n");
       output.append("with qty = 30 " + "\n");
       output.append("with unit = 04 " + "\n");
       output.append("with estimated cost = 15000 " + "\n");
       output.append("with actualcost = 8500 " + "\n");
       output.append("with description = Oracle-Support " + "\n");

       try {
           // Call the SQLJ method from the Java application
           sqljProc.addLineItem (aRequestno, aQuantity, aProjectNo,
               aUnit, anEstimatedcost, anActualcost, aDescription);
```

```
        }  // end try
      catch (SQLException ex) {
            output.append ("Error calling the SQLJ"
                 + " addLineItem() method : " + ex + "\n");
                 String sqlMessage = ex.getMessage();
                 output.append ("SQL Message: "
                 + sqlMessage + "\n");
        }  // end catch
  }  // End if

  output.append ("done.\n");

  return true;

  }  // End action()
}//end SqljInJavaApplet class
```

As the foregoing call demonstrates, the call to a SQLJ method from a Java applet is identical to the call from a Java application. This database connection is done via the Oracle JDBC Thin driver. This is a required "pure Java" driver for all Oracle Java applets. See steps 1–4 in "Deploying SQLJ in a Java Application," earlier in the chapter. Next, you will learn the remaining steps needed to run Java applets.

Step 5   Recompile the SQLJ application with the Java applet:

```
// At the command line
sqlj -profile=false PIManager.sqlj SqljInJavaApplet.java
```

Step 6   Translate the SQLJ .ser files into regular Java .class files. Create a root directory and retranslate the SQLJ .ser files. Make sure that you set up your path to point to this root directory. You may also need to put a copy of the JDBC driver and the SQLJ Translator into that directory. Failure to do so will generate the run-time error applet not initialized:

```
// At the command line
// directory. In NT, you can use the format: -d=c:\dist
sqlj -profile=false -ser2class -d=dist PIManager.sqlj
        SqljInJavaApplet.java
```

Step 7   Copy the SQLJ runtime.zip and classes111.zip in the same directory from step 6. Use your operating system command to do so.

Step 8   Set your system CLASSPATH to point to this directory.

Step 9   Create an HTML file for the Java applet.

Step 10   Run the Java applet by calling appletviewer:

```
// At the command line
AppletViewer SqljInJavaApplet.htm
```

Here is an example of an HTML file that calls the applet:

```
<HTML>
<HEAD>
<META HTTP-EQUIV="Content-Type"
CONTENT="text/html; charset=windows-1252">
<HTML>
<TITLE>
HTML Test Page
</TITLE>
</HEAD>
<BODY>
Chapter05.SqljInJavaApplet will appear below
in a Java enabled browser.<BR>
<APPLET CODE = "SqljInJavaApplet" CODEBASE = ".."
archive="I:\JDeveloper3.2\jdbc\lib\oracle8.1.7\classes12.zip"
WIDTH = 400 HEIGHT = 400 ALIGN = middle NAME = "TestApplet" >
</APPLET>
</BODY>
</HTML>
```

When you run the applet, you first get the screen shown in Figure 5-3. When you press the Insert Line_Item button, then you get the screen shown in Figure 5-4.

Deploying a SQLJ Applet

Deploying a SQLJ applet is almost identical to deploying SQLJ in a Java applet. You can use SQLJ source code in applets because the SQLJ run-time is pure Java. There are, however, a few considerations to be made. See the *Oracle9i SQLJ Developer's Guide and Reference* for more information about the SQLJ packages.

The following SQLJ packages must be packaged with your SQLJ applet:

- `sqlj.runtime`
- `sqlj.runtime.ref`
- `sqlj.runtime.profile`
- `sqlj.runtime.profile.ref`
- `sqlj.runtime.error`

Additionally, the packages here must be included if you are using Oracle customization:

- `oracle.sqlj.runtime`

- `oracle.sqlj.runtime.error`

Alternatively, since all these packages are included in the file `runtime.zip`, all you have to do is list the `runtime.zip` as a value for the archive key in your `<APPLET>` tag. The `runtime.zip` file comes with your Oracle SQLJ installation. You must also specify a pure Java JDBC driver, such as the Oracle JDBC thin driver, for your database connection. Furthermore, Oracle SQLJ requires the run-time environment of JDK 1.1.*x* or higher. You cannot employ browsers using JDK 1.0.*x*, such as Netscape Navigator 3.0 and Microsoft Internet Explorer 3.0, without either using a JRE plug-in or finding some other way of using JRE 1.1.*x* instead of the browser's default JRE.

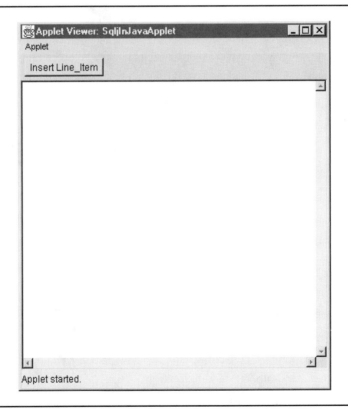

FIGURE 5-3.   *First screen when you run the applet*

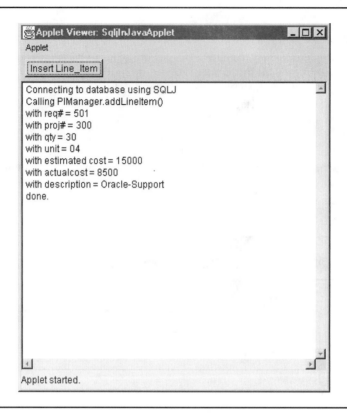

FIGURE 5-4. *Output from the applet when you click Insert Line_Item*

TIP
Remember to use `runtime11.zip` *to avoid Java reflection.*

Deploying SQLJ applets is almost identical to deploying SQLJ in Java applets. You will use the method from the `PIManager` class once more, but this time you will call it an SQLJ applet. The steps are

1. Create a stand-alone SQLJ application.

2. Compile the SQLJ application using the SQLJ Translator.

3. Run the SQLJ application.

4. Write a SQLJ applet. Call the SQLJ method within the program.

5. Recompile the SQLJ application with the SQLJ applet.

6. Translate the SQLJ .ser files into regular Java classes.

7. Copy the SQLJ runtime.zip and classes111.zip in the same directory from step 6.

8. Set your system CLASSPATH to point to this directory. This step is done only if you wish to use strictly the appletviewer utility program. To view the applet in a browser, make sure that the <APPLET> tag contains the following key/value pair: archive=classes111.zip,runtime.zip.

9. Create the HTML file for the Java applet.

10. Run the SQLJ applet by calling appletviewer.

Note that you can skip steps 1 to 3 and have all the SQLJ code from the PIManager class inside the SQLJ applet. Although it is not advisable, it can be done. The following SQLJ applet performs in a similar manner as the Java applet. In fact, SqljApplet.sqlj is exactly the same program as the SqljInJavaApplet.java; you only change the class name and, of course, store the program in a file bearing the same name as required for all Java and SQLJ programs.

```
/*
**  Program Name:        SqljApplet.sqlj
*/
// Import the JDBC classes
import java.sql.*;

// Import the java classes used in applets
import java.awt.*;
import java.io.*;
import java.util.*;

// Import the SQLJ class
import PIManager;

public class SqljInJavaApplet extends java.applet.Applet {

    // The button to call the SQLJ addLineItem() method
    Button execute_button;

    // The place to dump the applet actions
```

```
            TextArea output;

            // Create the User Interface
            public void init ()  {
              this.setLayout (new BorderLayout ());
              Panel p = new Panel ();
              p.setLayout (new FlowLayout (FlowLayout.LEFT));
              execute_button = new Button ("Insert Line_Item");
              p.add (execute_button);
              this.add ("North", p);
              output = new TextArea (10, 60);
              this.add ("Center", output);
            }  // End of init()

            public boolean action (Event ev, Object arg)  {
              if (ev.target == execute_button){
                 // Clear the output area
                 output.setText (null);

                // Connect to the database
                 PIManager sqljProc = new PIManager();

               // Stop program execution if we cannot connect to the database
               if  (DefaultContext.getDefaultContext() == null ) {
                      System.out.println("I cannot connect to the database "
                                        + "-- Stop Execution.");
                      System.exit(1);
               } // end if

                 output.append ("Connecting to database" +
                       " using SQLJ " + "\n");

              // Set Host Variables
                int aRequestno = 501;
                int aProjectNo = 300;
                int aQuantity = 30;
                String aUnit = "04";
                double anEstimatedcost = 15000;
                double anActualcost = 8500;
                String aDescription = "Oracle-Support";

                try {
                     // Call the SQLJ method from the Java application
```

```
           sqljProc.addLineItem (aRequestno, aQuantity, aProjectNo,
                aUnit, anEstimatedcost, anActualcost, aDescription);
        } // end try
        catch (SQLException ex) {
            output.append ("Error calling the SQLJ"
                + " addLineItem() method : " + ex + "\n");
                String sqlMessage = ex.getMessage();
                output.append ("SQL Message: "
                + sqlMessage + "\n");
        } // end catch
    } // End if

    output.append ("done.\n");
    return true;
  } // end action()
} // end SqljApplet class
```

In the "Deploying SQLJ in a Java Application" section of this chapter, you created a SQLJ application, the `PIManager.sqlj`, which you used to deploy SQLJ in a Java application, a Java applet, and a SQLJ applet. Next, you will deploy the SQLJ application, `PIManager.sqlj`, into the Oracle8*i*/9*i* JVM (see Chapter 1 to learn more about Oracle JVM).

Deploying SQLJ in an Oracle8*i*/9*i* Data Server: SQLJ Stored Procedures

SQLJ code can run in the Oracle8*i*/9*i* Server in the form of stored procedures, stored functions, triggers, Enterprise JavaBeans (EJB), and CORBA objects. See Chapter 4 for a detailed discussion on SQLJ and Java stored procedures, Chapter 9 to learn how to develop enterprise JavaBeans and CORBA objects using SQLJ, and *Oracle8i/9i Java Stored Procedures and Developer's Guide*.

There is very little difference between coding for server-side use as opposed to client-side use. The main differences involve database connections. Remember that SQLJ clients connect to an Oracle database via a JDBC thin or a JDBC OCI driver. SQLJ server-side programs connect through the JDBC server-side driver (see Chapters 1 and 4). The SQLJ client-side programs must explicitly establish a database connection either via an instance of the `DefaultContext` or a declared connection context class. On the server, the database connection is always implicit.

After you write your SQLJ program, you can translate and compile your code either on a client or in the server. You can load your SQLJ source code directly into the Oracle database, and you can specify that translation and compilation be done automatically. In fact, the Oracle8*i*/9*i* Server includes a SQLJ translator that can translate the SQLJ source files directly in the server. Alternatively, you can translate on the client and load in one step the `.class` and `.ser` files using the server-side SQLJ Translator. In either case, you use the Oracle `loadjava` utility program to load your SQLJ programs into the server. The recommended way is to have all of your SQLJ `.class` and `.ser` files in a single `.jar` file and then use `loadjava` to upload your SQLJ classes.

The characteristics of the Oracle JDBC server-side driver include the following:

- You only have one connection.

- The connection must be to the database in which the code is running.

- The connection cannot be closed—any attempt to close it will be ignored.

- The JDBC server-side driver does not support `auto-commit`. You must commit explicitly.

In this section, you will learn how to transform a SQLJ client-side program into a server-side stored procedure. You will use the SQLJ `PIManager.sqlj` application to do so. To create an SQLJ server-side program from a client-side program, you do the following:

Step 1   Edit the program and remove all explicit database connections and all SQLJ run-time classes.

```
/* Program Name:    PIManager.sqlj
**
*/
// Required Java classes
import java.sql.SQLException;

public class PIManager {

    public static void main (String argv[]) { // Main entry
    } // End Main

    public static void addLineItem
      ( int aRequestno,int aQuantity,int aProjectNo, String aUnit,
          double anEstimatedcost, double anActualcost,
            String aDescription ) throws SQLException {

      int aLineNo = 0;
      #sql {SELECT lineno_seq.NEXTVAL INTO :aLineNo FROM DUAL };

        try {
```

```
              #sql { INSERT INTO LINEITEM_LIST
                     ( requestno,lineno,projectno,quantity, unit,
                        estimatedcost, actualcost, description
                     )
                       VALUES
                         ( :IN aRequestno,:IN aLineNo,:IN aProjectNo,
                           :IN aQuantity,:IN aUnit, :IN anEstimatedcost,
                             :IN anActualcost,:IN aDescription
                         )
                     };
        } // End of try
        catch (SQLException er) {
             System.err.println(er.getMessage());
        }  // End of catch

        // Commit
        #sql {COMMIT};   // (See Note 1.)

     } // End addLineItem

} // End PIManager
```

Note in `PIManager.sqlj` as a SQLJ stored procedure:

1. This statement explicitly commits the changes to the database. Remember
that the Oracle JDBC server-side driver does not support `auto-commit`.
You may wish, however, to commit the change to the database in the
client-side program versus the server-side program. In this situation, you
can remove the `#sql {COMMIT}` statement from the `PIManager.sqlj`
and place it into your client-side program.

NOTE
*We could have left the `Oracle.connect()` calls
in our original code. Since the default context is
already initialized for server-side programs, running
this call in the server is not applicable. This is a neat
trick to write the exact same code for running in the
server, as well as on the client.*

Step 2   Translate the SQLJ source code. Use the SQLJ `ser2class` (see Chapter 4)
translator to do so.

```
// At the command prompt
sqlj -ser2class PIManager.sqlj
```

Step 3 Archive the generated classes and SQL profiles.

```
// At the command line
jar cvf0 PIManager.jar PIManager*.class PIManager*.ser
```

Step 4 Load the `PIManager.jar` file into the server.

```
// At the command line
loadjava -thin -verbose -resolve -user
    scott/tiger@haiti:1521:ORCL PIManager.jar
```

Step 5 Check the load in step 4 by running the `checkload.sql` script in SQL*Plus. You wish to find out if your SQLJ classes have been loaded with no error. We provide you with a script that does the work for you. The script uses the `user_objects` view to determine the status of your classes. Check the listing to find the name and the status of your SQLJ program. Proceed to step 6 if the status is valid.

```
-- In SQLPLUS
@checkload.sql
```

Step 6 Create a call specification for your SQLJ program using the following syntax:

```
-- Program Name: PI_Actions.sql
CREATE OR REPLACE PACKAGE PI_Actions AS
    PROCEDURE PI_main(p_entry     VARCHAR2);
    PROCEDURE add_Line_Item
        ( p_aRequestno NUMBER,p_aQuantity  NUMBER,
          p_aProjectNo NUMBER,p_aUnit VARCHAR2,
          p_anEstimatedcost NUMBER,p_anActualcost NUMBER,
          p_aDescription VARCHAR2
        );
END PI_Actions;
/
CREATE OR REPLACE PACKAGE BODY PI_Actions AS
    PROCEDURE PI_main(p_entry     VARCHAR2) AS LANGUAGE JAVA
        NAME 'PIManager.main(java.lang.String[])';
    PROCEDURE add_Line_Item
      ( p_aRequestno NUMBER,p_aQuantity  NUMBER,
        p_aProjectNo NUMBER,p_aUnit VARCHAR2,
        p_anEstimatedcost NUMBER,p_anActualcost NUMBER,
        p_aDescription VARCHAR2 ) AS LANGUAGE JAVA
        NAME 'PIManager.addLineItem(int,int,int,java.lang.String,
                          float,float,java.lang.String)';
END PI_Actions;
/
```

Step 7 Load the PL/SQL wrapper into the server.

```
-- IN SQLPLUS or server manager
@PI_Actions.sql
```

Step 8 Test your SQLJ stored procedure.

```
// In SQLPLUS
BEGIN
PI_Actions.add_Line_Item(501,300,30,'04',15000,8500,'DataBase
Support');
END;
/
```

Here is the output from step 8:

REQ#	L#	PR#	QTY	U#	EC	AC	WHAT
501	21	300	30	04	15000	8500	Datai-Consults
501	81	30	300	04	15000	8500	DataBase Support

The following SQLJ client applet will call a SQLJ stored procedure.

```
/***   Program Name:        SqljAppletCallsSqljSP.sqlj */

// Import the JDBC classes
import java.sql.*;

// Import the java classes used in applets
import java.awt.*;
import java.io.*;
import java.util.*;

// SQLJ-specific classes
import java.sql.SQLException;
import java.sql.DriverManager;
import sqlj.runtime.ExecutionContext;
import sqlj.runtime.ref.DefaultContext;
import oracle.jdbc.driver.OracleDriver;
import oracle.sqlj.runtime.Oracle;

// Import the Java Utility class
import ConnectionManager;

public class SqljAppletCallsSqljSP extends java.applet.Applet {
```

```
// The button to call the SQLJ addLineItem() method
Button execute_button;

// The place to dump the applet actions
TextArea output;

// Create the User Interface
public void init ()  {

  this.setLayout (new BorderLayout ());
  Panel p = new Panel ();
  p.setLayout (new FlowLayout (FlowLayout.LEFT));
  execute_button = new Button ("Insert Line_Item");
  p.add (execute_button);
  this.add ("North", p);
  output = new TextArea (10, 60);
  this.add ("Center", output);
}  // End of init()

public boolean action (Event ev, Object arg)  {
  if (ev.target == execute_button){

    // Clear the output area
     output.setText (null);

   // Connect to the database     (See Note 1.)
    DefaultContext sqljProcCtx = ConnectionManager.initContext();
    // Stop program execution if we cannot connect to the database
    if  (sqljProcCtx == null ) {
          System.out.println("I cannot connect to the database "
                        + "-- Stop Execution.");
          System.exit(1);
    } // end if
    // Create an execution context instance (See Note 2.)
    ExecutionContext sqljProcExecCtx = new ExecutionContext();

    output.append ("Connecting to database using SQLJ " + "\n");

    // Set Host Variables
    int aRequestno = 501;
    int aProjectNo = 300;
    int aQuantity = 30;
    String aUnit = "04";
    double anEstimatedcost = 15000;
    double anActualcost = 8500;
    String aDescription = "Oracle-Support";

    try {
```

```
        // Call the SQLJ method from the SQLJ applet
        #sql [sqljProcCtx,sqljProcExecCtx]     // (See Note 3.)
            { CALL PI_Actions.add_Line_Item
                ( :IN aRequestno, :IN aQuantity,
                    :IN aProjectNo, :IN aUnit, :IN anEstimatedcost,
                    :IN anActualcost, :IN aDescription
                )
            };
        output.append (" Record has been inserted " +
                                "- SUCCESS \n");
    }  // end try
    catch (SQLException ex) {
        output.append ("Error calling the SQLJ"
                + " addLineItem() method : " + ex + "\n");
        String sqlMessage = ex.getMessage();
        output.append ("SQL Message: " +
                sqlMessage + "\n");
    }  // end catch

  }  // End of if

  output.append ("Work completed \n");
  return true;

  }   // End of action() method

}    // End of SqljAppletCallsSqljSP class
```

Notes on `SqljAppletCallsSqljSP.sqlj` applet:
   This SQLJ applet inserts a record in the LINEITEM_LIST table via a SQLJ stored procedure in the Oracle8*i* data server.

   1. This statement creates an instance of the `DefaultContext` class by calling the `initContext()` method from the Java utility class `ConnectionManager`. Remember that the Oracle JDBC KPRB server-side driver does not support auto-commit. Therefore, you must establish a database connection in your client program prior to calling the SQLJ stored procedure.

   2. This statement creates an instance of the `ExecutionContext` class. You should always associate an explicit execution context instance to your SQLJ clause when you create your applet. You need to be in control of what the program is executing at the location specified in your connection context instance. More importantly, you may have several applets running and executing concurrently in the browser.

3. This statement calls the SQLJ stored procedure that inserts a record in the `LINEITEM_LIST` table.

Next, you will learn how to deploy SQLJ programs in the Oracle9i AS.

Deploying SQLJ in Oracle9i AS

In this section, you will learn the following:

- How to write the `LineItem` class, a Java serializable class that you can use as a return or input parameter to methods of another Java program.

- How to write the `PIManagerQueries` class, a SQLJ application that retrieves details from the LINEITEM_LIST table.

- How to write the `ServletCallSqljClass` class, a simple servlet that will call a method from the `PIManagerQueries` class and display the data in a Web browser.

- How to write a `WrapperForSCSC.jsp` program, a simple JavaServerPages application that will call the `ServletCallSqljClass` class.

First, we present here a brief overview of the Oracle Internet Application Server. To learn more about Oracle9i AS, see Oracle Technology Network (http://otn.oracle.com).

The Oracle Internet Application Server is part of the Oracle Internet Suite, which consists of the following:

- The Oracle8i database server. The next release of Oracle9i AS will be distributed with the Oracle9i database server.

- The Oracle Internet Developer Suite.

- The Oracle Internet Application Server.

Oracle9i AS is a middle-tier application that provides a set of services. Here is a partial list of its services:

- **Communication services**   Oracle HTTP Server (using Apache 1.3.12)
- **Content management services**   Oracle Internet File System

- **Business logic services** Oracle Business Components for Java (BC4J), Oracle8*i* JVM (Java Virtual Machine), Oracle8*i* PLSQL, and Oracle Forms Services

- **Presentation services** Apache Jserv, OracleJSP (JavaServer Pages), Oracle PL/SQL Server Pages, and Perl Interpreter

In this section, you will build an SQLJ application, the `PIManagerQueries.sqlj` that accesses the `PurchaseOrder` schema and retrieves the details of the `LineItem_List` table. The data retrieval is done via the `GetLineItemDetails()` method. When called, the `GetLineItemDetails()` method returns a Java object of type `LineItem`.

First, you will write the `LineItem` and the `PIManagerQueries` classes. In subsequent sections, you will build a Java servlet and a `JavaServerPages` application that will use the `PIManagerQueries` class.

Here is the complete definition of the `LineItem` class:

```
/*
** Program Name:     LineItem.java
** Description : A Java serializable class
**               that can be used as a parameter
**               to java methods.
*/
package Chapter05;
import java.io.*;
public class LineItem implements Serializable {
    // Data members
    int aRequestno;
    int aQuantity;
    int aLineno;
    int aProjectNo;
    String aUnit;
    double anEstimatedcost;
    double anActualcost;
    String aDescription;

    public int getRequestno() {
        return aRequestno;
    }
    public void setRequestno(int aRequestno) {
        this.aRequestno = aRequestno;
    }
    public int getLineNo() {
        return aLineno;
    }
    public void setLineNo(int aLineNo) {
```

```
            this.aLineno = aLineno;
      }
      public int getQuantity() {
         return aQuantity;
      }
      public void setQuantity(int aQuantity) {
            this.aQuantity = aQuantity;
      }
      public String getDescription() {
         return aDescription;
      }
      public void setDescription(String aDescription) {
            this.aDescription = aDescription;
      }
}  // End of LineItem class
```

Next, you will write the PIManagerQueries SQLJ application. The
PIManagerQueries SQLJ application consists of the following:

■ The PIManagerQueries() constructor that establishes a connection
   to the PurchaseOrder schema when you create an instance of the
   PIManagerQueries class. When invoked at run time, the constructor
   calls the initContext() method of the ConnectionManager class,
   which, in turn, creates a DefaultContext instance for you.

■ The main() method. Recall that a Java program that contains a main()
   method is called a Java application. Therefore, an SQLJ application must
   also have a main() method.

■ The GetLineItemDetails(aRequestno, aLineno) method that
   returns an object of type LineItem and whose definition requires two
   input parameters of type int.

Here is the complete definition of the PIManagerQueries.sqlj program:

```
/*
** Program Name:      PIManagerQueries.sqlj
*/
import sqlj.runtime.*;
import sqlj.runtime.ref.*;
import java.sql.*;
import oracle.sql.*;
import oracle.sqlj.runtime.Oracle;
import oracle.jdbc.driver.*;
import ConnectionManager;
public class PIManagerQueries {
```

```
   public  PIManagerQueries () {
      try {  // Establish a Connection
          ConnectionManager.initContext();
      } // End try
      catch (Exception ex) {
         System.err.println("Unable to connect "
             + "ConnectionManager : " + ex);
         System.exit(1);
      } // End catch
   }  // End Constructor

 // The main method is only used to test
 // the PIManagerQueries class without a
 // client.
public static void main (String argv[])
         throws SQLException  { // Main entry
      PIManagerQueries sqljApp = new PIManagerQueries();
      if  (DefaultContext.getDefaultContext() == null ) {
          System.out.println("I cannot connect to the database "
             + "-- Stop Execution.");
          System.exit(1);
      }
      // Create host variables
      int aRequestno = 500;
      int aLineno = 2;
      // Call the SQLJ method
      // Create an instance of the LineItem class
      LineItem item =
          sqljApp.GetLineItemDetails (aRequestno,aLineno);
      System.out.println(" " +item.getQuantity() +" "
                +item.getDescription());
} // End Main()
public LineItem GetLineItemDetails (
      int aRequestno,int aLineno) throws SQLException {
   LineItem aLineItem = new LineItem();
   int aQuantity = 0;
   String aDescription = null;
   try {
       #sql {
             SELECT QUANTITY, DESCRIPTION
                INTO   :aQuantity, :aDescription
             FROM LINEITEM_LIST
             WHERE   REQUESTNO = :aRequestno
                     AND lineno = :aLineno
           };  // End of SQLJ statement
   } // End of try
   catch (SQLException er) {
       System.err.println(er.getMessage());
```

```
        System.exit(1);
}    // End catch

// Set data members of the LineItem class
aLineItem.setRequestno(aRequestno);
aLineItem.setLineNo(aLineno);
aLineItem.setQuantity(aQuantity);
aLineItem.setDescription(aDescription);

// System.out.println(" " +aQuantity +" " +aDescription);
// Always close the connection
Oracle.close();

return aLineItem;
} // End GetLineItemDetails()

} // End PIManagerQueries class
```

Note that, like the PIManager class, the PIManagerQueries.sqlj program establishes a database connection via the ConnectionManager class. Next, compile all three classes.

At the prompt, type the following:

```
sqlj PIManagerQueries.sqlj LineItem.java ConnectionManager.java
```

If there is no error, create a .jar file of all .ser and .class files generated by the execution of the sqlj command:

```
// If all .ser and .class files exist in the same directory
// Type the following command to create a .jar file
jar cfv0 PimQry.jar  *.*

// Or, use full path and the file names
jar cfv0 PimQry.jar Chapter05\ConnectionManager.class
Chapter05\LineItem.class Chapter05\PIManagerQueries.class
Chapter05\PIManagerQueries_SJProfileKeys.class
Chapter05\PIManagerQueries_SJProfile0.ser
```

Next, you will write the ServletCallSqljClass class, a simple Java servlet that calls the GetLineItemDetails() method of the SQLJ PIManagerQueries application.

Java Servlets Using SQLJ Application

In this section, you will build the ServletCallSqljClass class. When you invoke the servlet, it will call the GetLineItemDetails method of the PIManagerQueries class to display the details of a row of the LINEITEM_LIST table. We provide here a brief overview of what is a Java servlet. Teaching you how to write Java servlets is beyond the scope of the book. To learn how to build Java servlets and JavaServerPages applications in the Oracle8*i* or Oracle9*i* database environment, see *Oracle8*i *Java Component Programming with EJB, CORBA, and JSP*, (9/2000), Oracle Press by Nirva Morisseau-Leroy, Martin Solomon, and Julie Basu.

What Is a Java Servlet?

A Java *servlet* is a server-side program that is invoked by a Web server to service HTTP requests. It runs on a Java Virtual Machine (JVM) in the Web server. Servlets are regular Java programs that are translated into platform-independent bytecode and are portable to any machine where Java is available. They run within the secure boundaries of the JVM and cannot cause memory access violations and server crashes. Importantly, servlets have full access to the APIs in the Java framework such as Enterprise JavaBeans, Java Mail, JNDI, and Java Remote Invocation Method (RMI). The Servlet 2.0 API Specification was finalized in 1998, and the Servlet 2.2 API was published in December 1999.

Here is the definition of the ServletCallSqljClass class. You can use your favorite editor to write the code or you can use Oracle JDeveloper 3.*x* to do so:

```
/*      Program Name: ServletCallSqljClass.java
**
**      Description:  This Java servlet does the following:
**      1. Create an instance of the PIManagerQueries class
**      2. Use the instance to call the GetLineItemDetails()
**         method of the PIManagerQueries class.
**      3. The GetLineItemDetails() method returns an object
**         of type LineItem.
**      4. The servlet displays the details of a row
**         of the LINEITEM_LIST table.
**
**
*/
import Chapter05.*;
import javax.servlet.*;
import javax.servlet.http.*;
import java.io.*;
import java.util.*;

public class ServletCallSqljClass extends HttpServlet {
   public void init(ServletConfig config) throws ServletException {
      super.init(config);
   } //End of init()
```

```java
/* Process the HTTP Get request */
public void doGet(HttpServletRequest request,
                  HttpServletResponse response)
           throws ServletException, IOException {

    //set the response to text/html
    response.setContentType("text/html");

    //set the outputStream
    OutputStreamWriter osw =
            new OutputStreamWriter(response.getOutputStream());
    PrintWriter out =
            new PrintWriter (response.getOutputStream());

    //html output
    out.println("<html>");
    out.println("<head><title>ServletCallSqljClass"
                      +"</title></head>");
    out.println("<body>");
    out.println("<h3>Output from ServletCallSqljClass</h3>");
    out.println(callSQLProcedure());
    out.println("</body></html>");
    out.close();

  } //End of doGet()


private String callSQLProcedure() {
   String OutputString = null;
   try {
       // Create an instance of the LineItem class
       PIManagerQueries sqljApp = new PIManagerQueries();

       int aRequestno = 500;
       int aLineno = 2;

       // Call the SQLJ method
       LineItem item =
               sqljApp.GetLineItemDetails (aRequestno,aLineno);

       OutputString = item.getRequestno() + " "
                    +item.getLineno() + " "
                    +item.getQuantity() +" "
                    +item.getDescription();
   }  //End of try
   catch(Exception e) {
       OutputString = "Error: " +e.getMessage();
   }//end catch
```

```
    // Return response to the browser
    return OutputString;
  }  //End of callSQLProcedure()

} // End of ServletCallSqljClass class
```

Compile the `ServletCallSqljClass` servlet to create the `.class` file. It is a good idea to compile and test your servlet before deploying it into the Oracle9*i* AS environment to avoid possible run-time errors. However, note that you do not need to compile the `servlet` class prior of deploying it into the Oracle9*i* AS environment. Since Oracle9*i* AS is distributed with the Oracle JVM, at run time, if the `.class` file of your servlet does not exist, Oracle JVM will compile your source code and create the Java `.class` file for you.

At the command prompt, invoke the Java compiler via the `javac` command:

 `javac ServletCallSqljClass.java`

There are two ways that you can invoke a Java servlet:

■ Via a static HTML page

■ Via a JSP program

You can invoke the servlet directly or you can invoke it via a JSP program. In either case, you do so by using a URL address. Figure 5-5 shows the output from the servlet when you invoke it via the Oracle JDeveloper (release 3.2) tool. In the next section, you will learn how to invoke a servlet via a JSP program while writing the `WrapperForSCSC.jsp` JSP program. JSP is very easy to use and provides a rapid design, development, and deployment cycle.

NOTE
The `WrapperForSCSC.jsp` is a wrapper for the `ServletCallSqljClass` class. A `.jsp` wrapper class is needed due to the Servlet 2.0 environment. Oracle9i AS uses the Apache webserver; and, at the time that they released the application server, Apache was servlet 2.0 compliant. In this environment, a JSP class is unable to call a servlet directly and can only call a JSP or an HTML page.

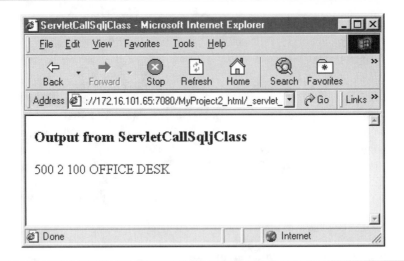

FIGURE 5-5. *Invoking a servlet in JDeveloper*

JavaServerPages (JSP) Using SQLJ Application

Before delving into the `WrapperForSCSC.jsp` program, we'll outline the basics of the JSP, including what it is and how it works.

What Is a JSP Program?

JavaServerPages is in a standard extension package and its root package is `javax` and not `java`. It is a subpackage of the servlet standard edition package, `javax.servlet`. JSP pages combine HTML and Java (or other languages that conform to the JSP model) into a single server processed file. JSP consists of a set of tags, which look similar to HTML tags. The Java code is distinguished by being enclosed in specific JSP tags. JavaServerPages is part of the Enterprise edition of the Java language. However, JSP is not included with the Standard edition of the Java language (J2SE).

Processing JSP Files

The very first time the JSP file is loaded by the JSP engine, it is initially processed in two stages:

- **The HTTP translation stage**   During this step, the file is processed; all HTML tags are processed; and the Java code is compiled into a Java `.class` file, which is generally a `Servlet` class.

■ **The request processing stage** When users make a request from the JSP page (for example, from a Web browser), the JSP engine processes the request by executing the compiled JSP file (that is, the servlet .class file). The Java code that is executed is known as a *scriptlet* and is dynamically executed with each user's request.

To learn more about JSPs, see the Bibliography at the end of the book. Next, you will write the WrapperForSCSC.jsp application.

The WrapperForSCSC.jsp is a very simple JSP application that calls the ServletCallSqljClass class. In this scenario, the user invokes the servlet indirectly via the WrapperForSCSC.jsp program. You invoke the JSP program from a browser via a URL address that you provide. The URL address is the location where the JSP program is located.

Here is the definition of the WrapperForSCSC.jsp program:

```
<%--
--      Program Name:    WrapperForSCSC.jsp
--      Description:      A JSP application that calls
--                       a servlet using Apache Jserv
--                       servlet2.0-compliant.
--%>
<%@ page isThreadSafe="true"
    import="ServletCallSqljClass" %>
<%! ServletCallSqljClass scsc = null;
    public void jspInit() {
        // Instantiate the servlet class: ServletCallSqljClass
        scsc  = new ServletCallSqljClass();
        try {
            scsc.init(this.getServletConfig());
        } // End of try
        catch  (ServletException se) {
            scsc  = null
        } // End of catch
    } // End of jspInit()
    public void jspDestroy() {
        if (scsc  != null) scsc .destroy();
    } // End of jspDestroy()
%>
<%if (scsc  != null)  {
    scsc.doGet(request, response);
}
else  {
    throw new JspException("Error initializing servlet!!");
}
%>
```

Note that you can test this code using any IDE that supports servlets and JSPs, any middle-tier application server of your choice, or Oracle9*i* AS. For example, you can use Oracle JDeveloper 3.*x* to test the servlet and the JSP code. We tested this code in JDeveloper 3.2. Figure 5-6 illustrates how to invoke `WrapperForSCSC.jsp` from JDeveloper 3.2. Also, we include in the CD-ROM the `DeployingInOracle9IAS.txt` file that provides detailed information on how to deploy servlets and JSPs in the Oracle9*i* AS environment.

Using `DataSource` in SQLJ Programs

In this section, you will learn how to use JNDI with the JDBC 2.0 API. You will build the `DataSource.sqlj` program, a very simple example that shows you how to use `DataSource` objects in the SQLJ program. We provide also the `DataSourceCF.sqlj` program that demonstrates how to build a Java `DataSource`. Teaching you how to build Java data sources is beyond the scope of the book.

Note that this program has been tested against Oracle release 8.1.7 using the JDK 1.3 execution environment. Recall that JNDI classes are distributed with JDK 1.3 and higher. If you wish to compile and run this application in earlier JDK releases, you will need to include in your `CLASSPATH` the `jndi.jar` file.

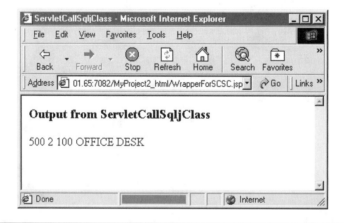

FIGURE 5-6. *Invoking a JSP program in JDeveloper*

To learn more about data source, see "Java Naming and Directory Interface Service Provider Interface (JNDI SPI) (http://java.sun.com/products/jndi/ index.html/ #download). Note that the source code for all the chapters of the book can be found at http://www.datai.com, http://www.osborne.com, or on the CD-ROM.

Here is the definition of the `DataSource.sqlj` program:

```
/*** Program Name: DataSource.sqlj */

// Import the JDBC classes
import java.sql.SQLException;
import sqlj.runtime.ref.DefaultContext;
import oracle.sqlj.runtime.Oracle;

/**
 - To run this example you must also have the javax.naming.*
   and javax.sql.* packages in your CLASSPATH.
**/

public class DataSource {

  // Declare the TestCtx context class.
  // Connections for this context are performed
  // by JNDI DataSource lookup
  #sql public static context TestCtx with (dataSource="jdbc/test");
  public static void main(String[] args)
        throws java.sql.SQLException {

    String platformDesc;
    String platformType;
    int keyid;

    // Retrieve details from the PLATFORM_TYPE_LIST table
    // using the SQLJ default data source, which is bound
    // to a default name called jdbc/defaultDataSource.
    // The connection to the database is performed
    // a JNDI DataSource looks up.
    #sql {
          SELECT P.key_id, P.type, P.description
            INTO :keyid, :platformType, :platformDesc
          FROM PLATFORM_TYPE_LIST P
          WHERE P.key_id = 4
        };

    System.out.println
```

```
          ("jdbc/defaultDataSource: Observation Platform #"
             +keyid +" " +platformType +" " +platformDesc);

     // Create an instance of the TestCtx class
     // Instances of TestCtx use the JNDI
     // DataSource from the context declaration:  "jdbc/test"
     TestCtx ctx = new TestCtx();
     #sql [ctx] {
                 SELECT P.key_id, P.type, P.description
                  INTO :keyid, :platformType, :platformDesc
                 FROM PLATFORM_TYPE_LIST P
                 WHERE P.key_id = 2
               };

     System.out.println ("jdbc/test: Observation Platform #"
             +keyid +" " +platformType +" " +platformDesc);

     // You can also use a dataSource connection context
     // and override its default username and passsword
     // by providing your own username and password to it.
     // "jdbc/test"
    TestCtx ctx2 = new TestCtx("scott","tiger");

     #sql [ctx2] {
                 SELECT P.key_id, P.type, P.description
                 INTO :keyid, :platformType, :platformDesc
                 FROM PLATFORM_TYPE_LIST P
                 WHERE P.key_id = 3
               };

   System.out.println (scott@jdbc/test: Observation Platform #
          +keyid +" " +platformType +" " +platformDesc);

     // Close all connections
     ctx.close();
     ctx2.close();
     Oracle.close();

   } // End of main()

 } // End of DataSource class
```

At the command prompt, compile the program:

```
I:>sqlj -status DataSource.sqlj DataSourceCF.sqlj
[Translating 2 files]
[Reading file DataSource]
```

```
[Reading file DataSourceCF]
[Translating file DataSource]
[Translating file DataSourceCF]
[Compiling 2 Java files]
```

At the command prompt, run the program:

```
I:>java -Djava.naming.factory.initial=DataSoureCF DataSource
```

The program produces the following output:

```
DataSourceCF.SimpleDataSource(
  "jdbc/defaultDataSource").getConnection()
jdbc/defaultDataSource:
Observation Platform #4 SURFACE MOORED_BUOY_OCEANIC
DataSourceCF.SimpleDataSource("jdbc/test").getConnection()
jdbc/test: Observation Platform #2 SURFACE CMAN_OCEANIC
DataSourceCF.SimpleDataSource("jdbc/test").getConnection("scott")
scott@jdbc/test: Observation Platform #3 OTHER SCIENTIST
```

In this chapter, you used a "pure" relational database, the financial PurchaseOrder schema, to implement some of the most advanced SQLJ concepts. You learned the following:

- How to manage single and multiple database connections via instances of the SQLJ DefaultContext and of a user-defined SQLJ declared ConnectionContext class.

- How to design complex SQLJ programs and how to deploy SQLJ in several scenarios:

  - Client-side applications using SQLJ:

    - SQLJ applications

    - SQLJ in Java applications and Java applets

    - SQLJ applets

    - SQLJ using Java DataSource objects

  - Server-side applications using SQLJ (inside the Oracle8*i*/9*i* database server):

    - SQLJ in stored procedures

  - Application server-side applications using SQLJ (inside the Oracle9*i* Internet Application server):

- SQLJ application.

- SQLJ in Java servlets

- SQLJ in JavaServerPages (JSP)

This concludes the chapter. In Chapter 6, you will learn how to use SQLJ scrollable iterators and dynamic SQL in SQLJ executable statements.

CHAPTER

6

Advanced SQLJ Functionality

tandard JDBC 2.0 features in JDK 1.2 and higher include enhancements for navigating through `java.sql.ResultSet`. These enhancements provide capabilities to move forward or backward, position relatively or absolutely, see changes to the database made internally or externally, and update result set data and then copy these changes to the database. Starting with Oracle8*i* SQLJ release 8.1.6, Oracle SQLJ supports JDBC 2.0 features. Note that these JDBC 2.0 features are also part of the SQLJ ISO Standard but not of the SQLJ ANSI Standard

In Chapter 7, JDBC interoperability features (capabilities that allow you to convert a JDBC `ResultSet` to an iterator) and subclassing iterator classes are discussed. This chapter discusses how iterator classes are implemented and what additional functionality they offer beyond the methods discussed in Chapters 2 and 3. Also, you will be introduced here to the latest features of Oracle9*i* SQLJ: support of dynamic SQL in SQLJ.

Specifically, you will learn how to

- Declare and use ResultSetIterator iterators

- Declare and use scrollable SQLJ iterators

- Declare and use scrollable named iterators

- Declare and use scrollable positional iterators

- Declare and use ScrollableResultSetIterator iterators

- Use embedded dynamic SQL in SQLJ

You learned in Chapter 3 some functionality of the SQLJ iterators. Recall that when you declare a named iterator in your program, the SQLJ translator generates a class that implements the `sqlj.runtime.NamedIterator` interface. Also, recall that when you declare a positional iterator in your program, the SQLJ translator generates a class that implements the `sqlj.runtime.PositionalIterator` interface. Important also, remember that both the `NamedIterator` and the `PositionedIterator` interface implement the `sqlj.runtime.ResultSetIterator` interface.

Declaring and Using ResultSetIterator **Iterators**

The `sqlj.runtime.ResultSetIterator` iterator defines the functionality of those objects used to navigate through a result set. It is a weakly typed iterator, as opposed to SQLJ named and positional iterators, which are strongly typed iterators. The `ResultSetIterator interface` provides the following:

- **public static final int ASENSITIVE**   Constant used by the "sensitivity" field indicating that the iterator is defined to have an asensitive cursor. `ASENSITIVE` means that the iterator may or may not pick up changes made to the result set by other statements and, depending on the `TRANSACTION ISOLATION` setting, perhaps even by other transactions.

- **public static final int FETCH_FORWARD**   The rows of the iterator can be processed from first to last. Note that in Oracle JDBC, the `FETCH_XXX` constant area really only hints for scrollable iterators. You can process a scrollable iterator in any fashion, regardless of the hint given.

- **public static final int FETCH_REVERSE**   The rows of the iterator can be processed from last to first.

- **public static final int FETCH_UNKNOWN**   The order in which the rows of the iterator will be processed is unknown.

- **public static final int INSENSITIVE**   Constant used by the "sensitivity" field indicating that the iterator is defined to have an insensitive cursor. `INSENSITIVE` means that the iterator will *not* pick up changes made to the result set.

- **public static final int SENSITIVE**   Constant used by the "sensitivity" field indicating that the iterator is defined to have a sensitive cursor. `SENSITIVE` means that the iterator *will* pick up changes to the result set and reflect them.

- **public java.sql.SQLWarning getWarnings()**   This method returns the first warning reported by calls on this iterator.

- **public void clearWarnings()**   After calling this method, a call to the `getWarnings()` method will return null until a new warning is generated.

- **public void close()**   This method closes the iterator object.

- **public int getFetchSize()**   This method returns the number of rows, that is, the current fetch size for this iterator object. See Chapter 10 to learn more about fetch size.

- **public java.sql.ResultSet getResultSet()**   This method returns the JDBC result set associated with this iterator.

- **public int getSensitivity()**   This method returns the sensitivity of this iterator object.

- **public boolean isClosed()**   This method checks whether the iterator is closed.

- **public boolean next()**   This method advances the iterator to the next row.

- **public void setFetchSize(int rows)**   This method gives the SQLJ run-time a hint as to the number of rows that should be fetched when more rows are needed from this iterator object.

To learn more about the preceding, see [...] \sqlj\doc\runtime\javadoc\ index.html, where [...] identifies the directory of ORACLE_HOME in your environment.

The ResultSetIterator iterator is useful when you do not need the functionality of a named or positional iterator. For example, you can use instances of the ResultSetIterator iterator to receive query data without having to declare a strongly typed iterator. In the SqljWithDynamicSql.sqlj program that you will develop later in this chapter, you will use an instance of the ResultSetIterator iterator to query the database.

In Oracle 8.1.7 and higher, Oracle has added the FETCH CURRENT FROM syntax. This permits you to use JDBC motion commands in conjunction with a positional iterator. In Oracle 9.0.1 and higher, Oracle provides the ScrollableResultSetIterator. Additionally, in 9.0.1, Oracle permits you to use a FETCH CURRENT FROM statement on either ResultSetIterator or on ScrollableResultSetIterator. These additional features complete the functionality for transforming JDBC programs on a one-to-one mapping basis into SQLJ programs.

Here is the syntax of a ResultSetIterator iterator:

```
#sql {FETCH CURRENT FROM :aResultSetIterator
        INTO :column1, :column2, :column3, ..., :columnN
    };
```

The following fragment code declares a ResultSetIterator iterator and populates data into it:

```
// Declare a ResultSetIterator
ResultSetIterator iter;
#sql {FETCH CURRENT FROM :iter
        INTO :column1, :column2, :column3
    };
```

where `column1`, `column2`, and `column3` are host variables. Recall that a SQLJ host variable is a non-dotted Java identifier. You learned these concepts in the "SQLJ Host Expression" section of Chapter 3.

Use the following fragment code to declare a `ResultSetIterator` object, using the iterator object to receive query data, and process data:

```
// Create a ResultSetIterator object
    ResultSetIterator iter;

    // Use of dynamic SQL in SQLJ.
    // See the "Meta Bind Expressions" section of this chapter.
    #sql iter = {SELECT :{selectList} FROM :{aTable} :{whereClause}
                };
    int accNoOutput;
    // Iterate
    while (iter.next()) {
        #sql {FETCH CURRENT FROM :iter
                INTO :accNoOutput, :projectno, :departmentno
                };
        System.out.println("Account No: " +accNoOutput
                +" Project No =  " +projectno
                +" Department No = " +departmentno);
    }  // End of while
```

The `ResultSetIterator` iterator is very useful also when you want to use concise SQLJ syntax to query the database and then process the data from a Java `ResultSet` object. For example, use the following fragment code to declare a `ResultSetIterator` object, query the database, convert the iterator object to a `ResultSet` object, and process the data using the `ResultSet` object:

```
...
// Declare a ResultSetIterator object
ResultSetIterator aResultSetIterator;

...
#sql aResultSetIterator = {SELECT * FROM ACCOUNT_LIST};
// Use the getResultSet() method to convert
// the aResultSetIterator object to a JDBC ResultSet object
ResultSet aResultSet = aResultSetIterator.getResultSet();

while (aResultSet.next()) {
    // process the data using the ResultSet instance
};
...
// Remember to always close an SQLJ iterator
aResultSetIterator.close();
```

The following rules apply when using a `ResultSetIterator` iterator:

■ No data access functionality, that is, no accessor methods, are available. You must convert the `ResultSetIterator` object to a JDBC `ResultSet` before processing the data. Alternatively, you can use the `FETCH CURRENT FROM` to navigate through the iterator.

CAUTION
FETCH CURRENT FROM on `ResultSetIterator` is available only in Oracle 9.0.1 and higher.

■ When you finish processing the data, close the `ResultSetIterator`. If you convert a `ResultSetIterator` object to a JDBC `ResultSet`, closing the iterator will automatically close the `ResultSet`. However, closing the `ResultSet` object will *not* close the `ResultSetIterator`.

■ The `ResultSetIterator` iterators are not supported as host expressions, whereas the named and positional iterators are. This holds through only for Oracle9i SQLJ release prior to 9.0.1.

See Chapter 7 to learn the interactions between SQLJ iterators and Java `ResulSet` objects.

CAUTION
Whenever you are using a weakly typed iterator instead of a strongly typed one, you are trading the strong type checking of the SQLJ `SELECT` operation for the convenience of not having to declare an iterator class.

Declaring and Using Scrollable SQLJ Iterators

The ISO standard for SQLJ has adopted support for scrollable iterators, which are patterned after the JDBC 2.0 specification for scrollable JDBC `ResultSet`. Starting with Oracle8i SQLJ release 8.1.7, Oracle SQLJ provides support for scrollable iterators.

SQLJ scrollable iterators are similar to scrollable JDBC result sets. Standard JDBC 2.0 features in JDK 1.2.x and higher include enhancements to result set functionality. These enhancements provide capabilities to navigate through the result set. For example, you can move forward or backward, position relatively or absolutely, see changes to the database made internally or externally, and update result set data. See the *Oracle8i/9i JDBC Developer's Guide & Reference* to learn more about scrollable JDBC result sets.

A SQLJ iterator is *scrollable* when it implements the `sqlj.runtime.Scrollable interface`. Use this syntax to declare a scrollable named iterator:

```
#sql public static iterator AccountIter implements
            sqlj.runtime.Scrollable  (int accountno,
                     int departmentno, int projno);
```

At compile time, the SQLJ translator generates an iterator class that implements the `Scrollable` interface. The generated class will support all the methods of the `Scrollable` interface.

The `Scrollable` Interface

The following methods are defined on scrollable iterators and execution contexts:

- **`getFetchDirection()`**   To retrieve the direction for fetching rows from database tables.

- **`setFetchDirection(int)`**   To give the SQLJ run-time a hint as to the direction in which rows are processed. The direction should be one of `sqlj.runtime.ResultSetIterator.FETCH_FORWARD`, `FETCH_REVERSE`, or `FETCH_UNKNOWN`.

The following methods will return false when there are no more rows:

- **`boolean isBeforeFirst()`**   To indicate whether the iterator object is before the first row in the result set.

- **`boolean isFirst()`**   To indicate whether the iterator object is on the first row of the result set.

- **`boolean isLast()`**   To indicate whether the iterator object is on the last row of the result set. Note that calling the method `isLast()` might be expensive because the SQLJ driver might need to fetch ahead one row to determine whether the current row is the last row in the result set.

- **`boolean isAfterLast()`**   To indicate whether the iterator object is after the last row in the result set.

You can use an ExecutionContext to provide the default direction when creating a scrollable iterator. However, if you do not specify a value for the direction on the ExecutionContext, then FETCH_FORWARD will be used as a default.

Scrollable Iterator Sensitivity

Scrollable iterators, like scrollable result sets, can be declared to have sensitivity to changes in the data of the underlying database. By default, scrollable iterators in Oracle SQLJ have a sensitivity setting of INSENSITIVE, meaning they do not detect any such changes in the database. However, you can use a declaration with clause to alter this setting. Use the SQLJ with clause as follows to specify sensitivity:

```
#sql public static iterator AccountIter
     implements sqlj.runtime.Scrollable

          with (sensitivity=SENSITIVE)
               (int accountno, int departmentno, int projno);
```

This declaration defines the AccountIter scrollable named iterator. All instances of the AccountIter iterator will be sensitive to data changes, subject to factors such as the fetch size window. To learn more about the behavior of sensitive scrollable result sets, and therefore sensitive scrollable iterators, see the *Oracle9i JDBC Developer's Guide and Reference*.

NOTE
The SQLJ standard also allows a setting of ASENSITIVE, but in Oracle SQLJ this is undefined. Trying to use a setting of ASENSITIVE will result instead in the default setting, INSENSITIVE.

Declaring and Using Scrollable Named Iterators

Use the following syntax to declare a scrollable named iterator:

```
#sql public static iterator Iterator_Name implements
     sqlj.runtime.Scrollable  (list_of_attribute_declarations);
```

For example, you can use this syntax to define the NamedScrollableIter scrollable named iterator:

```
#sql public static iterator NamedScrollableIter implements
                sqlj.runtime.Scrollable  (int accountno,
                            int departmentno, int projno);
```

Use an instance of the `NamedScrollableIter` iterator to query the `ACCOUNT_LIST` table:

```
// Create a variable of type NamedScrollableIter.
NamedScrollableIter s;
...
// Populate s.
#sql s = { SELECT ACCOUNTNO AS accountno,
                        PROJECTNO AS projectno,
                        DEPTNO AS departmentno
                FROM ACCOUNT_LIST
    };
```

Note that scrollable named iterators work with instances of either `DefaultContext` or `ConnectionContext`. The `UsingScrollableIterators` SQLJ class that you will develop later in this chapter demonstrates how to declare and use scrollable named iterators.

Nonscrollable iterators have only the `next()` method to move through the rows of a result set. Scrollable iterators use navigation methods defined in the `Scrollable interface` to do so. All the methods defined in the `Scrollable interface` are implemented in a scrollable named iterator.

TIP
A not-so-well-publicized secret is that the movement commands are also available on the positional scrollable iterators. Feel free to use these methods with positional scrollable iterators, if and only if you are also employing the FETCH CURRENT FROM syntax. If you are not employing the FETCH CURRENT FROM syntax, do not use these movement commands.

There are additional navigation methods applicable to scrollable named iterators:

- **previous()** This method moves the iterator object to the previous row in the result set. Note that `previous()` returns false if you try to execute it while positioned on the first row of the iterator.

- **first()** This method moves the iterator object to the first row in the result set.

- **last()** This method moves the iterator object to the last row in the result set.

- **absolute(int)** This method moves the iterator object to the given row number in the result set. The first row is row 1, the second is row 2, and so on. If the given row number is negative, the iterator object moves to an absolute row position with respect to the end of the result set. For example, calling absolute(-1) positions the iterator object on the last row, absolute(-2) indicates the next-to-last row, and so on.

- **relative(int)** This method moves the iterator object a relative number of rows, either positive or negative. Calling relative(0) is valid, but does not change the iterator object position.

CAUTION
If absolute() and relative() calls take you outside of the result set, SQLException will be raised.

The methods beforeFirst() and afterLast() return void because they never place the iterator object on an actual row of the result set.

- **void beforeFirst()** This method moves the iterator object to the front of the result set, before the first row. It has no effect if the result set contains no rows.

- **void afterLast()** This method moves the iterator object to the end of the result set, after the last row. It has no effect if the result set contains no rows.

Declaring and Using Scrollable Positional Iterators

Use the following syntax to declare a scrollable positional iterator:

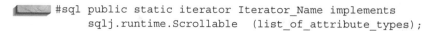

```
#sql public static iterator Iterator_Name implements
       sqlj.runtime.Scrollable  (list_of_attribute_types);
```

Use the above syntax to declare the `PosScrollableIter` scrollable positional iterator:

```
#sql public static iterator PosScrollableIter
          implements sqlj.runtime.Scrollable (int, int, int);
```

Use an instance of the `PosScrollableIter` iterator to query the `ACCOUNT_LIST` table:

```
// Create a variable of type PosScrollableIter
PosScrollableIter ps;
...
// Use ps to query the database.
#sql ps = { SELECT accountno, projectno, deptno
                    FROM ACCOUNT_LIST };
```

The scrollable positional iterator, like the scrollable named iterator, uses navigation methods defined in the `Scrollable` interface.

In the "Fetch Statement" section of Chapter 3, you learned about the `FETCH INTO` statement. Recall the syntax:

```
#sql { FETCH :aPositionalIterator INTO :x, :y, :z };
```

This is an abbreviated version of the `FETCH NEXT FROM` statement:

```
#sql { FETCH NEXT FROM :aPositionalIterator INTO :x, :y, :z };
```

The following `FETCH` statements apply to positional iterators:

- **FETCH PRIOR FROM**   Moves to the previous row of the result set
- **FETCH FIRST FROM**   Moves to the first row of the result set
- **FETCH LAST FROM**   Moves to the last row of the result set
- **FETCH ABSOLUTE :n FROM**   Passes numeric value to absolute movements
- **FETCH RELATIVE :n FROM**   Passes numeric value to relative movements

Note that you must use a host expression to specify the movement. You cannot simply use a constant for the numeric value.

```
#sql { FETCH RELATIVE 0 FROM :aPosIterator
          INTO :x, :y, :z }; // Incorrect
// The correct syntax is:
#sql { FETCH RELATIVE :(0) FROM :aPosIterator INTO :x, :y, :z };
```

In addition to the syntax noted here, you can navigate through a scrollable positional iterator through a combination of the navigation methods described in "Declaring and Using Scrollable Named Iterators," earlier in this chapter, and the FETCH CURRENT syntax described in "Declaring and Using ResultSetIterator Iterators."

Declaring and Using `ScrollableResultSetIterator` Iterators

Starting with Oracle9*i* SQLJ, support for the weakly typed `ResultSetIterator` iterator has been extended. Specifically, you can FETCH CURRENT FROM a `ResultSetIterator` iterator. Additionally, there exists now the `ScrollableResultSetIterator` interface that extends the `ResultSetIterator` interface and implements `Scrollable`, thus resulting in a scrollable result set iterator type:

```
package sqlj.runtime;
public interface ScrollableResultSetIterator
        extends ResultSetIterator implements Scrollable {

}
```

Because the `ScrollableResultSetIterator` extends the `ResultSetIterator` and implements `Scrollable`, it supports the methods described in the "Declaring and Using `ResultSetIterator` Iterators," "Declaring and Using Scrollable Named Iterators," and "Declaring and Using Scrollable Positional Iterators" sections of this chapter.
Use the following code to declare a `ScrollableResultSetIterator` object:

```
...
sqlj.runtime.ScrollableResultSetIterator aSrsi;
// Query the database using aSrsi
#sql aSrsi = { SELECT * FROM ACCOUNT_LIST };

// Position on the last row.
aSrsi.afterLast();
// Process the data
while (aSrsi.previous()) {
    #sql {FETCH CURRENT FROM :aSrsi
```

```
      INTO :accountno, :projectno, :deptno
   };
} // End of while
// Always close a SQLJ iterator
aSrsi.close();
```

CAUTION

Scrollability and FETCH CURRENT functionality for ResultSetIterator iterators are not supported in Oracle8i SQLJ releases.

You are now ready to develop a SQLJ program that implements the concepts that you learned regarding the advanced features of SQLJ iterators. You will apply this knowledge while writing the UsingScrollableIterators SQLJ class. The UsingScrollableIterators SQLJ class consists of the following:

- Three SQLJ scrollable iterators: The NamedScrollableIter scrollable named iterator, the PosScrollableIter scrollable iterator, and the aSrsi ScrollableResultSetIterator iterator. Here are the definitions:

  ```
  // A scrollable named iterator declaration
    #sql public static iterator NamedScrollableIter
           implements sqlj.runtime.Scrollable
              (int accountno, int projectno, int departmentno);
  ...
  // A scrollable positional iterator declaration
  #sql public static iterator PosScrollableIter
           implements sqlj.runtime.Scrollable (int, int, int);
  ...
  // A ScrollableResultSetIterator declaration
  // Oracle9i SQLJ (only)
  sqlj.runtime.ScrollableResultSetIterator aSrsi;
  ```

- The usingNamedScrollableIter() method uses an instance of the NamedScrollableIter iterator to store the results of a database query. It demonstrates how to use the different methods of a scrollable named iterator, whereas the following methods illustrate how to use methods of a scrollable positional and ScrollableResultSetIterator iterator, respectively.

- The usingPosScrollableIter() method uses an instance of the PosScrollableIter iterator to store the results of a database query.

■ The usingResultSetScrollableIter() method uses an instance of a ScrollableResultSetIterator iterator to store the results of a database query.

Here is the definition of the UsingScrollableIterators SQLJ class:

```
/* Program Name: UsingScrollableIterators.sqlj
**
** Purpose:      A SQLJ program that teaches how
**               to use SQLJ scrollable iterators.
**
** Important:    Scrollable iterators work with instances of
**               DefaultContext or ConnectionContext.
**
*/

import java.sql.SQLException;
import oracle.sqlj.runtime.Oracle;
import java.sql.*;
import oracle.sql.*;
import sqlj.runtime.*;
import sqlj.runtime.ref.*;
import oracle.jdbc.driver.*;

public class UsingScrollableIterators {

  // Create a variable of type DeclaredConnectionContext
  public static DeclaredConnectionContext conn;

  // Declare a named scrollable iterator
  // A named iterator is scrollable iFF
  // it implements sqlj.runtime.Scrollable
  #sql public static iterator NamedScrollableIter
        implements sqlj.runtime.Scrollable
            (int accountno, int projectno, int departmentno);

  public UsingScrollableIterators() {
          // Connect to the database
      try {
          // Initialize DefaultContext
          Oracle.connect
          ("jdbc:oracle:thin:@data-i.com:1521:ORCL",
                      "scott","tiger");

      } // End of try
      catch (SQLException ex) {
          System.out.println("I cannot Connect " +ex.getMessage());
```

```
        System.exit(1);
    } // End catch
} // End UsingScrollableIterators constructor

// Method that illustrates how to use scrollable named iterator
private static void usingNamedScrollableIter()
        throws SQLException {

System.out.println("Using a Scrollable Named SQLJ Iterator!!");

// Create a variable of type NamedScrollableIter
NamedScrollableIter s;

// Query the database
// using a scrollable named iterator
#sql s = { SELECT ACCOUNTNO AS accountno,
                          PROJECTNO AS projectno,
                          DEPTNO AS departmentno
                   FROM ACCOUNT_LIST
 };

// System.out.println("Using Named I selected!!");
printScrollable(s, 0, 0, 0);

// Use the next() method to get the data
s.next();
printScrollable(s, s.accountno(),s.projectno(),s.departmentno());
s.next();
printScrollable(s, s.accountno(),s.projectno(),s.departmentno());

// Use the previous() method to get the data
s.previous();
printScrollable(s, s.accountno(),s.projectno(),s.departmentno());

// Use the last() method to get the data
s.last();
printScrollable(s, s.accountno(),s.projectno(),s.departmentno());

// Use the first() method to get the data
s.first();
printScrollable(s, s.accountno(),s.projectno(),s.departmentno());

// Use the absolute() method to get the data
s.absolute(8);
printScrollable(s, s.accountno(),s.projectno(),s.departmentno());

// Use the relative() method to get the data
s.relative(-2);
```

```
    printScrollable(s, s.accountno(),s.projectno(),s.departmentno());

    // Use the afterLast() method to get the data
    s.afterLast();
    printScrollable(s, 0, 0, 0);

    // Of course, always close the iterator
    s.close();

}   // End of usingNamedScrollableIter() method

// Method that illustrates how to use scrollable positional iterator.
// As you can see, if you want your named and positional iterators
// to be scrollable, they must implement sqlj.runtime.Scrollable
#sql public static iterator PosScrollableIter
        implements sqlj.runtime.Scrollable (int, int, int);

private static void usingPositionalScrollableIter()
        throws SQLException {
  System.out.println("Using a Scrollable Positional"
                    +" SQLJ Iterator!!");
  int accountno = 0;
  int projectno = 0;
  int deptno =0;

    // Declare a scrollable positional iterator
    PosScrollableIter ps;

    // Query the database
    // using a scrollable positional iterator
    #sql ps = { SELECT accountno, projectno, deptno
                        FROM ACCOUNT_LIST };

    printScrollable(ps, 0, 0, 0);

    // Use the FETCH INTO to get the data
    #sql { FETCH :ps INTO :accountno, :projectno, :deptno };
    printScrollable(ps, accountno, projectno, deptno);

    // Use the FETCH NEXT INTO to get the data
    #sql { FETCH NEXT FROM :ps INTO :accountno, :projectno, :deptno };
    printScrollable(ps, accountno, projectno, deptno);

    // Use the FETCH PRIOR FROM INTO to get the data
    #sql {FETCH PRIOR FROM :ps INTO :accountno, :projectno, :deptno};
    printScrollable(ps, accountno, projectno, deptno);

    // Use the FETCH LAST INTO to get the data
```

```
#sql {FETCH LAST FROM :ps INTO :accountno, :projectno, :deptno};
printScrollable(ps, accountno, projectno, deptno);

// Use the FETCH FIRST FROM INTO to get the data
#sql {FETCH FIRST FROM :ps INTO :accountno, :projectno, :deptno};
printScrollable(ps, accountno, projectno, deptno);

// Use the FETCH ABSOLUTE FROM INTO to get the data
#sql { FETCH ABSOLUTE :(8) FROM :ps
          INTO :accountno, :projectno, :deptno
};
printScrollable(ps, accountno, projectno, deptno);

// Use the FETCH RELATIVE FROM INTO to get the data
#sql { FETCH RELATIVE :(-2) FROM :ps
          INTO :accountno, :projectno, :deptno  };
printScrollable(ps, accountno, projectno, deptno);

// Use the afterLast() method to get the data
ps.afterLast();
printScrollable(ps, 0, 0, 0);

// Again, always close the SQLJ iterator
ps.close();

}  // End of usingPositionalScrollableIter()

private static void usingResultSetScrollableIter()
          throws SQLException {
  System.out.println("Using a Scrollable ResultSetIterator "
                       +"SQLJ Iterator!!");
  int accountno = 0;
  int projectno = 0;
  int deptno =0;

  // Declare a ScrollableResultSetIterator
  sqlj.runtime.ScrollableResultSetIterator aSrsi;

  // Query the database using
  // a ScrollableResultSetIterator iterator
  #sql aSrsi = { SELECT * FROM ACCOUNT_LIST };

  // Position on the last row.
  aSrsi.afterLast();
  printScrollable(aSrsi, 0, 0, 0);

  // Use FETCH CURRENT FROM to process the data
  while (aSrsi.previous()) {
```

```
      #sql {FETCH CURRENT FROM :aSrsi
            INTO :accountno, :projectno, :deptno
      };

      printScrollable(aSrsi, accountno, projectno, deptno);
   } // End of while

   // Always close a SQLJ iterator
   aSrsi.close();

}  // End of usingResultSetScrollableIter()

public static void main(String[] args)
      throws SQLException {
   DriverManager.registerDriver
      (new oracle.jdbc.driver.OracleDriver());
   // Note that you could put the code to connect
   // to the database here avoiding instantiating
   // the class.  Instantiating the class is necessary just
   // to connect to the database.
   UsingScrollableIterators app =
               new UsingScrollableIterators();

   // System.out.println("I got connected");

   // Since all three methods below are static methods,
   // you can call them without the app instance of the
   // UsingScrollableIterators class
   usingNamedScrollableIter();
   usingPositionalScrollableIter();
   usingResultSetScrollableIter();

   // Always close your connection
   Oracle.close();

} // End of main()

// This method will print all data from instances of
// either a scrollable named or a positional iterator.
private static void printScrollable(sqlj.runtime.Scrollable s,
      int accountno, int projectno, int deptno)
         throws SQLException {

   /* Note that this method requires a sqlj.runtime.Scrollable
   ** instance instead of an instance of a
   ** scrollable named or positional iterator. Recall
```

```
** that a named or positional iterator becomes
** scrollable when it implements the
** sqlj.runtime.Scrollable interface.
*/

// This method will print the query results
if (s.isAfterLast()) {
    System.out.println("AfterLast.");
    return;
}  // End of if
if (s.isBeforeFirst()) {
    System.out.println("BeforeFirst.");
    return;
} // End of if
if (s.isFirst()) {
    System.out.print("First. ");
} // End of if

if (s.isLast()) {
    System.out.print("Last. ");
} // End of if

System.out.println("Account #: "+accountno +" Project #: "
              +projectno +" Department #: " +deptno);

}   // End of printScrollable()

} // End of UsingScrollableIterators class
```

Using Embedded Dynamic SQL in SQLJ

In the previous chapters of the book and the different sections of this chapter, you learned how to use SQLJ for the support of static embedded SQL. In Oracle8*i* SQLJ releases, you had to use JDBC code for dynamic SQL functionality. Starting with Oracle9*i* release 1, Oracle SQLJ includes extensions to support embedded dynamic SQL. Using JDBC is still an option, and may be preferable if code portability is a concern, but support for dynamic SQL permits use of SQLJ as a single, simplified API for database access.

You learned about embedded dynamic SQL in Chapter 1. Recall that in static embedded SQL, all the SQL statements embedded in the program are known at compile time, while in dynamic (embedded) SQL, at least some SQL statements are not completely known until run time.

Meta Bind Expressions

In this section, you will learn how to use Java *meta bind* expressions for the embodiment of dynamic SQL expressions in SQLJ statements. A meta bind expression contains a Java identifier of type `String` or a string-valued Java expression that is interpreted at run time. Meta bind expressions, like static embedded SQL clauses, appear in SQLJ executable statements.

In Chapter 1, you learned the syntax of a SQLJ executable statement:

```
#sql { sqlj clause };
```

where the `sqlj clause` can be of two kinds:

■ **An assignment clause**   A clause that contains a result expression because the clause delivers output, for example, a clause that contains a `SELECT` statement:

```
#sql aDnoAno = { SELECT departmentno, accountno FROM ACCOUNT_LIST
                     WHERE projectno = :projectno };
```

■ **A statement clause**   A clause that does not contain a result expression because it does not deliver output, for example, a clause that contains an `INSERT` or `DELETE` statement:

```
// Insert a new account into the ACCOUNT_LIST table
#sql { INSERT INTO ACCOUNT_LIST VALUES
           ( :accountno, :projectno, :departmentno) };
```

```
// Delete an account from the ACCOUNT_LIST table
#sql { DELETE FROM ACCOUNT_LIST WHERE accountno = :accountno };
```

A Java meta bind expression is enclosed in curly brackets or braces { } and is preceded by a colon (`:`) token. Use the syntax shown in Listing 6-1 to declare a meta bind expression:

Listing 6-1

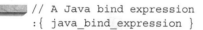
```
// A Java bind expression
:{ java_bind_expression }
```

Embed dynamic SQL into the `java_bind_expression` variable and use the variable in your SQLJ executable statement.

Optionally, the `java_bind_expression` can be followed by the `::` separator token to indicate that a SQL replacement code follows. Use the syntax shown in Listing 6-2 to declare a meta bind expression with SQL replacement code:

Listing 6-2

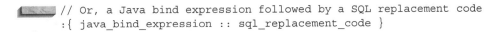

```
// Or, a Java bind expression followed by a SQL replacement code
:{ java_bind_expression :: sql_replacement_code }
```

NOTE
In either format, spaces are optional. Also, note that there can be multiple meta bind expressions in the SQL instructions of a SQLJ statement.

Java Bind Expression Usage

A Java bind expression can be either of the following:

- A Java identifier of type `String`

- A Java expression that evaluates to a character string

A Java bind expression has a syntax similar to that of SQLJ host expressions and is subject to standard Java syntactic rules. You learned about SQLJ host expressions in the "SQLJ Host Expression" section of Chapter 3. Recall the syntax for the SQLJ host expression:

```
:[ mode ] ( host_expression )
```

SQLJ host expressions are enclosed in parentheses, whereas Java bind expressions that are part of SQLJ meta bind expressions are enclosed within curly brackets or {braces}. The reason is that if there is SQL replacement code, the :: token acts as a separator between the Java bind expression and the SQL code; however, when there is no SQL replacement code, the closing } acts as a terminator.

SQL Replacement Code Usage

A SQL replacement code clause consists of a sequence of zero or more SQL tokens, with the following requirements and restrictions:

- It is subject to SQL syntax rules.

- Braces { and } must occur in matching pairs (with the exception of those that are part of a SQL comment, constant, or identifier).

- There can be no SQLJ host expressions or nested meta bind expressions within the SQL instructions.

Evaluation of Java Bind Expression at Translation Time

At translation time, there are two possible scenarios:

- The SQLJ statement does not contain a `sql_replacement_code`: If the SQLJ statement contains one or more meta bind expressions, then the SQLJ statement may only be checked syntactically, without using an exemplar schema. More important, the SQLJ translator does not perform online semantics checking on the statement.

- The SQLJ statement contains a `sql_replacement_code`. At translation time only, a SQLJ statement containing a `java_bind_expression` expression is replaced by the corresponding `sql_replacement_code`. If the `sql_replacement_code` is the empty sequence of SQL tokens, then the `java_bind_expression` expression is replaced with the empty string. The purpose of SQL replacement code is to enable the SQLJ translator to perform online semantics checking. Recall that one of the nice features of the SQLJ translator is the semantics checking of static embedded SQL clauses in SQLJ statements. At compile time, the SQLJ translator uses database connections to perform syntactic and semantics checking of the SQLJ executable statements. In dynamic embedded SQL such as JDBC, unlike in static embedded, semantics checking is performed only at run time. With Oracle9*i* SQLJ, the SQLJ translator permits semantics checking of embedded static SQL and dynamic SQL clauses at compile time. In the `SqljWithDynamicSql` SQLJ program that you will develop in this chapter, you will learn how to enable semantics checking of dynamic SQL clauses in SQLJ statements.

CAUTION
SQL replacement code works only at compile time. After you compile your SQLJ code, do not use the syntax shown in Listing 6-2. At run time, use the syntax shown in Listing 6-1.

Evaluation of Java Bind Expression Run-Time

At run time, each meta bind expression is replaced by the evaluation of its Java bind expression. If a Java bind expression evaluates to null, then the dynamic SQL statement, as a whole, becomes undefined.

Note that whenever there is SQL replacement code, even if the Java bind expression evaluates to an empty string, the meta bind expression is replaced by the SQL code during translation. The purpose of SQL replacement code is to enable the SQLJ translator to perform online semantics checking. If any meta bind expression within a SQLJ statement has no SQL replacement code clause, then the SQLJ translator cannot perform online semantics checking on the statement—it is only checked syntactically. More precisely, it can only be given a *superficial* syntax check; in general, it is *not* subject to full syntax checking at all.

Here is an example of the use of a SQL replacement code:

```
String aNewTable = "Non_existing_table";
#sql anAccountIter =
        {SELECT accountno AS accno,
               projectno AS projno, deptno AS departmentno
         FROM :{aNewTable :: ACCOUNT_LIST}
         WHERE deptno >= 200 :{andClause}
         };
// At compilation time, the above will be replaced with the following:
#sql anAccountIter =
        {SELECT accountno AS accno,
               projectno AS projno, deptno AS departmentno
         FROM ACCOUNT_LIST
         WHERE deptno >= 200 and deptno <= 201
```

CAUTION
This code works only at compile time. All it does is to enable semantics checking when you are compiling the program. You must replace this code with a Java bind expression that contains the name of an existing database table.

Meta Bind Expressions Usage

You can use a meta bind expression in place of any of the following:

- A table name. For example:

```
// SQLJ executable statements with no online semantics-checking
// Declare a Java variable to hold the name of a table.
String aTable = "ACCOUNT_LIST";
#sql { INSERT INTO :{aTable}
       VALUES (:accountno, :projectno, :departmentno )
       };

// Use of Java bind expression in SELECT statement
// Select account info
```

```
#sql {SELECT projectno, deptno INTO :projectno,:departmentno
         FROM :{aTable}
         WHERE accountno = :accountno
         };
// Assume that accountno, projectno, and departmentno are
// Java variables where
// accountno = 1020, projectno = 300, and departmentno = 200
// At runtime, the above SQL operation becomes:

INSERT INTO ACCOUNT_LIST VALUES ( 1020, 300, 200 );

// SQLJ executable statements with online semantics-checking
// Use :: sql_replacement_code to enable semantics-checking
// of dynamic SQL.
String anotherTable = "A_SPECIFIC_TABLE";
#sql { INSERT INTO :{ anotherTable :: ACCOUNT_LIST }
         VALUES (:accountno, :projectno, :departmentno )
      };
// At translation time, the above SQL operation becomes:
INSERT INTO ACCOUNT_LIST VALUES ( 1020, 300, 200 );

// At runtime, the above SQL operation becomes:
INSERT INTO A_SPECIFIC_TABLE VALUES ( 1020, 300, 200 );
// The above may NOT be what you want.
```

■ A column name in a SELECT list. Note that if you specify a column alias, you must use the meta bind variable without the column alias.

■ All or part of a WHERE clause condition. For example:

```
        // Part of WHERE clause
        String andClause = " and deptno <= 201";
        #sql anAccountIter =
              {SELECT accountno AS accno, projectno AS projno,
                    deptno AS departmentno
               FROM :{aTable}
               WHERE deptno >= 200 :{andClause}
              };


        // All of a WHERE clause
        String whereClause = " WHERE deptno >= 200 and deptno <= 201";
        #sql anAccountIter = {SELECT accountno AS accno,
                              projectno AS projno,
                              deptno AS departmentno
                          FROM :{aTable}
                          :{whereClause}
                        };
```

- An Oracle role, schema, catalog, or package name in a DDL or DML statement.

- A SQL literal value or SQL expression.

Meta Bind Expression Restrictions

Meta bind expressions are subject to the following restrictions:

- A java_bind_expression, unlike dynamic SQL in JDBC, cannot be the first non-comment of the SQL operation within a SQLJ statement. For example, the following fragment code will not compile.

```
// Declare a java_bind_expression
String query1 = "SELECT * FROM ";
String query2 = "ACCOUNT_LIST";
...

...
// This will not compile because
// of the query1
#sql result = { :{query1} :{query2} };

// sql_replacement_code using the following
// syntax will not compile either:
#sql result = { :{query1 :: SELECT * FROM ACCOUNT_LIST }
        :{query2 :: WHERE deptno IS NOT NULL } };
```

- A meta bind expression cannot contain the INTO token of a SQLJ SELECT...INTO statement, and cannot expand to become the INTO list of a SELECT...INTO statement.

- A meta bind expression cannot appear in any of the following kinds of SQL/SQLJ instructions or clauses: CALL, VALUES, PSM SET, COMMIT, ROLLBACK, FETCH...INTO, or CAST.

In this section, you will learn how to use dynamic SQL while writing the SqljWithDynamicSql class. It consists of the following:

- The public int createNewAccount (...) method inserts a new account in the database.

- The public void getAccountInfo() method retrieves data from the ACCOUNT_LIST table. It uses instances of a SQLJ named and ResultSetIterator iterators to populate the data from the database table. In this method, you also learn how to use the FETCH CURRENT FROM

:...INTO syntax to retrieve data from an instance of a
ResultSetIterator iterator.

Here is the definition of the SqljWithDynamicSql class:

```
/*
    ** Program Name:          SqljWithDynamicSql.sqlj
    **
    ** Purpose:               To demonstrate how Oracle9i
    **                        SQLJ supports dynamic SQL
    ** Required classes:      none
    **
*/

package chapter06;
import sqlj.runtime.*;
import sqlj.runtime.ref.*;
import java.sql.*;

/* oracle.sqlj.runtime.Oracle class
   contains connect() method for
   connecting to database.
*/
import oracle.sqlj.runtime.Oracle;

/**
 * A Sqlj class.
*/
public class SqljWithDynamicSql {
  // Create a SQLJ iterator
  #sql public static iterator AccountIter (int accno,
                                           int projno,
                                           int departmentno);

  /**
    ** Constructor
  */
  public SqljWithDynamicSql() throws SQLException {
      Oracle.connect( "jdbc:oracle:thin:@localhost:1521:ORCL",
                      "scott","tiger" );
  }  // End of default constructor

  public static void main( String args[] )
        throws SQLException {
    SqljWithDynamicSql app = new SqljWithDynamicSql();

    // Create a new acount
    int projectno = 300;
```

```
    int departmentno = 200;
    int accountno = 0;
    String aTable = "ACCOUNT_LIST";
    try {
        accountno = app.createNewAccount(projectno,
                                     departmentno,
                                     aTable);
    }  // End of try
    catch (SQLException ex) {
        System.out.println("unable to create new account!!"
                          +ex.getMessage());
        System.exit(1);
    }  // End of catch
    catch (java.lang.NullPointerException e) {
        System.out.println("unable to create a new account number!!"
                            +e.getMessage());
          System.exit(1);
    }  // End of catch

    // Get Account info
    try {
        app.getAccountInfo(accountno,aTable);
    }  // End of try
    catch (SQLException ex) {
        System.out.println("unable to get account info!!"
                          +ex.getMessage());
        System.exit(1);
    }  // End of catch
    finally {
        // Always close the database connection
        Oracle.close();
    } // End finally()

}  // End of main()

public int createNewAccount(int projectno,
             int departmentno, String aTable)
        throws SQLException {

    int accountno;
    try {
        #sql {SELECT ACCOUNTNO_SEQ.NEXTVAL
             INTO :accountno FROM DUAL
             };
    }  // End of try
    catch (java.lang.NullPointerException ex) {
        // quit. I need an accountno
        throw new java.lang.NullPointerException(
```

```
                         "Unable to create accountno, see DBA"
                      + " " +ex.getMessage());
    }  // End of catch()

    #sql { INSERT INTO :{aTable}
             VALUES (:accountno, :projectno, :departmentno )
          };
    // commit the changes
    #sql {COMMIT WORK};
    // return accountno
    return accountno;
}  // End of createNewAccount()

public void getAccountInfo(int accountno, String aTable)
          throws SQLException {
    int projectno;
    int departmentno;

    System.out.println("Use of meta bind in place of a table name!");
    // get account info
    #sql {SELECT projectno, deptno INTO :projectno,:departmentno
         FROM :{aTable}
         WHERE accountno = :accountno
         };
    System.out.println("I inside getAccountInfo "
                +"account no is: " +accountno +"projectno = "
                +projectno +" departmentno = " +departmentno);

    System.out.println("Use of part of a WHERE clause condition!");

    // Use of AND clause
    // Instantiate SQLJ iterator
    AccountIter anAccountIter = null;

    // Use andClause
    String andClause = " and deptno <= 201";
    #sql anAccountIter =
          {SELECT accountno AS accno, projectno AS projno,
                  deptno AS departmentno
            FROM :{aTable}
            WHERE deptno >= 200 :{andClause}
          };
    // Iterate
    while (anAccountIter.next()) {
          System.out.println(anAccountIter.accno() +" "
                             +anAccountIter.projno() +" "
                             +anAccountIter.departmentno());
    }  // End of while
```

```
System.out.println("Use of all a WHERE clause condition!");
String whereClause = " WHERE deptno >= 200 and deptno <= 201";
#sql anAccountIter = {SELECT accountno AS accno,
                             projectno AS projno,
                             deptno AS departmentno
                        FROM :{aTable}
                        :{whereClause}
                      };
while (anAccountIter.next()) {
      System.out.println(anAccountIter.accno() +" "
                        +anAccountIter.projno() +" "
                        +anAccountIter.departmentno());
}  // End of while

System.out.println("Use of column names in a SELECT-list!");
String selectList = " accountno AS accno, projectno AS projno, "
                   +" deptno AS departmentno ";
#sql anAccountIter = {SELECT :{selectList} FROM :{aTable}
                        :{whereClause}
                      };

while (anAccountIter.next()) {
      System.out.println(anAccountIter.accno() +" "
                        +anAccountIter.projno() +" "
                        +anAccountIter.departmentno());
}  // End of while

System.out.println("Use of FETCH CURRENT from a SQLJ iterator!");
// Create a ResultSetIterator object
ResultSetIterator iter;

#sql iter = {SELECT :{selectList} FROM :{aTable} :{whereClause}
            };
int accNoOutput;
// Iterate
while (iter.next()) {
    #sql {FETCH CURRENT FROM :iter
            INTO :accNoOutput, :projectno, :departmentno
         };
    System.out.println("Account No: " +accNoOutput
               +" Project No =  " +projectno
               +" Department No = " +departmentno);
}  // End of while

System.out.println("Use of SQL_REPLACEMENT_CODE!");

/*  Uncomment this fragment code to enable semantics_check
```

```
// Use of sql_replacement_code
// String aNewTable = "Non_existent_table";
#sql anAccountIter =
    {SELECT accountno AS accno,
            projectno AS projno, deptno AS departmentno
     FROM :{aNewTable :: ACCOUNT_LIST}
     WHERE deptno >= 200 :{andClause}
     };

*/
#sql anAccountIter =
    {SELECT accountno AS accno,
            projectno AS projno, deptno AS departmentno
     FROM :{aTable}
     WHERE deptno >= 200 :{andClause}
     };
while (anAccountIter.next()) {
        System.out.println(anAccountIter.accno() +" "
                          +anAccountIter.projno() +" "
                          +anAccountIter.departmentno());
} // End of while

// Always close iterators
if (anAccountIter != null) anAccountIter.close();
if (iter != null) iter.close();

} // End of getAccountInfo()
} // End of SqljWithDynamicSql class
```

In this chapter, you learned the following:

■ How to declare and use `ResultSetIterator` iterators

■ How to declare and use scrollable named and positional iterators

■ How to declare and use scrollable `ResultSetIterator` iterators

■ How to embed dynamic SQL in SQLJ executable statements

In Chapter 7, you will learn additional advanced SQLJ features. Specifically, you will learn how to use SQLJ stream classes, manipulate Large Objects (LOBs) in SQLJ, create multi-threaded SQLJ programs, JDBC interoperability features (capabilities that allow you convert a JDBC `ResultSet` to an iterator), and subclassing iterator classes.

CHAPTER
7

Advanced SQLJ Features

n the previous chapters, you developed SQLJ programs that manipulated several Oracle built-in SQL data types such as VARCHAR2, NUMBER, DATE, and CHAR. In this chapter, you will develop SQLJ programs to manipulate additional data types such as the Oracle datatypes LONG and LONG RAW, and the JDBC 2.0 BLOB, CLOB, and BFILE datatypes. SQLJ provides classes that allow you to store and retrieve objects in the database where the data can be ASCII, Unicode, or binary. Additionally, you will create a *multithreaded* SQLJ application, that is, a program that executes multiple tasks simultaneously, and a SQLJ program that demonstrates the interactions between SQLJ and JDBC constructs. Finally, you will write an application that subclasses an SQLJ iterator. While developing these programs, you will learn the following:

- How to use SQLJ stream classes

- How to manipulate Large Objects (LOBs) in SQLJ

- How to create multithreaded SQLJ programs

- The interactions between SQLJ and JDBC

- Subclassing of SQLJ iterators

SQLJ Streams

Most programming languages provide the mechanism to bring information from an external source or send information to an external destination. This information can be an object, a sequence of characters, a picture, sound, video, or database objects, and may reside in a file on disk, somewhere on the network, in memory, or in another program. Java provides stream classes as one of its mechanisms for moving data. Java programs use input streams for receiving information from external sources and output streams for moving information to external sources. A *stream* is a sequence of bytes, and a byte refers to eight contiguous bits starting on any addressable boundary. A *bit* or *binary digit* is the basic unit of computing.

The java.io package provides a collection of stream classes that are divided into two class hierarchies: character streams and byte streams. Character streams provide the API to read and write any character in the Unicode character set, whereas byte streams provide the API to read and write eight-bit bytes of information. The Reader and Writer classes are part of the character streams used for reading and writing character-based data. The InputStream and OutputStream classes are part of the byte streams used for reading and writing bytes. They are typically used to read and write binary data such as images and sounds. To learn more about Java streams, see *Java I/O* by Rusty Harold Elliotte (O'Reilly) and the Web site at http://java.sun.com/docs/books/tutorial/essential/io/index.html.

The sqlj.runtime SQLJ package provides stream classes, which are subclasses of the java.io.InputStream and java.io.OutputStream classes. They can be used to send and receive data from the database:

- The `BinaryStream` class is typically used to process binary files such as graphics, sounds, or documents. You will typically use this class with the `LONG RAW` Oracle data type, but you can also use it with the `RAW` data type.

- The `AsciiStream` class is used to process the ASCII character set, which is represented as ISO-Latin-1 encoding. You will typically use this class for the `LONG` Oracle data type, but you can also use it for the `VARCHAR2` Oracle data type.

- The `UnicodeStream` class is used to process the Unicode character set. Use this class with the `LONG` and the `VARCHAR2` Oracle data types. Note that Unicode is a 2-byte character set capable of having 65,536 possible characters. See http://www.unicode.org for further information on Unicode. Again, note that LONG is being deprecated.

NOTE
Oracle Corporation recommends that you use the Large Object (LOB) data types instead of the LONG and LONG RAW data types when you wish to store large data in the Oracle9 database. The "LOBs: Large Objects" section of this chapter introduces the SQLJ-supported LOB classes that include the BLOB, CLOB, and BFILE Oracle data types.

The supported SQLJ stream classes serve as wrappers to provide communication with your application and the database. You can use the classes as iterator columns to receive data from the database or as host variables to send data to the database. The SQLJ stream classes allow you to decompose large pieces of data into small and more manageable chunks, thereby getting better performance when information is transported to and from the database.

Sending Data to the Database with Streams

You can use instances of any of the SQLJ stream classes to transport data to the database by following these steps:

1. Determine the length of the data that you wish to send to the database. For example,

```
// Create an object of type java.io.File
File aFile = new File ("anAsciiFile.txt");
// Get and store the file length into an int variable
int length = (int)aFile.length();
```

2. Create an instance of the `java.io.InputStream` or one of its subclasses:

```
FileInputStream aFileInputStream = new FileInputStream(aFile);
```

3. Create an instance of one of the SQLJ stream classes:

```
AsciiStream anAsciiStream = new AsciiStream(aFileInputStream, length);
```

4. Use an instance of a SQLJ stream class as a host variable in a SQLJ executable statement:

```
#sql { INSERT INTO LONG_STREAM_TABLE (Filename, StreamData)
        VALUES (:fileName, :anAsciiStream) };
```

5. Close the stream objects of steps 2 and 3:

```
anAsciiStream.close();
aFileInputStream.close();
```

In the next section, you will develop a SQLJ application to store two ASCII files into the Oracle8*i*/9*i* data server.

Storing Files in the Database

You can use SQLJ streams to store ASCII, Unicode, and binary files in a database. The type of file you want to store in the database will determine the type of stream class you should use. Use the LONG data type to store an ASCII or Unicode data file into a table in the database, and use the LONG RAW data type to store a binary file.

The following `AsciiStreamInsert` SQLJ application creates the LONG_ STREAM_TABLE table. However, if the table exists, the application deletes the table before re-creating it. The table consists of two columns that are used to store the filename and the contents of the file, respectively. The application reads in ASCII files and stores the data in the database. Here is the listing of the program:

```
/* Program Name: AsciiStreamInsert.sqlj
**
** Purpose: A SQLJ application that will create a table named
** LONG_STREAM_TABLE for storing ASCII files. The program uses
** the SQLJ AsciiStream class to store ASCII files.
 */

// Import class for I/O operations
import java.io.*;

// Import required classes for SQLJ programs and database operations
import java.sql.*;
import oracle.sqlj.runtime.*;
import sqlj.runtime.*;

public class AsciiStreamInsert {
```

```
   public static void  main(String args[])  {
     AsciiStreamInsert streamApp = new AsciiStreamInsert();
     streamApp.connectDB();
     streamApp.createStreamTable();

     // Insert two ASCII files in the database
     // (See Note 1.)
 streamApp.insertAsciiStream("AsciiStreamInsert.sqlj");
     streamApp.insertAsciiStream("connect.properties");
   } // End of main

   // Method to connect to database.
   public void connectDB() {  // (See Note 2.)

     // Connect to the database using the connect.properties file.
     try { Oracle.connect(getClass(), "connect.properties"); }

     // Catch SQL exceptions error when connecting to database.
     catch (SQLException ex) {
       System.err.println( "Error connecting to database. " + ex);
       System.exit(1);  // Exit application
     } // End of catch block
   } // End of connectDB

   // Method to create the table for the stream
   public void createStreamTable() {  // (See Note 3.)

     // Delete LONG_STREAM_TABLE table if it already exists.
     try {
       #sql { DROP TABLE LONG_STREAM_TABLE };  // (See Note 4.)
     }
     catch (SQLException ex) {
      // Exception is raised if the table is not in the database.
      // Catch and ignore this exception and move to creating the table
      // to hold the streams.
     }
     // Create a table that will hold the filenames and the content
     try { // (See Note 5.)
       #sql { CREATE TABLE LONG_STREAM_TABLE(Filename   VARCHAR2 (56),
                         streamdata LONG) };
       System.out.println("Table LONG_STREAM_TABLE created.");
     }
     // Catch SQL exception error when creating the table
     catch (SQLException ex){
       System.err.println( "Could not Create table \n" + ex );
       System.exit(1);  // Exit application
     } // End of catch block
   } // End of createStreamTable method
```

```
void insertAsciiStream(String fileName) {
  try {
    File aFile = new File (fileName);  // (See Note 6.)

  int length = (int)aFile.length();  // (See Note 7.)

    // Create an instance of the FileInputStream class
    // (See Note 8.)
    FileInputStream aFileInputStream = new FileInputStream(aFile);

    // Create stream object to use as host variable
    // (See Note 9.)
    AsciiStream anAsciiStream =
                  new AsciiStream(aFileInputStream, length);

  // (See Note 10.)
  #sql { INSERT INTO LONG_STREAM_TABLE (Filename, StreamData)
                VALUES (:fileName, :anAsciiStream) };

    // Close stream AsciiStream and objects
    // (See Note 11.)
    anAsciiStream.close();
    aFileInputStream.close();

    #sql { COMMIT };  // Commit insert transaction to the database

    System.out.println("File: " + fileName + " has been inserted.");
  }
  catch (IOException ioe) {
    System.err.println("Error in reading " + fileName + "\n" + ioe);
    System.exit(1); // Exit application
  }
  catch (SQLException SQLe){
    System.err.println("Could not Insert into the table \n" + SQLe);
    System.exit(1);  // Exit application
  }  // End of try block
}  // End of insertAsciiStream method

}  // End of AsciiStreamInsert application
```

Notes on the `AsciiStreamInsert` application:

I. Pass the names of the two ASCII files that you wish to store in the database as the input parameters of the `insertAsciiStream()` method. This method will insert into the database the `AsciiStreamInsert.sqlj` and `connect.properties` files, respectively.

2. Use the `connectDB()` method to establish a connection with the database. It uses the `Oracle.connect()` method with the `connect.properties` properties file. Remember from Chapters 3 and 5 that the properties file contains the JDBC driver, URL, listener port, Oracle SID, username, and user password parameters. If this method is not able to connect to the database, it will print an error and the application will stop executing.

3. Use the `createStreamTable()` method to create a table that will hold the filenames and the contents of the ASCII files. This method deletes the table if it already exists and creates a new table.

4. This statement drops the `LONG_STREAM_TABLE` table from the database if it exists.

5. This statement creates the `LONG_STREAM_TABLE` table. The table uses the `VARCHAR2` SQL data type to store the filename and the `LONG` SQL data type to store the contents of the ASCII files. Note that this table is also capable of storing Unicode files.

6. This statement declares and creates a `java.io.File` object file handler that specifies the name of the file that you wish to store in the database.

7. This statement *casts* (that is, converts a data type to another) the length of the file returned by the `aFile.length()` method from a `long` to an `int` and then assigns the length to the length variable. The `aFile.length()` method returns a `long` value that you need to convert to an integer because the `AsciiStream` constructor that you will use later to create a stream object requires an `int` for the file's length. Note that the Java `long` value may be greater than the value that an `int` variable can hold. If this happens, the integer will contain an erroneous value. To avoid this problem, you may wish to check the length of the file against the largest possible integer value, which is the `java.lang.Integer.MAX_VALUE` (2147483647).

8. This statement creates a `java.io.FileInputStream` object by passing a `java.io.File` object to the constructor of the `FileInputStream` class. This new object holds the contents of the file.

9. This statement creates an `AsciiStream` object that you will use to insert the file into the database. The constructor of the `AsciiStream` requires that you supply a `FileInputStream` object and the length of the file as an integer. Note that you have to determine the type of file that you wish to store in the database. Choose a corresponding SQLJ stream class that matches the file type, and instantiate an appropriate object of the chosen class. For example, if the file is a Unicode file, you should instantiate a Unicode stream object. You can use one of the following constructors to create a SQLJ stream class object:

```
AsciiStream (InputStream in, int length);
     UnicodeStream (InputStream in, int length);
     BinaryStream (InputStream in, int length);
```

10. This statement inserts into the LONG_STREAM_TABLE table the name of the file and the file's content that you stored in the variables filename and anAsciiStream, respectively. Note that if the stream object is a UnicodeStream or an AsciiStream instance, you can also insert it into a table whose column is of the LONG or VARCHAR2 SQL data type. However, if the object is a BinaryStream instance, you should insert it into a LONG RAW or RAW column.

11. This statement and the one that follows it close the AsciiStream and the Java FileInputStream objects, respectively.

Next, you will learn how to retrieve data from the database using SQLJ stream classes.

Retrieving Data from the Database as Streams

SQLJ stream classes can be used to retrieve data from a database and populate a SQLJ named or positional iterator. (See Chapters 2 and 3 to learn more about SQLJ iterators.) Here is an example of a named iterator that uses the SQLJ BinaryStream class as an iterator column:

```
#sql iterator BinaryNamedIter (String filename,
                               BinaryStream streamdata);
```

The SQLJ stream classes allow you to retrieve different SQL data types from the database, such as LONG, LONG RAW, RAW, and VARCHAR2. Remember that you can use the AsciiStream and Unicode classes to retrieve data for a LONG SQL data type column and the BinaryStream class for a LONG RAW data type column.

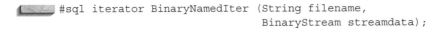

NOTE
Oracle9i and the Oracle JDBC drivers do not support the SQLJ SELECT INTO statement with the stream classes. Therefore, you must use an iterator.

Use the following steps to retrieve data from the database using SQLJ stream classes:

1. Declare a SQLJ iterator whose column is a SQLJ stream class. Note that if the iterator is a positional iterator, you can only have one stream column and it must be the last column of the iterator declaration. On the other hand, if the iterator is a named iterator, you may have more than one stream column. However, in this case, you must consume the iterator columns in the order in which they appear in the SELECT list. This is because stream columns must be read strictly in order. Also note that the row prefetch value is always internally reset to 1 whenever you have a stream column.

2. Create an instance of the SQLJ iterator as defined in step 1 of this section.

3. Create an instance of a stream class that corresponds to your file type. You can use the object as follows:

   ■ As a host variable in the FETCH INTO clause to retrieve data from a positional iterator. For example,

   ```
   #sql { FETCH :aHostVariable INTO :aFileName, :aBinaryStream };
   ```

   ■ As a host variable that stores query results from a named iterator. In this scenario, however, the type of the holding variable does not need to be of a SQLJ stream class type. It can be the java.io.InputStream class or a subclass of it, though not any subclass of the input stream class. Choose a stream class that makes sense for your application. For example,

   ```
   InputStream aBinaryStream;
   ```

4. Execute your query with a SQLJ execution statement that will populate the iterator from step 2.

5. Process the iterator by reading the stream and processing (writing) it to a local stream. After you call the accessor method of the iterator to access the stream column, you must read and process it in the same order that the columns were selected. If you do not, you may lose data.

6. Use the close() method of the input stream instance to close the local instance variable. Close the object immediately after processing the stream. In other words, close the stream object each time you iterate through the loop.

7. Use the close() method of the SQLJ iterator to close the iterator.

In the next section, you will develop a SQLJ application that will retrieve a file from the Oracle data server.

Retrieving Stored Files from a Database

You can use SQLJ stream classes to retrieve ASCII, Unicode, and binary files from a database. Remember that in situations in which you wish to transport information that resides in a file to or from a database, you need to determine the file type in order to choose the appropriate stream class in your program.

Next, you will create the `BinarySqljStream` SQLJ application to retrieve files stored as binaries in a database and use the steps you just read in the "Retrieving Data from the Database as Streams" section of this chapter while developing the program.

Before you run the application, create the database table from SQL*Plus that stores the names and the contents of binary files. The following table contains a `VARCHAR2` column for the filename and a `LONG RAW` column for the binary file:

```
CREATE TABLE BIN_STREAM_TABLE(Filename    VARCHAR2 (32),
                              streamdata LONG RAW);
```

Here is the listing of the `BinarySqljStream` SQLJ application:

```
/* Program Name: BinarySqljStream.sqlj
**
** Purpose: A SQLJ application to retrieve data, in the form
** of binary files, from a database to the disk of the local system.
**
** Create a table with SQL*Plus with the following command:
** CREATE TABLE BIN_STREAM_TABLE(Filename VARCHAR2 (32),
**                              streamdata LONG RAW);
**
// Import class for I/O operations
import java.io.*;

// Import required classes for SQLJ programs and database operations
import java.sql.*;
import oracle.sqlj.runtime.*;
import sqlj.runtime.*;

public class BinarySqljStream {

  // Iterator for binary files from the database
  // (See Note 1.)
  #sql iterator BinaryNamedIter (String          filename,
                                 BinaryStream streamdata);

  public static void  main(String args[])  {
    BinarySqljStream aBinaryStreamApp = new BinarySqljStream();
    aBinaryStreamApp.connectDB();
```

```java
  // (See Note 2.)
  // Insert binary file into the database.
  aBinaryStreamApp.insertBinaryStream("BinarySqljStream.class");

  // Insert this ASCII file into database as binary stream.
  aBinaryStreamApp.insertBinaryStream("connect.properties");

  // Retrieve all binary files from the database and save
  // them to disk. (See Note 3.)
  aBinaryStreamApp.retrieveBinFiles();
}

// Method to connect to database.
public void connectDB() {  // (See Note 4.)

  // Connect to the database using the connect.properties file.
  try {  Oracle.connect(getClass(), "connect.properties"); }

  // Catch SQL exceptions error when connecting to database.
  catch (SQLException ex) {
    System.err.println( "Error connecting to database. " + ex );
    System.exit(1);  // Exit application
  } // End of try block
} // End of connectDB

void insertBinaryStream(String filename) { // (See Note 5.)
  try {
    File aFile= new File (filename);
    int length = (int)aFile.length();

    // Create an input stream object from the File object
    FileInputStream aFileInputStream = new FileInputStream(aFile);

    // Create a stream object to use as a host variable
    BinaryStream aBinaryStream =
                    new BinaryStream(aFileInputStream, length);

    // Store the filename and the binary stream into the table
    #sql { INSERT INTO BIN_STREAM_TABLE (filename, streamdata)
                VALUES (:filename, :aBinaryStream) };

    // Close the objects
    aBinaryStream.close();
    aFileInputStream.close();

    #sql { COMMIT };          //Commit insert to the database
  }
  catch (IOException ioe) {
```

```
        System.err.println("Error in reading " + filename + "\n" + ioe);
        System.exit(1);  // Exit application
      }
    catch (SQLException ex){
        System.err.println("Could not Insert into the table \n" + ex);
        System.exit(1);  // Exit application
      }  // End of try block
  } // End of insertBinaryStream

  void retrieveBinFiles() {
    try {
      BinaryNamedIter aBinaryNamedIter = null; // (See Note 6.)
      String fname;

      // Stream variable to hold the retrieved
      BinaryStream aBinaryStream; // (See Note 7.)

      // Populate the iterator with data from the database
      // (See Note 8.)
      #sql aBinaryNamedIter =
                { SELECT filename, StreamData FROM BIN_STREAM_TABLE};

      // Iterate through the named iterator (See Note 9.)
      while (aBinaryNamedIter.next()) {
        fname = aBinaryNamedIter.filename(); // Get the filename

        // Get the stream object from the database (See Note 10.)
        aBinaryStream = aBinaryNamedIter.streamdata();
        // Method to store the retrieved files from the database
        //(See Note 11.)
        saveStreamToFile(aBinaryStream, "binary-directory\\" + fname);

        // With each iteration close the local stream (See Note 12.)
        aBinaryStream.close();
        System.out.println("File " + fname + " has been saved.");
      }

      // Close the named iterator
      aBinaryNamedIter.close();  // (See Note 13.)
    }
    catch (IOException ioe) {
      System.err.println("I/O error: \n" + ioe);
      System.exit(1);  // Exit application
    }
    catch (SQLException ex){
      System.err.println("Could not retrieve \n" + ex);
      System.exit(1);  // Exit application
    } // End of try block
  } // End of retrieveBinFiles
```

```
// Method to write an input stream to a file on the local system
// (See Note 14.)
public void saveStreamToFile(InputStream in, String filename)
                 throws IOException {

    // Create an output file to store the binary files retrieved
    // from the database
    FileOutputStream aFileOutputStream =
                    new FileOutputStream (filename);

    // Loop through stream, read stream and write the data a
    // character at a time to the output file (output stream).
    int ch;
    while ((ch = in.read()) != -1)
      aFileOutputStream.write (ch);

    // Close the output file
    aFileOutputStream.close ();
  } // End of saveStreamToFile
} // End of BinarySqljStream application
```

Notes on the `BinarySqljStream` application:

1. This statement declares the `BinaryNamedIter` named iterator, whose columns contain the filename and contents of the file.

2. These statements call the method to populate the database with the two files. The first file is the Java class file (bytecode) of the application, and the second one is the `connect.properties` file, which is an ASCII file stored as a binary stream in the database. The steps to store a binary file are similar to those used to store ASCII and Unicode files. Review the steps from the "Storing Files in the Database" section of this chapter.

3. This method invocation retrieves the files in the database and stores them on a local disk.

4. Use the `connectDB()` method to establish a connection with the database. It uses the `Oracle.connect()` method with the `connect.properties` properties file.

5. This method inserts files with the binary stream class into the `BIN_STREAM_TABLE` table of the database.

6. This statement declares the `BinaryNamedIter` iterator variable that will be used to query the database.

7. This statement declares the stream variable `aBinaryStream` that receives the stream data from the iterator. Note that the declaration data type could have also been the `java.io.InputStream` class or any of its subclasses.

8. This statement queries the database and populates the iterator with the filenames and files' content.

9. Iterate through the iterator and process the stream data from the iterator.

10. This statement uses the `streamdata()` accessor method from the iterator and assigns the instance to the local stream variable specified in note 7 of this section.

11. This method calls the `saveStreamToFile()` method, which writes the stream to a subdirectory on the local system disk.

12. The statement uses the `close()` method from the stream class to close the local stream instance. Note that it closes the instance after each iteration of the loop.

13. Use the `close()` method of the SQLJ iterator to close the iterator instance.

14. The `saveStreamToFile(...)` method takes a `String` and an `InputStream` object as its input parameters, where the first parameter is the name of the file and the second is an input stream object. The method then uses this information to write the data from the stream to a file on the local system.

In the next section, you will learn how to store large objects in a database and retrieve them from the database using the Oracle LOB SQL data types.

LOBs: Large Objects

In the previous section, you learned how to use SQLJ stream classes to transport data to and from an Oracle database. Remember that the stream classes provide the mechanism to manipulate the LONG and the LONG RAW SQL data types. Therefore, you can use them with Oracle7 and higher because the database supports these data types. However, Oracle Corporation recommends that you use LOBs (Large Objects) with Oracle8 or higher to store Java streams and large objects.

Since Oracle8i, the data server supports three types of LOB data types from the `oracle.sql` package:

- The BLOB (binary LOB) data type is used to store raw data such as video clips.

- The CLOB (character LOB) data type is used to store single-byte, fixed-width character data.

- The BFILE (binary file) data type is an external LOB that is used to store binary files outside of the database.

Note that The BLOB and CLOB data types implement the JDBC 2.0 LOB types, while BFILE is an Oracle-specific data type.

The CLOB and BLOB data types are called *internal LOBs* because they store their data in the database. The BFILE data type is called an *external LOB* because it stores its data in a file outside of the database.

LOBs provide several improvements over the LONG and LONG RAW data types:

- LOBs can store up to 4GB of data, whereas LONG and LONG RAW data types can only store up to 2GB of data.

- A table can have multiple LOB columns, whereas a table can only have one LONG or LONG RAW column.

- LOB data can be accessed incrementally and randomly, whereas LONG and LONG RAW data can only be accessed sequentially.

To manipulate LOBs from SQLJ, you can use either the routines of the DBMS_LOB package or one of the LOB classes from the oracle.sql package. Oracle recommends that you use the LOB classes from Java because they may provide better execution performance than the DBMS_LOB package. The oracle.sql package contains these LOB classes:

- **oracle.sql.BLOB**   Implements the JDBC 2.0 java.sql.Blob.

- **oracle.sql.CLOB**   Implements the JDBC 2.0 java.sql.Clob.

- **oracle.sql.BFILE**   An Oracle-specific data type.

See the *Oracle9i Application Developer's Guide—Large Objects (LOBs)* to learn more about LOBs.

Loading Files into BLOB Columns

In this section, you will use the BLOB class from the oracle.sql package to store files into a BLOB column of a database. The steps are as follows:

1. Execute a SQLJ or a SQL statement that creates a table that contains a BLOB column:

   ```
   CREATE TABLE LOBTABLE (blobfilename VARCHAR2 (32), blobdata BLOB);
   ```

2. Insert a record in the table and make the BLOB column non-null.

3. Before storing data into a BLOB column, you must first initialize it to make it non-null. If the column is not initialized, you will get an error message when you try to write to it. At initialization time, the database stores a

locator in the table that points to the storage address of the *LOB's value*—that is, it points to where the actual data is stored. The locator is always stored in the row, irrespective of the physical location of the LOB. Note that you will need to retrieve the LOB's locator prior to inserting the LOB value.

4. One way to initialize the BLOB column is to use the EMPTY_BLOB() method, which creates a locator. The BLOB column will not have any data in it after this method is executed.

5. The following code fragment initializes a BLOB column to give it a location:

```
#sql { INSERT INTO LOBTABLE(blobfilename, blobdata )
            VALUES ('blob-image.jpg', EMPTY_BLOB()) };
```

6. Note that the physical location of the internal LOB's value depends on its size and is completely transparent to you. Oracle will insert the internal LOB in the row-column of the table if its size is less than or equal to 3964 bytes, or outside the row-column but in the database if it is greater than 3964 bytes.

7. In order to store data into a BLOB column, you have to get the record locator of the BLOB. To do this, query the database with a SELECT INTO statement to retrieve the locator. This returns the locator to the host variable. In your SQLJ program, retrieve the LOB's locator into a BLOB host variable:

```
BLOB aBLOB;
#sql { SELECT blobdata INTO :aBLOB FROM LOBTABLE
            WHERE blobfilename = 'blob-image.jpg' FOR UPDATE };
```

8. Create a File type object, aFile, that holds the contents of the binary file you wish to insert:

```
// Create an object of type File
File aFile = new File(filename);
```

9. Steps 4 and 5 of this section are similar to steps 1 and 2 of the "Sending Data to the Database with Streams" section of this chapter. You may wish to review the previous section for clarity.

10. Create an instance of the java.io.InputStream or one of its subclasses of it:

```
FileInputStream aFileInputStream = new FileInputStream(aFile);
```

11. You will incrementally read chunks of data at a time from the file to store it into the database. So, use the getChunkSize() method of the BLOB class to determine an ideal chunk size (number of bytes) you should use to incrementally store data to the BLOB. You may choose and declare

your own chunk size if you wish; but for better performance, Oracle recommends that you use the value returned by the getChunkSize() method or a whole-number multiple of that value. The following statement stores the value returned by the method into the chunkSize variable:

```
int chunkSize = aBLOB.getChunkSize();
```

12. Create a byte array to retrieve the BLOB in incremental chunks. The following code fragment creates a byte array using the chunkSize variable you created in the previous step:

```
byte[] buffer = new byte [chunkSize];
```

13. Note that you should use a String array to store CLOB data instead of a byte array.

14. Read the contents of the file into the buffer[] array and use the putBytes() method from the oracle.sql.BLOB class to store the file into the database. The following code fragment illustrates the process:

```
// Create an int variable to hold the number of bytes read
int lenRead;
// Keep track of where next chunk of bytes are placed in BLOB
long offset = 1;

// Get the size (number of bytes) of the BLOB
long blobLength = aBLOB.length();

// Read data from the file and write the data to the BLOB. A -1 is
// returned when EOF is read from the read() method
while (lenRead = aFileInputStream.read(buffer)) != -1) {
    if ( blobLength < offset)
      buffer = new byte[lenRead];
    aBLOB.putBytes(offset, buffer); // Write to the database
    offset += lenRead;
}
```

15. Close the stream object.

NOTE
If you use the JDBC-OCI driver in 8.1.6 or later, you can stream directly into a LOB column, exactly like you did for LONG and LONG RAW. Unfortunately, this does not work with the thin or OCI drivers.

Next, you will learn how to retrieve a BLOB from the database, write its contents into a file, and store the file on a local system disk.

Retrieving Data from BLOB Columns and Writing It to Disk

The following SQLJ application, `BlobApplication`, uses the `oracle.sql.BLOB` class and its methods to store and retrieve a `BLOB` column from a database table. The program inserts three files into the `BLOB` column; then it retrieves them and writes the contents of the `BLOB` stored in the database as files on the local system disk. The listing of the program follows:

```
/* Program Name: BlobApplication.sqlj
**
** Purpose: A SQLJ application to store binary files into a BLOB
** column of the database. It will then retrieve and write the
** files from the database back to the disk of the local system.
**
*/

// Import class for I/O operations
import java.io.*;

// Import required classes for SQLJ programs and database operations
import java.sql.*;
import oracle.sql.*;
import oracle.sqlj.runtime.*;
import sqlj.runtime.*;

public class BlobApplication {

  // Named iterator that is used to retrieve BLOB objects (See Note 1.)
  #sql iterator NamedLOBIter (String blobfilename, BLOB blobdata);

  public static void  main(String args[])  {
    BlobApplication lobApp = new BlobApplication();
    lobApp.connectDB(); // Connect to the database

    // Load files specified in command line into the database
    // (See Note 2.)
    for (int i=0; i < args.length; i++)
      lobApp.insertIntoLobTable(args[i]);

    // Now write the files back to your local system disk
    lobApp.saveBlobTableToDisk(); // (See Note 3.)
  }  // End of main


  public void connectDB() { // Connect to database (See Note 4.)
```

```
    // Connect to the database using the connect.properties file.
    try { Oracle.connect(getClass(), "connect.properties"); }

    // Catch SQL exceptions error when connecting to database.
    catch (SQLException ex) {
      System.out.println( "Error connecting to the database. " + ex );
      System.exit(1);  // Exit application
    } // End of catch block
} // End of connectDB

void insertIntoLobTable( String blobFilename ) {
  try {

    // Insert the filename and initialize the BLOB column to null.
    // During this process, Oracle will store a LOB locator for you.
    // (See Note 5.)
    #sql { INSERT INTO LOBTABLE(blobfilename, blobdata)
            VALUES (:blobFilename, EMPTY_BLOB()) };


  // Method to insert the file into database
    insertBLOB(blobFilename);  // (See Note 6.)

    // Commit changes to the database (See Note 7.)
    #sql { COMMIT };

  }
  catch (SQLException ex){
    System.err.println( "Could not insert into the table \n" + ex );
    System.exit(1);  // Exit application
  } // End of catch block
} // End of insertIntoLobTable

void insertBLOB(String filename) throws SQLException {

  try {
    BLOB aBLOB;  // (See Note 8.)

    // Select the file to get the locator of the BLOB (See Note 9.)
    #sql { SELECT blobdata INTO :aBLOB FROM LOBTABLE WHERE
            blobfilename = :filename FOR UPDATE};

    // File from the local disk (See Note 10.)
    File aFile = new File (filename);
    FileInputStream aFileInputStream = new FileInputStream(aFile);
```

```
    int chunkSize = aBLOB.getChunkSize();  // (See Note 11.)

    long blobLength = aBLOB.length();

    // Buffer to hold chunk of data being read from the input stream
    byte[] buffer = new byte[chunkSize]; // (See Note 12.)

    int lenRead;  // For the number of bytes read in (See Note 13.)
    long offset = 1; // To keep track # of bytes read (See Note 14.)

    // Read data from the file and write the data to the BLOB
    // (See Note 15.)
    while ((lenRead = aFileInputStream.read(buffer)) != -1) {
      if ( blobLength < offset)
          buffer = new byte[lenRead];
      aBLOB.putBytes(offset, buffer); // Write to the database
      offset += lenRead;
    }

    // Close input file streams (See Note 16.)
    aFileInputStream.close();
  }
  catch (IOException e) {
    System.err.println("Error in reading " + filename + "\n" + e);
    System.exit(1);  // Exit application
  } // End of catch block
} // End of insertBLOB

void saveBlobTableToDisk() {
  try {
    NamedLOBIter aNamedLOBIter = null; // Iterator for BLOB

    // Populate the iterator with the filename and BLOB data from
    // the database (See Note 17.)
  #sql  aNamedLOBIter =
      { SELECT blobfilename, blobdata FROM LOBTABLE };

    // Process the iterator by writing the BLOB data to disk
    while ( aNamedLOBIter.next())  // (See Note 18.)
      writeBlobToDisk(aNamedLOBIter.blobfilename(),
                      aNamedLOBIter.blobdata());
  }
  catch (SQLException ex){
```

```
         System.err.println( "Could not insert into table \n" + ex );
         System.exit(1);  // Exit application
      } // End of catch block
   } // End of saveBlobTableToDisk method

   void writeBlobToDisk(String filename, BLOB readBlob)
                 throws SQLException {
      try {
        File aFile = new File ("blob_" + filename); // (See Note 19.)
        FileOutputStream aFileOutputStream = new FileOutputStream(aFile);
        long blobLength = readBlob.length();

        int chunkSize = readBlob.getChunkSize();
        // Buffer to hold chunk of data being read from the input stream
        byte[] buffer = new byte [chunkSize];

        // Read data from the BLOB and save data out to a file
        // (See Note 20.)
        for (long pos = 1; pos <= blobLength; pos += chunkSize) {
                chunkSize = readBlob.getBytes(pos, chunkSize, buffer);
                aFileOutputStream.write(buffer, 0, chunkSize);
        }

        aFileOutputStream.close(); // Close output file
      }
      catch (IOException e) {
        System.err.println("Error in writing " + filename + "\n" + e);
        System.exit(1);  // Exit application
      } // End of try-catch block
   } // End of writeBlobToDisk method
} // End of BlobApplication
```

Notes on the `BlobApplication` application:

1. This statement declares the `NamedLOBIter` named iterator whose columns
   are used for the filename and the contents of a binary file, respectively. Note
   that you can also use the SELECT INTO SQLJ clause for single-row queries
   on a table that contains LOB columns.

2. This statement stores the files specified on the command line to
   the database.

3. This statement calls the `saveBlobTableToDisk()` method to retrieve all files that are stored in the database and save their contents in files located on the local system disk.

4. This statement declares the `connectDB()` method to establish a connection with the database. It uses the `Oracle.connect()` method with the `connect.properties` properties file to do so. See Chapters 2 and 5 to learn more about SQLJ connections.

5. This statement uses a SQLJ executable statement to insert a filename and call the Oracle `EMPTY_BLOB()` function, which initializes and creates a locator.

6. This statement calls the `insertBLOB()` method to store the files in the database.

7. This statement commits the changes in the database.

8. This statement declares a `BLOB` variable that is used to insert data into the database.

9. This statement uses the `SELECT INTO` clause to query the database to retrieve the BLOB's column locator. The `FOR UPDATE` clause will implicitly begin a transaction for you. However, you can omit the `FOR UPDATE` clause if you are already in a transaction. In this statement, you can optionally remove the clause because you are in a transaction. This is because you have not executed the `COMMIT` statement since your last insert operation.

10. This statement opens the file.

11. This statement gets the optimal chunk size from the database. Remember that the `getChunkSize()` method returns the chunk data size you should use to store the data incrementally in the database.

12. This statement creates a `byte[]` array that is used to hold the contents of the file and to transport the data to the database.

13. This statement creates an `int` variable that holds the number of bytes that were read from the file.

14. This statement creates a `long` variable that keeps track of the number of bytes that have been read.

15. The statement uses a `while` loop to read the file and to insert the data in the database.

16. This statement uses the `close()` method to close the input stream object.

17. This statement queries the database and populates the iterator with the filenames and the BLOB data.

18. This statement calls the `writeBlobToDisk()` method to write the database files into files located on the system disk.

19. Create a file with a `blob_` prefix that will be used to store the data retrieved from the database.

20. The `while` loop iterates, reading chunks of data from the BLOB with the `putBytes()` method. This method reads `chunkSize` number of bytes into a byte array buffer, and returns the actual number of bytes read from the BLOB instance. The byte array buffer then writes its data to the output stream.

Using the `DBMS_LOB` Oracle Package with SQLJ

The `DBMS_LOB` package provides functions and procedures that allow you to manipulate LOBs. SQLJ executable statements can call these routines. In the previous section, you used the `oracle.sql.BLOB` class to manipulate BLOB columns; in this section, you will use the `DBMS_LOB` package to manipulate BLOB objects. However, remember that the LOB classes may provide better execution performance than the `DBMS_LOB` package.

For example, you can use the `DBMS_LOB.WRITE` procedure instead of the `putBytes()` method from the `BLOB` class to store `BLOB` data in the database. The following code fragment uses the `while` loop listed in the `BlobApplication` SQLJ application from the "Retrieving Data from BLOB Columns and Writing It to Disk" section of this chapter:

```
// while loop from the BlobApplication.sqlj file
while (lenRead = aFileInputStream.read(buffer)) != -1) {
    if ( blobLength < offset)
        buffer = new byte[lenRead];
    aBLOB.putBytes(offset, buffer); // Write to the database
    offset += lenRead;
}
```

The equivalent of the preceding code block using DBMS_LOB.WRITE is as follows:

```
// The DBMS_LOB.WRITE() is used in place of the aBLOB.putBytes().
while ( (lenRead = aFileInputStream.read(buffer)) != -1) {
  #sql { call DBMS_LOB.WRITE(:aBLOB, :lenRead, :offset, :buffer) };
  offset += lenRead;
}
```

The parameters of the DBMS_LOB.WRITE routine are as follows:

- **aBLOB**   Contains the locator for an internal LOB
- **lenRead**   Number of bytes to write or that was written
- **offset**   The offset position of the BLOB to begin writing
- **buffer**   An input byte array buffer that holds a chunk of BLOB data

You can use the Oracle DBMS_LOB.READ routine to read data from the database instead of the getBytes() method of the BLOB class. The following code fragment uses the for loop from the writeBlobToDisk() method of the BlobApplication SQLJ application:

```
// for loop from the BlobApplication.sqlj using the getBytes method

for (long pos = 1; pos <= blobLength; pos += chunkSize) {
        chunkSize = readBlob.getBytes(pos, chunkSize, buffer);
        aFileOutputStream.write(buffer, 0, chunkSize);
}
```

The preceding code block can be rewritten using the DBMS_LOB.READ procedure as follows:

```
// readBlob.getBytes() has been replaced with the DBMS_LOB.READ
  for (long pos = 1; pos <= blobLength; pos += chunkSize) {
  #sql {  CALL
     DBMS_LOB.READ(:readBlob, :INOUT chunkSize, :pos, :buffer) };
  aFileOutputStream.write(buffer, 0, chunkSize);
}
```

Here is a list of input parameters to the DBMS_LOB.READ method:

- **ReadBlob**   The locator for the LOB to be read
- **chunkSize**   The number of bytes to read or that were read
- **pos**   The offset in bytes from the beginning of the LOB
- **buffer**   A byte array buffer to read in the data

Using BFILE in SQLJ

In the previous sections, you learned how to manipulate the BLOB internal LOB SQL data type. Remember that the CLOB and BLOB are called internal LOBs because they store their data in the database. In this section, you will learn how to use the external

BFILE LOB, which stores its data outside of the database. BFILE files are read-only files and are located on storage devices such as hard drives, CD-ROMs, DVDs, and so on. There is one restriction for storing files as BFILE, however: the files have to be a single drive and cannot be striped across multiple disks.

The BFILE class provides the mechanism to manipulate the BFILE SQL data type. One fundamental difference between internal and external LOBs is that the former can be stored in the database and the latter cannot. In this section, you will learn how to retrieve BFILEs on a system disk and store their contents into a BLOB column in the database. The steps to do this are as follows:

1. Create a table that contains a BFILE column:

```
CREATE TABLE BFILE_LOB_TABLE (catalog VARCHAR2(32), classfile BFILE);
```

2. Use the catalog column name to catalog the bytecode files stored in the BFILE column.

3. Use the SQL*Plus or any other tool of your choice to create a directory alias that points to the directory where the binary files are located:

Listing 7-1

```
CREATE or REPLACE DIRECTORY "apps" AS 'c:\app\sqlj\files';
```

The CREATE DIRECTORY statement specifies the fully qualified directory path. Oracle uses the alias apps as its directory name. The c:\app\ sqlj\files specifies the directory path where the files are kept. Use the appropriate directory path for the UNIX operating systems, such as /home/app/sqlj/files. Modify the path in Listing 7-1 to reflect the location of your files. Note that you must have the CREATE ANY DIRECTORY system privilege in order for you to issue a CREATE DIRECTORY command.

4. Insert a BFILE object (Listing 7-2) in the BFILE_LOB_TABLE table that you created in step 1 of this section:

Listing 7-2

```
INSERT INTO BFILE_LOB_TABLE (catalog, classfile)
  VALUES ('bfile-1', BFILENAME('apps', 'BlobApplication.class'));
COMMIT;
```

As with the internal LOBs, you must initialize the BFILE's column in order to get a LOB locator. To initialize the BFILE object, use the BFILENAME function (Listing 7-2) whose parameters are the directory alias (Listing 7-1) and the BlobApplication.class BFILE file.

Next, you will create the copyBFILEToBlob() method that will use the BFILE class to read a file on the system and insert it into the BLOB column of the LOBTABLE table that you created in the BlobApplication SQLJ application.

You will also modify the application so that it can call the copyBFILEToBlob()
method. Remember that you created the BlobApplication application in the
"Retrieving Data from BLOB Columns and Writing It to Disk" section of this chapter.

    The copyBFILEToBlob() method is similar to the insertBLOB()
method of the BlobApplication program where the former uses the getBytes
method from the BFILE class to read the system file, and the latter uses the
FileInputStream stream method from the LOB class. Here is the modified
version of the BlobApplication SQLJ application that contains the new
copyBFILEToBlob() method:

```
/* Program Name: BlobApplication.sqlj
**
...
public class BlobApplication {

  // Named iterator that is used to retrieve BLOB objects
  #sql iterator NamedLOBIter (String blobfilename, BLOB blobdata);

  public static void  main(String args[])  {
    BlobApplication lobApp = new BlobApplication();

    lobApp.connectDB(); // Connect to the database
    // Load files specified in command line into the database
    for (int i=0; i < args.length; i++)
      lobApp. copyBFILEToBlob(args[i]);

    // Now write the files back to your local system disk
    lobApp.saveBlobTableToDisk();
  }  // End of main

    ...

void copyBFILEToBlob(String catalogName) {

    BLOB    aBLOB;   // Variable for the BLOB host variable
    BFILE   aBFILE; // BFILE variable for reading a file on the disk
    String filename;  // Variable for storing the retrieved BFILE

    try {
      // Select BFILE column from the database (See Note 1.)
      #sql { SELECT catalog INTO :aBFILE FROM BFILE_LOB_TABLE
        WHERE catalog = :catalogName};

      // Test to see if the BFILE is open. If it is not, then open it.
      if (!aBFILE.isFileOpen()) // (See Note 2.)
        aBFILE.openFile();
```

```
      // Get the file name of the retrieved file
      filename = aBFILE.getName(); // (See Note 3.)

      // Create a record in the LOBTABLE. The contents of the BFILE
      // will be inserted into this record.
      #sql { INSERT INTO LOBTABLE(blobfilename, blobdata)
                VALUES (:filename, EMPTY_BLOB()) };

      #sql {COMMIT}; // Commit insert transaction

      // Select the file to get the locator of BLOB
      #sql { SELECT blobdata INTO :aBLOB FROM LOBTABLE WHERE
                blobfilename = :filename FOR UPDATE };

      int chunkSize = aBLOB.getChunkSize();

      // Buffer to hold chunk of data being read from the input stream
      byte[] buffer = new byte[chunkSize];

      int lenRead;

      // Get the length of the binary file
      long blobLength = aBFILE.length();

      // Loop to insert data from the BFILE into the BLOB
      // (See Note 4.)
for (long offset = 1; offset<= blobLength; offset += chunkSize){
         chunkSize = aBFILE.getBytes(offset, chunkSize, buffer);
        if ( blobLength < offset)
           buffer = new byte[chunkSize];
        aBLOB.putBytes(offset, buffer);
      }
    } // End of try block
    // Catch SQL exception errors.
    catch (SQLException ex){
      System.err.println( "Could not insert into the table \n" + ex );
      System.exit(1);  // Exit application
    } // End of catch block
  } // End of copyBFILEToBlob method
} // End of BlobApplication
```

Notes on the copyBFILEToBlob method:

1. This statement gets the locator of the BFILE object.

2. This statement uses the Oracle isFileOpen() function to see whether the file is open.

3. This statement gets the filename of the locator of the aBFILE instance.

4. This statement uses a for loop to read the BFILE object and insert its contents in the BLOB column of the database. The first statement in the loop calls the getBytes() method to read the file and the putBytes() method to write the file in the database.

In the previous chapters of this book and in the previous sections of this chapter, you created many SQLJ programs that performed several tasks sequentially, that is, one at a time. How can you perform several tasks simultaneously in a single SQLJ program? The following section answers this question.

Multithreading

You can develop Java programs to perform several tasks simultaneously. For example, a Java program executing in a Web browser can play sounds, communicate with a database, and display images simultaneously. The Web browser program is performing multiple tasks, or *threads*, at the same time. The thread concept is a powerful feature of the Java language. A thread is a single sequential flow of execution within a program. The simultaneous processing of multiple threads in a single program is called *multithreading*.

In situations where you wish to accomplish several tasks simultaneously, such as data entry, retrieving data from the database, and so on, performance may be improved with the use of multithreading. You could develop a multithreaded application in which you create a thread to execute each of the preceding tasks. The performance gain comes from the fact that the CPU is not idle and is constantly being used.

Multithreading with SQLJ

You can develop SQLJ multithreaded applications that perform several tasks simultaneously. You can create SQLJ client-side and server-side multithreaded programs. SQLJ provides full support for multithreading. You can use multithreading in a SQLJ client-side program to gain *throughput* and performance. Throughput is the amount of data that is transferred or processed in a given amount of time. Although you can run multithreaded applications in the Oracle9*i* JVM, you will not necessarily gain throughput performance as you would with client-side programs, because SQLJ threads do not run simultaneously in the Oracle9*i* JVM but, rather, sequentially.

Multithreading with Execution Contexts

Recall that a SQLJ operation is always, implicitly or explicitly, associated with an instance of the `sqlj.runtime.ExecutionContext` class. Also, remember that an execution context provides a context in which SQL clauses are executed. You learned about execution and connection contexts in Chapter 5's "Relation of the Execution Context to the Connection Context in the SQLJ Executable Statement" section.

When you develop a SQLJ multithreaded application, if you wish the threads to share the same connection context instance (that is, you connect to the database only once in the program), you must create multiple execution context instances. If you use the same execution context instance for several threads that are retrieving data, you run the risk of overwriting the results from one thread to another. Moreover, the results from one thread may be visible to other threads sharing the same execution context.

You can create different execution context instances in multithreaded programs in two ways:

- You can use different connection context instances with each thread where each connection context object implicitly has its own execution context instance. Moreover, the connection context instance allows a SQLJ program to establish a single connection or multiple connections to a single database server.

- You can declare an execution context instance for each thread. Thus, each thread will have its own execution context instance. You can create an execution context instance with the `getExecutionContext()` method, which returns an `ExecutionContext` instance from a connection context instance.

The following code creates an `ExecutionContext` instance using the default connection context class:

```
String emp;

// Create an execution context instance from the default
// connection context
ExecutionContext anExecutionContext = new ExecutionContext();

// Use the previously declared execution context instance
#sql [anExecutionContext] { SELECT employee INTO :emp
                            FROM EMPLOYEE_LIST };
```

Alternatively, you can create an implicit execution context instance when you use a connection context instance:

```
EmployeeIterator empIter;

// Each thread will have its own default connection context class
dataiConnCtx = Oracle.getConnection
    ("jdbc:oracle:thin:@data-i.com:1521:ORCL","scott","tiger",false);

// Use the previously declared connection context instance
#sql [dataiConnCtx] empIter =
    { SELECT employee, employeeno FROM EMPLOYEE_LIST };
```

Multithreading with SQLJ Application

It is not difficult to create threads in Java. One way to do this is to declare a subclass of the `java.lang.Thread` class. The subclass that you declared should override the `run()` method of `Thread` class. After overriding the `run()` method, you can then create and start an instance of the subclass that you created. When the instance is started, it will initially execute the `run()` method. The initial execution of the `run()` method is similar to the `main()` method of a Java or SQLJ application and the `init()` method of a Java or SQLJ applet. Here is an example of a SQLJ class that extends the Java `Thread` class:

```
public class MultithreadApp extends Thread {
    ...
    public void run() {
        // This method is executed when the thread is started.
        // Put the code that you want to multi-thread in this method.
        ...
    }
}
```

The following `MultithreadApp` SQLJ application is a multithreaded program that queries the database and prints the employee data. It populates a named iterator with all the employee numbers, creates a `Thread` instance for each employee, and starts a thread for each instance. An explicit execution context instance is declared for each `Thread` instance. Here is the listing of the `MultithreadApp` application:

```
Program Name: MultithreadApp.sqlj
**
** Purpose: A SQLJ application that uses threads to print out
** the information of all employees of a schema.
*/

// Import required classes for SQLJ programs and database operations
import java.sql.SQLException;
```

```
import sqlj.runtime.ExecutionContext;
import sqlj.runtime.ref.DefaultContext;
import oracle.sqlj.runtime.Oracle;

public class MultithreadApp extends Thread { // (See Note 1.)

  // Iterator for retrieving employee's number to pass to each thread
  #sql iterator Employees (int employeeno);

  // Each thread will have its own employeeNo instance (See Note 2.)
  int employeeNo;

  //Constructor that establishes a connection to the database
  MultithreadApp() { // (See Note 3.)
    try {
      // set the default connection
      Oracle.connect(MultithreadApp.class, "connect.properties");
    }
    catch (SQLException e) {
      System.err.println("Error connecting to the database: " + e);
    }
  }

  // Constructor that assigns the employee number to the instance
  // variable. (See Note 4.)
  MultithreadApp(int employeeNo) {
    this.employeeNo = employeeNo;
  }

  public static void main (String args[]) { // (See Note 5.)
    MultithreadApp apps = new MultithreadApp();
    apps.processThreads();
  } // End of main method

  void processThreads()  {
    int numEmp;
    Employees empIter = null;

    try {
      // Get the number of employees in the database (See Note 6.)
      #sql { SELECT COUNT(employeeno) INTO :numEmp
             FROM EMPLOYEE_LIST };

      // Set isolation level to ensure that
      // ArrayIndexOutOfBoundsException does not occur. (See Note 7.)
      #sql { SET TRANSACTION ISOLATION LEVEL SERIALIZABLE };

      // Create an array of threads whose size is the # of employees
      Thread[] theThreads = new Thread[numEmp];
```

```
    // Get the employee numbers. Each thread will contain
    // an employee number instance. (See Note 8.)
    #sql empIter = { SELECT employeeno FROM EMPLOYEE_LIST };

    // Create a new thread for each employee record. (See Note 9.)
    for (int counter = 0; empIter.next(); counter++) {
     theThreads[counter] = new MultithreadApp(empIter.employeeno());
     theThreads[counter].start();
    }
   }
  catch (Exception e) {
    System.err.println("Error running the example: " + e);
  } // End of try-catch block
 } // End of processThreads constructor

public void run() { //(See Note 10.)
  int deptNo;
  String firstName, lastName, pos;

  // This randomly delays each thread (See Note 11.)
  try {
    Thread.sleep((int)(Math.random() * 2000));
  } catch (InterruptedException e) {}

  try {
    // Create an explicit execution context instance from the
    // default connection context (See Note 12.)
    ExecutionContext anExecutionContext = new ExecutionContext();

    // Use the execution context instance with the thread
    // (See Note 13.)
    #sql [anExecutionContext] {
                    SELECT deptno, firstname, lastname, type
                      INTO :deptNo, :firstName, :lastName, :pos
                       FROM EMPLOYEE_LIST
                         WHERE employeeno = :employeeNo };

    // Print information retrieved from the database.
    System.out.println("Employee Number: " + employeeNo);
    System.out.println("Name: " + firstName + " " + lastName);
    System.out.println("Title: " + pos + "\n");
  }
  catch (SQLException ex) {
    System.err.println("Database Error \n" + ex);
  } // End of try-catch block
 } // End of run method
}// End of MultithreadApp application
```

Notes on the `MultithreadApp` application:

1. This statement declares the `MultithreadApp` class as a subclass of the `Thread` class. This declaration allows you to create multiple instances of the `MultithreadApp` class as threads.

2. This statement declares an `int` variable to hold an employee number for each thread. This variable will be initialized when the thread is created.

3. This statement declares the `MultithreadApp()` default constructor to connect to the database. Note that it uses the `connect.properties` file. See Chapters 3 and 5 to learn more about connection context methods and the `connect.properties` file.

4. This statement declares the `MultithreadApp(int employeeNo)` parameterized constructor that is invoked each time a new thread is created. It assigns the value of the parameter `employeeNo` to the instance variable from note 2.

5. This statement creates the `main()` method that calls the default constructor from note 3 to establish a connection with the database and the `processThread()` method to create and execute the threads.

6. This statement gets the number of employee records in the database and assigns it to the `numEmp` host variable. The program will create threads based on this number.

7. You need to either run this with `TRANSACTION ISOLATION SERIALIZABLE` transaction control or make sure that nobody else is inserting additional records in the `EMPLOYEE_LIST` table, or you will get an `ArrayIndexOutOfBoundsException` exception.

8. This statement selects employee numbers from the `EMPLOYEE_LIST` table and stores the results in the `empIter` SQLJ iterator.

9. This statement uses a `for` loop to create a new `Thread` instance for each employee record and start the thread.

10. This statement declares the `run()` method. When a thread begins, it starts execution by invoking this method. This method is the starting point for threads the same way that the `main()` method is the starting point for applications.

11. This statement randomly delays the execution order of the threads. This is to ensure that the threads will not start their execution order sequentially, but will execute their code at a random interval between zero and two seconds.

12. This statement creates an execution context instance for each thread.

13. This statement uses an explicit execution context instance. Remember that you must create an execution instance for each thread to avoid possible conflicts during execution.

Note that instead of giving each thread its own `ExecutionContext` instance, you could also have given each thread its own `ConnectionContext` instance (for example, created on the same underlying JDBC connection).

Next, you will learn about the interoperability of SQLJ and JDBC.

Interoperability of SQLJ and JDBC

Recall that SQLJ provides a static embedded SQL interface for Java, whereas JDBC provides a dynamic SQL interface (see Chapter 1). JDBC is the way to use dynamic SQL operations in Java programs when details of database objects are known only at run time, and SQLJ when they are known at compile time. However, starting in Oracle 9.0.1 and later, SQLJ supports direct embedding of dynamic SQL in SQLJ statements. See Chapter 6 to learn how to write dynamic SQL statement within your SQLJ application.

SQLJ provides interoperability between SQLJ and JDBC—that is, static and dynamic SQL operations can reside in a single SQLJ program. SQLJ and JDBC interact in two ways:

■ Establishing a single or multiple connections to a database via JDBC and/or SQLJ connection objects

■ Casting JDBC result set objects into SQLJ iterator objects, that is, converting the former to the latter, and vice versa

Note that a good understanding of SQLJ connection contexts is a prerequisite for the subsequent sections of this chapter. See Chapter 5, particularly the "Using SQLJ Connection Context for Database Connections" section, and Appendix D. Next, you will learn how the SQLJ connection context interacts with the JDBC `Connection` class.

Converting a JDBC Connection to a SQLJ Connection

An investigation of the `ConnectionManager` class in the "Using the SQLJ `DefaultContext` Class" in Chapter 5 illustrates the interoperability between SQLJ connections and JDBC connections. The class converts a JDBC `Connection` object to a SQLJ `DefaultContext` object. The following shows a partial listing of the `ConnectionManager` class:

```
/*
** Class Name:     ConnectionManager.java
**
** Purpose:        This is a utility class that uses the
** same concepts, published in the ConnectionManager.class
** provided by Oracle Corporation to create a JDBC
** Connection and a SQLJ DefaultContext object using
** the values of its configuration attributes.
** Applications can use this class to establish a single
** database connection.…

public class ConnectionManager {
  /*
    Set up database connection information. Set these for your
    JDBC driver, database and account. If you leave them set
    to null, any program using this class will not run.
    */
    static public String DRIVER = null ;   //JDBC Driver class
    static public String DBURL  = null ;   //Database URL
    static public String UID    = null ;   //User ID
    static public String PWD    = null ;   //Password
...
  static public Connection aNewConnection() { // (See Note 1.)
    Connection aConnection = null;
    //Verify that the access parameters are defined.
    if (UID== null || PWD==null || DBURL==null || DRIVER==null) {
      System.err.println (
           "Please edit the ConnectionManager.java " +
             "file to assign non-null values " +
             "to the static string variables " +
             "DBURL, DRIVER, UID, and PWD. " +
              "Then recompile and try again." );
      System.exit(1);
    }
    try {
      Driver d = (Driver)(Class.forName( DRIVER ).newInstance());
      DriverManager.registerDriver(d);
    } // End of try
     catch (Exception e) {
      System.err.println( "Could not load driver: " + DRIVER );
      System.err.println(e);
      System.exit(1);
    } // End of catch
    try { // (See Note 2.)
      aConnection = DriverManager.getConnection (DBURL, UID, PWD);
    } // End of try
     catch (SQLException exception) {
      System.out.println("Error: could not get a connection");
```

```
        System.err.println(exception);
        System.exit(1);
      } // End of catch
      return aConnection; // (See Note 3.)
    } // End of aNewConnection()
    /**
       Returns the currently installed default context. If the current
       default context is null, a new default context instance is
       created and installed using a connection obtained from a call to
       getConnection.
    **/

    static public DefaultContext initContext() {
      // (See Note 4.)
      DefaultContext aDefaultContext =
            DefaultContext.getDefaultContext();
      if (aDefaultContext == null) {
        try {
            // (See Note 5.)
            aDefaultContext = new DefaultContext(aNewConnection());
        } // End of try
         catch (SQLException e) {
          System.out.println("Error: could not get a default context");
          System.err.println(e);
          System.exit(1);
        } // End of catch

        // (See Note 6.)
        DefaultContext.setDefaultContext(aDefaultContext);
      } // End of if
      // (See Note 7.)
      return aDefaultContext;
    }
}
```

Notes on the `ConnectionManager` class:

1. This statement creates the `aNewConnection()` method, which in turn creates and returns a new JDBC `Connection` object (from the `java.sql.Connection` class) using the current values of the `DRIVER`, `DBURL`, `UID`, and `PWD` attributes.

2. This statement instantiates the JDBC `Connection` object using the `getConnection()` method from the `java.sql.DriverManager` class.

3. This statement returns a JDBC `Connection` object to the method that called it.

4. This statement uses the getDefaultContext() method of the DefaultContext SQLJ class to get the default context and assigns it to the aDefaultContext variable. It will get the current default context if it exists.

5. This statement instantiates the aDefaultContext object by calling the parameterized constructor of the DefaultContext SQLJ classes and passing to the constructor a JDBC Connection object. In other words, a JDBC Connection object is converted to a SQLJ connection object. Finally, the first crumb related to the actual topic.

6. This statement sets the connection context as the current default context.

7. This statement returns the SQLJ DefaultContext object.

Note that SQLJ programs establish a single connection or multiple connections through an instance of the sqlj.runtime.ref.DefaultContext class, a declared connection context class, or the Oracle.connect() method. You learned in Chapter 5 that a declared connection context class implements the sqlj.runtime.ConnectionContext class. The getConnection() methods from both the DefaultContext and ConnectionContext classes return the underlying JDBC connection object associated with the connection context instance. That is, in both cases, a JDBC Connection object is converted to an instance of a SQLJ DefaultContext or ConnectionContext class. Remember also that you can use the connect() method of the oracle.sqlj.runtime.Oracle class to connect to a database that instantiates a DefaultContext object and implicitly installs this instance as the default connection. Therefore, the method also returns an underlying JDBC connection object.

Converting a SQLJ Connection to a JDBC Connection

A JDBC Connection object is necessary if you wish to use SQL operations dynamically in your program. In this section, you will instantiate JDBC objects from SQLJ connection context objects. You can do so by using the getConnection() method of a SQLJ connection context class that gets the underlying SQLJ Connection object from the DefaultContext or ConnectionContext class and returns to your program a JDBC Connection object. You can get the JDBC object several ways, as shown in Listings 7-3, 7-4, and 7-5:

Listing 7-3

```
// Declare an instance of the DefaultContext class
// to connect to the database.
DefaultContext aDefaultContext = Oracle.getConnection(
```

```
                "jdbc:oracle:thin:@data-i.com:1521:ORCL","scott","tiger");

// Use the declared connection context to get the underlying
// Connection instance of the DefaultContext instance
Connection aConnection = aDefaultContext.getConnection();
```

Alternatively, you can get a `DefaultContext` instance with the `getDefaultContext()` method of the `DefaultContext` class and then get its underlying `Connection` instance with the `getConnection()` method:

Listing 7-4

```
Connection aConnection =
        DefaultContext.getDefaultContext().getConnection();
```

Declare a JDBC `Connection` instance while establishing a `DefaultContext` connection by calling the `getConnection()` method of the `Oracle.connect()` method:

Listing 7-5

```
Connection aConnection = Oracle.connect(
    getClass(), "connect.properties").getConnection();
```

Sharing and Closing Connections

When JDBC and SQLJ are interspersed in the same program, the JDBC `Connection` instance and the connection context instance share the same underlying database connection, they inherit properties from each other, and any change to one affects the other. The JDBC `Connection` instance inherits all the properties of the `ConnectionContext` instance. Setting or changing connection properties specific to a SQLJ `ConnectionContext` instance, such as setting the `auto-commit` flag during creation and the `set/getStmtCacheSize()`, will directly set or change the property on the underlying connection. More precisely,

- The `ConnectionContext` instances inherit the properties of the JDBC `Connection` instance that was passed as a parameter to its constructor. No surprise here; they delegate to that connection instance, period.

- If the state of the `Connection` instance changes, those changes affect the state of the `ConnectionContext` instance, because they share the same connection session to the database. For instance, if the `rollback()` method from the `Connection` instance is invoked, any changes made from a previous commit or rollback will be dropped for both the `Connection` and the `ConnectionContext` instances.

NOTE
This is not such a great thing to do!!! The SQLJ
ExecutionContext will not know that a rollback
was issued and that, for example, it should clean
up a pending batch, and so on. Therefore, always
issue the COMMIT/ROLLBACK on the SQLJ side
whenever possible!

- When you close the JDBC Connection instance with the close() method, you close both the JDBC connection and the SQLJ connection. The resources of the connection context are not freed until the JVM runs the garbage collector. Even worse, in 8.1.7 and later, the JVM may not be able to free the connection context unless it has been closed, period. That's why it is important to clean up connection contexts as well! You will get an error if you try to access the data server with the connection context since the underlying connection is closed.

- When you close a SQLJ connection with the close() method of the context instance, you close both the SQLJ connection and the JDBC connection.

- By default, connection context closes all shared connections when the close() method is invoked.

If you declare JDBC and SQLJ connections in your SQLJ program, and they share the same connection, you can close the SQLJ connection without closing the JDBC connection. Recall the options of the close() method from the SQLJ connection classes:

```
close(boolean ConnectionContext.CLOSE_CONNECTION);
close(boolean ConnectionContext.KEEP_CONNECTION);
```

To keep the JDBC connection open, pass to the parameter of the close() method the static boolean constant KEEP_CONNECTION from the ConnectionContext class. The connection context instance will close and release its resources while the JDBC Connection instance will not close until it is explicitly closed or the finalizer() Java method is used:

```
aDefaultContext.close(ConnectionContext.KEEP_CONNECTION);
```

You can explicitly close the connection object with the static boolean constant CLOSE_CONNECTION from the ConnectionContext class:

```
aDefaultContext.close(ConnectionContext.CLOSE_CONNECTION);
```

Note that the previous statement has the same behavior as aDefault Context.close().

SQLJ Iterator and JDBC Result Set Interoperability

In this section, you will learn how to convert a JDBC `ResultSet` object to a SQLJ iterator object.

Converting SQLJ Iterators to JDBC Result Sets

You can develop a SQLJ program that contains static SQL operations (that is, SQLJ statements) that query a database by using iterators. You may wish to iterate the results via a JDBC `ResultSet` object versus a SQLJ iterator object with JDBC statements. You can use the `getResultSet()` method from a named or positional SQLJ iterator to get its underlying result set, thereby converting the SQLJ iterator to a JDBC result set. The following fragment code illustrates how to get the underlying result set:

```
// Declare a named SQLJ iterator
#sql iterator VendorIter (int vendorno, String name, String address);
...

VendorIter aVendorIter;
#sql aVendorIter = { SELECT vendorno, name, address FROM VENDOR_LIST };

// Convert the aVendorIter iterator object
// to the aVendorResultSet JDBC ResultSet
ResultSet aVendorResultSet = aVendorIter.getResultSet();

...

  (process the result set aVendorResultSet)

// close the iterator object and the result set instance
aVendorIter.close();
```

Rules for the result set after converting the iterator are

■ Do not access the iterator before or after you get and process the result set. Only access the data through the result set.

■ When you close the iterator instance, its underlying result set is also closed. You do not have to close the result set instance. In fact, if you do not close it through the iterator instance, the SQLJ run-time will not be able to clear SQL resources, and you may eventually run out of JDBC statement cursors. Always close the iterator and not the underlying result set!

Casting JDBC Result Sets to SQLJ Iterators

Recall that casting one object to another in effect converts that object type to another. Use the CAST operator in a SQLJ executable clause to populate a named or positional iterator from a JDBC ResultSet object. The CAST instance must be a ResultSet object:

```
// Declare a SQLJ iterator object
#sql iterator aPositionalIterator (int, String,  String);…

// A user-defined getMyResultSet() method that returns a ResultSet
// object. See the listing of the JdbcUsingSqljApp for the
// method's contents.
ResultSet aResultSetInstance = getMyResultSet();

// Convert the result set to a positional iterator. The result
// column must match the number and types of the iterator column.
#sql aPositionalIterator = { CAST :aResultSetInstance };
```

Rules for converting iterators to get a result set instance:

- The result set must have the *same* number of columns as the positional iterator columns, and its column types must match the column types of the iterator.

- The result set must have at *least* the same number of columns as the named iterator, and column types must match the column types of the iterator.

- The instance that is being converted must be a `java.sql.ResultSet` instance.

- When you use the CAST operator, the receiving iterator must be declared public.

  ```
  #sql public static iterator Employees (int, String, String );
  ```

- Do not access the result set before or after you get and procss the iterator. Access the data only through the iterator.

- When you close the iterator instance, the underlying result set is also closed. Therefore, you do not have to close the result set instance. If you do, the iterator will not be closed.

The following JdbcUsingSqljApp SQLJ application queries the database with a JDBC Connection instance. The results of the query are stored in a ResultSet instance. That ResultSet instance is converted with the CAST operator to a named iterator. Then the iterator's columns are processed and printed:

```
* Program Name: JdbcUsingSqljApp.sqlj
**
** Purpose: An application that gets a Connection instance from the
** DefaultContext connection. The Connection instance is used to
** query and get a JDBC result set. The result set is then cast to
** a named iterator that it printed.
*/

// Import required classes for SQLJ programs and database operations
import java.sql.*; (See Note 1.)
import oracle.sqlj.runtime.Oracle;
import sqlj.runtime.ref.DefaultContext;

public class JdbcUsingSqljApp {

  // Named iterator used to retrieve the department information
  // (See Note 2.)
  #sql public static iterator DepartmentIter
          (int deptno, String shortname, String longname);

  public static void  main(String args[])  {

    JdbcUsingSqljApp JdbcSqljApp= new JdbcUsingSqljApp();
    JdbcSqljApp.runApplication(); // This method begins the program

  } // End of main


  public void runApplication() {
    try {
      // Establish database connection and retrieve a JDBC Connection
      // instance (See Note 3.)
      Connection aConnection = connectDB();

      // (See Note 4.)
      ResultSet aResultset = getResultSetFromDatabase(aConnection);
      // (See Note 5.)
      processResultSetAsIterator(aResultset);
    }
    catch (SQLException ex) {
      System.err.println( ex );
      System.exit(1);  // Exit application
    }
  } // End of runApplication method

  // Method to connect to database
```

```
Connection connectDB() throws SQLException {

  // Connect to the database using the connect.properties file
  Oracle.connect(getClass(), "connect.properties");

  // Return the Connection instance from the DefaultContext instance
  // (See Note 6.)
  return DefaultContext.getDefaultContext().getConnection();

} // End of connectDB

ResultSet getResultSetFromDatabase(Connection aConnection)
                       throws SQLException{

  // Create Statement Object (See Note 7.)
  Statement aStatement = aConnection.createStatement();

  // Query the DEPARTMENT_LIST table (See Note 8.)
  return aStatement.executeQuery("SELECT * FROM DEPARTMENT_LIST");

} // End of getResultSetFromDatabase method

void processResultSetAsIterator(ResultSet aResultSet)
                                        throws SQLException {
  DepartmentIter aDepartmentIter;

  // Use the CAST operator to convert the result set to an Iterator
  // (See Note 9.)
  #sql aDepartmentIter = { CAST :aResultSet};

  // Process the iterator by printing out its value
  while(aDepartmentIter.next()){
    System.out.println( aDepartmentIter.deptno() + "   " +
                        aDepartmentIter.shortname() + "   " +
                        aDepartmentIter.longname());
  }

  // Close iterator. It will also close the result set object
  // (See Note 10.)
  aDepartmentIter.close();
} // End of processResultSetAsIterator method
} // End of JdbcUsingSqljApp application
```

Notes on the JdbcUsingSqljApp application:

  1. Import the java.sql package (JDBC API). This package provides the
   classes, libraries, and interfaces for accessing and writing Java applications
   that connect to databases.

2. Declare a named iterator that will be used to store the converted JDBC `ResultSet` objects. Remember that the iterator must be declared `public`.

3. The method `connectDB()` connects to the database and creates a `java.sql.Connection` instance of the `DefaultContext` class. The instance is returned and is assigned to the `aConnection` variable.

4. This method queries the database and populates a result set using the supplied JDBC `Connection` parameter. The `ResultSet` instance is returned and assigned to the `aResultSet` variable.

5. This method uses the result set from note 4 to convert the result set to an iterator instance. Then the method prints out the data of the iterator.

6. This statement gets the default connection context using the `DefaultContext.getDefaultContext()` method. The `getConnection()` method returns a `Connection` instance, which is the underlying connection.

7. The JDBC `Statement` class is responsible for sending dynamic SQL statements to the database. It has methods to update and query the database. Using the `Connection` instance of the parameter of the method, you create a `Statement` object with the `createStatement()` from the `Connection` instance. See Appendix C to learn more about JDBC.

8. This method uses the `Statement` object of note 7 to execute the dynamic SQL statement with the `executeQuery()` method. The method returns a `ResultSet` object that you will cast into an iterator.

9. This statement uses the `CAST` operator to convert the `aResultSet` JDBC `ResultSet` object to the `aDepartmentIter` SQLJ iterator object. The `CAST` operator binds the result set into the SQLJ executable statement. The `aDepartmentIter` named iterator instance is populated with the contents of the `aResultSet` object.

10. This statement closes the iterator object and the result set object.

Next you learn how to subclass iterators.

Subclassing SQLJ Iterator Classes

Oracle SQLJ provides the capability to subclass iterator classes. In Java, use the keyword `extends` to define a subclass. A subclass inherits all the public and protected members of its superclass or parent class. Like a Java subclass, an iterator subclass inherits all the public and protected members of its superclass. To define an iterator subclass, use the Java keyword `extends` follow by the iterator name. More importantly, the iterator subclass must contain a public constructor that takes an instance of `sqlj.runtime.RTResultSet` as its argument. At run time, the SQLJ run-time needs to call the constructor of your subclass. Note that you can still use all the functionality of the parent class. Defining an iterator subclass does not prevent you from using its parent class. If necessary, you can access the methods of the iterator with the keyword `super`. If you did not override a `super` class method in your subclass, you need not use the `super` qualifier. For example, you move to the next element of the iterator by invoking the `super.next()` method in the subclass.

The following are steps in subclassing an iterator:

1. Declare an iterator

   ```
   #sql public static iterator
               AccountIter (int accountno, int projno, int depno);
   ```

2. Declare an inner class and pass the iterator that you want to subclass as an argument to the constructor:

   ```
   public class Account {
     public Account(AccountIter aIter) throws SQLException {
       ...
     }
     ...
   } // End of Account class
   ```

3. Declare another inner class as a subclass of the iterator class `AccountIter`:

   ```
   public class AccountIterSubclass extends AccountIter
   ```

4. In the constructor of the subclass, `AccountIterSubclass`, pass an argument of type `sqlj.runtime.RTResultSet`:

   ```
   public AccountIterSubclass (RTResultSet rs) throws SQLException
   ```

5. Use the keyword `super` and pass `RTResultSet` instance as an argument to explicitly call the `AccountIter` iterator constructor:

   ```
   super(rs);
   ```

6. You can add functionalities to the subclass of the iterator by adding methods that can be accessed by instances of the subclass. You can also access methods of the parent iterator by using the keyword `super`. For example, the following code declares a method that advances to the next element of the iterator and gets an element from its parent:

   ```
   public Account getAccount() throws SQLException {
   Account acc = null;
   if (super.next()) {
   ```

```
        acc = new Account (this);
        }
        else {
        super.close();
        }
        return acc;
        }
```

In the next application, you will create two subclasses of the `EmployeeIter` iterator class. This program illustrates how you can add behavior and functionalities to SQLJ iterators by subclassing. The `Employee` class, an inner class of `SubclassIterator` application, contains a constructor that has an iterator as its parameter. The program also has two additional inner classes that subclass the iterator. The first inner class, `EmployeesList`, is a subclass of the `EmployeeIter` class. This class has the `getEmployees()` method, which returns a list of `Employee` objects. The second class returns a single `Employee` object from the iterator with each call to its `getEmployee()` method.

```java
import java.util.ArrayList;
import java.util.Enumeration;
import java.sql.SQLException;

import sqlj.runtime.profile.RTResultSet;
import oracle.sqlj.runtime.Oracle;

public class SubclassIterator {

  // Declare a named iterator -- Employee iterator
  #sql public static iterator EmployeeIter(String firstname, String lastname,
                                           String type);

  // Constructor for the SubclassIterator. Connect to DB
  // during instantiation
  SubclassIterator() throws SQLException {
    Oracle.connect(getClass(), "connect.properties");
  }

  // An employee class used for storing employee data
  public class Employee {

    private String firstName;
    private String lastName;
    private String title;

    // Employee constructor.  This constructor an iterator row as
    // it argument (See Note 1.)
    public Employee(EmployeeIter eIter) throws SQLException {
```

```java
      firstName = eIter.firstname();
      lastName = eIter.lastname();
      title = eIter.type();
  }

  // Create an accessor method to return the name of the employee
  public String getName() {
    return firstName + " " + lastName;
  }

  // Accessor method to return the title of the employee
  public String getTitle() {
    return title;
  }

} //End of Employee


// EmployeesList extends (subclass) the EmployeeIter iterator and it
// returns a ArrayList of Employee objects (See Note 2.)
public class EmployeesList extends EmployeeIter {

  // Pass a RTResultSet as the parameter of EmployeesList
  //(See Note 3.)
  public EmployeesList(RTResultSet rs) throws SQLException {
    super(rs);
  }

  // Return a list of Employee objects
  //(See Note 4.)
  public ArrayList getEmployees() throws SQLException {
    ArrayList emps = new ArrayList();

    while (super.next()) {
      emps.add(new Employee(this));
    }

    super.close();

    return emps;
  }
} // End of EmployeesList

// EmployeesObj also extends the EmployeeIter iterator and it
// returns an employee Object (See Note 5.)
 public class EmployeeObj extends EmployeeIter {

   public EmployeeObj(RTResultSet rs) throws SQLException {
```

```
    super(rs);
  }

  // Return a single Employee from the iterator
  // (See Note 6.)
  public Employee getEmployee()  throws SQLException {
   Employee emp = null;
   if (super.next()) {
     emp = new Employee(this);
   }
   else {
     super.close();
   }
   return emp;
  }
} // end of EmployeeObj

public static void main( String args[] ) {
  try {
    SubclassIterator aSubclassIterator = new SubclassIterator();
    aSubclassIterator.run();
  }
  catch( SQLException e ) {
    System.err.println( "Error running the SubclassIterator: " + e );
  }

}

private void run() throws SQLException {
  Employee emp = null;

  System.out.println("========================================");
  System.out.println("Printing employee list of each employee");
  System.out.println("========================================");

  EmployeeObj empIter;

  // Declare an instance of the EmployeeObj class, which is a
  // subclass of the EmployeeIter iterator.  (See Note 7.)
  #sql empIter = {select firstname, lastname, type from EMPLOYEE_LIST};

  emp = empIter.getEmployee();
  while (emp != null){
    System.out.println("Title: " + emp.getTitle() + "\t\t" +
                       "Name: " + emp.getName());
    emp = empIter.getEmployee();
  }
```

```
   System.out.println("\n\n");
   System.out.println("====================================");
   System.out.println("Printing employee list"    );
   System.out.println("====================================");

   emp = null;
   EmployeesList empsIter;

   // Declare  an instance of EmployeesList iterator, which is a
   // subclass of the EmployeeIter iterator
   #sql empsIter = {SELECT firstname, lastname, type
                    FROM EMPLOYEE_LIST};

   ArrayList emps = empsIter.getEmployees();

   for (int i = 0; i < emps.size(); i++) {
     emp = (Employee)emps.get(i);
     System.out.println("Title: " + emp.getTitle() + "\t\t" +
                        "Name: " + emp.getName());
   }
 } // End of run
} // End of SubclassIterator
```

Notes on the `SubclassIterator` application:

1. Declare an inner class and pass as its argument the iterator that you want to extend.

2. Extend the class with a named iterator. You can add functionalities to the iterator by declaring a `public` methods class.

3. Pass a `sqlj.runtime.RTResultSet` instance to the constructor of the inner class and pass that instance to the iterator's super class by calling the `super()` method.

4. Loop through the superclass (iterator) and add the elements of the iterator to the `ArrayList` Java collection class.

5. Extend the iterator as another class but with different sets of behavior. This class will return a single `Employee` object every time the `getEmployee()` method is called.

6. Get an `Employee` object from the iterator by making a call to the `super.next()` method.

7. Declare an instance of the EmployeeObj iterator, which is a subclass of the EmployeeIter iterator. You can make calls to the member methods of the EmployeeIter iterator, as well as the members of the EmployeeObj class.

In this chapter, you learned the following:

■ How to manipulate some of Oracle's data types, such as the LONG, LONG RAW, BLOB, CLOB, and BFILE data types, by using the SQLJ streams classes, LOB classes, and the Oracle DBMS_LOB package

■ How to insert ASCII, Unicode, and binary files into the Oracle database

■ How to convert SQLJ connection context objects to JDBC Connection objects, and vice versa

■ How to convert JDBC ResultSet objects to SQLJ iterator objects

This chapter concludes Part II. Chapter 8 marks the beginning of Part III, in which you will learn how to use an object-relational database, the scientific Observation schema, to implement SQLJ programs that access objects in the Oracle8*i*/9*i* data server.

PART
III

SQLJ and Object
Deployment

CHAPTER

8

Object-Relational
Processing Using SQLJ

ne of the major accomplishments of modern programming language technology is the emergence of object-oriented programming features. An object-oriented programming language must support

- **Composite data types** The nesting of arrays, records, sets, and the like.

- **User-defined abstract data types** Including in the data type definition both data and method members that can have the visibility levels of private or public, so as to separate the implementation of the data type from its use. Both composite and user-defined data types are available in all releases of Oracle8*i* database.

- **Inheritance** The ability to derive a new data type from an old one, appropriately inheriting data and method members. Note that, in addition to composite and user-defined data types, inheritance is now available in the Oracle9*i* database. See *Java with Object-Oriented Programming and World Wide Web Applications,* Wang, P., for a discussion.

Advantages of these features include improved data modeling, extensibility, and code reuse. In the mid-1980s, some researchers started investigating the extension of object-oriented programming languages (such as SMALLTALK and C++) to support database features for the purpose of gaining these advantages. Commercial versions of these systems, such as GEMSTONE and OBJECTSTORE, were available in the early 1990s. Notable features of these "pure object-oriented database systems" include the assignment of permanent object identifiers (OIDs) to records, and defining a relationship between two record types by including in one record type a field whose value is a set of OIDs for records in the other record type. The latter sets up a *containment hierarchy* (or a *has-a-set-of relationship*) between the two types of records. Containment hierarchies have the potential for providing a representation of relationships that is more convenient and efficient than the relational foreign-key technique, especially where structures with large shared substructures are involved. However, pure object-oriented database systems have been criticized as being too low level, and not comparable in database power to a mature relational DBMS such as Oracle.

In this chapter, you will examine the object-relational structures of Oracle8*i*/9*i* and the techniques for processing these structures in Oracle9*i* SQLJ. In particular, you will consider

- Oracle8*i*/9*i* SQL user-defined object types

- Processing SQL object types in Oracle9*i* SQLJ

- Oracle8*i*/9*i* SQL user-defined collection types
- Processing SQL collection types in Oracle9*i* SQLJ
- Using `SQLData` in SQLJ programs

Oracle8*i*/9*i* User-Defined SQL Object Types

Beginning with the release of Oracle8 in 1997, Oracle provided support for SQL-1999 structures known as *user-defined data types*. A user-defined data type is created by employing the SQL statements `CREATE TYPE` and `CREATE TYPE BODY`. With the `CREATE TYPE` statement, you define an *object type* or a *collection type*. An object type is analogous to a Java class. It contains data fields and methods, and can be used to implement abstract data types. A collection type is either a variable-length array (`VARRAY`) type or a `NESTED TABLE` type. The subject of this section is the object type. In this section, you will learn how to code

- `CREATE TYPE` and `CREATE TYPE BODY` statements for object types and `CREATE TABLE` statements for object tables
- `INSERT` statements for object tables
- `SELECT` and `UPDATE` statements for object tables

Creating Object Types and Object Tables

In this section, you will learn how to implement object types and object tables in Oracle database releases 8.*x*, 8.1.5, 8.1.6, and 8.1.7, and Oracle9*i*.

An *object type* is essentially a record type that can also include methods (that is, subprograms). These methods can be implemented in PL/SQL or Java. An object type can be used as the type of a table column, the type of a table row, or the type of a subprogram parameter or return value. Any table that has an object type as its row type is called an *object table*. Every instance of an object type in an object table is assigned a unique OID. Instances of object types that have an OID are said to be referenceable. Note, however, that if an object appears in a column of a "conventional" relational table, then the object is not referenceable, that is, has no OID. An object type has an OID only if it appears in an object table. OIDs provide a way of referencing rows in an object table that is potentially more efficient and convenient than the foreign-key technique.

You will learn how to create Oracle `TYPE` and object table definitions for an object-relational hurricane database that describes types of platforms where tropical weather observations are made, and that also describes the oceanic observations of

those tropical weather sightings. These statements can be submitted to SQL*Plus
for execution.

```
-- CREATE TYPE statement for object type declares data fields and
-- methods for type.
--
-- (See Note 1.)
CREATE TYPE platform_type AS OBJECT
  ( key_id number(8), type varchar2(50), description varchar2(50) );
/


-- Create object table.
CREATE TABLE PLATFORM_TYPE_LIST OF platform_type;


-- (See Note 2.)
CREATE TYPE oceanic_observation AS OBJECT (
    latitude_deg              number(10,4),
    longitude_deg             number(10,4),
    windspeed_mps             number(10,4),
    adj_windspeed_mps         number(10,4),
    wind_direction_deg        number(6),
    pressure_mb               number(6));
/


-- Create type that contains a method.


-- (See Note 3.)
CREATE TYPE oceanic_observation_type AS OBJECT (
    obs_id        number(8),
    when_t        date,
    at_time       char(8),
    station_id    number(6),
    produced_id   number(8),
    produced_by   REF platform_type,
    obsobj        oceanic_observation,
    member function get_platform_type
      return platform_type,
    pragma restrict_references( get_platform_type, wnds, wnps ) );
/
-- A function called from SQL statements must obey certain
-- rules meant to control side effects.
-- To check for violations of the rules, you can use the pragma
-- RESTRICT_REFERENCES. The pragma asserts that a function does
-- not read and/or write database tables and/or package variables.
-- By definition, autonomous routines never violate the
-- rules "read no database state" (RNDS) and
-- "write no database state" (WNDS) no matter what they do.
```

```
-- CREATE TYPE BODY statement will not compile without this pragma.
--
-- CREATE TYPE BODY statement for a type implements methods that are
--   declared in the CREATE TYPE statement for that type.
--
CREATE TYPE BODY oceanic_observation_type AS
  member function get_platform_type return PLATFORM_TYPE is
    pt platform_type;
  begin
    -- Select the PLATFORM_TYPE_LIST record whose OID matches the OID
    -- in the produced_by field of the oceanic_observation_type
    -- instance.
    --
    -- VALUE(ptl) returns the object type record from the
    -- table.  * wildcard or list of platform_type fields
    -- would be incompatible with pt variable.

    SELECT VALUE( ptl) INTO pt FROM PLATFORM_TYPE_LIST ptl
      WHERE REF( ptl ) = produced_by;
    return pt;
  end;
end;
/

-- Create object table.
-- (See Note 4.)
CREATE TABLE OCEANIC_OBSERVATION_LIST
  OF oceanic_observation_type;
```

Notes on the preceding statements:

1. **platform_type**   Is an object type for the types of platforms on which
   the tropical weather observations are recorded. PLATFORM_TYPE_LIST
   is an object table, whose rows are of the type platform_type, that
   contain a row for each platform type in the database.

2. **oceanic_observation**   Is an object type that consists of a field
   for each of the various measurements that could be taken for a tropical
   weather observation.

3. **oceanic_observation_type**   Is an object type for the combination
   of an oceanic_observation and the platform_type for the platform
   on which the observation was made. oceanic_observation_type
   contains two fields that merit further discussion: produced_by, which is
   a reference to a platform_type record, and obsobj, which is a nested

oceanic_observation record. In addition, the type contains a member function (that is, method), get_platform_type.

■ First, the produced_by field is discussed. produced_by is of type REF platform_type. Every object type has a REF type with which it is associated. The REF type is used to reference instances of the object type with which it is associated. The permissible values of a REF type field are OIDs of its associated object type instances. Thus, the value of the produced_by field must be an OID for a platform_type instance.

■ A REF type can be used anyplace in a SQL statement that a SQL type can be used. Using the produced_by field, you can get from an oceanic_observation_type record to a platform_type record without doing a join operation. Depending on the implementation of OIDs, this technique could be more efficient than the join operation.

■ The obsobj field represents a record of oceanic observations nested within the oceanic_observation_type record. An oceanic_observation_type record consists of data on where and when an observation was recorded, the OID of the type of platform on which the observation was recorded, and the actual observation itself. Both the platform type and the oceanic observation are represented by distinct records. The difference is that there is a separate table for the platform types, and produced_by will reference one of the records in that table; but there is not a separate table for the observations, so that obsobj is represented as a nesting of the observation within the oceanic_observation_type record. The justification for this difference is that many other oceanic_observation_type records share the same platform type, so that you don't want to repeat the platform_type within each of those records; but the oceanic observation data is unique to the oceanic_observation_type record, so that nesting won't cause any repetitions. It can be argued that the nested record representation is more natural than having the oceanic observation fields appear as top-level fields of the table, since in the nested representation those fields are cohesively grouped as a distinct object—just as they are in reality.

■ The CREATE TYPE statement for the oceanic_observation_type declares a member method get_platform_type that is implemented in the CREATE TYPE BODY statement for oceanic_observation_type. get_platform_type is a function that returns the platform_type record that is referenced by the oceanic_observation_type instance on which the method was invoked. Just as in Java, the method for a SQL user-defined type will be invoked on an instance of that type by using the dot operator (.). The instance that the method is "dotted with" acts like an implicit parameter for the method, and fields of that instance can be referenced within the method body without using the dot notation. If you wish, you can write self.produced_by within the method, instead of just produced_by, where self refers to the instance on which that method was invoked. The built-in REF function, which is invoked within the body of get_platform_type, can be applied to any referenceable object type instance and returns the OID of that instance. The REF function must be applied to an alias.

4. **OCEANIC_OBSERVATION_LIST** Is an object table whose rows are of type oceanic_observation_type, which contains a row for every observation in the database.

The following SELECT statement illustrates the invocation of the get_platform_type method on records from the OCEANIC_OBSERVATION_LIST table.

```
SELECT o.get_platform_type FROM OCEANIC_OBSERVATION_LIST o;
```

The get_platform_type method allows you to navigate from an OCEANIC_OBSERVATION_LIST record to a platform_type record without having to explicitly access the REF produced_by field—that is, the method serves to hide that REF field. Note that SQL object type methods are invoked using the dot notation, just as they are in Java, and that invocation must be done through an alias (o in this example).

INSERT **Statements for Object Tables**

The fields of the object table PLATFORM_TYPE_LIST are all of a simple type, so that you can insert records into PLATFORM_TYPE_LIST in a straightforward manner:

```
INSERT INTO PLATFORM_TYPE_LIST VALUES( 1056, 'SURFACE',
                                       'MOORED_BUOY_OCEANIC' );
```

However, the OCEANIC_OBSERVATION_LIST object table contains a nested record field and a REF field, and both require new techniques, as illustrated by the following INSERT statement:

```
INSERT INTO OCEANIC_OBSERVATION_LIST VALUES
   ( 2001, to_date( '11-DEC-1998', 'dd-mon-yyyy' ), 1212, 3000, 4000,
     ( SELECT REF( p ) FROM PLATFORM_TYPE_LIST p WHERE key_id = 1056 ),
       oceanic_observation(25.928, 270.367, 6.6731, 6.6731, 60, 1070)
   );
```

The OID of the desired `platform_type` record is obtained by a `SELECT` statement that invokes in its `select_list` the built-in `REF` function described earlier. The `REF` function, when applied to an alias for the `platform_type` table, returns the OID of the record selected by the `WHERE` clause. Recall that the `REF` function must always be invoked through an alias.

The nested `oceanic_observation` record is designated using the *constructor* for the `oceanic_observation` type. Every user-defined type in SQL has a method called a *constructor*, which is analogous to a Java constructor and is used to construct an instance of that type. The constructor has the same name as the type and, in the case of an object type, takes as its parameters the field values of the type instance being constructed. The constructor returns the instance that it has constructed. Note that the date is created by invoking the `to_date` function, in which the first parameter indicates a date, and the second parameter indicates the format of that date.

`SELECT` and `UPDATE` Statements for Object Tables

The following `SELECT` statement avoids the `get_platform_type` method to illustrate the explicit dereferencing of `REF` fields with the `DEREF` operator.

```
/* Print the PLATFORM_TYPE_LIST record and obsobj record for
     observation 2001.
*/
SELECT obsobj, DEREF( produced_by ) FROM OCEANIC_OBSERVATION_LIST
   WHERE obs_id = 2001;
```

The built-in `DEREF` function, when applied to an expression of type `REF`, returns the record being referenced by that expression. The `DEREF` function is the inverse of the `REF` function.

The next `SELECT` statement illustrates the implicit dereferencing of `REF` fields, and the accessing of fields in nested records using the cascaded dot notation.

```
/* Print the air temperature in centigrade degrees for oceanic
     observations made with platform_type 1056.
*/
SELECT o.obsobj.air_temperature_c FROM OCEANIC_OBSERVATION_LIST o
   WHERE o.produced_by.key_id = 1056;
```

Note that when you dot a `REF` field with a field in the record being referenced by that `REF` field (here, `o.produced_by.key_id`), you will automatically dereference that `REF` field and get the value of the designated field in the record being referenced (here, `key_id`). However, you must go through an alias (such as `o`) for this technique to work. Similarly, in order to access the fields in the nested `obsobj` record, you must go through an alias. Thus, the expressions `obsobj.air_temperature_c` and `produced_by.key_id` would be illegal in the SELECT statement, generating "Invalid column name" compilation errors. DEREF(produced_by).key_id would also be illegal. To retrieve a field in the record being referenced, as opposed to the entire record, you must use implicit dereferencing.

The last examples in this section illustrate the updating of object tables:

```
/* Change the degrees latitude to 105.2 in the
   OCEANIC_OBSERVATION_LIST record with obs_id 2001.
*/
UPDATE OCEANIC_OBSERVATION_LIST o SET o.obsobj.latitude_deg = 105.2
  WHERE o.obs_id = 2001;
```

Note again that the alias is required in order to access particular fields in the nested record.

```
( SELECT produced_by FROM OCEANIC_OBSERVATION_LIST
    WHERE obs_id = 2001 );
```

Observe that the following UPDATE statement would not work, because you are not allowed to update records through REFs to those records.

```
UPDATE OCEANIC_OBSERVATION_LIST o SET o.produced_by.type = 'balloon';
```

Processing SQL Object Types in Oracle9*i* SQLJ

In order to pass an object or collection between your Java code and your SQLJ statements using a host variable, result variable, or iterator attribute, you must have a Java class that corresponds to the type of that object or collection to use in the declaration of the host variable, result variable, or iterator attribute. The preferred way of implementing such a Java class is to have JPublisher generate it for you. These Java classes generated by JPublisher are called *Java custom classes*.

Another option is to use the generic oracle.sql classes: oracle.sql.STRUCT (for objects), oracle.sql.REF (for references), and oracle.sql.ARRAY (for collections). However, these classes do not provide the information SQLJ needs to perform strong type checking, and thus provides a less desirable option than the JPublisher-generated Java custom classes.

In this section, you will learn about

- Creating Java custom classes for user-defined types with JPublisher
- The Java custom class methods for SQL object types and reference types

■ `ObjectTypes.sqlj`: a SQLJ program that processes tables containing user-defined SQL object types

Using JPublisher to Create Java Custom Classes for User-Defined Types

You can run JPublisher on the operating system command line to create custom Java classes for the SQL user-defined types stored in Oracle database releases 8.*x* and 8*i*/9*i*. Note that JPublisher is also supported inside the JDeveloper IDE. The number of files JPublisher produces depends on whether you request `CustomDatum` classes or `SQLData` classes. `CustomDatum` classes modeled on the Oracle's API implement the `oracle.sql.CustomDatum` interface. `SQLData` classes modeled on the JDBC 2.0 API implement the `java.sql.SQLData` interface.

Note that, in the Oracle9*i* database, the `oracle.sql.CustomDatum` and `oracle.sql.CustomDatumFactory` interfaces have been replaced with the `oracle.sql.ORAData` and the `oracle.sql.ORADataFactory` interfaces, respectively. The `CustomDatum` and `CustomDatumFactory` interfaces, although deprecated in Oracle9*i*, will still be supported for backward compatibility. In Oracle8*i* JPublisher, the default setting is `CustomDatum`, whereas in Oracle9*i* JPublisher, the default setting is `ORAData`. However, Oracle9*i* JPublisher provides the `-compatible` option that allows you to generate `CustomDatum`, classes. The combined setting of `-compatible=customdatum` and `-usertypes=oracle` results in generated classes implementing the `CustomDatum interface`.

The `CustomDatum interface` supports object types and collection types such as Oracle `VARRAY` and `NESTED TABLE` in a strongly typed way. That is, for each specific `TYPE`, `REF`, or collection type in the database, there is a corresponding Java type. The `SQLData interface`, on the other hand, supports only object types in a strongly typed way.

In `SQLData`, all `REF` types are represented generically as instances of `java.sql.Ref`, and all collection types are represented generically as instances of `java.sql.Array`. In `CustomDatum`, all Oracle `REF` and collection types reside in their own classes and are represented as instances of their respective wrapper / custom classes.

NOTE
JPublisher generates wrapper / custom classes for REF and collection types only if it is generating CustomDatum classes.

Advantages of the Oracle CustomDatum Interface

CustomDatum has the following advantages:

- It does not require an entry in the type map for the Oracle object. When you use SQLData implementation classes, you must provide a type map resource properties file in which you list the SQL object types and their corresponding SQLData implementation classes. You will learn about type map resource properties files in the "Creating a Type Map for SQLData Classes" section of this chapter.

- It understands Oracle extensions.

- You do construct a CustomDatum from an oracle.sql.STRUCT. This is more efficient because it avoids unnecessary conversions to native Java types.

- It provides better performance: CustomDatum works directly with Datum types, which is the internal format used by the driver to hold Oracle objects.

One serious disadvantage of the CustomDatum interface is that classes that implement this interface are not serializable. The concept of serialization is very important when you want to ship Java objects across a network. Object components using derived classes of CustomDatum cannot be distributed on different computers, and thus cannot communicate across multiple systems in a network. In Chapter 9, you will learn how to develop Java serializable classes and SQLJ object components that use serializable classes. More important, you will learn how to distribute SQLJ object components to different computers over a network or different network systems using distributed technologies such as Java Remote Method Invocation (RMI), Enterprise JavaBeans (EJB), and Common Object Request Broker (CORBA).

Advantages of SQLData

SQLData has the following advantages:

- It is a JDBC standard, making your code more portable.

- It is much easier to write a class implementing SQLData by hand than one that implements ORAData/CustomDatum.

Requesting CustomDatum Classes from JPublisher

In this section, you will run JPublisher for a user-defined object type to request CustomDatum classes. Later on, in the "Requesting SQLData Classes from JPublisher" section of this chapter, you will run JPublisher for a user-defined object type to request `SQLData` implementation classes.

When you invoke JPublisher, it connects to the database and retrieves descriptions of the Oracle SQL object types or PL/SQL packages that you specify on the command line or from an input file. By default, JPublisher connects to the database by using the `oci` driver. However, JPublisher can also use the Oracle `thin` driver to connect to the database.

If you request `CustomDatum` classes, JPublisher automatically creates the following:

- A `.java` source file that defines the Java custom class for that object type. That is, an object class that represents instances of the Oracle object type in your Java program. The generation of `.java` source files is triggered by the value of the `method` option. By default, `-method= false`. However, if `-methods=true`, JPublisher generates `.sqlj` source files for your object types.

- A `.java` source file that defines the Java custom class for references to that object type.

- For each nested (directly or indirectly) object or collection of the top-level object type, a `.java` (or `.sqlj`) source file that defines the Java custom class for the type of that nested object or collection. These Java classes make it unnecessary to explicitly create custom classes for such nested types (by placing the name of the type on the JPublisher command line), but you can do so if you wish.

JPublisher Command-Line Syntax
The JPublisher command-line syntax consists of the keyword `jpub`, followed by a list of JPublisher options. Table 8-1, later in the chapter, presents a summary of JPublisher options.

Use the following syntax to run JPublisher:

 `jpub <jpublisher_option_settings>`

NOTE
The command-line syntax is platform dependent, so consult your platform-specific documentation for instructions on how to invoke JPublisher on your platform.

Appendix D lists the options that you can use on the JPublisher command line, their syntax, and a brief description. Detailed descriptions of each option can be found in the *Oracle8i/9i JPublisher User's Guide*.

In Listings 8-1 and 8-2, run JPublisher using the `jpub` keyword and specifying the `-sql`, `-user`, `-package`, and `-method` options to generate Java source files for the `Platform_Type` and the `Oceanic_Observation_Type` Oracle types that you created in the "Creating Object Types and Object Tables" section of this chapter:

Listing 8-1

```
// Using the default values for all the other
//  JPublisher options including the OCI driver
jpub -sql=Platform_Type:PlatWrap, OCEANIC_OBSERVATION:OceanicObs,
  Oceanic_Observation_Type:OceanicObsType -user=scott/tiger
  -method=false -package=chapter08
```

Alternatively, you can list the Oracle types in a file (see the `SchemaJpub.txt` in Listing 8-3) and invoke the tool with the `-input` option:

Listing 8-2

```
// Using the default values for all the other
//  JPublisher options including the OCI driver
jpub -user=scott/tiger
    -input=[input_file_directory]\SchemaJpub.txt
    -method=false -package=chapter08
```

Here is the file that holds the Oracle types:

Listing 8-3

```
-- SchemaJpub.txt
SQL PLATFORM_TYPE AS PlatWrap
SQL OCEANIC_OBSERVATION AS OceanicObs
SQL OCEANIC_OBSERVATION_TYPE AS OceanicObsType
```

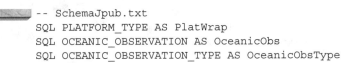

NOTE
You must add the option setting `-methods=false`. Otherwise, you will see the following extensions for the files `OceanicObs`, `OceanicObsType`, and `PlatWrap`: `.java` in 8.1.6 (default setting: `-methods=false`), `.sqlj` in 8.1.7 (and in 9.0.0 -default setting: `-methods=true`), and `.java`, except for `OceanicObsType.sqlj`, in 9.0.1 (default setting: `-methods=true`, but only classes that actually have methods will be generated as SQLJ files!).

The execution of the command shown in either Listing 8-1 or Listing 8-2 produces the following Java source files:

Listing 8-4

```
// OUTPUT
OceanicObs.java
OceanicObsRef.java
OceanicObsType.java
OceanicObsTypeRef.java
PlatWrap.java
PlatWrapRef.java
```

In Listing 8-4, all the classes that JPublisher generates for the `Platform_Type` and `Oceanic_observation_Type` types have `get` and `set` methods for the attributes of these types. Note that the `-package=chapter08` option specifies the name of the Java package for which JPublisher is generating a Java wrapper.

Here is an explanation of each of the classes:

■ A file named `PlatWrap.java` contains the definition of the Java custom class `PlatWrap` for the `platform_type` SQL object type. To get a Java custom class that is named according to Java conventions, when you specify the SQL user-defined type on the command line, you should capitalize the type name according to how you want the generated Java class name capitalized. JPublisher interprets dollar signs ($), underscores (_), and characters that are illegal in Java identifiers as word separators, and they are discarded (that is, they are not inserted into the generated Java class name). Note that if you want to specify the name for your generated `.java` file (and, therefore, also the name for your generated Java custom class) explicitly, you follow the SQL user-defined type name with a colon (`:`) and the class name you are explicitly assigning:

```
jpub -sql=platform_type:PlatWrap -user=scott/tiger
```

This explicit naming option offers a solution to the problem created by the inability of some JPublisher versions to strip the $ and _ from custom class names.

■ A file named `PlatWrapRef.java` contains the definition of the Java custom class `PlatWrapRef` for the SQL type `REF platform_type`.

■ A file named `OceanicObsType.java` contains the definition of the Java custom class `OceanicObsType.java` for the SQL object type `oceanic_observation_type`.

- A file named `OceanicObsTypeRef.java` contains the definition of the Java custom class `OceanicObsTypeRef` for the SQL type `REF oceanic_observation_type`.

- A file named `OceanicObs.java` contains the definition of the `OceanicObs` Java custom class. The `OceanicObs` class is a Java custom class for the `Oceanic_Observation` type corresponding to the type of the nested object `obsobj` of `oceanic_observation_type`. Note that if you did not explicitly request Java custom classes for the nested object `obsobj` in either of the first two listings here, JPublisher would have generated wrapper classes for the `Oceanic_Observation` type, but the name of the Java class that it generates for this class would be `OceanicObservation` and *not* `OceanicObs`. If you want to use specific names for generated custom classes, you must request them explicitly by listing it on the command line or in the `SchemaJpub.txt` file.

- A file named `OceanicObsRef.java` contains the definition of the Java custom class `OceanicObsRef` for the SQL type `REF oceanic_observation`.

Of course, each of the generated `.java` files must be compiled, using either `javac` or `sqlj` to generate the corresponding `.class` files so that the custom classes can be used in your SQLJ programs.

Understanding JPublisher Datatype Mappings

In this section, we first present a summary in Table 8-1 of JPublisher categories for SQL types, the mapping settings relevant for each category, and the default settings. Then, we elaborate on some of the JPublisher tool options, in particular the options that affect type mappings. Importantly, the type mappings control the types that the generated accessor methods support, that is, what types the `get` methods return and the `set` methods require.

SQL Type Category	Mapping Option	Mapping Settings	Default
UDT types	-usertypes	oracle, jdbc	oracle
Numeric types	-numbertypes	oracle, jdbc, objectjdbc, bigdecimal	objectjdbc
LOB types	-lobtypes	oracle, jdbc	oracle
Built-in types	-builtintypes	oracle, jdbc	jdbc

TABLE 8-1. *JPublisher SQL Type Categories, Supported Settings, and Defaults*

The following options control which type mappings JPublisher uses to translate object types, collection types, REF types, and PL/SQL packages to Java classes:

- **-builtintypes** Controls type mappings for nonnumeric, non-LOB, and predefined SQL and PL/SQL types.

- **-lobtypes** Controls type mappings for the BLOB and CLOB types.

- **-numbertypes** Controls type mappings for numeric types.

- **-usertypes** Controls JPublisher's behavior for user-defined types. It controls whether JPublisher generates CustomDatum classes or SQLData classes, and whether JPublisher generates code for collection and REF types. Use the mapping option value "oracle" to generate CustomDatum or ORAData classes or jdbc to generate SQLData classes.

Each type mapping option has at least two possible values: jdbc and oracle. The -numbertypes option has two additional alternatives: objectjdbc and bigdecimal.

Note the following:

- The JDBC mapping maps most numeric database types to Java primitive types such as int and float, and maps DECIMAL and NUMBER to java.math.BigDecimal.

- The Object JDBC mapping maps most numeric database types to Java wrapper classes such as java.lang.Integer and java.lang.Float, and maps DECIMAL and NUMBER to java.math.BigDecimal. It differs from the JDBC mapping only in that it does not use primitive types.

- The BigDecimal mapping, as the name implies, maps all numeric database types to java.math.BigDecimal. It supports NULL values and very large values.

Some other important options are

- **-case** This option for the JPublisher command line allows you to specify how JPublisher uses case in the naming of its generated fields, methods, and classes for nested types.

- **-case=mixed** This default indicates that the first character of every word is uppercase except for the first character in a method (underscore (_), dollar sign ($), and characters that are illegal in Java identifiers are treated as word separators, and are discarded).

- **-case=same** Indicates that the names should be the same as the SQL user-defined type.

- **-case=upper** Indicates that the names should be all uppercase.

- **-case=lower** Indicates that the names should be all lowercase.

You can use the -methods command-line option to have JPublisher generate Java wrappers for the methods in your SQL object type. Such a Java wrapper allows you to invoke the method through an instance of the generated custom class. In JPublisher release 8.1.5, the default setting for -methods is false (don't generate wrappers). Since 8.1.7, the default setting for –methods is now true. Note, however, that in Oracle9*i* JPublisher release 9.0.1, the true setting will generate .sqlj files only for those SQL types that actually define methods. You set -methods=true to enable the generation of Java wrappers for all the methods in your object type.

For example, to generate a Java wrapper for the get_platform_type method in oceanic_observation_type, you would enter

```
jpub -sql=oceanic_observation_type:OceanicObsType
-user=scott/tiger -methods=true
```

The preceding command would cause JPublisher to generate the following method for the OceanicObsType custom class:

```
PlatWrap getPlatformType()
```

When you have JPublisher generate Java method wrappers for your custom class, the custom class definition is placed in a .sqlj file, not a .java file, and you must use sqlj (not javac) to compile that file. If you have a SQLJ program that contains

```
OceanicObsType oot;
PlatWrap pt;
...
pt = oot.getPlatformType()
```

then getPlatformType() will appropriately invoke the get_platform_type SQL method so as to obtain the PlatWrap custom class version of the PLATFORM_TYPE record that is referenced by oot. It is important to realize that running a method on an object type instance means the following:

- The value of the instance is shipped to the DB server.

- The method is executed on the instance in the server.

■ The result(s), if any, and possibly the new value of the object are returned back to the client. Be aware, this is not a local call!

As noted in previous sections, by using the -input option on the jpub command line, you can specify a JPublisher input file that explicitly provides names for custom class fields and Java wrapper methods. For example, the following jpub command line specifies the file SchemaJpub.txt as being the input file for its invocation of JPublisher:

```
jpub -user=scott/tiger -methods=true
     -input=[input_directory]/SchemaJpub.txt
```

The file SchemaJpub.txt consists of a translation statement (in general, a JPublisher input file can contain one or more translation statements) that explicitly provides the custom class names ObsObj and getPlatformType, respectively, for the obsobj field and the get_platform_type method:

```
SQL Platform_Type AS PlatWrap
SQL oceanic_observation_type AS OceanicObsType
```

This translation statement indicates that for the SQL types Platform_Type and oceanic_observation_type, at least, two custom classes called PlatWrap and OceanicObsType, respectively, should be generated. When you run Oracle8*i* JPublisher releases 8.1.5, 8.1.6, and 8.1.7, with the -methods=true, the tool generates the following list of files:

Listing 8-5

```
PlatWrapRef.java
OceanicObsRef.java
OceanicObsTypeRef.java
PlatWrap.sqlj
OceanicObs.sqlj
OceanicObsType.sqlj
```

NOTE
In Oracle9i JPublisher release 9.0.1, the tool generates a .sqlj file only for oceanic_observation_type, since that is the only SQL object type that actually defines methods. To force the behavior shown here, you can use the new -methods=always setting option, which will force generation of .sqlj files regardless.

In addition to the methods listed in the `.java` source file shown in Listing 8-5, the `.sqlj` file contains the Java `getPlatformType ()` implementation method for the `get_platform_type` method of the `Oceanic_Observation_Type` type. You can call the `getPlatformType ()` in any Java or SQLJ program of your choice. Here is the definition of the `getPlatformType ()` method:

```
public  PlatWrap getPlatformType ()
  throws SQLException {
...

...
}  // End of getPlatformType ()
```

Java Custom Class Methods for Object Types and Reference Types

The most useful generated methods are described in this section. For more information on generated methods, see Chapter 6 of the *Oracle8i/9i SQLJ Developer's Guide and Reference*. For each field of an object type, there will be an accessor (`get`) method and a mutator (`set`) method generated for the custom class that can be used to, respectively, retrieve and change the value of that field in a custom class instance. The most useful methods in a REF type custom class are the `getValue ()` method, which returns the database object that is being referenced, and the `setValue ()` method, which can be used to change the field values of the database object that is being referenced. `setValue ()` changes the field values of the referenced database object so that they agree with the field values of the argument passed to `setValue ()`. Both of these involve a database round trip, so apply them carefully!

For example, the following methods will be contained in the custom class `PlatWrap`:

```
public java.math.BigDecimal getKeyId() throws SQLException,
public void setKeyId( java.math.BigDecimal x ) throws SQLException,
public String getDescription() throws SQLException,
public void setDescription( String x ) throws SQLException
```

Note that, by default, JPublisher treats all numeric fields as being of type `java.math.BigDecimal`.

The custom class `PlatformTypeRef` contains the following methods:

```
public PlatWrap getValue() throws SQLException,
public void setValue( PlatWrap x ) throws SQLException
```

Similar methods are generated for the `OceanicObs`, `OceanicObsREF`, `OceanicObsType`, and the `OceanicObsTypeRef` classes. The methods generated for the `OceanicObsType` class include accessor and mutator methods for the nested object:

```
OceanicObs getObsobj() throws SQLException
```

and

```
void setObsobj( OceanicObs x )
   throws SQLException
```

The program `ObjectTypes.sqlj`, in the following section, illustrates the use of these Java custom class methods.

`ObjectTypes.sqlj`: An Example SQLJ Program That Processes Tables Containing User-Defined SQL Object Types

The following is an example of a SQLJ program that processes tables containing user-defined SQL object types. The `ObjectTypes` SQLJ class consists of several methods that allow you to manipulate data in the `OCEANIC_OBSERVATION_LIST` table:

- **`insertObjects()`**   Use this method to insert data.
- **`removeObjects()`**   Use this method to delete data.
- **`updateObjects()`**   Use this method to update data.
- **`retrieveObjects()`**   In this method, you will use an instance of the `PlatObs` SQLJ named iterator and an instance of the `NamedScrollableIter` SQLJ scrollable named iterator to query data. In Chapter 6, you learned about the different types of SQLJ scrollable iterators. Specifically, you learned how to associate an instance of `DefaultContext` to scrollable iterators. Here, you will learn how to associate an instance of declared context class (`ConnectionContext` class) to SQLJ scrollable iterators. See Chapter 5, to learn about SQLJ non-scrollable iterators.
- **`usingTypeRef()`**   Use this method to learn how to manipulate Oracle REF types.

Here is the definition of the `ObjectTypes` class:

```
/*
** Program Name:  ObjectTypes.sqlj
```

```
**
** Purpose:  Illustrate the processing of object tables, REF fields,
**           and nested records in SQLJ.
**
*/
package chapter08;
import sqlj.runtime.*;
import sqlj.runtime.ref.*;
import java.sql.*;
import java.util.ArrayList;
import java.math.BigDecimal;

/* oracle.sqlj.runtime.Oracle class contains connect() method for
   connecting to database.
*/
import oracle.sqlj.runtime.Oracle;
import oracle.sql.*;

// Declare a ConnectContext class
// This is mandatory if you want to use
// scrollable named or positional iterators
#sql context DeclaredConnectionContext;

public class ObjectTypes {
    // Create a variable of type DeclaredConnectionContext
    public static DeclaredConnectionContext conn;

   /* The PlatObs named iterator will be used to hold a set of records
      consisting of a platform_type record and an oceanic_observation
      record, which have been retrieved using the
      OCEANIC_OBSERVATION_LIST table.
    */
   #sql public static iterator PlatObs( PlatWrap plat, OceanicObs obs );

   // Declare a scrollable named iterator
  #sql public static iterator NamedScrollableIter
       implements sqlj.runtime.Scrollable
             ( PlatWrap plat, OceanicObs obs );

   public ObjectTypes() {
      // Connect to the database
      connectDB();
      // Get an instance of the DeclaredConnectionContext
      // Note that, here, you could have easily used a
      // DefaultContext object instead of an instance
      // of a ConnectionContext class.
      // See Chapter 6, to learn how to use
      // DefaultContext object with scrollable iterators.
```

```
    try {
        conn =
         new DeclaredConnectionContext(
            Oracle.getConnection(ObjectTypes.class,
                         "connect.properties" ));
    } // End of try
    catch (SQLException e) {
       System.out.println("Unable to get a CTX instance");
       System.exit(1);
    } // End of catch block
} // End of constructor

public static void main( String[] args ) throws SQLException {
    // Connect to the database
    ObjectTypes app = new ObjectTypes();
    try {
        int [] oceanicObsId = insertObjects();
        removeObjects(oceanicObsId[0]);
        updateObjects(oceanicObsId[1]);
        retrieveObjects(oceanicObsId[2]);
        usingTypeRef(oceanicObsId[2]);
    }   // End of try
    catch (SQLException exn) { }
    // Close the connection
    finally {
        Oracle.close();
        if  (conn != null) conn.close();
    } // End of finally
} // End of main()

private static int[] insertObjects() throws SQLException {
    int [] obsids = new int[3];
    int obsid = 0;
    try {
        for (int i = 0; i < 3; i++) {
            // Create observation ids.
            // The OBSID_SEQ sequence is part of the
            // obsexample.SQL script listed in the
            // introduction of the book. You must run that
            // script prior of running this program.
            // (See Note 1.)
#sql { SELECT OBSID_SEQ.NEXTVAL INTO :obsid FROM DUAL
            };
            obsids[i] = obsid;
        }   // End for loop
    } // End of try
    catch (java.lang.NullPointerException ex){
        System.out.println("Unable to create Obs_id "
```

```
                                                  +ex.getMessage());
            System.exit(1);
        }   // End of catch

        // Insert 3 objects
        // Note this method would be more efficient
        // using SQLJ updateBatching. See Chapter 10
        // to learn about updateBatching
        try {
            for (int i = 0; i < 3; i++) {
                obsid = obsids[i];
                #sql { INSERT INTO OCEANIC_OBSERVATION_LIST
                        VALUES ( :obsid,'14-JUL-2001','000442',78,1,
                               (SELECT REF(P) FROM PLATFORM_TYPE_LIST P
                               WHERE P.KEY_ID = 1),
                               OCEANIC_OBSERVATION(12.2,128.7,
                                           16,16,50,NULL) )
                };
            }   // end of for loop
        } // End of try
        catch( SQLException e ) {
            System.out.println("Unable to insert observation "
                               +e.getMessage());
                    // Gentleman way of cleaning up
            #sql { ROLLBACK WORK };
            System.exit(1);
        } // End of catch
        // Commit the changes
        #sql {COMMIT WORK};
        return obsids;
    } // End of insertObjects()

    private static void removeObjects(int anOceanicObsId)
            throws SQLException {
        try {
            #sql {DELETE FROM OCEANIC_OBSERVATION_LIST O
                  WHERE O.obs_id = :anOceanicObsId
            };
        } // End of try
        catch (SQLException ex){
            System.out.println("Unable to delete observation "
                               +ex.getMessage());
            System.exit(1);
        }   // End of catch
        // Commit the changes
        #sql {COMMIT WORK};
    } // End of removeObjects()
    private static void updateObjects(int anOceanicObsId)
```

```
            throws SQLException {
        BigDecimal latitude = new BigDecimal(26.20);
        try {
            #sql { UPDATE OCEANIC_OBSERVATION_LIST O
                    SET O.obsobj.latitude_deg = :latitude
                    WHERE O.obs_id = :anOceanicObsId
            };
        } // End of try
        catch (SQLException ex){
            System.out.println("Unable to update observation "
                                +ex.getMessage());
            System.exit(1);
        }   // End of catch
        // Commit the changes
        #sql {COMMIT WORK};
    } // End of updateObjects()
    private static void retrieveObjects(int anOceanicObsId)
            throws SQLException {
        /* Declare custom class instances for platform_type and
           oceanic_observation object types.
        */

        PlatWrap pt;
        OceanicObs oo;
        OceanicObsType oo1;
        PlatObs aPlatObs = null;
        // Declare a scrollable named iterator
        NamedScrollableIter anScrollable = null;
        try {
            /* Select platform_type record that is referenced by, and
               oceanic_observation record that is contained in, the
               desired OCEANIC_OBSERVATION_LIST record.  Select these
               records into the custom class instances pt and oo.  The
               get_platform_type method is not used in this program so
               as to permit the illustration of explicit dereferencing.
            */
            #sql {select deref(O.PRODUCED_BY), O.OBSOBJ
                into :pt , :oo
                from oceanic_observation_list O
                where O.OBS_ID = :anOceanicObsId
            };

            /*  We can select an entire row from the
                the oceanic_observation_list table
            */
            #sql {select value(O) INTO :oo1
                from oceanic_observation_list O
                where O.OBS_ID = :anOceanicObsId
            };
```

```
/* We can use an iterator to get all observations. */
#sql aPlatObs = {select deref(O.PRODUCED_BY) AS plat,
                 O.OBSOBJ AS obs
              from oceanic_observation_list O
};
if  (pt == null) {
    System.out.println("NULL Platform");
}
else {
    // Print the obtained field values.
    System.out.println(
      (pt.getKeyId()==null) ? " " : pt.getKeyId().toString());
    System.out.println(
      (pt.getType()==null) ? " " : pt.getType());
    System.out.println(
      (pt.getDescription()==null) ? " " : pt.getDescription());
} // End if
if  (oo == null) {
    System.out.println("NULL Observation");
}
else {
    System.out.println
      ( "Latitude degrees = " + oo.getLatitudeDeg() );
    System.out.println
      ( "Longitude degrees = " + oo.getLongitudeDeg() );
} // End of if
if  (oo1 == null) {
    System.out.println("NULL OceanicObsType");
}
else {
    System.out.println(
      (oo1.getObsId()==null) ? " " : oo1.getObsId().toString());
    System.out.println(
      (oo1.getObsobj().getLatitudeDeg()==null)
         ? " " : oo1.getObsobj().getLatitudeDeg().toString());
    System.out.println(
      (oo1.getProducedBy().getValue().getDescription() == null)
         ? " " : oo1.getProducedBy().getValue().getDescription());
} // End if

while ( aPlatObs.next() ) {
   pt = aPlatObs.plat();
   oo = aPlatObs.obs();
   System.out.println( "Key id = " + pt.getKeyId() );
   System.out.println( "Type = " + pt.getType() );
   System.out.println( "Description = " + pt.getDescription() );
} // End of while
```

```
        /* We can use an scrollable named iterator
           to get all observations.
           Remember that you can also use instances
           of DefaultContext with scrollable
           iterators. See Chapter 6 to learn about
           scrollable iterators.
        */
        #sql [conn] anScrollable = {select deref(O.PRODUCED_BY) AS plat,
                                    O.OBSOBJ AS obs
                                     from oceanic_observation_list O
        };
        anScrollable.next();
        PlatWrap pt1 = anScrollable.plat();
        OceanicObs ooo = anScrollable.obs();
        System.out.println( "Latitude degrees = "
                            + ooo.getLatitudeDeg() );
        System.out.println( "Key id from scrollable = "
                            + pt1.getKeyId() );
        anScrollable.last();
        System.out.println
            ( "Latitude degrees = " + ooo.getLatitudeDeg() );
        System.out.println( "Key id from scrollable = "
                            + pt1.getKeyId() );

    } // End of try
    catch (SQLException ex){
        System.out.println("Unable to retrieve observation "
                            +ex.getMessage());
        System.exit(1);
    }   // End of catch
    finally {
        // Close iterator instance.
        if  (aPlatObs != null) aPlatObs.close();
        if  (anScrollable != null) anScrollable.close();
    } // End of finally

} // End of retrieveObjects()
private static void usingTypeRef(int anOceanicObsId)
        throws SQLException {
    PlatWrapRef ptr;
    try {
        /* Select desired produced_by value into REF custom class
           instance ptr.
        */
        #sql { SELECT produced_by INTO :ptr
               FROM OCEANIC_OBSERVATION_LIST
               WHERE obs_id = :anOceanicObsId
        };
```

```
     /* Use the getValue() method to get platform_type record that
        is referenced by selected produced_by field that is in ptr.
        Place this record in platform_type custom class instance pt
     */
     PlatWrap pt = ptr.getValue();

     /* Use mutator method in platform_type custom class instance pt
        to change the description value in that instance.
     */
     pt.setDescription( "METAR_OCEANIC" );

     /* Use the setValue() method in REF custom class instance to
        update the referenced record in the PLATFORM_TYPE_LIST table.
     */
     ptr.setValue( pt );
   }  // end of try
   catch (SQLException ex){
       System.out.println("Unable to retrieve observation "
                              +ex.getMessage());
       System.exit(1);
   }  // End of catch
 } // End of usingTypeRef()

 private void connectDB() {
   try {
      Oracle.connect( getClass(), "connect.properties" );
   }  // End of try
   catch( SQLException e ) {
     System.err.println( "Error connecting to database. \n" + e );
     System.exit(1);
   }  // End of catch
 }   // End of connectDB()

}  // End of ObjectTypes class
```

Note on the ObjectTypes class:

I. Because you know in advance that you want to store three rows of data, it would have been much more efficient (and a really good trick to learn and practice as well) to increment the sequence by 3 instead of 1, saving two out of three round trips to the database. Remember, round trips to the database are costly. In Chapter 10, you will learn how to save roundtrips to the database using mechanisms such as disabling auto-commit, row prefetching, update batching, statement catching, column definitions, and parameter size definitions.

Oracle8*i*/9*i* User-Defined SQL Collection Types

There are two kinds of collection types in Oracle, NESTED TABLEs and VARRAYs (variable-length arrays). In order for a table to contain a field that is of either of these collection types, a CREATE TYPE statement first has to be executed for the type. For example, suppose you wish to have a table of observations that passed quality control, which is to contain a field that itself is to be a table. Each record in the NESTED TABLE is to consist of an observation ID and a one-character code indicating how well the observation passed. You first create in SQL*Plus a type for the records in the NESTED TABLE and then a type for the NESTED TABLE. Only then can you create the table that contains the NESTED TABLE:

```
CREATE TYPE passedobs AS
  object( obsid number, passed char(1) ) ;
/

CREATE TYPE passedobsarray AS TABLE OF passedobs;
/

CREATE TABLE PASSED_OBSERVATION_LIST
  ( passed_id number(5),
    qcid      number(5),
    when_t    date,
    at_time   char(8),
    idobj     passedobsarray )
    NESTED TABLE idobj STORE AS POBSID_LIST;
```

Note that the table PASSED_OBSERVATION_LIST is not defined to be an object table (that is, there is no explicitly defined row type for it) because there will be no REF fields in the database that will reference its records, nor any other tables in the database having its record type as a field or a record type. Thus, there is no need to give the record type of PASSED_OBSERVATION_LIST a special name.

However, the question remains as to the advantages of nesting the idobj table in the PASSED_OBSERVATION_LIST table, as compared to implementing it as a separate table (which is how it will be physically implemented, anyway). It could be argued that the idobj information inherently belongs grouped with the other PASSED_OBSERVATION_LIST data, and that the naturalness of this representation is reflected in the relative simplicity of the "join-free" queries on this table given later in this section. The judgment concerning the validity of this argument is left up to you.

Another argument to justify the NESTED TABLE construct concerns the traffic between client programs and the Oracle server. NESTED TABLE types allow you to transfer a NESTED TABLE between the client and server as a single unit. Without such a construct, you would have to map complex structures into simple SQL types. The many separate components in the mapping would each require a separate trip to the server, appreciably degrading performance. In fact, this reduction of network traffic can be considered a general advantage of the object-relational approach, including not only collection types, but nested records and REFs as well. The Java custom classes can be viewed as an efficient, type-secure mechanism for providing a convenient unit of transfer between the SQLJ client program and the Oracle server.

The CREATE TABLE statement for a table that contains a NESTED TABLE must have a nested_table_clause that indicates which table will actually hold the records of the NESTED TABLE. In this case, POBSID_LIST will hold the records for the idobj field.

An alternative way of representing the passed observation information is as a variable-length array (VARRAY) within the PASSED_OBSERVATION_LIST record. The following statements are executed to create a table, PASSED_OBSERVATION_LIST2, that is analogous to PASSED_OBSERVATION_LIST, except that it contains a VARRAY instead of a NESTED TABLE. Note that the maximum size of the VARRAY (here, 100) must be supplied in the CREATE TYPE statement for the VARRAY.

```
CREATE TYPE passedobsarray2 AS VARRAY( 100 ) OF passedobs;
/

CREATE TABLE PASSED_OBSERVATION_LIST2
   ( passed_id number(5),
     qcid       number(8),
     when_t     date,
     at_time    char(8),
     idobj      passedobsarray2 );
```

How do you determine whether you should use a NESTED TABLE or a VARRAY? You do that by considering the two fundamental differences between a NESTED TABLE and a VARRAY:

- The NESTED TABLE is dynamic, whereas the VARRAY is static. This has several important implications. Records can be inserted, deleted, and updated in a NESTED TABLE after that table has been inserted into the outer record.

  In order to change a VARRAY in an outer record, the entire VARRAY has to be replaced. On the other hand, because of its static nature, a VARRAY can occupy less space than a NESTED TABLE. Also, if the VARRAY is small enough, its static nature allows it to be stored close to the rest of its outer record. This closeness can lead to a faster access time, as compared to the NESTED TABLE that is stored separately from its outer record. Note that up to a certain size (approximately 4K), a VARRAY column can be stored inline in a row, giving you faster access than if you used a NESTED TABLE.

■ Ordering has meaning for VARRAYs, but not for NESTED TABLEs. If ordering is important for your collection, you may prefer to implement it as a VARRAY. (Of course, the exploitation of ordering position at the logical level violates the relational philosophy.)

The following statements will insert records into the PASSED_OBSERVATION_LIST and PASSED_OBSERVATION_LIST2 tables:

```
// Insert data into the PASSED_OBSERVATION_LIST
INSERT INTO PASSED_OBSERVATION_LIST P
    SELECT 1,Q.qc_id,Q.WHEN_T,Q.at_time,
    passedObsArray(PASSEDOBS(1,'P'),
    PASSEDOBS(2,'P'),
    PASSEDOBS(3,'P'))
FROM QC_EVENT_LIST Q
WHERE Q.qc_id = 1
/
// Insert data into the PASSED_OBSERVATION_LIST2
INSERT INTO PASSED_OBSERVATION_LIST2 P
    SELECT 1,Q.qc_id,Q.WHEN_T,Q.at_time,
    passedObsArray2(PASSEDOBS(1,'P'),
    PASSEDOBS(2,'P'),
    PASSEDOBS(3,'P'))
FROM QC_EVENT_LIST Q
WHERE Q.qc_id = 1
/
```

Note that the QC_EVENT_LIST table is part of the Scientific Observation schema. See the Introduction of this book for a complete listing of that schema.

Processing SQL Collection Types in SQLJ

Your first step is to create Java custom classes for your SQL collection types using JPublisher. You execute JPublisher exactly as in the object type case. For example, here is what you would run to generate custom classes for the passedobsarray and passedobsarray2 types:

```
jpub -sql=PassedObsArray,PassedObsArray2 -user=scott/tiger
```

Capitalize just as you did in the object type case in the earlier section "Processing SQL Object Types in Oracle9*i* SQLJ." When you generate a custom class for a collection type, JPublisher automatically generates custom classes for your element types. Thus, in this example, JPublisher will automatically generate a custom class Passedobs for the SQL object type passedobs (and, therefore, also a REF custom class PassedobsRef). Each .java file generated for these classes—namely, PassedObsArray.java, PassedObsArray2.java, and PassedObs.java, PassedObsRef.java—must then be compiled using javac or sqlj. If you don't like the name JPublisher generated for the passedobs custom class (Passedobs), you can explicitly list PassedObs on the jpub command line to get the o capitalized:

```
jpub -sql=PassedObs,PassedObsArray,PassedObsArray2 -user=scott/tiger
```

For each collection custom class, the methods that JPublisher generates include

- **constructor** This method (of course, having the same name as the custom class) initializes the new custom class instance with an array that is passed in as an argument.

- **getArray()** This returns as an array the collection that is represented by the custom class instance.

- **setArray()** Replaces the collection that is represented by the custom class instance with the collection that is represented by an array passed as the argument to setArray().

- **length()** Returns the number of elements in the collection represented by the custom class instance.

- **getElement()** Returns an individual element in the collection represented by the custom class instance.

- **setElement()** Updates an individual element in the collection represented by the custom class instance.

In the current example, JPublisher will generate (among others) the following methods for the NESTED TABLE class PassedObsArray:

```
public PassedObsArray( Passedobs[] p );
public PassedObs[] getArray()throws SQLException;
public void setArray( PassedObs[] p ) throws SQLException;
public int length() throws SQLException;
public PassedObs getElement( long index ) throws SQLException;
public void setElement( PassedObs p, long index );
```

The index argument in getElement() and setElement() indicates which element in the collection is being retrieved or updated.

Methods with corresponding signatures are generated for the VARRAY class PassedObservationList2. In the next section, you will see a program, CollectionTypes.sqlj, that illustrates the use of these methods.

CollectionTypes.sqlj: An Example SQLJ Program That Processes Tables Containing NESTED TABLEs and VARRAYs

Following is an example of a SQLJ program that processes tables containing NESTED TABLEs and VARRAYs.

You will first create the PassedArray and PassedArray2 iterators that you will use to query the PASSED_OBSERVATION_LIST and PASSED_OBSERVATION_LIST2 tables, respectively. Each iterator declaration will reside in a file bearing the same name as the iterator. Recall, you learned these concepts in Chapter 3.

Here is the definition of the PassedArray iterator:

```
/*
** Program Name:  PassedArray.sqlj
**
** Purpose:   PassedArray is a named iterator used for the SELECT
**            statement in the selectNestedObjects() method of the
**            ObjectTypes.sqlj class. PassedArray will hold a set
**            of records from the PASSED_OBSERVATION_LIST.idobj
**            NESTED TABLE.
**
*/
package chapter08;
import sqlj.runtime.*;
import sqlj.runtime.ref.*;
import java.sql.*;
/* The following two iterators must be declared public. Because they
   will be nested in other iterators, you can define as nested inner
   classes or in their own files. If you define them as nested inner
   classes, use the public static attribute. This is the most
   convenient way to define an iterator type "just where you need it".
*/
#sql public iterator PassedArray( int aPassedId, PassedObsArr idobj );
```

Here is the definition of the PassedArray2 iterator:

```
/*
** Program Name:  PassedArray2.sqlj
**
** Purpose:  PassedArray is a named iterator used for the SELECT
**           statement in the selectVarrayObjects() method.
**           PassedArray will hold a set
**           of records from the PASSED_OBSERVATION_LIST2.idobj
**           VARRAY.
**
*/
package chapter08;
import sqlj.runtime.*;
import sqlj.runtime.ref.*;
import java.sql.*;
#sql public iterator PassedArray2( int aPassedId, PassedObsArr2 idobj );
```

The `CollectionTypes` class includes methods that allow you to manipulate the `idobj` (NESTED TABLE) of the `PASSED_OBSERVATION_LIST` and the `idobj` (VARRAY TABLE) of the `PASSED_OBSERVATION_LIST2` tables. It consists of the following:

- **insertObjects()** Use this method to insert data into a table that has a VARRAY table for one of its columns.

- **selectNestedObjects()** Use this method to retrieve data from a table that has a NESTED table for one of its columns.

- **selectVarrayObjects()** Use this method to retrieve data from a table that has a VARRAY table for one of its columns.

Here is the definition of the `CollectionTypes` class:

```
/*
** Program Name:  CollectionTypes.sqlj:
**
** Purpose:  Provide a series of examples that illustrate the use of
**           iterators and collection custom classes in inserting
**           and retrieving collections.
*/
/* java.math contains the BigDecimal class that is used by
   JPublisher generated code.
*/
package chapter08;
import sqlj.runtime.*;
```

```
import sqlj.runtime.ref.*;
import java.sql.*;
import java.math.*;
import java.math.BigDecimal;
/* oracle.sqlj.runtime.Oracle class contains connect() method for
   connecting to database.
*/
import oracle.sqlj.runtime.Oracle;

public class CollectionTypes {

  public CollectionTypes() {
     // Connect to the database
     connectDB();
  } // End of constructor

  public static void main( String[] args ) throws SQLException {
     // Connect to the database
     CollectionTypes app = new CollectionTypes();
     try {
          int passedId = insertObjects();
          selectNestedObjects(1,1);
          selectVarrayObjects(1,1);
     }  // End of try
     catch (SQLException exn) {
        System.out.println(exn.getMessage());
     } // End of catch
     // Close the connection
     finally {
        Oracle.close();
     } // End of finally
  } // End of main()

  private static int insertObjects() throws SQLException {
     int passedId = 0;
     try {
          // Create passed_id ids
          #sql { SELECT PASSED_ID_SEQ.NEXTVAL
                  INTO :passedId FROM DUAL
          };
     } // End of try
     catch (java.lang.NullPointerException ex){
          System.out.println("Unable to create passed_id "
                            +ex.getMessage());
          #sql { ROLLBACK WORK };
          System.exit(1);
     }  // End of catch
     // Insert data into the PASSED_OBSERVATION_LIST2 table
```

```
    try {
        #sql {INSERT INTO PASSED_OBSERVATION_LIST2 P
               SELECT :passedId, Q.qc_id,Q.WHEN_T,Q.at_time,
                  passedObsArray2(PASSEDOBS(1,'P'),
                    PASSEDOBS(2,'P'),PASSEDOBS(3,'P'))
                    FROM QC_EVENT_LIST Q
                       WHERE Q.qc_id = 2
        };
    } // End of try
    catch( SQLException e ) {
        System.out.println("Unable to insert observation "
                +e.getMessage());
        System.exit(1);
    } // End of catch
    // Commit the changes
    #sql {COMMIT WORK};
    return passedId;
} // End of insertNestedObjects()

private static void selectNestedObjects(int obsid, int passedId)
    throws SQLException {
    // Declare an array of PassedObs
    PassedObs[] po;
    PassedObsArr poa;
    // Declare an iterator
    PassedArray anPassedArray;

    /* Select the passed_id and nested idobj table of the
       OCEANIC_OBSERVATION_LIST record that contains the
       input observation id in its nested idobj table.
       (Assume that there is only one such record.)  idobj
       is selected into poa, an instance of the Java custom
       class instance that was generated for the NESTED TABLE
       type of idobj.
    */
    #sql { SELECT passed_id, idobj INTO :passedId, :poa
           FROM PASSED_OBSERVATION_LIST p
           WHERE passed_id = :passedId and
              :obsid IN
              ( SELECT i.obsid FROM TABLE( p.idobj ) i )
    };
    System.out.println( "passedid = " + passedId );
    /* Invoke the getArray() method on poa to move the nested
       table elements into the po array.
    */
    po = poa.getArray();
    /* In the for loop, the accessor methods for the NESTED TABLE
       elements are used to obtain and print the fields of the
```

```
        elements that were loaded into the po array.  Note that the
        array length attribute for po is used to terminate the loop.
     */
     for ( int i = 0; i < po.length; i++ ) {
          System.out.println( " obsid = " + po[i].getObsid()
                  + " passed code = " + po[i].getPassed() );
     } // End of for loop

     /* In the for loop, the getElement() method for poa is
        invoked to access the i-th record of the NESTED TABLE.
        getElement() enables you to access the records in a
        collection custom class directly, without first loading
        them into an array (as was done in Example 1). The generated
        custom class method is used to terminate the loop.
     */
     for ( long i = 0; i < poa.length(); i++ ) {
          System.out.println( " obs id = "
                  + poa.getElement(i).getObsid() +" passed code = "
                  + poa.getElement(i).getPassed() );
     } // End of for loop
     /* Use an iterator to query the Passed_observation_list
        Populate anPassedArray (outer iterator) with the passed_id
        and idobj field values from the PASSED_OBSERVATION_LIST table
        records that match the input quality control id.
     */
     /* The nested cursor must be used to extract the fields of idobj.
        If you merely place i.idobj in the select_list, there will be
        a type mismatch between that field and the iterator idobj
        attribute.
     */
     #sql anPassedArray =
         { SELECT p.passed_id AS aPassedId,
              CURSOR( SELECT i.obsid, i.passed
                    FROM TABLE( p.idobj ) i ) AS idobj
           FROM PASSED_OBSERVATION_LIST p
           WHERE p.qcid = 1
     };
     /* while loop uses iterator next() method to retrieve records
        from outer iterator.
     */
     while ( anPassedArray.next() ) {
        // Extract passed_id and print it.
        System.out.println
          ( "passed id = " + anPassedArray.aPassedId());
     }  // End of while
     // Close iterator
     anPassedArray.close();
   }  // End of selectNestedObjects()
```

```
private static void selectVarrayObjects(int obsid, int passedId)
     throws SQLException {
    // Declare an array of PassedObs
    PassedObs[] po;
    PassedObsArr2 poa;

    /* Select the passed_id and nested idobj table of the
       OCEANIC_OBSERVATION_LIST record that contains the
       input observation id in its VARRAY idobj table.
       (Assume that there is only one such record.)  idobj
       is selected into poa, an instance of the Java custom
       class instance that was generated for the VARRAY TABLE
       type of idobj.
    */
    #sql { SELECT passed_id, idobj INTO :passedId, :poa
          FROM PASSED_OBSERVATION_LIST2 p
          WHERE passed_id = :passedId and
             :obsid IN ( SELECT i.obsid FROM TABLE( p.idobj ) i )
    };
    System.out.println( "passedid = " + passedId );
    /* Invoke the getArray() method on poa to move the VARRAY
       table elements into the po array.
    */
    po = poa.getArray();
    /* In the for loop, the accessor methods for the VARRAY TABLE
       elements are used to obtain and print the fields of the
       elements that were loaded into the po array.  Note that the
       array length attribute for po is used to terminate the loop.
    */
    for ( int i = 0; i < po.length; i++ ) {
         System.out.println( " obsid = " + po[i].getObsid()
         + " passed code = " + po[i].getPassed() );
    } // End of for loop
    /* In the for loop, the getElement() method for poa is
       invoked to access the i-th record of the VARRAY TABLE.
       getElement() enables you to access the records in a
       collection custom class directly, without first loading
       them into an array (as was done in Example 1). The generated
       custom class method is used to terminate the loop.
    */
    for ( long i = 0; i < poa.length(); i++ ) {
         System.out.println
            ( " obs id = " + poa.getElement(i).getObsid()
             +" passed code = " +poa.getElement(i).getPassed() );
    } // End of for loop
 }  // End of selectVarrayObjects()
```

```
private void connectDB() {
  try {
      Oracle.connect( getClass(), "connect.properties" );
  } // End of try
  catch( SQLException e ) {
      System.err.println( "Error connecting to database. \n" + e );
      System.exit(1);
  } // End of catch
} // End of connectDB()

} // End of CollectionTypes class
```

Using SQLData Classes in SQLJ Programs

In this section, you will learn how to use SQLData classes in SQLJ programs. You will do so while developing the UsingSQLDataClasses SQLJ program.

The SQLData interface is standards based and potentially offers portability between different database systems. As noted in the "Advantages of the Oracle CustomDatum Interface" section of this chapter, the CustomDatum interface offers additional enhancements such as encapsulation of Oracle REF, NESTED TABLE, and VARRAY types.

You can use JPublisher to generate wrapper classes for either interface. You do so by using the tool with different options.

Requesting SQLData Classes from JPublisher

Here, you will run JPublisher requesting SQLData implementation classes. The strongly typed model, using either SQLData or CustomDatum/ORAData implementation classes, requires a Java class for each object type in the schema.

Like in the CustomDatum implementation, when you run JPublisher for a user-defined object type and choose the SQLData implementation for your custom object class, JPublisher generates a custom object class that corresponds to your Oracle object type.

The JPublisher generated class includes the following:

- get and set methods for each attribute

- Implementations of the standard SQLData interface readSQL() and writeSQL() methods

■ Wrapper methods that invoke the Oracle object methods executing in the server (unless you specify -methods=false when you run JPublisher)

Recall that the SQLData interface is intended only for object types and not for reference or collection types. Consequently, JPublisher will generate a custom class for Oracle object types only. To manipulate the Oracle REFs, you will need to use standard, weakly typed java.sql.Ref instances, or perhaps oracle.sql.REF instances if you do not require portability. Note that REF instances, like custom reference class instances, have Oracle extension methods getValue() and setValue() to read or write instances of the referenced object. For the Oracle collections such as NESTED TABLE and VARRAY, you will also use weakly type instances of java.sql.Array or oracle.sql.ARRAY. Array and ARRAY instances, like custom collection class instances, have getArray() functionality to read the collection as a whole or in part, but do not have the element-level access and writing flexibility offered by the custom collection class getElement() and setElement() methods.

NOTE
The SQLData interface is defined in the JDBC 2.0 specification to be portable. However, if you want the SQLData implementation produced by JPublisher to be portable, you must avoid using any Oracle-specific features and Oracle type mapping (which uses the Oracle-specific oracle.sql. classes).*

Use the JPublisher -usertypes option to specify which interface you want your classes to implement. A setting of -usertypes=oracle (the default) specifies the CustomDatum interface (or the ORAData interface in Oracle9i only), while a setting of -usertypes=jdbc specifies the SQLData interface.

The following JPublisher command-line syntax will result in implementation of SQLData:

```
jpub -usertypes=jdbc ... < other option settings>
```

In the "Requesting CustomDatum classes from JPublisher" section of this chapter, when you ran JPublisher using the keyword jpub specifying only the -sql, -user, -package options, you implicitly instructed to use the default options of the tool. You may want to review Table 8-1 so as to remember the default value of JPublisher options.

Use the syntax shown in Listing 8-6 to generate SQLData implementation classes:

Listing 8-6

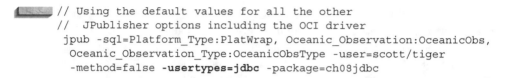

```
// Using the default values for all the other
//  JPublisher options including the OCI driver
  jpub -sql=Platform_Type:PlatWrap, Oceanic_Observation:OceanicObs,
  Oceanic_Observation_Type:OceanicObsType -user=scott/tiger
  -method=false -usertypes=jdbc -package=ch08jdbc
```

CAUTION
If you do not use the -usertypes=jdbc *option
explicitly with the value* jdbc, *JPublisher will
generate* CutomDatum *classes using the default
setting,* -usertypes=oracle.

Listing 8-7 shows the files that JPublisher generates when the command-line syntax shown in Listing 8-6 is executed:

Listing 8-7

```
// OUTPUT
PlatWrap.java
OceanicObs.java
OceanicObsType.java
```

Listing 8-8 shows a list of the methods that JPublisher generates for the OCEANIC_OBSERVATION_TYPE user-defined Oracle type. Method implementations are omitted for the sake of clarity:

Listing 8-8

```
package ch08jdbc;
public class OceanicObsType implements SQLData {
    // (See Note 1.)
    public static final String _SQL_NAME = "OCEANIC_OBSERVATION_TYPE";
    public static final int _SQL_TYPECODE = OracleTypes.STRUCT;
    private java.math.BigDecimal m_obsId;
    private java.sql.Timestamp m_whenT;
    private String m_atTime;
    private java.math.BigDecimal m_stationId;
    private java.math.BigDecimal m_producedId;
    // (See Note 2.)
    private java.sql.Ref m_producedBy;
```

```
    private OceanicObs m_obsobj;
    /* constructor */
    public OceanicObsType()
    public void readSQL(SQLInput stream,String type)throws SQLException
    public void writeSQL(SQLOutput stream) throws SQLException
    public String getSQLTypeName() throws SQLException
    /* accessor methods */
    public java.math.BigDecimal getObsId()
    public void setObsId(java.math.BigDecimal obsId)
    public java.sql.Timestamp getWhenT()
    public void setWhenT(java.sql.Timestamp whenT)
    public String getAtTime()
    public void setAtTime(String atTime)
    public java.math.BigDecimal getStationId()
    public void setStationId(java.math.BigDecimal stationId)
    public java.math.BigDecimal getProducedId()
    public void setProducedId(java.math.BigDecimal producedId)
    // (See Note 3.)
    public java.sql.Ref getProducedBy()
    public void setProducedBy(java.sql.Ref producedBy)
    public OceanicObs getObsobj()
    public void setObsobj(OceanicObs obsobj)
} // End of OceanicObsType class
```

Notes on the `OceanicObsType` class:

1. This statement and the one that follows it identify
   `OCEANIC_OBSERVATION_TYPE` and `OracleTypes.STRUCT` SQL
   types as public static final fields. Classes that implement `SQLData`
   must satisfy the requirements for type map definitions as outlined in the
   `SQLJ ISO` standard. Alternatively, `SQLData` wrapper classes can identify
   the associated SQL object type through a `public static final` field.
   This non-standard functionality was introduced in SQLJ version 8.1.6
   and continues to be supported. In both cases, you must run your SQLJ
   application under JDK 1.2 or later.

2. This statement declares the `PRODUCED_BY REF` attribute of
   `OCEANIC_OBSERVATION_TYPE` as a variable of weakly typed
   `java.sql.Ref`, as opposed to strongly typed using a `CustomDatum`
   implementation.

3. These statements declare the `getProducedBy()` and `setProducedBy()`
   methods, respectively. The former returns a `java.sql.Ref` object, and the
   latter requires a `java.sql.Ref` object as an input parameter.

Note that when you request SQLData classes for collections, no SQLData classes are generated. An attempt to request SQLData classes for collection types is shown in Listing 8-9:

Listing 8-9

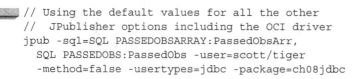

```
// Using the default values for all the other
//  JPublisher options including the OCI driver
jpub -sql=SQL PASSEDOBSARRAY:PassedObsArr,
   SQL PASSEDOBS:PassedObs -user=scott/tiger
   -method=false -usertypes=jdbc -package=ch08jdbc
```

The execution of the JPublisher command-line syntax shown in Listing 8-9 generates, rightfully so, a SQLData class for the PASSEDOBS Oracle type and no class is generated for the Oracle PASSEDOBSARRAY NESTED TABLE:

```
ERROR: When -usertypes=jdbc, nothing is generated for
collection types such as SCOTT.PASSEDOBSARRAY
SCOTT.PASSEDOBS
```

To manipulate Oracle collection types such as NESTED TABLE and VARRAY using SQLData implementation classes, you need to develop you own class using weakly typed instances of java.sql.Array or oracle.sql.ARRAY. If you do not want to do so, use the Oracle-specific CustomDatum or ORAData (Oracle9*i* only) interface.

The definition of the PlatWrap is shown in Listing 8-10. Like in Listing 8-8, method implementations are omitted for the sake of clarity.

Listing 8-10

```
package ch08jdbc;
public class PlatWrap implements SQLData {
  public static final String _SQL_NAME = "PLATFORM_TYPE";
  public static final int _SQL_TYPECODE = OracleTypes.STRUCT;
  private java.math.BigDecimal m_keyId;
  private String m_type;
  private String m_description;
  /* constructor */
  public PlatWrap(){
  }
  public void readSQL(SQLInput stream,String type) throws SQLException
  public void writeSQL(SQLOutput stream) throws SQLException
  public String getSQLTypeName() throws SQLException
  /* accessor methods */
  public java.math.BigDecimal getKeyId()
  public void setKeyId(java.math.BigDecimal keyId)
```

```
public String getType()
public void setType(String type)
public String getDescription()
public void setDescription(String description)

} // End of PlatWrap class
```

Requirements for Using SQLData Classes

SQLData implementation classes require the following:

- Use SQLData implementation classes only in statements that are explicitly associated with connection context instances of a declared connection context type.

- Declare a connection context class using the WITH attribute typeMap that specifies an associated class implementing a java.util.PropertyResourceBundle. For example:

  ```
  // Declare a ConnectionContext class
  #sql public static context CtxISO
          with (typeMap="ch08jdbc.PlatWrapTypeMap");

  // Retrieve a predefined DefaultContext instance
  // using an instance of the CtxISO context class
  CtxISO ctx =
          new CtxISO(DefaultContext.getDefaultContext());

  // Associate explicitly CtxISO instances
  // in all SQLJ statements that use
  // SQLData implementation classes:
  PlatWrap p1 = null;
  #sql [ctx] { :p1 …};
  ```

- A type map resource file that maps SQL object types to corresponding Java classes that implement the java.sql.SQLData interface.

Creating a Type Map for SQLData Classes

When you want to use java.sql.SQLData implementation classes, you must provide a type map resource properties file listing Java classes that implement the java.sql.SQLData interface and their corresponding SQL object types.

In the map resource file, the mapping is specified with entries of the following form:

```
// Use this format for Java classes
// residing in their specific file
class.<java_class_name>=STRUCT <sql_type_name>
```

```
// Use this format for inner classes
class.<outer_java_class_name>$<inner_java_class>=STRUCT <sql_type_name>
```

Use the following format to specify the mapping of the ch08jdbc.PlatWrap to the PLATFORM_TYPE:

```
class.ch08jdbc.PlatWrap=STRUCT SCOTT.PLATFORM_TYPE
```

The keyword STRUCT can also be omitted. Here, the PlatWrapMap.properties resource file contains the following entries:

```
class.ch08jdbc.PlatWrap=STRUCT SCOTT.PLATFORM_TYPE
# class.ch08jdbc.OceanicObs=STRUCT SCOTT.OCEANIC_OBSERVATION
# class.ch08jdbc.OceanicObsTyp=STRUCT SCOTT.OCEANIC_OBSERVATION_TYPE
```

CAUTION
Any class you mention in the .properties resource file must be available on the CLASSPATH or in source form on the SQLJ command line.

In this section, you will develop the UsingSQLDataClasses SQLJ class. This class demonstrates how to use SQLData implementation classes to send and receive instances of Oracle objects. Compiling and executing the UsingSQLDataClasses SQLJ class require the following:

- JDK 1.2 or higher

- Oracle JDBC 8.1.7 or higher (classes12.zip)

- Oracle SQLJ 8.1.7 or higher (runtime12.zip file and translator.zip file)

The UsingSQLDataClasses class includes the retrievePlatformDetails() method. To send and receive instances of the PlatWrap class, this method calls the GET_PLATFORM_DETAIL PL/SQL procedure.

Before developing the UsingSQLDataClasses SQLJ class, you will first write the GET_PLATFORM_DETAIL subprogram, a simple PL/SQL procedure that returns a PLATFORM_TYPE object containing the details of an atmospheric platform.

Here is the definition of the GET_PLATFORM_DETAIL PL/SQL procedure:

```
CREATE OR REPLACE PROCEDURE GET_PLATFORM_DETAIL(
                            p_platformid IN NUMBER,
```

```
                                p_inplatform IN PLATFORM_TYPE,
                                p_outplatform OUT PLATFORM_TYPE) AS
p_key NUMBER;
p_type VARCHAR2(50);
p_desc VARCHAR2(50);
BEGIN
    IF (p_platformid > 0) THEN
        SELECT P.key_id, P.type, P.description
            INTO p_key, p_type, p_desc
         FROM PLATFORM_TYPE_LIST P
         WHERE P.Key_id = p_platformid;
         p_outplatform := PLATFORM_TYPE(p_key, p_type, p_desc);
    ELSE
        p_outplatform := PLATFORM_TYPE(p_inplatform.key_id,
                                       p_inplatform.type,
                                       p_inplatform.description);
    END IF;
    END;
```

Notes on the GET_PLATFORM_DETAIL procedure:
   The GET_PLATFORM_DETAIL procedure includes the following:

- **The p_platformid IN parameter of type: Oracle NUMBER**   If
  p_platformid is greater than zero, you will query the database, use
  the query result to create a new PLATFORM_TYPE object, and return
  the object to the caller.

- **The p_inplatform IN parameter of type: PLATFORM_TYPE**   Recall
  that you created the PLATFORM_TYPE in the "Creating Object Types and
  Object Tables," earlier in this chapter. If p_platformid is not greater
  than zero, you will use the p_inplatform object to create a new
  PLATFORM_TYPE object and return the object to the caller.

- **The p_outplatform OUT parameter of type: PLATFORM_TYPE**   Use
  this parameter to return an object of type PLATFORM_TYPE and PlatWrap
  to the Java/SQLJ caller.

The following fragment code uses PlatWrap instances to call the
GET_PLATFORM_DETAIL PL/SQL procedure:

```
...
PlatWrap p1 = null;
PlatWrap p2 = null;
int keyId = 1;
// Note that, in this example, ctx is
```

```
// the instance of a declared ConnectionContext class
// Call the GET_PLATFORM_DETAIL PL/SQL procedure
#sql [ctx] { CALL GET_PLATFORM_DETAIL(:IN keyId,:IN p1, :OUT p2) };
```

Here is the definition of the UsingSQLDataClasses.sqlj program:

```
/*
** Program Name:  UsingSQLDataClasses.sqlj:
**
** Purpose:  Provide a series of examples that illustrate the use of
**           SQLData implementation classes.
**
*/
package ch08jdbc;
import sqlj.runtime.*;
import sqlj.runtime.ref.*;
import sqlj.runtime.ref.DefaultContext;
import java.sql.*;

/* oracle.sqlj.runtime.Oracle class contains connect() method for
   connecting to database.
*/
import oracle.sqlj.runtime.Oracle;

public class UsingSQLDataClasses {

   /*  Declaration of a connection context type
       to associate the type map with */
  #sql public static context CtxISO
           with (typeMap="ch08jdbc.PlatWrapTypeMap");
   protected static CtxISO ctx = null;

   public UsingSQLDataClasses() {
     // Connect to the database
     connectDB();
   } // End ofconstructor

   public static void main( String[] args ) throws SQLException {
     // Connect to the database
     UsingSQLDataClasses app = new UsingSQLDataClasses();
     try {
          retrievePlatformDetails();
     } // End of try
     catch (SQLException exn) {
          System.out.println(exn.getMessage() );
     } // End of catch
     // Close the connection
```

```
        finally {
            Oracle.close();
        } // End of finally

    }   // End of main()

    private static void retrievePlatformDetails()
            throws SQLException {
        PlatWrap p1 = null;
        PlatWrap p2 = null;
        int keyId = 1;

        // Call the GET_PLATFORM_DETAIL PL/SQL procedure
        // Associate explicitly a declared ConnectionContext instance
        #sql [ctx] {CALL GET_PLATFORM_DETAIL(:IN keyId,:IN p1, :OUT p2)};

        // Print the result
        System.out.println(
          (p2.getKeyId()==null) ? " " : p2.getKeyId().toString());
        System.out.println(
          (p2.getType()==null) ? " " : p2.getType());
        System.out.println(
          (p2.getDescription()==null) ? " " : p2.getDescription());

    }   // End of retrievePlatformDetails()

    private void connectDB() {
        try {
            Oracle.connect( getClass(), "connect.properties" );
            // ISO example using java.sql.SQLData
            ctx =
              new CtxISO(DefaultContext.getDefaultContext());

        }   // End of try
        catch( SQLException e ) {
          System.err.println( "Error connecting to database. \n" + e );
          System.exit(1);
        }   // End of catch
    }   // End of connectDB()

}   // End of UsingSQLDataClasses class
```

Some important points to note about compiling and running the
UsingSQLDataClasses class:

■ Make sure everything is in the same package (say, ch08jdbc) and everything
    is specified as belonging to that package (like the type map). For example,

because all program source code belongs to the `ch08jdbc` package, including the `PlatWrapMap.properties` resource file, you must fully qualify the properties file in the declaration of your context class:

```
#sql public static context CtxISO
        with (typeMap="ch08jdbc.PlatWrapTypeMap");  // CORRECT

// The following code will compile clean
// but will not run.
#sql public static context CtxISO
        with (typeMap="PlatWrapTypeMap");  // INCORRECT
```

- Make sure that the type map only references classes that actually exist on the `CLASSPATH` or that are being compiled.

- Place the source files in that package hierarchy, go to the root, and assuming that "." is in your `CLASSPATH`. For example:

```
sqlj -d . ch08jdbc/*.sqlj ch08jdbc/*.java
```

This command-line syntax will translate/compile the entire package.

- To run the `UsingSQLDataClasses` class, enter at the command line:

```
java ch08jdbc.UsingSQLDataClasses
```

In this chapter, you learned the following:

- How to create Oracle user-defined SQL object types

- How to use the Oracle JPublisher tool to generate Java custom classes for Oracle object and collection types using the Oracle-specific `CustomDatum interface`

- How to manipulate Oracle object and collection types using the `CustomDatum` implementation classes

- How to use the Oracle JPublisher tool to generate Java custom classes for Oracle object types using the `SQLData interface`

- How to manipulate Oracle object types using `SQLData` implementation classes

What you did not learn here was anything about inheritance. Note that Oracle9*i* and SQLJ 9.0.1/JPub 9.0.1 do support inheritance of SQL objects. At the time that we were publishing the book, Oracle9*i* database was not available. For updated information regarding Oracle9*i* products, see http://technet.oracle.com.

In Chapter 9, you will learn how to build SQLJ components and ship them over computer networks using RMI, EJB, and CORBA.

CHAPTER
9

SQLJ Business and Scientific Object Deployment

I n the previous chapters, you developed several SQLJ applications, applets, stored procedures, and database triggers. Moreover, you deployed SQLJ applications that encapsulate business logic into the Oracle8*i*/9*i* data server. When you were building these programs, you had the responsibility to design, create, and verify every piece. Your design structures had to capture enough detail to support the development of each line of code. In fact, you had complete control over every piece of the development process.

In this chapter, you will learn how to relinquish this control as you acquire the skills to design and develop software *components*. A component is a functional and operational piece of software consisting of several classes logically grouped together within a specific business task. More importantly here, you will learn how to decompose SQLJ applications into object components and distribute them to different computers over a network or different network systems.

During *object deployment,* you will ship a SQLJ component-based object—that is, a SQLJ component—across a network from one process to another using Java Remote Method Invocation (RMI), Enterprise JavaBeans (EJB), and Common Object Request Broker Architecture (CORBA). As you learned in Chapter 1, RMI is used to call Java remote objects, EJB allows you to create server-side Java remote objects, and CORBA gives you access to remote objects written in any language, including Java. As you go deeper into this chapter, you will learn more about these distributed paradigms.

While developing and deploying a SQLJ component-based object, you will learn the following:

- The basic concepts of distributed computing systems

- How to design and develop a SQLJ component-based object

- How to deploy a SQLJ component using the Java Remote Method Invocation

- How to deploy an Enterprise JavaBeans component object using a SQLJ implementation

- How to deploy a CORBA component object using a SQLJ implementation

Basic Concepts of Distributed Computing Systems

Large computer networks such as corporate and government intranets, the Internet, and the World Wide Web (WWW) have one common characteristic:

heterogeneity. Heterogeneous systems consist of a combination of hardware: heterogeneous networks—numerous operating systems (OSs) running on several different hardware configurations such as mainframes, UNIX workstations, PCs, and Apple Macintoshes, and software components where each of these components represents a valuable and indispensable portion of an enterprise as a whole. Presently, the challenge is to develop the software infrastructure to integrate or unify these components and enable communication between the objects that reside within them, in spite of their different designs and physical locations.

In response to this challenge, the concept of *distributed object* computing systems was born. Distributed object models are based on an object-oriented programming paradigm that allows the object components to be distributed on different computers throughout a heterogeneous network. In this scenario, each component remains within its own environment, occupies its own address space, and yet interoperates with other components as if each one were part of a unified whole.

The term *distributed computing,* illustrated in Figure 9-1, refers to programs or applications that make calls—that is, remote object invocation calls—to other programs located at different address spaces, possibly on different computers. In this situation, although each object may reside within its own address space—possibly on another computer, on a different network, or both—they appear as though they are local to the application that makes the calls. An *address space* is the range of memory locations to which a CPU can refer. Underlying all distributed computing architectures is the notion of communication between computers. In a distributed object model, server-side objects provide services, and client-side applications (which may reside on the same computer that provides the services) issue requests for those services to be performed on their behalf. More importantly, clients gain access to information transparently, without having to know on which software or hardware platform the information resides or where it is located on an enterprise's network.

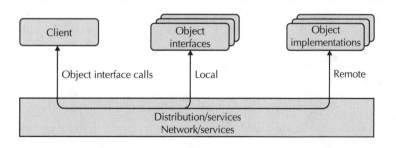

FIGURE 9-1. *Distributed object architecture*

Distributed computing systems have many advantages. They allow you to do the following:

■ Wrap legacy systems and enable communication with them. For example, CORBA provides mappings to specific languages such as C and C++ that permit you to *wrap* a FORTRAN application (that is, create C or C++ classes that publicly define the behavior of the FORTRAN application) so that a CORBA client application written in these languages can access the FORTRAN code. The code that is combined with another piece of code to determine how that code is executed is called a *wrapper.* This implies that the wrapped code (the FORTRAN code) can only be accessed via the wrapper (the C or C++ code).

■ Perform systems integration at many levels so that these systems may become less complex, thereby more efficient and flexible.

■ Decompose complex software applications into object components and distribute the objects to computers that best fit the task of each object.

■ Isolate software development as specific tasks that can be delegated to several developers concurrently and assembled together later during the development life cycle.

■ Allow components easily to be reused by multiple projects.

Standards to create and develop component-based applications in a distributed heterogeneous environment came about at the end of 1989 with the formation of the Object Management Group (OMG). OMG introduced an abstract object model for distributed systems, the Object Management Architecture (OMA). There now exists several distributed object paradigms, but the most popular ones are CORBA, the Distributed Component Object Model (DCOM), RMI, JavaBeans, and EJB:

■ CORBA, developed by OMG in the early 1990s, employs an Object Request Broker (ORB) to create and manage client and server communications between objects. Here, the terms *client* and *server* are not used in the traditional client-server sense, but relate rather to services. ORBs allow objects on the client side to make requests of objects on the server side without any prior knowledge of where those objects reside, in which language they are written, or on which hardware platform they are running. CORBA objects are packaged as binary components that remote clients can access via method invocations. CORBA uses the Internet Inter-ORB Protocol (IIOP) to access its remote objects. IIOP defines the way the bits are sent over a wire between CORBA clients and servers.

- DCOM is a component technology from Microsoft for distributing applications on the Windows (DNA) architecture. It uses a protocol called the Object Remote Procedure Call (ORPC) for "remoting" objects.

- The RMI system, from Sun JavaSoft, allows an object running in one Java Virtual Machine (JVM) to invoke methods on an object running in another JVM. RMI uses a protocol called the Java Remote Method Protocol (JRMP) for remote method invocation calls. The Java remote method invocation system described in the JDK 1.2 specification (October 1998) was designed to operate in the Java environment, and thus lacked interoperability with other languages. To address this problem, a solution known as RMI-IIOP was presented in the JavaOne Conference (June 1999). Presently, RMI objects can use the IIOP protocol to communicate with non-Java CORBA objects. The RMI-IIOP specification was developed jointly by Sun and IBM and runs on both JDK 1.1 (from release 1.1.6 onward) and Java 2. See http://java.sun.com/products/ rmi-iiop/ for more information regarding RMI-IIOP.

- JavaBeans is a component model/paradigm for Java. Components can be used in all sorts of things, not just distributed computing. It is used to build client-side applications by assembling visual (GUI) and nonvisual widgets, and server-side components. With the JavaBeans API you can create reusable, platform-independent components and combine them into Java servlets, JavaServerPages (JSP) applications, Java applets, Java applications, or a combination of any Java programs. To learn more about Java servlets and JSPs, see Oracle8i *Java Component Programming with EJB, CORBA, and JSP,* (Oracle Press, October, 2000).

- Enterprise JavaBeans, developed by numerous groups at Sun and its partner companies, extends the JavaBeans architecture to a higher level by providing an API optimized for building scientific and business applications as reusable server components. It is a server-side component model and is designed to address issues involved with managing distributed business objects in a three-tier architecture. Based conceptually on the RMI model, EJB is a cross-platform component architecture for the development and deployment of multi-tier, distributed, and object-oriented Java applications. EJB server components are application components that usually run in an application server. With the release of Oracle8i/9i, EJB components can now run in a database server. In EJB applications, object "remoting" follows the RMI specification, but vendors are not limited to the RMI transport protocol. For example, the Oracle8i/9i EJB server uses RMI over IIOP for its transport protocol. In the "Deploying an Enterprise JavaBeans Object Using a SQLJ Implementation" section of this chapter, you will develop an EJB application component that runs in the Oracle8i/9i data server (see "What Is Enterprise JavaBeans?" and "Developing an Enterprise Bean Application" to learn more about EJB).

See the Bibliography at the end of the book for more information regarding distributed computing systems.

In the following sections, you will use the Unified Modeling Language (UML) to design a SQLJ component, the Java programming language and SQLJ to develop the source code, and finally you will deploy the SQLJ component using RMI, EJB, and CORBA. UML is a language for constructing, modeling, and documenting software systems.

Designing and Developing a SQLJ Component-Based Object

In this section, you will create a SQLJ component-based object to manipulate an Oracle table, the PLATFORM_TYPE_LIST, of a user-defined datatype, PLATFORM_TYPE. Remember how you defined the PLATFORM_TYPE type and the PLATFORM_TYPE_LIST table (see the Introduction and Chapter 8 of this book). Listing 9-1 shows the SQL statements that created both the TYPE and the TABLE in the Oracle8i/9i data server.

Listing 9-1

```
-- In SQLPLUS or svrmgr
-- Create an Oracle type
CREATE TYPE PLATFORM_TYPE AS OBJECT(
    key_id      NUMBER(5),
    type        VARCHAR2(20),
    description VARCHAR2(50))
/
-- Create a table of PLATFORM_TYPE objects
CREATE TABLE PLATFORM_TYPE_LIST OF PLATFORM_TYPE
/
```

What Is a Component?

"A software component is a unit of composition with contractually specified interfaces and explicit context dependencies only. A software component can be deployed independently and is subject to composition by third parties." (Workshop on Component-Oriented Programming, ECOOP, 1996). An object is not necessarily a component. Nor is a component necessarily an object. An example of an object is an atmospheric observation object in the HRD Wind Analysis system (HWIND), developed at the Hurricane Research Division in Miami, where the attributes and operations associated with that observation object are designed solely with the HWIND application in mind. An example of a component is a SQLJ application that has been wrapped with an object interface and is being used to check business or scientific rules in an application or database server.

Component Composites

A component is the unit of work and distribution that packs together small, tightly coupled objects in larger units of independent deployment, as in Figure 9-2. It is a set of modules and consists, at a minimum, of the following:

- An object `interface` defines the behavior of the component. The behavior is the contract that the object `interface` offers publicly. The contract guarantees that the invocation of one of its `interface` methods produces either the result or one of the exceptions specified. A client that `wishes` to use a component will do so via the component `interface` that defines its access points. For example, a Java `interface` consists of a class name and a set of method signatures. A method signature consists of a method name and its parameter types along with its return values and exceptions. This `interface` must be declared public in order to be visible to a client; otherwise, a client gets an error when it invokes the object.

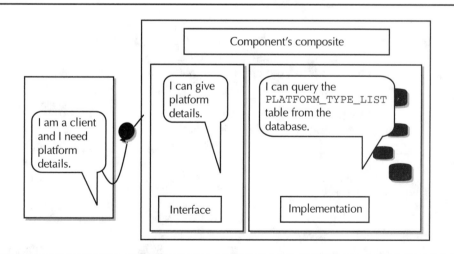

FIGURE 9-2. *Component composite*

■ An object *implementation* provides the method (behavior) definitions that precisely define the circumstances in which the object will react. The method implementation assures that, under the specified circumstances, the object will always produce a precisely defined result. Additionally, the component may be extended to include other classes that extend the implementation class.

What Is a Component Model?

Before software complexity becomes overwhelming, you should use modeling to stay in control. A component model defines a set of interfaces and classes that must be used in a particular way to isolate and encapsulate a set of functionality. In response to complexity, use component modeling to raise the level of abstraction in order to get a higher-level view of the software. You can use object modeling CASE tools that offer abstraction from the source code to create a model for your component. There are many modeling tools such as, Oracle Designer (database modeling, Oracle Corporation), Rational Rose (software systems modeling, Rational Software), Visio (general-purpose modeling, Visio Corporation), and so on. Most popular modeling tools use the UML methodology to create a component model. In Figure 9-3, you use UML to design the SQLJ component.

Notes on Figure 9-3: The SQLJ component-based object consists of the ObservationInterface interface, the ObservationAdaptor implementation class, the Platform DbObject child class, and the PlatWrap class. See Appendix B to learn more about interface, implements, and child classes.

■ The ObservationInterface interface consists of an interface name and a set of method signatures. The object's interface provides a public contract that describes the operations that are allowed on the PLATFORM_TYPE_LIST table. It defines the behavior of the SQLJ component.

■ The ObservationAdaptor implementation class provides, in this scenario, only the method definitions of the SQLJ component. You may create additional classes that extend the implementation class to provide the method bodies. The design offers a lot of flexibility, as you may decide to create several child classes where each provides a method body for a specific method definition.

■ The PlatWrap class is a Java class that wraps or maps the PLATFORM_ Type Oracle type. It provides a set of getter and setter methods that allow you to treat and manipulate the PLATFORM_TYPE SQL data type as a regular Java object. The getter and setter methods allow you to get and to set the value of data members, respectively.

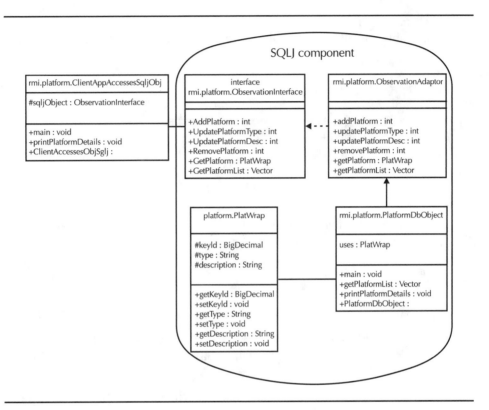

FIGURE 9-3. *High-level view of a client and a SQLJ component-based object*

■ The PlatformDbObject child class is a subclass of the
ObservationAdaptor class. The class provides a method body for the
getPlatformList() method. Note that users can examine and manipulate
the SQLJ component only via the public methods defined in the object
interface, and are therefore unaware of how it is implemented.

■ The ClientAppAccessesSqljObj class is a client-side SQLJ application
that uses the SQLJ component.

Developing a SQLJ Component

Here, you will create a SQLJ component and a SQLJ client-side application to
access the component. Note that a software component is also called a *business
object.* In this scenario, the term *business object,* like the term *component,* refers
to an object that performs a set of tasks associated with a particular business
process. Throughout the remainder of this chapter, the terms *SQLJ object, SQLJ*

business object, SQLJ component-based object, or *SQLJ component* will be used interchangeably and all of them will refer to a software component written in SQLJ.

NOTE
All Java programs using JDBC or SQLJ implementation have been recompiled in JDK 1.1.x, 1.2.x, and 1.3 run-time environments using Oracle JDBC drivers (classes111.zip for JDK 1.1.x and classes12.zip for Java 2). All programs have been tested against Oracle8i (releases 8.1.5, 8.1.6, and 8.1.7).

Use the steps listed here to create a SQLJ business object and a client-side SQLJ application that uses the business object:

1. Create the directories that you wish to use to build and deploy your SQLJ component.

2. Create an object `interface: ObservationInterface`.

3. Create an implementation class: `ObservationAdaptor`. Note that both the interface and the implementation class could have been defined in files with the `.sqlj` extension.

4. Create the `PlatWrap` Java class that maps the `PLATFORM_TYPE` Oracle type. This class provides all the `getter` and `setter` methods to manipulate the `PLATFORM_TYPE` SQL data type. Remember that you defined the `PLATFORM_TYPE` in Listing 9-1.

5. Create the `PlatformDbObject` SQLJ class, defined in a file with the `.sqlj` extension, which extends the implementation class. This SQLJ application provides the method body for the `getPlatformList()` method defined in the `ObservationInterface` interface.

6. Compile the classes from steps 2 to 5. Use the `javac` compiler and the SQLJ translator to do so.

7. Run the `PlatformDbObject` class to make sure it delivers the expected result. You do so either at the command line by invoking the JVM (for example, `java PlatformDbObject`) or by using the facility of the tool that you use to develop the source code.

8. Create the `ClientAppAccessesSqljObj` SQLJ client-side application that uses the SQLJ business object.

9. Recompile all the programs as you did in step 6.

10. Run the client-side application, the `ClientAppAccessesSqljObj`.

Step 1 Create the directories that you wish to use to build and deploy your SQLJ component.

```
// Create the directories to store the Java and SQLJ source code
mkdir buildobjects\rmi\platform

// Create the directories to store
// the Java classes and the SQLJ .ser classes
mkdir deployobjects\rmi\platform
```

Step 2 Create an object interface: `ObservationInterface`. As you create a program, you might wish to compile it immediately so that you can correct any syntax errors. If you decide to do so, remember to set your CLASSPATH as specified in step 6 of this section.

```
/*      Program Name: ObservationInterface.java   (See Note 1.)
**      Purpose:      A java interface to query the
**      obsschema schema stored in Oracle8i data server.
*/

package rmi.platform;            // (See Note 2.)

import java.sql.SQLException;
import java.util.*;

public interface ObservationInterface {   // (See Note 3.)

    int addPlatform (PlatWrap p)
            throws SQLException; // (See Note 4.)

    int updatePlatformType (int platformId, String type)
            throws SQLException; // (See Note 5.)

    int updatePlatformDesc (int platformId, String desc)
            throws SQLException;

    int removePlatform (int platformId)
            throws SQLException;  // (See Note 6.)

    PlatWrap getAPlatform(int platformId)
            throws SQLException; // (See Note 7.)
```

```
    Vector getPlatformList()
            throws SQLException;  // (See Note 8.)
}  // End of ObservationInterface interface
```

Notes on the `ObservationInterface` interface:

1. Program documentation. This section is optional but is highly recommended.

2. This statement defines the package name, `rmi.platform`. The Java programming language requires a mapping between the fully qualified package name of a class and the directory path to that class. This mapping lets the Java compiler know the directory in which to find the class files mentioned in a program. Before you begin writing any code in Java, you should decide on package and directory names. Do not be surprised, however, if you need to change your design in the future.

3. This statement declares the `ObservationInterface` interface. Remember that the behavior of an object is defined and possibly described in its `interface`, remember also that client-side programs can only access the object via the entry points defined in the object's `interface`.

4. This statement defines a method signature to add a row of data of type `PlatWrap` to the `PLATFORM_TYPE_LIST` table stored in the Oracle8*i*/9*i* data server. Note the clause `throws SQLException`, which defines the exception mechanism for database applications. Remember that a method signature consists of a method name and its parameter names and types, along with its return values and exceptions.

5. This statement and the one that follows it define two method signatures that can change the values of the column attributes `type` and `description`, respectively.

6. This statement defines a method signature that removes a row of data from the `PLATFORM_TYPE_LIST` table.

7. This statement defines a method that returns an object of type `PlatWrap`.

8. This statement defines a method that returns a Java `Vector` of `PlatWrap` objects.

Step 3   Create an implementation class: `ObservationAdaptor`. Remember that both the interface and the implementation class could have been defined in files with the `.sqlj` extension.

```
/*    Program Name: ObservationAdaptor.java
**    Purpose:      A java Class that implements
```

```
** the ObservationInterface class to
** query the obsschema stored in Oracle8i. This
** implementation class provides ONLY the method
** definitions for all the methods specified
** in the ObservationInterface interface
*/

package rmi.platform;

import java.sql.SQLException;
import java.util.*;

public class ObservationAdaptor
     implements ObservationInterface  {    // (See Note 1.)
//  Method definition to add a new PlatWrap object in the database.
    public int addPlatform (PlatWrap p)
          throws SQLException {

       return 0;
    }    // End of addPlatform
//  Method definition to change the type attribute in the database.
    public int updatePlatformType (int platformId, String type)
          throws SQLException {

       return 0;
    }    // End of updatePlatformType
//  Method definition to change the description attribute.
    public int updatePlatformDesc (int platformId, String desc)
           throws SQLException {

       return 0;
    }    // End of updatePlatformDesc
//  Method definition to remove a PlatWrap object.
    public int removePlatform (int platformId)
          throws SQLException {

       return 0;
    }    // End of removePlatform
//  Method definition to get a specific PlatWrap object
//  whose key_id = platformId.
    public PlatWrap getAPlatform(int platformId)
          throws SQLException {

       return null;
    }   // End of getAPlatform

//  Method definition to get a list of all the PlatWrap objects.
    public Vector getPlatformList()
```

```
      throws SQLException {

   return null;
 }   // End of getPlatformList
}    // End of ObservationAdaptor class
```

Note on the `ObservationAdaptor` class:

I. This statement declares an implementation class for the SQLJ object.
   Note that the implements clause is part of the class definition. For more
   flexibility, the `ObservationAdaptor` class provides only the method
   definitions for the `ObservationInterface` interface. Remember that
   in Java, when a class declares that it implements an interface, a contract is
   formed between the class and the compiler. By entering into this contract,
   the class agrees that it will provide method bodies or definitions for each of
   the method signatures declared in that interface.

Step 4   Create the `PlatWrap` Java class that maps the `PLATFORM_TYPE` Oracle
type. This class provides all the `getter` and `setter` methods to manipulate the
`PLATFORM_TYPE` SQL data type.

```
/*      Program Name:      PlatWrap.java
**
**      Purpose:           Serialize the PlatformType class
**
*/

package rmi.platform;

import java.math.BigDecimal;

public class PlatWrap
     implements java.io.Serializable {    // (See Note 1.)

 // Declare data members
 protected BigDecimal keyId;
 protected String type;
 protected String description;

 // Default constructor
 public PlatWrap() {
 }   // End of constructor

 // Parameterized constructor that initializes
 // the data members with the input parameters.
 public PlatWrap(BigDecimal keyId,
```

```
                  String type, String description ) {
  this.keyId = keyId;
  this.type = type;
  this.description = description;
}    // End of constructor

// getter method returns the value of the keyId
// data member that has been previously set
// by the setKeyId() method
public java.math.BigDecimal getKeyId() {
  return keyId;
}

// setter method that assigns the input parameter
// to the keyId data member.
public void setKeyId(BigDecimal keyId) {
  this.keyId = keyId;
}
// getter method returns the value of the type
// data member that has been previously set
// by the setType() method
public String getType() {
  return type;
}
// setter method that assigns the input parameter
// to the type data member.
public void setType(String type) {
  this.type = type;
}
// getter method returns the value of the description
// data member that has been previously set
// by the setDescription () method
public String getDescription() {
  return description;
}
 // setter method that assigns the input parameter
// to the description data member.
public void setDescription(String description) {
  this.description = description;
}
} // End of PlatWrap class
```

Note on the `PlatWrap` class:

This class provides a getter and a setter method for each column attribute of the `PLATFORM_TYPE_LIST` table. Note the use of the `this` Java keyword in the parameterized constructor, as well as in the `getter` methods. Remember that the keyword `this` refers to the immediate object and removes the ambiguity between the member variables of the class and the arguments of the constructor and the methods. (See Appendix B to learn more about the `this` keyword and other Java constructs.)

1. This statement defines the `PlatWrap` class as a Java serializable object. A Java class becomes a serializable object when it implements the `java.io.Serializable` interface. When you create a serialized object, Java stores the state of the object in a stream—a sequence of bytes. It does so with sufficient information so that the object can be reconstructed at the receiving end of the stream. The concept of serialization is very important when you want to ship Java objects across a network. For example, Java requires processes called *marshaling* and *unmarshaling* in order to send data across different address spaces. Marshaling packs a method call's parameters (at a client's space) or return values (at a server's space) into a standard format for transmission. Unmarshaling, the reverse operation, unpacks the standard format to an appropriate data presentation in the address space of a receiving process. Marshaling and unmarshaling can only be used on serialized objects. The SQLJ application that you are developing does not require that the `PlatWrap` be a serialized object, but the RMI and the EJB applications that you will develop in the subsequent sections do require a serialized object.

Step 5   Create the `PlatformDbObject` SQLJ class, defined in a file with the `.sqlj` extension, that extends the implementation class. This SQLJ application provides the method body for the `getPlatformList()` method defined in the `Observation Interface` interface. Note that the class also provides the `print Platform Details()` method for displaying the column attributes of the table. This method is only visible within the scope of the `PlatformDbObject` class. No other program can access it. This method was created only to enable you to test the SQLJ application before creating the client application. After testing the output from the class, you may remove it from the `PlatformDbObject` class if you want.

```
/*     Program Name: PlatformDbObject.sqlj
**     Purpose:      A SQLJ Class that extends the
**  ObservationAdaptor and fully implements the
**  getPlatformList(): Vector from the ObservationInterface
**  to query the obsschema schema stored in Oracle8i/9i
*/

package rmi.platform;

// Required SQLJ classes for any SQLJ program
import sqlj.runtime.*;
import sqlj.runtime.ref.*;
```

```
// Required Oracle classes for Oracle database
import oracle.sql.*;
import oracle.sqlj.runtime.Oracle;
import oracle.jdbc.driver.*;

import java.sql.*;
import java.math.BigDecimal;
import java.util.Vector;

// (See Note 1.)
public class PlatformDbObject extends ObservationAdaptor {

    // Declare a named iterator
    #sql iterator PlatformColumnIter (int  aPlatformId,
      String aType, String aDesc); // (See Note 2.)

    public PlatformDbObject () {
      try {
          // Instantiate Default Context for the database server
          Oracle.connect(PlatformDbObject.class,
            "connect.properties");  // (See Note 3.)
      } // end try
      catch (Exception ex) {
        System.err.println(" Contructor Error from "
          + "PlatformDbObject: " + ex);
      } // end catch
    } // end constructor

  public static void main(String [] args)
     throws SQLException {

    PlatformDbObject app = new PlatformDbObject();

    // Stop program execution because I cannot connect to DB.
    // (See Note 4.)
    if ( DefaultContext.getDefaultContext() == null ) {
        System.out.println("I cannot connect to the database"
            + " -- Stop executing PlatformDbObject.sqlj");
        System.exit(1);
    } // End if

    // Retrieve platform data from the database (See Note 5.)
    Vector platformVector = app.getPlatformList();
    if (platformVector == null) {
        System.out.println("No records found ");
        System.exit(1);
    } // End if
```

```
    // Create an array of PlatFormType
    PlatWrap[] platformTypes =
      new PlatWrap[platformVector.size ()];   // (See Note 6.)

    // Copy the vector content into the PlatFormType[]
    platformVector.copyInto(platformTypes);    // (See Note 7.)

    // Print the details
    printPlatformDetails(platformTypes);      // (See Note 8.)
  }  // End main()

public Vector getPlatformList()throws SQLException {

    // Use platformVector to store PlatFormType objects
    Vector platformVector = new Vector();

    // Use PlatformColumnIter to retrieve
    // rows of data from PLATFORM_TYPE_LIST table
    PlatformColumnIter aPlatformColumnIter = null;

    try {
        #sql aPlatformColumnIter =          // (See Note 9.)
            { SELECT P.key_id AS aPlatformId,
                     P.type AS aType,
                     P.description AS aDesc
              FROM PLATFORM_TYPE_LIST P
            };

        while (aPlatformColumnIter.next()) {  // (See Note 10.)

          int keyId = aPlatformColumnIter.aPlatformId();
          String type = aPlatformColumnIter.aType();
          String description = aPlatformColumnIter.aDesc();

          // Instantiate aPlatformType  (See Note 11.)
          PlatWrap aPlatformType = new PlatWrap();

          // Set the data members of the aPlatformType object
          // (See Note 12.)
          aPlatformType.setKeyId(new BigDecimal(keyId));
          aPlatformType.setType(type);
          aPlatformType.setDescription(description);

          // add a PlatformType object to the platformVector
          // (See Note 13.)
          platformVector.addElement(aPlatformType);
        }  // End while
```

```
        // Close the SQLJ iterator
        aPlatformColumnIter.close();
    }   // End of try
    catch (SQLException e) {
            e.printStackTrace();
    }   // End of catch

    System.out.println("Number of records found: "
            + platformVector.size());
    return platformVector;   // (See Note 14.)

}   // End getPlatformList()

public static void printPlatformDetails(PlatWrap[] p)
    throws SQLException {
    if ( p[0].getKeyId()== null )  {
        System.out.println("Platforms do not exist ");
        return;
    }   // End if

    int i;
    for (i = 0; i < p.length; i++) {    // (See Note 15.)
        System.out.println(
          ((p[i].getKeyId()==null) ?
              "NULL keyId" : p[i].getKeyId().toString())
              + " " + ((p[i].getType()==null) ?
              "NULL type" : p[i].getType())
              + " " + ((p[i].getDescription()==null) ?
              "NULL description" : p[i].getDescription()) );
    } // End of for loop

}   // End printPlatformDetails ()

}  // End of PlatformDbObject class
```

Notes on the `PlatformDbObject` SQLJ application:

1. This statement declares the `PlatformDbObject` class as a subclass of
the `ObservationAdaptor` class (see Appendix B for a definition and
examples of Java subclasses).

2. This iterator declaration clause declares a named iterator, the
`PlatformColumnIter`, which is used to select rows from the
`PLATFORM_TYPE_LIST` table. Remember that when you specify
an iterator in a SQLJ application, SQLJ generates a class named

`PlatformColumnIter`. (See Chapters 2 and 3 to learn more about SQLJ iterators.)

3. This statement uses the `Oracle.connect()` method to create an instance of the `DefaultContext` class. The method installs the new connection as the static default context. The database connection uses the JDBC driver, URL, listener port, Oracle SID, username, and user password parameters listed in the properties file. (See Chapters 2 and 5 to learn more about the `Oracle.connect()` method.)

4. This statement uses the `getDefaultContext()` method from the `DefaultContext` class to determine whether a connection instance exists. You will want to stop program execution if the program did not establish a database connection.

5. This statement calls the `getPlatformList()` method and stores the results into a `Vector` variable. The method returns a `Vector` (set) of `PlatWrap` objects.

6. This statement creates an array of `PlatWrap` objects. Note that the array length is equal to the size of the vector that is returned by a call to the `platformVector.size()`. (See Appendix B to learn about Java arrays.)

7. This statement uses the `copyInto()` method from the Java `Vector` class to copy all the vector's elements into the `platformTypes[]` array.

8. This statement calls the `printPlatformDetails()` method to print the objects' values from the `platformTypes[]` array. Note that a class can define methods that are not specified in the `interface`. These methods, however, can only be invoked within the JVM that is running these services. If you later decide to use the SQLJ object as a remote object, the methods that you declare in this class that are not specified in the `interface` cannot be invoked remotely.

9. This assignment clause executes a `SELECT` statement, constructs an iterator object that contains the result table for the `SELECT` statement, and assigns the iterator object to the variable `aPlatformColumnIter`. Note that an execution context instance is associated implicitly with this SQL operation. Also, because the application is using a default connection, it is not necessary to specify a connection context instance. (See Chapters 3 and 5 to learn more about SQLJ iterator, connection, and execution context statements.)

10. The `next()` method, which belongs to the generated class, `PlatformColumnIter`, advances the iterator to successive rows in the SQLJ result set. This method is similar to the `next()` method for the JDBC

ResultSet. The next () method returns a value of true when the next row is available or a value of false when all table rows have been fetched from the iterator. (See Appendix C to learn more about JDBC ResultSet.)

11. This statement creates an instance of the PlatWrap class. You need to store a set of these objects in the platformVector variable.

12. This statement and the two that follow it use the setKeyID(), setType(), and setDescription() methods from the PlatWrap class to set the values for the keyId, type, and description, respectively. Remember that those methods are called setters.

13. This statement adds a PlatWrap object into the platformVector Vector variable.

14. This statement returns a vector of PlatWrap objects.

15. This statement prints all the objects' values from the PlatWrap object array. Note the use of the Java tertiary operator, the "expression ? op 1: op 2," to test for null values. After evaluating the expression p[i].getKeyId()==null, the tertiary operator returns op 1 if the expression evaluates to true or op 2 if it evaluates to false. Remember also that SQL nulls from the database are converted to Java null values. Also note that if the receiving Java type is primitive and an attempt is made to retrieve a SQL null, then a sqlj.runtime.SQLNullException is thrown, and no assignment is made.

Step 6 Compile the classes from steps 2 to 5. Use the javac compiler and the SQLJ translator to do so. Your connect.properties file must reside in the same directory as the .class files that the programs generated. The .class files are located in the device:\deployobjects\rmi\platform directory, where device is a driver letter (see Listing 9-2).

Listing 9-2

```
// At the command line
// First:   Set your CLASSPATH.
set CLASSPATH=%CLASSPATH%;device:\buildobjects

// Go to the directory that you created in Step 1
cd device:\buildobjects\rmi\platform

// Compile all programs using the SQLJ Translator.
// The *.java allows you to compile all Java source code.
// The "-d" option sends the classes to the deployobjects directory
sqlj -profile=false -d=device:\deployobjects
  PlatformDbObject.sqlj *.java
```

Step 7 Run the `PlatformDbObject` class to make sure it delivers the expected result. You do so either at the command line by invoking the JVM (for example, `java PlatformDbObject`) or by using the facility of the tool that you use to develop the source code (see Listing 9-3).

Listing 9-3
Here is the generated output that will be created when you run the `PlatformDbObject` SQLJ application:

```
// At the command line
// First:   Set your CLASSPATH.
set CLASSPATH=%CLASSPATH%device:\deployobjects;

// Go to the deployobjects directory
cd device:\deployobjects\rmi\platform

// Execute the following command to run the SQLJ application
java rmi.platform.PlatformDbObject
```

Note that you must qualify the name of the program with its package name. This maps the fully qualified package name of a class and the directory path to that class. The mapping lets the Java compiler know the directory in which to find the class files mentioned in a program. In Listing 9-3, you run the program using the package name, `rmi.platform`. When you run the `rmi.platform.PlatformDbObject`, you get the following output:

```
// Resuting output after running
// the rmi.platform.PlatformDbObject class
Number of records found: 6
1   SURFACE MOORED_BUOY_OCEANIC
2   SURFACE CMAN_OCEANIC
3   OTHER SCIENTIST
4   SURFACE MOORED_BUOY_OCEANIC
5   SURFACE CMAN_OCEANIC
6   OTHER SCIENTIST
```

Step 8 Create the `ClientAppAccessesSqljObj` SQLJ client-side application that uses the SQLJ business object. Note that you could easily write the `ClientAppAccessesSqljObj` class using a JDBC implementation versus a SQLJ implementation. The point in this book is to teach you how to write Java programs using SQLJ.

```
/*    Program Name:      ClientAppAccessesSqljObj.sqlj
**
**    Purpose:           This SQLJ application will access
**    the SQLJ object via the interface ObservationInterface.
```

```
*/

package rmi.platform;

// Required SQLJ classes for any SQLJ program
import sqlj.runtime.*;
import sqlj.runtime.ref.*;

// Required Oracle classes for Oracle database
import oracle.sql.*;
import oracle.sqlj.runtime.Oracle;
import oracle.jdbc.driver.*;

import java.sql.*;
import java.math.BigDecimal;
import java.util.*;
import java.util.Vector;

public class ClientAppAccessesSqljObj {

  // (See Note 1.)
  protected static ObservationInterface sqljObject;
  public ClientAppAccessesSqljObj()
    throws SQLException {

    // Connect to the database
    sqljObject = new PlatformDbObject();    // (See Note 2.)
  } // End of constructor

  public static void main(String[] args)
    throws SQLException  {

    ClientAppAccessesSqljObj app =
            new ClientAppAccessesSqljObj();

    if  (DefaultContext.getDefaultContext() == null ) {
        System.out.println("I cannot connect to "
                   + "the database "
                   + "-- Stop Execution.");
        System.exit(1);
    }    // End if

    // Declare a platform vector
    Vector platformVector = null;

    try {
        platformVector =
          sqljObject.getPlatformList();  // (See Note 3.)
```

```
    }     // End of try
    catch (SQLException ex) {
        System.out.println("Error calling the SQLJ"
                + " object " + ex + "\n");
        String sqlMessage = ex.getMessage();
        System.out.println("SQL Message: "
                + sqlMessage + "\n");
        System.exit(1);
    }   // end of catch

    try {
        // Print the details
        printPlatformDetails(platformVector); // (See Note 4.)
    }   // End of try
    catch (SQLException ex) {
        System.out.println("Error printing platform"
                + " details " + ex + "\n");
        String sqlMessage = ex.getMessage();
        System.out.println("SQL Message: "
                + sqlMessage + "\n");
    }   // end of catch
}   // End of main()

public static void printPlatformDetails(Vector platformVector)
    throws SQLException {
    if (platformVector == null) {
        System.out.println("No Data FOUND");
        return;
    }   // End if

    PlatWrap p = null;
    Enumeration enum = platformVector.elements();

    // Iterate to get the column
    // attributes from the table
    while (enum.hasMoreElements()) {    // (See Note 5.)
        // Get PlatformType from the platformVector
        p = (PlatWrap)enum.nextElement();

        // Get the column values
        System.out.println(
            ((p.getKeyId()==null) ? " " : p.getKeyId().toString())
                + " " + ((p.getType()==null) ? " " : p.getType()) + " "
                +((p.getDescription()==null) ? " " : p.getDescription()
                    ) );
    }     // End of while

}   // End of printPlatformDetails()

}   // End of ClientAppAccessesSqljObj class
```

Notes on the `ClientAppAccessesSqljObj` application:

This client application uses the `getPlatformList()` method defined in the SQLJ object's interface, `ObservationInterface`, to query the `PLATFORM_TYPE_LIST` table. It calls the `getPlatformList()` method whose body is in the `PlatformDbObject` SQLJ program. The `ClientAppAccessesSqljObj` application uses its own method, `printPlatformDetails()`, to print the values from a `Vector` variable.

1. This statement declares an instance of the ObservationInterface interface, the `sqljObject`.

2. This statement instantiates `sqljObject` to an object of type `Platform DbObject`. You need to do this because you wish to access the `getPlatformList()` method specified in the interface, ObservationInterface, whose method body resides in the `PlatformDbObject` class.

3. This statement calls the `getPlatformList()` method in the `PlatformDbObject` program.

4. This statement calls the local function `printPlatformDetails()` from the `ClientAppAccessesSqljObj` application to print the values of the objects from the `platformVector` variable. It does *not* call the `printPlatformDetails()` method from the `PlatformDbObject` class. Remember that the latter method is visible only within the scope of the `PlatformDbObject` class. See Note 8 from the "Notes on the `PlatformDbObject` SQLJ application" section of this chapter.

5. This statement uses an object of the Java `Enumeration` type to print the values from the `platformVector` variable.

Step 9 Recompile all the programs as you did in step 6.

```
// Review Step 6 to set your classpath
sqlj -profile=false -d=path\deployobjects PlatformDbObject.sqlj *.java
```

Step 10 Run the client-side application, `ClientAppAccessesSqljObj`.

```
// Set your classpath. Review Step 7 to do so.
java rmi.platform.ClientAppAccessesSqljObj
```

```
// Resulting output
```

```
// Note that you get the same output
// when you ran the rmi.platform.PlatformDbObject class
Number of records found: 6
1   SURFACE MOORED_BUOY_OCEANIC
2   SURFACE CMAN_OCEANIC
3   OTHER SCIENTIST
4   SURFACE MOORED_BUOY_OCEANIC
5   SURFACE CMAN_OCEANIC
6   OTHER SCIENTIST
```

In the next section, you will develop an RMI application that uses the SQLJ business object that you created in the "Designing and Developing a SQLJ Component-Based Object" section of this chapter.

Deploying a SQLJ Component Using the Java Remote Method Invocation

In the previous section, you created a SQLJ component-based object and a client program that uses the object. In that scenario, both the client and SQLJ object resided on the same machine, the `datai` server. In this section, you will develop an application in which a client located on any machine on a network will use a business object that resides on a different machine, possibly on the same network or on a different network. In the situation in which the two objects reside on different machines, you need a mechanism by which these objects can communicate. The Java Remote Method Invocation provides that mechanism.

What Are the Needs of RMI Distributed Object Applications?

The needs of distributed object applications are as follows:

- **Locating remote objects** In this scenario, the remote object can reside in any address space, that is, in any computer on a network. RMI distributed objects use the naming mechanism provided by the `rmiregistry`. You will learn more about the `rmiregistry` in the upcoming, "What Is RMI?", section of this chapter.

- **Communicating with remote objects** RMI handles all communication details for you.

- **Loading class bytecodes that are shipped around** RMI provides the mechanisms to load class bytecodes of your server-side objects. Note that the terms server-side objects refer to Java bytecodes residing in an address space other than the client address space.

Recall that the RMI system allows Java objects running in one Java Virtual Machine (JVM) to invoke Java objects running in another JVM. You learned about this concept in "Basic Concepts of Distributed Computing Systems," earlier in this chapter. Before delving into code, a brief overview of RMI is important.

What Is RMI?

Java RMI provides distributed facilities for software components written in Java. Developing and deploying a distributed application using RMI is fairly quick and easy. RMI uses a network-based registry to keep track of the distributed objects. It depends on a naming mechanism called the *rmiregistry*. RMI allows you to locate Java server-side objects. It transparently handles the details of communication between remote objects so that remote communication looks to the programmer like a standard Java method invocation. One of the central and unique features of RMI is its ability to download the *bytecodes* (or simply *code*) of an object's class without having to define the class in the receiver's JVM. RMI provides the mechanisms for loading an object's code, as well as for transmitting its data. Importantly, RMI passes objects by their true type, thus the behavior of those objects is not changed when they are sent to another JVM. This mechanism allows new types to be introduced into a remote JVM, thus extending the behavior of an application dynamically.

RMI applications can use one of two mechanisms to obtain references to remote objects:

- Register remote objects with the rmiregistry.

- Pass and return remote object references as part of the application's operations.

The rmiregistry runs on a server machine and holds information about the available server objects. A server object makes a method available for remote invocation by binding it to a name in its registry. A Java/RMI client accesses the remote server object by acquiring an object reference to a Java/RMI server object, as illustrated in Figure 9-4. For remote invocation, RMI uses a stub class to call remote objects. The stub acts as a proxy for the remote object. To locate a server object, a client first does a lookup for a server object reference and then invokes methods on the server object as if the server object resided in the client's address space. Alternatively, another Java class can do the lookup. A stub for a remote object implements the same set of remote interfaces that the remote object implements. This allows a stub to be cast to any of the interfaces that the remote object implements.

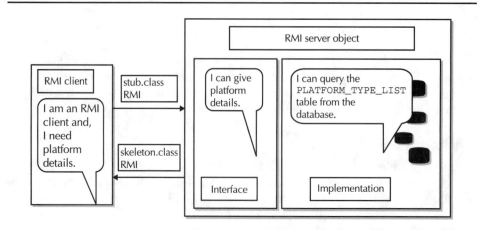

FIGURE 9-4. *RMI client invoking RMI server object*

In this section, you will develop an RMI-based application in which a Java class other than the client, the `RmiPlatformDbObject` class (Figure 9-5), will do the object lookup for you. Note that a Java class acquires a server object via a URL address. You will use a URL to name your server objects the same way you would name an HTML page. For example, the `rmi://datai/PlatformServer` specified in the listing of the `RmiPlatformDbObject` class is the URL address of the server object that you will create. For more information concerning the RMI distributed model, see the Java Remote Method Invocation Specification, http://java.sun.com/ products/jdk/1.2/docs/guide/rmi/spec/rmiTOC.doc.html.

RMI Object Composites

A distributed application built using Java RMI consists, at the minimum, of the following:

- A remote interface that, as in the SQLJ component, specifies the behavior of the RMI object. An object becomes remote by implementing a remote interface. An RMI remote interface must extend the `java.rmi.Remote` interface. The following fragment code defines the `RmiPlatformServer Interface` interface:

```
public interface RmiPlatformServerInterface
        extends java.rmi.Remote {
  // List of methods signatures
  Vector getPlatformList()
     throws RemoteException, SQLException;
    ...
} // End of RmiPlatformServerInterface interface
```

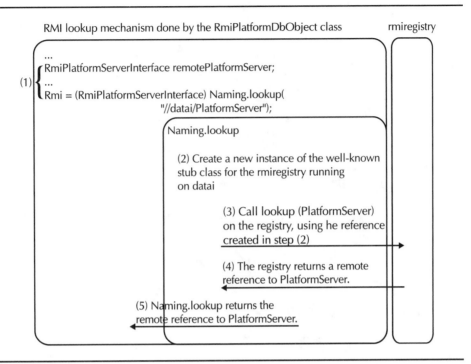

RMI lookup mechanism done by the RmiPlatformDbObject class   rmiregistry

```
...
RmiPlatformServerInterface remotePlatformServer;
(1) ...
Rmi = (RmiPlatformServerInterface) Naming.lookup(
            "//datai/PlatformServer");
```

Naming.lookup

(2) Create a new instance of the well-known
stub class for the rmiregistry running
on datai

(3) Call lookup (PlatformServer)
on the registry, using he reference
created in step (2)

(4) The registry returns a remote
reference to PlatformServer.

(5) Naming.lookup returns the
remote reference to PlatformServer.

FIGURE 9-5.   *RMI lookup mechanism*

NOTE
Each method of the interface must declare
`java.rmi.RemoteException` *in its*
`throws` *clause, in addition to any*
application-specific exceptions.

■ *An implementation class* that specifies the behavior definitions specified by
the object interface and, perhaps, additional methods not published in the
interface. Any object that implements the `RmiPlatformServerInterface`
`interface` becomes a remote object. The following code defines the
`RmiPlatformServerImplementation` implementation class:

```
public class RmiPlatformServerImplementation
    extends java.rmi.server.UnicastRemoteObject
    implements RmiPlatformServerInterface {
    // define in this class all the methods
    // advertised in the RmiPlatformServerInterface
    // and, perhaps, additional methods that you
    // wish to define.
```

```
...
Vector getPlatformList()
  throws RemoteException, SQLException {

    // Method definitions of the same method defines in the
    // RmiPlatformServerInterface interface

    ...
  }
} // End of RmiPlatformServerImplementation class
```

NOTE
Methods of the implementation class not advertised in the interface are not accessible by the client. That is, only those methods defined in a remote interface are available to be called in the receiving JVM.

■ A *client class* that makes requests by invoking methods on the remote objects.

Developing an RMI Object

The RMI object that you will develop here accepts tasks from clients, runs the tasks, and returns the results. The steps to create a distributed version of your SQLJ component using RMI are as follows:

1. Create a high-level view of the RMI-based application.

2. Create a Java `interface` server object, `RmiPlatformServerInterface`.

3. Create a Java implementation server object, `RmiPlatformServerImplementation`.

4. Create a Java class, `RmiPlatformDbObject`, to do the object lookup in the `rmiregistry` located on the `datai` server, get a reference to the SQLJ object, and load its class.

5. Create the `ClientAppAccessesRmiObj` client-side application that uses the remote service.

6. Compile all the classes from steps 2 to 6 including the classes for the SQLJ object.

7. Run the implementation class through the `rmic` compiler to create the stub and skeleton classes for the client and the server.

8. Start the RMI registry.

9. Start the `rmi.platform.RmiPlatformServerImplementation` implementation server class.

10. Start the client.

Step 1 Create a high-level view of the application. Figure 9-6 illustrates this.

Step 2 Create the `RmiPlatformServerInterface` interface. The primary function of the `interface`, like the `ObservationInterface` of the SQLJ business object, is to inform the clients of available methods on the server. The RMI interface defines the remotely accessible operations of your server-side object.

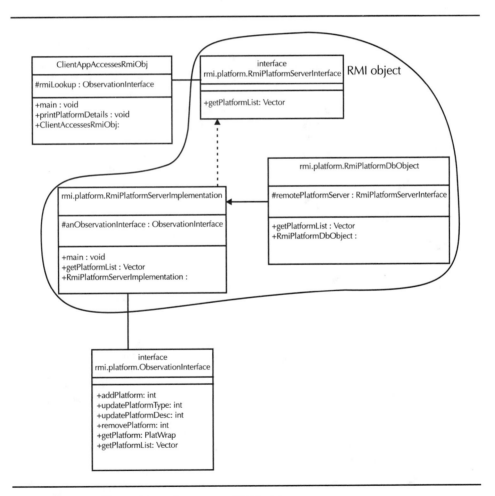

FIGURE 9-6. *RMI object that uses a SQLJ object*

There exists a protocol between an RMI client and the RMI object that allows requests to be submitted to the RMI object, the RMI object to execute the requests, and the results of the request to be returned to the client. This protocol is expressed in interfaces that you design for your object. A client can use the RMI interface, the `RmiPlatformServerInterface`, to submit a query to the RMI object. Your RMI interface consists of one remote method: the `getPlatformList()` method. Note that you may specify as many methods as you wish. If you do so, do not forget to provide the method bodies. Recall that you created the `getPlatformList()` method body in the `PlatformDbObject` SQLJ application in "Designing and Developing a SQLJ Component-Based Object," earlier in this chapter.

```
/*       Program Name: RmiPlatformServerInterface.java   */

package rmi.platform;     // (See Note 1.)

import java.rmi.*;      // (See Note 2.)
import java.sql.SQLException;
import java.util.*;

public interface RmiPlatformServerInterface
    extends java.rmi.Remote { // (See Note 3.)
  // This interface advertises only the getPlatformList() method.
  // When you design an RMI remote interface, you must include
  // in this class all the methods that you want to be accessed by
  // your RMI client.
  Vector getPlatformList()
    throws RemoteException, SQLException;  // (See Note 4.)
}  // End of RmiPlatformServerInterface interface
```

Notes on the `RmiPlatformServerInterface` interface:

1. This statement specifies that the class reside in the same package as the SQLJ business object interface, the `rmi.platform` package.

2. These statements, `java.rmi.*` and `java.sql.SQLException`, make the `java.rmi.*` package and the `java.sql.SQLException` class available to the `RmiPlatformServerInterface` interface.

3. This statement declares a `public interface`. Remember that you must declare this `interface public`, or an error will be generated when a client calls the `getPlatformList()` method. More importantly, an RMI `interface` must extend the `java.rmi.Remote` interface. By extending the `Remote` interface, the `RmiPlatformServerInterface` interface marks itself as one whose methods can be called from any JVM.

4. This statement declares the remote method that can be invoked by a client. Each method specified in the `interface` class must declare `java.rmi.RemoteException` or a superclass of `RemoteException` in its `throws` clause. With RMI-based applications, the Java language reports network-related communication and server problems by throwing `java.rmi.RemoteException` exceptions. In addition to the `RemoteException` in the `throws` clause, you also need to specify any application-specific exceptions. For example, you have to add the `SQLException` in the `throws` clause because the `getPlatformList()` method accesses a database. Also remember that you need to declare the data type of the remote object as the remote interface type. In this program, the Java `Vector` is the return data type.

Step 3   Create the `RmiPlatformServerImplementation` server class. The functions of an RMI remote implementation class are as follows:

■ Implement a remote `interface`.

■ The server needs to create and install the remote objects and get the object ready so that it can accept incoming remote calls. To get the object ready, it needs to be "exported" when the client instantiates the object. The superclass `UnicastRemoteObject` supplies implementations for a number of `java.lang.Object` methods (`equals`, `hashCode`, `toString`) that are defined appropriately for remote objects. It also includes constructors and static methods used to *export* a remote object, that is, make the remote object available to receive incoming calls from clients. To create and install the remote objects, your program needs to use a specific setup procedure. This setup procedure can be encapsulated in a `main()` method in the remote object implementation class itself, or it can be included in another class entirely. Here, we used a `main()` method to do so.

The steps to create and install a remote object are as follows:

1. Create and install a security manager. For example,

```
if (System.getSecurityManager() == null) {
        System.setSecurityManager(new
RMISecurityManager());
}  // End if
```

2. Create one or more instances of the remote object. For example,

```
// Create an instance of the remote object
// located in the rmiregistry
```

```
RmiPlatformServerImplementation myServer =
            new RmiPlatformServerImplementation();
```

3. Register at least one of the remote objects with the rmiregistry. Note that you could use another naming service such as Java Naming and Directory Interface (JNDI). You will use JNDI when you develop your Enterprise JavaBeans and CORBA objects later on in this chapter. For example,

```
Naming.rebind("//data-i.com/PlatformServer", myServer);
```

NOTE
With Java 2, you can extend the `java.rmi.activation.Activatable` *class (used to construct remote objects that can execute on demand) instead of* `UnicastRemoteObject`. *If you extend* `Activatable` *you need to export the remote object by calling either the* `Unicast RemoteObject.exportObject` *or* `Activatable.exportObject` *method explicitly from your class's constructor (or another initialization method, as appropriate).*

4. Declare a constructor that throws a `java.rmi.RemoteException` and any application-specific exceptions. For example,

```
public RmiPlatformServerImplementation ()
    throws RemoteException, SQLException {
    ...
}  // End of constructor
```

Here is the listing of the `RmiPlatformServerImplementation` class:

```
/*      Program Name:    RmiPlatformServerImplementation.java
**
**      Purpose:         This is the RMI implements class.
*/

package rmi.platform;

import java.rmi.server.*;        // (See Note 1.)
import java.rmi.*;
import java.sql.SQLException;
import java.util.*;

public class RmiPlatformServerImplementation
```

```
  extends java.rmi.server.UnicastRemoteObject
  implements RmiPlatformServerInterface {  // (See Note 2.)
// (See Note 3.)
protected ObservationInterface anObservationInterface;

public RmiPlatformServerImplementation ()
  throws RemoteException, SQLException {  // (See Note 4.)
  // (See Note 5.)
  anObservationInterface = new PlatformDbObject();
}  // End of constructor

public Vector getPlatformList()
  throws RemoteException, SQLException {  // (See Note 6.)

  Vector platformVector = null;
  // (See Note 7.)
  platformVector = anObservationInterface.getPlatformList();
  return platformVector;
}  // End of getPlatformList()

public static void main(String[] args) {

  // Create and install a security manager
  if (System.getSecurityManager() == null) {  // (See Note 8.)
     System.setSecurityManager(new RMISecurityManager());
  }  // End if

  try {
     // Create an instance of the remote object
     // located in the rmiregistry
     // (See Note 9.)
     RmiPlatformServerImplementation myServer =
              new RmiPlatformServerImplementation();
     System.out.println("Binding the object");

     // Bind this object instance to the name PlatformServer.
     // Add the name that identifies the remote object in the
     // registry to the RMI registry running on the server
     // DO NOT FORGET TO CHANGE 'data-i.com' TO YOUR HOST NAME.
     // (See Note 10.)
     Naming.rebind("//data-i.com/PlatformServer", myServer);
     System.out.println("Platform Server ready!");
  }  // End of try
  catch (Exception e) {
     System.out.println(e.getMessage());
     e.printStackTrace();
  }  // End of catch
```

```
    }   // End of main()

}   // End of RmiPlatformServerImplementation class
```

Notes on the `RmiPlatformServerImplementation` class:

1. This statement makes the `java.rmi.server.*` and the `java.rmi.*` packages available to the class.

2. In the Java language, a remote object implementation must implement, at a minimum, one remote `interface`. This statement implements the `RmiPlatformServerInterface` interface and extends the `java.rmi.server.UnicastRemoteObject` interface class. `UnicastRemoteObject` is a convenience class, defined in the RMI public API, that can be used as a superclass for remote object implementations. The superclass `UnicastRemoteObject` supplies implementations for a number of `java.lang.Object` methods (`equals`, `hashCode`, `toString`) so that they are defined appropriately for remote objects. `UnicastRemoteObject` also includes constructors and static methods used to make the remote object available to receive incoming calls from clients. The `java.rmi.server.UnicastRemoteObject` class provides the capability to create a remote object that can use RMI's default socket-based transport for communication between a client and a server and also enables the `RmiPlatformServerImplementation` class to run all the time. A remote object implementation does not have to extend `UnicastRemoteObject`, but any implementation that does not must supply appropriate implementations of the `java.lang.Object` methods. Alternatively to extending `UnicastRemoteObject`, you may extend `java.rmi.activation.Activatable` (JDK 1.2, used to construct remote objects that can execute on demand). In this scenario, you export the remote object by calling either the `UnicastRemoteObject.exportObject` or `Activatable.exportObject` method explicitly from your class's constructor (or another initialization method, as appropriate).

3. This statement creates a variable of type `ObservationInterface`. Remember that you should use the SQLJ object you created in the "Designing and Developing a SQLJ Component-Based Object" section of this chapter. Note that you can only access the object via its access points as specified in the object's interface.

4. This statement declares the constructor for the remote object. This constructor, like any other Java constructor, calls the constructor of its superclass, `java.rmi.server.UnicastRemoteObject`, which allows an instance of the class to be exported. Exporting a remote object makes

the object available to accept incoming remote requests by listening for incoming calls to the remote object on an anonymous or designated port number. When you instantiate the `RmiPlatformServerImplementation` class via a call to its constructor, the class will automatically be exported. Remember that Java requires that you include the `RemoteException` in the `throws` clause, even if the constructor does nothing else. If you forget the constructor, the `javac` compiler will generate an error.

5. This statement creates an instance of the `PlatformDbObject` class and stores the result in a variable of type `ObservationInterface`. You can use the instance to call the `getPlatformType()` method, whose method body resides in the `PlatformDbObject` class.

6. This method declaration includes the `RemoteException` and the application-specific exception, the `SQLException`. This class provides the method body as required.

7. This statement calls the `getPlatformList()` method of the `PlatformDbObject` using RMI. This method implements the protocol between the RMI object and its clients. Clients (or callers) submit a request (in this example, making a query), and the RMI object executes the query and returns the results directly to the callers.

8. First, the `main()` method of the class must create and install a security manager. This is done by invoking the `System.getSecurity Manager()` method from the `RmiSecurityManager` class. The security manager guarantees that the loaded class performs only the allowed operations. RMI clients or servers cannot load a class when there is no security manager. Second, the `main()` creates an instance of the remote object implementation and binds that instance to a name in the rmiregistry.

9. The first statement in the `try` block creates an instance of the remote object. Upon instantiation, the remote object is exported and is, therefore, ready to receive incoming requests from clients.

10. This statement registers the remote object in the rmiregistry on the `datai` server with the name `PlatformServer`. Remember that an rmiregistry is a server name service that allows remote clients to get a reference to a remote object. Also, the rmiregistry binds a URL-formatted name of the form `"//localhost/YourObjectBindingName"`, where `localhost` is your host, like `data-i`, and `YourObjectBindingName` is a user-defined string, like the `PlatformServer` string. Once you register a remote object in the rmiregistry, clients can do object lookups using the URL-formatted name that you defined in the program. In this example, clients will use the

//datai/PlatformServer URL to get a reference to the remote object associated with this name. Note that the rmiregistry runs on a default port number, 1099. You may use a port number other than the default, but then you will need to specify the port number explicitly. For example, you could use port number 1620. If you do, you must specify the 1620 port in your program: "//datai:1620/PlatformServer". The myServer is a reference to the object implementation on which remote methods will be invoked. Remote implementation objects never leave the JVM where they are created. Clients that do remote requests always get a serialized instance of the implementation stub class and never get an actual copy of the object. For example, clients will get an instance of the RmiPlatformServer Implementation_Stub class. The stub and the skeleton classes will be generated in step 7 of this section, in which you will invoke the rmic compiler. Since clients get a reference to the remote object instead of an actual copy, they need to reconstruct the object in their address space. This is one of the reasons why Java requires that the object be serialized. Remember that Java stores a serializable object in a stream with sufficient information to reconstruct the object. Note that for security reasons in the Java language, an application can only bind or unbind an object on the rmiregistry running on the same host. Object lookups, however, can be done from any host.

Step 4   Create a Java class, the RmiPlatformDbObject class, to get a reference to the SQLJ object and load its class.

```
/*      Program Name:    RmiPlatformDbObject.java
**
**      Purpose:         This class does a lookup to
** get the server object reference.
*/

package rmi.platform;

import java.rmi.*;      // (See Note 1.)
import java.sql.SQLException;
import java.util.*;

public class RmiPlatformDbObject
        extends ObservationAdaptor {    // (See Note 2.)

  protected RmiPlatformServerInterface remotePlatformServer;

  public RmiPlatformDbObject ()
        throws RemoteException, SQLException {  // (See Note 3.)
```

```
    try {
        if (System.getSecurityManager() == null) { // (See Note 4.)
            System.setSecurityManager(new RMISecurityManager());
        }    // End if

        // (See Note 5.)
        remotePlatformServer =
            (RmiPlatformServerInterface)
              Naming.lookup("rmi://data-i.com/PlatformServer");

        System.out.println ("Naming lookup WORKED");
    }   // End of try
    catch (Exception e) {
        System.out.println ("Naming lookup did not work");
        e.printStackTrace();
    }   // End of catch()

  }   // End of constructor

  public Vector getPlatformList()
      throws SQLException {

    Vector platformVector = null;
    try {      // (See Note 6.)
        platformVector =
            remotePlatformServer.getPlatformList();
    }   // End of try
    catch (RemoteException e) {    // (See Note 7.)
        e.printStackTrace();
    }   // End of catch

    return platformVector;

  }   // End of getPlatformList()

}   // End of RmiPlatformDbObject class
```

Notes on the `RmiPlatformDbObject` class:

1. This statement makes the `java.rmi` package available to the program. RMI clients need some classes from this package such as the `Naming` and `RemoteException` classes.

2. This statement extends the `ObservationInterface` interface of the SQLJ object.

3. This statement creates a Java variable, the remotePlatformServer, of type RmiPlatformServerInterface.

4. This statement will create and install a security manager if none is present.

5. This statement does an object lookup by calling the Naming.lookup() method. This method will return a reference to the remote object implementation from the rmiregistry on the data-i server. The Naming. lookup() method uses a format similar to the Naming.rebind() method from Note 10 in the "Notes on the RmiPlatformServerImplementation class" part of this section. The string, "rmi://data-i/PlatformServer", specifies that you wish to get a reference of the remote object called PlatformServer from the rmiregistry located on the datai server. The Naming.lookup() method, with the arguments that you provide, will construct an instance of the RmiPlatformServerImplementation_ Stub class and will return this instance to the program. Then the program will use the stub instance to load the stub class from the CLASSPATH. The RmiPlatformServerImplementation_Stub class will be generated in step 7 when you run the RmiPlatformServerImplementation class through the rmic compiler.

6. This statement calls the getPlatformList() method specified in the RmiPlatformServerInterface interface class, whose body resides in the PlatformDbObject class.

7. The method does not use the RemoteException in its throws clause, but instead it does so in a catch block.

Step 5   Create the ClientAppAccessesRmiObj client-side application that uses the remote service.

The ClientAppAccessesSqljObj SQLJ client that you created in the "Designing and Developing a SQLJ Component-Based Object" section, earlier in this chapter is similar to the RMI client, but these clients differ from each other in the way that each accesses the business object. In the previous section, you created an application in which both client and business objects resided in the same address space, in the same computer. If you want to move the client code to another computer, you have to move the business object code to the same computer because you did not provide the mechanism for the client to remotely access the SQLJ component.

In this application, you use RMI, which provides the mechanism to remotely access the SQLJ component, where both client and server objects reside in different address spaces. In this scenario, the RMI client code can reside anywhere on a network (possibly in another computer), independent of the location of the SQLJ component code. RMI allows the client to invoke a remote method by making a call to a client stub class (referred to as a *proxy*). The client proxy packs the call parameters into a request message and invokes the JRMP wire protocol to ship the message to the server. The server-side stub, called a *skeleton,* unpacks the message and calls the actual method on the object.

```
/*      Program Name:       ClientAppAccessesRmiObj.java
**
**      Purpose:            This Java application will access
**  a remote object using JAVA RMI.
*/
package rmi.platform;

import java.awt.*;
import java.io.*;
import java.sql.*;
import java.util.*;

// Mandatory Java classes for RMI calls
import java.rmi.Naming;
import java.rmi.RemoteException;

public class ClientAppAccessesRmiObj {

  protected static ObservationInterface rmiLookup;  // (See Note 1.)

  public ClientAppAccessesRmiObj()
      throws RemoteException, SQLException {

    // Connect to the database
    rmiLookup = new RmiPlatformDbObject();  // (See Note 2.)

  }  // End of constructor

  public static void main(String[] args)
      throws RemoteException, SQLException  {

    try {
        ClientAppAccessesRmiObj app =
              new ClientAppAccessesRmiObj();
    }  // End of try
    catch (Exception ex) {
       System.out.println("Cannot Instantiate  "
           + "the RmiPlatformDbObject class ");
       System.exit(1);
    }  // End of catch

    // Declare a platform vector
```

```
    Vector platformVector = null;

    try {
        platformVector =
            rmiLookup.getPlatformList();   // (See Note 3.)
    }    // End of try
    catch (SQLException ex) {
        System.out.println("Error calling the SQLJ"
                + " object " + ex + "\n");
        String sqlMessage = ex.getMessage();
        System.out.println("SQL Message: "
                + sqlMessage + "\n");
        System.exit(1);
    }   // End of catch

    try {
        // Print the details
        printPlatformDetails(platformVector);
    }   // End of try
    catch (SQLException ex) {
        System.out.println("Error printing platform"
                + " details " + ex + "\n");
        String sqlMessage = ex.getMessage();
        System.out.println("SQL Message: "
                + sqlMessage + "\n");
    }   // End of catch

}   // End of main()

public static void printPlatformDetails(Vector platformVector)
    throws SQLException {
  if  (platformVector == null) {
        System.out.println("No Data FOUND");
        return;
  }  // End if

  PlatWrap p = null;
  Enumeration enum = platformVector.elements();

  // Iterate to get the column
  // attributes from the table
  while (enum.hasMoreElements()) {
     // Get PlatformType from the platformVector
     p = (PlatWrap)enum.nextElement();
     // Get the column values
     System.out.println(
       ((p.getKeyId()==null) ? " " : p.getKeyId().toString())
          + " " + ((p.getType()==null) ? " " : p.getType()) + " "
```

```
                + ((p.getDescription()==null) ? " " : p.getDescription()
                ) );
    }     // End of while

  }   // End of printPlatformDetails()

} // End of ClientAppAccessesRmiObj class
```

Notes on the `ClientAppAccessesRmiObj` client:

1. This statement creates a Java variable of type `ObservationInterface` named `rmilookup`. Remember that you want to access the SQLJ object from this client.

2. This statement creates an instance of the `RmiPlatformDbObject` class and stores it in the `rmilookup` variable.

3. This statement calls the `getPlatformList()` method, whose body resides in the `PlatformDbObject` class. When a client invokes the remote `getPlatformList()` method, the client's JVM looks at the `RmiPlatformServerImplementation_Stub` class. The class defined within the stub is an image of the server class. The client's request is then routed to the skeleton class located on the server, the `RmiPlatform-ServerImplementation_Skel` class, which in turn calls the appropriate method on the server. In this scenario, the stub acts as a proxy to the skeleton and the skeleton is a proxy to the actual object's method. Finally, RMI serializes the `PlatWrap` objects and returns them to the client.

Step 6   Compile all the classes from steps 2 to 6 including the classes for the SQLJ object (see Listing 9-4). Set your `CLASSPATH` and recompile all the programs in the `rmi.platform` package. To do so, review step 6 from the "Designing and Developing a SQLJ Component-Based Object" section of this chapter.

Listing 9-4

```
// Set your CLASSPATH in a similar manner as you did in Step 6
// of the previous section. Then recompile all classes.
sqlj -profile=false -d=path\deployobjects
    PlatformDbObject.sqlj *.java
```

Step 7   Run the implementation class through the `rmic` compiler to create the stub and skeleton classes for the client-side and server-side object, respectively. Run the compiler on the fully qualified class filename, `rmi.platform.RmiPlatform ServerImplementation`, that contains the remote object implementation. When you invoke the `rmic` compiler (Listing 9-5), the compiler generates the class files `RmiPlatformServerImplementation_Stub.class` and `RmiPlatform`

`ServerImplementation_Skel.class`. The generated stub classes implement exactly the same set of remote interfaces as the remote object itself. Remember that an RMI client uses a reference to the stub class to load the remote object class. In fact, the stub acts as a proxy for the remote object.

Listing 9-5

```
// run the rmic compiler. Don't forget to set your CLASSPATH
// review Step 7 from the previous section
rmic -d -vcompat D:\deployobjects
        rmi.platform.RmiPlatformServerImplementation

// The rmic compiler generates the stub and the skeleton classes
RmiPlatformServerImplementation_Stub.class
RmiPlatformServerImplementation_Skel.class
```

Step 8   Start the RMI registry (see Listing 9-6) on the `data-i` server. At the command line, set your path and start the registry. Note that if you use a port number other than the default one, you need to specify it when you start the registry. For example, if you use port number 1620, enter **rmiregistry 1620** at the command line.

Listing 9-6

```
// Get a new window and Set your CLASSPATH.
set CLASSPATH=%CLASSPATH%device:\deployobjects;

// Go to the directory where your classes are located
cd device:\deployobjects\rmi\platform

// start the rmiregistry (UNIX)
rmiregistry &

// Windows NT
rmiregistry
```

Step 9   Start the `rmi.platform.RmiPlatformServerImplementation` server class (see Listing 9-7).

Listing 9-7

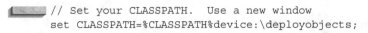

```
// Set your CLASSPATH.  Use a new window
set CLASSPATH=%CLASSPATH%device:\deployobjects;

// Go to the directory where your classes are located
cd device:\deployobjects\rmi\platform
```

```
// Start the server class
java rmi.platform.RmiPlatformServerImplementation
```

When you start the server in Listing 9-7, you will get the following output:

```
// Output when you start the server
Binding the object
Platform Server ready!
```

Step 10 Start the client (see Listing 9-8). Once the registry and the server are up and running, then you can start the client.

Listing 9-8

```
// Set your CLASSPATH
set CLASSPATH=%CLASSPATH%device:\deployobjects;

// Go to the directory where your classes are located
cd device:\deployobjects\rmi\platform

// Start the client
java rmi.platform.ClientAppAccessesRmiObj

// Using the data from the PLATFORM_TYPE_LIST table
// Resulting output
1   SURFACE MOORED_BUOY_OCEANIC
2   SURFACE CMAN_OCEANIC
3   OTHER SCIENTIST
4   SURFACE MOORED_BUOY_OCEANIC
5   SURFACE CMAN_OCEANIC
6   OTHER SCIENTIST
```

In the remaining sections of this chapter, you will develop distributed applications where the business objects reside in the Oracle database. You will use EJB and CORBA to do so. In Chapters 4 and 5, you stored Java and SQLJ logic into the Oracle8*i*/9*i* data server. With Java and SQLJ stored procedures and call specifications, you were limited to the set of Java classes that represent some SQL data types. With CORBA and EJB, methods take objects as arguments and return objects. Moreover, these objects maintain object identity during the entire database session.

Next, you will develop an EJB application and you will deploy the EJB object in the Oracle8*i*/9*i* data server. For more information on EJB technology, consult the *Oracle8i Java Component Programming with EJB, CORBA, and JSP*, the *Enterprise JavaBeans and CORBA Developer's Guide,* the Bibliography at the end the book, and the Enterprise JavaBeans Specification Version 1.0 and 1.1 (http://java.sun.com/products/ejb/docs10.html).

Deploying an Enterprise JavaBeans Object Using a SQLJ Implementation

In the previous section, you developed an RMI-based application that allowed a RMI client to use the SQLJ object you created in "Designing and Developing a SQLJ Component-Based Object," earlier in the chapter. The ClientApp-AccessesRmiObj client used the Java Remote Method Invocation to remotely invoke the getPlatformList() method of the SQLJ object. In this section, you will develop an Enterprise JavaBeans object that resides in the Oracle8*i*/9*i* database and an EJB client application program (that can reside anywhere on the network) that uses the EJB object.

What Is Enterprise JavaBeans?

Enterprise JavaBeans (EJB) is a component architecture for developing and deploying distributed transaction-oriented applications written in Java. EJB is based on the RMI specification model. Remoting EJB objects is supported through the standard Java API for remote method invocation. Remember that the remote invocation method is done via the Java Remote Method Invocation. You learned about RMI in "Deploying a SQLJ Component Using the Java Remote Method Invocation," earlier in this chapter. The Java API, as in the RMI-based applications, allows a client to invoke an EJB object using any distributed object protocol, including the IIOP protocol (TCP/IP with some CORBA-defined message exchanges). The EJB specification defines a standard mapping of EJB to CORBA that enables a non-Java CORBA client to access EJB objects and any other client that uses an ORB to access EJB objects that reside on CORBA-based EJB servers (see Figure 9-7). Also, Web browser clients can use the HTTP protocol (set of rules for exchanging files over the World Wide Web) to invoke *servlets* that invoke EJB objects. Servlets are Java modules that extend request/response-oriented servers, such as Java- enabled Web servers. They provide a way to generate dynamic documents. The javax.servlet package provides interfaces and classes for writing servlets. Servlets can be embedded in many different servers but are mostly embedded within HTTP servers.

Enterprise JavaBeans Roles

The EJB architecture defines six roles in the development and deployment of enterprise Beans. Each role can be performed by a different party, but also a single party may perform several roles. The roles are as follows:

1. An *enterprise Bean provider* develops a component called an *enterprise Bean* that implements a business task. In this section, you will assume

the role of an enterprise Bean provider and, as such, you will develop an enterprise Bean that produces a listing of the platforms from the Observation schema.

2. An *application assembler* composes applications (for example, GUI, servlets, applets, or scripts) that use the enterprise Bean.

3. A *deployer* is responsible for the deployment of enterprise Beans and their containers. An enterprise Bean lives in a container and a container lives in an application or database server.

4. An *EJB server* provider is usually an operating system, middleware, or a database vendor. An EJB server is a collection of services for supporting EJB installations. An EJB server manages the resources needed to support EJB components.

5. An *EJB container provider* provides an API that insulates the enterprise Bean from the specifics of an underlying EJB server. EJB components reside in an EJB container. An EJB container is a system that manages the life of an enterprise Bean. It provides the environment in which the Beans can operate, and handles the object life cycle, including creating and destroying an object, and the state management of the Beans. In the next section, you will learn about the state management of an enterprise Bean.

6. A *system administrator* is responsible for monitoring the system on which the enterprise Beans are running.

Types of Enterprise JavaBeans

The EJB 1.1 architecture defines two types of enterprise Beans: the session object type and the entity type Bean. In April 2001, Sun Microsystems released the proposed final draft of the EJB Specification Version 2.0. EJB 2.0 defines, in addition to the session and entity Beans specified in EJB 1.1, the message-driven Bean.

A session Bean lives in an EJB session container, whereas an entity Bean resides in an EJB entity container:

■ A *session object type* is a logical extension of a single-client program and executes on behalf of the client that creates it. It is relatively short-lived—that is, its life is that of its client, and it is removed when the client quits or the EJB server crashes. EJB server providers, like Oracle, provide session containers where an EJB session is just a database session. A fundamental characteristic of a database session is that the session dies when the user disconnects with the database or when the data server crashes.

In order to manage the session Bean container (Figure 9-7), one must know its *state management mode.* At deployment time, a session Bean is specified as having either a STATELESS or a STATEFUL state management mode. A session Bean is said to be STATELESS when the Bean can be used by any client (moreover, its state is not retained across methods and transactions), or STATEFUL when the session Bean does retain its state. A STATELESS session Bean is referred to as a Bean that contains no conversational state, whereas a STATEFUL session Bean contains a conversational state. Note that the Oracle8*i* EJB server release 8.1.5 and 8.1.6 implement only the EJB session container contract as specified by the EJB specification 1.0, whereas the Oracle8*i* release 8.1.7 and Oracle9*i* EJB servers are EJB 1.1 compliant.

- An *entity enterprise Bean* is a remote object that manages persistent data. It is a persistent object, uniquely identified by a primary key, that represents an object view of an entity stored in a persistent storage (for example, a database) or an entity that is implemented by an application. Unlike an enterprise session Bean, an entity Bean can be accessed concurrently by multiple clients, its client object view is location independent, and its lifetime is not limited by the lifetime of the JVM process in which it executes—that is, an entity Bean does not die when the EJB server crashes. Starting with Oracle8*i* release 8.1.7, you can build entity Beans and deploy them in the Oracle8*i* and Oracle9*i* database servers.

- A *message-driven Bean* is a stateless component that is invoked by the container as a result of the arrival of a Java Message Service (JMS) message.

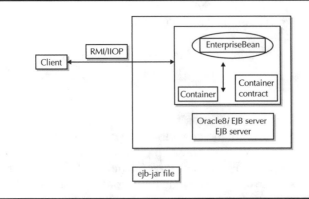

FIGURE 9-7. *Enterprise JavaBeans container contract (specification)*

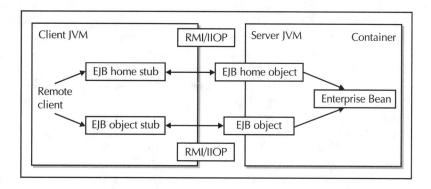

FIGURE 9-8. *EJB client-side and server-side objects*

The integration between JMS and EJB is used to perform asynchronous work within the EJB server.

Enterprise JavaBeans Object Composites

An EJB object consists of four major components (see Figure 9-8):

- **The Bean home `interface`** An EJB container implements the home interface for the EJB objects that it provides. A client accesses an enterprise Bean, irrespective of its implementation and its container, via the enterprise Bean home `interface`. The home interface allows the client to create, look up, and remove EJB objects. The following fragment code defines a Bean home interface for a session Bean and an entity Bean, respectively:

```
// session Bean home definition
public interface PlatformHome extends EJBHome {
  public Platform create()
    throws CreateException, RemoteException;
}
// entity Bean home definition
public interface PurchaseOrderHome extends EJBHome {
  public Purchase create()
    throws CreateException, RemoteException;
  public PurchaseOrder findByPrimaryKey (String aPrimaryKey)
    throws FinderException, RemoteException;
}
```

A client uses the Java Naming and Directory Interface (JNDI) to locate the home interface. The JNDI architecture (developed by Sun and the other partners such as IBM, Hewlett-Packard, Netscape, and Novell) provides naming and directory functionality to Java applications, and consists of an Application Programming Interface (API) and a Service Provider Interface (SPI). Remember that the EJB container is a system that manages the life of an enterprise Bean. The EJB container also provides the Bean instances with a `SessionContext` interface class, which consists of several methods that allow a client to manipulate `Context` instances maintained by the container. The notion of a context, defined by the `Context` package, is the core interface for clients to look up, bind, unbind, and rename EJB objects, as well as create and destroy subcontexts. For example, a client uses an instance of the `InitialContext` class to look up an EJB home interface. One context might require a specification of security credentials in order to access a service, whereas another might require a specification of the server configuration. The required specifications are referred to as the environment of a `Context`. The `Context` interface also provides methods for retrieving and updating the environment of a `Context`. For example, the `ClientJavajForEjbPlatform` client, which you will develop in this section, uses the following code segment to locate the container for the `PlatformDb` EJB object:

```
serviceURL = "sess_iiop://haiti:2481:orcl";
objectName = "/test/PlatformDb";
// where "/test" is the directory where you
// published the PlatformDb EJB object.

// Create an instance of the Context class
Context ic = new InitialContext (env);
// Use the lookup method of the Context class
// to get a reference of the PlatformHome interface object.
PlatformHome home =
        (PlatformHome)ic.lookup (serviceURL + objectName);
```

For more information regarding JNDI, see http://java.sun.com/products/jndi/ and the Bibliography at the end of the book.

■ **The EJB container** This provides the enterprise Bean remote `interface`. A client uses an instance of an enterprise Bean remote `interface` to create an instance of an EJB object. The following fragment code defines a remote interface:

```
public interface Platform extends EJBObject {
  // Define here the operations that
  // you wish your users to invoke
}
```

- **The enterprise Bean implementation class**   This is the actual class that implements the Bean remote `interface`. The business logic methods reside in the implementation class. The following fragment code defines an implementation class for a session Bean and an entity Bean, respectively:

```
// Session Bean class
public class PlatformDb extends SessionBean {
  // provide here the method bodies
  // of all the methods advertised in the remote interface.
}


// Entity Bean class
public class PurchaseBean extends EntityBean {
  ...

  ...

}
```

- **The Bean deployment descriptor**   To deploy Enterprise JavaBeans into a database server or an application server, the Bean provider must provide the appropriate deployment descriptor file. Importantly, if you develop several Enterprise JavaBeans, you must include a deployment descriptor for each of your enterprise Beans. Deployment descriptors are serialized classes that serve a function similar to property files. They allow you to describe and customize run-time attributes, that is, run-time behaviors of server-side components (security, transactional context, and so on) without having to change the Bean class or its interfaces. Deployment descriptors are created after you create the interfaces and the Bean class for your enterprise Bean. In the EJB 1.0 Specification, a deployment descriptor is an ASCII file (`.ejb` file); whereas in EJB 1.1, the deployment descriptor (`.xml` file) is written using XML notation. Note that the EJB 1.1 Specification defines two types of deployment descriptors, one for each type of Beans: the session Bean and the entity Bean.

NOTE

If you are developing Enterprise JavaBeans for Oracle8i releases 8.1.5 and 8.1.6, use an ASCII file (`.ejb` file) for your deployment descriptor file. For Oracle8i release 8.1.7 and Oracle9i, you must use a deployment descriptor file written in XML notation to deploy your EJBs.

Developing an Enterprise Session Bean Application

The steps to develop an EJB session Bean are as follows:

1. Create a high-level view of the EJB-based application.

2. Create the directories that you wish to use for your package name.

3. Create a Bean remote `interface` server object, the `Platform` interface.

4. Create a Bean home `interface` server object, the `PlatformHome` `interface`.

5. Create a Java class to map the Oracle `PLATFORM_TYPE` type. You will use the `PlatWrap` class that you created for your SQLJ component-based object.

6. Create the Bean itself, `PlatformDb` class. This class, like the `PlatformDbObject`, implements the business logic. Remember that `PlatformDbObject` implements the `getPlatformList()` method in the "Designing and Developing a SQLJ Component-Based Object" section of this chapter. The `PlatformDb` class implements the identical business logic and will use the `PlatWrap` class to ship the EJB object to the client.

7. Set your `CLASSPATH` and compile all the classes from steps 3 to 6.

8. Create the deployment descriptor file, the `Platform.ejb` file.

9. Create a JAR file of the classes that you created from steps 3 to 6. See Chapters 4 and 5 for more information on JAR files.

10. Load and deploy the EJB object into the Oracle8i/9i EJB server.

11. Create the EJB client, `ClientJavaForEjbPlatform`, to use the EJB object.

12. Set your `CLASSPATH` and compile the client class.

13. Run the EJB client.

CAUTION
The length of an object name that resides in the Oracle8i/9i database is limited to 30 characters. Oracle stores the fully qualified name of the object, that is, the path and the object name. For example, the Platform interface *is stored in the database under the* platform\Platform *name. Also note that the* PIter *SQLJ iterator declared in the* PlatformDb *class is stored under the* plat Server\Piter *name. Remember this limitation when you name your server-side programs.*

Step 1 Create a high-level view of the EJB-based application (see Figure 9-9).

Step 2 Create the directories you wish to use for your package name.

```
// Create the directories to store the Java and SQLJ source code
// if you have not yet created it
mkdir deployobjects\platform
```

Step 3 Create a Bean remote interface server object, the Platform interface:

```
/*      Program Name:     Platform.java
**
**      Purpose:     EJB remote interface
*/
package platform;
import javax.ejb.*;
import java.rmi.RemoteException;
import java.util.Vector;

public interface Platform extends EJBObject  {  // (See Note 1.)

  // Note that the Platform EJB remote interface is
  // advertising the getPlatformList() in a similar manner
  // to the RmiPlatformServerInterface in the
  // "Deploying a SQLJ Component Using the Java
  // Remote Method Invocation" section of this chapter.
  public Vector getPlatformList()
    throws java.sql.SQLException,
        RemoteException;  // (See Note 2.)

} // End of Platform interface
```

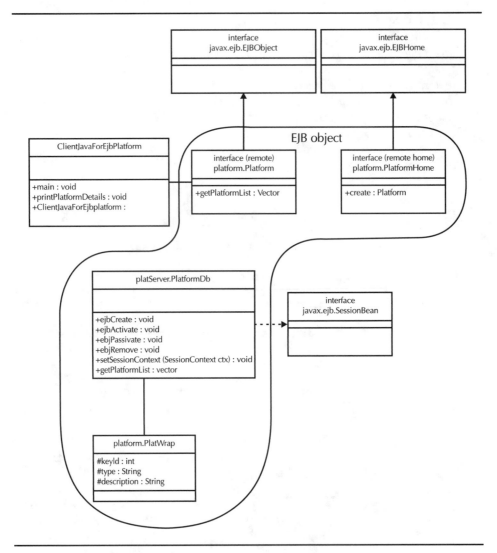

FIGURE 9-9. *High-level view of the PlatformDB EJB object*

Notes on the remote `Platform interface`:

  I. The Bean remote interface must be a subclass of the
  `javax.ejb.EJBObject` class. The `EJBObject` interface must be
  extended by all EJB remote interface classes. The EJB remote interface,
  like the RMI interface, defines the methods that are callable by an EJB

client. The `EJBObject` is an object that exposes only the remote interface that you specified. It acts like a proxy, intercepting the remote object invocations and calling the appropriate methods on the enterprise Bean instance.

2. This statement defines only the method that implements the business logic, which the Bean contains. As in the RMI-based applications, you must declare all the methods you want EJB clients to have access to, and the methods must include in their `throws` clause the Java `RemoteException` and any application-specific exceptions. In this example, the `java.sql.SQLException` exception for database applications is included in the `throws` clause of the method.

Step 4 Create a Bean home `interface` server class, the `PlatformHome` class:

```
/*      Program Name:     PlatformHome.java
**
**      Purpose:          EJB home interface
*/

package platform;
import javax.ejb.*;
import java.rmi.RemoteException;

public interface PlatformHome extends EJBHome {  // (See Note 1.)

  public Platform create()
    throws CreateException, RemoteException;    // (See Note 2.)

}  // End of PlatformHome EJB home interface
```

Notes on the `PlatformHome` interface:

1. This interface must be declared as a subclass of the `EJBHome` interface and must define the enterprise Bean type-specific `create()` method. An EJB container implements the `EJBHome` interface of each enterprise Bean installed in the container. It makes the `EJBHome` interfaces available to the client through JNDI, allowing the client to create and delete Beans, and query information or "metadata" about the Beans. You will need to publish the enterprise Bean home interface in order for a client to access the class. You do so with the `deployejb` tool provided by Oracle. The `deployejb` tool publishes in the database a reference to the home object, as well as the EJB object, and the EJB client looks up at the home reference object to create instances of the Bean. (See Appendix D to learn more about this tool.)

2. This statement declares the `create()` method that returns a type of the EJB `Platform interface` object. EJB clients use the Bean home interface to create a Bean instance. For each create method in the home interface, there must be a corresponding method called `ejbCreate()` specified in the implements class, with the same signature (see the listing of the `PlatformDb` class following step 6). The `create()` method is specified to return the Bean type, whereas the `ejbCreate()` is a void method (see Appendix B to learn more about Java void methods). When a client invokes the `create()` method on the home, the container invokes the corresponding `ejbCreate()` method in the Bean itself. Note that the method declaration must include the `CreateException` and the `RemoteException` exceptions in its `throws` clause.

Step 5 Create a Java class to map the Oracle `PLATFORM_TYPE` type. You will use the `PlatWrap` class that you created for your SQLJ component-based object. See the listing for the `PlatWrap` class in step 4 of the " Developing a SQLJ Component" section, earlier in this chapter.

Step 6 Create the Bean itself, `PlatformDb` class. This class, like the `PlatformDbObject`, implements the business logic. Remember that `PlatformDbObject` implements the `getPlatformList()` method in the "Designing and Developing a SQLJ Component-Based Object" section, earlier in this chapter. The `PlatformDb` class implements the identical business logic and will use the `PlatWrap` class to ship the EJB object to the client:

```
/*      Program Name: PlatformDb.sqlj
**      Purpose:      A SQLJ Class that implements the
**   SessionBean interface and fully implements the
**   getPlatformList(): Vector from the EJB remote
**   interface, the platform.java class
**   The class implements the logic to query
**   the PLATFORM_TYPE_LIST table.
**
*/
package platform;

// import the serializable object
import platform.PlatWrap;

import java.rmi.RemoteException;
import java.sql.*;

import java.math.BigDecimal;
import java.util.Vector;
import javax.ejb.*;
```

```java
public class PlatformDb implements SessionBean {    // (See Note 1.)
  SessionContext sessionCtx;

  public void ejbCreate()
    throws CreateException, RemoteException {   // (See Note 2.)
  }
  public void ejbActivate() { // (See Note 3.)
  }
  public void ejbPassivate() {
  }
  public void ejbRemove() {
  }
  public void setSessionContext(SessionContext ctx) {
      this.sessionCtx = ctx;
  }

  // Declare a named iterator
  #sql iterator PIter (int  aPlatformId,
          String aType, String aDesc);

  // This is the method body for the method
  // specified in the EJB remote interface: platform.java
  public Vector getPlatformList()
      throws SQLException, RemoteException {

    // Use platformVector to store PlatFormType objects
    Vector platformVector = new Vector();

    // Use PIter to retrieve
    // rows of data from PLATFORM_TYPE_LIST table
    PIter anPIter = null;

    try {
        #sql anPIter =
            { SELECT P.key_id AS aPlatformId,
                     P.type AS aType,
                     P.description AS aDesc
              FROM PLATFORM_TYPE_LIST P
            };

      while (anPIter.next()) {

        int keyId = anPIter.aPlatformId();
        String type = anPIter.aType();
        String description = anPIter.aDesc();

        // Instantiate aPlatformType
```

```
                PlatWrap aPlatformType = new PlatWrap();

                // Set the data members of the aPlatformType object
                aPlatformType.setKeyId(new BigDecimal(keyId));
                aPlatformType.setType(type);
                aPlatformType.setDescription(description);

                // add a PlatformType object to the platformVector
                platformVector.addElement(aPlatformType);

            }   // End of while

            // Close the iterator
            anPIter.close();

        }   // End of try
        catch (SQLException e) {
                e.printStackTrace();
        }   // End of catch

        return platformVector;

    }    // End of getPlatformList()
}   // End of PlatformDb class
```

Notes on the `PlatformDb` class:

This Bean implementation class shows the minimum methods required for an EJB implementation method. Note that the enterprise Bean class does not implement the Bean's remote `interface`, the `EJBObject` class does so when you install the EJB object. At invocation time, the `EJBObject` acts as a proxy, passing method invocations through to the Bean instance installed on the server.

1. Every enterprise session Bean implementation class must implement the `SessionBean interface`. The container uses the `SessionBean` methods to notify the EJB instances of the instance's life cycle events.

2. This statement implements the method that will be invoked on the server when the EJB client invokes the `create()` method from the Bean home interface.

3. This statement and the ones that follow it implement the four required methods specified by the `javax.ejb.SessionBean interface` class:

   ■ **ejbActivate()** This method is called when the instance is activated from its "passive" state. Note that the temporary transfer of the state of an idle session Bean to some form of secondary storage is called *passivation,* and the transfer back is called *activation.* At activation time, the EJB instance will acquire any resource that it had released earlier with the `ejbPassivate()` method. Oracle8*i*/9*i* EJB server does not use the `ejbActivate()` or the `ejbPassivate()` method.

- **`ejbPassivate()`** This method is called before the instance enters the "passive" state. It will release any resource that it can reacquire later in the `ejbPassivate()` method.

- **`ejbRemove()`** A container invokes this method before it ends the life of a session object to release system resources and destroy a Bean instance at the client's request.

- **`setSessionContext (SessionContext ctx)`** The container can use this method to store a reference to the context object into a variable. This method is called at Bean's creation.

Step 7   Set your `CLASSPATH` and compile all the classes from steps 3 to 6.

NOTE
Use JDK 1.1.6 or JDK 1.1.8 and `classes111.zip` *(JDBC driver) to compile and deploy the EJB applications in the Oracle8i release 8.1.5. Use JDK 1.2.x (Java 2) and* `classes12.zip` *(JDBC driver) to compile and deploy the EJB applications in the Oracle8i release 8.1.6 and 8.1.7 and Oracle9i. Also remember that you need to have the commands java and javac from the JDK in your PATH in order for you to deploy EJBs in the Oracle environment.*

```
// At the command line
set ORACLE_HOME=C:\Oracle\Ora81
// Use your database server name, your iiop port listener number.
// This is a default port number that you find in the
// listener.ora file. If you do not have access to this
//   file, ask your DBA.
set ORACLE_SERVICE=sess_iiop://datai:2481:orcl

// Use the JDK 1.1.6 or 1.1.8
set JDK_CLASSPATH=D:\jdk1.1.8\lib\classes.zip
// For jdk1.2 use the following:
// set JDK_CLASSPATH=[jdk1.2_HOME]\lib\dt.jar;
```

```
//              [jdk1.2_HOME]\lib\tools.jar;
// and %ORACLE_HOME%\jdbc\lib\classes12.zip;

// get to the directory that you created in step 2
cd deployobjects\platform

// Set the CLASSPATH
set CLASSPATH=.;D:\deployobjects;% \
  ORACLE_HOME%\lib\aurora_client.jar; \
 %ORACLE_HOME%\jdbc\lib\classes111.zip; \
 %ORACLE_HOME%\sqlj\lib\translator.zip; \
 %ORACLE_HOME%\lib\vbjorb.jar;   \
 %ORACLE_HOME%\lib\vbjapp.jar;%JDK_CLASSPATH%

// NOTE: For SQLJ 8.1.7 or 9i you must add ...\sqlj\lib\runtime12.zip
// Compile the classes in the platform directory
javac -g *.java

// Compile the sqlj class
cd platform
sqlj -ser2class PlatformDb.sqlj

// Alternatively, you could compile all classes
// Using the sqlj command. For example:
// sqlj -ser2class PlatformDb.sqlj [list of java classes]
```

Step 8   Create the deployment descriptor file. Here we provide two deployment descriptor files:

- ■ The Platform.ejb ASCII file that allows you to deploy EJBs in Oracle8*i* release 8.1.5. By convention, you use the .ejb extension. The EJB container provider will provide a deployment tool that can read the descriptor file, parse it, signal parse errors, and then verify that the descriptor file, the interface declaration, and the Bean implementation declaration meet the EJB standard. Oracle provides the deployejb tool to do the task for you. This tool accepts ASCII (Oracle8*i* releases 8.1.5 and 8.1.6) and XML (Oracle8*i* release 8.1.7 and Oracle9*i*) formatted files.

- ■ The Platform.xml XML file that allows you to deploy EJBs in the Oracle8*i* release 8.1.7 and Oracle9*i* environments. If you are not very familiar with XML, you can still write an ASCII file as your deployment descriptor and use the Oracle ejbdescriptor tool to translate your .ejb file to an XML file. To learn more about the Oracle tools, see the *Oracle8*i */9*i Java Tool Reference and Appendix D of this book.

Next, you will write the ASCII `Platform.ejb` deployment descriptor file.

```
// File Name:   Platform.ejb
// platform EJB deployment descriptor.

SessionBean platServer.PlatformDb {  // (See Note 1.)

  BeanHomeName = "test/PlatformDb";   // (See Note 2.)
  // (See Note 3.)
  RemoteInterfaceClassName = platform.Platform;
  HomeInterfaceClassName = platform.PlatformHome;

  AllowedIdentities = {OBSSCHEMA};  // (See Note 4.)

  // SessionTimeout = 20; (See Note 5.)
  StateManagementType = STATELESS; // (See Note 6.)

  RunAsMode = CLIENT_IDENTITY; // (See Note 7.)

  TransactionAttribute = TX_REQUIRED; // (See Note 8.)
} // End of platServer.PlatformDb
```

Notes on the `Platform.ejb` deployment descriptor file:

1. This statement declares the `PlatformDb` EJB object as a `SessionBean`. Note that the name of the object is fully qualified with the directory in which the class resides.

2. This statement declares the name of the EJB published object and the directory associated with the object. When you install Oracle8*i*, the software automatically creates a directory called `test` that you can use to store the published EJB home class of the EJB object. Use the `sess_sh` tool provided by Oracle to create directories of your choice. (See Chapter 6 of the *Enterprise JavaBeans and CORBA Developer's Guide* to learn more about EJB and CORBA tools.) Note that if you are using an Oracle8*i* release 8.1.7 client against earlier releases of the Oracle database (Oracle8*i* releases 8.1.5 or 8.1.6), Oracle provides the `sess_sh_816` and the `publish_816` tools to maintain backward compatibility with Oracle8*i* 8.1.7. The `sess_sh` (session shell) tool is an interactive interface to a database instance's session namespace. You specify database connection arguments when you start `sess_sh`. It then presents you with a prompt to indicate that it is ready for commands. Each database instance running the Oracle8*i*/9*i* JVM software has a *session namespace,* which the Oracle8*i* ORB uses to activate CORBA and EJB objects. A session namespace is a hierarchical collection of objects known

as `PublishedObjects` and `PublishingContexts` and is analogous to UNIX file system files and directories. A namespace incorporates the idea of a session directly in the URL, allowing the client to easily manipulate multiple sessions. In the string `"test/PlatformDb"`, the `test` directory is the namespace and `PlatformDb` is the name of the `PublishedObject`. Each `Published-Object` is associated with a class schema object that represents a CORBA or EJB implementation in the database. From the `PublishedObject`, the Oracle8*i*/9*i* ORB obtains the information necessary to find and launch the corresponding class schema object. Use the following syntax to invoke the session shell:

```
// At the command line
sess_sh [options] -user <user> -password <password>
   -service <serviceURL>
  [-d | -describe]  [-h | -help]
  [-iiop]  [-role <rolename>]  [-ssl]  [-version]
```

3. Use the `RemoteInterfaceClassName` and `HomeInterfaceClassName` variables to store the name of the remote `interface` and the remote home `interface` of the EJB object.

4. This statement specifies which user is allowed to access the enterprise Bean. In this example, only the `obsschema` user can use the Bean.

5. This commented statement indicates that you can set the session timeout value. You set the value in seconds. In this scenario, the session will use the EJB container-specific default value.

6. This statement declares an enterprise Bean State Management Mode. The argument to the method is `STATEFUL_SESSION` or `STATELESS_SESSION`.

7. The `CLIENT_IDENTITY` attribute instructs the container to run the EJB method with the client's security identity.

8. The `TX_REQUIRED` attribute specifies that the enterprise Bean requires that the method be executed in a global transaction. In other words, if the caller is associated with a transaction, the EJB method will be associated with the caller's transaction; otherwise, start a new global transaction.

Note that the Oracle `ejbdescritor` tool is used to translate the `Platform.ejb` to the `Platform.xml` file. To learn more about XML, see the *Oracle XML Reference Guide, Oracle8i/9i Java Tools Reference,* and the Bibliography at the end of this book.

NOTE
Oracle8i release 8.1.7 and Oracle9i are EJB 1.1-compliant. Both database servers require that the deployment descriptor file be written in XML notation.

Writing Deployment Descriptor Using XML Notation

In this section, you will convert the `Platform.ejb` descriptor file into the `Platform.xml` descriptor file using XML notation. You will use the Oracle `ejbdescriptor` tool to do so. For more information regarding this tool, see Appendix D and the *Oracle8i/9i Java Tool Reference Guide*.

Here is a list of the options of the `ejbdescriptor` tool:

```
ejbdescriptor [-options] <infile> <outfile>
[-parse]
[-parsexml]
[-dump]
[-dumpxml]
[-encoding]


// To get description of each options:
// At the command line, type the following:

ejbdescriptor
// Resulting output
usage: ejbdescriptor [-parse | -dump] in out
Options:
-parse: parse a deployment descriptor and output a serialized object.
-parsexml: parse a xml deployment descriptor and output a textual
form.
-dump: get a serialized object and dump it in textual form
-dumpxml: get a texual form deployment descriptor and dump
it in xml form
-encoding: specifies the encoding for the deployment descriptor
in: a filename or - or nothing for stdin.
out: a filename or - or nothing for stdout.
```

Use the `ejbdescriptor` tool to convert the `Platform.ejb` ASCII file to the `Platform.xml` file using the XML notation:

```
// Make sure you are at the root directory
// of where all your .class files are located
ejbdescriptor -dumpxml Platform.ejb Platform.xml
```

Here is a listing of the `Platform.xml` file:

```
<?xml version = '1.0' encoding = 'Cp1252'?>
<!DOCTYPE ejb-jar PUBLIC
"-//Sun Microsystems Inc.//DTD Enterprise JavaBeans 1.1//EN"
"ejb-jar.dtd">
<ejb-jar>
    <enterprise-beans>
        <session>
            <description>no description</description>
            <ejb-name>test/PlatformDb</ejb-name>
            <home>platform.PlatformHome</home>
            <remote>platform.Platform</remote>
            <ejb-class>platform.PlatformDb</ejb-class>
            <session-type>Stateful</session-type>
            <transaction-type>Container</transaction-type>
        </session>
    </enterprise-beans>
    <assembly-descriptor>
        <security-role>
            <description>no description</description>
            <role-name>OBSSHEMA</role-name>
        </security-role>
        <method-permission>
            <description>no description</description>
            <role-name>OBSSHEMA</role-name>
            <method>
                <ejb-name>test/PlatformDb</ejb-name>
                <method-name>*</method-name>
            </method>
        </method-permission>
        <container-transaction>
            <description>no description</description>
            <method>
                <ejb-name>test/PlatformDb</ejb-name>
                <method-name>*</method-name>
            </method>
            <trans-attribute>Required</trans-attribute>
        </container-transaction>
    </assembly-descriptor>
</ejb-jar>
```

Note that the very first line of the `Platform.xml` file generated by the Oracle `ejbdescriptor` tool is incorrect. If you use this file as is, when you invoke the Oracle `deployejb` tool, you get the following error:

Reading Deployment Descriptor...
<Line 1, Column 1>: XML-0231: (Error) Encoding 'Cp1252' is
not currently supported.

Here is the first line:

`<?xml version = '1.0' encoding = 'Cp1252'?>` `-- `**INCORRECT**

To avoid this error, before invoking the `deployejb` tool, replace the first line with the following:

`<?xml version = '1.0' encoding = 'UTF-8'?>`

Step 9   Create the `platform.jar` JAR file (see Listing 9-9) of the classes that you created from steps 3 to 6:

Listing 9-9

```
// At the command line, do the following:
// Set your CLASSPATH if you have not done so yet.
// Review Step 7 of this section.

jar cvf0 platform.jar platform\Platform.class \
  platform\PlatWrap.class   \
  platform\PlatformHome.class   \
  platform\PlatformDb$PIter.class   \
  platform\PlatformDb.class \
  platform\PlatformDb_SJProfile0.class \
  platform\PlatformDb_SJProfileKeys.class
```

Step 10   Load and deploy the EJB object into the Oracle8*i*/9*i* EJB server (see Listing 9-10). Use the Oracle tool, `deployejb`, to load and publish the EJB object in the Oracle8*i*/9*i* EJB server. (See Appendix D for a list of the Oracle tools and their associated options.) The `deployejb` tool "publishes" the EJB object into a namespace using the `platformDb` name that you declared in the `Platform.ejb` (Oracle8*i* releases 8.1.7 and 8.1.6) or `Platform.xml` (Oracle8*i* release 8.1.7 and Oracle9*i*) file. Recall that you used the `PlatformServer` name to "publish" the RMI object into the server's `rmiregistry`, whereas you use the `platformDb` name to publish your EJB object into a namespace. When you install Oracle8*i*/9*i*, the software creates the test directory as a default namespace, which you can use to publish your EJB and CORBA objects. At deployment time, the `deployejb` tool reads the deployment descriptor file (`Platform.ejb` or `Platform.xml`) that you created in step 8 and the JAR file (`platform.jar`) in step 9 of this section to create the `platform_generated` JAR file. The EJB client that you will develop later

in this section uses the `platform_generated` JAR file to access your
`PlatformDb` Bean.

At the command line:

Listing 9-10

```
// First set your CLASSPATH - review Step 7 of this section
// Go to the directory where the files are
// located and invoke the EJB tool
// Oracle8i releases 8.1.7 and Oracle9i
cd device:\deployobjects\platform
deployejb -republish -temp temp \
    -u obsschema -p obsschema -s %ORACLE_SERVICE% \
   -descriptor Platform.xml platform.jar
Reading Deployment Descriptor...done
Verifying Deployment Descriptor...done
Gathering users...done
Generating Comm Stubs.........done
Compiling Stubs...done
Generating Jar File...done
Loading EJB Jar file and Comm Stubs Jar file...done
Generating EJBHome and EJBObject on the server...done
Publishing EJBHome...done

//     OR
// Oracle8i releases 8.1.5 and 8.1.6 only
cd device:\deployobjects\platform
deployejb -republish -temp temp \
    -u obsschema -p obsschema -s %ORACLE_SERVICE% \
   -descriptor Platform.ejb platform.jar

// Output file from deployejb using either
// the Platform.xml or Platform.ejb deployment descriptor file.
platform_generated.jar
```

Note that if the deployment is not successful, you may use the `dropjava` tool
to remove all the Java classes that you loaded via the `deployejb` tool and the
`sess_sh` tool to remove the Bean home interface name from the published object
namespace (see Listing 9-11). You can also create new directories under the root
directory to hold objects for separate projects, but, to do so, you must have access
as database user `SYS`:

Listing 9-11

```
// Remove all the classes using the JAR file that deployejb
// tool created for you. For example, the platform_generated.jar.
// You can use the Oracle oci8 driver or the Oracle JDBC-THIN driver
// The following example uses the THIN driver. At the command line:
```

```
dropjava -thin -u obsschema/obsschema@datai:1521:orcl   \
   platform_generated.jar

// Open a shell session:
sess_sh -user obsschema -password obsschema \
  -service sess_iiop://datai:2481:orcl
// go to the test directory
cd test
// Remove the PublishedObject name
rm -r /test/PlatformDb
```

Step 11   Create the `ClientJavaForEjbPlatform` EJB client that will use the
`Platform` EJB object:

```
/*      Program Name: ClientJavajForEjbPlatform.java
**      Purpose:     A Java client to access Platform EJB
**   object stored in Oracle8i/9i data server.
**      Client tasks:
**      1. Locates the remote home Bean interface.
**      2. Authenticates the client to the server.
**      3. Activates an instance of the Platform bean.
**      4. Invokes the getPlatformList() method on the bean
*/

// import the EJB platform remote interface   (See Note 1.)
import platform.Platform;
// import the EJB  platform home interface
import platform.PlatformHome;
// import the serializable object
import platform.PlatWrap;

// import the ServiceCtx class from the Oracle package
// (See Note 2.)
import oracle.aurora.jndi.sess_iiop.ServiceCtx;

// import the Java mandatory classes to use JNDI   (See Note 3.)
import javax.naming.Context;
import javax.naming.InitialContext;

// import application-specific Java classes
import java.util.Hashtable;
import java.sql.*;
import java.math.BigDecimal;
import java.util.*;
import java.util.Vector;

public class ClientJavaForEjbPlatform {
```

```
public static void main(String[] args)
    throws Exception  {
if (args.length != 4) {
    System.out.println("usage: Client "
        +"serviceURL objectName user password");
    System.exit(1);
}  // End if

String serviceURL = args [0];
String objectName = args [1];
String user = args [2];
String password = args [3];

Hashtable env = new Hashtable();

// Set the JNDI environment for the client
// to locate the EJB object (See Note 4.)
env.put(Context.URL_PKG_PREFIXES, "oracle.aurora.jndi");
env.put(Context.SECURITY_PRINCIPAL, user);
env.put(Context.SECURITY_CREDENTIALS, password);
env.put(Context.SECURITY_AUTHENTICATION,
    ServiceCtx.NON_SSL_LOGIN);

// Create an instance of the Context class. (See Note 5.)
Context ic = new InitialContext (env);

// Create an instance of the EJB object home interface.
PlatformHome home = null;
// Create an instance of the EJB Bean class.
Platform myPlatformBean = null;

try {
    // Use the home interface to
    // locate the EJB object (See Note 6.)
    home =
        (PlatformHome)ic.lookup (serviceURL + objectName);

    // Create a Bean instance  (See Note 7.)
    myPlatformBean = home.create();

}  // End of try
catch ( Exception ex ) {
    System.out.println("Cannot locate"
        +" or create Platform home");
    System.exit(1);
}  // End of catch

Vector platformVector = null;
```

```
    try {
        // Invoke the EJB object's method   (See Note 8.)
        platformVector =
            platformVector = myPlatformBean.getPlatformList();
    }   // End of try
    catch ( Exception ex ) {
        System.out.println("Cannot locate or "
            + "getPlatformList()");
        System.exit(1);
    }   // End of catch

    // Print the details. Code REUSE! (See Note 9.)
    printPlatformDetails(platformVector);
}   // End of main()

public static void printPlatformDetails(Vector platformVector)
        throws SQLException {

    if  (platformVector == null) {
        System.out.println("No Data FOUND");
        return;
    }   // End if

    PlatWrap p = null;
    Enumeration enum = platformVector.elements();
    // Iterate to get the column attributes from the table
    while (enum.hasMoreElements()) {
        // Get PlatformType from the platformVector
        p = (PlatWrap)enum.nextElement();
        // Get the column values
        System.out.println(
            ((p.getKeyId()==null) ? " " : p.getKeyId().toString())
            + " " + ((p.getType()==null) ? " " : p.getType()) + " "
            + ((p.getDescription()==null) ? " " : p.getDescription()
                ) );
    }       // End of while

  }   // End of printPlatformDetails()
}   // End of ClientJavaForEjbPlatform class
```

Notes on the `ClientJavajForEjbPlatform` client application:

1. The import `platform.Platform`, import
   `platform.PlatformHome`, and import `platform.PlatWrap`
   statements import in the program the EJB remote `interface`, remote
   home `interface`, and the serialized class of the EJB object.

2. You must import this class from the
   `oracle.aurora.jndi.sess.sess_iiop` package.

3. This statement and the one that follows it import the Java classes specified
   in the `javax` package. You must import these classes if you wish to use the
   JNDI API.

4. The following four statements store the environment parameters in a Java
   `HashTable`. The JNDI `Context` object needs these parameters. Use the
   `put()` method provided by the `HashTable` class to store the parameters in
   a hash table. For more information regarding JNDI, see the first bullet in the
   section "Enterprise JavaBeans Object Composites," earlier in this chapter.

5. To get the root of the JNDI naming hierarchy, create an instance of the
   `Context` class using the JNDI `InitialContext()` method.

6. The first thing a client does is to locate the enterprise Bean home interface.
   Remember that the client uses the home interface to look up, create, and
   remove EJB objects. Once you acquire an initial context, you can invoke its
   methods to get a reference to the EJB home interface. To look up the Bean,
   you need a URL address and the published full path name of the EJB
   object. Use the following syntax to construct a URL for the `Platform`
   enterprise Bean:

```
<service_name>://<hostname>:<iiop_listener_port>:<SID>
  /<published_obj_name>

// Use the following for your Platform EJB object
// 2481 is a default listener port for IIOP and is configured
// in the listener.ora file.
sess_iiop://yourHost:2481:ORCL/test/PlatformDb
```

   Note that, because the actual location of the EJB container is transparent to
   the client, a client that uses JNDI might be written to include EJB containers
   that are located on multiple machines.

7. Once you get the Bean, create a new session Bean by invoking the
   `create()` method of the `PlatformHome` home remote interface
   class. The `create()` method returns a reference to the program.

8. Use the reference to invoke the `getPlatformList()` method of the
   EJB object.

9. This statement calls your client method to print the platform details.

Step 12   Set your `CLASSPATH` and compile the client class:

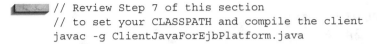

```
// Review Step 7 of this section
// to set your CLASSPATH and compile the client
javac -g ClientJavaForEjbPlatform.java
```

Step 13   Run the EJB client. When you set the CLASSPATH to run the client, you must include the file that the deployejb tool had generated for you in step 10 of this section. The client needs the file to locate your EJB object. Use the following syntax to set your CLASSPATH and run the client program (see Listing 9-12).

Listing 9-12

```
// Set your variables as you did in Step 7 of this section.

// Then set your CLASSPATH. Please note that the JAR file
// generated at deployment time,
// the platform_generated.jar, has been added.

set CLASSPATH=.;D:\deployobjects; \
%ORACLE_HOME%\lib\aurora_client.jar; \
%ORACLE_HOME%\jdbc\lib\classes12.zip; \
%ORACLE_HOME%\sqlj\lib\translator.zip; \
%ORACLE_HOME%\lib\vbjorb.jar; \
%ORACLE_HOME%\lib\vbjapp.jar;%JDK_CLASSPATH%; \
platform_generated.jar

// CAUTION: In 8.1.7 and later you must add the sqlj runtime12.zip

// Run the client program using the following arguments:
// 1.   Oracle service name
// 2.   The EJB object and its full path
// 3.   Username (owner or authorized user)
// 4.   password
java ClientJavaForEjbPlatform
   %ORACLE_SERVICE% /test/PlatformDb obsschema obsschema

// Using the data from the PLATFORM_TYPE_LIST table
// Resulting output
1   SURFACE MOORED_BUOY_OCEANIC
2   SURFACE CMAN_OCEANIC
3   OTHER SCIENTIST
4   SURFACE MOORED_BUOY_OCEANIC
5   SURFACE CMAN_OCEANIC
6   OTHER SCIENTIST
```

Note that we provide a makeit.bat file to compile and load all the programs and publish the EJB object, and also a runit.bat file to run the client.

Java Servlets Using EJBs

In this section, you will write the `ServletEJBClient` class, a simple Java servlet that invokes the method of the `test/PlatformDb`, which you previously deployed in the Oracle database server. Here is the definition of the `ServletEJBClient` class:

```
/*      Program Name: ServletEJBClient.java
**
**      Description:  This Java servlet uses the PlatformDb
**      EJB object.
*/

package servlet;

// import the EJB platform remote interface
import platform.Platform;
// import the EJB  platform home interface
import platform.PlatformHome;
// import the serializable object
import platform.PlatWrap;

// import the ServiceCtx class from the Oracle package
import oracle.aurora.jndi.sess_iiop.ServiceCtx;

// import the Java mandatory classes to use JNDI
import javax.naming.Context;
import javax.naming.InitialContext;

// import application-specific Java classes
import java.util.Hashtable;
import java.sql.*;
import java.math.BigDecimal;
import java.util.*;
import java.util.Vector;

// Import packages to run servlets
import javax.servlet.*;
import javax.servlet.http.*;
import java.io.*;
import java.util.*;

public class ServletEJBClient
    extends HttpServlet {
  /**
   * Initialize global variables
   */
```

```java
public void init(ServletConfig config)
    throws ServletException {

  super.init(config);

} // End init() method

/**
 * Process the HTTP Get request
 */
public void doGet (
        HttpServletRequest request,
        HttpServletResponse response)
    throws ServletException, IOException {

  response.setContentType("text/html");
  OutputStreamWriter osw =
        new OutputStreamWriter(response.getOutputStream());
  PrintWriter out =
        new PrintWriter (response.getOutputStream());
  out.println("<html>");
  out.println("<head><title>ServletEJBClient</title></head>");
  out.println("<body>");
  out.println("<h1>The ServletEJBClient "
        +"Class Using EJB Object </h1>");
  out.println(getEJBInfo());
  out.println("</body></html>");
  out.close();

} // End doGet() method

/**
 * Get Servlet information
 * @return java.lang.String
 */
private String getEJBInfo() {

    String OutputString = null;
    String serviceURL = "sess_iiop://data-i.com:2481:ORCL";
    String objectName = "/test/PlatformDb";
    String user = "obsschema";
    String password = "obsschema";

    Hashtable env = new Hashtable();

    // Set the JNDI environment for the client
    // to locate the EJB object
```

```
env.put(Context.URL_PKG_PREFIXES, "oracle.aurora.jndi");
env.put(Context.SECURITY_PRINCIPAL, user);
env.put(Context.SECURITY_CREDENTIALS, password);
env.put(Context.SECURITY_AUTHENTICATION,
        ServiceCtx.NON_SSL_LOGIN);

Context ic = null;
// Create an instance of the Context class
try {
    ic = new InitialContext (env);
} // End of try()
catch (javax.naming.NamingException nex) {
      OutputString = "Cannot instantiate Context "
                     +nex.getMessage();
      return OutputString;
} // End of catch()

// Create an instance of the EJB object home interface.
PlatformHome home = null;

// Create an instance of the EJB Bean class.
Platform myPlatformBean = null;

try {
    // Use the home interface to
    // locate the EJB object
    home =
        PlatformHome)ic.lookup (serviceURL + objectName);

    // Create a Bean instance
    myPlatformBean = home.create();
}  // End of try
catch ( Exception ex ) {
      OutputString =
            "Cannot locate"
            +" or create Platform home"
            +ex.getMessage();
      return OutputString;
}  // End of catch()

Vector platformVector = null;
```

```
     try {
         // Invoke the EJB object's method
         platformVector =
              platformVector = myPlatformBean.getPlatformList();
     }   // End of try
     catch ( Exception ex ) {
          OutputString =
                  "Cannot locate or " +"getPlatformList()"
                  +ex.getMessage();
          return OutputString;
     }   // End of catch()

     OutputString = " ";
     PlatWrap p = null;
     Enumeration enum = platformVector.elements();

     // Iterate to get the column attributes from the table
     while (enum.hasMoreElements()) {
         // Get PlatformType from the platformVector
         p = (PlatWrap)enum.nextElement();
         // Get the column values
         OutputString = OutputString
             +((p.getKeyId()==null) ? " " : p.getKeyId().toString())
             + " " + ((p.getType()==null) ? " " : p.getType()) + " "
             + ((p.getDescription()==null) ? " " : p.getDescription())
             + "<br>";
     }     // End of while

     return OutputString;

   } // End of getEJBInfo() method

} // End of ServletEJBClient class
```

When you run the `ServletEJBClient` class, you get the output shown in Figure 9-10.

The definition of the `ServletEJBClient` class concludes the section on Enterprise JavaBeans in this chapter. Next, you will learn how to write a CORBA object and deploy it in the Oracle8*i*/9*i* data server. To learn more about CORBA, see *Oracle CORBA Developer's Guide*.

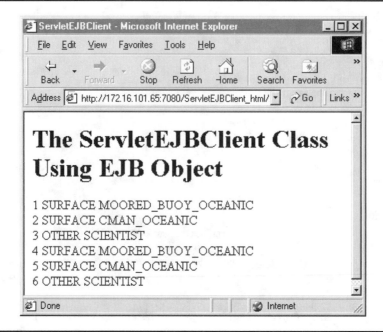

FIGURE 9-10. *ServletEJBClient invokes EJB method*

Deploying a **CORBA** Object Using a **SQLJ** Implementation

In the previous sections of this chapter, you developed a SQLJ business object and a SQLJ client that uses the object where both the client and object reside in the same address space. Next, you created an RMI object and an RMI client that uses the SQLJ object by making a remote invocation call on its getPlatformList() method. Finally, you developed an EJB object that resides in the Oracle8i/9i data server and an EJB client that also remotely invoked the EJB object's method, getPlatformList(). In both cases, the RMI and EJB applications, you use SQLJ to implement the business logic. More importantly, you use distributed object technologies, RMI and RMI/IIOP, respectively, to establish communication between client and components that reside in different address spaces.

In this section, you will develop a CORBA distributed application consisting of a CORBA object that encapsulates the business logic that you implemented in the previous sections and a CORBA client, like the SQLJ client, the RMI client, and the EJB client, that will use the object.

What Is CORBA?

Underlying distributed object paradigms is the notion of establishing the relationships between objects that live in different address spaces. It is hard to develop distributed objects that communicate transparently, efficiently, and reliably. CORBA specification addresses this challenge.

As previously stated in the "Basic Concepts of Distributed Computing Systems" section of this chapter, CORBA is a distributed object architecture that allows business objects to interoperate (communicate) across network systems, regardless of the programming language in which they are written or the platform on which they are running. CORBA supports remote, local, and client/server object collaboration. CORBA clients and servers use IIOP to communicate. The separations of interface and implementation objects and location and access transparency are the fundamental design principles behind CORBA. Interfaces to remote objects are described in a platform-neutral interface definition language (IDL). Mappings from IDL to specific programming languages are implemented, binding the language to CORBA/IIOP. Today, over 800 companies—such as hardware, software, and database vendors—support CORBA.

CORBA specifies a set of bus-related services for creating and deleting objects, accessing them by name, and storing them in persistent storage. The CORBA specification contains several components (see Figure 9-11):

- *The Object Request Broker (ORB)* core is responsible for client and server object communication. ORB is the object bus that lets objects make

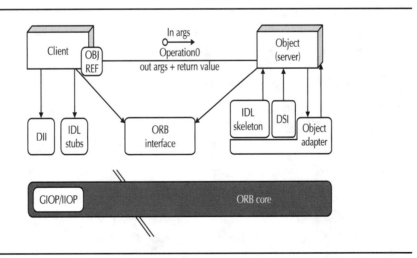

FIGURE 9-11. *CORBA component architecture*

requests to, and receive responses from other objects located in the same address space or remotely.

■ *The Interoperability Specification*, whose elements are the General and Internet Inter-ORB (GIOP and IIOP), defines the elements of interoperability between independently produced ORBs.

■ *Interface Definition Language (IDL)* defines the interfaces and the types of objects that the interfaces they use. IDL provides operating system—and programming language—independent interfaces to all the services and components that reside on a CORBA bus, allowing client and server objects written in different programming languages to interoperate.

■ *The Programming language mappings for IDL* (for example, C, C++, Java, and so on) include definition of the language-specific data types and interfaces to access CORBA objects through the ORB.

■ *The Static Invocation Interface (SII)* is a programming interface to the stub class that provides communication between client and server objects written in non-object-oriented languages.

■ *Dynamic Invocation Interface (DII)* allows the dynamic construction of object invocations rather than calling a stub class that is specific to a particular operation. DII lets you discover methods to be invoked at run time. Dynamic invocations are difficult to program, but they provide maximum flexibility and are very useful tools to discover services at run time.

■ *Static Skeleton Interface (SSI) and Dynamic Skeleton Interface (DSI)* allow static and dynamic handling of objects.

■ *Portable Object Adapter (POA)* provides an object adapter that can be used with multiple ORBs. An ORB provides services through an object adapter (generation and interpretation of object references, method invocations, and so on). Object implementations use object adapters to access the ORB.

■ *ORB Interface and Implementation Repositories (IR)*, respectively, are the interface that goes directly above the ORB and the repository of information for the ORB to locate and activate implementation objects. The Interface Repository APIs allow you to obtain and modify the descriptions of the registered component interfaces, the methods they support, and the parameters they require.

This section provides a short introduction on the ORB component. Detailed discussion of all CORBA components is beyond the scope of this book. For more information on CORBA components, see the Bibliography at the end of the book, particularly the CORBA 2.2 Specification, Client/Server Programming with Java *and* CORBA, and Instant CORBA.

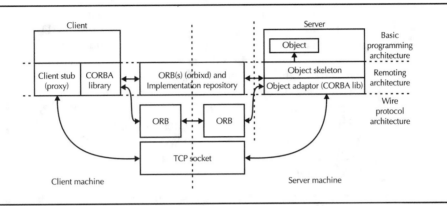

FIGURE 9-12. *CORBA ORB architecture*

Object Request Broker

CORBA uses an ORB (Figure 9-12) middleware that handles the communication details between client and server objects. The ORB is structured to provide a high degree of interoperability of a wide variety of object systems. It is responsible for the mechanisms that locate the object's implementation, activate the object, and communicate the requested data to the client. The CORBA client communicates via the object interface, which is completely independent of where the object is located. Like the RMI and the EJB clients, the CORBA client uses a stub class to invoke remote objects. Additionally, it can use the Dynamic Invocation Interface (DII) or can directly interact with the ORB for some functions. In CORBA, the term *Dynamic Invocation* refers to a client's request being constructed at run time, instead of being known at compile time.

CORBA Object Composites

The CORBA object components are similar to the RMI and EJB object components and consist of the following:

- An application `interface` source file defined in the OMG Interface Definition Language (OMG IDL) that must have an `.idl` extension. The IDL file describes the interfaces that client objects call and object implementations provide. When you write the IDL `interface` file, you need to specify the interfaces, the interfaces' operations (that is, the method definitions or the behavior of the object), and the data types used in these interfaces. The OMG IDL grammar is a subset of the ANSI C++ standard and supports C++ syntax for constant type and operation declarations. Client programs are not written in OMG IDL, but in languages for which

IDL mappings have been defined. For example, IDL mappings exist for programming languages such as C, C++, Smalltalk, COBOL, ADA, and Java. After you create the IDL file, the next step is to run the file through the IDL compiler. The IDL compiler generates the "type" information for each interface's method and stores it in a repository called the Interface Repository (IR). The interface's information is generated in the programming language of your choice, depending on the IDL mapping, that you have in your system. For example, Inprise provides a mapping of IDL for Java, the VisiBroker for Java. To map IDL files to Java, you can use the `idl2java`, `java2idl`, and `java2iiop` tools (Inprise's VisiBroker for Java) that are distributed with Oracle8i/9i.

■ An `interface implementation`, like an RMI or an EJB implementation class, provides the actual state and behavior of an object. The object implementation interacts with the ORB to establish its identity, create new objects, and obtain ORB services.

■ A client object sends a request, during which it obtains an Object Reference for the CORBA object. A client initiates the request when it calls either the stub class that is specific to the object or uses the Dynamic Invocation Interface (DII). Note that the new release of Oracle8i/9i supports requests only via a stub class. When a client makes a request, it first gets an Object Reference, which it then uses to activate the object. Object activation (that is, preparing an object to execute an operation) is done when the client invokes an object's method. The client knows how to find or create the CORBA objects and, like the RMI and the EJB clients, can access the object's functionality only via the object's public interface. Note that CORBA server objects are located by name through the CORBA Naming Service. Also, note that CORBA clients, like EJB clients, use the JNDI to locate CORBA objects stored in the Oracle8i/9i database, as in Figure 9-13. Remember that the CORBA ORB is an object bus. The CORBA Naming Service allows components on the bus to locate other components by name.

Next, you will develop a CORBA object and deploy it into the Oracle8i/9i data server.

Developing a CORBA Object

The steps to develop and deploy a CORBA object using a SQLJ implementation are as follows:

   I. Create the directories that you wish to use to store and deploy your object.

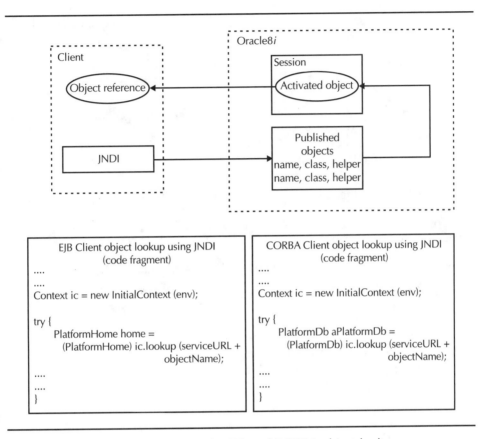

Figure content:

Client

Object reference

JNDI

Oracle8*i*

Session

Activated object

Published
objects
name, class, helper
name, class, helper

EJB Client object lookup using JNDI
(code fragment)

....

....

Context ic = new InitialContext (env);

try {
    PlatformHome home =
        (PlatformHome) ic.lookup (serviceURL +
            objectName);

....

....
}

CORBA Client object lookup using JNDI
(code fragment)

....

....

Context ic = new InitialContext (env);

try {
    PlatformDb aPlatformDb =
        (PlatformDb) ic.lookup (serviceURL +
            objectName);

....

....
}

FIGURE 9-13.   *Client using JNDI for EJB and COBRA object lookup*

2. Create a high-level view of your object.

3. Create the OMG IDL file, `platform.idl`.

4. Generate the stub and the skeleton classes. The IDL compiler will generate
   the stub and the skeleton classes for you when you run the `platform.idl`
   file through the compiler (see Listing 9-9, earlier in this chapter). The client
   IDL stubs provide the static interfaces to object services. These precompiled
   stubs define how clients invoke corresponding services on the servers and
   act like local proxy for a remote server object. Static invocations are easier
   to program, faster, and self-documenting. The server IDL stubs (skeletons)
   provide static interfaces to each service exported by the server.

5. Create the server object implementation class, the `PlatformCorbaImp` class.

6. Create the `ClientJavaForCorbaPlatform` CORBA client that will use the CORBA object.

7. Set your CLASSPATH and compile all the programs.

8. Create the `CorbaPlat.jar` JAR file.

9. Load the programs into the Oracle8*i*/9*i* data server.

10. Publish the CORBA object.

11. Run the CORBA client.

Step 1 Create the directories that you wish to use to store your source code:

```
// Create the directories to store the Java and SQLJ source code
mkdir deployobjects\platServer
```

Step 2 Create a high-level view of your object, as in Figure 9-14.

Step 3 Create the IDL file, `platform.idl`. An OMG IDL specification consists of type, constant, exception, and/or module definitions. The `platform.idl` file is a very basic IDL file:

```
//      File Name:      platform.idl                    */
//      Purpose:    OMG IDL file for the
//                  Platform CORBA Object
//

module corbaPlatform { // (See Note 1.)
  struct PlatWrapper {  // (See Note 2.)
    long keyId;
    wstring aType;
    wstring aDescription;
  };  // End of PlatWrapper struct

  typedef sequence <PlatWrapper> PlatformArr; // (See Note 3.)

  exception SQLError {  // (See Note 4.)
    wstring message;
  };  // End of SQLError exception

  interface PlatformCorba {  // (See Note 5.)
    // (See Note 6.)
    PlatformArr getPlatformList () raises (SQLError);
  };  // End of PlatformCorba interface

}; // End of CORBA module
```

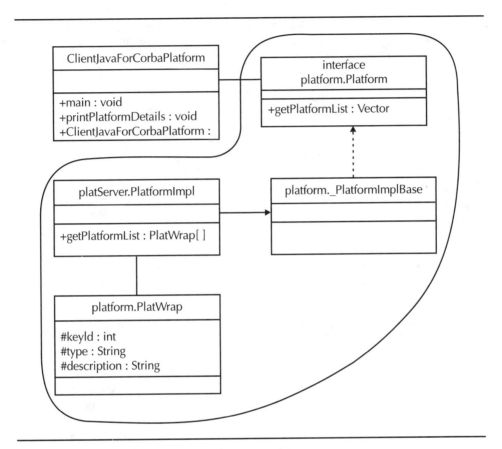

FIGURE 9-14. *High-level view of CORBA object*

Notes on the `platform.idl` file:

1. This statement declares a CORBA module. A module consists of a group of usually related object interfaces. The CORBA module is used to prevent name clashing between CORBA and other programming languages. Note that an IDL module is mapped to a Java package with the same name. Also, note that all IDL type declarations within the module generate corresponding Java class or interface declarations within the generated package.

2. This statement declares a CORBA *struct*. A struct is mapped to a `final` Java class with the same name. The `keyId`, `aType`, and `aDescription`

fields are called *attributes* and correspond to Java instance variables. An attribute is made visible to clients as a pair of operations, get_*XXXX* and set_*XXXX*, and consequently, are mapped to a pair of Java accessor and modifier methods. When you compile the IDL file, the compiler also generates a *holder* and a *helper* class for the struct. For example, the IDL compiler will generate the PlatWrapperHolder and the PlatWrapperHelper classes for the PlatWrapper struct. See Note 5 below for more information regarding generated helper and holder classes. See the upcoming Listing 9-13 for a listing of the Java classes generated by the IDL compiler.

3. This statement declares a CORBA *sequence* that maps to a Java array with the same name. Consequently, the PlatformArr sequence defines a Java array of PlatformWrapper objects.

4. This statement declares the SQLError user-defined exception. IDL exceptions are mapped very similarly to CORBA struct. User-defined exceptions are mapped to final Java classes that extend the org.omg. CORBA.UserException class. A holder and a helper class, as for the struct, are also generated. They are the SQLErrorHolder and the SQLErrorHelper classes, respectively.

5. This statement declares an IDL interface header that consists of an interface name and an optional inheritance specification (that is, an interface can be derived from another interface; it is called a *single inheritance*). Also, CORBA allows an interface to inherit from multiple interfaces; it is called *multiple inheritances*. The interface declaration may include constant, type, exception, and operation declarations. An IDL interface is mapped to a public Java interface with the same name that contains the mapped operation signatures. Clients use the object interface to look up an object. The lookup method returns a reference to the interface and clients use the reference to invoke methods on the object. In addition to the Java interface, the IDL compiler generates two other Java classes, the PlatformCorbaHelper helper and the PlatformCorbaHolder holder classes. A helper class contains methods that read and write the object to a stream and cast the object to and from the type of the base class, whereas a holder class is used by the application when parameters in the interface operation are of type out or inout.

6. This statement declares an operation in the `interface` body. Operation declarations in OMG IDL are similar to C function declarations. You normally declare the published operations on the object in the `interface` body.

Step 4   Generate the `_st_PlatformCorba` stub and the `_PlatformCorbaImplBase` skeleton classes (see Listing 9-13). The `_<interfaceName>ImplBase` skeleton class, like the EJB Object's implementation class, is installed on the server and communicates with the stub file on the client side. The server skeleton also returns parameters and return values to the client. The CORBA ORB handles the communication between the client's stub and the server's skeleton. The IDL compiler will generate the Java classes corresponding to the declarations specified in the `platform.idl` file including the stub and the skeleton classes. Refer to the preceding "Notes on the `platform.idl` file" part of this section for more information regarding the generated Java classes. Note that the `_example_` `PlatformCorba` (`_st_` is a VisiBroker-specific prefix) class is also included. This class gives you an example of how you should implement the interface on the server. See the listing of the `_example_PlatformCorba` in Listing 9-14. Use the `idl2java` tool to compile the OMG IDL file.

Listing 9-13

```
// First, set the following variables. At the command prompt:
set ORACLE_HOME=Device:\Oracle\Ora81
// Please edit the host name to correspond to your host name:
set ORACLE_SERVICE=sess_iiop://datai:2481:orcl

// Set a variable to hold your JDK 1.1.x path and
// ORACLE file %ORACLE_HOME%\jdbc\lib\classes111.zip;
set JDK_CLASSPATH=Device:\jdk1_1_8\jdk1.1.8\lib\classes.zip

// Set a variable to hold your JDK 1.2.x path
// ORACLE file %ORACLE_HOME%\jdbc\lib\classes12.zip;
// set JDK_CLASSPATH=Device:\java2\lib\dt.jar;
// Device:\java2\lib\tools.jar;

// Get to the directory where you stored your platform.idl file
// Review Step 1 of this section.
cd Device:\deployobjects\corbaPlatform

// Set your CLASSPATH.
```

```
set CLASSPATH=.;Device:\deployobjects; \
%ORACLE_HOME%\lib\aurora_client.jar; \
%ORACLE_HOME%\jdbc\lib\classes111.zip; \
%ORACLE_HOME%\sqlj\lib\translator.zip;  \
 %ORACLE_HOME%\lib\vbjorb.jar; \
%ORACLE_HOME%\lib\vbjapp.jar;%JDK_CLASSPATH%

// CAUTION: with SQLJ 8.1.7 or later,
// add either runtime11.zip or runtime12.zip
// Compile the OMG IDL file
idl2java -no_comments platform.idl

// Expected Java output files from compiled IDL file:
Traversing platform.idl
Creating: corbaPlatform\PlatWrapper.java
Creating: corbaPlatform\PlatWrapperHolder.java
Creating: corbaPlatform\PlatWrapperHelper.java
Creating: corbaPlatform\PlatformArrHolder.java
Creating: corbaPlatform\PlatformArrHelper.java
Creating: corbaPlatform\SQLError.java
Creating: corbaPlatform\SQLErrorHolder.java
Creating: corbaPlatform\SQLErrorHelper.java
Creating: corbaPlatform\PlatformCorba.java
Creating: corbaPlatform\PlatformCorbaHolder.java
Creating: corbaPlatform\PlatformCorbaHelper.java
Creating: corbaPlatform\_st_PlatformCorba.java
Creating: corbaPlatform\_PlatformCorbaImplBase.java
Creating: corbaPlatform\PlatformCorbaOperations.java
Creating: corbaPlatform\_tie_PlatformCorba.java
Creating: corbaPlatform\_example_PlatformCorba.java
```

Note that the `_tie_PlatformCorba.java` class generated by the IDL compiler provides you with an alternative means to implement a server object, other than extending the generated skeleton class.

Listing 9-13

```
//     File Name:    _example_PlatformCorba.java
package platform;
public class _example_PlatformCorba
      extends corbaPlatform._PlatformImplBase {  // (See Note 1.)
  public _example_PlatformCorba(java.lang.String name) {
    super(name);
  }
  public _example_PlatformCorba() {
    super();
```

```
   }
   public corbaPlatform.PlatWrapper[] getPlatformList()
          throws corbaPlatform.SQLError {
     // IMPLEMENT: Operation
     return null;
   }
}
```

Note on Listing 9-14:

1. The implementation class must be a subclass of the
   _PlatformCorbaImplBase skeleton class. Remember
   that the client uses the _st_PlatformCorba stub class on the
   client side to communicate with the _PlatformCorbaImplBase
   server skeleton class.

Step 5   Create the PlatformCorbaImp server object implementation class.
   The PlatformCorbaImp, like the PlatformDbObject from the SQLJ
component and the Platform from the EJB object, implements the application-
specific business logic. It provides the information needed to create an object
and the services to invoke its methods. The following is a listing of the
PlatformCorbaImp class:

```
/*      Program Name: PlatformCorbaImp.sqlj
**      Purpose: A SQLJ Class that extends the
**   _PlatformCorbaImplBase interface generated by
**   IDL compiler and fully implements the
**   getPlatformList(): Array from the IDL
**   interface Platform declaration
**   The class implements the logic to query

**   the PLATFORM_TYPE_LIST table.
*/
package platServer;

import corbaPlatform.*;
import corbaPlatform.PlatWrapper;

import java.sql.*;
import java.util.Vector;

// Declare a named iterator
#sql iterator PIter (int  aPlatformId,
```

```
                String aType, String aDesc);
// (See Note 1.)
public class PlatformCorbaImp
   extends corbaPlatform._PlatformCorbaImplBase {

  public corbaPlatform.PlatWrapper[] getPlatformList ()
     throws corbaPlatform.SQLError {   // (See Note 2.)
    try {
        Vector platformVector = new Vector ();

        // Use the PIter SQLJ iterator to retrieve
        // rows of data from the PLATFORM_TYPE_LIST table
        PIter anPIter = null;

        #sql anPIter =
           { SELECT P.key_id AS aPlatformId,
                    P.type AS aType, P.description AS aDesc
             FROM PLATFORM_TYPE_LIST P
           };

        // Store the contents of the SQLJ iterator in
        // the platformVector object
        while (anPIter.next()) {   // (See Note 3.)
            platformVector.addElement
             ( new PlatWrapper
               ( anPIter.aPlatformId(),anPIter.aType(),
                 anPIter.aDesc()
               )
             );
        }   // End of while

        // Always close your SQLJ iterator
        anPIter.close();

        // Create an array of PlatWrapper objects whose
        // length is equal to the vector length
        PlatWrapper[] queryResult =
              new PlatWrapper[platformVector.size()];
        // Copy the contents of the platformVector object
        platformVector.copyInto(queryResult);
        // Return an array of PlatWrapper objects to the caller
        return queryResult;

     }   // End of try
```

```
    catch (SQLException e) {
       throw new SQLError (e.getMessage ());  // (See Note 4.)
    }  // End of catch

  }  // End of getPlatformList ()

}  // End of PlatformCorbaImp class
```

Notes on the `PlatformImpl` class:

1. This statement declares a subclass of the
   `corbaPlatform._PlatformImplBase` class generated
   by the IDL compiler in step 4. Remember that the generated
   class mapped the operation signatures for the CORBA object. The
   `PlatformCorbaImp` class provides the operation body for the object.

2. This statement declares the `getPlatformList ()` method. Note that
   the user-defined error is included in the method's `throws` clause.

3. This statement declares a `while` loop to retrieve the column values of the
   database table, the `PLATFORM_TYPE_LIST` table, stored in the `anPIter`
   iterator variable. The `platformVector.addElement (...)` statement
   first constructs a `PlatWrapper` object by calling the parameterized
   constructor of the `PlatWrapper` class using the accessor methods of
   the SQLJ `iterator`, and then it inserts the newly created object into
   the `platformVector` variable. The remaining code of the program is
   identical to the `PlatformDbObject` class in the section "Designing
   and Developing a SQLJ Component-Based Object," earlier in this chapter.

4. This statement raises the `SQLerror` user-defined error in its
   `throws` clause.

Step 6   Create the `ClientJavaForCorbaPlatform` CORBA client that will
use the CORBA object.

```
/*      Program Name: ClientJavaForCorbaPlatform.java
**      Purpose:      A Java client to access CORBA
**  object stored in Oracle8i/9i data server.
*/

// Import the CORBA platform interface
```

```
import platform.*;
import platServer.*;

import oracle.aurora.jndi.sess_iiop.ServiceCtx;
import javax.naming.Context;
import javax.naming.InitialContext;

import java.util.Hashtable;
import java.sql.*;
import java.math.BigDecimal;
import java.util.*;
import java.util.Vector;

public class ClientJavaForCorbaPlatform {

  public static void main(String[] args) throws Exception {

    if (args.length != 4) {
       System.out.println("usage: Client "
          + "serviceURL objectName user password");
       System.exit(1);
    }  // End if

    String serviceURL = args [0];
    String objectName = args [1];
    String user = args [2];
    String password = args [3];

    // Setup environment for JNDI   (See Note 1.)
    Hashtable env = new Hashtable();
    env.put(Context.URL_PKG_PREFIXES, "oracle.aurora.jndi");
    env.put(Context.SECURITY_PRINCIPAL, user);
    env.put(Context.SECURITY_CREDENTIALS, password);
    env.put(Context.SECURITY_AUTHENTICATION,
        ServiceCtx.NON_SSL_LOGIN);

    // Get an initial context instance
    Context ic = new InitialContext (env);
    PlatformCorba aPlatform = null;
    try {
        // Create a PlatformCorba object and invoke
        // the lookup() method to get a reference
        // of the PlatformCorba interface.
        // (See Note 2.)
        aPlatform =
           (PlatformCorba)ic.lookup (serviceURL + objectName);
```

```
        // Use the instance to invoke
        // the remote object's method   (See Note 3.)
        PlatWrapper[] platformArray = aPlatform.getPlatformList();

        // Print the details. Code REUSE!
        printPlatformDetails(platformArray);

    }   // End of try
    catch ( Exception ex ) {
        System.out.println("== Cannot locate"
            +" or create Platform == "
            +ex.getMessage());
        System.exit(1);
    }   // End of catch

}   // End of main()

public static void printPlatformDetails(PlatWrapper[] p)
    throws SQLException {
    int i;
    for (i = 0; i < p.length; i++) {
        System.out.println(p[i].keyId + " "
            + p[i].aType + " "   +p[i].aDescription );
    } // End of for loop

}    // End printPlatformDetails()

}   // End of ClientJavaForCorbaPlatform class
```

Notes on the `ClientJavaForCorbaPlatform` application:

The CORBA client is almost identical to the EJB client that you created
in "Deploying an Enterprise JavaBeans Object Using a SQLJ Implementation,"
earlier in this chapter.

  1. This statement and the ones that follow it are identical to the statement in
      the EJB client in the "Deploying an Enterprise JavaBeans Object Using a SQLJ
      Implementation" section of this chapter. You use JNDI to look up a CORBA
      object that resides in the Oracle8*i*/9*i* data server the same way that you look
      up an EJB object. Note that a CORBA application requires that an ORB be
      active on both the client system and the system running the server. The
      client-side ORB is normally initialized as part of the processing that
      goes on when the client invokes the `lookup()` method on the JNDI
      `InitialContext` object that it instantiates. The ORB on the server is

started by the presentation that handles IIOP requests. Oracle8*i*/9*i* JVM provides a JNDI interface to CosNaming (CORBA naming service) so that you use URL-based naming to refer to, and activate, CORBA objects in a session. For information regarding JNDI environment settings, see the Oracle *CORBA Developer's Guide, the* "Notes on the `ClientJavajForEjbPlatform` client application" part of the "Deploying an Enterprise JavaBeans Object Using a SQLJ Implementation" section of this chapter, and the Bibliography at the end of the book.

2. This statement creates an instance of the `Platform` interface that the IDL compiler generated for you in step 4 of this section. When you call the `lookup` method, it returns an object reference to the `interface`.

3. This statement invokes the `getPlatformList()` method of the CORBA object using the object reference from the previous statement. Note that CORBA objects are activated on demand, that is, the client activates the object when it invokes the method; at invocation time, the ORB loads the object into memory and caches it. A cache is a buffer of high-speed memory filled often with instructions from main memory. In CORBA, to invoke a remote function, the client makes a call to the client stub. The stub packs the call parameters into a request message and invokes a wire protocol to ship the message to the server. At the server side, the wire protocol delivers the message to the server stub, which then unpacks the request message and calls the actual function on the object.

Step 7   Set your `CLASSPATH` and compile all the programs generated by the IDL compiler from step 4, including your CORBA client and your SQLJ class:

```
// Review Step 4 of this section to set your CLASSPATH
// and then compile all Java source code. At the command line:
javac -g  corbaPlatform\PlatWrapper.java
javac -g  corbaPlatform\PlatWrapperHolder.java
javac -g  corbaPlatform\PlatWrapperHelper.java
javac -g  corbaPlatform\PlatformArrHolder.java
javac -g  corbaPlatform\PlatformArrHelper.java
javac -g  corbaPlatform\SQLError.java
javac -g  corbaPlatform\SQLErrorHolder.java
javac -g  corbaPlatform\SQLErrorHelper.java
javac -g  corbaPlatform\PlatformCorba.java
javac -g  corbaPlatform\PlatformCorbaHolder.java
javac -g  corbaPlatform\PlatformCorbaHelper.java
javac -g  corbaPlatform\_st_PlatformCorba.java
javac -g  corbaPlatform\_PlatformCorbaImplBase.java
javac -g  corbaPlatform\PlatformCorbaOperations.java
javac -g  corbaPlatform\_tie_PlatformCOrba.java
```

```
// Compile the platServer\PlatformCorbaImp.sqlj program
sqlj -ser2class platServer\PlatformCorbaImp.sqlj

// Compile the  CORBA client
javac -g ClientJavaForCorbaPlatform.java
```

Alternatively, you could use the following format to compile all SQLJ and Java source code at once:

```
// At the command line:
sqlj -C-g -ser2class corbaPlatform\*.java platServer\*.sqlj
ClientJavaForCorbaPlatform.java
```

Step 8   Create a JAR file of all your .class files from platform and platServer directories. Oracle recommends using a JAR file consisting of .class files to load SQLJ and Java into the Oracle8*i*/9*i* data server. See Appendix D to learn more about the jar tool.

```
// Set your CLASSPATH if you have not done so.
// Create the CorbaPlat.jar JAR file
jar cvf0 CorbaPlat.jar corbaPlatform\PlatWrapper.class \
 corbaPlatform\PlatWrapperHolder.class \
 corbaPlatform\PlatWrapperHelper.class \
 corbaPlatform\PlatformArrHolder.class \
 corbaPlatform\PlatformArrHelper.class \
 corbaPlatform\SQLError.class \
 corbaPlatform\SQLErrorHolder.class \
 corbaPlatform\SQLErrorHelper.class \
 corbaPlatform\PlatformCorba.class \
 corbaPlatform\PlatformCorbaHolder.class \
 corbaPlatform\PlatformCorbaHelper.class \
 corbaPlatform\_st_PlatformCorba.class \
 corbaPlatform\_PlatformCorbaImplBase.class \
 corbaPlatform\PlatformCorbaOperations.class \
 corbaPlatform\_tie_PlatformCorba.class \
 platServer\PIter.class \
 platServer\PlatformCorbaImp.class \
 platServer\PlatformCorbaImp_SJProfile0.class \
 platServer\PlatformCorbaImp_SJProfileKeys.class
```

Step 9   Load the programs into the Oracle8i/9i data server using the CorbaPlat JAR file that you created in step 8. You do so with the Oracle loadjava tool. To learn more about the loadjava tool, see Chapter 3, Appendix D, and the *Oracle8i Java Tools Reference* manual.

At the command line:

```
// At the command line:
loadjava -verbose -resolve -thin -u \
  obsschema/obsschema@datai:1521:orcl CorbaPlat.jar
```

Step 10 Publish the CORBA object into Oracle8*i*/9*i*. This is the final step in preparing a CORBA object. When you publish a CORBA object, you are "*physically*" putting a CORBA object into the namespace. Objects are published in the Oracle database using the OMG CosNaming service and can be accessed using Oracle's JNDI interface to CosNaming. Remember that the namespace in the database looks just like a typical file system, and also, you can examine and manipulate objects in the publishing namespace using the session shell tool (sess_sh). See step 10 of the "Deploying an Enterprise JavaBeans Object Using a SQLJ Implementation" section of this chapter for more information regarding the Oracle namespace. Use the publish tool specifying the CorbaPlatformObj user-defined name for the CORBA object that you wish to publish or any name of your choice, the platServer.PlatformCorbaImp implementation class, and the corbaPlatform.PlatformCorbaHelper class.

```
// Set your CLASSPATH and publish the object into the database
publish -republish -u obsschema \
  -p obsschema -schema OBSSCHEMA -s %ORACLE_SERVICE%  \
  /test/CorbaPlatformObj platServer.PlatformCorbaImp \
  corbaPlatform.PlatformCorbaHelper
```

Step 11 Run the ClientJavaForCorbaPlatform CORBA client. If you have no error from the preceding steps, then run the client:

```
// Please, set your CLASSPATH. Review Step 4 to do so.
// Add the following to your
// CLASSPATH (Oracle8i release 8.1.7 and Oracle9i only):
// [ORACLE_HOME]\lib\mts.jar
Java ClientJavaForCorbaPlatform sess_iiop://datai:2481:orcl \
  /test/PlatformCorbaObj obsschema obsschema
```

As you would expect, the resulting output after the execution of the ClientJavaForCorbaPlatform class is as follows:

```
1    SURFACE MOORED_BUOY_OCEANIC
2    SURFACE CMAN_OCEANIC
3    OTHER SCIENTIST
4    SURFACE MOORED_BUOY_OCEANIC
5    SURFACE CMAN_OCEANIC
6    OTHER SCIENTIST
```

Note that a `makeit.bat` file is provided to compile and load all the programs and publish the CORBA object, and also a `runit.bat` file to run the CORBA client.

In this chapter, you used an object-relational database, the scientific Observation schema, to develop components implemented in SQLJ. While developing a software component, you learned the following:

- Basic concepts of distributed objects.

- How to design and develop a SQLJ component and a client that uses the component, in a scenario where both component and client reside in the same address space.

- How to design and develop distributed objects and clients that use these objects by making remote invocation calls on the components' methods. While the object and the client were located on different address spaces, it appears as though they were local to the clients that make the call. You created the RMI, EJB, and CORBA objects to demonstrate this concept, and also, in all three cases, you used SQLJ to implement the business logic encapsulated in the object. In addition, you learned that EJB and CORBA clients use database sessions, just like any other Oracle client, but, unlike a session in which the client communicates through SQL*Net, you access CORBA and EJB sessions through IIOP.

This chapter concludes Part III. Chapter 10 marks the beginning of Part IV, where you will learn performance-tuning techniques that will help you use SQLJ effectively.

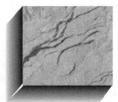

PART
IV

Effective Use of SQLJ

CHAPTER
10

SQLJ Applications:
Performance Tuning

n the previous chapters, you learned how to design, implement, and deploy SQLJ programs. In this chapter, you will learn how to tune your SQLJ source code and thereby improve performance.

Oracle provides two JDBC implementations: one that supports the Sun Microsystems JDK 1.2.*x* and complies to the JDBC 2.0 standard, and one that supports JDK 1.1.*x* and complies with the Sun JDBC 1.22 standard. Note that the Oracle JDK 1.1.*x*–compatible driver is functionally "equivalent" to the JDK 1.2–compatible driver. Also, notice that if you use APIs on Oracle-specific classes, you can write code that uses JDK 1.2 features but that runs under both JDK 1.1.*x* and 1.2. Using SQLJ, however, makes it almost transparent to produce a cross-compatible program.

In addition to the standard JDBC support, Oracle JDBC drivers are further enhanced with the Oracle-specific type extensions for Oracle datatypes; Oracle objects; and specific schema naming and performance extensions for update batching, row prefetching, and so on.

The Oracle extensions include two packages: the `oracle.sql.*` and the `oracle.jdbc.driver.*` Java packages. The former includes classes to support all Oracle type extensions, and the latter includes classes to support database access and updates in Oracle type formats. Note that, in Oracle9*i* JDBC drivers release 9.0.1, the second package has been deprecated in favor of interfaces in the `oracle.jdbc.*` package. Important here is that the `oracle.jdbc.driver.*` package (in 9.0.1, `oracle.jdbc.*`) includes the `OracleConnection` class, which implements the `java.sql.Connection interface` and provides methods to set values to the Oracle performance extensions for SQL statements executing in a current connection.

In this chapter, you will revisit the `ConnectionManager` class that you created in Chapter 5 and extend its capability to connect to the Oracle8*i*/9*i* data server using the `OracleConnection` class. More important here, you will learn how to write efficient SQLJ programs that use the features provided by the Oracle JDBC drivers, Oracle-defined extensions, and Oracle8*i*/9*i* SQLJ to improve your application performance.

Specifically, in this chapter you will

■ Extend the `ConnectionManager` class created in Chapters 5 and 6 so that it can be used as a utility class that includes methods that convert an instance of the `sqlj.runtime.ref.DefaultContext`, `sqlj.runtime.ConnectContext`, and `java.sql.Connection` classes to instances of the `oracle.jdbc.driver.OracleConnection` class. See Chapter 5 to learn more about SQLJ connection classes.

■ Learn about the support features of Oracle performance enhancements.

- Develop efficient SQLJ programs that implement the Oracle performance enhancements.

- Tune SQL statements from SQLJ with the Oracle Optimizer.

- Consider other ways to improve performance by reducing network traffic.

Extending the `ConnectionManager` Class

In this section, you will create additional methods in the ConnectionManager class that convert an instance of the SQLJ DefaultContext, ConnectionContext, or the JDBC java.sql.Connection classes to an instance of the OracleConnection class.

In the previous chapters, you use the Oracle connect.properties file to establish connections to the database. Remember that a *properties* file is a text file in which you specify a connection URL, username, and password. You learned about the connect.properties file in the "Connecting to the Database" section of Chapter 2. In this chapter, you will learn how to use the ConnectionManager class to connect to the database. The ConnectionManager class that you will develop here does something similar to what the connect.properties file does.

A partial listing of the ConnectionManager class is presented in Chapter 6; you might want to review it before proceeding. Here is the listing of the modified version of the class that uses the OracleConnection class:

```
/*   Class Name: ConnectionManager.java
**
**   Purpose:   Java utility program to establish
**     connections to Oracle databases
*/

import oracle.jdbc.driver.OracleConnection;
import sqlj.runtime.ref.DefaultContext;
import sqlj.runtime.ConnectionContext;
import oracle.sqlj.runtime.Oracle;
import java.sql.Connection;
import java.sql.SQLException;

public class ConnectionManager {

  // An instance variable used to hold an OracleConnection instance
  private OracleConnection anOracleConnection = null;

  /*
```

```
   Set up database connection information. Set these variables for
   your JDBC driver, database and account. If you leave them set
   to null, any program using this class will not run
*/

static private String DBURL  = null ;  //Database URL
static private String UID    = null ;  //User ID
static private String PWD    = null ;  //Password

static {
   /* Start of Oracle configuration
      Modify the DBURL, UID, and PWD variables to reflect the
      user, driver, and database that you wish to connect to
   */

   //  Required for programs using OCI 7 driver
   //  DBURL = "jdbc:oracle:oci7:@" ;

   //  Required for programs using OCI 8 driver
   //  DBURL = "jdbc:oracle:oci8:@" ;
   //  The Oracle OCI 9 driver accepts the designation oci8
   //  as well as oci. Thus people may want to use oci8 if
   //  they write for both 8i and 9i databases.

   //  Required for programs using oracle thin driver
   //  DBURL = "jdbc:oracle:thin:@localhost:port#:SID" ;

   // (See Note 1.)
   DBURL = "jdbc:oracle:thin:@data-i.com:1521:ORCL";
   UID   = "scott";
   PWD   = "tiger";
   // End of Oracle configuration
} // End of static initializer

public ConnectionManager() {
   try {
      // Get a Connection instance from the underlying JDBC
      // connection. Cast the returned Connection to an
      // OracleConnection instance (See Note 2.)
      anOracleConnection = (OracleConnection)
        DefaultContext.getDefaultContext().getConnection();
   } // End of try block
   // (See Note 3.)
   catch (java.lang.NullPointerException e) {
      // An exception is raised if there is no previous connection
      // to the database. The following method establishes a
      // connection and test to see if the DBURL, UID, and PWD
      // variables are defined. It then establishes a connection with
```

```
      // the database
      connectDB();
    } // End of catch block
} // End of ConnectionManager() constructor

public ConnectionManager(Connection aConnection) {
    if  (aConnection == null ) {
        // Establish a connection if there is no
        // associated connection with the Connection
        // parameter object
        connectDB();
    }
    else
        // Cast the Connection parameter to an OracleConnection
        // instance (See Note 4.)
        anOracleConnection = (OracleConnection)aConnection;
} // End of ConnectionManager() constructor

public ConnectionManager(DefaultContext aDefaultContext) {
  try {
    // Cast the underlying JDBC connection of the DefaultContext
    // object to the OracleConnection instance variable
    anOracleConnection =
      (OracleConnection)aDefaultContext.getConnection();
  } // End of try block
  catch (java.lang.NullPointerException e) {
    // Establish a connection if there is no associated connection
    // with the DefaultContext parameter object.
    connectDB();
  } // End of catch block
} // End of ConnectionManager() constructor

public ConnectionManager(ConnectionContext aConnectionContext) {
  try {
    // Cast the underlying JDBC connection of a declared
    // ConnectionContext object to the OracleConnection
    // instance variable.
    anOracleConnection =
      (OracleConnection)aConnectionContext.getConnection();
  } // End of try block
  catch (java.lang.NullPointerException e) {
    // Establish connection if there is no associated connection
    // with the ConnectionContext parameter object
    connectDB();
  } // End of catch block
} // End of ConnectionManager() constructor

/*
```

```
      Creates a new OracleConnection object using the current values
      of the DBURL, UID, and PWD variables, or the installed
      default context. If any of the needed attributes is null, or a
      connection is not able to be established, an appropriate error
      message is printed to System.out and the programs exits.
*/
private void connectDB() {
  // Verify that the access parameters are set. (See Note 5.)
  if (UID==null || PWD==null || DBURL==null) {
    System.err.println (
      "Please edit the ConnectionManager.java file to assign " +
      "non-null values to the static string variables " +
      "DBURL, UID, and PWD. Then recompile and try again." ) ;
    System.exit(1) ;
  } // End of if

  try {
    // If there is no connection to the database, establish one
    // while converting and casting the underlying JDBC connection
    // to an OracleConnection instance
    //   (See Note 6.)
    anOracleConnection = (OracleConnection)
      Oracle.connect(DBURL, UID, PWD, false)
        .getDefaultContext().getConnection();
  } // End of try block
  catch (SQLException e) {
    System.err.println("Error connecting to the database");
    System.err.println(e);
    System.exit(1) ;
  } // End of catch block
} // End of connectDB() method

public void resetOracleConnection(Connection aConnection) {
  // Using the Connection or an OracleConnection object from the
  // parameter, reset the anOracleConnection instance variable
  anOracleConnection = (OracleConnection)aConnection;
} // End of resetOracleConnection() method

public void resetOracleConnection(DefaultContext aDefaultContext) {
  // Using the DefaultContext object parameter, reset the
  // anOracleConnection instance variable
  anOracleConnection =
    (OracleConnection)aDefaultContext.getConnection();
} // End of resetOracleConnection() method

public void resetOracleConnection(ConnectionContext
                                    aConnectionContext) {
  // Using the ConnectionContext object parameter, which
```

```
    // represents a declared connection context object, reset
    // the anOracleConnection instance variable
    anOracleConnection =
      (OracleConnection)aConnectionContext.getConnection();
} // End of resetOracleConnection() method

public Connection getConnection() {
    // Return a java.sql.Connection object by casting it from the
    // OracleConnection instance variable
    return (Connection)anOracleConnection;
} // End of getConnection() method

public OracleConnection getOracleConnection() {
    // Return the OracleConnection instance variable
    return anOracleConnection;
} // End of getOracleConnection() method

public DefaultContext getDefaultContext() {
    // Return the current installed DefaultContext instance
    return DefaultContext.getDefaultContext();
} // End of getDefaultContext() method

// (See Note 7.)
public void closeConnection() {
    try {
        DefaultContext aDefaultContext =
                    getDefaultContext();
    } // End of try block
    catch (java.lang.NullPointerException e) {
        throw e;
    } // End of catch block
    finally {
        try {
            Oracle.close();
        }  // End of try
        catch (SQLException e) {
            System.err.println("Error closing connection");
            System.err.println(e);
            System.exit(1) ;
        } // End of catch()
    }  // End of finally
}  // End of ConnectionManager class
```

Notes on the `ConnectionManager` class:

    1. Set the database access information by assigning values to the DBURL
(database URL), UID (user ID), and PWD (password) instance variables of

this `ConnectionManager` class. These variables are used to establish connections to the database.

2. This statement gets a `Connection` object from the installed `DefaultContext` and then casts the returned instance to an `OracleConnection` object.

3. This `catch` block catches a `java.lang.NullPointerException` exception error that is thrown if there were no previous connections made to the database. In this case, the program will call the `connectDB()` method to establish a connection to the database.

4. This statement converts a `java.sql.Connection` object to an `OracleConnection` object and assigns the `Connection` to the `OracleConnection` instance variable.

5. This statement checks whether the `DBURL`, `UID`, and `PWD` variables have been set. The method will print an error message and exit the program if any of the variables are not defined.

6. Using the `DBURL`, `UID`, and `PWD` class variables, establish a connection to the database with the `Oracle.connect()` method. Use the `getConnection()` method of the `DefaultContext` connection to get the underlying JDBC connection. Cast the returned `Connection` instance to an `OracleConnection` instance and assign it to the `anOracleConnection` variable.

7. This method closes the SQLJ connection context along with the JDBC connection. Closing the `OracleConnection` would have closed only the JDBC connection. You should always close the SQLJ connection context (which will also close the JDBC connection, unless you use the `ConnectionContext.KEEP_CONNECTION` flag). If you do not close the SQLJ connection context, then the cached SQLJ statements will linger around and leak SQL cursors, a rather unfortunate event that will cause major problems—foremost in server-side code, where the same session hangs around for a while.

Support Features of Oracle Performance Enhancements

One possible way to improve the performance of database applications written in Java and using a JDBC or SQLJ implementation is to reduce the number of round trips made to the database. In this section, you will learn the features provided by the Oracle JDBC drivers, Oracle-defined extensions, and Oracle8*i*/9*i* SQLJ to reduce the number of round trips made to the database thereby improve performance.

There are two performance enhancements available under JDBC 2.0: row fetching and update batching. These performance enhancements, known as Oracle extensions, were available since Oracle8*i* release 8.1.5. Since Oracle8*i* release 8.1.6, the Oracle JDBC drivers provide these performance features at three different levels:

■   For client-side JDBC and SQLJ programs, Oracle provides the JDBC-OCI and JDBC-THIN drivers.

■   For server-side JDBC and SQLJ stored procedures, including Enterprise JavaBeans (EJB) and CORBA objects, Oracle provides the THIN and INTERNAL drivers.

■   For middle-tier JDBC and SQLJ programs, developers can use the JDBC-OCI and JDBC-THIN drivers. Specifically for the Oracle9*i* Application Server (Oracle9*i* AS), in addition to the client-side JDBC drivers, developers can also use the THIN and INTERNAL drivers.

To learn how to use the Oracle JDBC drivers in the Oracle9*i* AS, EJB objects, and CORBA objects, see Chapters 5 and 9, respectively. Note that with Oracle8*i* release 8.1.6 and higher, you have the option of using the standard JDBC API, standard JDBC batching API, or the Oracle extensions. However, Oracle recommends that you do not mix, in a single application, both the JDBC 2.0 standard model and the Oracle batching API.

To use the Oracle performance extensions with Oracle SQLJ, your code requires the following:

■   Your source code must be written using an Oracle SQLJ implementation. In order words, your Java class must reside in a `.sqlj` file.

■   Your JDBC driver must be an Oracle JDBC driver. You can use any Oracle client-side or server-side JDBC driver.

■   You must customize the SQLJ profiles appropriately. To do so, Oracle recommends that you use the default customizer, `oracle. sqlj. runtime.util.OraCustomizer`. Important to note is that if you want to customize profiles with the Oracle customizer, you must use the Oracle SQLJ run-time and an Oracle JDBC driver, even if you do not actually use Oracle extensions in your code.

The Oracle JDBC drivers, Oracle-defined extensions, and Oracle8*i*/9*i* SQLJ provide the following features to improve the performance of your JDBC (Oracle8*i* release 8.1.5) or SQLJ (Oracle8*i* SQLJ releases 8.1.6 and 8.1.7 and Oracle9*i* SQLJ) program:

■ **Disabling the `auto-commit` mode** Use this feature to avoid committing implicitly in your programs. When `auto-commit` mode is enabled (that is, the `auto-commit` flag is set to true), it tells the database to commit the transaction after every SQL statement is executed. When the `auto-commit` mode is enabled, program execution can be quite expensive in terms of time and processing efforts. When `auto-commit` mode is disabled, the JDBC driver groups the connection's SQL statements without committing the statements. By disabling `auto-commit`, you combine the set of SQL statements into a single transaction. You can commit or discard the transaction by either specifying an explicit `COMMIT` or `ROLLBACK` statement in the program. See Chapter 3 to learn more about the `auto-commit` flag in SQLJ connections. This feature is implemented in all Oracle SQLJ releases and Oracle JDBC drivers. In SQLJ programs, you can enable or disable `auto-commit` mode as follows:

■ `auto-commit` mode is disabled by default when you use the `Oracle.connect()` method to establish a database connection.

■ Use the `auto-commit` flag parameter in the `getConnection()` method of the `sqlj.runtime.ref.DefaultContext` class or the `sqlj.runtime.ConnectContext` class to enable or disable the `auto-commit` mode. Remember the syntax for this method (see Chapter 5):

```
getConnection(String   URL,
              String   username,
              String   password,
              boolean  auto-commit-flag)
```

■ Use the `setAutoCommit(false/true)` method of the `java.sql.Connection` or the `OracleConnection` classes to disable or enable `auto-commit` mode.

■ **Row prefetch** Use the row prefetch to retrieve a group of rows in one round trip to the database. The `prefetchWithSqlj()` method of the `PerformanceApp` SQLJ program demonstrates how to use the SQLJ row prefetching mechanism. This feature is supported by all releases of Oracle JDBC drivers and Oracle8*i*/9*i* SQLJ. Note that setting the row prefetch size is also supported on the `ExecutionContext` class with SQLJ 8.1.7 and later (this is a portable SQLJ standard feature).

■ **Update batching**   Use this feature to batch an accumulated number of `INSERT`, `DELETE`, or `UPDATE` statements in one batch and send these statements in one round trip to the database. The `insertWithSqljBatch ()` and `insertWithJdbcBatch()` methods of the `PerformanceApp` SQLJ program illustrate how to use the JDBC and SQLJ update batching mechanisms. This feature is supported by all releases of Oracle JDBC drivers and Oracle8*i* SQLJ releases 8.1.6 and higher. It is not supported by Oracle8*i* SQLJ release 8.1.5.

■ **Statement caching**   Use statement caching to save prepared statements in memory and reuse these statements, thereby avoiding repeated processing in the server. (This feature is supported by all releases of Oracle JDBC drivers and Oracle8*i* SQLJ releases 8.1.6 and higher. It is not supported by Oracle8*i* SQLJ release 8.1.5.)

■ **Column definitions**   Use this feature to define column types and sizes before executing a SQL operation in your source code. This feature may be able to save round trips to the database, since column types and sizes are predefined. In a SQLJ program, the column definition feature has rather small-to-negligible performance improvement. (This feature is supported by all releases of Oracle JDBC drivers and Oracle8*i* SQLJ releases 8.1.6 and higher. It is not supported by Oracle8*i* SQLJ release 8.1.5.)

■ **Parameter size definitions**   Use this feature to define the sizes of your host variables prior of executing an SQL operation. Predefined sizes of host variables provide more efficient memory usage. In a SQLJ program, the parameter size definition feature, like the column definition feature, has rather small-to-negligible performance improvement. (This feature is supported by all releases of Oracle JDBC drivers and Oracle8*i* SQLJ releases 8.1.6 and later. It is not supported by Oracle8*i* SQLJ release 8.1.5.)

■ **SQLJ translator `-codegen=oracle` option**   Use this option when compiling your SQLJ source code to instruct the SQLJ translator to use Oracle-specific code generation. When you use this option, the generated codes are optimized with direct calls to Oracle JDBC, thereby eliminating the overhead of intermediate calls to the SQLJ run-time. Supported with Oracle 9.0.1 and higher.

Row Prefetching with SQLJ

When you have to retrieve a large number of records from the database or perform many updates and inserts in the database, one way to improve performance is to reduce the number of round trips to the database server. For performance improvements, the Oracle JDBC drivers provide the row prefetching mechanism. See the *Oracle8i/9i JDBC Developer's Guide and Reference* for more information on the Oracle JDBC row prefetching feature.

Fetch Size

By default, standard JDBC receives the results of a query one row at a time, with each row requiring a separate round trip to the database. With JDBC 2.0, you can specify for a query the number of rows fetched with each database round trip. In the Oracle environment, this number is referred to as the *row prefetch value,* whereas in JDBC 2.0 it is referred to as the *fetch size.* By default, when Oracle JDBC executes a query, it receives ten rows at a time (in one round trip) from the database cursor. You can change the number of rows retrieved with each trip from the database cursor by changing the default Oracle row prefetch value.

The fetch size is used implicitly in a JDBC `ResultSet` or a SQLJ `iterator` object. When your statement object executes a query against the database, the fetch size of the statement object is passed to the resulting result set object produced by the query. You can explicitly override the implicit fetch size of a `ResultSet` or `iterator` object. In the `PerformanceApp` SQLJ application, you will learn how to override the default fetch size of an `iterator` object while writing the `prefetchWithSqljUsingEcObject()` method.

The fetch size of the `ResultSet` or an `iterator` object, either set explicitly or by default (implicitly), determines the number of rows that are retrieved in any subsequent trips to the database. In the Oracle JDBC drivers, the row prefetch value is used as the default fetch size in a statement object. Setting the fetch size overrides the row prefetch setting and affects subsequent queries executed through that statement object. The fetch size includes any trips that are still required to complete the original query, as well as any refetching of data into the `ResultSet` object. It is important to note that data can be refetched, either explicitly or implicitly, to update a `scroll-sensitive` or `scroll-insensitive/updatable` `ResultSet` object. To learn more about these types of result sets, see the *Oracle8i/9i JDBC Developer's Guide Reference* and the Bibliography at the end of this book.

NOTE
*When you query an Oracle database with no
prefetch value, SQLJ retrieves ten rows at a time.
Row prefetch uses the JDBC default value for row
prefetch, which is 10 by default. Also note that
neither Oracle SQLJ nor Oracle JDBC supports
batch fetches, which is the fetching of sets of rows
into arrays of values.*

You can set the fetch size and get its value. In Oracle JDBC 8.1.6 and higher,
the following methods of the `OracleConnection` class are available for setting
and getting the fetch size in all JDBC `Statement`, `PreparedStatement`,
`CallableStatement`, and `ResulSet` objects and SQLJ statements:

- `void setFetchSize(int rows) throws SQLException`

- `int getFetchSize() throws SQLException`

Note that the `setFetchSize()` and `getFetchSize()` methods of the
`OracleConnection` class are also available in the SQLJ `ExecutionContext`
class. Oracle recommends that you use the methods of the SQLJ `ExecutionContext`
class. The other two ways of accomplishing essentially the same thing would be nice
to know if you are using SQLJ 8.1.6 or earlier. However, the `ExecutionContext`
`get/setFetchSize()` API is SQLJ standard, and thus portable.

In the `prefetchWithSqljUsingEcObject()` method of the `PerformanceApp`
class that you will develop later in this chapter, you will use the methods of the
`ExecutionContext` class to set and get the fetch size, respectively.

Use the following fragment code to set and get the fetch size:

```
// Use the default ExecutionContext instance of a default
// connection context instance to set the fetch size.
// The following statement is too long. So we split it.
DefaultContext.getDefaultContext().
    getExecutionContext().setFetchSize(20);

// Use the default ExecutionContext instance of a default
// connection context instance to get the fetch size.
```

```
// The following statement is too long. So we split it.
int fetchSize =
   DefaultContext.getDefaultContext().
      getExecutionContext().getFetchSize();

// Use the methods of an OracleConnection instance
// to set and get the fetch size
anOracleConnection.setFetchSize(20);
int anotherFetchSize = anOracleConnection.getFetchSize();

// Create an ExecutionContext object
ExecutionContext ec = new ExecutionContext();

// Use the methods of the ExecutionContext instance
// to set and get the fetch size
ec.setFetchSize(100);
int anotherFetchSize ec.getFetchSize();
```

NOTE
Using the JDBC 2.0 fetch size is fundamentally similar to using the Oracle row prefetch value. However, do not mix the JDBC 2.0 fetch size API and the Oracle row prefetching API in your program. You can use one or the other, but not both.

Note that the Oracle row prefetch value can be affected in the following circumstances:

- **Query executions**   At run time, the fetch size value of a JDBC `ResultSet` or SQLJ `iterator` object is automatically updated.

- **Explicit refetching rows in a result set through the result set `refreshRow()` method**   This method is available in JDBC 2.0 and applies only to scroll-sensitive/read-only, scroll-sensitive/updateable, and scroll-insensitive/updateable result sets. See Chapter 6 and *Oracle8i/9i JDBC Developer's Guide* to learn more about SQLJ scrollable iterators and scrollable result sets, respectively.

- **Fetch size setting**   The Oracle row prefetch value will be overridden by any setting of the fetch size. Also, note that the prefetch value will be (internally) reset to 1 if you are fetching a LONG column.

You can refetch data into a `ResultSet` object either explicitly or implicitly. You do so via the `refreshRow()` method of the `ResultSet` object. Here is the definition of the `refreshRow()` method:

```
void refreshRow() throws SQLException
```

Note that the `refreshRow()` method is supported only by some types of `ResultSet` objects such as (Oracle8*i* release 8.1.6 and later):

- Scroll-sensitive/read-only

- Scroll-sensitive/updateable

- Scroll-insensitive/updateable

Overriding Row Prefetching Default Value

The `OracleConnection` class provides methods that allow you to set the number of rows to prefetch in the client. To use the methods of the `OracleConnection` class, you must create an instance of it. You can get an instance of this class from the underlying JDBC `Connection` instance. Recall that in Chapter 6 you created SQLJ connection objects by converting a JDBC `Connection` object from the underlying connection. Listing 10-1 illustrates how to convert a `DefaultContext` object to a JDBC `Connection` object and then convert the latter to an `OracleConnection` object. Use the `setDefaultRowPrefetch()` method of the `OracleConnection` object to override the default prefetch value. For example, override the default prefetch value with a value of 20:

Listing 10-1

```
// Get an OracleConnection object by first converting the installed
// DefaultContext object to a java.sql.Connection object with the
// DefaultContext.getDefaultContext().getConnection() method, then
// cast the returned java.sql.Connection object to an
// OracleConnection object. Finally, use the setDefaultRowPrefetch()
// method to set the prefetch value to 20.
(OracleConnection)
  DefaultContext.getDefaultContext().getConnection()
    .setDefaultRowPrefetch(20);
```

Note that, in addition to the SQLJ `DefaultContext` class, you can convert an instance of the SQLJ `ConnectionContext` class to an instance of the `OracleConnection` class. The following fragment code converts an instance of a declared connection context class to a JDBC `Connection` object, casts the `Connection` object to an `OracleConnection` object, and then uses the setDefaultRowPrefetch() method of the OracleConnection object to specify the prefetch value (see Listing 10-2):

Listing 10-2

```
// Assume that you have created an instance
// of a declared ConnectionContext class named declaredCtx.
// Use the declaredCtx.getConnection() method to convert the
// declaredCtx object to a JDBC Connection object, cast
// the latter to an OracleConnection object, and use the
// setDefaultRowPrefetch() method to specify a
// prefetch value of 100.

( (OracleConnection)
  declaredCtx.getConnection() ).setDefaultRowPrefetch(100);
```

When you want to know the current setting of the row prefetch value, use the getDefaultRowPrefetch() method of an OracleConnection instance to do so:

```
int current_value;
current_value = anOracleConnection.getDefaultRowPrefetch();
```

The steps for using the row prefetching mechanism in SQLJ programs are as follows:

1. Convert an instance of the DefaultContext class or a declared connection context class (see Listing 10-3) to a java.sql.Connection object and cast the latter to an OracleConnection object. See the "Interoperability of SQLJ and JDBC" section of Chapter 6 to learn more about converting SQLJ connection objects to JDBC Connection objects.

   Listing 10-3

   ```
   // Cast a DefaultContext object to a java.sql.Connection object
   OracleConnection anOracleConnection = (OracleConnection)
     DefaultContext.getDefaultContext().getConnection();

   // Cast the declared ConnectionContext object named declaredCtx
   // to a java.sql.Connection object.
   OracleConnection anOracleConnection = (OracleConnection)
       declaredCtx.getConnection();
   ```

2. Specify the row prefetch value with the setDefaultRowPrefetch() method of the OracleConnection instance:

   ```
   // This statement sets the default row prefetch value to 20 by
   // calling the method and passing it the value 20.
   anOracleConnection.setDefaultRowPrefetch(20);
   ```

NOTE
The default prefetch value will automatically be set to 1 when you retrieve data from an iterator that contains the LONG or the LONG RAW data types, regardless of the prefetch value you pass to the setDefaultRowPrefetch() method.

Update Batching

JDBC's *update batching* allows UPDATE, DELETE, and INSERT statements that are "batchable" and compatible (that is, identical statements including white space) to be collected into a batch and sent to the database for execution at once, saving round trips to the database. SQLJ update batching is somewhat different. SQLJ batches occurrences of the same statement, that is, a statement at a particular line in a particular source file. Even if you have 50 statements that are identical (white space and all), these would *not* get batched together.

Typically, you use update batching for an operation that is executed repeatedly within a loop. Update batching is especially useful with prepared statements, when you are repeating the same statements with different variable values.

In the Sun Microsystems JDBC 2.0 specification, update batching is referred to as batch updates. Since Oracle8*i* release 8.1.5, the update batching feature was supported as an Oracle JDBC extension and was not supported by Oracle SQLJ. Starting with Oracle8*i* release 8.1.6, this feature is supported by all client-side and server-side Oracle JDBC drivers, Oracle8*i* SQLJ releases 8.1.7, and Oracle9*i* SQLJ.

Oracle update batching uses a batch value mechanism that typically results in implicit processing of batches of statements. SQLJ permits implicit processing of batches. Note that the JDBC 2.0 batch API requires the explicit specification and use of batching. This makes it easy to add batching performance improvements to an existing SQLJ program (whereas a JDBC program would require extensive rewrite to make use of batching). A batch limit is the number of SQL operations that you want to batch for each trip to the database.

In Oracle SQLJ, update batching is tied to the execution context usage. An execution context is an instance of the sqlj.runtime.ExecutionContext class. Recall that you learned about the ExecutionContext class in Chapter 5. A SQLJ operation is always associated with an instance of the ExecutionContext class. If you do not associate an execution context object explicitly with your SQLJ clause, SQLJ will implicitly use the default instance of this class that is associated with the connection context you are using with the SQLJ clause. The following code fragment demonstrates how ExecutionContext instances are associated to a SQLJ operation either explicitly or implicitly:

```
// Create an ExecutionContext object
ExecutionContext ec = new ExecutionContext();
```

```
// Explicit association of the "ec" object
// with the SQLJ operation.
#sql [ec] { INSERT INTO PERF_TABLE VALUES(:20) };

// Implicit association of the default ExecutionContext object
// of a preset DefaultContext instance
// with the SQLJ operation.
#sql { INSERT INTO PERF_TABLE VALUES(:30) };
```

Controlling Update Batching

The ExecutionContext class provides several methods that allow you to control update batching:

- **setBatching (true/false)**   Use the true or false value to enable or disable update batching in your program.

- **isBatching()**   Use this method to determine whether batching is enabled. Note that this method does not indicate whether there is currently a pending batch.

- **getBatchLimit()**   Use this method to get the current batch limit.

- **setBatchLimit()**   Use this method to set the batch limit or override the default batch limit.

- **executeBatch()**   Use this method to execute a pending batch, explicitly.

- **getBatchUpdateCount()**   Use this method to get an array of update counts of successful statements for the last batch that was executed. This is a very useful method in situations where the batch was executed implicitly.

In a batch-enabled situation, the value returned by the getUpdateCount() status method of the ExecutionContext class is modified after each statement is encountered. Use the following constant values to decode the value returned by the getUpdateCount() method:

- **NEW_BATCH_COUNT**   Indicates that a new batch was created in the last statement encountered

- **ADD_BATCH_COUNT**   Indicates that the last statement encountered was added to an existing batch

- **EXEC_BATCH_COUNT**   Indicates that after the last statement encountered, a pending batch was executed either implicitly or explicitly

To refer to the NEW_BATCH_COUNT, ADD_BATCH_COUNT, and ADD_BATCH_
COUNT constants, use the ExecutionContext qualified name. For example,

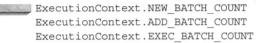

```
ExecutionContext.NEW_BATCH_COUNT
ExecutionContext.ADD_BATCH_COUNT
ExecutionContext.EXEC_BATCH_COUNT
```

Note the following:

- Update batching is disabled by default.

- The update batching feature is enabled or disabled in each execution context independent of any other execution context, and each execution context instance maintains its own batch.

- To use update batching, you must customize your application with the Oracle customizer.

The following fragment uses the update batching mechanism to repeatedly insert rows into the PERF_TABLE table:

```
// Create an ExecutionContext object
ExecutionContext ec = new ExecutionContext();

// Enable batching.
// See the "Enabling and Disabling Update Batching" section
// of this chapter for detailed explanations on this method.
ec.setBatching(true);

// Use a user-defined value to set the batch limit
// See the "Setting A Batch Limit" section
// of this chapter for detailed explanations on this method.
ec.setBatchLimit(100);

// Associate the SQLJ operation with the "ec" object
// and use it in a for loop to insert values
// repeatedly into the PERF_TABLE table
for(int i= 1; i <= insertMax; i++)
    #sql [ec] { INSERT INTO PERF_TABLE VALUES(:i) };
```

Enabling and Disabling Update Batching

You have read that Oracle SQLJ enables update batching via an instance of the ExecutionContext class. You can use the execution context instance associated with the connection context instance being referenced, explicitly or implicitly, by the SQLJ statement. More important, SQLJ performs update batching separately for each execution context instance. Each one can have update batching enabled and pending independent of your other execution context instances, and each maintains its own batch.

Use the `setBatching(true/false)` method to enable or disable update batching:

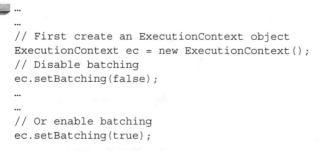

```
...

...

// First create an ExecutionContext object
ExecutionContext ec = new ExecutionContext();
// Disable batching
ec.setBatching(false);

...

...

// Or enable batching
ec.setBatching(true);
```

Note the following:

- The `setBatching()` method does not affect an existing statement batch.

- Neither enabling nor disabling update batching causes an existing batch to be executed or canceled.

Use the `isBatching()` method to determine whether batching is enabled or disabled. For example,

```
// Create an ExecutionContext object
// if you have not previously done so.
ExecutionContext ec = new ExecutionContext();

// Declare a boolean variable
// and use the isBatching() method.
// The method returns true if batching
// is enabled or false otherwise
boolean batchingOn = ec.isBatching();
```

NOTE
The `isBatching()` method does not indicate whether or not a batch is currently pending. The `getUpdateCount()` method will determine this.

Setting a Batch Limit

In a batch-enabled situation, you can specify that each update batch be executed after a predefined number of SQLJ operations. To do so, use the `setBatchLimit( int )` method of the `ExecutionContext` class. The `setBatchLimit()` method accepts the following input parameters:

- **User-defined value** Any user-defined value.

- **AUTO_BATCH** A static constant that allows the SQLJ run-time to determine the batch limit. In Oracle SQLJ, it is currently treated as if you had specified a batch limit of 20.

- **UNLIMITED_BATCH** A static constant that specifies that there is no batch limit. When batch is enabled, the default is unlimited batch.

The following fragment code shows how to use the `setBatchLimit()` method of an `ExecutionContext` object:

```
// Create an ExecutionContext object
    ExecutionContext ec = new ExecutionContext();

// Use a user-defined value to set the batch limit
ec.setBatchLimit(100);
// Let the SQLJ runtime determine the batch limit
ec.setBatchLimit(ExecutionContext.AUTO_BATCH);
// Use the UNLIMITED_BATCH value to set the batch limit
ec.setBatchLimit(ExecutionContext.UNLIMITED_BATCH);
```

Note that the constants live in `ExecutionContext`. Therefore, you must qualify the constants with `ExecutionContext`. However, you do not need to qualify the constants if your program extends `sqlj.runtime.ExecutionContext`. For example,

```
ExecutionContext.UNLIMITED_BATCH
```

Executing Batching Explicitly

Use the `executeBatch()` method of the execution context instance to explicitly execute a pending batch:

```
    // Create an ExecutionContext object
ExecutionContext ec = new ExecutionContext();

    // Set bacthing options using the ExecutionContext object
ec.setBatching(true);
```

```
ec.setBatchLimit(insertMax);

…
…

// Add 'insertMax' number of rows into the database
for(int i= 1; i <= insertMax; i++)
   #sql [ec] { INSERT INTO PERF_TABLE VALUES(:i) };

// Execute any pending batch explicitly
ec.executeBatch();
```

Executing Batching Implicitly

Pending update batches execute implicitly in the following circumstances:

■ The predefined batch limit is reached. For example,

```
// Create an ExecutionContext object
ExecutionContext ec = new ExecutionContext();

// Set bacthing options using the ExecutionContext object
ec.setBatching(true);
ec.setBatchLimit(insertMax);
…
…

// Add 'insertMax' number of rows into the database
// Assume that insertMax = 100 and predefined batch limit = 20
// When the limit is reached, the statement sends 20 insert
// statements in one round trip to the database. Insertion
// of 100 rows will cost 5 round trips versus 100 ones.
for(int i= 1; i <= insertMax; i++)
   #sql [ec] { INSERT INTO PERF_TABLE VALUES(:i) };
```

■ A different executable statement is encountered. It does not matter whether the statement is batchable or not. Whether the batch size limit has been reached or not, the existing batch is executed first, and then the different executable statement is executed.

```
// Encounter a batchable statement
for(int i= 1; i <= insertMax; i++) {
   #sql [ec] { INSERT INTO PERF_TABLE VALUES(:i) };
}
// Batch limit may have not been reached.
// Encountering a different statement causes
// a pending batch to be executed
#sql [ec] { INSERT INTO ANOTHER_TABLE VALUES(20) };
```

In summary, Oracle SQLJ only batches the same statement. If a statement is batchable and batching is enabled, then a new batch is created. Only the same statement will be added to this batch. Whenever a different statement (batchable or not) is encountered, then any pending batch is executed first. Thus, Oracle SQLJ might not be performing batching in as many scenarios as other JDBC drivers might perform batching (for example, other drivers might be able to batch different, batch-compatible statements). Whether or not the batch size limit of the first batch has been reached, the first batch is executed, and then a new batch is created, starting with the incompatible statement.

```
// Assume that the following statement is
// using update batching
for(int i= 1; i <= insertMax; i++)
  #sql [ec] { INSERT INTO PERF_TABLE VALUES(:i) };

// Assume that the following statement is also
// using update batching. Two imcompatible batchable
// statements cause the first batchable statement
// to be executed.
for(int j= 1; j <= insertMax; j++)
  #sql [ec] { INSERT INTO ANOTHER_TABLE VALUES(j) };
```

- Use COMMIT explicitly. For example,

```
for(int j= 1; j <= insertMax; j++)
  #sql [ec] { INSERT INTO ANOTHER_TABLE VALUES(j) };

// Implicitly execute the batch and commit
#sql { COMMIT };
```

Controlling Implicit Batching

You can avoid implicit update batching of batchable and nonbatchable SQLJ statements or noncompatible batchable statements by using several ExecutionContext objects. For example,

```
// Create two ExecutionContext objects
ExecutionContext ec1 = new ExecutionContext();
ExecutionContext ec2 = new ExecutionContext();

// Set bacthing options using the ExecutionContext object
ec1.setBatching(true);
ec1.setBatchLimit(100);
ec2.setBatching(true);
ec2.setBatchLimit(100);
```

```
// Assume that insertMax = 2000
for(int i= 1; i <= insertMax; i++) {
    #sql [ec1] { INSERT INTO PERF_TABLE VALUES(:i) };
    #sql [ec2] { INSERT INTO ANOTHER_TABLE VALUES(i) };
}  // End of for loop
```

Canceling Batching Explicitly

You can explicitly cancel pending batches or batches that have executed. You do so via the cancel() method of the execution context instance. For example,

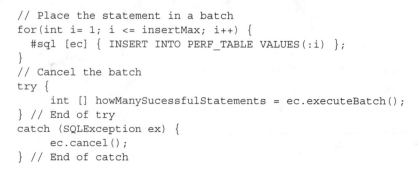

```
// Place the statement in a batch
for(int i= 1; i <= insertMax; i++) {
  #sql [ec] { INSERT INTO PERF_TABLE VALUES(:i) };
}
// Cancel the batch
try {
    int [] howManySucessfulStatements = ec.executeBatch();
} // End of try
catch (SQLException ex) {
    ec.cancel();
} // End of catch
```

You should note the following:

■ When you cancel a batch, the next batchable statement will start a new batch.

■ Calling cancel() will also cancel any statement currently executing.

■ Canceling a batch does *not* disable update batching.

Update Batching Limitations

Here is a list of the limitations of the Oracle update batching feature:

■ If a nonbatchable statement depends on a batchable statement, make sure that the batchable statement is executed prior to the nonbatchable statement.

■ A JDBC COMMIT or ROLLBACK operation does not execute pending batches. It is important to note that the SQLJ COMMIT or ROLLBACK statement will execute pending batches. Oracle recommends that you always use #sql {COMMIT} or #sql {ROLLBACK} to appropriately clean up both SQLJ resources and JDBC resources.

■ Implicit execution of nonbatchable or incompatible batchable statements results in the automatic execution of previously encountered batchable statements before the nonbatchable or incompatible statements, but after that statement's input parameters have been evaluated and passed to the statement.

■ Free resources by executing or canceling, explicitly, any batch-enabled execution context instance no longer needed.

■ If a statement causes an exception, batchable statements following this statement will not be executed. However, batchable statements that had already been executed prior to the exception are not rolled back.

■ If a batch in which the exception occurred was executed implicitly as the result of another (unbatchable or incompatible) statement being encountered, the latter is not executed.

Statement Caching

Situations in which you need to use identical SQLJ executable statements repeatedly, you can use the statement caching feature of Oracle8i/9i SQLJ to improve your application performance. Note that, in batching-enabled situations, there is also an underlying JDBC statement cache. In some cases, the SQLJ and JDBC statement caches are used separately, and in other circumstances SQLJ uses the JDBC cache instead of maintaining its own.

SQLJ and JDBC statement caching mechanisms allow you to cache (save) the executable statements. Performance gains are shown in subsequent executions of cached statements in contrast to repreparing noncached ones. When repreparing a statement instead of reusing an already prepared one, execution can take up to 100 percent longer. Statement caching is beneficial for saving executable statements that are used repeatedly. There is no benefit in using statement caching when executable statements are used only once. Note that, in Oracle SQLJ, caching (cache size of 5) is the default setting since SQLJ version 8.1.6.

Subsequent executions of cached statements have the following advantages:

■ The code does not have to be reparsed.

■ The statement object does not have to be re-created.

■ The parameter size definitions do not have to be recalculated.

Implementing Robust Caching in SQLJ

The statement caching mechanism is a standard feature of Oracle SQLJ and can be used with any Oracle JDBC driver. However, for more robust caching, Oracle recommends using a driver that implements the `sqlj.runtime.profile.ref.ClientDataSupport interface`. Starting with Oracle8i release 8.1.6, the Oracle JDBC drivers implement this `interface`, which provides the following features:

- A separate cache for each database connection that your application establishes instead of a single cache for your entire application. This feature prevents cached statements executed in one connection to be flushed by another connection because each connection is using its own cache.

- The capability for your application to share cached statements between multiple instances of a connection context class that share the same *underlying* connection. Important here is that cached statements executed in one connection can be reused by another connection without being flushed.

NOTE
The performance of your SQLJ program can be increased, even when the cache size is a value of 1.

Statement Caching with the Oracle Customizer

When you use the Oracle SQLJ translator, it automatically executes the Oracle customizer, which, by default, enables statement caching in your application. However, with Oracle-specific code generation in Oracle 9.0.1 or later, statement caching is implemented through the JDBC statement cache and controlled through connection context methods. Recall that you get Oracle-specific code generation when you use the `-codegen=oracle` option to compile your SQLJ source code.

The default value of the cache size is 5. That is, enabling statement caching means that automatically a cache that can hold a maximum of five executable statements for each database connection is available to your program.

To enable statement caching, at the command line, use the `stmtcache` option of the Oracle customizer to alter the default value. For example,

```
// Set the statement cache size on the
// command line or in a properties file.
sqlj -P-Cstmtcache=15 PerformanceApp.sqlj

// Disable statement caching, set the cache size to 0
```

```
sqlj -P-Cstmtcache=0 PerformanceApp.sqlj

// Use the Oracle customizer force option to
// force a re-customization
sqlj -P-Cforce -P-Cstmtcache=0 PerformanceApp_SJProfile0.ser


// Set individual statement cache
// for several profiles. Compile each profile
// separately.
sqlj -P-Cstmtcache=10 PerformanceApp_SJProfile0.ser
sqlj -P-Cstmtcache=15 PerformanceApp_SJProfile1.ser
sqlj -P-Cstmtcache=0 PerformanceApp_SJProfile1.ser
```

Note the following:

- Statement cache size setting is determined according to how you set the Oracle customizer `stmtcache` option when you customized the profile.

- At run time, the statement cache size for a connection is set when the first statement on that connection is executed

- If you use the SQLJ translator with the –codegen=oracle option, there is no profile customization, and, therefore, the `stmtcache` option is not available. With this option, SQLJ uses the JDBC statement cache instead of a separate SQLJ statement cache.

- Choose the cache size limit appropriately. If it is too small, then the cache might fill up, resulting in statements being flushed before they are reexecuted. If it is too large, then database resources or program resources might be exhausted.

The `OracleConnection` class provides methods that allow you to set and get the cache size value. Use `setStmtCacheSize(int)` and `getStmtCacheSize()` to set and get the cache size, respectively. In Oracle9*i* SQLJ, similar methods have been added to the `sqlj.runtime.ref.DefaultContext` and `ConnectionContext` classes:

- **public static void setDefaultStmtCacheSize(int)** Use this method to change the default statement cache size for all connection contexts. Recall that the default statement cache size is five statements. When you use this method, the new cache size value becomes the initial statement cache size for any subsequently created instance of any connection context class, not just the class upon which you call the method. It is important to note that the method call does not affect connection context instances that already exist.

- **`public static int getDefaultStmtCacheSize()`** Use this method to retrieve the current default statement cache size for connection contexts.

- **`public void setStmtCacheSize(int)`** Use this method to set the statement cache size for the underlying connection of the particular connection context instance and override the default statement cache size of five statements.

- **`public int getStmtCacheSize()`** Use this method to retrieve the current statement cache size for the underlying connection of the connection context instance.

Statement Caching Limitations

Here is a partial list of some limitations of the SQLJ statement caching feature:

- Avoid using the same connection context object for statements executed once with statements executed multiple times. In this scenario, the cache size limit might be reached, and executable statements might unnecessarily be flushed.

- Do not use distinct executable statements. Put the SQL operations in a method, and call the method repeatedly, instead of using distinct statements.

Column Definitions

Oracle SQLJ, like Oracle JDBC, supports column type and size definitions. This feature allows the user to specify the types under which to retrieve column data in a query. When standard JDBC performs a query, it first uses a round trip to the database to determine the types that it should use for the columns of the result set. Column definitions save a round trip to the database that would otherwise be necessary to describe the table. This is particularly true for the Oracle JDBC THIN driver. In SQLJ, the column definition feature has rather small to negligible performance improvement.

If you enable column type and size definitions in your SQLJ source code, Oracle SQLJ will automatically register your column types and sizes for you. Oracle SQLJ does it in the following manners:

- During translation (customization), the Oracle customizer connects to a specified database schema that determines types and sizes of columns that need to be retrieved, and then writes this information to the SQLJ profile.

This can be accomplished at compile-time during separate customization of an existing profile.

■ At run time, the SQLJ run-time will use the information in the profile to register the column types and sizes with the JDBC driver, using a call to the defineColumnType() method available in the Oracle JDBC statement classes.

NOTE
To learn more about the Oracle customizer, see the
Oracle8i/9i SQLJ Developer's Reference Guide.

Enabling Column Definition in SQLJ Programs

Use the following option of the Oracle customizer to enable column definitions:

■ Enable the Oracle customizer optcols flag (-P-Coptcols on the SQLJ command line). This option enables SQLJ iterator column type and size definitions to optimize performance. Column definitions require the customizer to make a database connection to examine columns of tables being queried, so the customizer harness user, password, and url options must be set appropriately (as well as the customizer harness driver option if you are not using the default OracleDriver class). This flag is disabled by default, but you can also disable it explicitly. Note that you can set customizer-specific options, such as options for the Oracle customizer, on the SQLJ command line or in a SQLJ properties file. For example,

```
// Set it at the command line
// when you are compiling your program
 sqlj < SQLJ Options >
   -P-Coptcols PerformanceApp_SJProfile*.ser

// or
 sqlj -P-Coptcols=true

// or in a SQLJ properties files
profile.C

// Disable the flag, explicitly
 sqlj -P-Coptcols=false
```

- Set the user, password, and URL for the database connection during
customization (-P-user, -P-password, and -P-url on the SQLJ
command line). In addition, set the JDBC driver class (-P-driver on the
SQLJ command line) if you are not using the default OracleDriver class.

```
// Set it at the command line
// when you are compiling your program
 sqlj < SQLJ Options >
    -P-user=scott/tiger@jdbc.oci8@
    -P-Coptcols PerformanceApp_SJProfile*.ser

// Use the -P-Cforce option to
// insert column definitions into an existing profile
sqlj < SQLJ Options >
    -P-user=scott/tiger@jdbc.oci8@
    -P-Cforce -P-Coptcols PerformanceApp_SJProfile*.ser

// // Use the -P-Cforce option to
// insert column definitions into existing
// profiles in a .jar file
sqlj < SQLJ Options >
    -P-user=scott/tiger@jdbc.oci8@
    -P-Cforce -P-Coptcols MyAppProfiles.jar
```

Note the following:

- When you construct your SQL operation, it is advisable that you explicitly
select the columns you will use, rather than using a SELECT *, because
you might not actually use all the columns selected. You might want to
translate with the SQLJ -warn=strict flag set, which will warn you if
additional (unwanted) columns will be selected by your query. Note that
the -warn=strict setting is part of the default warning setting.

- Column definitions are not possible for any iterator or result set that
includes one or more object or collection columns.

Parameter Size Definitions

Oracle SQLJ and Oracle JDBC allow you to optimize your JDBC resources by
defining parameter sizes of your host variables in a Java program. In SQLJ, the
parameter definition feature has rather small to negligible performance improvement.
To learn more about parameter size definitions, see Appendix A of the *Oracle8i/9i
SQLJ Developer's Guide*.

Use the parameter size definition feature in the following circumstances:

■   Input or output parameters in stored procedure or function calls

■   Return values from stored function calls

■   Input or output parameters in SET statements

■   Input or output parameters in PL/SQL blocks

SQLJ implements parameter size definitions through customizer option settings in combination with "hints" embedded in source code comments. If you do not enable the parameter definition flag, then parameter size defaults and source code hints will be ignored, and maximum or default resources will be allocated according to the JDBC implementation. Unlike the `optcols` option, the `optparams` option does not require a database connection by the customizer, because you are providing the size specifications yourself.

Use these options and hints as follows:

■   Enable parameter size definitions, through the Oracle customizer parameter definition flag.

■   Specify default sizes for particular datatypes through the Oracle customizer parameter default size option.

■   Override datatype default sizes for particular parameters by embedding hints in source code comments, following a prescribed format.

■   Enable parameter size definitions through the Oracle customizer parameter definition flag.

■   Specify default sizes for particular datatypes through the Oracle customizer parameter default size option.

Override datatype default sizes for particular parameters by embedding hints in source code comments, following a prescribed format. For any given host variable, when parameter size definitions are enabled, resources are allocated according to the source code hint if there is one. If there is no source code hint, then the default size for the corresponding datatype is used if one was specified. If there is no source code hint or appropriate default size, then maximum resources are allocated according to the JDBC implementation.

At the SQLJ command line, use the following Oracle customizer options to enable parameter size definitions:

■   `optparams` flag to enable parameter size definitions. This flag is disabled by default. For example,

```
// Enable it on the command line
-P-Coptparams

// OR
-P-Coptparams=true

// Disable parameter size, explicitly
-P-Coptparams=false
```

■ `optparamdefaults` option to set default sizes for particular datatypes. You must use this option in conjunction with `optparams`. For example,

```
// Here is the complete command line syntax
sqlj <...SQLJ options...>
   -P-Coptparams
   -P-Coptparamdefaults=defaults-string
      PerformanceApp.sqlj

// Enable parameter size definitions for
// existing profiles
sqlj <...SQLJ options...>
   -P-Coptparams
   -P-Coptparamdefaults=defaults-string
      PerformanceApp_SJProfile.ser

// Enable parameter size definitions for
// existing profiles in a jar file
sqlj <...SQLJ options...>
   -P-Coptparams
   -P-Coptparamdefaults=defaults-string
      MyProfilesFiles.jar
```

Source Code Hints for Parameter Size Definitions

When the Oracle customizer `optparams` flag is enabled, you can embed hints in your SQLJ statements. Use the following format to embed hints for parameter size definition in SQLJ programs:

```
// Assign a size in byte
   /*(size_in_bytes)*/
```

The specification `/* () */` means that even if there is a default parameter size for this type set, do *not* provide any parameter size hint for this particular parameter. For example,

```
// Override the default parameter size
/*()*/
```

> **NOTE**
> *If any parameter size is altered such that its actual size exceeds its registered size at run time, a SQL exception will be thrown.*

This ends the section regarding the support features of Oracle performance enhancements. In the next section, you will learn how to write efficient SQLJ programs that use these performance features. You will do so while developing the `PerformanceApp` SQLJ application.

Developing Efficient SQLJ Programs

In the previous sections of this chapter, you learned the performance enhancements that Oracle provides. Here, you will learn how to use these features while developing the `PerformanceApp` SQLJ application.

The `PerformanceApp` SQLJ application illustrates how to use Oracle JDBC drivers and SQLJ classes to perform row prefetch and update batching in SQLJ. More specifically, it performs the following tasks:

- Inserts records with different batch values using SQLJ statements

- Inserts records with different Oracle JDBC batch values using JDBC statements

- Retrieves rows of data by setting different prefetch values using SQLJ statements and the methods of an `OracleConnection` instance

- Retrieves rows of data by setting different prefetch values using SQLJ statements and the methods of an `ExecutionContext` object

```
/* Program Name: PerformanceApp.sqlj
** Purpose:     A SQLJ application that demonstrates how to
** insert records as a batch and query the database by setting
** prefetch values.
**
*/

import oracle.jdbc.driver.OracleConnection;
import oracle.jdbc.driver.OraclePreparedStatement;
import java.sql.PreparedStatement;
```

```
import java.sql.SQLException;

public class PerformanceApp {

  #sql public static iterator PrefetchIter (int anumber);

  public static void main(String[] args)
          throws SQLException {
    PerformanceApp Prefetchapp = new PerformanceApp();
    ConnectionManager aConnectionManager = new ConnectionManager();

    // Establish connection with the database and return an
    // OracleConnection instance. This instance is used to set values
    // of the JDBC row prefetch and the batch. (See Note 1.)

    OracleConnection anOracleConnection =
      aConnectionManager.getOracleConnection();

    Prefetchapp.runApplication(anOracleConnection);

    // Always close the connection
    // This method closes both the SQLJ connection context
    // and the JDBC connection.  See Note 7 in the
    // "Notes on the ConnectionManager class" section.
    aConnectionManager.closeConnection();

  } // End of main() method

void runApplication(OracleConnection anOracleConnection) {
    // The number of rows to insert into the database (See Note 2.)
    int rowsToInsert = 1000;
    try {
      #sql { DROP TABLE PERF_TABLE}; // (See Note 3.)
    }
    catch (SQLException ex){ }

    try { // (See Note 4.)
      #sql { CREATE TABLE PERF_TABLE(anumber NUMBER)};

      System.out.println("*** Inserting rows in the database ***\n");
      System.out.println("********* Please Wait ********\n");

      System.out.println("******** Inserting with SQLJ BATCH "
                   +"********\n");
      // Insert an additional 1000 records with a batch value of 10
      // (See Note 5.)
      insertWithSqljBatch(rowsToInsert, anOracleConnection, 10);
      // Insert an additional 1000 records with a batch value of 100
```

```
    insertWithSqljBatch(rowsToInsert, anOracleConnection, 100);
    // Insert an additional 1000 records with a batch value of 1000
    insertWithSqljBatch(rowsToInsert, anOracleConnection, 1000);

    System.out.println("\n**** Inserting with JDBC BATCH ****\n");
    // (See Note 6.)
    // Insert an additional 1000 records with a batch value of 10
    insertWithJdbcBatch(rowsToInsert, anOracleConnection, 10);
    // Insert an additional 1000 records with a batch value of 100
    insertWithJdbcBatch(rowsToInsert, anOracleConnection, 100);
    // Insert an additional 1000 records with a batch value of 1000
    insertWithJdbcBatch(rowsToInsert, anOracleConnection, 1000);

    System.out.println("\n********* Query the table *********\n");

    System.out.println("*** Querying the database by" +
                    " row prefetching *\n");
    // Query database using the default prefetch value of 10
    // (See Note 7.)
    prefetchWithSqlj(anOracleConnection,
                    anOracleConnection.getDefaultRowPrefetch());
    // Query database with SQLJ by setting the prefetch value to 100
    prefetchWithSqlj(anOracleConnection, 100);
    // Query and set database row prefetch value to 1000
    prefetchWithSqlj(anOracleConnection, 1000);

    // Query and set database row fetch to 1000
    // Using the methods of the ExecutionContext instance
    // (See Note 8.)
    prefetchWithSqljUsingEcObject(anOracleConnection, 1000);

  } // End of try block
  catch (SQLException e){
    System.out.println(e);
    System.exit(1);
  } // End of catch block

} // End of runApplication() method

static void insertWithSqljBatch(int insertMax,
        OracleConnection anOracleConnection,
            int batchNumber) throws SQLException {

  System.out.flush();

  // (See Note 9.)
  // Create an ExecutionContext object
  ExecutionContext ec = new ExecutionContext();
```

```
    // (See Note 10.)
    // Set batching options using the ExecutionContext object
    ec.setBatching(true);
    ec.setBatchLimit(insertMax);

    // Get the time when record insertions begin (See Note 11.)
    long start = System.currentTimeMillis();

    // Add 'insertMax' number of rows into the table (See Note 12.)
    for(int i= 1; i <= insertMax; i++)
      #sql [ec] { INSERT INTO PERF_TABLE VALUES(:i) };

    // Execute the batch
    ec.executeBatch();

    // Get the time it took to insert the rows (See Note 13.)
    long finish = System.currentTimeMillis() - start;

    // Print the number of records inserted in the database and the
    // time it took to insert those records.
    System.out.print("** With SQLJ, " + insertMax
             + " records inserted ");
    System.out.println("in " +(finish / 1000.0)+ " seconds.\n");
} // End of insertWithSqljBatch() method

static void insertWithJdbcBatch(
               int insertMax,
               OracleConnection anOracleConnection,
               int batchNumber)  throws SQLException {

    // Set the batch value with the value of the parameter
    // (See Note 14.)
    anOracleConnection.setDefaultExecuteBatch(batchNumber);

    long start = System.currentTimeMillis(); // Get the start time

    // Get a PreparedStatement object for sending the insertions
    // to the database (See Note 15.)
    PreparedStatement aPreparedStatement =
      anOracleConnection.prepareStatement(
        "INSERT INTO PERF_TABLE VALUES (?)");

    // Insert new records into the database (See Note 16.)
    for (int i=1; i <= insertMax; i++) {
      aPreparedStatement.setInt(1,i);
      aPreparedStatement.execute();
    }
```

```
    // Send the inserted records to the database in batches
    // (See Note 17.)
    ((OraclePreparedStatement)aPreparedStatement).sendBatch();

    // Get the time that it took for the record insertions
    long finish = System.currentTimeMillis() - start;

    aPreparedStatement.close(); // Close statement object

    System.out.print("** With JDBC BATCH set to " +
         anOracleConnection.getDefaultExecuteBatch() + " rows. ");
    System.out.println(insertMax + " rows inserted in " +
         (finish / 1000.0)+ " seconds.\n");
} // End of insertWithJdbcBatch() method

static void prefetchWithSqlj(OracleConnection anOracleConnection,
                             int prefetchValue)
                                 throws SQLException {
    int rows = 0;
    // Set the row prefetch value (See Note 18.)
    anOracleConnection.setDefaultRowPrefetch(prefetchValue);

    PrefetchIter aPrefetchIter = null;

    long start = System.currentTimeMillis(); // Get the start time

    #sql aPrefetchIter = { SELECT anumber FROM  PERF_TABLE };

    // Iterate through the iterator (See Note 19.)
    while (aPrefetchIter.next()){
      rows++;      // Count the number of rows read
    }

    // The time it took to accomplish the retrieve and process the
    // iterator
    long finish = System.currentTimeMillis() - start;

    aPrefetchIter.close();

    System.out.print("** PREFETCH value set to " +
         anOracleConnection.getDefaultRowPrefetch() + " rows. ");
    System.out.println(rows + " rows retrieved in " +
                      (finish / 1000.0)+ " seconds.\n");
} // End of prefetchWithSqlj() method

static void prefetchWithSqljUsingEcObject(
                      OracleConnection anOracleConnection,
                      int prefetchValue) throws SQLException {
```

```
// Create an ExecutionContext object (See Note 20.)
ExecutionContext ec = new ExecutionContext();

int rows = 0;

// Use the setFetchSize() method of the ec object (See Note 21.)
ec.setFetchSize(prefetchValue);

PrefetchIter aPrefetchIter = null;
long start = System.currentTimeMillis();

 // (See Note 22.)
 #sql [ec] aPrefetchIter = { SELECT anumber FROM  PERF_TABLE };

 while (aPrefetchIter.next()){
     rows++;
 }  // End of while

long finish = System.currentTimeMillis() - start;
aPrefetchIter.close();

// Use the getFetchSize() method of the ec object
// (See Note 23.)
System.out.print("** PREFETCH value set to " +
                ec.getFetchSize() + " rows. ");
System.out.println(rows + " rows retrieved in " +
                (finish / 1000.0)+ " seconds.\n");

 } // End of prefetchWithSqljUsingEcObject() method

} // End of PerformanceApp class
```

Notes on the `PerformanceApp` SQLJ application:

1. Call the `connectDB()` method to connect to the database. This method returns an `OracleConnection` instance. Later in the program, you will use methods provided by this instance to specify values to the row prefetch and the batch update values.

2. The `rowsToInsert` variable holds the number of insertions to be made in the database. You can change this value to insert more or less rows into the database.

3. This statement drops the table if it exists. If the table does not exist, a `SQLException` error is raised and caught by the `catch` block.

4. Create a table that will be used for inserting data into the database.

5. Use the `insertWithSqljBatch()` method to insert 1000 records in the database. Remember that the `rowsToInsert` parameter holds the value of the number of rows to insert. This method is used to show the amount of time it takes to insert records with SQLJ versus inserting records with JDBC batch update.

6. Insert rows in the database with the `insertWithJdbcBatch()` method. The last parameter of this method is the value for the JDBC batch. The method is called three times with update batch values of 10, 100, and 1000 passed as its parameter.

7. This method will query the database using an `OracleConnection` object and a prefetch value as its parameters. In the first method call, the `prefetchWithSqlj()` method uses the default row prefetch value of 10. The method does so by calling the `getDefaultRowPrefetch()` method. In the second and third call, the prefetch value is set to 100 and 1000, respectively.

8. This method will query the database using a prefetch value of 1000. It uses the `setFetchSize()` and the `getFetchSize()` of an `ExecutionContext` object to set and get the fetch size, respectively.

9. This statement creates an instance of the `ExecutionContext` class.

10. These statements use the `setBatching()` and the `setBatchLimit()` methods of the `ExecutionContext` class to enable update batching and set the batch limit.

11. This statement gets the current time in milliseconds. This time is used with the stop time in note 13 to calculate the time it takes the insert operations to complete.

12. This statement inserts records into the database with a SQLJ executable statement using explicitly the `ExecutionContext` object created in note 9.

13. This statement gets the stop time and calculates the time it took, in milliseconds, to complete the insert operations with SQLJ.

14. Set the batch value to the number supplied by the parameter of the `insertWithJdbcBatch()` method.

15. The `PreparedStatement` class extends the JDBC `Statement` class (see Appendix C). It is responsible for sending information to the database.

The question mark (?) refers to the placeholder for the data that will be inserted into the database with the `setInt()` method in note 13.

16. This loop inserts data into the database. When the `execute()` method is called and when the batch value is reached, it will automatically send and insert the data as a batch to the database. The `setInt()` method refers to the question mark of note 12. The value that is sent to the database is passed as a parameter to this method.

17. The `sendBatch()` method will flush and send any remaining statements waiting to be sent to the database.

18. Using the `prefetchValue` variable of the `prefetchWithSqlj()` method, set the row prefetch value with the `setDefaultRowPrefetch()` method by passing to it the `prefetchValue` variable parameter.

19. This loop statement iterates through the result set. The data from the database is retrieved a batch at a time. When the default row prefetch value is reached, it will go to the database and retrieve the default prefetch number of rows.

20. This statement creates a new `ExecutionContext` object whose methods will be used to set and get the prefetch value, respectively.

21. This statement uses the `setFetchSize()` method of the `ExecutionContext` object to set the fetch size. Remember that the `OracleConnection` class has a similar method to set the fetch size.

22. This statement explicitly associates the `ec` object to the SQLJ executable statement to execute a query against the database.

23. This statement uses the `setFetchSize()` method of the `ExecutionContext` object to get the current fetch size and prints it.

Tuning SQLJ Statements with the Oracle Optimizer

The Oracle SQL *optimizer* provides an efficient way to execute SQL statements in the Oracle database. The optimizer selects the best access path for your SQL statements by using either the rule-based or the cost-based approach.

See *Oracle8i/9i Tuning* and the *Oracle8i/9i SQL Reference* for further information on the Oracle optimizer:

- The *rule-based* approach is based on the access paths available and the ranks of these access paths.

- Using the *cost-based* approach, the optimizer determines which execution plan is most efficient by considering available access paths and factoring in information based on statistics for the schema objects (tables or indexes) accessed by the SQL statement. The cost-based approach also considers *hints*, which are optimization suggestions to the optimizer placed in a comment in the statement.

Since you, the Oracle database designer or implementer, may have more information on the data than the Oracle optimizer and know how you wish the database to handle the data, you can pass hints to the optimizer to tune your SQL statements. For instance, you might know that a certain index is more selective for certain queries. Based on this information, you might be able to choose a more efficient execution plan than the optimizer. In such a case, use hints to force the optimizer to use your optimal execution plan.

Oracle SQLJ allows you to pass hints to the Oracle optimizer to tune your SQL statements. You pass the hints with a comment (/* or «--) notation, followed by a plus sign (/*+ or «--+). The comments containing hints must follow the Oracle keyword DELETE, SELECT, or UPDATE statement block. At run time, the SQLJ translator will recognize the hints, combine them with your SQL statement, and send them to the database. For example, you can use a /*+ ORDERED */ or a «--+ ORDERED hint in your SQLJ executable statement to tell the Oracle optimizer to join tables in the order in which they appeared in the FROM clause. Listing 10-4 illustrates this concept:

Listing 10-4

```
#sql static iterator EmployeeIter (String lastname, String longname);
...

EmployeeIter anEmployeeIter;

// Pass a hint to the Oracle optimizer to first join the EMPLOYEE_LIST
// table and then join the department_list table.
#sql anEmployeeIter = { SELECT /*+ ORDERED */ lastname, longname
                        FROM EMPLOYEE_LIST emp, DEPARTMENT_LIST dept
                        WHERE emp.deptno = dept.deptno };
... (process iterator)
```

Considering Other Ways to Reduce Network Traffic

An important performance consideration that may be particularly useful in server-side programs: avoid conversions into JDBC types, particularly if data is primarily moved around, and you do not need to perform computations/logic on the data. Thus, instead of using `java.lang.`*Xxxx* or `java.sql.`*Xxxx* classes, use instances of corresponding `oracle.sql.`*XXXX* classes. The overhead of converting from SQL to Java and back can be significant, particularly in server-side applications.

Also, note that when you use two-tier client/server applications whose processing is performed on the client's machine, you can experience network bottleneck. You can reduce or possibly eliminate this problem by using a three-tier approach. Remember that in the three-tier architecture, the processing of the data from the database is done on an application server versus a client's machine. In this scenario, the client (first tier) connects to an application server (middle tier). See Chapters 1 and 5 to learn more about application servers. The middle tier processes clients' requests by handling and processing data from and to a database server (third tier). In a three-tier approach, only the processed results of the middle tier are sent over the network to the client, thus eliminating the need for the client to retrieve and process data from the database. The three-tier architecture can also eliminate some of the restrictions of the network connections and security imposed by Java applets and Web browsers.

SQLJ can be deployed in various scenarios, including in a three-tier architecture. Instead of processing the database business logic from a SQLJ client, you can reduce the client's processing by removing the business logic that processes database data and moving that logic from the client to an application server. Note that the application server can be located on a stand-alone server or on a database server.

As you learned in Chapter 9, you can develop Java RMI, Enterprise JavaBeans (EJB), and CORBA objects using SQLJ. Moreover, with the Oracle8*i*/9*i* data server, your SQLJ applications can reside inside the Oracle8*i*/9*i* JavaVM in the form of Java stored procedures, EJB, and CORBA objects. More importantly, the performance techniques that you learned in the previous sections of this chapter, such as row prefetching and JDBC batching, can be implemented in SQLJ applications residing either internally or externally to the Oracle8*i*/9*i* database. (See Chapter 9 to learn how to develop RMI, EJB, and CORBA objects.)

In this chapter, you learned the following:

- How the SQLJ connection contexts and JDBC connections interact. You acquire the skills to convert SQLJ `DefaultContext`, `ConnectionContext`, or the JDBC `java.sql.Connection` classes to an instance of the `OracleConnection` class while writing the `ConnectionManager` class.

■ How the Oracle JDBC, Oracle extensions, and Oracle performance enhancements further enhanced the standard JDBC. You learned that you can use the Oracle performance features such as row prefetching, update batching, and statement caching to reduce the number of round trips to the database, and database processing time (in the case of statement caching), thereby improving your application performance.

■ How to write efficient SQLJ programs that use the support features of Oracle performance enhancements.

In Chapter 11, you will learn about the Oracle Internet development tools. In particular, you will be acquainted with the Oracle *JDeveloper* tool, a user-friendly development tool that allows you to build, debug, and deploy database applications written in Java and SQLJ.

CHAPTER
11

Oracle9i
Development
Tools

racle provides several Internet development tools, such as Designer, WebDB, JDeveloper, Developer (formerly Developer/2000), JPublisher, and so on. This chapter provides a brief overview of these tools, particularly Oracle Designer, WebDB, and JDeveloper. Remember that JPublisher enables you to specify and customize the mapping of database object types, reference types, and collection types (varrays or nested tables) to Java classes. See Chapter 8 to learn more about the JPublisher tool.

In this chapter, you will find the following:

- A brief overview of Oracle Internet development tools.

- A description of some features of the JDeveloper tool.

- A step-by-step walkthrough that demonstrates how to create, compile, and run a SQLJ application using the JDeveloper Integrated Development Environment (IDE).

Brief Overview of Oracle Internet Development Tools

Oracle provides several tools that you can use to develop and deploy database applications over the Web. The following section introduces some of them. Note that you can get a free evaluation copy of most Oracle products. You can either download them from http://technet.oracle.com or order the CDs from the Oracle store, whose link is found at the same address.

Oracle Designer Tool

Designer is a visual development modeling tool that provides an environment to model database applications. It allows you to generate server-side Database Definition Language (DDL) statements that can be used to create new schemas or update old ones. You can use Designer to develop database applications for many databases such as Oracle7, Oracle8, Oracle8*i*, Oracle9*i*, Oracle Lite, Oracle Rdb, IBM DB/2, Sybase Adaptive Server, Microsoft SQL Server, or any ODBC-compliant database. Applications designed with Designer for an Oracle database are stored in a repository in the Oracle database. Additionally, you can create architectures for client/server or Web-based application deployment, Dynamic HTML, Visual Basic, or C++.

You can use Designer to model "pure" relational databases using Entity Relationship (ER) modeling techniques and object-relational databases using features of the Unified Modeling Language (UML) object analysis and design methodology. The UML features are part of the *Designer Object Extension* tool formerly called *Object Database Designer*. Remember that UML features notation for analyzing and designing software components. (See Chapter 9 for more information regarding UML.)

Designer Generators

You can use Designer to automatically generate the following:

- *Oracle Developer Forms Generator* creates screen layouts, client-side application logic, and database access definitions.

- *Oracle WebServer Generator* produces applications to run over the Web.

- *C++ Generator* generates C++ classes that map the Oracle types that you wish to access from a C++ client-side application. (See Chapters 8 and 9 to learn how to develop and access Oracle types for Oracle8 and Oracle8*i*/9*i* databases.)

- *Visual Basic Generator* generates Visual Basic applications based on module and database design specifications recorded in the repository.

- *Oracle Report Generator* defines report modules and their usage.

- *Oracle Server Generator* creates server-side components such as SQL DDL that include the table, column, Foreign Key constraint, Check constraint, and Primary Key constraint definitions.

See http://technet.oracle.com for technical information on Oracle Internet tools.

Oracle WebDB

WebDB is an HTML-based development tool for building Web database applications (for example, HTML forms, reports, charts, menus, and so on) and Web sites. It is easy to use, easy to access, and easy to administer. The tool provides many wizards that guide the user during the entire development process. WebDB is a solution for building, deploying, and proactively monitoring Web database applications and content-driven Web sites.

WebDB contains many tools that DBAs can use to manage a Web site, such as

- The capability to create database users and assign roles and development privileges to them

■ The capability to configure the WebDB Listener and PL/SQL gateway

■ The capability to organize the structure of WebDB sites

Both types of users, Oracle application developers and database administrators (DBAs), can use WebDB to build applications over the Web. WebDB applications are stored in the Oracle database and can be used with Oracle 7.3.4 or later. When you build a Web site with WebDB, all the maintenance tools are included in the site itself—that is, you can change the site wherever you are (for example, in your office or on the road). WebDB also includes an HTTP listener that you can install to act as a Web server and a PL/SQL interface to the database. Use WebDB to browse databases over the Web, build components (for example, reports, menus, and so on), and monitor users and database activity.

Oracle JDeveloper

JDeveloper is a user-friendly development tool that allows you to build, debug, and deploy database applications written in Java and SQLJ. Starting with release 3.*x*, JDeveloper enables you to develop, debug, and deploy Java client applications, dynamic HTML applications, Web and application server components, and database stored procedures based on industry-standard models. JDeveloper also supports XML. It uses XML internally and enables development of XML applications. JDeveloper enables developers to create business-to-consumer and business- to-business XML applications. You can use the tool to write XML documents and XSL Stylesheets; to generate XML on-the-fly using the Business Components for Java Framework or the database directly; and to transform XML into HTML, WML, XML, or any other format. For detailed descriptions of JDeveloper, see the *Oracle JDeveloper Guide*, from Oracle Press.

When you wish to develop Java or SQLJ client-side and server-side programs, you may use your favorite editor or the Oracle JDeveloper tool. In this chapter, you will use JDeveloper to develop the `MySqljAppUsingJDev` SQLJ application.

JDeveloper Features
Use the Oracle JDeveloper to:

■ Create Oracle Business Component For Java (BC4J). BC4J is Oracle JDeveloper's programming framework for building scalable, multiple-tier database applications from reusable business components. BC4J is a 100 percent Java, XML-powered framework that enables productive development, portable deployment, and flexible customization of multiple-tier. Use JDeveloper to assemble and test application services from reusable business components. You then deploy these application services as either Common Object Request Broker Architecture

(CORBA) server objects or Enterprise JavaBean (EJB) session beans on enterprise-scale server platforms supporting Java technology.

■ Build Oracle XML applications.

■ Build component-based applications with JavaBeans.

■ Create Java and SQLJ client-side applications and applets.

■ Create and deploy Java and SQLJ server-side applications to Oracle8*i* and Oracle9*i*.

■ Build dynamic JSP Servlet applications. JSP is a technology that simplifies the process of building Web-based applications containing dynamic content by allowing you to embed dynamic content in a standard HyperText Markup Language (HTML) or XML Web page. The JavaServer Pages standard is based on the Java servlet standard for writing dynamic server-side Web service modules in pure Java. They allow you to create dynamic Web pages and Web-based applications by applying special XML-like tags and embedding pure Java code scriptlets in a Web page. Remember that servlets are Java programs that extend request/response-oriented servers such as Java-enabled Web servers.

■ Create, debug, and deploy Enterprise JavaBeans (EJB) applications to Oracle8*i* and Oracle9*i*. (See Chapter 9 to learn more about EJB applications.)

■ Create, debug, and deploy CORBA applications to Oracle8*i* and Oracle9*i*. (See Chapter 9 to learn more about CORBA objects.)

■ Generate InfoBus data forms using JFC/Swing components.

■ Switch JDK versions between 1.1.*x*, 1.2, and 1.3.

This section provides you with a brief overview of the JDeveloper IDE. While reading this section, you will learn how to use the Navigator component to create, organize, and access workspaces, projects, packages, and Java and SQLJ classes. See the "Developing a SQLJ Application Using JDeveloper" section of this chapter to learn more about these components.

Primary Components of the JDeveloper IDE

When you open JDeveloper, you see its command, development, and message areas, as shown in Figure 11-1.

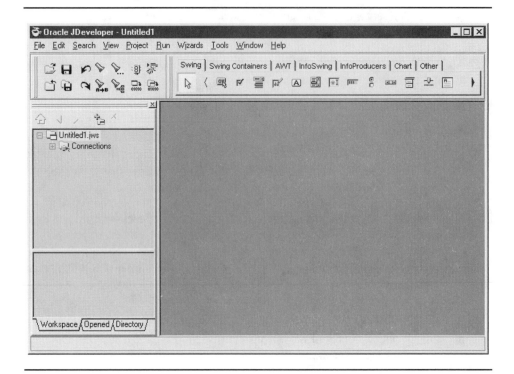

FIGURE 11-1. *Oracle JDeveloper tool*

Command Area

The *command area* in Figure 11-1 contains the following components:

- The menu bar displays a list of the available commands within the tool, such as File, Edit, Search, View, Project, Run, Wizards, Tools, Windows, and Help.

- The toolbar displays the shortcut keys to open and save a file, save all files, undo an operation, search, search again, debug a program, redo an operation, replace, browse a symbol, make and rebuild a program.

- The component palette displays the Java Beans that reside in the tool library. It allows you to add components to your user interface, install custom or third-party components, and customize the palette.

Development Area

You use the *development area* (refer to Figure 11-1) to access your Java and SQLJ source files. In other words, you can create, edit, and view your source code in that area.

Message Area

The *message view* area at the bottom of the JDeveloper window displays errors and messages during a debugging session.

Developing a SQLJ Application Using JDeveloper

The steps to develop a SQLJ application are as follows:

1. Create a workspace.

2. Create a project.

3. Add a SQLJ file to your project to create the source code file.

4. Set project properties so that JDeveloper can check SQLJ syntax at compile time. This step is optional, but highly recommended.

5. Compile the program.

6. Run the program.

Creating a New Workspace

In JDeveloper IDE, a *workspace* keeps track of the projects and environment settings that you use while developing your Java or SQLJ program. When you start JDeveloper, the tool navigator automatically displays the last project that you created—that is, the last workspace is opened by default, enabling you to pick up where you left off. If you wish to create a new workspace and a new project, you need to close the current workspace. You do so by clicking File | Close Workspace. After you close the workspace, the screen looks like the one in Figure 11-1. Workspaces are stored in files with the extension .jws.

The steps to create a workspace are as follows:

1. Choose File | New Workspace.

2. If prompted, select the files in the current workspace that you wish to save and click OK.

Alternatively, you can rename the default workspace. See the "Renaming a Workspace" section, later in this chapter.

Creating a New Project

To create a project, use the Project Wizard that creates a project file with the file extension .jpr. This project file contains the project properties and a list of all the files in the project. The tool uses the list of files and the project settings when you load, save, or build a project. You can see the project file at the top node of the project tree in the Navigation pane. The Project Wizard creates a project file, which stores the project properties, and an optional HTML file that contains default project information. You can edit the HTML page to record pertinent information about the project. Here are the steps to create a new project:

1. Click File | New Project. You'll see the Project Wizard screen shown here:

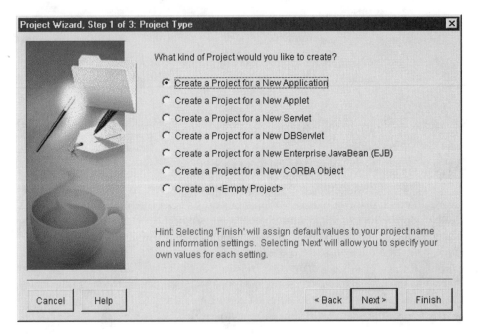

2. Select "Create an <Empty Project>" and click Next. The second wizard screen appears with a default project and package names, as shown next:

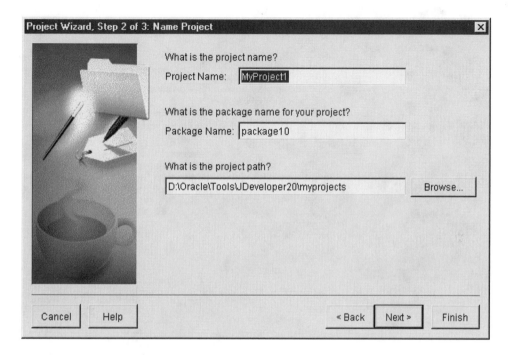

3. Enter new project and package names if you wish to override the defaults. For example, enter **MySqljAppUsingJDev** and **sqljproject** for the project name and the package name, respectively, and click Next to continue. Alternatively, you may click Next without entering additional information to accept the default project and package names. By default, JDeveloper stores the source code files that you created in the `myprojects` directory and the class files in the `myclass` directory. If you wish to store your projects in a different directory path, click Browse, select your directory path, and then click OK.

4. JDeveloper allows you to document your application. If you want to accept the default, click Next. Otherwise, edit the necessary fields such as Title, Author, and Description (as shown next), and click Next.

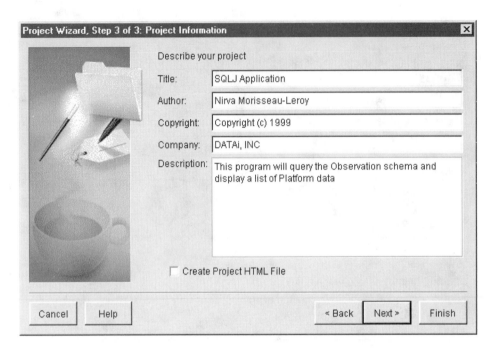

5. The tool displays the Finish screen, shown next. Click Finish to create the project.

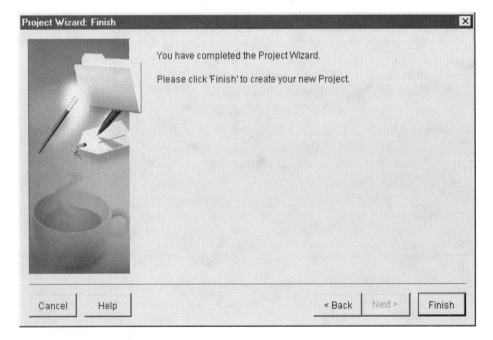

Note that a project is created using the name that you entered in step 3. The navigator reflects these changes, as shown in Figure 11-2.

Renaming a Workspace

In Figure 11-2, the navigator displays the Untitled1.jws filename of the default workspace. Follow these steps to rename the workspace:

1. Click Untitled1.jws.

2. Click File | Rename. You'll see a Save As dialog box like the one shown here:

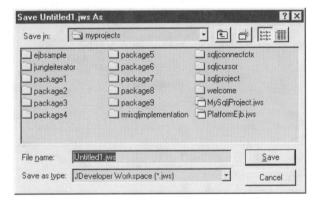

3. Change Untitled1.jws to MySqljAppUsingJDev, select the sqljproject package, and click Save to save the workspace file in the sqljproject package.

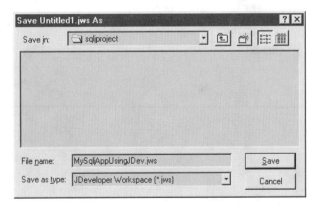

Note that the navigator reflects the changes that you make (see Figure 11-3).

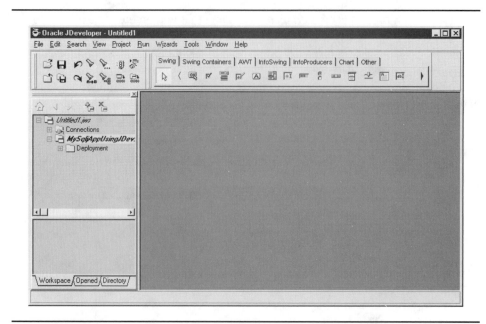

FIGURE 11-2. *Navigator shows the new project.*

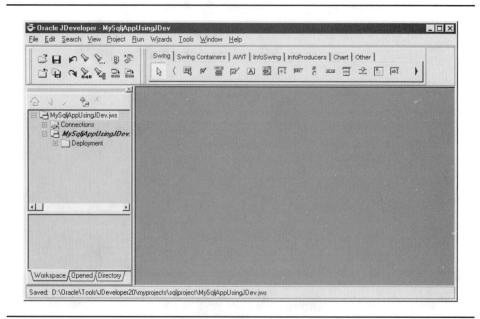

FIGURE 11-3. *Navigator shows the new name of the workspace.*

Adding a SQLJ Source File to the Project

In this section, you will create your SQLJ source file. The steps are as follows:

1. Click File | New. JDeveloper displays the New panel and its icons.

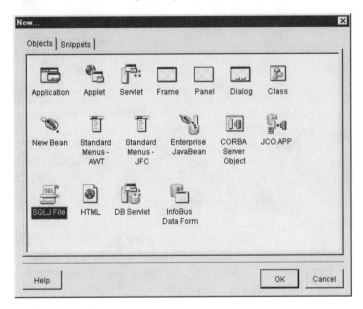

2. You can select the icon that corresponds to your need—in this case, the SQLJ File icon—and then click OK. The tool creates the `Untitled1.sqlj` file, as shown next.

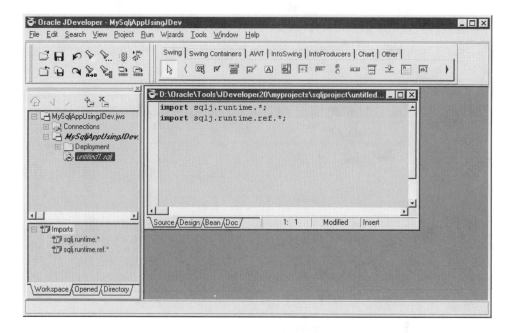

3. Double-click to display the Untitled1.sqlj source file. By default, JDeveloper inserts two import statements to make the sqlj.runtime.* and the sqlj.runtime.ref.* available to your SQLJ program.

4. Rename the file by entering **MySqljAppUsingJDev**, and save the new file in the sqljproject package. Note that the navigator reflects your changes, as shown next.

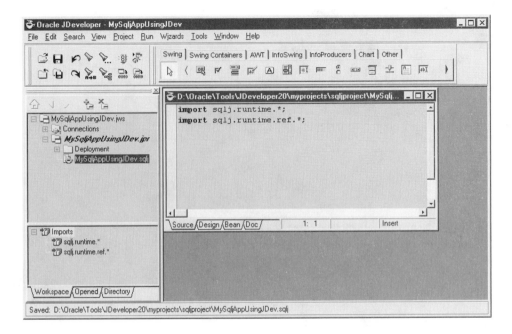

Congratulations. You have just created an empty SQLJ program. The next step is to enter your SQLJ source code, as shown in Figure 11-4 (see the listing of the `MySqljAppUsingJDev` SQLJ application at the end of this chapter).

Setting the Project Properties

JDeveloper allows you to set the project properties so that the SQLJ translator can connect to the database and check SQLJ semantics at compile time. To enable this functionality, you need to create a connection object in the tool. To do so, follow these steps:

1. Click Project | Project Properties to open the Properties dialog box shown next.

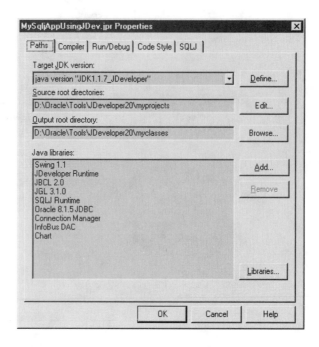

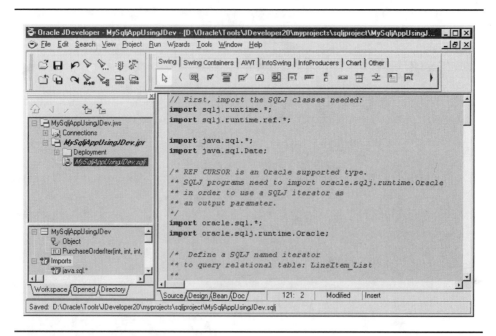

FIGURE 11-4. *SQLJ source code*

2. Click SQLJ, and then click "Check SQL semantics against database schema," as shown here:

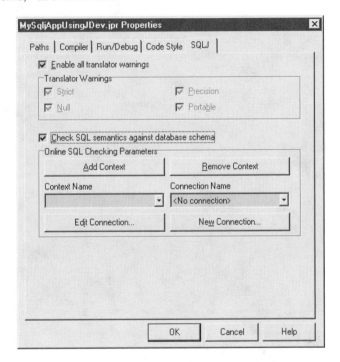

3. Click New Connection.

4. Enter username and password. The default is your local host. If the database is not on your local host, then replace the `localhost` string with the URL address of your database—for example, `data-i.com`. Note that the name of the connection object is `Connection2`; you may change it to a more meaningful name if you wish.

5. Click Test Connection to connect to the database and test your connection. If the test is successful, the connection object named `Connection2` appears, as shown next.

6. Click OK.

Next, you will learn how to compile a SQLJ program using JDeveloper.

Compiling a SQLJ Program

Compiling a program in JDeveloper is very easy. To do so,

1. Click the name of the SQLJ program you wish to compile.

2. Click `Project | Rebuild`.

JDeveloper invokes the SQLJ translator that compiles your program. If compilation errors are generated (warning or fatal), JDeveloper will list them in the message area at the bottom of the screen. Note that in Figure 11-5 the program was compiled successfully and a list of warning messages is presented in the message area. Note that if you wish

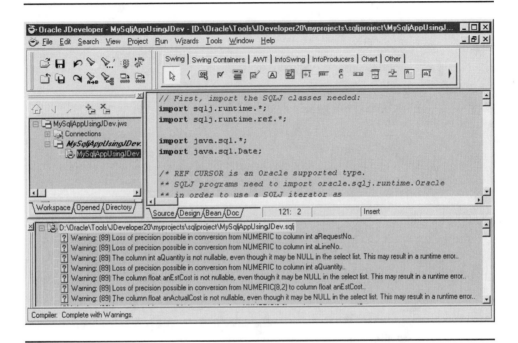

FIGURE 11-5.   *List of warning messages generated at compilation time*

to see generated errors at translation time, you may modify a line in the `.sqlj` program, for example, change `L.lineno AS aLineNo` to `L.lineo AS aLineNo` and recompile the program. When you recompile the program, you will see the error message produced by the SQLJ translator when it is connected to the database.

Remember that when you compile a SQLJ program, the SQLJ translator generates a Java source file and a class file. By default, JDeveloper stores the Java source file in the package directory that you created in step 2 in the "Creating a New Project" section of this chapter. If you wish to run the SQLJ program from the Navigator tree, you need to include the Java source file in your project. To do so, you can click the green plus sign (+) in the Navigator tree, select the file `MySqljAppUsingJDev.java`, and click Open (see Figure 11-6). You are now ready to run the SQLJ program.

Running a SQLJ Program

In the previous section, you learned how to compile a SQLJ program using JDeveloper. Fortunately, you had no syntax errors while compiling the program. In situations in which the translator generates fatal errors, you need to edit the source code, correct the

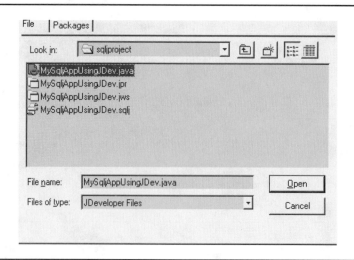

FIGURE 11-6. *Add a Java source file to your project*

errors, and recompile the program using the steps listed in the preceding section, "Compiling a SQLJ Program." Next, you will run the program.

Before you do so, however, JDeveloper's documentation suggests that you rebuild the entire project, particularly in a situation in which you have compiled each program individually, as in the scenario described in the preceding section. When you rebuild the project, the tool creates the appropriate file dependencies and ties any loose ends that may exist. To rebuild the project:

1. Click the MySqljAppUsing.jpr file.

2. Click Project | Rebuild MySqljAppUsing.jpr or click the Rebuild icon on the toolbar. JDeveloper will recompile all programs within the project, as shown in Figure 11-7.

Hopefully, you have no errors. You can, therefore, run the program. To do so, follow these steps:

1. Click the MySqljAppUsing.java file.

2. Click Run | Run using the options from the command area, or alternatively click Run on the toolbar. Note that when you use the run option to execute the program, JDeveloper recompiles the program before running it. So, at subsequent times when you wish to recompile a program, you only need to click the program name and then click Run.

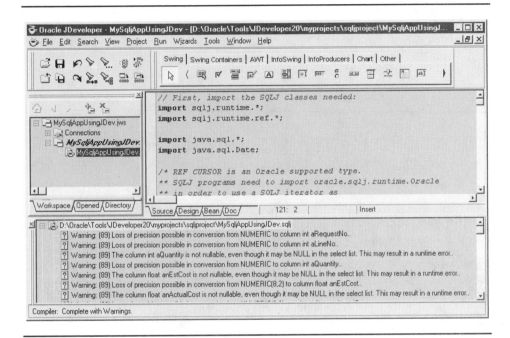

FIGURE 11-7.   *JDeveloper recompiles all programs in the project*

Figure 11-8 shows that the output of the program is listed in the window named *Compiler* associated with the `MySqljAppUsing` program located at the bottom of the tool main window. This SQLJ application accesses the Purchase Order schema and retrieves the details from the LINEITEM_LIST table. See the "Introduction" in this book for a complete listing of the Purchase Order schema or the CD-ROM distributed with the book.

Use the Compiler window's scroll bar to view the results generated by the SQLJ application. Note that this program has been tested with the latest release of JDeveloper, that is JDeveloper 3.2.

Here is the listing of the `MySqljAppUsingJDev` SQLJ application:

```
/*  Program Name: MySqljAppUsingJDev.sqlj
**
**  Purpose:      Use a SQLJ named iterator to
** retrieve purchase orders and their associated
** line items.
*/

// Import the SQLJ runtime classes
import sqlj.runtime.*;
```

```
import sqlj.runtime.ref.*;

// Import the Java classes
import java.sql.*;
import java.sql.Date;

import oracle.sql.*;
import oracle.sqlj.runtime.Oracle;

public class MySqljAppUsingJDev {

    /*  Declare a public SQLJ named iterator
    ** to query the LineItem_List relational table.
    **
    ** Columns listed in the SQLJ named iterator
    ** must match directly the database name columns.
    ** Database data type must also match iterator
    ** data type.  */
    #sql public iterator PurchaseOrderIter
            ( int aRequestNo, int aLineNo,
              int aQuantity, String aUnit,
              float anEstCost, float anActualCost,
              String aDesc
            );
// Default constructor
public MySqljAppUsingJDev(){  // (See Note 1.)
    try {
        /* Register the driver and set the default context
        ** The constructor is the best place to do this.
        ** Edit the setDefaultContext call for a URL
        ** appropriate to your system. */

        // (See Note 2.)
        DriverManager.registerDriver
            (new oracle.jdbc.driver.OracleDriver());
        DefaultContext.setDefaultContext
            (new DefaultContext
              ("jdbc:oracle:thin:@data-i.com:1521:ORCL",
                "scott","tiger",false)
            );
    } // End try
    catch (Exception ex) {
        System.err.println("Database Connection failed: " + ex);
        } // end catch
    }  // End constructor

  public static void main (String [] args) throws SQLException {
     // Instantiate MySqljAppUsingJDev()     (See Note 3.)
```

```
    MySqljAppUsingJDev app = new MySqljAppUsingJDev();

    // Stop program execution if we cannot connect to the database
    // (See Note 4.)
    if  (DefaultContext.getDefaultContext() == null ) {
         System.out.println("I cannot connect to the database "
                               + "-- Stop Execution.");
         System.exit(1);
    } // End if
    try {
        app.runMySqljAppUsingJDev ();  // (See Note 5.)
    } // End try
    catch (SQLException ex) { // (See Note 6.)
      System.err.println("Error running the " +
            "MySqljAppUsingJDev application: " + ex);
      String sqlState = ex.getSQLState();
      System.err.println("SQL State: " + sqlState);
      String sqlMessage = ex.getMessage();
      System.err.println("SQL Message: " + sqlMessage);
      int errorCode = ex.getErrorCode();
      System.err.println("SQL Error Code: " + errorCode);
    }  // End catch
} // End main()

 void runMySqljAppUsingJDev () throws SQLException {
   // Instantiate PurchaseOrderIter iterator
   // and initialize it: purchaseOrder
   PurchaseOrderIter aPurchaseOrderIter = null;

  // Query Purchase_List database table using
  // aPurchaseOrderIter. (See Note 7.)
  #sql aPurchaseOrderIter =
      { SELECT L.requestno AS aRequestNo,
            L.lineno AS aLineNo,
            L.quantity AS aQuantity,
            L.unit AS aUnit,
            L.estimatedcost AS anEstCost,
            L.actualcost AS anActualCost,
            L.description AS aDesc
        FROM lineitem_list L
        ORDER BY L.requestno
      };  // end of SQLJ statement

    // Iterate and print purchase order info. (See Note 8.)
    while (aPurchaseOrderIter.next() ) {
       System.out.println("Request No: " +
            aPurchaseOrderIter.aRequestNo() );
       System.out.println("Line Item No: " +
```

```
                    aPurchaseOrderIter.aLineNo() );
          System.out.println("Quantity: " +
                    aPurchaseOrderIter.aQuantity() );
          System.out.println("Unit: " +
                    aPurchaseOrderIter.aUnit() );
          System.out.println("Estimated Cost: " +
                    aPurchaseOrderIter.anEstCost() );
          System.out.println("Actual Cost: " +
                    aPurchaseOrderIter.anActualCost() );
          System.out.println("Quantity: " +
                    aPurchaseOrderIter.aDesc() );
      }  // End while

      /* Close the iterator
      **
      ** Iterators should be closed when you no longer need them
      */
      aPurchaseOrderIter.close();
  } // End runMySqljAppUsingJDev()

} // End MySqljAppUsingJDev.class
```

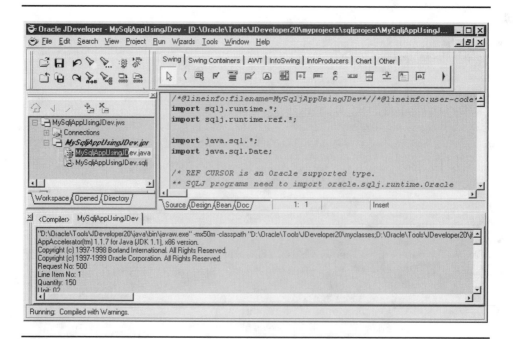

FIGURE 11-8. *Program output is listed in the window named Compiler*

Notes on the `MySqljAppUsingJDev` SQLJ application:

1. This statement creates a default constructor that, when invoked, will automatically connect to the Oracle database. See Chapters 2, 5, and 7 to learn more about SQLJ connection objects and Appendix B for Java default constructors. Remember that a SQLJ constructor is identical to a Java constructor.

2. The semantics of the next seven lines could be replaced with the following:

```
oracle.sqlj.runtime.Oracle("jdbc:oracle:thin:"
  +"@data-i.com:1521:ORCL","scott","tiger");
```

3. This statement instantiates the `MySqljAppUsingJDev` SQLJ class.

4. This statement ensures that the program stops execution if it fails to connect to the database.

5. This statement calls the `runMySqljAppUsingJDev` method.

6. The `catch` block includes several statements:

   ■ The first statement prints a user-defined error message.

   ■ The following statements use the methods from the `java.sql.SQLException` class and its subclasses to provide more information on the SQL errors generated by the program (see Chapters 2 and 4 to learn more about generated SQL errors):

      ■ The next statement calls the `getSQLState()` method that returns a five-digit string containing the SQL state.

      ■ The next statement prints the SQL state retrieved from the previous statement.

      ■ The next statement calls the `getMessage()` method that returns an error message.

      ■ The next statement prints the error message.

      ■ The next statement calls the `getErrorCode()` method that returns 0. This information is really meaningless.

      ■ The next statement prints the error code.

7. This statement selects all purchase orders and their associated line items and stores the results in a SQLJ iterator object. Remember that multi-row queries are stored in SQLJ iterator objects. See Chapters 2, 3, and 6, and Appendix D to learn more about SQLJ iterators.

8. This statement uses a `while` loop to iterate the results stored in the iterator object.

This chapter concludes Part IV. It introduced some of the Oracle Internet development tools such as Oracle Designer, Oracle WebDB, and JDeveloper. Additionally, it presented a step-by-step walkthrough that taught you how to create, compile, and run a SQLJ program.

Appendix A marks the beginning of Part V, where you will learn basic SQL and PL/SQL concepts that will help you understand SQLJ constructs.

PART
V

Appendixes

APPENDIX

A

Oracle SQL Basics

n this Appendix, you will find

- Some basic material on the relational database model

- A tutorial for the SQL relational database language

- A discussion of embedded SQL, the approach that allows SQL statements to be executed from general-purpose programming languages such as C and C++

- A discussion of PL/SQL, Oracle's procedural extension of SQL

The Relational Model for Databases

Clearly, the seminal advance in database technology was the creation of the relational model for databases by E. F. Codd as presented in *A Relational Model of Data for Large Shared Data Banks*. The basic advantage of the relational model is that it provides power through simplicity. In particular, the model is based on a simple data structure, the table, and simple very high-level database languages such as SQL, in which the user indicates what is to be done instead of how to do it. You are referred to Chapter 3 of *An Introduction to Database Systems, Sixth Edition*, Date, C.J., for a description of the advantages provided by such simplicity.

NOTE
Some fundamental definitions for the relational model are now presented here. A file *is a set of records, where a* record *is a set of fields, and a* field *is the smallest unit of named data in the file.*

Figure A-1 illustrates a file, called `EMPLOYEE_LIST`, that contains a record for each employee in a company, containing the fields `employeeno`, `lastname`, `firstname`, `phone`, and `departmentno`.

employeeno	lastname	firstname	phone	departmentno

FIGURE A-1. *EMPLOYEE_LIST*

This EMPLOYEE_LIST file enjoys a special property that is very important in the relational model; it is an example of a *table*. A *table* is a file in which every record has the same structure, that is, the same number, and the corresponding semantic type, of fields. The *semantic type* of a field is the meaning of the field. EMPLOYEE_LIST is a table, since each record in it contains exactly the same semantic type (although not necessarily the same values) of fields. Specifically, each EMPLOYEE_LIST record consists of an employee number, a last name, a first name, a phone number, and a department number.

In the relational model, each table should be equipped with a *primary key*, that is, a field (or collection of fields) that satisfies the following two properties:

■ **Uniqueness**   No two records in the table will have the same primary-key values.

■ **Fully defined**   Every record in the table must have a value for each field in its primary key. This means that when a record is inserted into a table, a value must be given to each field in the primary key.

The primary key is the principal means of identifying a record in a table.

The primary key for the EMPLOYEE_LIST table consists of one field, the employeeno field. This is designated in Figure A-1 (and generally in this appendix) by circling the primary-key field.

The MARRIAGE table in Figure A-2 represents the marriages, both past and present, between a set of men and a set of women. Since it is possible for a person to have ex-spouses, both the husband_ssn and the wife_ssn are required fields in the primary key. Such a primary key that contains more than one field is called a *composite primary key*.

A *relational database* is a logically related collection of tables. In general, a database describes *entities* (that is, distinguishable objects) and relationships between entities (see *The Entity-Relationship Model—Toward a Unified View of Data* by P. Chen).

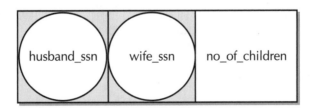

FIGURE A-2.   *MARRIAGE*

For example, the database in Figure A-3 describes the entities `employee`, `department`, and `project`, as well as the relationship between employees and departments, and the account relationship between projects and departments.

As is typical in relational databases, each entity is represented by its own table. The relationship between departments and employees is represented by placing departmentno, the primary key of the DEPARTMENT_LIST table, in the EMPLOYEE_LIST table. The account relationship between departments and

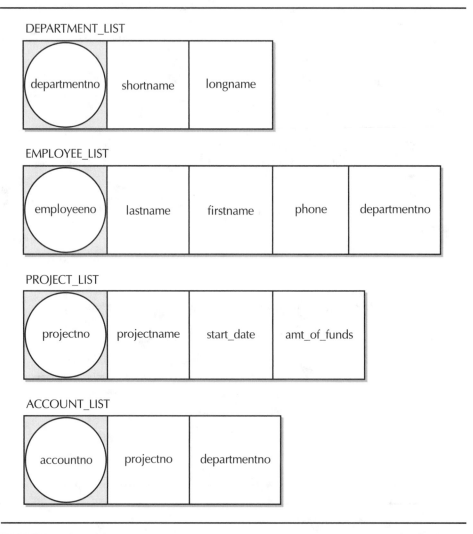

FIGURE A-3. *The DEPARTMENT-EMPLOYEE-PROJECT-ACCOUNT database*

projects is represented by its own table, ACCOUNT_LIST, containing the primary keys of the DEPARTMENT_LIST table (departmentno) and the PROJECT_LIST table (projectno). Thus, in both of these relationships, the primary keys of the entities being related are used to define the relationships.

However, the account relationship gets its own table while the department-employee relationship does not. The reason for this difference is that the account relationship is a many-to-many relationship (each department can have an account with many projects, and each project can have an account with many departments), whereas the department-employee relationship is a one-to-many relationship (each department can have many employees, but each employee works in only one department). Since placing the departmentno in the PROJECT_LIST table, or placing the projectno in the DEPARTMENT_LIST table, would generate too much redundancy, it is indeed desirable to represent the account relationship as a separate table.

As you have seen in the preceding discussion, relationships are represented in the relational model by using the primary keys of the entities being related (actually, *alternate keys,* keys that could have been chosen to be the primary key but were not, can also be used). The primary key of one table (the referenced table) that appears in another table (the referencing table) is called a *foreign key* for the referencing table. The *referential integrity rule* states that no foreign key can reference a nonexistent record in the referenced table. Hence, if departmentno 100 appears in an EMPLOYEE_LIST record, there must be a departmentno 100 in a DEPARTMENT_LIST record. Most relational database systems support the referential integrity rule. You will see later how this rule is enforced in SQL.

A *relational database language* is a language for setting up the structure of and manipulating relational databases. The commands in a relational database language that are used to set up the structure of a database (for example, creating a new table) are called *DDL (Data Definition Language) commands.* The commands for manipulating a database (for example, inserting, deleting, updating, and retrieving records) are called *DML (Data Manipulation Language) commands.* SQL is by far the most widely used relational database language.

A *relational database management system* (RDBMS) is an implementation of one or more relational database languages. Most RDBMSs implement SQL, but some implement other relational database languages as well. The first two significant RDBMSs were the research systems INGRES (see *The Design and Implementation of INGRES*), developed at the University of California at Berkeley, and System R (see *System R: Relational Approach to Database Management*), developed at IBM Research, San Jose. System R was based on SQL, while INGRES was based on the relational database language QUEL. However, the commercial version of INGRES, available in the early 1980s, supported both SQL and QUEL, with SQL being the principal language for the system.

The first commercially available RDBMS, and the first commercial implementation of SQL, was the Oracle RDBMS, which was available by 1979.

SQL

In the next two sections, you will consider the DDL and DML commands of SQL, respectively. You are referred to *An Introduction to Database Systems, Sixth Edition, Date,* C.J., and *Oracle8i/9i SQL Reference Manual* for more information on these commands.

In Oracle, you can submit SQL commands interactively to the SQL*Plus and SQL*DBA utilities.

SQL DDL Commands

The most important SQL DDL command is the CREATE TABLE command, which creates a new database table. A simplified syntax of the CREATE TABLE command is

```
CREATE TABLE tablename ( list_of_field_definitions_and_constraints )
```

where a `list_of_field_definitions_and_constraints` is a *field definition,* or a sequence of field definitions and constraints separated by commas. Each field definition consists of a *field name* followed by a *field data type.* A *constraint* is a condition that the database must satisfy in order to be consistent, such as a primary-key constraint or a foreign-key constraint. For example, the following CREATE TABLE command creates the database table described in Figure A-1.

```
CREATE TABLE
   EMPLOYEE_LIST
      ( employeeno    number(5),
        lastname      varchar2(30),
        firstname     varchar2(30),
        phone         varchar2(13),
        departmentno  number(5),
        PRIMARY KEY   ( employeeno ),
        FOREIGN KEY   ( departmentno ) REFERENCES DEPARTMENT_LIST )
```

number is the SQL numeric data type, which includes integers and floats, with number(5) indicating an integer with a maximum of five digits and varchar2 as the SQL data type for variable length strings. The primary-key constraint ensures that

- No two records in EMPLOYEE_LIST can have the same employeeno value.

- Every record inserted into EMPLOYEE_LIST must have a non-NULL employeeno value. Note that when a field has not been given a value in a record, SQL by default will assign a special NULL value to the field in that record.

The foreign-key constraint ensures the enforcement of the referential integrity rule by constraining operations on both the referencing table (EMPLOYEE_LIST) and the referenced table (DEPARTMENT_LIST). Specifically, the RDBMS will not allow an EMPLOYEE_LIST record to be inserted if it contains a departmentno that is not in the DEPARTMENT_LIST table. Similarly, the departmentno field of an already existing record cannot be changed to a departmentno that is not in the DEPARTMENT_LIST table. Also, the RDBMS will not allow a DEPARTMENT_LIST record to be deleted if the departmentno of that record is still in the EMPLOYEE_LIST table (that is, if there is still an employee in that department). Similarly, an update of a departmentno field in the DEPARTMENT_LIST table is not allowed if that update would cause a departmentno to "disappear" from the DEPARTMENT_LIST table, and if that departmentno is still in the EMPLOYEE_LIST table. However, SQL allows foreign keys to be NULL and, therefore, reference no record at all.

The inverse of the CREATE TABLE command is the DROP TABLE command, which purges a table from the database. For example,

```
DROP TABLE EMPLOYEE_LIST
```

purges the EMPLOYEE_LIST table from the database.

Other SQL DDL commands include the ALTER TABLE command, which changes the logical structure of an already existing table; the CREATE VIEW command, which creates a virtual table (one that exists as a stored definition instead of a stored set of records in the database); and the CREATE INDEX command, which creates a B-tree index on a table to speed up retrievals. Refer to *An Introduction to Database Systems, Sixth Edition,* by C.J. Date, and *Oracle8i/9i SQL Reference Manual* for information on these commands.

SQL DML Commands

SQL contains four DML commands:

- **INSERT statement**   Use to insert records into a table

- **DELETE statement**   Use to delete records from a table

- **UPDATE statement**   Use to change the field values of already existing records in a table

- **SELECT statement**   Use to retrieve data from the database

The syntax of the DELETE and UPDATE statements and the syntax of one of the two types of INSERT statements, the INSERT SELECT statement, are based on the syntax of the SELECT statement. Therefore, these statements will be discussed after the SELECT statement.

First, the INSERT VALUES statement, the type of INSERT statement that is *not* based on the SELECT statement, is discussed. A CREATE TABLE statement creates an empty table. The INSERT VALUES statement can be used to load a record into a table. The syntax of the INSERT VALUES statement is

```
INSERT INTO tablename ( field_list ) VALUES ( values_list )
```

The field_list indicates the order in which field values will be inserted, and values_list contains those field values. For example,

```
INSERT INTO EMPLOYEE_LIST
    ( employeeno, lastname, firstname, phone, departmentno )
        VALUES ( 1056, 'Jones', 'Rachel', '(305)555-0359', 15 )
```

inserts the indicated record into the EMPLOYEE_LIST table. Note that string literals are delimited by single quotes (') in SQL.

SELECT Statements

First, the simplest kind of SELECT statement—namely, a SELECT statement that involves only one table—is considered.

One-Table SELECT Statements

The simplified syntax of a one-table SELECT statement is

```
SELECT expression_list FROM tablename [ where_clause ]
```

where the square brackets indicate that the where_clause is optional. The expression_list is a list of expressions, with each expression built up using operators, constants, and the fields from tablename. A where_clause is the keyword WHERE, followed by a Boolean combination of comparison_clauses using the Boolean operators AND, OR, or NOT, where a comparison_clause has this form:

```
expression1 comparison_operator expression2
```

expression1 and expression2 are as in the expression_list, and the comparison_operators are <, <=, >, >=, =, and <> (inequality operator). For example,

```
SELECT employeeno, phone
  FROM EMPLOYEE_LIST
```

```
WHERE departmentno = 15
   AND firstname = 'Michelle'
```

prints the employeeno and phone number for each employee with the first name Michelle who works in department number 15. The comparison clauses in the preceding example can be called compare-against-constant clauses, as they each compare the value of a specific field to a specific constant. Such compare-against-constant clauses are very common in SELECT statements.

In general, the one-table SELECT statement will print the indicated expressions from the indicated table for records that satisfy the WHERE clause condition. The * wildcard may appear in place of the expression_list in the SELECT statement, indicating that all the fields in the table should be printed; and a missing where_clause indicates that each record in the table will contribute output. For example,

```
SELECT * FROM EMPLOYEE_LIST
```

prints the entire EMPLOYEE_LIST table.

Multiple-Table SELECT Statements

Next, SELECT statements that involve more than one table are considered. These are true database commands in that they act across tables at the database level. Consider the following query:

```
Print the project names of projects that have an account
with department number 15.
```

This query involves both the ACCOUNT_LIST table to find the project numbers of projects that have an account with department number 15, and the PROJECT_LIST table, to "translate" the project numbers found in ACCOUNT_LIST into the project names that are to be printed. This query can be coded as the following SELECT statement:

```
SELECT PROJECT_LIST.projectname
   FROM PROJECT_LIST, ACCOUNT_LIST
      WHERE ACCOUNT_LIST.departmentno = 15
         AND ACCOUNT_LIST.projectno = PROJECT_LIST.projectno
```

Note that field names are modified with table names, using the dot (.) operator to protect against the ambiguity that would arise when the same field name appears in different tables in the query.

The compare-against-constant clause ACCOUNT_LIST.departmentno = 15 can be thought of as identifying the desired ACCOUNT_LIST records. The join clause ACCOUNT_LIST.projectno = PROJECT_LIST.projectno can be thought of as obtaining the `PROJECT_LIST` record that "matches" such an `ACCOUNT_LIST` record, in that it contains the same `projectno`. In general, a join clause has the form

```
fieldreference1 comparison_operator fieldreference2
```

where a `fieldreference` has the form `[ tablename. ]fieldname`, and the referenced fields come from different records.

A special type of join clause involves fields from different records in the same table. This type of join clause requires the *alias* construct. For example, consider the next query:

```
Print the pairs of first names of employees who have the same
last names, but different first names.
```

This query can be expressed in SQL as

```
SELECT EX.firstname, EY.firstname
   FROM EMPLOYEE_LIST EX, EMPLOYEE_LIST EY
      WHERE EX.lastname = EY.lastname
         AND EX.firstname <> EY.firstname
```

In the `FROM` clause, `EX` and `EY` are assigned as two aliases for `EMPLOYEE_LIST` records that can be used in the `WHERE` clause, allowing you to compare different records from the `EMPLOYEE_LIST` table. Specifically, the two join clauses obtain `EMPLOYEE_LIST` records `EX` and `EY` for different employees (their first names are different) who have the same last names.

Nested `SELECT` Statements

A *nested* `SELECT` statement is a `SELECT` statement that contains another `SELECT` statement in its `WHERE` clause. A subquery is a `SELECT` statement that is contained in the `WHERE` clause of a nested `SELECT` statement. A common reason for including a subquery in the `WHERE` clause of a `SELECT` statement is that the `WHERE` clause contains the `IN` operator. You can use the `IN` operator to test whether a value belongs to a set of values that is designated by a subquery. For example, consider the problem, which was solved previously without subqueries, of printing the project names of projects that have an account with department number 15. A nested solution to this problem is

```
SELECT projectname FROM PROJECT_LIST
   WHERE projectno IN
      ( SELECT projectno FROM ACCOUNT_LIST
         WHERE departmentno = 15 )
```

Here, we print the names of projects whose project number belongs to the set of numbers of projects that have an account with department number 15. In general, the form of such a *membership test* is

expression IN (subquery)

where the IN operator returns true if the value of the indicated expression belongs to the set designated by the indicated subquery.

Some prefer a nested solution of a query to a flat (that is, nonnested) solution because the nested solution can be a simple connection of simple (often one-table) selects. When the nesting structure does provide a sequence of one-table SELECT statements, as in the preceding example, it is not necessary to qualify field names with table names. Also, there are some queries that do not have flat solutions. These are queries that involve the NOT IN operator in a negative membership test. The *negative membership test* has the form

expression NOT IN (subquery)

which returns true if the value of the expression does not belong to the set designated by the subquery, and returns false otherwise. For example, the query

Print the project names of projects that do not have an account with department number 15.

does not have a flat solution. However, this query has the following nested solution:

```
SELECT projectname FROM PROJECT_LIST
    WHERE projectno NOT IN
      ( SELECT projectno FROM ACCOUNT_LIST
          WHERE departmentno = 15 )
```

Observe that the following query prints the project names of projects that have an account with at least one department number other than 15, instead of the desired output:

```
SELECT PROJECT_LIST.projectname
    FROM PROJECT_LIST, ACCOUNT_LIST
      WHERE ACCOUNT_LIST.departmentno <> 15
        AND PROJECT_LIST.projectno = ACCOUNT_LIST.projectno
```

In general, the inequality operator cannot be used to simulate the NOT IN operator.

Aggregate Functions

Roughly speaking, an *aggregate function* is a function that assigns a number to a set of field values or a set of records. In the SELECT statement, aggregate functions can appear in the expression_list after the keyword SELECT, or in a HAVING clause (which will soon be introduced). The aggregate functions supported by SQL include AVG, SUM, MAX, MIN, and COUNT. Oracle SQL supports additional aggregate functions, namely, VARIANCE and STDDEV (standard deviation).

For example, you can code the query

Print how many accounts involve department number 15.

as

```
SELECT COUNT(*) FROM ACCOUNT_LIST
   WHERE departmentno = 15
```

where COUNT(*) indicates that you are counting records. The other form of the COUNT aggregate function is

```
COUNT( DISTINCT expression )
```

where you are counting distinct expression values.

Each of the other aggregate functions takes an expression, optionally prefixed with the keyword DISTINCT or the keyword ALL, as its argument. For example, AVG(DISTINCT qty) indicates that duplicate qty values should be removed before computing the average qty. AVG(ALL qty) indicates that the average should be computed for all the qty values, including duplicates. ALL is the default for the SUM, AVG, MAX, MIN, VARIANCE, and STDDEV aggregate functions.

Suppose you are required to print, for each department, the department number and the number of accounts that involve that department. You can do this using the GROUP BY clause:

```
SELECT departmentno, COUNT(*) FROM ACCOUNT_LIST
   GROUP BY departmentno
```

Here, the GROUP BY clause partitions the ACCOUNT_LIST table into groups, with one group for each departmentno, and generates one line of output—namely, the departmentno and number of accounts—for each group. You can modify this query so that only groups that satisfy a specified condition generate output. You accomplish this with the HAVING clause. For instance, the following SELECT statement prints the department number and number of accounts for each department that has more than ten accounts:

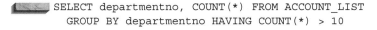

```
SELECT departmentno, COUNT(*) FROM ACCOUNT_LIST
   GROUP BY departmentno HAVING COUNT(*) > 10
```

In closing, please note that Oracle SQL aggregate functions are referred to as group functions.

UNION, INTERSECT, and MINUS Operators

Please observe that all the SELECT statements that you have seen so far take each field from a designated table. However, suppose you want to print the department numbers that appear in either the ACCOUNT_LIST table or the EMPLOYEE_LIST table. You cannot do this using the constructs discussed thus far. However, SQL supports a UNION operator, the output of which is the set-theoretic union of the outputs of the SELECT statements that are its operands, that you can use to solve this problem.

```
SELECT departmentno FROM EMPLOYEE_LIST
   UNION
SELECT departmentno FROM ACCOUNT_LIST
```

This query will print the department numbers that are in the ACCOUNT_LIST table or in the EMPLOYEE_LIST table, with duplicate records removed.

SQL also provides the INTERSECT and MINUS operators. The department numbers common to the ACCOUNT_LIST and the EMPLOYEE_LIST table are given by

```
SELECT departmentno FROM ACCOUNT_LIST
   INTERSECT
SELECT departmentno FROM EMPLOYEE_LIST
```

Similarly, the department numbers that are in the ACCOUNT_LIST table but are not in the EMPLOYEE_LIST table will be printed by

```
SELECT departmentno FROM ACCOUNT_LIST
   MINUS
SELECT departmentno FROM EMPLOYEE_LIST
```

Observe that the MINUS and NOT IN operators provide alternative solutions to the same type of problem. For example, the preceding query can also be expressed as

```
SELECT departmentno FROM ACCOUNT_LIST
   WHERE departmentno NOT IN
      ( SELECT departmentno FROM EMPLOYEE_LIST )
```

The query that was previously solved with the `NOT IN` operator, namely,

> Print the project names of projects that do not have an account with department number 15.

has the following solution with the `MINUS` operator:

```
SELECT projectname FROM PROJECT_LIST
    WHERE projectno IN
      ( SELECT projectno FROM PROJECT_LIST
          MINUS
        SELECT projectno FROM ACCOUNT_LIST
          WHERE departmentno = 15 )
```

DISTINCT and ORDER BY

Finally, the keyword `DISTINCT` and the `ORDER BY` clause are discussed. In order to suppress duplicate records in the output from a `SELECT` statement, follow the keyword `SELECT` with the keyword `DISTINCT`. For example,

```
SELECT DISTINCT departmentno FROM ACCOUNT_LIST
```

will print the department numbers in the `ACCOUNT_LIST` table without duplication.

In order to guarantee that the output from a `SELECT` statement is sorted on one or more fields, you use an `ORDER BY` clause following the `WHERE` clause in the `SELECT` statement. For example, the following query prints the `ACCOUNT_LIST` records involving department number 15, sorted on the `accountno` and `projectno` fields:

```
SELECT * FROM ACCOUNT_LIST WHERE departmentno = 15
    ORDER BY accountno, projectno
```

INSERT SELECT, DELETE, and UPDATE Statements

The `SELECT` statement syntax is used in the `INSERT SELECT` statement, the `DELETE` statement, and the `UPDATE` statement. The syntax of the `INSERT SELECT` statement is

```
INSERT INTO tablename ( field_list ) select_statement
```

where the `expression_list` in the `SELECT` statement must be type compatible with the `field_list` after the `tablename`. When you execute the `INSERT SELECT` statement, the records delivered by the `SELECT` statement are inserted into the indicated table. For example,

```
INSERT INTO ACCOUNT_LIST( accountno, projectno, departmentno )
   SELECT * FROM NEW_ACCOUNTS
```

will insert the NEW_ACCOUNTS records into the ACCOUNT_LIST table, where NEW_ACCOUNTS is a table that has the same structure as the ACCOUNT_LIST table.

The syntax of the DELETE statement is

```
DELETE FROM tablename [ where_clause ]
```

The optional where_clause has the same syntax as the WHERE clause in a one-table SELECT statement on tablename (however, it can contain subqueries). When executed, the records in tablename that satisfy the where_clause are deleted from tablename. For example, the following statement will delete the ACCOUNT_LIST records for department number 15:

```
DELETE FROM ACCOUNT_LIST WHERE departmentno = 15
```

Similarly, the UPDATE statement can contain a WHERE clause that indicates which records should be updated. For example, the following UPDATE statement changes the last name of employee 1056 to Smith and changes the phone number to (305)555-0873:

```
UPDATE EMPLOYEE_LIST
   SET lastname = 'Smith', phone = '(305)555-0873'
     WHERE employeeno = 1056
```

The general form of the UPDATE statement is

```
UPDATE tablename SET set_list [ where_clause ]
```

where set_list is a list of elements of the form

```
field  = expression
```

When you execute the UPDATE statement, the values of the indicated fields will be changed to the indicated expressions on the records in tablename that satisfy the WHERE clause.

Transaction Control Commands

In addition to DDL and DML commands, SQL supports *transaction control commands*. A *transaction* is a unit of database work (that is, a section of an embedded SQL program or online session that is guaranteed, among other things, to be completely done or completely undone). Examples of transaction control commands are the COMMIT WORK statement

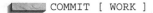 COMMIT [WORK]

which makes all database changes in the transaction permanent, and the ROLLBACK statement

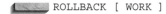 ROLLBACK [WORK]

which undoes all database changes in the transaction. Typically, the COMMIT WORK and ROLLBACK statements divide the program or session into transactions.

Embedded SQL

An *embedded SQL program* is a program in a general-purpose programming language, such as C or C++, that directly contains SQL statements within it. An embedded SQL program in a general-purpose programming language is processed by a precompiler that translates it into a program in the general-purpose programming language without SQL statements. In particular, the SQL statements are translated into function calls to a SQL run-time library for the programming language. The Oracle precompiler for C is called Pro*C. SQL statements are specially marked in the embedded SQL program by prefixing them with the keywords exec sql. Most SQL statements can be directly placed in such an exec sql statement. A notable exception, as you will see, is the SELECT statement.

Embedded SQL Example Program

The following is a Pro*C—acceptable embedded SQL program that inserts records into the ACCOUNT_LIST table from a data file called ACCT_DATA (Pro*C source files have the extension .pc).

```
/*
** Program Name:  load_acctlist.pc
**
** Purpose:  Load the ACCOUNT_LIST table from the text file ACCT_DATA.
**
*/
#include<stdio.h>
#include<string.h>
#include<stdlib.h>

/* (See Note 1.) */
exec sql include sqlca;

main()
{ /* Declare host variables (C variables that will appear
     in exec sql statements) in the declare section.
```

```
*/
/* (See Note 2.) */
exec sql begin declare section;
  int accountno, projectno, departmentno;
  varchar2 user[21], pass[20];
exec sql end declare section;

/* Declare C variables that won't appear in exec sql statements.
*/
/* fp is a standard I/O file pointer that will be used to read
   the ACCT_DATA file.
*/
FILE * fp;
int i;

/* Connect to the database with username = scott and
   password = tiger.
*/
strcpy( user.arr, "scott" );
user.len = strlen( user.arr );
strcpy( pass.arr, "tiger" );
pass.len = strlen( pass.arr );
exec sql CONNECT :user IDENTIFIED BY :pass;

/* Test sqlcode to see if connected.  If not connected,
   terminate program.
*/
if ( sqlca.sqlcode != 0 )
  { fprintf( stderr, "Sorry, cannot connect to database,
                      program terminated. \n" );
    return;
  }

/* Open data file. */
if ( ( fp = fopen( "ACCT_DATA", "r" ) == NULL ) );
  { fprintf
     ( stderr, "Cannot open data file, program terminated. \n" );
    return;
  }

/* Read data file records, and insert them into the
   ACCOUNT_LIST table.
*/
/* Fields in the data file are separated by blanks, and records
   are terminated with newlines.
*/
while( fscanf
  ( fp, "%d%d%d", &accountno, &projectno, &departmentno) != EOF )
```

```
{ exec sql INSERT INTO ACCOUNT_LIST
    VALUES ( :accountno, :projectno, :departmentno );

  /* Test sqlcode to see if insert worked.
     If it worked, commit the insert.
  */
  if ( sqlca.sqlcode != 0 )
    { fprintf( stderr, "%d%d%d could not be inserted\n",
             accountno, projectno, departmentno );
    } else COMMIT WORK;
}
printf ( "Program complete. \n" );
fclose(fp);
}
```

Notes on `load_acctlist.pc`:

1. The SQL communications area `sqlca` (a `struct`) is included into the program by the `exec sql include sqlca` statement. One of the fields in `sqlca` is the `sqlcode` field, which is set to zero by the system whenever a SQL statement successfully executes, and is set to a nonzero value whenever the execution of a SQL statement generates a warning or an error. `sqlca. sqlcode` should be checked after the execution of each SQL statement.

2. C variables that appear in `exec sql` statements are called *host variables* and must be declared in the declare section of the program. When host variables appear in `exec sql` statements, a colon must prefix them (for example, `:accountno`). You can use host variables any place in an `exec sql` statement that an expression can appear.

The SQL `varchar2` variable-length data type is implemented as a `struct` with a data field (`arr`) that contains a pointer to a string, and a length field (`len`) that contains the logical length of the string referenced by `arr`.

Cursors

A `SELECT` statement cannot be directly executed as an `exec sql` statement. The reason for this is that the designers of embedded SQL decided that they wanted the output from the `SELECT` statement to be automatically buffered and then read by the program from the buffer one record at a time. Such a transparent buffer is called a *cursor,* and is manipulated by several types of statements. The `DECLARE CURSOR` statement attaches a `SELECT` statement to a cursor identifier. The `OPEN` statement activates a cursor and binds the values of any host variables that appear in the `DECLARE CURSOR SELECT` statement. The `FETCH` statement reads the next record from the cursor into host variables (the SELECT statement output records are fetched from the cursor sequentially, one record at a time). The CLOSE statement deactivates the cursor.

The following embedded SQL program repeatedly reads a project number and prints the department numbers and account numbers for accounts involving that project. When the program reads -1 instead of a valid project number, it terminates.

```
/*
** Program Name:  accts_for_projs.pc
**
** Purpose:  Prints department numbers and account numbers for
**           accounts involving the input project.
*/
#include<stdio.h>
#include<string.h>
#include<stdlib.h>
exec sql include sqlca;
main()

{ /* Declare host variables. */
  exec sql begin declare section;
  int accountno, projectno, departmentno;
  varchar2 user[21], pass[20];
  exec sql end declare section;

  /* Declare cursor. */
  /* (See Note 1.) */
  exec sql DECLARE xa CURSOR FOR
     SELECT departmentno, accountno FROM ACCOUNT_LIST
        WHERE projectno = :projectno;

  /* Connect to the database with username = scott and
     password = tiger.
  */
  strcpy( user.arr,"scott" );
  strcpy( pass.arr,"tiger" );
  user.len=strlen( user.arr );
  pass.len=strlen( pass.arr );
  exec sql CONNECT :user IDENTIFIED BY :pass;

  /* Check sqlcode to see if connected. */
  if( sqlca.sqlcode !=0 )
    { fprintf ( stderr, "Sorry, cannot connect to database,
                        program terminated. \n" );
      return;
    }
```

```
/* Main loop. */
for( ; ; )
  { printf( "Please enter a project number
            (enter -1 to terminate)>>\n " );
    scanf( "%d", &projectno );
    if( projectno == -1 ) { printf( "BYE\n" );
                            return;
                          }

    /* Open cursor, which binds projectno value to cursor
       SELECT statement, and fetch records for that projectno.
    */
    exec sql OPEN xa;

    /* Fetch loop. */
    for( ; ; )
      { exec sql FETCH xa INTO :departmentno, :accountno;

        /* sqlcode is nonzero when there are no more records
           to be fetched.
        */
        if( sqlca.sqlcode !=0 ) break;
        printf( "Department number = %d Account number = %d /n",
              departmentno, accountno );
      }

    /* Close cursor, so it can be reopened at the beginning
       of the main loop.
    */
    /* (See Note 2.) */
    exec sql CLOSE xa;
  }
}
```

Notes for `accts_for_projs.pc`:

1. The SELECT statement that is attached to the cursor xa contains a host variable `:projectno`. The values of host variables are bound to cursors at OPEN time, not at DECLARE CURSOR time, and not at FETCH time. Therefore, it is irrelevant that `projectno` has not been given a value at the point where the DECLARE CURSOR appears; and if you changed the value of the `projectno` variable in the FETCH loop, that will not affect the records that are fetched in the FETCH loop.

2. You cannot open a cursor if it is already open. This is the reason for closing the cursor at the end of the main loop.

This discussion of embedded SQL is closed by considering why a facility for invoking SQL from a host programming language is even needed. Why is a stand-alone interactive interface like SQL*Plus not sufficient? First, a program, such as a process control system (instead of a human end user) may need direct access to a database. Second, SQL was not initially intended to be computationally complete. SQL is considered a data sub-language that specializes in data retrieval facilities, at the expense of omitting computational structures such as looping statements. Thus, the computational facilities of a language such as C complement the very high-level data access facilities of SQL.

For more information on embedded SQL, you are referred to *Oracle Developer's Guide* and *Oracle8i/9i Pro*C Manual*.

PL/SQL

PL/SQL is Oracle's procedural extension to SQL, which was strongly influenced by the Ada programming language. SQL and PL/SQL are the basic languages used throughout the Oracle RDBMS. However, starting with the Oracle8i/9i releases, SQLJ has begun to offer PL/SQL some competition for its central position in the Oracle RDBMS.

In some cases, PL/SQL provides an easier-to-use alternative to embedded SQL, which is more tightly integrated to SQL than the latter approach. In other cases, it can be used in conjunction with embedded SQL.

PL/SQL Block

The basic unit of PL/SQL is the *PL/SQL block*. You can submit a PL/SQL block interactively to SQL*Plus and SQL*DBA, as well as invoking it from embedded SQL. A PL/SQL block has this form:

```
[ declare section ]
begin
  list_of_statements
  [ exception section ]
end;
```

The optional `declare section` contains declarations that are local to the block. The `list_of_statements` is a sequence of one or more PL/SQL statements, each of which is terminated by a semicolon (`;`). The optional `exception section` starts with the keyword `exception` and contains exception handlers for the block that handle user-defined or predefined exceptions (*exceptions* are identifiers that correspond to error conditions).

A PL/SQL statement can be any transaction control command, any SQL DML command except a `SELECT` statement (SQL DDL commands are not allowed), a

SELECT INTO statement, a control statement (loop, if, exit, or return), an assignment statement, a procedure call, a cursor manipulation statement (OPEN, FETCH, or CLOSE), a raise statement (to raise an exception), or a (nested) PL/SQL block. You are referred to *Oracle8 PL/SQL Programming* and *Oracle8i/9i PL/SQL Manual* for extensive treatments of PL/SQL statements, and to *Oracle8i/9i Application Developer's Guide Fundamentals* for helpful information on the effective use of PL/SQL. In this appendix, you will find a few key examples.

The following PL/SQL block, which prints the department numbers of departments that have an account with every project, illustrates the SELECT INTO, if, and for loop statements:

```
declare
nprojs number(5); nprojsd number(5);
begin

  /* Count the total number of projects. */
  SELECT COUNT(*) INTO nprojs FROM PROJECT_LIST;

  /* For each department, check if the number of projects supplied
     by the department equals the total number of projects, that is,
     if the department has an account with each project.  If so,
     print the department number.
  */
  for i in ( SELECT departmentno FROM DEPARTMENT_LIST )
    loop

      /* Count the number of projects with which the current
         department has an account.
      */
      /* Note that expressions involving PL/SQL variables, such as
         i.departmentno, can appear any place in a SQL statement that
         an expression is expected.
      */
      SELECT COUNT( DISTINCT projectno ) INTO nprojsd
        FROM ACCOUNT_LIST
          WHERE departmentno = i.departmentno;

      /* If the department has an account with each project,
         use the put_line procedure of the dbms_output package
         to print the department number.
      */
      if nprojs = nprojsd
        then dbms_output.put_line( i.departmentno );
      end if;
    end loop;
end;
```

The constructs used in this PL/SQL block are discussed here. In the `declare` `section` of this PL/SQL block, number PL/SQL variables are declared that will hold the total number of projects (`nprojs`) and the number of projects that have an account with a particular department (`nprojsd`). Note that most of the SQL data types, in addition to other data types, are supported in PL/SQL.

A `SELECT INTO` statement, which can be directly used in embedded SQL and in PL/SQL, is a `SELECT` statement whose `WHERE` clause returns a single record, and such a statement stores the field values of that record in the variables listed in the `INTO` clause. Here, the first `SELECT INTO` statement in the PL/SQL block computes the total number of projects, and stores that value in `nprojs`.

Next, there is a `for` `loop` that iterates over the department numbers in the `ACCOUNT_LIST` table. Before discussing the exact type of loop used in the preceding PL/SQL block, a few statements about PL/SQL loops in general are made. PL/SQL supports a `loop` statement with the following syntax:

```
loop
    list_of_statements
end loop
```

This construct sets up an infinite loop (a do forever), that must be terminated by the execution of an exit statement (`exit`), which, like the `break` statement in C, will cause control to be transferred out of the loop to the first statement following the loop. Optionally, the keyword `loop` can be prefixed with a `while` clause or a `for` clause. A `while` clause has the syntax

```
while Boolean_condition
```

which converts the loop into a `while` `loop` as in C, that is, a pretest loop in which the loop is terminated when the Boolean condition evaluates to false.

There are several types of `for` clauses. One type has the form

```
for var in initial_expression ... final_expression
```

which sets up a counter-driven `for` `loop`, with integer counter in `var`, in which the `list_of_statements` is repeatedly executed, with `var` taking on, in successive iterations, `initial_expression`, `initial_expression+1`, ..., `final_expression`. The form of the `for` clause used in the preceding PL/SQL block has the syntax

```
for var in ( subquery )
```

where the `list_of_statements` is repeatedly executed for each record generated by the subquery, with the `var` taking on, in successive iterations, each of the records generated by the subquery. In either form, the for var is implicitly declared, and should not be explicitly declared in a declaration section.

The syntax of the PL/SQL if statement is

```
if condition then list_of_statements
zero-or-more [ elsif condition then list_of_statements ]
   [ else list_of_statements ]
end if
```

An if statement can contain zero or more elsif clauses. When an if statement is executed, if the Boolean condition before the first then evaluates to true, the list_of_statements following the first then is executed. Otherwise, the list_of_statements following the then of the first elsif whose condition evaluates to true is executed. If all the conditions evaluate to false, the list_of_statements following the else is executed.

In the if statement in the preceding PL/SQL block, the put_line procedure of the dbms_output package is used to print the department number. put_line takes one argument, which it prints followed by a newline, and is overloaded to take as an argument various built-in SQL types. The dbms_output package is a collection of procedures that are useful for accomplishing "quick and dirty" output. You will see more about procedures and packages in the next two subsections.

PL/SQL Subprograms

A *PL/SQL subprogram* is a named, parameterized PL/SQL block that can be called (invoked) from various places, including other PL/SQL blocks. When a subprogram is called, *actual parameters* are passed that are matched up with the corresponding formal parameters in the subprogram declaration in a manner indicated by the *mode* of the formal parameters.

The PL/SQL blocks that you have seen so far have not been named and are, therefore, referred to as *autonomous PL/SQL blocks*.

There are two kinds of subprograms in PL/SQL: procedures and functions. A *procedure* does not return a value, and a *procedure call* must be used as a statement (not as an expression). On the other hand, a *function* returns a value, and a *function call* must be used as an expression and cannot stand by itself as a statement. Thus, a function call must be used as part of a statement, for example, as the right-hand side of an assignment statement. A subprogram can be declared local to a PL/SQL block in the declaration section of that block, or it can be directly stored globally in the database; or, as you will see, it can be stored globally in the database by including it in a package that is stored globally in the database.

The Oracle SQL CREATE FUNCTION (CREATE PROCEDURE) statement is used to store a function (procedure) in a database. You can submit such a statement, as you can any Oracle SQL statement, to SQL*Plus. A stored subprogram can be called from any PL/SQL block that has access to the database in which the subprogram is stored. In addition, stored functions can be used any place in a SQL statement that an expression is expected. Here is a slightly simplified syntax of the CREATE FUNCTION statement (the CREATE PROCEDURE syntax is similar):

```
CREATE FUNCTION functionname ( formal_parameter_list )
    return returntype is declaration_list
      begin
        statement_list
[ exception_section ]
      end [ functionname ] ;
```

A formal_parameter_list element has the form

```
formal_parameter_name [ mode ] type
```

The mode can be in (the value of the formal parameter is initialized to the value of the corresponding actual parameter, that is, the parameter in the function call, at call time, but trying to change the formal parameter value results in a PL/SQL syntax error); out (the actual parameter is set to the value that the formal parameter has at return time); or in out (the combination of the in mode and out mode). If the mode is missing for a formal parameter, the in mode is assumed.

The following CREATE FUNCTION statement stores a function named insertemp in the database. This function inserts a new employee record into the EMPLOYEE_LIST table and returns true if EMPLOYEE_LIST does not already contain an employee record with the same employeeno, and false otherwise.

```
CREATE FUNCTION insertemp
    ( empno         EMPLOYEE_LIST.employeeno%type,
      lastname      EMPLOYEE_LIST.lastname%type,
      firstname     EMPLOYEE_LIST.firstname%type,
      phone         EMPLOYEE_LIST.phone%type,
      departmentno EMPLOYEE_LIST.departmentno%type ) return Boolean is
x integer;
begin

  /* Check for duplicate employee number. */
  /* Return false, if a duplicate exists. */
  SELECT COUNT(*) INTO x FROM EMPLOYEE_LIST
    WHERE employeeno = empno;
  if x > 0 then return false;
  end if;

  /* Otherwise, insert employee record, commit insert and return
     true.
  */
```

```
/* PL/SQL variables can be used any place in a SQL statement that
   an expression is expected.
*/
INSERT INTO EMPLOYEE_LIST
  VALUES ( empno, lastname, firstname, phone, departmentno );
COMMIT WORK;
return true;
end insertemp;
```

Note that in the preceding example, the data types of the formal parameters are inherited from the corresponding EMPLOYEE_LIST field data types, by using the type attributes of the EMPLOYEE_LIST fields (field name followed by %type). The data type number could have been directly used here, but it is safer (in lieu of the possibility of table field type change) to use the %type attributes. A type attribute expression can be used anywhere in PL/SQL that a data type is expected. Observe also that the keyword declare is omitted in the declare section of subprograms.

An example of a PL/SQL block that calls the preceding insertemp function is

```
begin
  if not insertemp ( 1111, 'Smith', 'Michelle', '(305)555-0359', 15 )
  then dbms_output.put_line ( 'Employee 1111 already exists.' );
end;
```

In this example, each actual parameter of the insertemp function call is matched up with its corresponding formal parameter in the insertemp function definition by these parameters having the same position in their respective parameter lists. There is also a facility in PL/SQL for matching up actual and formal parameters by name. Refer to *Oracle8i/9i PL/SQL Manual* for a description of this facility.

Advantages of using subprograms in PL/SQL, as in any other programming language, include modularity, extensibility, reliability, maintainability, and abstraction (see *Oracle Developer's Guide* for details). The specific advantages of using stored subprograms in Oracle include higher productivity (applications can exploit a central repository of common code), better performance (to execute ten individual SQL statements involves ten database calls, but to execute a stored subprogram containing ten SQL statements causes one database call), and conservation of memory (the shared memory capability of Oracle allows for only one copy of a stored subprogram to be loaded into memory for all applications that access it). See *Oracle Developer's Guide* for more details.

PL/SQL Packages and Exceptions

In this section, an example illustrating packages and exceptions is presented. A PL/SQL *package* is a construct that groups together logically related resources such as variables, subprograms, cursors, and exceptions. If the `package` is stored in a database, all these resources are available to any SQL or PL/SQL construct that has access to the database. A package consists of two units: a required package specification and an optional package body. The package specification is the interface to the `package` in that it declares the variables, exceptions, cursors, subprograms, and so on, that are available for use by clients of the package. The package body fully defines subprograms that are specified in the package specification, and so implements the specification (only subprogram specifications, and not the complete subprogram, can appear in a package specification). A package specification is stored in a database by the SQL CREATE PACKAGE statement. A package body is stored in a database by the CREATE PACKAGE BODY SQL statement.

Consider a package emppak that provides resources for the manipulation of the EMPLOYEE_LIST table.

```
CREATE PACKAGE emppak is
norec exception;
procedure deleteemp ( empno EMPLOYEE_LIST.employeeno%type );
function insertemp
   ( empno          EMPLOYEE_LIST.employeeno%type,
     lastname       EMPLOYEE_LIST.lastname%type,
     firstname      EMPLOYEE_LIST.firstname%type,
     phone          EMPLOYEE_LIST.phone%type,
     departmentno EMPLOYEE_LIST.departmentno%type )
     return number;
end emppak;

CREATE PACKAGE BODY emppak is
  procedure deleteemp ( empno EMPLOYEE_LIST.employeeno%type ) is x integer;
  begin

    /* Check if employee record exists. */
    SELECT COUNT(*) INTO x FROM EMPLOYEE_LIST
      WHERE employeeno = empno;

    /* If it doesn't exist, raise an exception, terminating
       the procedure.
    */
    /* If it does exist, delete employee, and commit the delete.
    */
    if x = 0 then raise norec;
    end if;
    DELETE FROM EMPLOYEE_LIST WHERE employeeno = empno;
    COMMIT WORK;
  end deleteemp;
```

```
function insertemp
  ( empno        EMPLOYEE_LIST.employeeno%type,
    lastname     EMPLOYEE_LIST.lastname%type,
    firstname    EMPLOYEE_LIST.firstname%type,
    phone        EMPLOYEE_LIST.phone%type
    departmentno EMPLOYEE_LIST.departmentno%type ) return boolean is  x integer;
begin

  /* Check for duplicate employee number. */
  /* Return false, if a duplicate exists. */
  SELECT COUNT(*) INTO x FROM EMPLOYEE_LIST
    WHERE employeeno = empno;
  if x > 0 then return false;
  end if;

  /* Otherwise, insert employee record, commit insert, and
     return true.
  */
  /* Recall that PL/SQL variables can be used any place in a
     SQL statement that an expression is expected.
  */
  INSERT INTO EMPLOYEE_LIST
    VALUES ( empno, lastname, firstname, phone, departmentno );
  COMMIT WORK;
  return true;
end insertemp;
/* Local block in package body. */
begin
  CREATE TABLE EMPLOYEE_LIST
    ( employeeno    number(5),
      lastname      varchar2(30),
      firstname     varchar2(30),
      phone         varchar2(13),
      departmentno  number(5),
      PRIMARY KEY  ( employeeno ),
      FOREIGN KEY  ( departmentno ) REFERENCES DEPARTMENT_LIST );
  end;
end emppak;
```

This package specification for `emppak` exports three resources: the `norec` exception, the `deleteemp` procedure, and the `insertemp` function.

An *exception* is a PL/SQL identifier that corresponds to an error. There are only two operations that can be applied to an exception: an exception can be *raised* (that is, activated), and an exception can be *handled*. When an exception is raised in a PL/SQL block, that block is terminated, and a handler is sought in the exception section of that block. If a handler is found, the exception is deactivated and control is passed to the statement following the one that invoked the block (the statement following the block, if the block is not the outer block of a subprogram, or the statement following the subprogram call, if the block is the outer block of a subprogram).

If a handler is not found in the exception section of the block, the exception remains active, and a handler is searched for (and executed, if found) in the block containing the statement that invoked the block (that is, the invoking block), followed by the termination of the invoking block. This method is repeated until a handler is found or there are no more blocks left. In our case, the norec exception is raised in the deleteemp procedure and is intended to be handled by the block that invoked the deleteemp procedure, since a handler is not provided in the deleteemp procedure. norec is an example of a user-defined exception, that is, declared by the programmer in an exception declaration, and is explicitly raised by a raise statement.

The other type of exception is a predefined exception that corresponds to an Oracle internal error, and is automatically raised by the system (or also can be explicitly raised). An example of a predefined exception is no_data_found, which is automatically raised by the system when a SELECT INTO statement does not retrieve any data. Predefined exceptions are handled just like user-defined exceptions.

The procedure deleteemp and the function insertemp illustrate two different ways of reporting errors. The function insertemp returns an error code, while the procedure deleteemp raises an exception. It is probably best to use the return code technique, unless the error is a serious one, because the user-defined exception method suffers a performance overhead. On the other hand, the repeated explicit checking of error codes can make the PL/SQL code harder to read.

Note that the package body can contain its own local block that is executed when the package is created. You can use such a local block to accomplish initializations. This local block is analogous to a Java constructor. In our case, the EMPLOYEE_LIST table is created when the package is created. The reason for this is to try and use the emppak package to encapsulate the EMPLOYEE_LIST table as much as possible, encouraging the users of the package to go through the exported subprograms as much as possible.

The following PL/SQL block illustrates how the resources of the package emppak can be used.

```
begin
  /* Insert a new employee record with emppak.insertemp. */
  if not emppak.insertemp
    ( 3000, 'Smith', 'Damon', '(954)555-0172', 15 )
    then dbms_output.put_line
      ( 'Employee 3000 already exists in table.' );
      else dbms_output ( 'Employee 3000 inserted' );
```

```
/* Now delete the 3000 record. */
emppak.deleteemp( '3000' );

/* Exception handler for norec exception. */
when emppak.norec then dbms_output.put_line
   ('Employee 3000 cannot be fired since employee does not exist.' );
end;
```

Notes:

1. An emppak resource is referenced by "dotting" the package name with the resource name (for example, emppak.norec). In particular, this is exactly what is done when put_line is referenced (dbms_output.put_line).

2. An exception handler has the syntax

   ```
   when exceptionname then list_of_statements
   ```

3. The statements in the list are executed, and then control is passed out of the block, as previously described.

Finally, it should be remarked that PL/SQL blocks can be invoked from Oracle-embedded SQL programs. The syntax for invoking a PL/SQL block from a Pro*C program is

```
exec sql execute

   PL/SQL_block

end-exec;
```

For example,

```
exec sql execute
  begin

     /* Select number of accounts into the C host variable naccts. */
     SELECT COUNT(*) INTO :naccts FROM ACCOUNT_LIST;

     /* Select number of employees into C host variable nemps. */
     SELECT COUNT(*) INTO nemps FROM EMPLOYEE_LIST;
  end;
end-exec;
```

A performance advantage of including a PL/SQL block in an `exec sql` statement is that the entire block is passed to the Oracle server in one call, as opposed to requiring multiple calls, which would be the case if each SQL statement in the block were coded in its own `exec sql` statement.

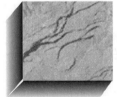

APPENDIX
B

Java Basics

his appendix is an introduction to the Java programming language. You will learn about the following:

- Java constructs to develop an application: `JavaApplication`

- The concepts of classes and objects in the Java language

- Java constructs to develop the applet `MyJavaAppletFromOracle8iBook`

The Java Application

This section examines and explains an application called `JavaApplication`, which is a simple Java program consisting of one method called `main()`. Through a line-by-line investigation of this program, you will learn some basic features of Java, such as variables, operators, expressions, and control flow statements. In the sections that follow the Java application, you will learn more about the syntax and semantics of the Java language.

An *application* is a stand-alone program that runs independent of any Java-compatible browser. At run time, a Java Virtual Machine (JVM) invokes the `main()` method for program execution. If this method is not found, an error message will be generated.

The source code for a Java class resides in a file with the same name as the class and with the `.java` extension. For example, the source code of the `JavaApplication` class resides in a file named `JavaApplication.java`.

In this section, you will use the `JavaApplication` application to print out the parameters supplied at the command line. These parameters are passed to the application as an array of strings.

```
//Program name: JavaApplication.java
public class JavaApplication {

  public static void main(String[] args){

    //Loop control variable.
    int loopVar = 0;

    // Loop to print words from the command line argument iterate
    // until there are no elements left in the array
    for (loopVar = 0; loopVar<args.length; loopVar++){
      System.out.println(args[loopVar]);
```

```
    }
  }
}
```

Variables and Data Types

Java allows the declaration of variables in programs. All variables in Java have a data type, a name, and a scope. When a variable is declared, it must be associated with a data type.

Java supports a complete set of *primitive* data types and *reference* (nonprimitive) data types. The primitive data types are handled by value, that is, the actual values are stored in the variable. The nonprimitive data types, such as objects and arrays, are handled *by references,* that is, the address of an object or an array is stored in the variable. Table B-1 lists Java's primitive data types and the range of their values.

The following code fragment demonstrates how to declare Java variables and their associated data types:

```
// Create the loopVar int primitive data type variable and
// assign to it the value of 0
int loopVar = 0;

// Create the args reference variable
// to store the address of an array of strings
String[] args;
```

Table B-1 presents a list of Java primitive data types and a range of their values.

Type	Size	Minimum Value	Maximum Value
boolean	1 bit	n/a	n/a
char	16 bits	\u0000 (0)	\uFFFF (65535)
byte	8 bits	−128	128
short	16 bits	−32768	32768
int	32 bits	−2147483648	2147483648
long	64 bits	−9223372036854775808	9223372036854775807
float	32 bits	±1.40239846E-45	±3.4028236E+38
double	64 bits	±4.9E-324	±1.798E+308

TABLE B-I. *Primitive Data Types*

Arrays and Strings

Two important data types in any programming language are *arrays* and *strings*.
Like most programming languages, Java provides a mechanism for collecting and
managing a set of values through an array. In Java, both arrays and strings are
objects. In the subsequent sections of this appendix, you will learn more about
the concept of objects. The `main()` method accepts as a parameter an array that
holds a set of strings as its argument:

```
public static void main(String[] args){
...
}
```

Operators and Expressions

Java provides a set of *operators* that you can use to perform functions on variables.
Some examples of operators are **+** (addition), **++** (increment), and **=** (assignment).
Java *expressions* combine a sequence of operators, variables, and method calls.
They are used to help with the execution control within a program to compute
and assign values to variables. The following code fragment lists some examples
of Java operators and an expression:

```
// Assignment operator: '='
// Assign the value of 0 to the integer variable loopVar
int loopVar = 0;   // An expression
```

Control Flow Statements

Java provides support for two types of control flow statements: *branching* and
looping. These statements control the flow of the program, that is, the sequence in
which the program's statements are executed. The branching control flow statements
include the `if-then-else` and the `switch` statements. The looping control flow
statements include the `for`, `while`, and `do-while` loops.

The `JavaApplication` application uses a `for` statement to iterate through
the `args` array and print its value. A `for` loop iterates and repeatedly executes
statements until a boolean expression is evaluated to false (condition not met).
The following iterates through statements until `loopVar` is evaluated to be greater
than or equal to `args.length`, where `.length` is the size of the `args` array:

```
for (loopVar = 0; loopVar<args.length; loopVar++){ ... }
```

Compilation and Execution

Now that you have written a Java application, the next step is to compile the program. You can do so with the javac compiler. You can invoke it at the command line:

```
javac JavaApplication.java
```

If the compilation is successful, the javac compiler will generate a `.class` file (bytecode) Java `Application.class` for the source file `JavaApplication.java`. You can run the application using a Java interpreter program by issuing the following command at the command line:

```
java JavaApplication position department company
```

After executing the previous command, the output of the application displays the following on your console:

```
position
department
company
```

Java Classes and Objects

The Java programming language is an object-oriented programming language that is based on *classes* and *objects*. A class is a collection of attributes and methods that serves as a blueprint for creating objects, and an object is an instance of a class. Since Java is based on objects and classes, you will need to understand some basic object-oriented programming concepts to write good Java programs.

The topics covered in this section will help you learn how to build and construct Java classes and objects. The topics discussed are

- Creating and using objects
- Creating and using constructors
- Using `this`
- Class members
- Access modifiers
- Method return types

- Creating subclasses
- Creating packages
- Importing classes and packages
- Abstract classes
- Interfaces

You will use the following `Employee` class to learn how to create and use Java classes and objects throughout this section by adding some additional functionality to the class. As in the section "The Java Application," earlier in this appendix, you will learn more about Java through a line-by-line investigation of the `Employee` class as you build it.

```
//Program name: Employee.java
public class Employee {
  public String name;
  public double salary;
  public double hours;
}
```

Creating and Using Objects

An *object* is an instance of a class, in which each object has its own copy of the attributes and methods of a class. In Java, an object needs to be *instantiated,* which dynamically allocates memory for the object and creates an instance of a class.

Creating Objects

Now that you have the `Employee` class, you can create an instance of the class by declaring a variable and instantiating an `Employee` object:

- **Declaration** Before creating an object, however, you must *declare* a variable that will refer to an `Employee` object.

  ```
  Employee emp;
  ```

  The emp variable refers to the data type `Employee`. It is important to understand that emp is not an object. It is a reference to an `Employee` data type. You need an instance of the class to have an object.

- **Instantiation** After you have declared a variable, you have to use a class constructor to instantiate or allocate memory for an object. This is accomplished by using the operator `new`, followed by a constructor of the class:

  ```
  emp = new Employee();
  ```

Alternatively, the declaration and instantiation can be accomplished all in one statement:

```
Employee emp = new Employee();
```

Note that in Java, since strings are so commonly used, you do not have to use the new operator to instantiate them. You can create an instance of the String class simply by enclosing the characters between double quotes. For example,

```
String name = "John";
```

is equivalent shorthand for

```
String name = new String(new char[]{'J','o','h','n'});
```

Note that fields in Java are initialized to default values (unless specified otherwise) when a new instance is created: objects are initialized to null; byte, short, and int to 0; float and double to 0.0; boolean to false; and char to \u0000.

Deleting Objects

Java will automatically delete any object that is no longer being referenced by a variable. This memory cleanup is called *garbage collection*. The garbage collector runs in a low-priority thread, usually when the system is idle. However, when the JVM runs out of memory, the garbage collector will run in higher priority mode to reclaim resources. Setting a variable to null will eliminate the reference to the object, assuming that the object is not referenced somewhere else. If the object is no longer referenced, the garbage collector will run the object's finalize() method, if it has one, and delete it from memory.

Accessing Member Variables of Objects

After you have created an object, use the dot member separator (.) to access the members of the class. The following example uses the member separator to assign values to the member attributes of the object:

```
emp.name = "John";     // Set value of name
emp.salary = 11.50;    // Assign the hourly salary
emp.hours = 40.0;      // Set value to 40 hours
```

The following ObjectClassProgram is an application that instantiates the Employee class, assigns values to its data members, and prints the values:

```
// Program name: ObjectClassProgram.java
public class ObjectClassProgram {
  public static void main(String[] args){
```

```
// Create a new Instance of the Employee class
Employee emp = new Employee();
emp.name = "John";   // Set the value of name
emp.salary = 11.50; // Assign the hourly salary
emp.hours = 40.0;     // Set value to 40 hours
System.out.println( "Name: " + emp.name + " | Hourly salary: $" +
                    emp.salary + " | Hours worked " + emp.hours);
  }
}
```

Creating and Using Constructors

Every object has a constructor when it is instantiated. If you do not declare a constructor explicitly, Java will create an implicit, public, 0-argument constructor for you. An object's constructor is usually a good place to perform initialization.

Default Constructor

If you look at the declaration and the instantiation of the emp object in the ObjectClassProgram application, you will notice that a call is made to the Employee() constructor. The Employee() constructor is the *default constructor* for the Employee class and has no arguments. The following example illustrates the way to call the default constructor:

```
Employee emp = new Employee();
```

Constructor Overloading

Overloading is when you create more than one constructor or method with the same name, but with different signatures. The Java compiler is able to differentiate between the methods or constructors that have been overloaded because its arguments are different.

The following is a listing of the Employee class that has been modified to include a new explicit default constructor, or 0-argument constructor, and an overloaded constructor with three arguments. Note that the default constructor does not come implicitly for free any longer, since it has been explicitly defined. Also, both constructors' names are the same as the class name:

```
//Class name: Employee.java
public class Employee {
  public String name;
  public double salary;
  public double hours;

  public Employee(){   //Default constructor
      name = "";        //Initialize name to an empty string
      salary = 5.50;   //Initialize salary to the minimum wage
```

```
    hours = 0.0;
}

//Constructor that takes in three arguments for initializing
public Employee(String name, double salary, int hours){
    this.name = name;
    this.salary = salary;
    this.hours = hours;
}
}
```

Initializing the Constructors

The following example illustrates two examples of how to declare and initialize data members listed in the two constructors of the Employee class:

```
//Create an object using the default constructor of the Employee data
//type.
Employee emp1 = new Employee();

//Initialize the variables of the object
emp1.name = "John";  // Initialize value of name
emp1.hours = 40.0;   // Initialize value to 40 hours

// Create another object and initialize the
// constructor with three arguments

Employee emp2 = new Employee("Jill", 15.50, 25);
```

Using the this Keyword

If you look at the Employee constructor that has the three arguments, you will notice that it uses the keyword this. In the Employee constructor, the keyword this refers to the variable of the immediate object, and removes the ambiguity between the member variables of the class and the arguments of the constructor:

```
public Employee(String name, double salary, int hours){
   this.name = name;
   this.salary = salary;
   this.hours = hours;
}
```

In the previous example, if you were to code the assignment of name = name, at compilation time, the compiler would not know which name variable belongs to the argument and which name belongs to the member field of the class. In this scenario, the use of the keyword this is necessary to differentiate the class members and the constructor arguments. You can avoid ambiguity and the use of the `this` keyword by using unique identifiers in the constructor arguments:

```
public Employee(String empName, double empSalary, int empHours){
  name = empName;
  salary = empSalary;
  hours = empHours;
}
```

Class Members

An *instance variable,* also called *instance field,* is created every time a new object of a class is instantiated. Conversely, a *class variable* is one in which only one copy of the variable is created at run time. Instance variables and class variables are collectively called *member variables.* In addition, the term *member of a class* refers collectively to the instance variables, class variables, and the methods of a class.

Class Variables and Class Methods

Use the `static` keyword to declare a class variable or a class method:

```
//A class variable
public static double minimumWage = 5.50;

//A class method
public static Employee WorkedMost(Employee emp1, Employee emp2){
   ...
  }
```

When you declare a class variable or a class method with the `static` keyword, there is only one copy of the variable or the method associated with the class for the JVM, rather than many instances of the variable.

In the following example, the `Employee` class has been modified to include a class variable `minimumWage` and a class method `WorkedMost()`. The `minimumWage` variable is assigned the value of $5.50. The `WorkedMost()` method uses two employee objects as its input arguments, compares the number of hours of each employee object, and returns the `Employee` object that worked the most hours.

```
// Program name: Employee.java
public class Employee {
  public String name;
  public double salary;
  public double hours;
```

```
// This creates a class variable
public static final double minimumWage = 5.50;

public Employee(){  //Default constructor
    name = "";        //Initialize name to empty string
    salary = minimumWage;  //Initialize salary to the minimum wage
    hours = 0.0;
}

// Constructor that takes in three arguments for initializing its
// instance variables
public Employee(String name, double salary, int hours){
    this.name = name;
    this.salary = salary;
    this.hours = hours;
}
public void PrintPay(){
    System.out.println("The salary this week for " + name + " is $"
                        + salary*hours);
}

//This method is a Class method
public static Employee WorkedMost(Employee emp1, Employee emp2){
    //Returns the employee who worked the most hours
    if (emp1.hours > emp2.hours)
      return emp1;
    else
      return emp2;
  }
}
```

You can access class variables and class methods through either the class name or an instance variable:

```
// Create instances of the Employee class
Employee emp = new Employee("Jill", 15.50, 25);

// You can access WorkedMost and minimumWage via class method
// and class variable
System.out.println("The minimum wage is $" + Employee.minimumWage);

// You can also access the WorkedMost() method and the minimumWage
// variables through the declared variable

System.out.println("The minimum wage is $" + emp.minimumWage);
```

Constants

Use the `final` keyword to declare variables as constants. The variable must be initialized to a value when it is declared `final`. Once you declare a variable as `final`, it cannot be changed. Therefore, it makes sense for you to declare a `final` member variable as a class variable with the keyword `static`. If you do not, you will create a new copy of the variable or method every time a new object is created. In the `Employee` class, the `minimumWage` class variable is declared as a constant variable by using the keyword `final`:

```
public static final float minimumWage = 5.50f;
```

`final` Class

If a class is declared as `final`, then the class cannot become a superclass of another class (see the "Creating Subclasses" section of this appendix). You can declare the `Employee` class as `final` if you do not wish this class to be subclassed:

```
final class Employee {
... //Method body omitted
}
```

Method Return Types

Every method declared in Java requires a method return type. Methods must return an object of the method's declared return type. To return an object from a method, use the `return` keyword, followed by an instance of the return type within the body of the method. When the `return` keyword is encountered, the method stops execution and, if the return type is not `void`, returns the return object back to the method that called it. A method of return type `void` does not return anything. If the method returns type is `void`, you have the option of not returning anything or simply using the `return` keyword by itself to stop execution of the method. Since the return type of the `WorkMost()` method is the `Employee` class, it has to return an `Employee` object to the method that called it.

Creating Subclasses

Let us say that you want the `Employee` class to include two types of employees: some who require a license for their occupation and some who do not. The employees who have licenses get an extra 10 percent bonus. To store the license number as a string and print the weekly salary for these employees, an additional instance variable for the license number and another print method could have been added to the `Employee` class. Subclassing provides a more elegant way for you to add these additional features. This will permit you to use all the members of the

`Employee` class method without having to make additional changes to the `Employee` class just for the employees who have licenses.

A subclass inherits all the `public`, `protected`, and default members of its superclass (parent class). Use the keyword `extends` to define a subclass. The following class `LicenseEmployee` defines a subclass of its `Employee` superclass:

```
//Program name: LicenseEmployeeeloyee.java
public class LicenseEmployee extends Employee {
  public String license;  //License Number of the employee
  //10% extra pay for employee with license
  private static double bonus = 1.10;

  //Constructor method of the subclass
  public LicenseEmployee(String name, double salary, int hours,
                  String license){

    //Call the constructor of the super class
    super(name, salary, hours);
    this.license = license;
  }

  //A Method that overrides the PrintPay method in the Employee class
  public void  PrintPay(){
    System.out.println("The salary this week for " + name
                       + " is $" + salary*hours*bonus);
  }

  //A Method that is in the subclass but not the super class
  public void PrintSubclass(){
    System.out.print("License " + license + "; and ");
    super.PrintPay();
  }
}
```

A subclass can call its parent members. In this situation, the subclass can use the keyword `super` to explicitly invoke the superclass members. For example, the `LicenseEmployee` constructor from the `LicenseEmployee` class invokes its parent constructor to initialize its arguments, and the `PrintSubclass()` method invokes its parent method to print the employee's salary.

Creating Packages

A *package* is a bundle or collection of related classes. The Sun JDK contains various packages for performing different functions. The JDK `java.sql` package, for example, contains the set of classes that defines the JDBC API.

You are not limited to the packages provided by Java; you can also create your own packages by following these rules:

- The optional `package` keyword, followed by a package name, must be the first statement at the beginning of your source code file.

- There can be only one `public` top-level class, but there can be many `public` inner classes.

- The filename must have the `.java` extension.

The following code fragment shows an example of how to declare a package called `com.data-i.humanResource` for the `Employee` class:

```
package com.data_i.HumanResource;

public class Employee {
  ... //Class body omitted
}
```

Access Modifiers

The member variables and methods of the `Employee` class are all declared `public`. This means that all classes and packages have access to their members. However, this may yield some undesirable results. For example, if you created `Employee` objects with the salary information of the employees from a database, programmers who use the class might not need to know the salary of the employees, or worse, have the privilege to change the salary. This information should be encapsulated and protected from the programmer. You could declare some member variables of the class with access modifiers so that they cannot be accessed or modified by other classes, subclasses, or packages.

Java provides access modifiers as an encapsulation mechanism to protect classes and class members from being accessed. The access modifiers are placed at the beginning of variables and methods. The access modifiers use the keywords `private`, `protected`, and `public`. The fourth access protection, called the "default package," does not have any explicit access modifier.

Table B-2 shows the access protection level of each of these access modifiers:

- **`private`** Member variables and methods are only visible within the class in which they are specified. The `private` members are not available to their subclasses or other packages. Other classes cannot access the `private` members of the class, even if they are within the same package.

Type	Access Modifier			
	`public`	`protected`	`package`	`private`
Class	Yes	Yes	Yes	Yes
Package	Yes	Yes	Yes	No
Subclass	Yes	Yes	No	No
Different package	Yes	No	No	No

TABLE B-2.   *Access Protection and Visibility*

- ■ **`protected`**   Member methods and variables of a class that are protected are only accessible from its class, subclasses, and the classes in the same package. In addition, the class members are available to its subclasses in other packages but not classes in other packages.

- ■ **`public`**   This modifier makes members visible to all classes and packages.

- ■ **default package**   This modifier hides members from other packages, but classes in the same package have access to such members.

Importing Classes and Packages

Use the `import` statement to make members of an entire class or package available to your program. By using the `import` statement, you just have to specify the class name and not the full package and class name.

```
//Import all classes in the package by specifying the '*'
import java.sql.*;
//Import the ResultSet class
import java.sql.ResultSet;
```

Importing classes and packages saves you from having to type the fully qualified name of the class whenever it is used. For example, if you import the `java.sql` package, there is a class in this package called `ResultSet`. You can use `ResultSet` by itself instead of the fully qualified name of `java.sql.ResultSet` in your program.

Note that Java implicitly imports the classes of the `java.lang` package into your program, so you do not have to explicitly import this package.

Abstract Classes

Java provides the `abstract` class mechanism for representing the concept of abstraction. It allows you to specify requirements for a class that has to be extended and implemented. In the employee example, if you wanted to include the identification of an employee, you could not do it because you cannot instantiate the identification of an employee. It is an abstract concept. You can, however, instantiate the social security number of the employee as a string. Additionally, you can instantiate different types of identification numbers as strings or other data types.

Use the `abstract` keyword to declare a class as an abstract class. Within an abstract class, you can also have abstract method declarations without implementing the method's body. The method body of an abstract class is implemented in the classes that extend them. The rules for abstract classes are these:

- Abstract classes cannot be instantiated.

- An abstract class can have abstract method declarations with no implementation of the method bodies.

- A subclass of an abstract class is abstract if it does not implement all abstract methods of the abstract class.

The following example, `IDAbstract`, is an abstract class that returns the identification number of its workers. For this example, the company hires permanent employees, as well as independent contractors. Permanent employees use their social security number, and contractors use an Employee Identification Number (EIN) for their identification. The following example illustrates classes that use the `IDAbstract` abstract class to create two new classes, the `Employee` and `Contractor` classes. These two classes implement the abstract method `ID()` from the abstract class, with each class returning its own identification number.

```
//declare an abstract class
public abstract class IDAbstract{
  private String name = null;

  public abstract String ID();

  public void setName(String name) {
    this.name = name;
  }
  public String getName() {
    return name;
  }
}
```

A class such as the preceding would much more typically be declared as an interface. The idea of an abstract class is that you can provide an implementation of some of the methods, but other methods only have the requirement of their existence. You can immediately replace abstract class with interface.

```
class Employee extends IDAbstract{
  protected String SSN;
  … //Other methods of the Employee class omitted
  public String ID(){ return SSN; }
}

class Contractor extends IDAbstract{
  protected String EIN;
  … //Other methods of the Contractor class omitted
  public String ID(){ return EIN; }
}
```

Interfaces

An `interface`, like an abstract class, defines a set of methods or constant declarations with no implementation of the method bodies. Unlike the abstract class, however, all the method declarations of the interface are automatically abstract and public. Any member variables declared in an interface are implicitly `static` and `final` (constant). In addition, a class can implement multiple interfaces, whereas a class can only extend one abstract class.

An interface declaration is similar to a class declaration, except that an interface uses the keyword `interface` instead of the `class` or `abstract` clauses. Methods of the interface are implicitly abstract, even if the keyword `abstract` is not part of the method declaration. Use the `implements` clause on a new class to implement a declared interface. Every method of an interface must be implemented in the new class.

```
public interface Profile {
  public void PrintProfile();
}

class EmployeeProfile extends Employee implements Profile {
  public void PrintProfile(){
    //Must provide this class with a method body for the interface.
    }
}
```

In the example, the `EmployeeProfile` class is a subclass of the `Employee` class, and it implements the `Profile` interface. For every method declaration in the

`Profile` interface, in this example `PrintProfile()`, the `EmployeeProfile` class has to provide a method body.

Next, you will learn about Java applets.

Introduction to Java Applets

A *Java applet* is a program written in the Java programming language and executed from a browser or an AppletViewer, which is a utility program for executing applets from Sun Microsystems. The browser invokes an applet's `init()` method to start program execution in the same way that the JVM invokes the application's `main()` method to run a Java application.

Once an applet is developed, the path to the applet bytecode is added to an HTML page so that a browser can run it. An AppletViewer can also be used to run the applet from the command line.

The source code of a Java applet, as in the Java application, is stored in a file with the `.java` extension. The source code is compiled into a binary bytecode file with a `.class` extension. Follow these steps to create and run an applet:

1. Create a Java applet source code file with a `.java` extension, such as `MyJavaAppletFromOracle8iBook.java`.

2. Compile the source code that will generate the `.class` file.

3. Create a Web page with your favorite HTML editor.

4. Use the HTML `<APPLET>` tag to point to the `.class` file.

5. Run the applet in a browser or with the AppletViewer utility.

In this section, you will create the `MyJavaAppletFromOracle8iBook` applet, compile it, and learn the steps required to run it.

To create a Java applet, you must first import the necessary Java classes. When writing applet source code, you should import at least two classes:

- **`java.awt` (Abstract Windowing Toolkit) class**   Use this class to design the user interface (see "Brief Overview of the Java `AWT` Class" in this section).

- **`java.applet.Applet` class**   Extend this class to create the functionality of the applet and to run it.

The following example illustrates how to import the necessary Java classes:

```
import java.awt.*;
import java.applet.Applet;
```

A Java applet is made up of at least one public class. The following declaration is used to create the applet class:

```
import java.awt.*;
import java.applet.Applet;
public class MyJavaAppletFromOracle8iBook extends Applet {
    ...
}
```

If you choose not to import the `java.applet.Applet` class, you can subclass the `MyJavaAppletFromOracle8iBook` class by using the fully qualified name of the class after the `extends` keyword:

```
import java.awt.*;
public MyJavaAppletFromOracle8iBook extends java.applet.Applet {
    ...
}
```

The class declaration defines the `MyJavaAppletFromOracle8iBook` class as `public`. The access modifier `public` indicates that the class can be extended and accessed by other Java classes and packages. The keyword `extends` causes the class to inherit all of the data members and methods of its superclass, the `Applet` class in this case.

The `Applet` class is a subclass of the Java AWT `Panel` class. Consequently, both the Java `Applet` and the `MyJavaAppletFromOracle8iBook` class participate in the AWT event and drawing model of their superclasses. The AWT is the user interface toolkit that is provided as part of the Java language class library. Figure B-1 shows the inheritance hierarchy of the `Applet` class. This hierarchy determines the functionality of the `Applet` class.

An applet uses the `Applet` API, which is a set of methods and interfaces that allows the applet to take advantage of the close relationship between applets and Web browsers. This API is provided by the `java.applet` package, specifically the `Applet` class and the `AppletContext` interface of the package.

The `Applet` API can do the following:

- Notify the API of the *milestone* methods: `init()`, `start()`, `stop()`, and `destroy()`.

- Display short status strings.

- Enable document display in a browser.

- Find other applets running on the same page.

- Play sounds.

- Get parameters from the `<APPLET>` tag.

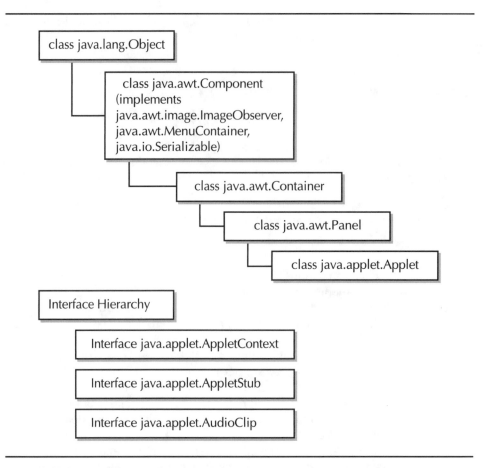

FIGURE B-1. *Applet class hierarchy*

In addition to the Applet API, an applet can use several other User Interface (UI) classes, depending on the kind of information it needs to represent. Applets can play sounds, and display videos, movies, documents, and so on.

There are four *milestone methods* from the java.applet.Applet class that allow applets to respond to major events:

■ **The init() method**   Use this method to initialize the applet each time it is loaded. This is useful for any initialization that needs to be completed. Because it is similar to the Java constructor, include the init() method where you would normally put in the constructor. Note that constructors should be avoided in an applet because the init() method must first run before the full environment becomes available to the applet. For quicker response, the `init()` method is a good place to have methods that load images.

- **The `start()` method**   Use this method to start program execution and use it to load or reload the applet.

- **The `stop()` method**   Use this method to stop program execution when the user leaves the applet page or quits the browser.

- **The `destroy()` method**   Use this method to clean up the environment and to free up any resources that the applet is holding.

The following example declares an `init()` method. This declaration tells the Java Virtual Machine (JVM) to override the `init()` method from the `Applet`. A browser controls an applet's behavior by executing milestone methods.

```
import java.awt.*;
public class MyJavaAppletFromOracle8iBook extends java.applet.Applet {
   public void init() {
     ...
   }
   ...
}
```

In order for the applet to respond to events, it needs to override either some or all of the milestone methods. Your applet can override the `start()` method. This method performs the applet's work. Subsequently, if this method is overridden, the `stop()` method should also be overridden. The `stop()` method suspends the applet's execution so that it does not take up system resources when the user is not on the page where the applet is being executed. Furthermore, the `stop()` method does everything necessary to shut down the applet's thread of execution. Finally, applets do not need to override the `destroy()` method, particularly when the applets override the `stop()` method. Instead, use the `destroy()` method to release additional resources.

A graphical user interface is made up of elements called *components*. Components allow users to interact with programs, whether the program is a Java applet or an application. In the `AWT` package, all the user interface components are instances of the class container or of its subclass. These components must fit completely within the boundary of the container that holds them. In this example, the components are nested into the container and the result is a tree of elements, shown in Figure B-2, starting with the container as the root.

Because the `Applet` class inherits from the `AWT Container` class, it contains `Components` and other user interface objects such as buttons, labels, pop-up lists,

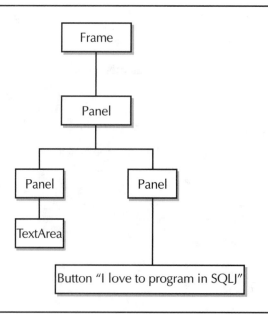

FIGURE B-2. *Component tree*

and scrollbars (see the section "Brief Overview of the Java AWT Class"). In this example, an instance of the Button class is created:

```
import java.awt.*;
public class MyJavaAppletFromOracle8iBook extends java.applet.Applet {
   public void init() {
      add( new Button("I love to program in SQLJ"));
      ...
   }
   ...
}
```

So far, you created an applet class with an inert user interface. In order to add more functionality to the MyJavaAppletFromOracle8iBook class, you need to understand the AWT package.

Brief Overview of the Java AWT Class

The Java AWT is a package of classes for building graphical user interfaces. It provides nine basic noncontainer component classes, as shown in Figure B-3. They are Button, Canvas, Checkbox, Choice, Label, List, Scrollbar, TextArea, and TextField. Additionally, there are four top-level display surfaces: the Window, the Frame, and the Dialog, which have borders and a title, and the Panel, which

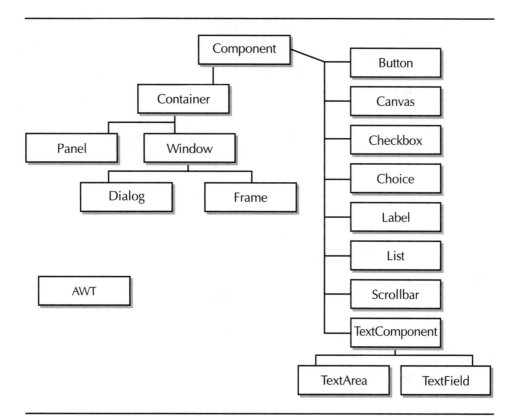

FIGURE B-3. *Java AWT package*

is used to hold other components. You first create a container, and then create components to place in it.

When building a user interface, first create an instance of the Window class or the Frame class. The frame, in the case of an applet, is the browser window. Since all applets subclass the Panel class, components can be added to instances of the Applet class itself.

Typically, a user interface has more than one container and component. To add components to a container, use the container's add() method. The code here adds a Button component to the MyJavaAppletFromOracle8iBook class:

```
add( new Button("I love to program in SQLJ"));
```

Note that the creation of the component is in the init() method and that this method is automatically invoked during the initialization of the applet. Therefore, the buttons will be drawn and displayed as soon as the browser is notified by the init() milestone method.

In the previous statements, an object of type Button was created. You need to lay out the button after it is created. You can use the layout manager associated with the container to control the layout. In the AWT package, the layout manager classes implement the LayoutManager interface. The AWT provides five layout managers that are used to place components in a container. Each container has a default layout manager. The default layout manager for the Panel class is the FlowLayout manager. The BorderLayout manager is the default layout manager for both the Frame and the Dialog classes. Use the BorderLayout manager to adjust the placement of components within the regions North, South, East, West, and Center. Use the FlowLayout manager to arrange the components from left to right. Other layout managers provide additional layout flexibility.

```
import java.awt.*;
public class MyJavaAppletFromOracle8iBook extends java.applet.Applet {
    public void init() {
        // First create a variable of type Panel
        Panel aPanel;

        // Use the setLayout() method to use the BorderLayout Manager
        setLayout(new BorderLayout());

        // Instantiate your panel
        aPanel = new Panel();
        ...
        // add button to your applet
        add( new Button("I love to program in SQLJ"));
    }
    ...
}
```

You may wish to add a text area to the panel in your applet. This is accomplished by creating an instance of the TextArea class and adding it to the panel using the add() method from the Panel class.

```
import java.awt.*;
public class MyJavaAppletFromOracle8iBook extends java.applet.Applet {
    public void init() {
        Panel aPanel;
        // Use the setLayout method to use the BorderLayout Manager
        setLayout(new BorderLayout());

        // Instantiate your panel
        aPanel = new Panel();

        // Add a text area
        aPanel.add(new TextArea);
```

```
        // Place your text area in the south side of the panel
        add("South", aPanel);

        // add button to the applet
        add( new Button("I love to program in SQLJ"));
    }
    ...
}
```

So far you have an inert interface—that is, the applet does not do much. In order for the applet to do something, the user interface must take some action. This is accomplished through an *event*. Event handling is done by the action() method of the Component class and is beyond the scope of this book. To complete the applet, however, you will learn to handle at least one event through the action() method. The Component class is the superclass of the Panel class that handles events for basic components such as Button, Checkbox, Choice, and TextField. The MyJavaAppletFromOracle8iBook class overrides the action() method. This method has two objects as its arguments:

```
public boolean action (Event anEvent, Object anObject)
```

The anEvent parameter object describes the event that occurred, and the anObject parameter object contains different values, depending on the type of event that occurred.

```
import java.awt.*;
public class MyJavaAppletFromOracle8iBook extends java.applet.Applet {
    TextArea aTextArea;
    public void init() {
        // Use the setLayout method to use the BorderLayout Manager
        setLayout(new BorderLayout());

        // Instantiate your panel
        Panel aPanel = new Panel();

        // Create a text area
        aTextArea = new TextArea();

        // Add a text area
        aPanel.add(aTextArea);

        // Place your text area in the south of the panel
        add("South", aPanel);

        // add a button to your applet
        add( new Button("I love to program in SQLJ"));
    }
```

```
    // Add an action() method to handle an event
    public boolean action (Event anEvent, Object anObject) {
        String aString = (String)anObject;

        // Use the method from the TextArea class to add a text
        aTextArea.appendText(aString + "\n");
        return false;
    }
}
```

Now that you have created the applet, it can be compiled. At the command line, type the following command:

```
javac MyJavaAppletFromOracle8iBook.java
```

Once the applet is compiled successfully, create an HTML file using your favorite editor to run the applet. The HTML file should be in the same directory as the compiled bytecode file MyJavaAppletFromOracle8iBook.class.

The applet may be customized with the many attributes of the <APPLET> tag. The following is an example of an HTML tag that tells the viewer or browser to load the applet with the initial size of the applet set to 500 pixels wide and 250 pixels high:

```
<APPLET code="MyJavaAppletFromOracle8iBook.class" width="500" height="250"></APPLET>
```

To run an applet in a browser, a Java-enabled browser is needed, such as Netscape 2.0 or later or Internet Explorer 3.0 or later. You can also use the AppletViewer to run the applet.

When using a browser to view a page that contains an applet, the bytecode of the applet is downloaded to the browser and is executed on the client's computer. The applet is an independent program running within the browser. Web browsers execute the applet when the browser loads an HTML document that contains an applet tag.

The AppletViewer can also be used to run the applet:

```
AppletViewer MyJavaAppletFromOracle8iBook.html
```

In this appendix, you learned the basic features of the Java language—such as variables, operators, expressions, classes, and objects—through the investigation of a Java application and a Java applet. In Appendix C, you will learn about Java Database Connectivity (JDBC).

APPENDIX
C

Introduction to Java Database Connectivity (JDBC)

JDBC application is a Java program that invokes SQL statements through JDBC method calls to access relational databases. The communication between the program and the data server is done via the JDBC API (a set of Java interfaces, classes, and exceptions to support database connections) and multiple low-level drivers for connecting to different databases. See the "Basic JDBC Concepts" section in Chapter 1.

In this appendix, you will create the following JDBC programs to access a database:

- A JDBC application
- A JDBC applet that calls a PL/SQL stored procedure

Please refer to the *Oracle8i/9i JDBC Developer's Guide and Reference* and the *JDBC Database Access with Java* for further information on how to program with JDBC.

Creating a JDBC Application

In this section, you will create a JDBC application to

- Create a table, the DEPARTMENT_LIST, in the Oracle relational database
- Insert data into the DEPARTMENT_LIST table
- Query the DEPARTMENT_LIST table
- Display the query results via a JDBC ResultSet object

There is a standard organization to JDBC programs:

1. Import the JDBC API package, the java.sql package.

2. Load and register the JDBC driver with the JDBC DriverManager class. You can obtain connection objects from the DriverManager after the driver has been registered. When you use JDBC to create a connection, auto-commit is on by default! This behavior is different than the default SQLJ behavior with Oracle.connect() or Oracle.getConnection(). No explicit commit() is needed to commit the following DML statements to the database.

3. Create a Connection object to connect to the database.

4. Create a `Statement` instance to send SQL statements to the database. This object can execute dynamic or static embedded SQL statements.

5. Use the JDBC `Statement` instance to execute database tasks.

6. Use the JDBC `ResultSet` instance to obtain the results of a database query and retrieve the data via its `next()` method.

7. Close the `Statement` and the `ResultSet` instances.

8. Close the connection to the database.

Using the JDBC API, you will write `JdbcApplication`, an application to create a table, insert data into it, and then query the data from an Oracle database:

```
// Program name: JdbcApplication.java

// Import packages necessary for the application
import java.sql.*;

class JdbcApplication {
    public static void main (String args []) throws SQLException {

        // Load and register the Oracle JDBC driver
        DriverManager.registerDriver(
                    new oracle.jdbc.driver.OracleDriver());
        /* Alternatively, instead of using the DriverManager class, you
         * could also use the following statement to register the
         * the driver
         * Class.forName("oracle.jdbc.driver.OracleDriver").newInstance();
         */
        // Connect to the database
        String anURL = "jdbc:oracle:thin:@data-i.com:1521:ORCL";
        Connection conn =
            DriverManager.getConnection(anURL, "scott", "tiger");

        // Create Statement Object
        Statement stmt = conn.createStatement ();

        // Create a table and Insert records into the table
        stmt.executeUpdate("CREATE TABLE DEPARTMENT_LIST(" +
                        "deptno NUMBER," +
                        "shortname VARCHAR2(8)," +
                        "longname   VARCHAR2(20))");
        stmt.executeUpdate("INSERT INTO DEPARTMENT_LIST " +
                        "VALUES(200, 'ACNT','Accounting')");
        stmt.executeUpdate("INSERT INTO DEPARTMENT_LIST " +
```

```
                              "VALUES(240, 'HR','Human Resource')");

      // Query the table
      ResultSet rset =
              stmt.executeQuery("SELECT * FROM DEPARTMENT_LIST");

      // Process the Result Set
      while (rset.next())
        System.out.println(rset.getInt(1)+ " " +
              rset.getString("shortname") + " " + rset.getString(3));

      // Close the Result Set and Statement object
      rset.close();
      stmt.close();

      // Close connection to the database
      conn.close();
    }
}
```

1. Import the JDBC Package

Use the following syntax to make the JDBC class immediately available to your program:

```
import java.sql.*;
```

Additionally, you may need to import vendor-specific driver packages for the database that you wish to access. For example, you have to import the `oracle.sql` package to access the Oracle-specific types such as BLOB, DATE, and RAW.

2. Load and Register the JDBC Driver

You must tell the JDBC program how to manage driver communication with the database. This is accomplished by loading the vendor-specific driver manager and registering it with the `registerDriver()` method provided by the `DriverManager` class of the JDBC API:

```
DriverManager.registerDriver (new oracle.jdbc.driver.OracleDriver());
```

The driver manager is responsible for connecting to the database with a specified URL. It is also responsible for searching for an appropriate driver when the `getConnection()` method from step 3 is called.

More importantly, note that you meant to say that you need to register every vendor-specific driver once, regardless of the number of DB connections you obtain from each.

Alternatively, in theory, you can use the following syntax to load and register the vendor's driver:

```
Class.forName("oracle.jdbc.driver.OracleDriver");
```

The `registerDriver()` method explicitly creates an instance of the vendor-specific driver to register the driver, whereas the `forName()` method implicitly does it for you. In practice, initializing the `OracleDriver` class may not properly register itself with the `DriverManager` in all Java environments. However, the following does work:

```
Class.forName("oracle.jdbc.driver.OracleDriver").newInstance();
```

This permits you to obtain and subsequently use the JDBC driver class in the form of a `String` instead of hard coding the driver into the application.

3. Create the Connection Object to Connect to the Database

Once the driver has been loaded, a `Connection` instance must be created in order for the program to connect to the database. A connection object from the `java.sql.Connection` class is instantiated through the `getConnection()` method of the `DriverManager` class. The `Connection` object is established by passing the `get Connection()` method a JDBC URL. The `DriverManager` passes this URL to the different drivers that are registered with it. The driver that recognizes the URL will return an instance of a class implementing the `java.sql.Connection` interface, which then the `DriverManager` returns. The vendor-specific component of the JDBC URL (such as *oracle* in jdbc:oracle:oci8:@) permits the JDBC driver to determine whether it is responsible for a particular JDBC URL.

The `Connection` class contains methods to control connections to the database. The `getConnection()` method can be called with arguments specifying the database URL for the connection, the password, and the username. Other parameter signatures of this method accept different parameters. See Chapter 5 and the *Oracle 9i JDBC Developer's Guide and Reference* to learn more about the `getConnection()` method and the various lists of its input arguments.

```
String anUrl = "jdbc:oracle:thin:@data-i.com:1521:ORCL";
Connection conn = DriverManager.getConnection(anURL, "scott", "tiger");
```

By default, the `auto-commit` mode is set on (to `true`) in JDBC. You have to explicitly set `auto-commit` to `false` if you want to control the transaction of your SQL statements with `commit()` or `rollback()` methods of the `Connection` class.

```
// Set the auto-commit mode on.  This is the default when a
// Connection object is obtain.
conn.setAutoCommit(true);

// Set the auto-commit mode off
conn.setAutoCommit(false);

// Commit SQL transactions to the database
conn.commit();

// Undo previous SQL transactions
conn.rollback();
```

4. Create the Statement Instance to Perform Database Tasks

Now that you have established a database connection to the data-i database server, you need to instantiate objects to manage the SQL statements that will be executed against the database. Use the `createStatement()` method of the `Connection` class associated with a `Connection` object to create a statement object:

```
Statement stmt = conn.createStatement ();
```

5. Use the Statement Instance to Execute Database Tasks

The `executeQuery()` method of the `Statement` class is used to send query requests to a database, whereas the `executeUpdate()` method of the `Statement` class is used for sending SQL statements that modify the state of the database (DDL statements and DML statements such as `INSERT`, `UPDATE`, and `DELETE`). In the following example, create the table `DEPARTMENT_LIST` and insert two rows of data into it.

```
stmt.executeUpdate("CREATE TABLE DEPARTMENT_LIST( " +
                                "deptno NUMBER," +
                                "shortname VARCHAR2(8)," +
                                "longname  VARCHAR2(20))");
stmt.executeUpdate("INSERT INTO DEPARTMENT_LIST " +
                   "VALUES( 200, 'ACNT','Accounting')");
```

```
stmt.executeUpdate("INSERT INTO DEPARTMENT_LIST " +
                    "VALUES( 240, 'HR','Human Resource')");
```

6.Use the JDBC `ResultSet` Object

Use the `executeQuery()` method to retrieve the data and then return it via a JDBC `ResultSet` object:

```
ResultSet rset = stmt.executeQuery ("SELECT * FROM DEPARTMENT_LIST");
```

After you execute your query, use the `next()` method of the `ResultSet` object to get the values of the row. The `next()` method advances the `rset` object to successive rows of the JDBC `ResultSet`. This method returns a value of true while rows are still available, or a value of false if there are no more rows (that is, when all table rows have been fetched from the result set). Use the `next()` method to iterate through the `ResultSet` object:

```
while (rset.next())
    System.out.println(rset.getInt(1)+ " " +
            rset.getString("shortname") + " " + rset.getString(3));
```

Use the various JDBC get*Xxx* methods such as `getString()` and `getInt()` to retrieve column values from the current row of the result set. You can use either the table column name or the column index number as the input parameter to these methods. Note that the column index number refers to the position of the column of the result set and not the column of the database table.

In the `rset.getString("shortname")` statement, the parameter `shortname` is the column name of the result set; whereas in `rset.getString(3)`, it is the relative position of the result set column. The 3 is the third column of the result set, which is the `longname` column.

7. Close the Statement Instances and the `ResultSet`

Use the `close()` method to close any `Statement` and `ResultSet` objects that you created. You should always explicitly close all `Statement` and `ResultSet` objects. If you do not explicitly close these objects, cursor leaks in your database session will occur, and you will soon encounter an ORA-01000—maximum open cursors exceeded!

```
// Close the rset ResultSet and the stmt Statement objects
rset.close();
stmt.close();
```

8. Close the Connection to the Database

You must close your connection once you finish with the database connection. This is accomplished via the `close()` method of the `Connection` class:

```
// Close connection to the database
conn.close();
```

Java Applet Calls a PL/SQL Stored Procedure

A *JDBC applet* is a Java applet that uses the JDBC API to access a database. See Appendix B to learn more about Java applets.

In this section, you will create a Java applet, the JdbcApplet. This applet calls a PL/SQL stored procedure to retrieve a list of vendors' names from the VENDOR_LIST table. Note that PL/SQL is an Oracle RDBMS procedural language extension to SQL. If you wish to access stored procedures from databases other than Oracle, you should consult your vendor's manual to learn how to create server-side stored procedures in your environment. See Appendix A to learn more about PL/SQL procedures, functions, and packages.

The JdbcApplet applet calls the Oracle PL/SQL purchase_queries.select-VendorName stored procedure to select the name of the vendors from the VENDOR_LIST table and displays the results:

```
//Program Name: JdbcApplet.java

// Import Oracle jdbc driver (See Note 1.)
import oracle.jdbc.driver.*;

// Import the package necessary for the JDBC applet
import java.sql.*;

// Import the Java classes needed for the in applet
import java.awt.*;

public class JdbcApplet extends java.applet.Applet {
   // The button of the applet for executing the query
   Button execute_button;

   // The query displays its result in this text area
   TextArea output;

   // Use for connecting to the database
   Connection conn;
```

```java
// Create the User Interface
public void init () {
  this.setLayout (new BorderLayout ());
  Panel p = new Panel ();
  p.setLayout (new FlowLayout (FlowLayout.LEFT));
  execute_button = new Button ("JDBC Applet");
  p.add (execute_button);
  this.add ("North", p);
  output = new TextArea (10, 60);
  this.add ("Center", output);
}

public boolean action (Event ev, Object arg) {
  if (ev.target == execute_button) {
    try {
      // Clear the output area
      output.setText (null);
        // Load the JDBC driver
      DriverManager.registerDriver(
              new oracle.jdbc.driver.OracleDriver());

      // Connect to the database
      conn = DriverManager.getConnection(
          "jdbc:oracle:thin:@data-i.com:1521:ORCL","scott", "tiger");
       // Create a callable statement object
      CallableStatement cstmt;  // (See Note 2.)
      // Prepare the call
      cstmt = conn.prepareCall  // (See Note 3.)
          ( "{call purchase_queries.SelectVendorName(?)}" ) ;

      // Register the output parameter (See Note 4.)
      cstmt.registerOutParameter(1, OracleTypes.CURSOR);

      // Execute the callable statement
      cstmt.execute();          // (See Note 5.)

      // Get the results into an Oracle result set (See Note 6.)
      OracleResultSet anOracleResultSet = (OracleResultSet)
              ((OracleCallableStatement)cstmt).getCursor (1);

      // Process the Oracle Result Set like you would process a
      // JDBC result set process the Result Set
      while (anOracleResultSet.next())
              output.appendText(anOracleResultSet.getString(1)+ "\n");

      // Close the Result Set
```

```
        anOracleResultSet.close();
        // Close connection to the database
        conn.close();
      }
      catch (Exception e) {
            output.appendText (e.getMessage() + "\n");
      }
      return true;
    }
    else
      return false;
  }
}
```

Notes on the `JdbcApplet` applet:

1. Starting with Oracle 9.0.1, you should be using `oracle.jdbc.*` instead of `oracle.jdbc.driver.*`.

2. To access a PL/SQL procedure from a Java program, you must create a `CallableStatement` object. The `java.sql.CallableStatement` interface provides a way for you to call stored procedures. Callable statements also provide you with a way to obtain an OUT or IN OUT parameter from your statement execution. This can be from calling a stored procedure, but it could also come from an OUT or IN OUT in a PL/SQL block.

3. This statement prepares the call to the procedure. The procedure returns an Oracle object of type REF CURSOR. See Appendix A to learn about Oracle REF CURSOR.

4. The `registerOutParameter()` method registers all OUT or IN/OUT parameters. You would use the set*Xxx*() method for INs or IN/OUTs.

5. This statement executes the procedure call.

6. This statement retrieves an `OracleResultSet` as an out parameter from a PL/SQL procedure, and you must cast your callable statement to an `OracleCallableStatement`. You have to use the Oracle-specific API on the `ResultSet` object to retrieve the REF CURSOR.

Refer to Appendix B and the *Oracle8i/9i JDBC Developer's Guide and Reference* to learn more about Java applets and Java programs calling PL/SQL stored procedures.
   In this appendix, you created two JDBC programs, an application and an applet; in each, you used the JDBC API to connect to the database and execute dynamic SQL operations to manipulate the database. Appendix D presents a SQLJ quick reference guide.

APPENDIX
D

SQLJ Quick
Reference Guide

his appendix gives you a summary of SQLJ. You can come here to look up SQLJ syntax, refresh your memory on concepts that you learned in the different chapters of the book, or get an overview of the fundamentals of SQLJ.

Here, you will encounter

- Setting the SQLJ environment

- SQLJ iterations

- Java host expressions

- Executable statement clause

- Database connections

- Selected `sqlj.runtime` classes

- Supported types for host expressions

- Tools

Setting the SQLJ Environment

Developing SQLJ database applications requires the following:

- The Java Development Kit (JDK) version 1.1 or later from JavaSoft, or an equivalent Java interpreter and compiler. You can download the JavaSoft JDK from Sun Microsystems at http://java.sun.com/j2se/. After downloading it, follow the instruction that comes with the JDK to install it. The Java JDK may already be on your system, especially if you are on a multiuser system such as UNIX, or you have installed a Java Development Environment tool such as the Oracle JDeveloper or the Visual Café from Symantec. Test to see whether the interpreter is installed on your system by typing at the command line:

    ```
    java -version
    ```

    If a version number of 1.1.*x* or later is returned, then you may not have to install a Java compiler and interpreter.

- A JDBC driver implementing the standard `java.sql` JDBC interfaces from Sun Microsystems. Note that if you are developing applications for an Oracle database (Oracle7 or later), you should get the Oracle JDBC drivers.

NOTE
*Oracle SQLJ supports any standard-compliant
JDBC driver. Therefore, if you are connecting to a
database other than the Oracle data server, install
the JDBC API supplied by the database vendors.*

■   Oracle SQLJ. You can install the Oracle SQLJ by downloading it from
    Oracle's Web site at http://technet.oracle.com, or you can choose to install
    it when you install the Oracle8*i* JServer. The installation includes the class
    files for the SQLJ translator, SQLJ profile customizer, and SQLJ run-time.
    These class files are available in the file `translator.zip` file. Note
    that, with Oracle SQLJ release 8.1.7 or later, there is also an independent
    run-time library: `runtime.zip` / `runtime11.zip` / `runtime12.zip`.

Setting the `CLASSPATH` and `PATH` Environment Variables

Set the `CLASSPATH` environment variable after SQLJ has been installed on your
system. The `CLASSPATH` environment variable tells the Java compiler, the Java
interpreter, and the SQLJ translator where to search for Java class libraries. In order
to compile Java source codes and/or SQLJ source codes or run Java programs, you
have to make sure that the `CLASSPATH` environment variable is set correctly. Do
the following to set the `CLASSPATH`:

For Oracle8*i* SQLJ releases 8.1.5 and 8.1.6, you need two files to set the
`CLASSPATH` environment variable:

■   **`classes[ver].zip`**   Contains the JDBC API class files, where the `ver`
    is the Oracle JDBC API version, such as `classes111.zip` for use with
    JDK 1.1.*x*.

■   **`translator.zip`**   Has the class files for the SQLJ translator, the SQLJ
    profile customizer, and the SQLJ run-time.

For Oracle8*i* SQLJ release 8.1.7 and Oracle9*i*, you need three files to set the
`CLASSPATH` environment variable:

■   **`classes[ver].zip`**   Contains the JDBC API class files, where the `ver`
    is the Oracle JDBC API version, such as `classes12.zip` for use with JDK
    1.2 and later. You use `classes111.zip` for JDK 1.1.*x*, and with Oracle 9*i*
    you use `classes12.zip` for JDK 1.1.3.

■   **`translator.zip`**   Has the class files for the SQLJ translator, the SQLJ
    profile customizer, and the SQLJ run-time.

■ **`runtime[ver].zip`** Where `ver` is 11 for JDK 1.1, 12 for JDK 1.2, or `" "` (empty String) when using Oracle SQLJ releases prior to 8.1.7 or Oracle JDBC drivers releases prior to 9*i*. For Oracle SQLJ release 8.1.7 and later, the combination of the `runtime12.zip` and the SQLJ `translator.zip` files gives your program access to all necessary SQLJ files that you need to compile and run it.

Note that with Oracle9*i* release 9.0.1 and later the libraries for JDBC and SQLJ also come in `.jar` format (in addition to the `.zip` format). The content is, however, the same in the two formats.

Do the following to set the CLASSPATH on the different operating system (note that `jdbcdir` is the directory in which you installed the JDBC drivers, and `sqljdir` is the directory in which the `translator.zip` and the `runtime12.zip` files reside):

■ For JDK 1.1.*x* and Oracle SQLJ prior to release 8.1.7, on the Microsoft Windows 95/98 operating systems, type the following at the command line:

```
SET CLASSPATH =
%CLASSPATH%;[jdbcdir]\lib\classes111.zip;[sqljdir]\lib\translator.zip;
```

■ For Java 2, on the Microsoft Windows 95/98 operating systems, type the following at the command line:

```
SET CLASSPATH = %CLASSPATH%;[jdbcdir]\lib\classes12.zip;
[sqljdir]\lib\translator.zip;[sqljdir]\lib\runtime12.zip;
```

■ In Microsoft Windows NT, you can set the CLASSPATH variable each time you open an MS-DOS window as follows:

```
SET CLASSPATH =
%CLASSPATH%;[jdbcdir]\lib\classes111.zip;[sqljdir]\lib\translator.zip;
```

1. Open the Control Panel and double-click the System icon.

2. Choose the Environment tab, and under System Variables choose CLASSPATH from the list. Append the following to the end of the line in the Values box:

```
[sqljdir]\lib\classes111.zip;[sqljdir]\lib\translator.zip;
```

■ In the UNIX operating system, you can set the CLASSPATH variable each time you open a session using the following command:

```
setenv CLASSPATH
${CLASSPATH}:[sqljdir] /classes111.zip:[sqljdir]/translator.zip
```

Note that SQLJ works with any standard-compliant JDBC driver. Therefore, if you are connecting to a database other than the Oracle data server, follow the instructions and include in your CLASSPATH the JDBC API supplied by the database vendors.

Another issue with the CLASSPATH—particularly when trying to execute demo programs—is that it should have a dot (.) (the current directory) as a component. This will permit classes and sources in the current directory to be found by SQLJ and JavaC.

Setting the CLASSPATH can be very confusing and frustrating. If you run into trouble and need assistance, consult README files that come with the 8*i* release 8.1.7 and 9*i* SQLJ distributions. Alternatively, you can go to the SQLJ FAQ at the Oracle Web site http://www.oracle.com/java/sqlj/faq.html or the Oracle Technology Network (OTN) Web site at http://technet.oracle.com.

Set the PATH environment variable so that the operating system will know where to find the SQLJ executable files. The procedure to set the path is similar to the setting of the CLASSPATH environment variable previously discussed. Set the PATH by following the steps of setting the CLASSPATH and replacing instances of CLASSPATH with PATH. For example, this will set the PATH on the Microsoft operating systems:

```
SET PATH = %PATH%[Oracle Home]\bin;
```

Replace [Oracle Home] with your actual Oracle Home directory.

SQLJ Declarations

There are two types of SQLJ declarations: iterator and connection context declarations. A SQLJ declaration is made up of a #sql token, followed by a class declaration, as described in Chapters 1 and 3.

Iterator Declaration

A SQLJ iterator is similar to a Java ResultSet, which is described in Appendix C, in that it is used to store query results from a database. Use the following syntax to declare a basic SQLJ iterator:

```
#sql <modifier> iterator Iterator_ClassName ( type_declarations );
```

The modifier can be any standard Java class modifier, such as public, static, private, or protected, or it can be the default package. SQLJ modifier rules correspond to the Java modifier rules, as in Appendix B. The type_declarations are separated by commas.

In any iterator declaration, you may optionally include the following:

- **`implements clause`**   Use this clause to specify one or more interfaces that the generated class will implement.

- **`with clause`**   Use this clause to specify one or more initialized constants to be included in the generated class.

Use the following syntax to declare a SQLJ iterator with `implements` and `with` clauses:

```
#sql <modifier> iterator Iterator_ClassName
  implements intfc1,…,intfcN
    with (var1=value1,…,varn=valueN)
( type declarations );
```

The portion `intfc1,…,intfcN` is known as the `implements` clause. The portion `with (var1=value1,..., varN=valueN)` is known as the `with` clause. Where there is both a `with` clause and an `implements` clause, the `implements` clause must come first. Note that parentheses are used to enclose `with` lists, but not `implements` lists.

There are two types of SQLJ iterators: *named* and *positional,* as described in Chapters 1, 2, and 3.

SQLJ Named Iterator
When declaring a named iterator, you specify column names and types. For example,

```
// A named iterator declaration
#sql public iterator Employee(int employeeno, String name);
```

SQLJ Positional Iterator
Unlike a named iterator, when declaring a positional iterator, you specify column types. For example,

```
// A positional iterator declaration
#sql public iterator Employee(int, String);
```

Scrollable Iterators
The ISO standard for SQLJ has adopted support for scrollable iterators. SQLJ scrollable iterators are patterned after the JDBC 2.0 specification for scrollable JDBC `ResultSets`. A SQLJ iterator is scrollable when it implements the `sqlj.runtime.Scrollable` interface. Use the following syntax to declare a scrollable iterator, described in Chapter 6:

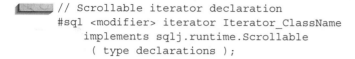

```
// Scrollable iterator declaration
#sql <modifier> iterator Iterator_ClassName
   implements sqlj.runtime.Scrollable
     ( type declarations );
```

There are three types of SQLJ scrollable iterators:

- **Scrollable named iterator**   Use the following syntax to declare a scrollable named iterator:

```
#sql public static iterator NamedScrollableIter
    implements sqlj.runtime.Scrollable
      (int accountno, int projectno, int departmentno);
```

- **Scrollable positional iterator**   Use the following syntax to declare a scrollable positional iterator:

```
#sql public static iterator PosScrollableIter
    implements sqlj.runtime.Scrollable
      ( int , int , int );
```

- **ScrollableResultSetIterator iterator** (Oracle9i SQLJ only)   Use instances of this iterator to populate data from the database. For example,

```
// Declare a ScrollableResultSetIterator
sqlj.runtime.ScrollableResultSetIterator aSrsi;

// Populate data from the ACCOUNT_LIST table.
#sql aSrsi = { SELECT * FROM ACCOUNT_LIST };
```

The Scrollable Interface

The following methods are defined on scrollable iterators, as well as on execution contexts. Use an ExecutionContext to provide the default direction when creating a scrollable iterator.

- **getFetchDirection()**   Retrieves the direction for fetching rows from database tables.

- **setFetchDirection(int)**   Gives the SQLJ run-time a hint as to the direction in which rows are processed. The direction should be one of sqlj.runtime.ResultSetIterator.FETCH_FORWARD, FETCH_REVERSE, or FETCH_UNKNOWN.

NOTE
*If you do not specify a value for the direction on the
ExecutionContext, then FETCH_FORWARD will
be used as a default.*

Scrollable Iterator Methods

Named iterators use movement methods to navigate through the rows of a result set.
Most movement methods for scrollable iterators work like the next () method of
nonscrollable iterators. Here is a list of the methods:

- **previous ()** Moves the iterator object to the previous row in the
  result set.

- **first ()** Moves the iterator object to the first row in the result set.

- **last ()** Moves the iterator object to the last row in the result set.

- **absolute (int)** Moves the iterator object to the given row number in the
  result set. The first row is row 1, the second is row 2, and so on. If the given
  row number is negative, the iterator object moves to an absolute row position
  with respect to the end of the result set. For example, calling absolute (-1)
  positions the iterator object on the last row, absolute (-2) indicates the
  next-to-last row, and so on.

- **relative (int)** Moves the iterator object a relative number of rows,
  either positive or negative. Calling relative (0) is valid, but does not
  change the iterator object position.

There are also a number of predicates on scrollable iterators. All these methods
will return false whenever the result set underlying the iterator contains no rows.

- **isBeforeFirst ()** Indicates whether the iterator object is before the first
  row in the result set.

- **isFirst ()** Indicates whether the iterator object is on the first row of the
  result set.

- **isLast()** Indicates whether the iterator object is on the last row of the result set. Note that calling the method isLast() can be expensive because the SQLJ driver might need to fetch ahead one row to determine whether the current row is the last row in the result set.

- **isAfterLast()** Indicates whether the iterator object is after the last row in the result set.

Subclassing Iterators

SQLJ supports the ability to subclass iterator classes. This feature can be very useful in allowing you to add functionality to your queries and query results. For example,

```
public class SubclassIterator {
   // Declare an iterator
   #sql public static iterator EmployeeIter
      (String firstname, String lastname, String type);

   // Declare an iterator subclass.
// EmployeesList extends (subclass) the EmployeeIter iterator
   // and it returns a ArrayList of Employee objects
   public class EmployeesList extends EmployeeIter {
      // One very important requirement is:
      // The iterator subclass must implement the constructor
      public EmployeesList (sqlj.runtime.profile.RTResultSet rs)
         throws SQLException {
         super(rs);
      }
      ...
   } // End of EmployeesList class

} // End of SubclassIterator class
```

See Chapter 7 to learn more about subclassing iterators.

Connection Context Declaration

Declare and use ConnectionContext classes to establish database connections to schemas located on different data servers. See Chapters 3 and 5 and the "Database Connections" section of this appendix. In any connection context declaration, like in any iterator declaration, you may optionally include an `implements` and/or `with` clause:

```
#sql <modifier> context Context_ClassName implements intfc1,...,intfcN
    with (var1=value1,...,varn=valueN);
```

The `modifier`, as in an iterator declaration, can be any standard Java class modifier, such as `public`, `static`, `private`, or `protected`, or the default package. The SQLJ modifier rules correspond to the Java modifier rules (see Appendix B). The optional portion `intfc1,...,intfcN` is known as the `implements` clause. In the following, `LocalHostConnectionContext` is a user-defined `ConnectionContext` class name:

```
#sql public context LocalHostConnectionContext;
```

`implements` Clause

You may use the Java `implements` clause with both the iterator and the connection context declaration types, as described in Chapters 3 and 5. The following declaration of the `ConnectionContext` class, `Context_Classname`, specifies one or more interfaces to be implemented by the generated class:

```
#sql <java_modifiers> context Context_Classname
        implements InterfaceClass1, ... , InterfaceClassN;
```

The `implements` clause, `implements InterfaceClass1...
InterfaceClassN`, derives one or more classes from a Java interface.

`with` Clause

The SQLJ `with` clause allows you to declare a SQLJ iterator or `ConnectionContext` class by specifying one or more constants that will be in the generated class (see Chapters 3, 5, and 6 for more information). The generated constants will be `public static final`. The syntax is

```
// A connection context declaration and the with clause
#sql public static context TestCtx with (dataSource="jdbc/test");
```

Note that the `with` clause is unique to SQLJ and does not exist in Java. The following example demonstrates the use of a `with` clause in a named iterator declaration:

```
#sql public iterator Employee with (TYPECODE=OracleTypes.NUMBER)
        (int employeeno, String name);
```

The `Employee` iterator will define the `public static final` attribute `TYPECODE` and initialize it to the value of the `typecode` for the `NUMBER` datatype, as defined in the Oracle JDBC `oracle.jdbc.driver.OracleTypes` class.

Java Host Expressions

SQLJ uses Java *host expressions* interspersed within the SQL statement to pass arguments between Java source code and SQL operations, as described in Chapter 3. A host expression is any legal Java variable or complex expression that is preceded by a colon (`:`). Complex expressions must be enclosed in parentheses ().

```
String emp;
int empNo = 1056;
...
// The following SQLJ statement uses the Java variables emp and empNo
// as host expressions. Note that a colon precedes the Java variables
// emp and empNo to make them host variables. In addition, variable
// emp maps SQL data to Java, and empno maps Java data to SQL.
#sql {SELECT lastname INTO :emp FROM EMPLOYEE_TABLE
            WHERE employeeno = :empNo };
```

Executable Statement Clause

A SQLJ executable statement clause is prefixed with the `#sql` token, followed by a SQLJ clause, and is terminated with a semicolon, as described in Chapters 3 and 5.

The SQLJ Clause

A SQLJ clause is the executable part of a statement (everything to the right of the `#sql` token). It consists of embedded SQL inside curly braces, preceded by a Java result expression. There are two types of SQLJ clauses:

- A *statement clause* is a clause without a result expression. For example,

  ```
  #sql { sql_operation };
  ```

- An *assignment clause* is a clause with a result expression. For example,

  ```
  #sql anIteratorInstance = { sql_operation };
  ```

The SQL clause is used in processing DML statements such as the standard SQL `SELECT`, `UPDATE`, `INSERT`, and `DELETE`, as described in Chapter 3):

```
#sql { INSERT INTO EMPLOYEE_LIST
        (employeeno, lastname, firstname, phone, departmentno )
          VALUES ( 1056, 'Jones', 'Rachel', '(305)555-0359', 15 ) };
```

Single-Row Query Results:
The `SELECT` ... `INTO` Clause

The `SELECT` ... `INTO` clause is used to retrieve a single row of data into one or more host variables, as described in Chapter 3:

```
#sql { SELECT expression1,…, expressionN
          INTO :host_exp1,…, :host_expN
            FROM datasource [optional clauses] };
```

Here is an example:

```
#sql { SELECT lastname, firstname,
          INTO :firstName, :lastName
            FROM EMPLOYEE_LIST
              WHERE employeeno = 1056 };
```

The `FETCH` ... `INTO` Clause

The `FETCH` ... `INTO` clause is used to retrieve multirow data from positional iterators. The following example illustrates how to use the `FETCH` ... `INTO` clause (see Chapters 3, 5, and 6 for more information):

```
//Declare the positional iterator EmployeeIter
#sql public iterator EmployeeIter (int, String, String);
…

// Then declare an iterator instance emps
EmployeeIter emps;
//Query to put data in the positional iterator 'emps'
#sql emps = { SELECT employeeno, lastname, firstname
                FROM employee_list };
…
String firstName;
String lastName;
int id;

while (true) {
  // Use FETCH INTO to retrieve data from the emps positional iterator
  #sql { FETCH :emps INTO :id, :firstName, :lastName };
  // Use the endFetch() method to determine the end.
  if (emps.endFetch()) break;   // This test must be AFTER fetch
  System.out.print("The Employee number: " + id);
  System.out.println( " and Name: " + firstName + " " + lastName );
}
emps.close();  // Close the iterator
…
}
```

Use the following statements to move to the current, prior, previous, first, and last row in the result set. Use the prior(), previous(), first(), and last() movement methods on named scrollable iterators. Note that you should never use the movement commands on a scrollable positional iterator unless you use the FETCH CURRENT FROM clause to populate from the iterator (all other FETCH clauses do a movement *and* a population together).

The FETCH CURRENT ... INTO Clause

Here is the syntax for FETCH CURRENT ... INTO:

```
#sql { FETCH CURRENT FROM :iter INTO :x  };
```

FETCH CURRENT FROM is supported on scrollable and nonscrollable iterators, and since Oracle9*i* SQLJ release 9.0.1, on ResultSetIterators as well. (See Chapters 6 and 7 for more information.)

The FETCH PRIOR ... INTO Clause

Here is the syntax for FETCH PRIOR ... INTO:

```
#sql { FETCH PRIOR FROM :iter INTO :x  };
```

The FETCH FIRST ... INTO Clause

Here is the syntax for FETCH FIRST ... INTO:

```
#sql { FETCH FIRST FROM :iter INTO :x  };
```

The FETCH LAST ... INTO Clause

Here is the syntax for FETCH LAST ... INTO:

```
#sql { FETCH LAST FROM :iter INTO :x  };
```

Absolute and Relative Movements

Here is the syntax for FETCH ABSOLUTE ... FROM ... INTO and FETCH RELATIVE ... FROM ... INTO, respectively:

```
#sql { FETCH ABSOLUTE :n FROM :iter INTO :x  };
#sql { FETCH RELATIVE :n FROM :iter INTO :x  };
#sql { FETCH RELATIVE (0) FROM :iter INTO :x  };
```

Note that this is semantically equivalent to

```
FETCH CURRENT FROM :iter INTO :x
```

SET TRANSACTION Syntax

In SQLJ, the SET TRANSACTION statement has the following syntax:

```
#sql { SET TRANSACTION <access_mode>,
    <ISOLATION LEVEL isolation_level> };
```

If you do not want to use the default connection for your transaction, you can specify a particular connection context instance for a SET TRANSACTION statement. For example,

```
// Declare a ConnectionContext class
sql context MyCtx;
MyCtx myCtx = new MyCtx( …);
// Use an instance of the context class
// in your set transaction statement
#sql [myCtxt] { SET TRANSACTION ISOLATION LEVEL SERIALIZABLE };
```

In a standard SQLJ SET TRANSACTION statement, you can optionally specify the isolation level first, or specify only the access mode, or only the isolation level. For example,

```
#sql { SET TRANSACTION READ WRITE };
#sql { SET TRANSACTION ISOLATION LEVEL SERIALIZABLE };
#sql { SET TRANSACTION READ WRITE, ISOLATION LEVEL SERIALIZABLE };
#sql { SET TRANSACTION ISOLATION LEVEL READ COMMITTED, READ WRITE };
```

NOTE
In SQLJ, both the access mode and the isolation level can be set in a single SET TRANSACTION statement.

Transaction Access Mode Settings

The access_mode settings are as follows:

- **READ WRITE (default)**   In a READ WRITE transaction, the user is allowed to update the database. SELECT, INSERT, UPDATE, and DELETE are all legal.

- **READ ONLY (not supported by Oracle JDBC)**   In a READ ONLY transaction, the user is not allowed to update the database. SELECT is legal, but INSERT, UPDATE, DELETE, and SELECT FOR UPDATE are not.

Transaction Isolation Level Settings

The READ COMMITTED, SERIALIZABLE, READ UNCOMMITTED, and REPEATABLE READ isolation level settings (where supported) operate in the following fashion:

- **READ COMMITTED (default for Oracle8***i***)**   Dirty reads are prevented; non-repeatable reads and phantom reads are allowed. If the transaction contains DML statements that require row locks held by other transactions, then any of the statements will block until the row lock it needs is released by the other transaction.

- **REPEATABLE READ (not supported by Oracle8***i***)**   Dirty reads and non-repeatable reads are prevented; phantom reads are allowed.

- **SERIALIZABLE**   Dirty reads, nonrepeatable reads, and phantom reads are all prevented. Any DML statements in the transaction cannot update any resource that might have had changes committed after the transaction began. Such DML statements will fail.

The COMMIT and ROLLBACK Clauses

The COMMIT and ROLLBACK clauses are used for transaction control. You can use these transaction control statements if auto-commit is set to false (see "Database Connections" in this appendix):

```
// USE COMMIT to commit any changes that have been executed since
// the last commit.
#sql { COMMIT };
// Use ROLLBACK to cancel any changes that have been executed since
// the last commit.
#sql { ROLLBACK };
```

NOTE
Do not use the COMMIT or ROLLBACK clauses if the auto-commit flag is enabled. This will result in unspecified behavior (or perhaps SQL exceptions). See Chapter 10 for more information.

The Procedure Clause

You can use the CALL token to call stored procedures from a database, as described in Chapters 1 and 3:

```
#sql { CALL PROCEDURE_NAME(<PARAM_LIST>) };
```

As in the example:

```
// Assume that there is a PL/SQL stored procedure named
// InsertPurchaseOrder() in the database. Use CALL to access it.
int newOrderNbr;
...
#sql {CALL InsertPurchaseOrder ( :newOrderNbr ) };  // Procedure call
```

The Function Clause

You can use the VALUES token to call stored functions from a database. Because functions have return values, you have to have a result expression in your SQLJ executable statement (see Chapters 1 and 3 for more on functions):

```
#sql result = { VALUES(FUNCTION_NAME(<PARAM_LIST>)) };
```

As in the example:

```
...
// Assume that there is a stored function named InsertPurchaseOrder()
// in the database. Use VALUES to call it.
int empInsertSuccess;
#sql empInsertSuccess = { VALUES (InsertPurchaseOrder
                ( 1111, 'Smith', 'Michelle', '(305)555-0359', 15 ) };
```

The Assignment Clause: SET

The *assignment* statement allows you to assign Java host variable values to the SET token, as described in Chapter 3:

```
// SQLJ executable statements setting host variables
#sql { SET :hostvariable = expression };
```

The following example uses two stored functions to calculate the cost of an item and assign the results in the host variable cost:

```
double cost;
...
#sql { SET :cost = GetUnitPrice() * GetQuantity()};
```

PL/SQL Blocks

SQLJ allows you to include PL/SQL blocks as executable statements. The PL/SQL block is contained within the curly braces (see Chapters 1 and 2 and Appendix A for more information):

```
// The <DECLARE ...> statement is optional for PL/SQL blocks
#sql { <DECLARE ...> BEGIN ... END; };
```

Here is an example of a PL/SQL block:

```
// SQLJ executable statement using an Oracle PL/SQL block
// to create observation ids in the OceanicObservationList table
#sql {
     DECLARE
          incrementNo   NUMBER;
     BEGIN
          incrementNo := 1;
          WHILE incrementNo <= 100 LOOP
               INSERT INTO OceanicObservationList(obs_id)
                    VALUES (2000 + incrementNo);
                incrementNo := incrementNo + 1;
          END LOOP;
     END;
     };
```

Database Connections

In this section, you will find topics for connecting and controlling database connections (see Chapters 2 and 5 for more details):

- Connections with the `DefaultContext` class
- Connections with the `ConnectionContext` class
- Control SQL operations with the `ExecutionContext` class
- Connection properties file

The `DefaultContext` Class

Use an instance of the `DefaultContext` class or one of the methods of the `oracle.sqlj.runtime.Oracle` class, the `connect()` or the `getConnection()` methods, to establish database connections, as described in Chapter 5.

A Single, Static Connection

This sets *the* SQLJ default context instance. There is only one such static instance per JavaVM. For single connections, you can use the `Oracle.connect()` method by specifying the URL, username, password, and the optional `auto-commit` flag, or by specifying a connect.properties file (see the "Connection Properties File" section of this appendix and Chapters 2 and 5 for details):

```
Oracle.connect(NameOfClass.class, "connect.properties");
```

The NameOfClass.class in the previous example is the name of your class. You can also use the getClass() method from java.lang.Object in lieu of specifying the name of your class:

```
Oracle.connect(getClass(), "connect.properties");
```

The following statement uses the Oracle thin driver and specifies a URL, username, and password, respectively. By default, the auto-commit flag is set to false, as described in Chapters 2 and 5:

```
Oracle.connect(
    "jdbc:oracle:thin:@data-i.com:1521:ORCL", "scott", "tiger");
```

You can also specify the setting of the auto-commit flag. The following statement uses the Oracle oci8 driver and specifies a URL, username, password and auto-commit flag.

```
Oracle.connect(
    "jdbc:oracle:oci8:@data-i.com:1521:ORCL", "scott", "tiger", true);
```

Multiple Connections

You can create multiple instances of the DefaultContext class to connect to one or more schemas. You can use the oracle.getConnection() method to do so. See the "Selected sqlj.runtime Classes" section of this appendix and Chapter 5. For example,

```
DefaultContext conn1 =
    Oracle.getConnection("jdbc:oracle:thin:@data-i.com:1521:ORCL1",
        "username1", "password1");

DefaultContext conn2 =
    Oracle.getConnection("jdbc:oracle:thin:@db:1521:ORCL2",
        "username2", "password2");
```

Use the conn1 and the conn2 objects with square braces to execute SQL operations in different schemas located on data-i.com and db, respectively.

```
#sql [conn1] { SQL operation };
#sql [conn2] { SQL operation };
```

Use the `setDefaultContext()` method of the `DefaultContext` class to switch the (single, `static`) default connection from one schema to another:

```
// Set the default connection to conn2
DefaultContext.setDefaultContext(conn2);
#sql { SQL operation };  // This statement uses conn2

// Set the default connection to conn1
DefaultContext.setDefaultContext(conn1);
 #sql { SQL operation }; // This statement uses conn1
```

The `ConnectionContext` Interface

By declaring a context type, you obtain a class that implements this interface. Use a user-defined SQLJ context type to connect to a single database, as well as to several databases, described further in the "SQLJ Declarations" and "Connection Context Declaration" sections of this appendix and Chapter 5):

```
// A declared ConnectionContext class
#sql public context LocalHostConnContext;

// Syntax to instantiate a user-defined context class
LocalHostConnContext connDeclared = new LocalHostConnContext
    (url, username, password, autocommit);

//  For example,
LocalHostConnContext connDeclared = new LocalHostConnContext
  ("jdbc:oracle:thin:@localhost:1521:orcl", "scott", "tiger", true);

//  Associate the connection object with a SQL operation
#sql [connDeclared] { SQL operation };
```

The `ExecutionContext` Class

An *execution context* is an instance of the `sqlj.runtime.ExecutionContext` class, described in the "Selected `sqlj.runtime` Classes" section of this appendix and Chapter 5. The `ExecutionContext` class contains methods to help you control the execution of your SQL operations. A SQLJ operation is always associated with an instance of the `ExecutionContext` class. If you do not associate an `ExecutionContext` object explicitly with your SQLJ clause, the execution context instance associated with the connection context instance is used to execute this clause:

```
// Create an instance of the ExecutionContext class from the
// default connection.
```

```
ExecutionContext anExecCtx = new ExecutionContext();

// Explicit association of an instance of a connection context class
// and an explicit instance of an instance of the ExecutionContext
// class with a SQLJ statement
#sql [connDeclared, anExecCtx] emps =
    { SELECT lastname from EMPLOYEE_LIST};

// Implicit association of an instance of the default context class
// and an explicit instance of an instance of the ExecutionContext
// class with a SQLJ statement
#sql [anExecCtx] emps = { SELECT lastname from EMPLOYEE_LIST};

// Use the following statement to retrieve the current instance of
// the ExecutionContext class that is associated with the single,
// static instance of the DefaultContext.
ExecutionContext anExecCtx =
    DefaultContext.getDefaultContext().getExecutionContext();

// Wait only 3 seconds for operations to complete
anExecCtx.setQueryTimeout(3);

// Select employees using the execution context of default connection
// context
#sql [anExecCtx] emps = { SELECT lastname from EMPLOYEE_LIST};

// The statement above is equivalent to:
#sql emps = { SELECT lastname from EMPLOYEE_LIST};

System.out.println("There are " + anExecCtx.getUpdateCount() +
                   " employees");
```

Connection Properties File

You can set the parameters of the connect() method in a properties file, as described in Chapters 2 and 5. You use the connect() method to establish a connection with the database:

```
# An example of a properties file called "connect.properties"

# Filename: connect.properties
# A line that begins with a '#' is a comment line.
# Users should uncomment one of the following URLs or add their own.
# This example uses the oracle thin driver to connect to the database
sqlj.url=jdbc:oracle:thin:@localhost:1521:ORCL
```

```
#sqlj.url=jdbc:oracle:oci8:@
#sqlj.url=jdbc:oracle:oci7:@
#
# In the following two lines, enter the username and password
sqlj.user=scott
sqlj.password=tiger
```

Oracle9*i* SQLJ Support for Dynamic SQL

Oracle9*i* SQLJ includes extensions to support dynamic SQL. Dynamic SQL expressions embedded in SQLJ statements are referred to as *meta bind* expressions. To learn more about meta bind variables, see Chapter 6 and the *Oracle9*i *SQLJ Developer's Guide and Reference* manual.

Meta Bind Expressions

Use meta bind expressions for dynamic SQL in SQLJ statements where you would use static SQL clauses. A meta bind expression contains a Java identifier of type `String` or a string-valued Java expression that is interpreted at run time. If you want SQLJ to perform online semantics checking, you can optionally include in a meta bind expression some static SQL replacement code to be used for online checking during translation.

You can use a meta bind expression in place of any of the following:

- A table name

- A column name in a `SELECT` list (without the column alias, if one was specified)

- All or part of a `WHERE` clause condition

- A role, schema, catalog, or package name in a DDL or DML statement

- A SQL literal value or SQL expression

Meta Bind Syntax

Here is the general syntax of meta bind variables (spaces are optional):

```
:{ Java_bind_expression }
// or:
:{ Java_bind_expression :: SQL_replacement_code }
```

Java Bind Expression

A Java bind expression can be either of the following:

- A Java identifier of type `String`

- A Java expression that evaluates to a character string

The Java bind expressions within meta bind expressions are not enclosed within parentheses. This is because if there is SQL replacement code, the :: token acts as a separator between the Java bind expression and the SQL code; if there is no SQL replacement code, the closing (}) acts as a terminator. In either case, there is no ambiguity.

SQL Replacement Code

A SQL replacement code clause consists of a sequence of zero or more SQL tokens, with the following requirements and restrictions:

- It is subject to SQL syntax rules.

- Braces—{ and }—must occur in matching pairs (with the exception of those that are part of a SQL comment, constant, or identifier).

- There can be no SQLJ host expressions or nested meta bind expressions within the SQL instructions.

Here are some examples of SQLJ dynamic SQL:

```
String aNewTable = "Non_existing_table";
#sql anAccountIter =
            {SELECT accountno AS accno,
                     projectno AS projno, deptno AS departmentno
             FROM :{aNewTable :: ACCOUNT_LIST}
             WHERE deptno >= 200 :{andClause}
             };
// At compilation time, the above will be replaced with the following:
#sql anAccountIter =
            {SELECT accountno AS accno,
                     projectno AS projno, deptno AS departmentno
             FROM ACCOUNT_LIST
             WHERE deptno >= 200 and deptno <= 201
```

```
// SQLJ executable statements with no online semantics-checking
// Declare a Java variable to hold the name of a table.
String aTable = "ACCOUNT_LIST";
#sql { INSERT INTO :{aTable}
       VALUES (:accountno, :projectno, :departmentno )
     };

// Use of Java bind expression in SELECT statement
// Select account info
#sql {SELECT projectno, deptno INTO :projectno,:departmentno
          FROM :{aTable}
          WHERE accountno = :accountno
          };
// Assume that accountno, projectno, and departmentno are
// Java variables where
// accountno = 1020, projectno = 300, and departmentno = 200
// At runtime, the above SQL operation becomes:

INSERT INTO ACCOUNT_LIST VALUES ( 1020, 300, 200 );

// SQLJ executable statements with online semantics-checking
// Use :: sql_replacement_code to enable semantics-checking
// of dynamic SQL.
String anotherTable = "A_SPECIFIC_TABLE";
#sql { INSERT INTO :{ anotherTable :: ACCOUNT_LIST }
        VALUES (:accountno, :projectno, :departmentno )
     };
// At translation time, the above SQL operation becomes:
INSERT INTO ACCOUNT_LIST VALUES ( 1020, 300, 200 );

// At runtime, the above SQL operation becomes:
INSERT INTO A_SPECIFIC_TABLE VALUES ( 1020, 300, 200 );
// The above may NOT be what you want.
```

Selected `sqlj.runtime` Classes

This section lists the methods of the following classes. See the [ORACLE_HOME]/
sqlj/doc directory to learn about all the SQLJ classes.

- `sqlj.runtime.ref.DefaultContext`
- `sqlj.runtime.ExecutionContext`

The `sqlj.runtime.ref.DefaultContext` Class

The `DefaultContext` class provides a complete implementation of the `ConnectionContext` interface. This is the same class definition that would have been generated by the reference translator from the following declaration:

```
// Remember: You must import this package.
import sqlj.runtime.ref;
#sql public context DefaultContext;
```

The `DefaultContext` class contains the following useful methods:

- **getConnection()** Gets the underlying JDBC `Connection` object. You can also use the `setAutoCommit()` method of the underlying JDBC Connection object to set the `auto-commit` flag for the connection.

- **setDefaultContext(DefaultContext ctx)** This is a static method that sets the single, static default context instance your application uses; it takes a `DefaultContext` instance as input. SQLJ executable statements that do not specify a connection context instance will use the default context that you define with this method (or that you define using `Oracle.connect()`).

- **getDefaultContext()** This is a static method that returns the `DefaultContext` instance currently defined as the default context for your application (through the earlier use of the `setDefaultContext()` class method). The `getDefaultContext()` method returns `null` if `setDefaultContext()` was not previously called. Note that, when you are executing in the server-side JavaVM, the `getDefaultContext()` method does not return `null`, even if `setDefaultContext()` was not previously called.

- **getExecutionContext()** A method that returns the default `ExecutionContext` instance for this connection context instance.

- **close(boolean [CLOSE_CONNECTION/KEEP_CONNECTION])** Use this method to close a connection and release all resources.

The `sqlj.runtime.ExecutionContext` Class

The `ExecutionContext` class contains methods for execution control, execution status, and execution cancellation. See Chapters 5, 7, and 10 for more information.

This section lists the methods of the `ExecutionContext` class and categorizes them as

- Status methods
- Control methods
- Cancellation methods

Status Methods

You can use the following methods to obtain status information about the most recent SQL operation:

- **`getWarnings()`** Returns a `java.sql.SQLWarning` object containing the warnings reported by the last SQL operation that completed using this context, or returns `null` if no warning occurred. The SQL Warning object ultimately represents all warnings generated during the execution of the SQL operation and the subsequent outputting of parameters to the output host expressions. Note that the Oracle JDBC driver does not return SQLWarnings.

- **`getUpdateCount()`** Returns the number of rows updated by the last SQL operation executed using this execution context instance. Zero (0) is returned if the last SQL operation was not a DML statement. The value of the constant `QUERY_COUNT` is returned if the last SQL operation produced an iterator or result set. The constant value of the `EXCEPTION_COUNT` is returned if the last SQL operation terminated before completing execution, or if no operation has yet been attempted using this execution context instance.

Use the following constant values to decode the value returned by the `getUpdateCount()` method:

- **`NEW_BATCH_COUNT`** Indicates that a new batch was created in the last statement encountered

- **`ADD_BATCH_COUNT`** Indicates that the last statement encountered was added to an existing batch

- **`EXEC_BATCH_COUNT`** Indicates that after the last statement encountered, a pending batch was executed either implicitly or explicitly

To refer to the NEW_BATCH_COUNT, ADD_BATCH_COUNT, and ADD_BATCH_COUNT constants, use the ExecutionContext qualified name. For example,

```
ExecutionContext.NEW_BATCH_COUNT
ExecutionContext.ADD_BATCH_COUNT
ExecutionContext.EXEC_BATCH_COUNT
```

Control Methods

Use the following methods of an execution context instance to control the operation of future SQL operations executed using that instance (operations that have not yet started).

- **getMaxFieldSize()** Returns an int specifying the maximum amount of data (in bytes) that would be returned from a SQL operation subsequently using this execution context. This applies only to columns of type BINARY, VARBINARY, LONGVARBINARY, CHAR, VARCHAR, or LONGVARCHAR (see tables in the "Supported Types for Host Expressions" section of this appendix). By default, this parameter is set to zero (0), meaning there is no size limit.

- **setMaxFieldSize()** Takes an int as input to modify the field-size maximum.

- **getMaxRows()** Returns an int specifying the maximum number of rows that can be contained by any SQLJ iterator or JDBC result set created using this execution context instance. If the limit is exceeded, the excess rows are silently dropped without any error report or warning. By default, this parameter is set to zero (0), meaning there is no row limit.

- **setMaxRows()** Takes an int as input to modify the row maximum.

- **getQueryTimeout()** Returns an int specifying the timeout limit, in seconds, for any SQL operation that uses this execution context instance. (This can be modified using the setQueryTimeout() method.) If a SQL operation exceeds this limit, a SQL exception is thrown. By default, this parameter is set to zero (0), meaning there is no query timeout limit.

- **setQueryTimeout()** Takes an int as input to modify the query timeout limit.

Cancellation Method

The cancel() method can be used to cancel SQL operations in a multithreading environment. This method is used by one thread to cancel a SQL operation currently being executed by another thread. It cancels the most recent operation that has started but not completed using this execution context instance. This method has no effect if no statement is currently being executed using this execution context instance.

Supported Types for Host Expressions

In this section, you will find the following supported SQLJ type host expressions:

- Standard JDBC types
- Java wrapper classes
- Oracle extensions
- SQLJ stream classes

Standard JDBC Types and JDBC 2.0 Types

Oracle JDBC and SQLJ support JDBC 2.0 types in the standard `java.sql` package. Table D-1 summarizes the JDBC types that are supported by SQLJ.

Standard JDBC 1.1.x Types	Oracle Java Type Constant	Oracle SQL Type
Boolean	BIT	NUMBER
Byte	TINYINT	NUMBER
Short	SMALLINT	NUMBER
int	INTEGER	NUMBER
Long	BIGINT	NUMBER
Float	REAL	NUMBER
Double	FLOAT, DOUBLE	NUMBER
java.lang.String	CHAR	CHAR
java.lang.String	VARCHAR	VARCHAR2
java.lang.String	LONGVARCHAR	LONG
Byte[]	BINARY	RAW
Byte[]	VARBINARY	RAW
Byte[]	LONGVARBINARY	LONGRAW

TABLE D-1.   *Standard JDBC and JDBC 2.0 Types*

Standard JDBC 1.1.x Types	Oracle Java Type Constant	Oracle SQL Type
java.sql.Date	DATE	DATE
Java.sql.Time	TIME	DATE
Java.sql.Timestamp	TIMESTAMP	DATE
Java.math.BigDecimal	NUMERIC	NUMBER
Java.math.BigDecimal	DECIMAL	NUMBER
Standard JDBC 2.0 Types	**Oracle Java Type Constant**	**Oracle SQL Type**
java.sql.Blob	BLOB	BLOB
java.sql.Clob	CLOB	CLOB
java.sql.Struct	STRUCT	STRUCT
java.sql.Ref	REF	REF
java.sql.Array	ARRAY	ARRAY
Custom object classes implementing java.sql.SQLData	STRUCT	STRUCT

TABLE D-1. *Standard JDBC and JDBC 2.0 Types* (continued)

Java Wrapper Classes

Since Java primitive types cannot contain null values, you can use the corresponding Java classes, as shown in Table D-2, when the database may return a null value.

Java Type	Oracle Java Type Constant	Oracle SQL Type
java.lang.Boolean	BIT	NUMBER
java.lang.Byte	TINYINT	NUMBER

TABLE D-2. *Java Wrapper Classes*

Java Type	Oracle Java Type Constant	Oracle SQL Type
java.lang.Short	SMALLINT	NUMBER
java.lang.Integer	INTEGER	NUMBER
java.lang.Long	BIGINT	NUMBER
java.lang.Float	REAL	NUMBER
java.lang.Double	FLOAT, DOUBLE	NUMBER

TABLE D-2.   *Java Wrapper Classes* (continued)

Oracle Extensions

The oracle.sql classes are wrappers for the SQL data and provide appropriate mappings and conversion methods to Java formats. Because data in an oracle.sql.* object remains in SQL format, no precision information is lost. When you use Java variables in your SQLJ program, the SQL output is converted to a corresponding Java data type, shown in Table D-3, and the SQL input is converted to a corresponding Oracle data type. Note that, in Oracle 9*i* and later CustomDatum is being deprecated in favor of ORAData.

Oracle Extensions	OracleTypes Definition	Oracle SQL Type
oracle.sql.NUMBER	NUMBER	NUMBER
oracle.sql.CHAR	CHAR	CHAR
oracle.sql.RAW	RAW	RAW

TABLE D-3.   *Oracle Extensions*

Oracle Extensions	OracleTypes Definition	Oracle SQL Type
oracle.sql.DATE	DATE	DATE
oracle.sql.ROWID	ROWID	ROWID
oracle.sql.BLOB	BLOB	BLOB
oracle.sql.CLOB	CLOB	CLOB
oracle.sql.BFILE	BFILE	BFILE
oracle.sql.STRUCT	STRUCT	STRUCT
oracle.sql.REF	REF	REF
oracle.sql.ARRAY	ARRAY	ARRAY
Custom object classes implementing oracle.sql.CustomDatum	STRUCT	STRUCT
Custom object classes implementing oracle.sql.CustomDatum	REF	REF
Custom object classes implementing oracle.sql.CustomDatum	ARRAY	ARRAY
Any other custom Java classes implementing oracle.sql.CustomDatum (to wrap any oracle.sql type)	Any	Any
QUERY RESULT OBJECTS		
java.sql.ResultSet	CURSOR	CURSOR
SQLJ iterator objects	CURSOR	CURSOR

TABLE D-3.   *Oracle Extensions* (continued)

NOTE
Numeric types in the Oracle database are stored as a NUMBER. When retrieving data from the Oracle database and converting to Java types, precision may be lost when using the Oracle JDBC drivers. Therefore, depending on the use, you might want to use the oracle.sql.NUMBER *to preserve the precision.*

Oracle SQLJ Support for JDBC 2.0 Types

The following JDBC 2.0 types are currently *not* supported in Oracle JDBC or SQLJ:

- ■ **JAVA_OBJECT**   Represents an instance of a Java type in a SQL column.
- ■ **DISTINCT**   A distinct SQL type represented in or retrievable from a basic SQL type (for example, SHOESIZE --> NUMBER).

Table D-4 lists the JDBC 2.0 types that Oracle SQLJ supports.

JDBC 2.0 Types	Oracle Extensions
java.sql.Blob	oracle.sql.BLOB
java.sql.Clob	oracle.sql.CLOB
java.sql.Struct	oracle.sql.STRUCT
java.sql.Array	oracle.sql.ARRAY
java.sql.Ref	java.sql.REF
java.sql.SQLData	oracle.sql.CustomDatum (where_SQL_TYPECODE = OracleTypes.STRUCT)

TABLE D-4.   *Correlation Between Oracle Extensions and JDBC 2.0 Types*

Requirements for Classes Implementing `SQLData`

Classes that implement `SQLData` must satisfy the requirements for type map definitions as outlined in the SQLJ ISO standard. Alternatively, `SQLData` wrapper classes can identify the associated SQL object type through a `public static final` field. This nonstandard functionality was introduced in SQLJ version 8.1.6 and continues to be supported. In both cases, you must run your SQLJ application under JDK 1.2 or later.

Note that `SQLData`, unlike `CustomDatum`, is for mapping structured object types only. It is not for object references, collections/arrays, or any other SQL types. If you are not using `CustomDatum`, then your only choices for mapping object references and collections are the weak types `java.sql.Ref` and `java.sql.Array`, respectively (or `oracle.sql.REF` and `oracle.sql.ARRAY`). `SQLData` implementations require a JDK 1.2.*x* environment. Although Oracle JDBC supports JDBC 2.0 extensions under JDK 1.1.*x* through the `oracle.jdbc2` package, Oracle SQLJ does not.

SQLJ Stream Classes

Standard SQLJ provides Binary, ASCII, and Unicode classes (Table D-5), for convenient handling of long data in streams (see Chapter 7).

Java Type	OracleTypes Definition	Oracle Datatype
`sqlj.runtime.` `BinaryStream`	LONGVARBINARY	LONG RAW
`sqlj.runtime.` `AsciiStream`	LONGVARCHAR	LONG
`sqlj.runtime.` `UnicodeStream`	LONGVARCHAR	LONG

TABLE D-5. *SQLJ Stream Classes*

Tools

This section discusses the SQLJ, EJB, and CORBA tools. For more information, see the *Oracle Java Tools Reference Guide*.

- SQLJ Translator tool: `sqlj`
- Java Archive tool: `jar`
- JPublisher tool: `jpub`
- Load Java tool: `loadjava`
- Drop Java tool: `dropjava`
- Enterprise JavaBeans tool: `deployejb`
- Session Namespace tool: `publish`

NOTE
The tables presented in this appendix list the options of Oracle8i release 8.1.7. For a list of options for earlier releases of the Oracle database, please consult the Oracle documentation related to your specific release.

SQLJ Translator Tool: `sqlj`

The Oracle `sqlj` tool is used for translating SQLJ source codes and invoking the Java compiler (see Chapter 2). The syntax for the `sqlj` tool at the command line is

```
sqlj <option-list> file-list
```

The `option-list` is a list of SQLJ option settings separated by spaces (see Table D-6). The `file-list` is the list of files, `.sqlj`, `.java`, `.ser`, or `.jar`, separated by spaces. The `*` wildcard entry can be used in filenames.

The following example does not run the customize profile; it converts the `.ser` files to `.class` files, and sets the output directory for the `.class` files to `dist` (see Chapters 4 and 5 for more information):

```
sqlj -profile=false -ser2class -d=dist PIManager.sqlj
SqljInJavaApplet.java
```

Options	Descriptions	Default
-C <option>	Passes <option> to javac compiler.	n/a
-cache	Enables caching of the results generated by the online checker. This avoids additional database connections during subsequent SQLJ translation runs. The analysis results are cached in a file, SQLChecker.cache, which is placed in your current directory.	false
-checkfilename	Specifies whether a warning is issued during translation if a source file name does not correspond to the name of the public class (if any) defined there true Environment.	true (Oracle9*i*)
-checksource= true/false	Instructs SQLJ type resolution. To examine source files as well as class files or files specified on the SQLJ command line.	true
-classpath command- line only)	Specifies CLASSPATH to Java VM and Java compiler (passed to javac).	None
-codegen	Specifies type of code generation: Iso for standard SQLJ code generation; oracle for Oracle-specific code generation with direct Oracle JDBC calls Iso Basic.	Iso (Oracle9*i*)
-compile=false	Do not compile generated Java files.	true (Oracle9*i*)
-compiler- executable	Specifies the Java compiler to use javac Environment.	javac (Oracle9*i*)
-compiler- encoding-flag	Tells SQLJ whether to pass the flag to tell SQLJ whether to pass the encoding setting (if that option is set) to the Java compiler.	true (Oracle9*i*)

TABLE D-6. *sqlj* *Options List*

Options	Descriptions	Default
-d=<directory>	Sets output directory for profile (`.ser`) files generated by SQLJ and `.class` files generated by the compiler (passed to `javac`) empty (use directory of `.java` files for `.class` files; use directory of `.sqlj` files for `.ser` files).	Empty
-dir	Sets output directory for generated `.ser` and `.class` binary files	Empty
-driver	Specifies JDBC driver to register.	oracle.jdbc. driver. OracleDriver
-explain= true/false	The –explain flag instructs the SQLJ translator to include "cause" and "action" information (as available) with translator error message output (for the first occurrence of each error).	False
-encoding -encoding=SJIS -encoding SJIS	Specifies encoding for SQLJ input and output source files, if setting `sqlj.encoding` in a properties file.	
-g	(Command line only) passed to `javac`; enables `-linemap` n/a `javac` compatible.	
-help	Instructs SQLJ to display varying levels of information about SQLJ options.	
-help-long	Instructs SQLJ to display varying levels of information about SQLJ options.	
-help-alias	Instructs SQLJ to display varying levels of information about SQLJ options.	
-P-help -C-help	Requests help through –P and –C to receive information about the profile customizer or Java compiler.	
-profile= true/false	Limits this processing, directing the SQLJ startup script to skip the indicated process. To enable or disable processing of generated profile (`.ser`) files by the SQLJ profile customizer.	

TABLE D-6. *sqlj* Options List (continued)

Options	Descriptions	Default
`-linemap=` `true/false`	Enables line mapping from the generated Java `.class` file back to the `.sqlj` source file	False
`-jdblinemap=` `true/false`	Use `-jdblinemap` in conjunction with the Sun Microsystems `jdb` debugger; otherwise, use `-linemap`.	False
`-n`	Instructs the `sqlj` script to construct the full command line that would be passed to the SQLJ translator, including any `SQLJ_OPTIONS` settings, and echo it to the user without having the SQLJ translator execute it. This includes capturing and echoing the name of the JVM that would be launched to execute the SQLJ translator and echoing the full class name of the translator. This does not include settings from properties files.	

`-offline`	Specifies characteristics of online and offline semantics checking. It specifies a Java class that implements the semantics checking component of SQLJ for offline checking.	`Oracle.sqlj.`
		`checker.`
		`OracleChecker`

`-online`	Specifies characteristics of online and offline semantics checking	`oracle.sqlj.`
		`checker.`
		`OracleChecker`

`-optcols`	Enables iterator column type and size definitions to optimize performance (used with Oracle-specific code generation only; otherwise, use equivalent Oracle customizer option).	`false` (Oracle9*i*)
`-optparams`	Enables parameter size definitions to optimize JDBC resource allocation (used with `-optparamdefaults`; used with Oracle-specific code generation only; otherwise, use equivalent Oracle customizer option).	`false` (Oracle9*i*)
`-optparamdefaults`	Sets parameter size defaults for particular datatypes (used with `-optparams`; used with Oracle-specific code generation only; otherwise, use equivalent Oracle customizer option).	`false` (Oracle9*i*)

TABLE D-6.   `sqlj` *Options List* (continued)

Options	Descriptions	Default
`-vm=echo`	Alternative to –n option.	
`-P<option>`	Prefix that marks options to pass to SQLJ profile customizer.	n/a
`Password= <password>`	Sets user password for database connection for online semantics checking.	None
`-profile=false`	Do not customize generated `*.ser` profile files.	True
`-props`	Specifies properties file (see SQLJ properties files).	None
`-ser2class`	Converts generated `*.ser` files to `*.class` files.	False
`-status, -v`	Prints status during translation.	False
`-url=<url>`	Specifies URL for online checking.	`jdbc:oracle: oci8:@`
`-user, -u- password-default- url-prefix`	Enables online checking.	none (no online semantics checking)
`-verbose` (command line only)	Passed to `javac`; enables –`status`.	n/a
`-version`	Displays varying levels of information about SQLJ and JDBC driver versions.	
`-version-long`	Displays varying levels of information about SQLJ and JDBC driver versions.	
`-warn`	Comma-separated list of flags to enable or disable various warnings—individual flags are `precision/noprecision`, `nulls/nonulls`, `portable /noportable`, `strict/nostrict`, and `verbose/noverbose`; global flag is `all/none`.	`Precision nulls noportable strict noverbose`
Advanced Translator Options	Flags marking options to be passed to the Java interpreter, Java compiler, and SQLJ profile customizer.	
`-J`	Marks options for Java interpreter from which SQLJ was invoked.	

TABLE D-6. *sqlj Options List* (continued)

Options	Descriptions	Default
-C	Marks options for Java interpreter invoked from the sqlj script.	
-P	Marks options for profile customizer. To pass generic options to the customizer harness that apply regardless of the customizer.	
-P-C	Passes vendor-specific options to the particular customizer you are using.	

TABLE D-6. *sqlj Options List* (continued)

Translator Properties File

You can supply a SQLJ properties file to the SQLJ translator instead of supplying options as arguments at the command line. When the SQLJ translator is invoked, it always searches for the *default* properties file sqlj.properties. The translator looks for this properties file in the following order: the Java home directory, the user home directory, and the current directory.

The properties.file rules and syntax are these:

■ You cannot use the following options in the sqlj.properties files: -classpath, -help, -help-long, -help-alias, -C-help, -P-help, -J, -n, -passes, -props, -version, -version-long, and -vm.

■ Each SQLJ option is prefixed by sqlj, for example,

```
sqlj.warn=none
sqlj.linemap=true
```

■ Each Java compiler option is prefixed by compile, instead of -C-, for example,

```
compile.verbose
```

■ General profile customization options are prefixed by profile, instead of -P-, for example,

```
profile.backup
```

The following is a sample sqlj.properties file that uses the default context:

```
# A line that begins with a '#' is a comment line.
# Set user/password and JDBC driver
sqlj.user=scott/tiger
sqlj.driver=oracle.jdbc.driver.OracleDriver
# Turn on the compiler verbose option
compile.verbose
```

Java Archive Tool: `jar`

The `jar` tool, whose options are shown in Table D-7, is an archive utility that combines (archives) multiple files into a single file with a `.jar` extension. This Java application tool is mainly used to facilitate the packaging of Java applets or applications into a single archive file. The following is the syntax for the SUN JDK `jar` utility:

```
jar {ctxu}[vfmOM] [jar-file] [manifest-file] file1, file2, …
```

Option	Description
-c	Create new archive.
-C	Change to the specified directory and include the following file.
-t	List table of contents for archive.
-u	Update existing archive.
-x filename	Extract named (or all) files from archive.
-v	Generate verbose output on standard error.
-f	Specify archive filename.
-m	Include manifest information from specified manifest file.
-0	Store only; use no ZIP compression; `.jar` file that can be put in your CLASSPATH.
-M	Do not create a manifest file for the entries.

TABLE D-7. *jar Options List*

The following example combines all the files containing .class and .ser extensions into an uncompressed .jar archive file named Platform.jar (see Chapter 5):

```
jar -cvf0 Platform.jar *.class *.ser
```

The following example creates a .jar archive file called jarfile2.jar and combines all the files of directory dir1 and all the files with the extension of .class from the directory dir2:

```
jar -cvf0 jarfile2.jar dir1 dir2/*.class
```

JPublisher Tool: jpub

The jpub tool (see Table D-8) is used to automatically generate custom Java classes For more information, see Chapters 7 and 8 and the *Oracle JPublisher User's Guide*. This tool connects to a database and retrieves the declarations of the SQL object types or PL/SQL packages that you specify on the command line or from an input file. The syntax for invoking the JPublisher tool is

```
jpub <options>
```

Option	Description	Default Value
-access	Determines the access modifiers that JPublisher includes in generated method definitions.	public (JPublisher 9*i*)
-builtintypes	Specifies the type mappings (jdbc or oracle) for non-numeric, non-LOB, built-in database types.	jdbc
-compatible	Specifies the interface to implement in generated classes for Oracle mapping of user-defined types— ORAData or CustomDatum (supported for backward compatibility); modifies the behavior of -usertypes=oracle.	Oradata (JPublisher 9*i*)

TABLE D-8.   *jpub Options List*

Option	Description	Default Value
-case=<case>	The Java identifiers that JPublisher generates. The <case> are mixed, same, lower, and upper, where the default is mixed.	mixed
-dir	The directory that holds generated packages.	Current directory
-driver	The JDBC driver JPublisher uses to connect to the database. The default driver is oracle.jdbc.driver.OracleDriver.	oracle.jdbc.driver.OracleDriver
-encoding	Specifies the Java encoding of JPublisher's input files and output files.	The value of the System property file.encoding
-input	The file that lists the types and packages JPublisher translates.	n/a
-lobtypes	Specifies the type mappings (jdbc or oracle) that JPublisher uses for BLOB and CLOB types.	oracle
-mapping	Specifies which object attribute type and method argument type mapping the generated methods support. The mapping types are oracle, jdbc, or objectjdbc. If no type is specified, then it assumes objectjdbc.	objectjdbc
-methods	Determines whether JPublisher generates classes for PL/SQL packages and wrapper methods for methods in packages and object types. If -methods=false, JPublisher does not generate PL/SQL classes and methods. The default is −methods=false.	all
-numbertypes	Specifies the type mappings (jdbc, objectjdbc, bigdecimal, or oracle) JPublisher uses for numeric database types.	objectjdbc

TABLE D-8.   *jpub Options List* (continued)

Option	Description	Default Value
`-omit_schema_` `names`	Specifies whether all object type and package names generated by JPublisher include the schema name.	Do not omit schema names
`-package`	The name of the Java package for which JPublisher is generating a Java wrapper.	n/a
`-props=<filename>`	Specifies a file that contains JPublisher options in addition to those listed on the command line.	n/a
`-sql`	Specifies object types and packages for which JPublisher will generate code.	n/a
`-types`	Specifies object types for which JPublisher will generate code. Note that the `-types` parameter is currently supported for compatibility, but deprecated in favor of `-sql`.	
`-url`	Specifies the URL JPublisher uses to connect to the database. The default is `-url=jdbc:oracle:` `oci8:@sid`.	`jdbc:oracle:oci8:@`
`-user=<user/` `password>`	An Oracle username and password. This must be supplied.	n/a
`-usertypes`	Specifies the type mappings (`jdbc` or `oracle`) JPublisher uses for used-defined database types	`oracle`

TABLE D-8.   *jpub Options List* (continued)

The following example causes JPublisher to connect to the database with username `scott` and password `tiger`. The `-mapping` option instructs JPublisher to map the object attribute types from the Oracle database into Java classes. Note that the `-mapping` option is being deprecated for `jpub`. With the `-package` option, JPublisher places the Java-generated classes in the package `corp`. The `–dir` places all output in the `demo` directory:

```
jpub -user=scott/tiger -dir=demo -mapping=oracle -package=com.data-i
-types=PlatformType
```

JPublisher Properties File

Aside from passing command-line parameters to the `jpub` tool, you can optionally use a properties file to specify parameters. This is accomplished by specifying the `-props` parameter with a text file:

```
jpub -props=jpublisher.properties
```

The following shows an example of the `jpublisher.properties` file:

```
# Filename: jpublisher.properties
# A line that begins with a '#' is a comment line.
jpub.user=scott/tiger
jpub.types=Employee
jpub.mapping=oracle
jpub.case=lower
jpub.package=corp
jpub.dir=demo
```

Using the previous `jpublisher.properties` file with the `jpub` tool is equivalent to the following:

```
jpub -user=scott/tiger -types=Employee -mapping=oracle -case=lower
-package=corp -dir=demo
```

Load Java Tool: `loadjava`

Use the `loadjava` tool, whose options are listed in Table D-9, to load resource files into the Oracle8*i* or 9*i* database. The `loadjava` tool creates schema objects from files and loads them into a schema, as described in Chapters 4, 5, and 8. You must have the CREATE PROCEDURE privilege to load files into your schema, and the CREATE ANY PROCEDURE privilege to load files into another schema. The syntax for the `loadjava` tool is

```
loadjava {-user | -u} <user>/<password>[@<database>] [options]
<file>.java | <file>.class | <file>.jar | <file>.zip |
<file>.sqlj | <resourcefile> …

   [-debug]
   [-d | -definer]
   [-e | -encoding <encoding_scheme>]
   [-f | -force]
   [-g | -grant <user> [, <user>]…]
   [-help]
   [-nohelp]
   [-o | -oci8]
```

```
[ -order ]
[-noverify]
[-r | -resolve]
[-R | -resolver "resolver_spec"]
[-S | -schema <schema>]
[ -stdout ]
[-s | -synonym]
[-tableschema <schema>]
[-t | -thin]
[-v | -verbose]
```

Option	Description
`<filenames>`	You can specify any number and combination of `.java`, `.class`, `.sqlj`, `.jar`, `.zip`, and resource filenames in any order. `.jar` and `.zip` files must be uncompressed.
`-debug`	Directs the Java compiler to generate debug information.
`-definer`	By default, class schema objects run with the privileges of their invoker. This option confers definer privileges upon classes instead.
`-encoding`	Identifies the source file encoding for the compiler, overriding the matching value, if any, in the `JAVA$OPTIONS` table. Values are the same as for the `javac –encoding` option. If you do not specify an encoding on the command line or in a `JAVA$OPTIONS` table, the encoding is assumed to be `latin1`. The –encoding option is relevant only when loading a source file.
`-force`	Forces files to be loaded even if they match digest table entries.
`-grant <grants>`	Grants the EXECUTE privilege on loaded classes to the listed users and/or roles. Any number and combination of user and role names can be specified, separated by commas but not spaces (`-grant Bob,Betty` not `-grant Bob, Betty`).
`-help`	Prints the usage message on how to use the `loadjava` tool and its options.
`-nohelp`	Suppresses the usage message that is given if either no option is specified or the –help option is specified.
`-noverify`	Causes the classes to be loaded without bytecode verification. You must be granted oracle.aurora.security.JserverPermission(Verifier) to execute this option. In addition, this option must be used in conjunction with –r.

TABLE D-9. *loadjava Options List*

Option	Description
-oci8	Use the OCI JDBC driver. −oci8 and −thin are mutually exclusive; if neither is specified, -oci8 is used by default.
-order	Directs loadjava to load the classes in an order that facilitates resolution of those classes. Classes are loaded in a manner where any dependent class is loaded before the class that includes it as a dependency.
-resolve	Compiles (if necessary) and resolves external references in classes after all classes on the command line have been loaded. −andresolve and −resolve are mutually exclusive.
-resolver \<resolver>	Use a resolver that requires all referred to classes to be found.
-schema	Designates the schema where schema objects are created. If not specified, the logon schema is used. To create a schema object in a schema that is not your own, you must have the CREATE PROCEDURE or CREATE ANY PROCEDURE privilege.
-stdout	Causes the output to be directed to stdout, rather than to stderr.
-synonym	Creates a PUBLIC synonym for loaded classes, making them accessible outside the schema into which they are loaded. You must have the CREATE PUBLIC SYNONYM privilege.
-tableschema \<schema>	Creates the loadjava internal tables within this specified schema, rather than in the Java file destination schema.
-thin	Use the thin JDBC driver. −oci8 and −thin are mutually exclusive; if neither is specified, -oci8 is used by default.
-user, -u	Specifies a user, password, and database connect string. The argument has the form \<username>/\<password> [@\<database>].
-verbose	Directs loadjava to emit detailed status messages while running.

TABLE D-9. *loadjava Options List* (continued)

The following example makes a connection to the default database with the default oci8 driver, loads the files contained in the PurchaseItems.jar file into the EMPLOYEE_LIST schema, and then resolves them:

```
loadjava −user scott/tiger −resolve
−schema EMPLOYEE_LIST PurchaseItems.jar
```

Next, connect with the thin driver and then load `TheSqljFile.sqlj` file, resolving it as it is loaded:

```
loadjava -thin -user scott/tiger@data-i.com:1521:ORCL
-resolve TheSqljFile.sqlj

// Use loadjava to upload a CORBA object
// into Oracle8i/Oracle9i database server
loadjava -verbose -resolve -thin -u
  obsschema/obsschema@datai:1521:orcl CorbaPlat.jar
```

Drop Java Tool: `dropjava`

Use the `dropjava` tool, whose options are listed in Table D-10, to remove Java schema objects from the data server. Chapters 4 and 8 of this book and the *Oracle8i Enterprise JavaBeans and CORBA Developer's Guide* can give you more information. This tool accomplishes the opposite of the `loadjava` tool. The syntax is

```
dropjava [options] {<file>.java | <file>.class | file.sqlj |
  <file>.jar | <file.zip> | <resourcefile>} …
-u | -user <user>/<password>[@<database>]
[-o | -oci8]
[-S | -schema <schema>]
[ -stdout ]
[-s | -synonym]
[-t | -thin]
[-v | -verbose]
```

Option	Description
`-user`	Specifies a user, password, and optional database connect string.
`<filenames>`	You can specify any number and combination of `.java`, `.class`, `.sqlj`, `.jar`, `.zip`, and resource filenames in any order. `.jar` and `.zip` files must be uncompressed.

TABLE D-10. *dropjava Options List*

Option	Description
-oci8	Use the OCI JDBC driver. −oci8 and −thin are mutually exclusive; if neither is specified, −oci8 is used by default.
-schema	Designates the schema from which schema objects are dropped. If not specified, the logon schema is used. To drop a schema object from a schema that is not your own, you need the DROP ANY PROCEDURE system privilege.
-stdout	Causes the output to be directed to stdout, rather than to stderr.
-synonym	Drops a PUBLIC synonym that was created with loadjava.
-thin	Use the thin JDBC driver. The -oci8 and -thin options are mutually exclusive; if neither is specified, then -oci8 is used by default.
-verbose	Directs dropjava to emit detailed status messages while running.

TABLE D-10.   *dropjava Options List* (continued)

The following example removes the objects created by loading the TheSqljFile.sqlj file with the loadjava tool. The database connection is made through the default oci8 driver.

```
dropjava -user scott/tiger TheSqljFile.sqlj
```

If you translated your program on the client and loaded it using a .jar file containing the generated components, then use the same .jar file to remove the program:

```
dropjava -user scott/tiger -schema EMPLOYEE_LIST PurchaseItems.jar
```

Enterprise JavaBeans Tool: `deployejb`

The deployejb tool, whose options are listed in Table D-11, reads the deployment descriptor and the bean .jar file containing interfaces and classes, as described in Chapter 8. The tool converts the text descriptor to a serialized object, generates and compiles classes that affect client-Bean communication, and loads compiled classes into the database. It also publishes the Bean's home interface name in the session namespace so clients can look it up through JNDI. Table D-11 lists the options of Oracle8*i* release 8.1.7. For a list of options for earlier releases of the Oracle database, please consult the Oracle documentation related to your specific release.

```
deployejb {-user | -u} <username> {-password | -p} <password>
{-service | -s} <serviceURL> -descriptor <file>
    -temp <work_dir> <beanjar>
    [-addclasspath <dirlist>]
    [-beanonly]
    [-credsFile <credentials>]
    [-describe | -d]
    [-generated <clientjar>]
    [-help | -h]
    [-iiop]
    [-keep]
    [-oracledescriptor <file>]
    [-republish]
    [-resolver "resolver_spec"]
    [-role <role>]
    [-ssl]
    [-useServiceName]
    [-verbose]
    [-version | -v]
```

Option	Description
-user <username>	Username.
-password <password>	Specifies the password for <username>.
-service	URL identifying database in whose session namespace the EJB is to be published. The service URL has the form sess_iiop://<host>:<lport>:<sid>.
-credsFile	Supply a text file with credentials instead of a username and password for the connect. You create this file by exporting a wallet into a text version.

TABLE D-11. *deployejb* Options List

Option	Description
-descriptor	Specifies the text file containing the EJB deployment descriptor.
-temp	Specifies a temporary directory to hold intermediate files deployejb creates. Unless you specify -keep, deployejb removes the files and the directory upon completion.
<beanjar>	Specifies the name of the .jar file containing the Bean interface and implementation files.
-addclasspath <dirlist>	Lists table of contents for archive.
-beanonly	Skips generation of interface files. Basically, this option enables you to reload the Bean implementation if none of the interfaces has changed.
-describe	Summarizes the tool's operation, and then exits.
-generated <clientjar>	Specifies the name of the output (generated) .jar file, which contains communication files Bean clients need.
-help	Summarizes the tool's operation, and then exits.
-iiop	Connects to the target database with IIOP instead of the default session IIOP.
-keep	Do not remove the temporary files generated by the tool.
-oracledescriptor	Specifies the text file containing the Oracle-specific deployment descriptor.
-republish	Replaces the published BeanHomeName attributes if it has already been published.
-resolver	Specifies an explicit resolver spec, which is bound to the newly loaded classes. If -resolver is not specified, the default resolver spec, which includes current user's schema and PUBLIC, is used. For more information, see the discussion on -resolve and -resolver in the earlier section "Load Java tool: loadjava."

TABLE D-11. *deployejb Options List* (continued)

Option	Description
-role \<role\>	Specifies role to assume when connecting to the database; no default.
-ssl	Connects to the database with SSL authentication and encryption.
-useServiceName	If you are using a service name instead of an SID in the URL, you must specify this flag. Otherwise, the tool assumes the last string in the URL is the SID.
-verbose	Emits detailed status information while running.
-version	Shows the tool's version, and then exits.

TABLE D-11. *deployejb* Options List (continued)

The following example uses the deployejb tool to generate the .jar file to use on the client side to access the Bean (see Chapter 8):

```
// Oracle8i release 8.1.5 and 8.1.6
deployejb -republish -temp /temp -u obsschema -p obsschema
-service sess_iiop://data-i.com:1521:ORCL
-descriptor Platform.ejb Platform.jar

// Oracle8i release 8.1.7 and Oracle9i
deployejb -republish -temp /temp -u obsschema -p obsschema
-service sess_iiop://data-i.com:1521:ORCL
-descriptor Platform.xml Platform.jar
```

ejbdescriptor Tool

The ejbdescriptor tool, whose options are listed in Table D-12, transforms a serialized deployment descriptor to text, and vice versa. Developers are most likely to use ejbdescriptor to extract the deployment descriptor data from an EJB developed for a non-Oracle environment. The deployejb tool calls ejbdescriptor to build a deployment descriptor from the text file you specify in the -descriptor argument.

```
ejbdescriptor [-options] <infile> <outfile>
    [-parse]
    [-parsexml]
```

```
[-dump]
[-dumpxml]
[-encoding]
```

Create a release 8.1.7 XML deployment descriptor from a release 8.1.6 .ejb deployment descriptor, as described in Chapter 9:

```
ejbdescriptor -dumpxml Platform.ejb Platform.xml
```

Option	Description
-parse	Creates serialized deployment descriptor <outfile> from a release 8.1.6 and previous .ejb text deployment descriptor specified in <infile>.
-parsexml	Creates the release 8.1.6 .ejb text deployment descriptor <outfile> from an XML deployment descriptor specified in <infile>.
-dump	Creates a release 8.1.6 .ejb deployment descriptor text file <outfile> from serialized deployment descriptor <infile>.
-dumpxml	Creates the release 8.1.7 XML deployment descriptor file <outfile> from a release 8.1.6 text deployment descriptor <infile>.
-encoding	Identifies the source file encoding for the compiler, overriding the matching value, if any, in the JAVA$OPTIONS table. Values are the same as for the javac -encoding option. If you do not specify an encoding on the command line or in a JAVA$OPTIONS table, the encoding is assumed to be latin1. The -encoding option is relevant only when loading a source file.
<infile>	Name of the file to parse or read. The default is standard in. The conventional suffix for a deployment descriptor file is .ejb or .xml; for a serialized descriptor, it is .ser.
<outfile>	Name of file to dump or write. The default is standard out. The conventional suffix for a deployment descriptor file is .ejb or .xml; for a serialized descriptor, it is .ser.

TABLE D-12. *ejbdescriptor Options List*

Create a release 8.1.6 deployment descriptor from an XML deployment descriptor:

```
ejbdescriptor -parsexml Platform.xml Platform.ser
```

Create a text file representation of a release 8.1.6 deployment descriptor:

```
ejbdescriptor -dump Platform.ser Platform.ejb
```

Create a serialized deployment descriptor from a release 8.1.6 deployment descriptor file:

```
ejbdescriptor -parse Platform.ejb Platform.ser
```

Display the contents of a release 8.1.6 deployment descriptor:

```
ejbdescriptor -dump Platform.ser
```

Session Namespace Tool: `publish`

The `publish` tool, whose options are listed in Table D-13, creates or replaces (republishes) a `PublishedObject` in a `PublishingContext`. For more information, see Chapter 9 and the *Oracle8i/9i Enterprise JavaBeans and CORBA Developer's Guide*. Use the command-line `publish` tool to create (publish) `PublishedObjects`:

```
publish [options] <name> <class> [<helper>]
      -user | -u <username> -password |-p <password>
      -service |-s <serviceURL>
```

where options are

```
[-describe | -d]
   [-g | -grant {<user> | <role>}[,{<user> | <role>}]...]
   [-recursiveGrant | -rg | -rG
      {<user> | <role>}[,{<user> | <role>}]...]
   [-h | -help]
   [-idl]
   [-iiop]
   [-replaceIDL]
   [-resolver]
   [-role <role>]
   [-republish]
   [-schema <schema>]
   [-ssl]
```

```
[-useServiceName]
[-version | -v]
```

Option	Description
<name>	Name of the `PublishedObject` being created or republished; `PublishingContexts` are created if necessary.
<class>	Name of the class schema object that corresponds to `<name>`.
<helper>	Name of the Java class schema object that implements the `narrow()` method for `<class>`.
-user <username>	Username.
-password <password>	Specifies authenticating password for specified `<username>`.
-service	URL identifying database whose session namespace is to be "opened" by `sess_sh`. The service URL has the form `sess_iiop://<host>:<lport>:<sid>`.
-describe	Summarizes the tool's operation and then exits.
-grant <schemas>	Grants read and execute rights to the list of schemas.
-help	Summarizes the tool's syntax and then exits.
-iiop	Connects to the target database with IIOP instead of the default session IIOP.
-role	Role to assume while publishing; no default.
-republish	Republish if object already exists. If the `PublishedObject` does not exist, `publish` creates it.
-schema schema	The schema containing the Java `<class>` schema object.
-ssl	Connects to the database with SSL server authentication.
-version	Shows the tool's version and then exits.

TABLE D-13. *publish Options List*

The following example publishes the CORBA server implementation
`platServer.PlatformCorbaImp` and its helper class `/test/`
`CorbaPlatformObj` in the tool invoker's schema:

```
publish -republish -u obsschema -p obsschema -schema OBSSCHEMA
-service sess_iiop://data-i.com:1521:ORCL
/test/CorbaPlatformObj platServer.PlatformCorbaImp
 corbaPlatform.PlatformCorbaHelper
```

Bibliography

A Brief Overview of JDBC, http://java.sun.com/products/jdbc/overview.html

Albertson, Tom, *Best Practices in Distributed Object Application Development: RMI, CORBA and DCOM (Part 1 of 4),* http://www.developer.com/news/techfocus/022398_dist1.html, February 1998

Albertson, Tom, *Distributed Object Application Development: The Java-RMI Solution (Part 2 of 4),* http://www.developer.com/news/techfocus/030298_dist2.html, March 1998

Albertson, Tom, *Distributed Object Application Development: The Java-CORBA solution (Part 3 of 4),* http://www.developer.com/news/techfocus/030998_dist3.html, March 1998

Astrahan, M.M. et al, *System R: Relational Approach to Database Management,* ACM TODS 1, No. 2 (June 1976)

Austin, Calvin and Monica Pawlan, *Writing Advanced Applications for the Java Platform,* http://developer.java.sun.com/developer/onlineTraining/Programming/JDCBook/index.html#contents, August 1999

Bauer, Mark, *Oracle8i/9i Tuning,* Oracle Corporation

Burghart, Ted, *Distributed Computing Overview,* http://www.quoininc.com/quoininc/dist_comp.html, 1998

Cafe au Lait Java FAQs, News, and Resources, http://metalab.unc.edu/javafaq

Chen, Peter Pin-Shan, *The Entity-Relationship Model—Toward a Unified View of Data,* ACM TODS 1, No. 1 (March 1976)

Coad, Peter, Mark Mayfield, and Jon Kern, *Java Design, Building Better Apps & Applets, Second Ed.,* Yourdon Press Computing Series, 1999

Codd, E.F., *A Relational Model of Data for Large Shared Data Banks,* CACM 13, No. 6 (June 1970)

CORBA 2.2 Specification, http://www.omg.org/corba/cichpter.html#idls&s, February 1998

Database Languages—SQL—Part 10: SQL/OLB (ANSI X3.135.10), American National Standards Institute, 1998

Date, C.J., *An Introduction to Database Systems, Sixth Ed.,* Addison-Wesley, 1995

Enterprise JavaBeans Tutorial: Building Your First Stateless Session Bean, http://developer.java.sun.com/developer/onlineTraining/Beans/EJBTutorial/index.html

Feldmann, Bronya and Jeff Stein, *Oracle 8i ProC Manual,* Oracle Corporation, 1999

Flanagan, David, *Java In A Nutshell,* O'Reilly, 1997

Gosling, James, Bill Joy, and Guy Steele, *The Java Language Specification, Version 1.0,* http://asuwlink.uwyo.edu/sun-jws/, 1996

Gray, Jim and Andreas Reuter, *Transaction Processing: Concepts and Techniques,* Morgan Kaufmann Publishers, San Mateo, CA, 1993

Hamilton, Graham, Rick Cattell, and Maydene Fisher, *JDBC Database Access with Java, A Tutorial and Annotated Reference,* Addison-Wesley, 1997

Harold, Elliotte Rusty, *Java I/O,* O'Reilly, 1999

Harris, Steven G., *Oracle 8i/9i Java Developer's Guide and Reference,* Oracle Corporation

Heller, Philip et al., *Java 1.1 Developer's Handbook,* Sybex, 1997

Java Naming Directory Interface (JNDI), http://java.sun.com/products/jndi/

Java Remote Method Invocation Specification 1.50, JDK 1.2, October 1998, http://java.sun.com/products/jdk/1.2/docs/guide/rmi/spec/rmiTOC.doc.html

JNDI 1.1 and 1.2 Documentation, http://java.sun.com/products/jndi/docs.html#12

Lorentz, Diana and Denise Oertel, *Oracle8i/9i SQL Reference,* Oracle Corporation

McClanahan, David, *Oracle Developer's Guide,* Oracle Press, Osborne/McGraw-Hill, 1996

Mohseni, Piroz, *Exploit Distributed Java Computing with RMI, NC World,* http://www.ncworldmag.com/ncw-01-1998/ncw-01-rmi.html, January 1998

Mohseni, Piroz, *Exploit Distributed Java Computing with RMI, Part II, NC World,* http://www.ncworldmag.com/ncw-02-1998/ncw-02-rmi2.html, February 1998

Momplaisir, Gerald, *Design of a Financial Administrative System Using the Semantic Binary Model,* Master's thesis, School of Computer Sciences, Florida International University, 1997

Monson-Haefel, Richard, *Enterprise JavaBeans,* O'Reilly & Associates, Inc., June 1999

Monson-Haefel, Richard, *Enterprise JavaBeans,* O'Reilly & Associates, Inc., June 2000

Morisseau-Leroy, Nirva, *Atmospheric Observations, Analyses, and The World Wide Web Using a Semantic Database,* Master's thesis, School of Computer Sciences, Florida International University, 1997.

Morisseau-Leroy, N., Solomon, M., Basu J., *Oracle8i Java Components,* Osborne/McGraw-Hill; ISBN: 0072127376, October 2000

Morisseau-Leroy, N., Solomon, M., Momplaisir, G., *Oracle8i SQLJ Programming,* Osborne/McGraw-Hill; ISBN: 0072121602, November 1999

Orfali, Robert, and Dan Harkey, *Client/Server Programming with Java and CORBA, Second Ed.,* John Wiley & Sons, 1998

Orfali, Robert, et al., *Instant CORBA,* John Wiley & Sons, 1997

Part 1—The Stored Procedure Specification, Part 2—The Stored Java Class Specification, http://www.oracle.com/java/sqlj/standards.html

Pfaeffle, Thomas, *Oracle8i/9i JDBC Developer's Guide and Reference,* Oracle Corporation, 2000-2001

Portfolio, Tom, *Oracle8/9ii Java Stored Procedures and Developer's Guide,* Oracle Corporation, 2000-2001

Portfolio, Tom, *PL/SLQ User's Guide and Reference,* Oracle Corporation, 2000-2001

Raphaely, Denis and Susan Kotsovolos, *Oracle8i/9i Application Developer's Guide—Large Objects (LOBs),* Oracle Corporation, 2000-2001

Raphaely, Denis, *Oracle8i/9i Application Developer's Guide— Fundamentals,* Oracle Corporation, 2000-2001

RMI over IIOP, http://java.sun.com/products/rmi-iiop/, June 1999

Schlicher, Bob, *Applying CORBA in the Enterprise,* http://developer. netscape.com/viewsource/schlicher_corba.html, 2/98

Schlicher, Bob, *CORBA in the Enterprise, Part 2: Prerequisites and Analysis,* http://developer.netscape.com/viewsource/schlicher_corba2/schlicher_ corba2.html

Schlicher, Bob, *CORBA in the Enterprise, Part 3: Object-Oriented System Design,* http://developer.netscape.com/viewsource/schlicher_corba3.html

Schlicher, Bob, *CORBA in the Enterprise, Part 4: Applying Object-Oriented and Component Design,* http://developer.netscape.com/viewsource/ schlicher_corba4/schlicher_corba4.html

Shah, Rawn, *Bean Basics: Enterprise JavaBeans Fundamentals, NC World,* http://www.ncworldmag.com/ncw-04-1998/ncw-04-ejbprog2.html, April 1998

Shah, Rawn, *Bean Basics: Enterprise JavaBeans Programming, NC World,* http://www.ncworldmag.com/ncworld/ncw-03-1998/ncw-03-ejbprog.html

Shah, Rawn, *Enterprise JavaBeans: Industrial-Strength Java, NC World,* http://www.ncworldmag.com/ncworld/ncw-01-1998/ncw-01-ejbeans.html, January 1998

Siple, Matthew, *The Complete Guide to Java Database Programming, JDBC, ODBC, and SQL,* Computing McGraw-Hill, 1998

Smith, Tim and Bill Courington, *Oracle8i/9i CORBA Developer's Guide,* Oracle Corporation, 2000-2001

Smith, Tim and Bill Courington, *Oracle8i/9i Enterprise JavaBeans,* Oracle Corporation, 2000-2001

SQLJ Availability in DB2 for OS/390, http://www.software.ibm.com/data/db2/os390/sqlj.html

SQLJ, http://www.sqlj.org/

Stonebraker, Michael, Eugene Wong, Peter Kreps, and Gerald Held, *The Design and Implementation of INGRES,* ACM TODS 1, No. 3 (September 1976)

Sun Microsystems Enterprise JavaBeans Specification 1.0, 1.1, and 2.0, 1998-2001, http://java.sun.com/products/ejb/docs10.html

Sun Microsystems Glossary, http://www.sun.com/glossary/glossary.html

Sun Microsystems JavaBeans Specification 1.01, http://java.sun.com/beans/spec.html, December 1996

Unicode Consortium, http://www.unicode.net

Valesky, Tom, *Enterprise JavaBeans, Developing Component-Based Distributed Applications,* Addison-Wesley, 1999

Wang, Paul S., *Java with Object-Oriented Programming and World Wide Web Applications*, Brooks/Cole Publishing, Pacific Grove, CA, 1999

Wright, Brian, *Oracle 8/0ii SQLJ Developer's Guide and Reference* Oracle Corporation, 2000-2001

Index

INTERNATIONAL CONTACT INFORMATION

AUSTRALIA
McGraw-Hill Book Company Australia Pty. Ltd.
TEL +61-2-9417-9899
FAX +61-2-9417-5687
http://www.mcgraw-hill.com.au
books-it_sydney@mcgraw-hill.com

CANADA
McGraw-Hill Ryerson Ltd.
TEL +905-430-5000
FAX +905-430-5020
http://www.mcgrawhill.ca

**GREECE, MIDDLE EAST,
NORTHERN AFRICA**
McGraw-Hill Hellas
TEL +30-1-656-0990-3-4
FAX +30-1-654-5525

MEXICO (Also serving Latin America)
McGraw-Hill Interamericana Editores S.A. de C.V.
TEL +525-117-1583
FAX +525-117-1589
http://www.mcgraw-hill.com.mx
fernando_castellanos@mcgraw-hill.com

SINGAPORE (Serving Asia)
McGraw-Hill Book Company
TEL +65-863-1580
FAX +65-862-3354
http://www.mcgraw-hill.com.sg
mghasia@mcgraw-hill.com

SOUTH AFRICA
McGraw-Hill South Africa
TEL +27-11-622-7512
FAX +27-11-622-9045
robyn_swanepoel@mcgraw-hill.com

**UNITED KINGDOM & EUROPE
(Excluding Southern Europe)**
McGraw-Hill Education Europe
TEL +44-1-628-502500
FAX +44-1-628-770224
http://www.mcgraw-hill.co.uk
computing_neurope@mcgraw-hill.com

ALL OTHER INQUIRIES Contact:
Osborne/McGraw-Hill
TEL +1-510-549-6600
FAX +1-510-883-7600
http://www.osborne.com
omg_international@mcgraw-hill.com

Get Your FREE Subscription to *Oracle Magazine*

Oracle Magazine is essential gear for today's information technology professionals. Stay informed and increase your productivity with every issue of *Oracle Magazine*. Inside each **FREE,** bimonthly issue you'll get:

- Up-to-date information on Oracle Database Server, Oracle Applications, Internet Computing, and tools
- Third-party news and announcements
- Technical articles on Oracle products and operating environments
- Development and administration tips
- Real-world customer stories

Three easy ways to subscribe:

1. Web Visit our Web site at www.oracle.com/oramag/. You'll find a subscription form there, plus much more!

2. Fax Complete the questionnaire on the back of this card and fax the questionnaire side only to **+1.847.647.9735.**

3. Mail Complete the questionnaire on the back of this card and mail it to P.O. Box 1263, Skokie, IL 60076-8263.

If there are other Oracle users at your location who would like to receive their own subscription to *Oracle Magazine*, please photocopy this form and pass it along.

☐ YES! Please send me a FREE subscription to *Oracle Magazine*.   ☐ NO

To receive a free bimonthly subscription to *Oracle Magazine*, you must fill out the entire card, sign it, and date it (incomplete cards cannot be processed or acknowledged). You can also fax your application to +1.847.647.9735. Or subscribe at our Web site at www.oracle.com/oramag/

SIGNATURE (REQUIRED) X _____ **DATE** _____

NAME _____ TITLE _____

COMPANY _____ TELEPHONE _____

ADDRESS _____ FAX NUMBER _____

CITY _____ STATE _____ POSTAL CODE/ZIP CODE _____

COUNTRY _____ E-MAIL ADDRESS _____

☐ From time to time, Oracle Publishing allows our partners exclusive access to our e-mail addresses for special promotions and announcements. To be included in this program, please check this box.

You must answer all eight questions below.

1 What is the primary business activity of your firm at this location? *(check only one)*
- ☐ 03 Communications
- ☐ 04 Consulting, Training
- ☐ 06 Data Processing
- ☐ 07 Education
- ☐ 08 Engineering
- ☐ 09 Financial Services
- ☐ 10 Government—Federal, Local, State, Other
- ☐ 11 Government—Military
- ☐ 12 Health Care
- ☐ 13 Manufacturing—Aerospace, Defense
- ☐ 14 Manufacturing—Computer Hardware
- ☐ 15 Manufacturing—Noncomputer Products
- ☐ 17 Research & Development
- ☐ 19 Retailing, Wholesaling, Distribution
- ☐ 20 Software Development
- ☐ 21 Systems Integration, VAR, VAD, OEM
- ☐ 22 Transportation
- ☐ 23 Utilities (Electric, Gas, Sanitation)
- ☐ 98 Other Business and Services _____

2 Which of the following best describes your job function? *(check only one)*
CORPORATE MANAGEMENT/STAFF
- ☐ 01 Executive Management (President, Chair, CEO, CFO, Owner, Partner, Principal)
- ☐ 02 Finance/Administrative Management (VP/Director/ Manager/Controller, Purchasing, Administration)
- ☐ 03 Sales/Marketing Management (VP/Director/Manager)
- ☐ 04 Computer Systems/Operations Management (CIO/VP/Director/ Manager MIS, Operations)

IS/IT STAFF
- ☐ 07 Systems Development/ Programming Management
- ☐ 08 Systems Development/ Programming Staff
- ☐ 09 Consulting
- ☐ 10 DBA/Systems Administrator
- ☐ 11 Education/Training
- ☐ 14 Technical Support Director/ Manager
- ☐ 16 Other Technical Management/Staff
- ☐ 98 Other _____

3 What is your current primary operating platform? *(check all that apply)*
- ☐ 01 DEC UNIX
- ☐ 02 DEC VAX VMS
- ☐ 03 Java
- ☐ 04 HP UNIX
- ☐ 05 IBM AIX
- ☐ 06 IBM UNIX
- ☐ 07 Macintosh
- ☐ 09 MS-DOS
- ☐ 10 MVS
- ☐ 11 NetWare
- ☐ 12 Network Computing
- ☐ 13 OpenVMS
- ☐ 14 SCO UNIX
- ☐ 24 Sequent DYNIX/ptx
- ☐ 15 Sun Solaris/SunOS
- ☐ 16 SVR4
- ☐ 18 UnixWare
- ☐ 20 Windows
- ☐ 21 Windows NT
- ☐ 23 Other UNIX _____
- ☐ 98 Other _____
- 99 ☐ **None of the above**

4 Do you evaluate, specify, recommend, or authorize the purchase of any of the following? *(check all that apply)*
- ☐ 01 Hardware
- ☐ 02 Software
- ☐ 03 Application Development Tools
- ☐ 04 Database Products
- ☐ 05 Internet or Intranet Products
- 99 ☐ **None of the above**

5 In your job, do you use or plan to purchase any of the following products or services? *(check all that apply)*
SOFTWARE
- ☐ 01 Business Graphics
- ☐ 02 CAD/CAE/CAM
- ☐ 03 CASE
- ☐ 05 Communications
- ☐ 06 Database Management
- ☐ 07 File Management
- ☐ 08 Finance
- ☐ 09 Java
- ☐ 10 Materials Resource Planning
- ☐ 11 Multimedia Authoring
- ☐ 12 Networking
- ☐ 13 Office Automation
- ☐ 14 Order Entry/Inventory Control
- ☐ 15 Programming
- ☐ 16 Project Management
- ☐ 17 Scientific and Engineering
- ☐ 18 Spreadsheets
- ☐ 19 Systems Management
- ☐ 20 Workflow

HARDWARE
- ☐ 21 Macintosh
- ☐ 22 Mainframe
- ☐ 23 Massively Parallel Processing
- ☐ 24 Minicomputer
- ☐ 25 PC
- ☐ 26 Network Computer
- ☐ 28 Symmetric Multiprocessing
- ☐ 29 Workstation

PERIPHERALS
- ☐ 30 Bridges/Routers/Hubs/Gateways
- ☐ 31 CD-ROM Drives
- ☐ 32 Disk Drives/Subsystems
- ☐ 33 Modems
- ☐ 34 Tape Drives/Subsystems
- ☐ 35 Video Boards/Multimedia

SERVICES
- ☐ 37 Consulting
- ☐ 38 Education/Training
- ☐ 39 Maintenance
- ☐ 40 Online Database Services
- ☐ 41 Support
- ☐ 36 Technology-Based Training
- ☐ 98 Other _____
- 99 ☐ **None of the above**

6 What Oracle products are in use at your site? *(check all that apply)*
SERVER/SOFTWARE
- ☐ 01 Oracle8
- ☐ 30 Oracle8*i*
- ☐ 31 Oracle8*i* Lite
- ☐ 02 Oracle7
- ☐ 03 Oracle Application Server
- ☐ 04 Oracle Data Mart Suites
- ☐ 05 Oracle Internet Commerce Server
- ☐ 32 Oracle *inter*Media
- ☐ 33 Oracle JServer
- ☐ 07 Oracle Lite
- ☐ 08 Oracle Payment Server
- ☐ 11 Oracle Video Server

TOOLS
- ☐ 13 Oracle Designer
- ☐ 14 Oracle Developer
- ☐ 54 Oracle Discoverer
- ☐ 53 Oracle Express
- ☐ 51 Oracle JDeveloper
- ☐ 52 Oracle Reports
- ☐ 50 Oracle WebDB
- ☐ 55 Oracle Workflow

ORACLE APPLICATIONS
- ☐ 17 Oracle Automotive
- ☐ 35 Oracle Business Intelligence System
- ☐ 19 Oracle Consumer Packaged Goods
- ☐ 39 Oracle E-Commerce
- ☐ 18 Oracle Energy
- ☐ 20 Oracle Financials
- ☐ 28 Oracle Front Office
- ☐ 21 Oracle Human Resources
- ☐ 37 Oracle Internet Procurement
- ☐ 22 Oracle Manufacturing
- ☐ 40 Oracle Process Manufacturing
- ☐ 23 Oracle Projects
- ☐ 34 Oracle Retail
- ☐ 29 Oracle Self-Service Web Applications
- ☐ 38 Oracle Strategic Enterprise Management
- ☐ 25 Oracle Supply Chain Management
- ☐ 36 Oracle Tutor
- ☐ 41 Oracle Travel Management

ORACLE SERVICES
- ☐ 61 Oracle Consulting
- ☐ 62 Oracle Education
- ☐ 60 Oracle Support
- ☐ 98 Other _____
- 99 ☐ **None of the above**

7 What other database products are in use at your site? *(check all that apply)*
- ☐ 01 Access
- ☐ 02 Baan
- ☐ 03 dbase
- ☐ 04 Gupta
- ☐ 05 IBM DB2
- ☐ 06 Informix
- ☐ 07 Ingres
- ☐ 08 Microsoft Access
- ☐ 09 Microsoft SQL Server
- ☐ 10 PeopleSoft
- ☐ 11 Progress
- ☐ 12 SAP
- ☐ 13 Sybase
- ☐ 14 VSAM
- ☐ 98 Other _____
- 99 ☐ **None of the above**

8 During the next 12 months, how much do you anticipate your organization will spend on computer hardware, software, peripherals, and services for your location? *(check only one)*
- ☐ 01 Less than $10,000
- ☐ 02 $10,000 to $49,999
- ☐ 03 $50,000 to $99,999
- ☐ 04 $100,000 to $499,999
- ☐ 05 $500,000 to $999,999
- ☐ 06 $1,000,000 and over

If there are other Oracle users at your location who would like to receive a free subscription to *Oracle Magazine*, please photocopy this form and pass it along, or contact Customer Service at +1.847.647.9630

Form 5   OPRESS

Knowledge is power. To which we say,

crank up the power.

Are you ready for a power surge?

 Accelerate your career—become an **Oracle Certified Professional** (OCP). With Oracle's cutting-edge *Instructor-Led Training*, *Technology-Based Training*, and this *guide*, you can prepare for certification faster than ever. Set your own trajectory by logging your personal training plan with us. Go to **http://education.oracle.com/tpb**, where we'll help you pick a training path, select your courses, and track your progress. We'll even send you an email when your courses are offered in your area. If you don't have access to the Web, call us at 1-800-441-3541 (Outside the U.S. call +1-310-335-2403). **Power learning has never been easier.**

University